Beyond the Fifth Century

Beyond the Fifth Century

Interactions with Greek Tragedy from
the Fourth Century BCE to the Middle Ages

Edited by
Ingo Gildenhard and Martin Revermann

De Gruyter

ISBN 978-3-11-048234-8
e-ISBN 978-3-11-022378-1

Library of Congress Cataloging-in-Publication Data

Beyond the fifth century : interactions with Greek tragedy from
  the fourth century BCE to the Middle Ages /
edited by Ingo Gildenhard and Martin Revermann.
     p. cm.
  Includes bibliographical references and index.
  ISBN 978-3-11-022377-4 (hardcover : alk. paper) -- ISBN
  978-3-11-022378-1 (ebk.) 1. Greek drama (Tragedy)--History
  and criticism. 2. Greek drama (Tragedy)--Appreciation--His-
  tory. 3. Classical literature--Greek influences. 4. Literature,
  Medieval--Greek influences. 5. Intertextuality. I. Gildenhard,
  Ingo, 1970- II. Revermann, Martin. III. Title: Beyond
the 5th century.
     PA3136.B49 2010
     882'.009--dc22
                                                        2010017824

Bibliographic information published by the Deutsche Nationalbibliothek

The Deutsche Nationalbibliothek lists this publication in the Deutsche
Nationalbibliografie; detailed bibliographic data are available in the Internet
at http://dnb.d-nb.de.

Cover Image: Mihály Zichy, Charcoal Illustration of Imre Madách,
The Tragedy of Man: In Athens (1887). Hungarian National Gallery, Budapest
Typesetting: Bernd Burkart, Winnenden; www-form-und-produktion.de
Printing: Hubert & Co. GmbH & Co. KG, Göttingen
∞ Printed on acid-free paper

Printed in Germany

www.degruyter.com

Acknowledgements

The idea for this volume was hatched in the summer of 2000, after a study day devoted to "Greek tragedy – beyond the fifth century", which Martin Revermann organized at Merton College Oxford. It took some time to mature; but five years later, the workshop "Points of Contact – Greek tragedy in the Western tradition up to the 17th century" took place at the Institute of Classical Studies in London, with generous financial support from the British Academy. Most of the papers collected in the present volume (and some others) were first delivered at this occasion. To ensure both coherence and coverage, we subsequently recruited further contributors; four of them presented preliminary versions of their chapters at a workshop organized by Ingo Gildenhard at Durham University in the spring of 2007. To round out the volume, we decided to add two further pieces, which are in part re-publications: Timothy Barnes' wide-ranging chapter on "Christians and the Theater", which remains fundamental for our understanding of the wider ideological and material context of the "reverberations" of Greek tragedy in the late Roman Empire, first appeared in *Roman Theater and Society: E. Togo Salmon Papers I*, edited by Wiliam J. Slater (Ann Arbor 1996), and we thank the University of Michigan Press for the permission to reprint it here. An earlier and significantly shorter version of Martin Revermann's chapter appeared in *Theatre Research International* 30 (2005).

The core of the book derives from the London workshop, which could not have happened without the generous award of a small conference grant from the British Academy, and we are profoundly grateful for its financial support. Ingo Gildenhard would also like to acknowledge the *Exzellenzcluster 16* of the *Deutsche Forschungsgemeinschaft* "Kulturelle Grundlagen von Integration" at the Universität Konstanz for the award of a fellowship during which the volume assumed its final shape. Our contributors have been a model of patience and good humour, and as editors we feel privileged to have had the opportunity to work with, and learn from, such a fine group of scholars.

Finally, we would like to express our gratitude to Caroline Reich for indispensable help with the index (which was generously funded by the Graduate Centre for the Study of Drama at the University of Toronto) and, especially, Sabine Vogt, Katrin Hofmann, and Maria Erge at de Gruyter, who saw the volume through press with admirable patience and efficiency.

Ingo Gildenhard, Durham University
Martin Revermann, University of Toronto

Table of Contents

INGO GILDENHARD AND MARTIN REVERMANN
Introduction 1

A. Getting the Show on the Road

JOHANNA HANINK
The Classical Tragedians, from Athenian Idols
to Wandering Poets 39

MARTIN REVERMANN
Situating the Gaze of the Recipient(s): Theatre-Related
Vase Paintings and their Contexts of Reception 69

PAOLA CECCARELLI
Changing Contexts: Tragedy in the Civic and Cultural Life
of Hellenistic City-States 99

B. From Greece to Rome

INGO GILDENHARD
Buskins & SPQR:
Roman Receptions of Greek Tragedy 153

ALISON KEITH
Dionysiac Theme and Dramatic Allusion
in Ovid's *Metamorphoses* 4 187

JENNIFER INGLEHEART
"I'm A Celebrity, Get Me Out of Here":
the Reception of Euripides' *Iphigenia among
the Taurians* in Ovid's Exile Poetry 219

C. The Roman Empire

ANNETTE M. BAERTSCHI
Drama and Epic Narrative: The Test Case
of Messenger Speech in Seneca's *Agamemnon* 249

ALESSANDRA ZANOBI
Seneca and Pantomime 269

THOMAS SCHMITZ
A Sophist's Drama: Lucian and Classical Tragedy 289

D. Late Antiquity and the Middle Ages

TIMOTHY BARNES
Christians and the Theater 315

CAROL SYMES
The Tragedy of the Middle Ages 335

ANDREW WHITE
Adventures in Recording Technology:
The Drama-as-Performance in the Greek East 371

DOMENICO PIETROPAOLO
Whipping Jesus Devoutly:
The Dramaturgy of Catharsis and the Christian Idea
of Tragic Form 397

List of Contributors 425

Index 429

Introduction

INGO GILDENHARD AND MARTIN REVERMANN

1 Taking tragedy beyond the fifth century

No sub-field in the discipline of Classics has experienced such growth, in both quantitative and qualitative terms, over the past fifteen or so years as the study of the reception of classical material.[1] This applies both to the Anglophone and the continental European academic traditions. The reasons for this remarkable phenomenon are not entirely intellectual in nature (reception sells, after all – to students, administrators and funding bodies alike). But this does not detract in any way from the fundamental intellectual merit of such studies: they communicate, to everyone who is willing to listen, that and how classical antiquity *matters*. Who in the incipient 21st century could, or even would want to, detract from the significance of studies in the dynamics of cultural transfer and interaction?

The academic study of Greek drama, tragedy in particular, has been spearheading this development. Early and isolated research set aside[2], it was the publication of Flashar's *Inszenierung der Antike* in 1991[3] and the foundation, in 1996, of the Oxford-based *Archive of Performances of Greek and Roman Drama*[4] with its important conferences and an impressive string of publications that made work on the reception of Greek drama the powerhouse of reception studies in the discipline of Classics as a whole. If the contemporary significance of Homer can be said to play itself out between "world literature" and the "Western canon", as the subtitle of a recent edited volume has it, the same applies to the surviving corpus of Greek tragic scripts (as well as, one might add, the tragic plays of Seneca, even though their appeal has rather waned since early modern times).[5] Apart from being

---

1   For a programmatic assessment see Hardwick 2009.
2   The 1911-book by Wilhelm Süss (*Aristophanes und die Nachwelt*) comes to mind.
3   A second edition came out in 2009.
4   See http://www.apgrd.ox.ac.uk/.
5   For Homer, see Graziosi and Greenwood 2007. Even in collected volumes on classical receptions more generally, receptions of Greek drama (and more specifically

in and of themselves a part of the global repertory, the ancient plays, via direct or indirect intertextual dialogue, have also entered into the dramatic traditions of the European vernaculars as well as non-Western traditions of drama – from William Shakespeare to Wole Soyinka.[6] In a recent book on "how the ancient world shapes our lives", "tragedy" figures as the climactic third element in a tricolon that starts with "love" and "sex";[7] and "how to stage a Greek tragedy" continues to be a topical challenge.[8] Provocatively pronounced dead since Racine and Milton[9], Tragedy has nonetheless continued to show the strongest of vital signs in all strata of cultural life, if only we have the receptivity to pick them up.[10] And Greek tragedy lurks behind it all. One of the reasons for this continued vitality is the genre's ability to thematize issues in a way that is at once topical and universal, not least in terms of politics – both the political semantics of tragic scripts and the political dimension of tragic performances (two related, but distinct phenomena), from the fifth century to the present, has been an abiding concern of critical discourse for a while now.[11]

In this intellectual climate, what makes *Beyond the Fifth Century* different? How does our volume seek to advance scholarship in the area and make an impact on the sub-field as a whole? Two differentiators are key to

---

    Greek tragedy) tend to command the lion's share of the contributions. See e.g. Stray 2007 or Hardwick and Stray 2008. But as Barner 1973, 12 recalls, almost everywhere in Europe "die lateinische wie die nationalsprachliche Tragödie" began "im Zeichen Senecas": "von Mussatos *Ecerinis* im Jahr 1314 über Trissino, Jodelle und Garnier, Kyd und Marlowe bis hin zu Shakespeare und Calderón, bis hin auch zu Opitz, Gryphius und Lohenstein".

6   See Etman 1981 for a study of the influence of ancient Greek and classicizing drama on Arab theatre; Goff and Simpson 2007 as well as Hardwick and Gillespie 2007 for African and African-American engagements with Greek tragedy; and, more generally, the papers collected in Decreus and Kolk 2004.

7   Goldhill 2004.

8   For a recent view see Goldhill 2007. (The ways it has been met over the last four centuries is the focus of a vibrant scholarly industry that has its centre in the abovementioned *Archive of Performances of Greek and Roman Drama*.)

9   By George Steiner in his influential *The Death of Tragedy* 1961, re-visited (and expressly re-iterated) in Steiner 2008.

10   Poole 2005 is an inspiring and ambitious narrative about the continued cultural significance, indeed necessity, of tragedy. The articles assembled in Felski 2008 similarly demonstrate the continuous vitality inherent in discussing tragedy. More localized general discussions by classicists are Goldhill 2008b and Hall 2010, 1–11 and 328–46.

11   The so-called "civic ideology" debate, see e.g. Goldhill 1990, Griffin 1998 and Rhodes 2003 for fifth-century Athens. Hardwick 2007 discusses the explosive politics of some recent "post-colonial" productions, while politics (especially of gender) loom large in the magisterial account of Greek tragedy on the British stage by Hall and Macintosh 2005.

our project. The first is chronological. Given the vitality of ancient Greek drama in the modern theatre, it is small wonder that the recent slate of companions to (Greek) tragedy, designed to introduce a wider readership to the genre and all featuring sections on reception, think about reception along a typical chronological profile. Some (though not all) include a nod to Rome and then jump straight to the Renaissance, with a special emphasis on tragedy in nineteenth- and twentieth-century productions. Of the twenty-eight contributions in Bushnell 2005, for instance, all are either on tragedy in fifth-century Athens or on tragedy from the Renaissance onwards – with the exception of Schiesaro's lone (if excellent) chapter 16 on "Roman tragedy".[12] All of this is indicative of the fact that so far the study of tragedy reception in general has focused mainly on reception since the early modern period, with a strong emphasis on the 19th and, especially, the 20th century. Reception in antiquity has only recently started to receive sustained attention, and there continues to be extremely little on reception in late antiquity or the Middle Ages. The chronology of our volume, spanning as it does the period from the fourth century BCE to the Middle Ages, joins others in the attempt to start filling precisely this enormous gap.[13]

The second differentiator is of at least equal importance. Rather than focusing, as it is usually done, almost exclusively on performance reception (in the form of re-performances or theatrical adaptations), our volume examines a whole range of different modes of reception or engagement. Performance reception is, of course, one of them, and features prominently in a number of contributions.[14] But there is also much of what may be branded inter-generic reception, the interaction of tragedy with other, non-performative, genres (e.g. Keith, Ingleheart, Baertschi). Inter-medial reception is at the core of Revermann's paper, which analyses and contextualizes the appropriation of tragedy in the medium of theatre-related vase paintings of the fourth century BCE. Other contributions also analyze inter-medial reception, even if the mediation may be of a different sort: through the biographical tradition (thematized by Hanink) or festival inscriptions (which are at the heart of Ceccarelli's paper), or through recording technology itself (as discussed in White's

---

12   Cf. also Easterling 1997a and Gregory 2005.
13   Notably, the *Archive of Performances of Greek and Roman Drama* has begun work on a second database "which strives to map performance in antiquity". See Hall and Wyles 2008 for the first corresponding edited volume.
14   There are healthy signs of growing methodological awareness: Hall 2004 is a significant first step towards theorizing performance reception, while Hardwick's important *Greece & Rome* survey on reception studies (= Hardwick 2003) is continually aware of hermeneutics (her more recent work explores the value of postcolonial studies for work in reception studies). See also Schmitz 2007 ch. 6 (on the reader-response aspect of reception studies) and Revermann 2008. Holub 1984 is a much-quoted but outdated theoretical account.

contribution). Contextual reception, that is the interface between tragedy and society-at-large (festival culture and entertainment (both public and private), education, religious practice, even life-style) finds extensive discussion in a substantial number of papers in this volume (Hanink, Ceccarelli, Gildenhard, Schmitz, Barnes, Symes, Pietropaolo). Last but certainly not least there is a strong, and novel, emphasis on the comparative study of traditions, where the focus is less on genealogical influences (although such may be present) than on the close study of equivalences (Symes, Pietropaolo). We should add that compartmentalizing in this way various modes of reception, while heuristically helpful, is somewhat artificial, as in the practice of cultural studies these modes of analysis are frequently combined. Performance reception, inter-generic and contextual reception, for instance, regularly go hand in hand (as they do in, for instance, Gildenhard's chapter on Roman receptions of Greek tragedy). But the point, and with it the specific nature of our volume, is clear enough and remains valid.

Tragedy, then, is an art form created in classical antiquity that has outlived and transcended its context of origin to shape (Western) cultural history *tout court*, and in various ways, including the (roughly) two millennia between its heyday in fifth-century Athens and the first re-performance of an ancient tragic script on a modern stage in 1585, Sophocles' *Oedipus the King* at the Teatro Olimpico in Vicenza.[15] While few (one would assume) still subscribe to the once fashionable set of preconceptions and prejudices about the "barbarian" playwrights of republican Rome, the decline and fall of the tragic sublime in the Roman empire (obsessed as it was with brutal and blood-thirsty spectacles) or the "dark" ages of dominant Christianity, the "immensely complex story" (to cite Pat Easterling) about "the wider impact of Greek tragedy on the culture of antiquity" is arguably still "waiting to be told" – to say nothing of the Middle Ages and the Renaissance.[16] Indeed, Easterling identifies the "task of capturing in detail the reverberations of tragedy in later antiquity" (and, one may add, beyond) as "one of the most interesting challenges for contemporary critics".[17]

Neither this introduction nor the papers that follow have the ambition to come up with the master narrative of this story, or even substantial parts of it. Our aim is more modest: what we try to offer is a range of specific case studies which trace some of the "reverberations" of Greek tragedy from the fourth century BCE to the Middle Ages. All of the chapters contribute to current scholarship (in Classics, but also in a range of cognate disciplines)

---

15   On which see Macintosh 2009, 70–3.
16   Easterling 1997b, 226.
17   Easterling 1997b, 226. Easterling 2005 and 2006 tackle the challenge for Aeschylus and Sophocles respectively.

by offering original research and often challenging established views. That said, we also entertain hopes that the volume may fulfill at least some of the functions usually ascribed to "Companions" (that newly popular genre of publication) for graduate students and adventurous undergraduates. This, we hope, will especially apply to those with an interest in literary history, comparative literature, cultural poetics, historical genealogies and ideological contexts of the sort frequently neglected in guides that pursue mainstream approaches and which feature significantly more reductionist formats than the longer and fully annotated papers collected in our volume.[18]

The volume proceeds in chronological order to trace tragic receptions in the fourth century and the Hellenistic Period (A), the Rome of the republic and the Augustan principate (B), the Roman Empire (C), and late antiquity and the Middle Ages (D). In the remainder of this introduction, we will set out to map the field (in an admittedly rudimentary fashion) by situating the individual chapters within broader thematic and historical contexts. Prior to this, however, we wish to identify and discuss, at a general level, some of the overarching and recurrent themes that inform, shape and guide thinking about the reception of tragedy, especially in the time-period under consideration here.

2   Recurrent themes in tragic receptions

(a) *Re-instantiation through re-performance.* While it is reasonable, though not absolutely safe, to assume that all of the surviving tragic scripts were originally designed for the specific competition at one of the Athenian dramatic festivals (the Lenaea or the Great Dionysia), the recycling of tragic plays was a common feature, so much so that we have to reckon with "a vibrant re-performance culture by the last quarter of the fifth century at the very latest".[19] Then, in the archonship of Theodotus (i.e. 387/6), so the Athenian *Fasti* inform us, "the tragedians for the first time presented an old drama" (παλαιὸν δρᾶμα πρῶτον παρεδίδαξαν οἱ τραγωιδοί) at the Great Dionysia. This piece of evidence, which says nothing of full-scale competitions, does not seem to bear out the popular claim, enshrined in Pickard-Cambridge, that "the plays of the three tragedians started being re-performed from 386 BC with the introduction of a theatrical competition for the 'classical' plays of the fifth century" (if anything, the term παρεδίδαξαν would seem to suggest re-performances, initiated by actors ("the tragedians"), outside

---

18   For companions (good and bad) see Goldhill 2008a, with its programmatic opening citation from Homer's *Odyssey*: "The Companions perished because of their own outrages."

19   Revermann 2006, 68.

of the regular competition).[20] As Ceccarelli argues, such a competition of "classics" was most likely a later development, to be dated to the reign of Demetrius Poliorketes.[21] But in conjunction with the canonization (which included re-performance) into a classic triad of the tragic playwrights Aeschylus, Sophocles and Euripides which underlies Aristophanes' *Frogs* (of 405), this is the first evidence we have of fifth-century tragic scripts officially re-entering the stage as precious cultural artifacts, endowed with a special authority, patina and prestige.[22] To what extent the Athenians took care that the re-performances of their classics from the "golden age" consisted of a *verbatim* reproduction of the original scripts is difficult to determine, and we should probably reckon with some significant tweaking (not least as a consequence of the documented impact which star actors with their big egos could have). In some ways, surely, re-performance is a "live", rather than "archival", tradition that not just allows for but even demands continual adaptation to remain relevant and successful.[23]

For just how long re-performances of fifth-century tragedy, and tragedy in general, continued is not entirely clear. Re-performances are safely attested, by literary and epigraphical sources, for the second century CE, after which the evidence currently available peters out. The second century CE certainly had a functional and well-developed infrastructure to support the drama business: the extremely interesting letters from Hadrian to the guild of the Artists of Dionysus (preserved as inscriptions which were published in 2006) provide fascinating glimpses into the organizational structure of what appears to be a vibrant performance circuit throughout the Mediterranean.[24] How exactly this re-performance culture manifested itself is a matter of dispute.[25] While tragedies appeared on stage well into the imperial period, they increasingly had to jostle with other performance genres, such as pantomime, for stage time. The impact of pantomime may also account for the fact that in later antiquity impresarios came to stage "digest versions" of tragic plays, which consisted of a sequence of highlights. In fact, for some time the "extract theory", as formulated by Gentili, which assumes as the norm performances of isolated bits and pieces of the classics, had

---

20 So, most recently, Michelakis 2008, 221, Webb 2008, 63 and Csapo 2010, 106f.
21 See below, chapter 3.
22 For the political ideology of Athens' cultural conservatism in the fourth century, see more generally the study of Menandrian comedy by Lape 2003.
23 Revermann 2006, 66–95 discusses this "fundamental problem", with the (perhaps surprising) result that the authenticity assumption is significantly easier to justify for (topical) comedy than (by and large universalist) tragedy.
24 Petzl / Schwertheim 2006.
25 In this volume, the phenomenon is discussed for specific periods by Ceccarelli, Zanobi and Barnes.

come close to orthodoxy, but it has recently been challenged quite pow-
erfully.[26] Performances of full texts, with many (if perhaps not all) of the
bells and whistles that were standard in fifth-century Athens, may well have
been much more frequent, and enduring, than has previously been assumed.
Whether it was the sphere of public performance or symposiastic staging,
until at least the second century CE there continued to be plenty of contexts
where tragedy could be encountered, as live drama and in full.

(b) *Evolution*. The phenomenon of re-performance ought not to obfuscate the equally important fact that new tragic plays continued to be written. *Pace* Aristotle, tragedy as a performance genre kept evolving even after
the death of Sophocles. The details of this process are virtually impossible
to reconstruct – the only surviving specimen of fourth-century tragedy, for
instance, is the pseudo-Euripidean *Rhesus*, though even its dating has been
controversial.[27] The same is true of Hellenistic tragedy: apart from the fragments of Ezekiel's *Exagoge* and Lycophron's "monodramatic" *Alexandra*
virtually nothing has survived.[28] But it is safe to assume that its poetics will
have differed in important respects from classical precedents and that this
stage in the evolution of tragedy in turn influenced later playwrights, in particular Seneca.[29] The creative interactions between tragedy and other genres
of performance (such as mime and pantomime) is as important here as the
much more radical transformations of the tragic heritage in Christian contexts[30] – such as, for instance, the *Christus Patiens* cento, written, so the
author informs us, "in the fashion of Euripides" (κατ' Εὐριπίδην; 3).[31]

(c) *Dispersal and translation*. Like no other genre fifth-century Athenian
tragedy outgrew its local origins and became a truly ecumenical phenomenon. Already in the (early) fifth century tragedy and tragic playwrights were
export hits: witness Aeschylus' stint in Sicily and Euripides' departure to
Macedonia at the end of his life.[32] Just like the death of the polis in the Helle-

---

26 Nervegna 2008, taking issue with Gentili 1979. See also Csapo 2010, 168–204.
27 See Ritchie 1964 and Fraenkel 1965, more recently Thum 2005 and Feickert 2005.
    Marco Fantuzzi's major new commentary on the play is eagerly awaited. For fourth-
    century tragedy more generally, see Xanthakis-Karamanos 1980, Easterling 1993 (a
    reference we owe to Johanna Hanink), and Hall 2007.
28 Tragic remnants are briefly discussed by Fantuzzi and Hunter 2004, ch. 9. A few
    lines of Carcinus' *Medea* have recently become known, see West 2007. For Ezekiel,
    see Jacobson 1983 and Kannicht 1991.
29 The best treatment of the problem is still Tarrant 1978.
30 See Lada-Richards 2007.
31 Dating and attribution of the work are controversial. For a survey of the scholarship,
    see Pollmann 1997 who argues against the authorship of Gregory of Nazianz and in
    favour of a dating of the work not before the eleventh or twelfth century.
32 For a discussion of the biographical traditions that accrued around those departures
    see Hanink's chapter.

nistic age has been greatly exaggerated, so too tragedy continued to flourish, and on a vast scale, with the rise of acting as a profession and tragic shows being staged in every self-respecting Greek city-state across the Mediterranean.[33] In the wake of the conquest of Alexander the geographical scope of tragic performances stretched from Sicily in the West to Ai-Khanum in the East.[34] A crucial chapter in the wider dissemination of the genre was its circulation in translations and creative adaptations (the boundaries were fluid, even within a single script) during the last three centuries BCE, when the Romans began to domesticate Greek textual artifacts more generally.[35] Since then, translation has remained a vital medium for keeping the ancient plays alive for changing audiences.[36]

(d) *Material culture and cultural poetics*. In addition to the theatre, tragedy and its accoutrements also left traces in other contexts and media. The perhaps most notable instance of such inter-medial reception is the dialogue that developed between "pots" and "plots", i.e. the representation of, and commentary on, tragic scripts and *sujets* in Greek vase painting.[37] The great tragedians received statues in fifth-century Athens;[38] and the tragic mask acquired an all but ubiquitous presence in ancient culture.[39] Tragedy also furnished inspiration for funerary art[40], and wall paintings or mosaics of tragic scenes would decorate homes in order to signal the connoisseurship (real or alleged) of their owners. Some tragic scripts, such as Euripides' *Phoenissae*, played a significant role in Greco-Roman education as welcome repositories of correct Attic elocution.[41] And in the ancient world a tight connection existed between education in rhetoric and eloquence and public performance, or, to use a more fashionable term, the "theatricality" of political life.[42] The

---

33 For ancient actors see the papers collected in Easterling and Hall 2002, further Ceccarelli 2004, and Csapo 2010, 83–116.
34 For drama in the Hellenistic period, see Sifakis 1967, Gentili 1979, Le Guen 1995 and Revermann 1999/2000, as well as the more recent volumes edited by Battezzato 2003a, Martina 2003 and Vox 2006 (with the review by Hanink 2007).
35 See below for more extensive comments on this extraordinary phenomenon.
36 See e.g. Hardwick 2000 and Walton 2006.
37 See Revermann's chapter below. The most comprehensive account, lavishly illustrated, is Taplin 2007. For an idiosyncratic formulation of the "iconocentric" view (which denies any link between performance and pictorial representation) see Small 2003.
38 See Hanink's contribution below.
39 The most impressive finds come from Lipari. See Bernabò Brea and Cavalier 2001 with Battezzato 2003b, Wiles 2007.
40 See Sista 2003 with further bibliography.
41 For the role of tragic scripts in educational contexts see e.g. Cribiore 1996 and 2001 as well as Morgan 1998.
42 From the vast literature on theatricality, not all of it specifically concerned with tragedy, see e.g. Burns 1972, Turner 1974, Kolb 1981, Schechner 1985, Bartsch

two rhetorical handbooks that survive from the late Roman republic, for instance, i.e. the *Rhetorica ad Herennium* and Cicero's de *Inventione*, as well as Cicero's dialogue *de Oratore*, resort repeatedly to tragic citations to illustrate aspects of (faulty) argumentation and delivery.

(e) *Cross-generic dialogue.* From its very beginnings, tragedy defined itself through dialogue with other poetry (narrative elegy and choral lyric, but most of all Homeric epic), and it soon became itself a partner in intertextual conversation.[43] Aristophanes' comedies maintain a sustained dialogue with tragedy and the tragic playwrights, to the point of putting them repeatedly on stage[44], while conversely tragedy's incorporation of comic themes and techniques is much less pronounced and, nearly exclusively (for us, at any rate), the preserve of (late) Euripides.[45] From the fourth century onwards, tragic scripts were chosen as a point of allusive reference by authors writing in virtually every other genre of Greek or Roman literature at one point or another – from epic to oratory, from philosophy to historiography, from elegy to the novel.[46] As Easterling points out, "this intense penetration of the language and literature of antiquity gave tragedy a special imaginative status that did not ultimately depend on performance traditions for its survival".[47] From the point of view of literary tradition, the survival of tragic subject matter in non-dramatic genres enabled its re-emergence in the form of a tragic play – a point paradigmatically illustrated by the story of Tereus, Procne, and Philomela. While some authors of the archaic period (notably

---

1994 and Chaniotis 1997. Rehm 2003, 13 nicely points to the current situation in performance studies, which lives by the tenet that "all that matters is performed, and only performance really matters" – with the potentially paradoxical result that the original site of performance – the theatre – gets decentered.

43 Justly famous is Aeschylus' claim that his plays were "slices from the banquet of Homer" (Athen. 8, 347D = test. 112a Radt). In some theorists of the genre (such as Aristotle) "tragic" is a trans-generic quality. See his discussion (*Poetics* 1448a25ff., 1448b38ff.) of the difference between *Odyssey* and *Iliad*. For inflections of Archaic lyric in the tragic playwrights see Bagordo 2003 and especially Swift 2010, for reflections of tragic lyrics in later literature Karanasiou 2002. A test case for tragedy (Aeschylus' *Persians*) taking on narrative elegy (Simonides) as the proper genre for celebratory poetry in the wake of the Persian Wars is explored by Taplin 2006.

44 For tragedy and Aristophanes, see Silk 2000, 42–97.

45 Seidensticker 1982.

46 The literature on the subject is accordingly vast. See e.g. Hardie 1997 for tragedy in Virgil, Hardie 1990, Gildenhard and Zissos 1999, as well as Keith and Ingleheart below, for tragedy in Ovid (both the *Metamorphoses* and the exile poetry), Ripoll 2004 for tragedy in Valerius Flaccus, Wilson 1996 and Hanink (below) for tragedy in the Attic orators, Nightingale 1995 for tragedy and Plato, Walbank 1955 and 1960 and Chiasson 2003 for tragedy and historiography, and Letoublon 1990, Paulsen 1992, Pattoni 2005 as well as May 2006 for tragedy and the novel.

47 Easterling 1997 226.

Homer) allude to the myth, it received its defining literary treatment in the *Tereus* of Sophocles. This tragedy, though lost to us save some meager fragments, spawned an impressive intertextual afterlife and thus offers an intriguing example of the importance of later authors and periods for the codification, transmission and continued vitality of Athenian tragedy. For the disappearance of Sophocles' play from our literary record is more than made up for by its rich history of cross-generic reception. Already Aristophanes, in his *Birds*, engaged with the play extensively, and through the Latin version of *Tereus* by the playwright Accius, the myth entered Roman literature and received its "classic" formulation in Ovid's *Metamorphoses* (6.424–674). Ovid, in turn, inspired Seneca, who patterned his tragedy *Thyestes* on the Ovidian model, and Ovid and Seneca together served as models for Gregorio Correr's tragedy *Progne* (1428) and Shakespeare's *Titus Andronicus*.[48]

(f) *Tragedy, myth, and the classical tradition.* Over the centuries, Greek and Roman mythology has proved to be a remarkably flexible multi-purpose medium: it is a source of sheer aesthetic pleasure, offers inexhaustible conceptual challenges, and provides an idiom in which to negotiate reality. Myths, however, are never free-floating but are articulated in various genres. Tragedy contributed significantly to shaping the ways we think about a wide range of mythic figures. Many heroes (as well as lesser mortals) carry the imprint of the genre as an indelible part of their history – none more so than Oedipus. But even Achilles, the epic hero par excellence, acquired a genuinely tragic complexion over time: tragedy deformed him in its own image, initiating a hostile history of reception that stretches from Aeschylus to Shakespeare and beyond.[49] When Aeschylus, in his Achilles-trilogy, the so-called "tragic *Iliad*", turned Achilles into a despicable traitor of the common cause, threatened with stoning for his refusal to fight, the best of the Achaeans in Homer had turned, at least momentarily, into the worst of the Greeks in tragedy: "Stoning is essentially the punishment by the community of the individual who has sinned against it."[50] If Aeschylus left the "truth" of the primordial epic by and large intact, Shakespeare, in *Troilus and Cressida*, went a shocking step further: he casts him as a

---

48   The sequence continues right up to the present: see Timberlake Wertenbaker's *The Love of the Nightingale* (1989) and Sarah Kane's *Cleansed* (1998).

49   Achilles' history of reception is traced in detail by Callen King 1987 and Latacz 1995; see also the entries in Reid 1993.

50   Parker 1983, 194–5. West 1987, 184 uses even stronger language: stoning is "the traditional form of communal execution of an abominated criminal, where everyone and no one takes responsibility for the killing." It is, in other words, the most unheroic death that one can suffer. See further Michelakis 2002, 56: "Aeschylus' Achilles is as much a hero of the Homeric past as an aristocrat of the Athenian present, both an example and a problem, a hero and a villain."

brazen-faced liar and a treacherous coward who has his Myrmidons ambush and kill a disarmed and defenseless Hector, only to take credit for the deed: "On, Myrmidons, and cry you all amain,/ 'Achilles hath the mighty Hector slain!'"[51] This rewriting of the Iliadic encounter between the Trojan prince and the son of Peleus is also an assault on Homer: "In addition to deflating the epic account, the passage purports to explain how that false account arose in the first place."[52] In other words, rather than perpetuating the *kleos aphthiton* of his hero, Homer, according to Shakespeare, is a singer of lies, and Achilles' reputation for heroic greatness a fraud. Shakespeare knew how to put classical authorities into their place.[53] With *Troilus and Cressida*, the tragic descent of Homer's semi-divine figure into infamy and disgrace has reached its nadir. There are little signs of recovery.[54]

(g) *Literary and cultural theory.* Tragedy presumably provoked and invited theorizing fairly early on. Aristophanes' *Frogs* is the first manifestation for us of such a discourse, but tantalizing bits such as the information that Sophocles wrote a treatise "On the chorus" (*Peri chorou*) or the amount of previous theorizing that must underlie some works by Plato (the *Symposium* and the *Republic*, for instance, but also the *Ion*) are (frustrating) hints at lost debates that were in all likelihood quite lively and engaging.[55] Aristotle's *Poetics*, probably the product of the second half of the fourth century BCE, is, (again) for us, the landmark study (a status which it cannot possibly have had in antiquity).[56] And since Aristotle, theorizing about tragedy has continued apace, especially from the Renaissance onwards – from Sir Philip Sidney's reflections on "high and excellent Tragedy" in his *The Arte of English Poesie* (1589) to Friedrich Nietzsche's *The Birth of Tragedy* (1872), from George Steiner's *The Death of Tragedy* (1961) and Raymond Williams' *Modern Tragedy* (1966) to Terry Eagleton's *Sweet Violence* (2003) or Adri-

---

51   *Troilus and Cressida* 5.9. "Audiences or readers who come to *Troilus and Cressida* (1601–02) from the *Iliad* may be in for a shock" – so W. Cohen in his introduction to the play in *The Norton Shakespeare* (New York and London, 1997) 1823–34, here 1823. See Bevington 1998, 390 for a discussion of Shakespeare's possible sources for this scene and Shirley 2005, 233–6 for an illuminating account of this scene's production history.

52   Cohen 1997, 1824.

53   For an elaboration of this theme, see Lyne 2000.

54   A telling example is Christa Wolf's *Kassandra* (1983).

55   Bagordo 1998 collects and discusses the preserved fragments of theoretical writing on tragedy.

56   The best comprehensive discussion of Aristotle's *Poetics* continues to be Halliwell 1998. Brink 1971 (on Horace's *Ars Poetica*) is crucial for Hellenistic literary theory about drama. Laird 2006 collects a number of seminal articles on ancient literary criticism (some of them in revised and updated form).

an Poole's *Tragedy: A Very Short Introduction* (2005).[57] And the chapters by Symes, White, and Pietropaolo amply illustrate that critical thought on tragedy, over and above Horace's *Ars Poetica*, did not cease during the millennium and a half between Aristotle and the Renaissance, but formed an integral aspect of Christian discourse throughout the Middle Ages – even though Christian authors often thought with, about, and against tragedy in ways profoundly alien to contemporary humanist, existentialist, or political understandings of the genre.[58]

(h) *The transmission of texts*. With very few exceptions, the journey of classical texts from antiquity to the present has been a precarious one. Sobering is the difference between the large number of playwrights active in fifth-century Athens and the vast number of plays they composed for performance on the one hand, and the handful of plays that has survived from the canonical triad on the other. Much fell by the wayside on the long road from the archives of Athens, via the library of Alexandria and the scholars of Byzantium, before a few remaining scripts made the crucial transition from manuscript to print.[59] Only few plays survived the centuries more or less intact, owing to a long tradition of scribes and commentators that bestowed longevity to performance scripts beyond their ephemeral enactment on stage.[60] And a quarter of a century after the first Greek text saw a print edition (*The Battle of the Mice and Frogs* at Brescia, c. 1474), the Venetian Aldus Manutius saw to the *editio princeps* of Sophocles (August 1502), soon to be followed by those of Euripides and Aristophanes. In 1518, three years after Manutius' death, that of Aeschylus appeared as well. From ca. 1600 onwards, the tragedies of Aeschylus, Sophocles and Euripides, the

---

57　This (selective) list indicates that tragedy has clearly remained good to think with, whether in a conservative or a revolutionary key – even though, at least for one observer, this has primarily been a continental European, rather than an Anglo-American phenomenon. See the observation by Steiner 1996, 545 that "Hölderlin, Hegel, Schelling, Nietzsche, Walter Benjamin, and Heidegger play almost no part in British academic-professional discussions of Greek tragic drama." Exceptions are Williams and Silk and Stern 1981 as well as Eagleton 2003 and 2008, who writes, like Williams before him, from an emphatically Marxist perspective and with little sympathy for Steiner's work. Collections of modern theorizing about tragedy include Drakakis and Conn Liebler 1998. See also Lambropoulos 2006.

58　See Kelly 1993 for a survey of ideas and forms of tragedy from Aristotle to the Middle Ages and Pace 2003 for Tzetzes' views on tragedy. The first three chapters of Barish's classic 1981-monograph on the "antitheatrical prejudice" are also most relevant in this context. See, for instance, his spirited (and good-humoured) engagement with Tertullian's *De spectaculis* (44–51).

59　See generally Reynolds and Wilson 1991 and, more specifically, Garland 2004.

60　For the distinction between commenting on and enacting tragedy, see Falkner 2002. Another extra-theatrical context that proved instrumental in preserving tragic scripts was education. See note 41 above.

three playwrights who had already attained canonical status in ancient Athens, started to reappear on stage, often in Latin translations.[61]

(i) *Transhistorical and cross-cultural perspectives.* A different line of enquiry from historical reception is the comparison between Greek tragedy and other tragic traditions, or, more generally, other cultural traditions that show thematic affinities with (Greek) tragedy. What are the features that unify Sophocles and Shakespeare?[62] Is "true" tragedy inconceivable in a Judeo-Christian context?[63] To what extent do Job and Philoctetes resemble each other?[64] These questions to do with equivalences broaden a concern with the reception of tragedy into a more general exploration of poetics and comparative literature, literary anthropology and the anthropology of literature.[65] There is still a significant amount of research to be done on the interactions between classical Greek tragedy and the Christian dramatic tradition, from the Middle Ages to the Counter-Reformation[66], and the papers by Symes and Pietropaolo in this volume are important contributions which, we hope, will help initiate a broader discussion that needs to take place.[67] One certainly need not presuppose genealogical links to render the comparative analysis of the dramatic representation of violence across different theatrical traditions a promising area of investigation: comparative analysis along the lines of equivalences does much to throw light on all traditions that serve as *comparanda*.

---

61 See Flashar (²2009, a general account), Hall, Macintosh and Taplin 2000 (on Euripides' *Medea*), Hall, Macintosh and Wrigley 2004 (on reception of Greek tragedy in the late 20th century), Macintosh and Hall 2005 (on Greek tragedy in Britain from the Restoration to the beginning of WW1), Macintosh, Michelakis, Hall and Taplin 2005 (on Aeschylus' *Agamemnon*), and Macintosh 2009 (on Sophocles' *Oedipus the King*).

62 See Silk 1996 and 2004.

63 Steiner 1961. See also Steiner 1996.

64 Daube 1996.

65 For the approach (though without specific case studies concerning tragedy), see Assmann, Gaier and Trommsdorff 2004.

66 See Hardison 1965 for Christian drama in the Middle Ages. Stroh 2007, 217 estimates that in German speaking countries alone, Jesuit educational institutions produced more than 20,000 plays in the sixteenth and seventeenth centuries. He concludes: "Die paar hundert Texte …, die wir heute noch lesen können, waren nach Schätzung ihres besten Kenners, Fidel Rädle, nur zwei bis drei Prozent der Gesamtproduktion. Wann gab es je in Deutschland eine so furiose Theaterbegeisterung!"

67 The most sophisticated discussion known to us of equivalences (including the limits of this concept) is by the comparatist Natalie Melas in her 2007-book *All the Difference in the World. Post-Coloniality and the Ends of Comparison*. Melas devotes an intriguing chapter to Walcott's *Omeros*.

3   Chapters in tragic receptions:
from the fourth century BCE to the Middle Ages

A: Getting the show on the road

When does "reception" start? Are the people who watched the very first performance of a fifth-century play recipients – instead of, or in addition to, spectators (A)? Are those who attended re-performances of tragedies and comedies, during their authors' lifetime and beyond, recipients (B)? Is it legitimate to use the term recipients for the readers of a dramatic script on a papyrus-roll, the purchasers of vases with theatre-related pictorial programmes or those who put comic terracotta figurines into their homes (C)?

In important ways, yes, in all the scenarios outlined above. Reception, first of all, can be synchronic (scenario A above). There seems to be the assumption, widespread and usually unarticulated, that reception by definition is something "after the fact", a response that needs time to "kick in" and therefore cannot possibly be synchronic. On this view, it is only key events such as the death of a playwright or, in exceptional circumstances, a particularly exposed first performance which become "traumatic", so to speak, and induce over time a paradigm change in how the public (or relevant parts of it) responds to a cultural artifact and its producer(s). But "receptivity", the readiness to respond on the part of the consumer of a cultural commodity, is an ongoing process, even if it may vary in degree over time. Sophocles' Athenian contemporaries are recipients, engaging with the artist and his products in continuous negotiations over value, acceptance and rejection. Similarly, those exposed to reperformances, during or after the playwright's life-time (scenario B), are part of these negotiations (and this includes negotiating with other recipients). The same dynamics, finally, apply to those whose access to the original (and by definition ephemeral) performance is mediated in one way or another, through writing or artistic representation of any description (scenario C).

The articles assembled in this section investigate instances of the scenarios B and C, and invariably focus on reception of tragedy subsequent to the deaths of the three now-canonical tragedians. Different as they are in tone and subject matter, two features unite all three papers. One is that they, invariably and exclusively, utilize not the plays themselves but mediated evidence: the biographical tradition, theatre-related iconography, and festival inscriptions. All of this is material that, until quite recently, has not or not fully been mined for information about tragedy and its reception. Secondly, all three contributions acknowledge that, while the process of reception was initiated during the artists' life-time, the traumatic caesura of their passing away resulted in a different quality of reception and new modes of "receptivity": the emergence of the playwrights as classics and their *post mortem* canonization as cultural icons; the creation of fetishes (or "sacred objects" in the Durkheimian sense) associated with those icons (tombs, play texts, objects from their personal belongings); and, as a consequence, new kinds of symbolic interaction with those uncontested masters of the craft. These dynamics, and the "end-of-an-era" feeling, are forcefully articulated by the tone of Aristophanes' *Frogs* (405), which both pre-supposes and celebrates the canonization of the triad of classical tragedians, and sets the tone for the decades, even centuries, to follow.

Johanna Hanink follows up precisely those threads in the first piece of this section. To explore the dynamics of cultural memory (and amnesia) regarding fifth-century tragedy, she zooms in on an often forgotten, or rather an easily discarded, type of evidence: the ancient biographical tradition. Hanink is interested less in the historical truth value of the lives of the poets than in their status as documents which attest to contests over cultural ownership. Whose Euripides, for example, is being constructed in those sources? And especially, how do geography and localization serve as strategic weapons in those struggles of ownership? In several instances Hanink is able to unearth what she calls "discursive substitutions". Thus Euripides is launched by Lycurgus as an Athenian patriot at a time when the city's actual political power is in undeniable decline.[68] Conversely, there is an even stronger tradition that emphasizes Euripides' non-Athenian impact and connections, thereby asserting claims of ownership made by the Macedonian and Alexandrian rulers. The "de-Athenianization" of Euripides (and Aeschylus, for that matter) stands in stark contrast with the (hyper?)-Athenianization of Sophocles, and finds symbolic expression in the acquisition of sacred, i.e. fetishized, objects (Euripides' lyre, for instance) by non-Athenian monarchs.

In the second contribution, Revermann looks at another case of mediated reception, through tragedy-related vase paintings. Painted pottery with theatrical motifs, the vast majority of which does not come from Athens but from South Italy, is a kind of evidence unparalleled in the history of world theatre. This article focuses not, as is often done, on the iconography itself but on the rapport it establishes with its viewers: the gaze of the recipient(s). This gaze is conditioned, not least by its situational context. Arguing against current orthodoxy, Revermann maintains that the theatre-iconography of most vessels makes best sense not in a funerary but a symposiastic context, for which, he argues, many vases were primarily intended (which does not at all preclude additional use as part of a funeral). Indeed, the very notion of "context" for theatre-related iconography needs to be fine-tuned to accommodate for the range of uses that these vessels could, and would, be

---

68 This strategy of cultural displacement is foreboding of what will happen centuries later in the Second Sophistic. See Swain 1996 and Whitmarsh 2001.

put. Using the splendid *Cleveland Medea* crater as his central case study, Revermann attempts to think through the context of this vessel's use at the symposium. These vases and their pictorial programmes respond to intellectual and emotional needs of their purchasers and onlookers from their peer groups alike. In this function, they establish matrices of competition, and serve to integrate as well as differentiate their recipients on a variety of emotional, educational and cognitive levels. As artifacts which do not just invite but in fact require such levels of engagement, these vessels serve not simply to "illustrate" the experience of tragedy: they deepen and enrich it.

Ceccarelli, finally, explores a vast, unwieldy and, until recently, largely unexplored corpus of evidence, festival inscriptions.[69] Looking for traces that tragedy left on stone, she focuses on honorific inscriptions which announce and celebrate in the context of competitive public performance honours that were bestowed on outstanding individuals (citizens and foreigners). In her detailed and nuanced analysis, which predominantly explores a significant amount of non-Athenian evidence (especially from Kos and Priene), Ceccarelli arrives at differentiated, and quite surprising, conclusions. While in Athens the tragic competitions continued to be the high-profile slot during which, as part of the pre-play ceremonies, the *polis* celebrated its power to bestow honours on individuals, this is not the case elsewhere. Even more, there are documented instances of a shift from dramatic performances as honorific occasions towards choral and gymnic competitions. The underlying reasons must, given the present state of the evidence, remain unclear and may be fiscal in nature (dramatic competitions were expensive, conceivably much more so than choral or gymnic ones[70]). But Ceccarelli's piece is a healthy reminder that while tragedy undoubtedly remained a major force in Greek cultural and political life in Hellenistic times and beyond, it continually needed to re-assert its position within a competitive market-place of rival cultural commodities.

---

69   The first systematic attempt at utilizing inscriptional evidence are the articles collected in Wilson 2007. The recently discovered letters from Hadrian to the guilds of the artists of Dionysus, published with commentary by Petzl / Schwertheim 2006, are a very important addition to the tally.

70   Wilson 2008 makes the detailed case for the costs associated with one particular (and arguably the most important) dramatic festival, the Great Dionysia in Athens at the end of the fifth century. He arrives at a total cost (from both the private and public sector, in a roughly equal split) of ca. 30 talants – an enormous sum.

B: From Greece to Rome

In 240 BCE, so our records of literary history have it, Livius Andronicus translated a Greek drama, most likely a tragedy, into Latin for performance at the *Ludi Romani* – a deed of linguistic pioneering that caught on. Tragedy became, and remained, a vibrant presence in ancient Rome throughout the republican and imperial periods, and the near-complete loss of Roman tragedy (apart from Seneca) is a most significant gap in our knowledge not just of the literary but also the socio-cultural dynamics of republican and imperial Rome.[71] For various reasons, the Roman reception and practice of tragedy is an arresting phenomenon.[72]

To begin with, for the first time this decisively Greek "system of the imagination"[73] with its highly contingent origins in fifth-century Athens reached new audiences, not just across distances of space and time but of language and culture. With the translation of Greek scripts into Latin, tragedy finally relinquished the confines of linguistic solipsism and became part of a much wider *oikumene* of literature and thought. Such instances of cross-cultural reception have been crucial for the expansion of the "hypoleptic horizon" of the Western tradition – as Jan Assmann has dubbed the nexus of cultural continuity and coherence in which texts refer to other texts in the form of controlled variation.[74]

Secondly, the Roman reception of Greek tragedy raises very interesting questions about the dynamics of intercultural encounters and the limits and possibilities of cross-cultural communication and acculturation, the shifts in

---

71 Attempts at a synthetic monograph-length discussion of the genre are rare and not always successful: see e.g. Erasmo 2004 with the reviews by Cowan 2005 and Leigh 2006. Boyle 2006, on the other hand, is by and large excellent.

72 Milestones in scholarship, including bibliographical ones, include the editions by Jocelyn 1967, Dangel 1995 and Schierl 2006 of the tragic fragments of, respectively, Ennius, Accius and Pacuvius; Lennartz 1994 on the playwrights as translators; the relevant entries in Suerbaum 2002; and the Forschungsbericht by Manuwald 2004. See further Goldberg 2007, who surveys recent trends in the study of Roman tragedy (including Seneca).

73 One of Gian Biagio Conte's paraphrases for "genre". He defines the concept as "a discursive form capable of constructing a coherent model of the world in its own image. It is a language, that is, a lexicon and style, but also a system of the imagination and a grammar of things" (Conte 1994, 132).

74 Assmann ²1997, 281. Despite the fact (or, perhaps, because of it?) that Latin literature has been, from the start, a literature defined by reception (and has been studied as such for centuries), it often gets short thrift in "classical reception studies". The new *Blackwell Companion to Classical Receptions*, for instance, fashionably Hellenocentric in outlook overall, has four chapters on Greek material and one on Achaemenid Persia in its opening section on 'Reception within Antiquity and Beyond' – and none on Rome. See Hardwick and Stray 2008.

meaning texts undergo as they travel across culture, the (literary) representation of "the other", and the interface between discourse and practice in societal
evolution – in short, an entire hosts of issues that are key areas of debate in
contemporary cultural studies. Today, we think we know that meaning is not an
inherent quality of literary artifacts. Rather, readers or theater audiences ascribe
significance to a text or a play on the basis of their interests, knowledge, and
preconceptions. And in Republican Rome, tragic scripts were not only rendered
into a different tongue, with its specific resources of signification, but began to
percolate within conditions of apprehension and intelligibility radically different
from those for which they were initially intended. Moreover, the various uses
to which the Romans put tragic texts and the ideas contained within them – not
just in the theater, but also the schools, the law courts, and other poetry and
prose – afford prime evidence for the constructivist truism that we need to look
at literary texts the way Malinowski does at sticks (which might be used for very
different purposes, such as digging, walking, punting, or fighting): "In each of
these specific uses, the stick is embedded in a different cultural context; that is,
put to different use, surrounded with different ideas, given a different cultural
value and as a rule designated by a different name."[75] As Goldhill puts it, with
specific reference to our genre: "It is extremely hard to decide in general or in
specific cases to what degree the placing of Athenian tragedy in other cities,
other times, allows for other modes of representation [and we might add, recep-
tion]. ... When the characters of fiction are set in an other place and other time,
it is especially hard to articulate securely these differences and similarities."[76]

Thirdly, there is a sense in which receptivity to drama (of any kind)
must have been especially high in Roman society, of all periods. The notion
of a "theatre state"[77] seems particularly applicable in the Roman context
where there were ample opportunities for highly theatrical interactions at
various levels. Intriguingly, the Latin *persona* denotes both "social role" and
"theatrical masks", and it is not all that far-fetched to call Rome a "mask-
to-mask" society in which social interactions often implied the acting out of
specific roles, such as *patronus* or *cliens, pater familias, patruus* or *avuncu-
lus*, consul or tribune of the people.[78] The affinities between orator and actor

---

75   Malinowski 1931, quoted by Burke 1997, 186.
76   Goldhill 1990, 110–1.
77   An expression coined by the anthropologist Clifford Geertz 1980.
78   See Bettini 1991. For the semantics of *persona*, see e.g. the succinct discussion by
     Berry 1996, 146: "The primary meaning of *persona* is an actor's mask representing
     a particular type of character; by extension the word comes to mean a character in
     a play, and then a man's character or personality. ... Later it indicated, in legal con-
     texts, the person involved in a case, and finally an individual person in the modern
     sense", with some further bibliography.

were a source of considerable anxiety during the republic.[79] More generally, public life often had a highly dramatic quality, as during the various processions that crisscrossed the cityscape on a regular basis. Their theatrical nature is particularly apparent in the funeral procession (*pompa funebris*) of former office-holders, which featured actors, wearing masks (*imagines*), who impersonated those forebears of the deceased who had also reached a curule office. Once the procession reached the forum they would take a seat on their curule chairs and form the imaginary audience of the funeral oration, delivered by a close kin of the deceased.[80] These and other features of Roman culture formed the complex matrix for tragedy's "transculturation" or "indigenization" at Rome, resulting in a transformation and evolution of both the genre and Rome's cultural imaginary.[81]

Fourthly, tragedy played an important role in the evolution of a Latin literature on the basis of Greek models, "an undertaking", as Denis Feeney puts it, "which no one in the Mediterranean had ever contemplated before, but which became a paradigm for later literary history."[82] It was Livius who was responsible for the 'big bang' that initiated this fascinating, virtually unique, and certainly uniquely influential process, putting into motion a cross-cultural and trans-linguistic dynamic that would come to characterize all subsequent literary efforts in Latin and, centuries later, the emerging European vernaculars. In helping to initiate and define a hybrid literature, partly Greek and partly Roman, tragedy contributed to the larger cultural configuration that goes by the name of "Greco-Roman civilization", which has played a major role in debates over the cultural identity of Europe. To cite, summarily, one such plot-construction: "Leo [sc. Friedrich, 1851–1914] had in practice founded Latin studies as we know them when he defined Livius Andronicus as the first translator of Western literature. His influential sentence about Andronicus, 'He is the beginner of the first derivative literature of our cultural universe' (p. 59) harks back to p. 3 'Roman literature is the first literature dependent on the Greeks, the first secondary, non home-grown literature', and this in turn presupposes p. 1 'Western civilization depends on Graeco-Roman culture, and so does the spread of Christianity through Roman and German peoples … Roman culture is the spiritual link between

---

79 See e.g. Edwards 1993, 98–136 and Fantham 2002. The interchange between stage and politics, or, indeed, their conflation, became only more complex during the empire: see introduction to Section D.

80 Flower 1996. Another obvious example of the 'theatrical' element in Roman public life was the triumph. After the classic study of Versnel 1970, see now the groundbreaking work of Flaig 2003, Rüpke 2006, and Beard 2007.

81 The terms in quotation marks are those of Hutcheon 2006, xvi.

82 Feeney 1998, 53; cf. Fantham 1989, 220.

the ancient and the modern worlds … The dynamics of civilization was from East to West …'."[83]

Finally, in the late republican and Augustan period tragedy, more insistently and thoroughly than in Greece, entered into allusive dialogue with other genres. From Plautus to Virgil, from Catullus to Ovid, Latin authors decided to enrich their texts by engaging with tragic scripts (in Greek and Latin).[84] This, in turn, has helped tragedy to survive and evolve, in a process for which Ovid's *Metamorphoses* proved pivotal. Like no author before or after, Ovid managed to outfit a comprehensive compendium of myth with a literary format of the highest sophistication that would continue to resonate with ever-changing audiences. The Roman reception of Greek tragedy, then, offers rich territory for exploring cross-cultural and cross-generic dynamics, and the three chapters in this section do precisely that.

Gildenhard's chapter "Buskins & SPQR: Roman receptions of Greek tragedy" surveys the cultural standing of tragedy in republican Rome, with a special emphasis on what plays about Greek mythic characters may have meant to a Roman audience and the strategies of translation employed by the Roman playwrights to render the tragic worlds of Greece intelligible to new audiences. He also maps the diffusion of tragic thought in Roman society beyond the context of the theatre and explores possible correlations between the semantics of tragedy and the larger political culture.

In Keith's paper, entitled "Dionysiac theme and dramatic allusion in Ovid's *Metamorphoses* 4", which focuses on the presence of tragic elements in the *Metamorphoses*, this linguistic crossing is explored alongside a generic crossing. Awareness of tragic elements in inter-generic dialogue is a fairly recent critical development. In studies of Latin intertextuality, the interface between epic and elegiac modes has always attracted the lion's share of critical attention. There are, however, promising signs in the recent scholarly literature (especially on Virgil and Ovid) that tragedy is poised to take center stage in the next wave of intertextual studies on Latin literature.[85] Keith offers a detailed reading of tragic allusions in books 3 and 4 of Ovid's *Metamorphoses*, with a particular emphasis on the episode of the daughters of Minyas that opens the fourth book of the poem. She shows how Bacchus, the patron deity of the tragic theatre, establishes a powerful and ominous presence in the *Metamorphoses* that does not only manifest itself in the transformation into bats of the sisters who defy his divinity, but also in the thematic design of the tales they tell. Keith demonstrates how their stories, told in lieu

---

83   Barchiesi 2002, quoting from F. Leo's *Geschichte der römischen Literatur, Erster Band: die archaische Literatur*, Berlin 1913.
84   For the notion of generic enrichment see Harrison 2007.
85   See in particular Hardie 1990 and 1997, further Gildenhard and Zissos 1999, 2007.

of participation in the Dionysiac rituals, reverberate with tragic themes, such as the contrast between city and country, man and beast, the related themes of exile and wandering in the wilds, the repeated intervention of a vengeful divinity, and spectacle, recognition and reversal. Her study illustrates paradigmatically how Ovid in and through the *Metamorphoses* codified and preserved much of Athens' tragic legacy, making it accessible to later ages in what should become the "bible of artists and painters".

Finally, Ingleheart, in "'I'm a celebrity: get me out of here!': the reception of Euripides' Iphigenia in Tauris in Ovid's exile poetry", shows how Ovid's engagement with tragedy continues in his *Tristia* and *Epistulae* ex Ponto in a sadly autobiographic vein, as the poet models his experiences in Tomi on tragic (and geographically apposite) precedents.

C: The Roman Empire

Apart from fifth-century Athens, Rome of the first century CE is the only place from which tragic scripts have survived by and large intact. Seneca wrote tragedy in a peculiarly Roman key, and overall his tragic idiom has remained as influential as that of his Greek predecessors, especially during early modern times.[86] As Miola puts it:[87]

> To imagine the unthinkable, speak of the unspeakable, and portray the impossible, European writers of tragedy looked to the ten plays of Lucius Annaeus Seneca. There they admired a swelling, superheated rhetoric for outsized rage and grief as well as rhetorical forms – the soliloquy, stichomythia (line by line exchange), *sententia* (wise saying), and choral reflection. There they also found useful stock characters – nurse, tyrant, ghost, and messenger – as well as thrilling protagonists like Phaedra, Hercules, Medea, and Atreus, who acted out forbidden desires and impulses. Seneca especially inspired one popular and lurid kind of Renaissance tragedy, the tragedy of revenge.

The association with the depiction of atrocity has not served Seneca's reputation well in more recent times (the notable exception being Antonin Artaud who considered Seneca the closest precursor to his own "Theatre of Cruelty"[88]). Not too long ago, the equivalent to Miola's new-historicist move

---

86   Earlier scholarship includes Regenbogen 1930, Charlton 1946, Barner 1973, Lefèvre 1978, Schmidt 1978, who calls Seneca the "Vater der neuzeitlichen europäischen, insbesondere der mythologischen Tragödie" (13). See now also Staley 2009.

87   Miola 2000, 116.

88   Artaud in a letter to his friend Jean Paulham (16 December 1932): "(...) he [Seneca] seems to me to be the greatest tragic author in history (...). You can't find a better *written* example of what is meant by cruelty in the theatre than in *all* the Tragedies of Seneca, but especially in Atreus and Thyestes. (...) In Seneca the primordial forces resound in the spasmodic vibration of the words" (quoted from Schumacher 2004, 82).

to associate Shakespeare's representation of violence on stage with "the Elizabethan appetite for blood spectacle" (he cites public executions, cock-fighting, and bearbaiting), was the *old*-historicist move in Senecan studies to explicate his penchant for reveling in outrage with reference to the bloody-mindedness of the age. Indeed, gladiatorial shows, the burning of Christians on the cross, the butchery of wild animals on a vast scale in the arena (with the occasional mauling of an unfortunate hunter thrown in for good measure), and mythological snuff-shows would seem to outclass the Elizabethan pastimes in cruelty. The seemingly "rhetorical" (in contrast to genuinely dramatic) quality of Seneca's tragedies, including his perceived penchant for bombastic hyperbole, did its part to have generations of modern critics throw the book at him. But as with so many canonical authors, Seneca's appreciation is rhythmical, oscillating as it does between sympathetic exegesis and hostile dismissals, and over the last thirty years or so, scholars such as Richard Tarrant, Anthony Boyle and Alessandro Schiesaro have done much to rehabilitate his reputation.[89]

All three critics are unanimous in granting Seneca a supreme degree of literary sophistication, and have done much to illuminate his extraordinary complex dialogue not just with his Greek models or the tragic tradition of republican and early imperial Rome (in particular Accius), but Greek and Latin literature *tout court*, especially the authors of the Augustan period. The epics of Virgil and Ovid, in particular, are omnipresent in Seneca's tragedies, and if Keith in her paper traces the journey of tragic material into epic, the chapter by Annette Baertschi, "Messenger speeches in Senecan drama and the dramatic quality of epic", considers the impact of epic on Senecan tragedy. While the adoption of epic narrative strategies in the messenger-speeches of Greek tragedy has been the subject of several studies in recent years, a similar analysis and examination of the messenger's performance in Senecan drama is still lacking. Through a close look at the messenger-speech in Seneca's *Agamemnon* Baertschi demonstrates that, apart from reworking the Greek tragic heritage, the passage also shows a sustained engagement with epic, appropriating its poetic and specifically narrative techniques and, in doing so, increasing the dramatic impact.

By way of contrast, Alessandra Zanobi's chapter on "Seneca and panto-mime" explores a dimension of Seneca's dramatic art that derives from his dialogue with the most popular performance genre of the imperial period, pantomime. Her thought-provoking thesis is that many of the idiosyncrasies of Seneca's poetics – structural looseness, a free-standing chorus, or "running commentaries", i.e. extended descriptions of one actor by another while both are on stage – betray the influence of pantomime. Zanobi further

---

89   Tarrant 1976, 1978; Boyle 1983, 1997; Schiesaro 2003.

argues that Seneca had good reasons for enriching the tragic genre by what she calls the "aesthetics of pantomime". Those formal choices enhance key aspects of the thematic economy of his plays. Zanobi's insistence on the importance and impact of pantomine is indicative of current attempts to give this genre, finally, the sustained scholarly attention it deserves and without which any history of performance in antiquity will remain inadequate.[90]

No equivalent to Seneca's tragic corpus has survived from the Greek half of the Roman empire, but this does not mean that engagement with the legacy of Attic tragedy did not continue. Thomas Schmitz' chapter on "Lucian and classical tragedy" focuses on the Second Sophistic and one of its main representative, Lucian, asking what "tragedy" meant for this author in particular and, more generally, for the culture of the second century CE. Schmitz' answer is multi-layered. He begins with a philological investigation of the use of the words "tragedy" and "tragic" in Lucian's *oeuvre*, both in the literal and the metaphorical sense. The following sections broaden the investigation. Schmitz traces the special fascination of the authors of the Second Sophistic with the theatrical and histrionic aspects of Greek tragedy, shows how tragedy came to stand in for a repertory of fictional tales, or mythology more generally, works out the specific ethos ("seriousness") that tragedy carried (by contrast with comedy), and analyses tragic discourse as a prime instance of literature from the past that at the time of Lucian was studied as "classic" in school. Schmitz concludes by demonstrating that dialogue with tragedy played an important role in the self-definition and the self-fashioning of the cultural elite in the Greek East during the Roman empire. As a cultural manifestation of the classical past it commanded respect not only as text but also as an antiquarian phenomenon – as an integral part of this most important and the most mythical of all sophistic places, classical Athens.

D: Late Antiquity and the Middle Ages

Tragic drama was one element of the classical heritage that provoked extensive and productive tussles with Christianity.[91] Christian anxieties crystalized around "morality" and "mimesis".[92] A hostile discourse on the theatre that revolved around negative stereotyping of actors as immoral or effeminate and theater-buildings as sites of vulgar pleasures dates of course back as far as the Roman republic. Actors carried a social stigma; dancers, especially

---

90 The monograph by Lada-Richards 2007 and the collection of articles in Hall / Wyles 2008 are major steps in this direction.

91 For Christian reactions to the ancient theatre more generally, see Dox 2004 as well as Barish 1981 (still the standard work on anti-theatrical polemics).

92 Webb 2008.

pantomimes, were considered effeminate; and the distinction between orator and actor caused much ideological fretting, especially in the imperial period when even emperors were known to switch position, moving from the *cavea* onto the stage. The church fathers, from Tertullian onwards, picked up on and amplified these concerns from a Christian point of view.[93] Concerns about the transformative power of mimesis, too, had pagan precedents, in particular, of course, in the philosophy of Plato.

But the two worlds of the pagan stage and Christian dogma did not always stand in stark, unmediated opposition, in part perhaps because the theater was too powerful and alluring an institution to reject it wholesale. As with any other element or institution of paganism endowed with cultural prestige, Christians developed ways of incorporating a radically refashioned version of it into their own outlook on the world. A good example is the reconfiguration of the mime-actor as a martyr.[94] Eusebius detected in tragic passages indications of theodicy and the second coming of Christ.[95] The confrontation produced some graphic and memorable vignettes. And Augustine used Virgil's tragedy of Dido as his starting point for Christian soul-searching: "I was forced to memorise the wanderings of Aeneas – whoever he was – while forgetting my own wanderings; and to weep for the death of Dido who killed herself in love, while bearing dry-eyed my own pitiful state, in that among these studies I was becoming dead to You, O God, my life."[96] In other words, he crucified himself for his inability to weep for his own sins while being moved to tears and pity by a fictional character from pagan lore – a rhetorical self-fashioning perhaps based on the story of the tyrant Alexander of Pherae who is said to have left the theatre in the middle of a tragic performance, because he would not wish to be seen to be moved to pity for characters on stage, given his gruesome and merciless track-record in his dealings with his subjects.[97]

Christian attitudes towards the pagan theater more generally and tragedy specifically changed over time. If initially the church fathers rejected this part of the classical heritage, most church authorities realized the benefits of a classical education, and as sources of linguistic competence, style and eloquence, if not as repositories of knowledge, the pagan classics (including

---

93 See e.g. Weismann 1972, Brown 1989, 305–22, Mayer and Allen 2000, 118–25, Webb 2008, Barnes, below with further bibliography.
94 See Panayotakis 1997, Lim 2003, Elm von der Osten 2004, 2005, 2006.
95 See *Praeparatio Evangelica* 13.13.48 with von Haehling 2005, 350 who also discusses Eusebius' hostile reception of the tragic heritage.
96 Augustine, *Conf.* 1.13.20–1. See MacCormack 1998 for Vergil and Augustine more generally.
97 See Jacobson 1972, 297: "In each case the 'villain' weeps for fictional creations in a work of art but is unable to show the same sympathy and remorse in real life."

tragic scripts) retained a place in educational settings. In time, Christians ex-
egetes of classical literature developed a range of interpretative techniques,
foremost among them allegory, for the resourceful appropriation of unpalatable pagan content into their own ideological (or theological) universe. For
tragedy, this process arguably culminates in Chapter 83 of the first book of
Honorius Augustodunensis' *Gemma Animae* (1100), which allegorically relates Christian liturgy in "the theatre of the church" (*in theatro Ecclesiae*) to
the staging of a tragic play. As Dox notes: "*De tragoediis* sets out to define
classical tragedy in terms of the celebration of the mass. Honorius's analogy
demonstrated that Christianity had redeemed the theatrical performances of
the Greco-Roman past."[98] By that time, of course, Christianity had evolved
its own traditions of performance, with only the vaguest genealogical links
to the performance culture of pagan antiquity.[99]

Christians too participated in the dialogue with tragic scripts. An intertextual shade of Euripides' *Bacchae* haunts the Acts of the Apostles.[100]
And some gestures of tragic protagonists appealed to Christian sensibilities,
while also serving to spice up accounts of martyrdom. Thus the author of
the *Passio Perpetuae* has his heroine re-enact the death of Polyxena, who in
Euripides, Ovid and elsewhere had attained renown for taking care to cover
her body modestly in the very act of falling under the sacrificial knife.[101] As
Jan Bremmer notes, "Perpetua even outdoes Polyxena by also asking for a
comb to readjust her hair (!)."[102]

The papers in this section all reassess the transition from pagan to Christian culture, putting equal weight on continuity as well as change. In his
wide-ranging chapter "Christians and the theater" Timothy Barnes delineates the impact of Christianity on pagan performance culture more generally, in particular mime and pantomime, giving due attention to the fact
that tragic performances had already been in significant decline before the
advent of Christianity. Symes advances a similar argument. She first interro-
gates the critical responses to medieval ideas of tragedy and medieval treatments of genres analogous to tragedy in order to expose the anachronistic
premises and unsuitable methodologies that have governed scholarly evalu-

---

98   Dox 2002, 52. See further the chapters by Symes and Pietropaolo below.
99   See e.g. Hardison 1965, Simon 1991, and Enders 1992, 1999 for dramatic perfor-
      mances in the Middle Ages and Valentin 2001 for Jesuit theater.
100 See Dormeyer 2005 with further bibliography.
101 See Eur. *Hec.* 568–70, Ovid, *Met.* 13.479–80: *tunc quoque cura fuit partes velare
      tegendas,/ cum caderet, castique decus servare pudoris.* Secondary literature in-
      cludes Braun 1983 and Habermehl 2004.
102 In his review of Habermehl 2004, *BMCR* 2006.01.34. He continues: "In short, the
      conclusion seems inescapable that the editor did not give a trustworthy account of
      the deaths of Perpetua and her fellow martyrs but wanted to please his readers with
      a description that catered to the taste of the times for violence and pornography."

ations of the available sources. The article then looks at what is currently
known about the processes by which tragedies and other theatrical texts
were preserved, copied, edited and anthologized from antiquity to the advent of print. The main aim of this part is to demonstrate that the allegations
of censorship or carelessness regularly leveled against Christian theologians
or the scribes and scholars of Byzantium are largely groundless, and that the
canon of Greek tragedy had already been fatally narrowed before the end
of the second century. The second part of the paper takes a fresh look at the
ways in which medieval theorists and performers adapted and appropriated
the texts and ideas of tragedy which they inherited. Rather than expecting
them to conform to Aristotelian or Renaissance notions of classical texts,
Symes discusses her authors from within medieval sensibilities. Overall, she
aims to look beyond the anti-theatrical discomfiture of Tertullian and Augustine, and the anti-medieval polemics of modernity. Against a sketch of the
vibrancy of medieval theatrical activity she comes up with a more balanced
account of the significance of tragedy in particular and ancient theatre more
generally for the Middle Ages.

Andrew White's "Adventures in recording technology: the drama-as-
performance in the Greek East" complements Symes' chapter (with its focus
on the Latin West) by exploring the significant continuities, especially on
the level of language and music, between classical Greece and Byzantium,
and the place of tragedy within this cultural continuum – in particular the
connection between Byzantine hymnography and the (lost) music that accompanied Greek tragic performances. Key sources for his explorations are
the scholiasts and the rhetoricians who display a broad-ranging knowledge
of the tragic heritage.

In the final chapter of the volume, Domenico Pietropaolo examines how,
in the transitional period between the Middle Ages and the Renaissance,
prior to the humanistic rediscovery and idealization of Greek philosophy
and just before the triumph of classical academicism in art, Christians understood the issue of moral catharsis before spectacles of re-enacted suffering. The body of dramatic texts on which the paper is based consists for the
most part of passion plays performed in church but also includes edifying
accounts of martyrdom and meditation on the experience of suffering. The
theoretical underpinnings of the argument are found (i) in the theology of the
cathartic emotions of pity and fear, as expounded chiefly, though not exclusively, by St. Thomas Aquinas, (ii) in the Islamic interpretation of Aristotle's
Poetics, from Avicenna to Averroes, and in the subsequent Christianization
of its main themes, (iii) in the allegorical interpretation of the liturgy offered by William Durandus, (iv) in the contemporary theory of genre, and
(v) in various theoretical inferences drawn from what was then known of
Greek tragic heroes. In this paradigm, the liturgy of the Eucharist serves as
the text's ultimate referent and as the audience's source of enlightenment

along each stage of the reception process. By issuing this call to introspection in light of the liturgy, these Christian tragedies achieve their effects by the excitation and development of pity and fear as positive and edifying emotions. When the process is over, cathartic pity becomes *misericordia*, or the impulse to alleviate the unjust pain of others by suffering along with them. Cathartic fear, on the other hand, becomes a reminder that the predicament of tragic characters is an ever- present possibility in our lives, and tragic form emerges redesigned as an aesthetic structure meant to show that re-enactments of history and faith, that is to say plays and the liturgy, are related by continuity and reciprocal implication. The paper thus provides a fitting closure to the story of tragic reception our volume tells, by analyzing the transformation of fifth-century BCE tragic practice and fourth-century BCE tragic theory into a thoroughly Christian mode of theatrical representation and spectator response.

Bibliography

Allan, William (2001), "Euripides in Megale Hellas: Aspects of the Early Reception of Greek Tragedy", in: *G&R* 48, 67–86.

Assmann, Aleida / Gaier, Ulrich / Trommsdorff, Gisela (eds.) (2004), *Positionen der Kulturanthropologie*, Frankfurt a. M.

Assmann, Jan (²1997), *Das kulturelle Gedächtnis. Schrift, Erinnerung und politische Identität in frühen Hochkulturen*, Munich.

Bagordo, Andrea (1998), *Die antiken Traktate über das Drama (mit einer Sammlung der Fragmente)*, Stuttgart.

—— (2003), *Reminiszenzen früher Lyrik bei attischen Tragikern*, Munich.

Barchiesi, Alessandro (2002), "Review of Jörg Rüpke (ed.) *Von Göttern und Menschen erzählen. Formkonstanzen und Funktionswandel vormoderner Epik*, Stuttgart 2001", in: *BMCR* 2002.06.26.

Barish, Jonas (1981), *The Antitheatrical Prejudice*, Berkeley / Los Angeles / London.

Barner, Wilfried (1973), *Produktive Rezeption: Lessing und die Tragödien Senecas*, Munich.

Bartsch, Shadi (1994), *Actors in the Audience: Theatricality and Doublespeak from Nero to Hadrian*, Cambridge/ MA.

Battezzato, Luigi (2003a), *Tradizione testuale e ricezione letteraria antica della tragedia greca: atti del convegno, Scuola Normale Superiore, Pisa 14–15 Giugno 2002*, Amsterdam.

—— (2003b), "Review of L. Bernabò Brea and M. Cavalier (2001) *Maschere e personaggi del teatro greco nelle terracotte liparesi*, Rome", in: *JHS* 123, 247–50.

Beard, Mary (2007), *The Roman Triumph*, Cambridge/ Mass.

Bernabò Brea, Luigi / Cavalier, Madeleine (2001), *Maschere e personaggi del teatro greco nelle terracotte liparesi*, Rome.

Berry, D. H. (1996), *Cicero pro P. Sulla oratio* (= Cambridge Classical Texts and Commentaries 30), Cambridge.

Bettini, Maurizio (1991), *Anthropology and Roman Culture: Kinship, Time, Images of the Soul*, translated by John Van Sickle, Baltimore.

Bevington, David (ed.) (1998), *Troilus and Cressida*, London.

Boyle, A. J. (ed.) (1983), *Seneca tragicus: Ramus Essays on Senecan drama*, Berwick, Vic.

—— (1997), *Tragic Seneca: an Essay in the Theatrical Tradition*, London.

—— (2006), *An Introduction to Roman Tragedy*, London and New York.

Braden, Gordon (1985), *Renaissance Tragedy and the Senecan Tradition: Anger's Privilege*, New Haven and London.

Braun, René (1983), "'*Honeste cadere*': un topos d'hagiographie antique", *Bulletin du Centre de Romanistique et de Latinité Tardive* (Nice) 1, 1–12.

Brink, C. O. (1971), *Horace on Poetry: the Ars poetica*, Cambridge.

Brown, Peter (1989), *The Body and Society: Men, Women and Sexual Renunciation in Early Christianity*, London.

Burke, Peter (1997), *Varieties of Cultural History*, Oxford.

Burns, Elizabeth (1972), *Theatricality: a Study of Convention in the Theatre and in Social Life*, London.

Bushnell, Rebecca (ed.) (2005), *A Companion to Tragedy*, Oxford.

Callen King, Katherine (1987), *Achilles. Paradigm of the War Hero from Homer to the Middle Ages*, Berkeley/ Los Angeles/London.

Ceccarelli, Paola (2004), "'Autour de Dionysos': remarques sur la dénomination des artistes dionysiaques", in: Christophe Hugoniot et al. (eds.), *Le statut de l'acteur dans l'antiquité grecque et romaine*, Tours, 109–142.

Cairns, Douglas / Liapis, Vayos (eds.) (2006), *Dionysalexandros* (FS Garvie), Swansea.

Champlin, Edward (2003), "Agamemnon at Rome: Roman Dynasts and Greek Heroes", in: David Braund and Christopher Gill (eds.), *Myth, History and Culture in Republican Rome: Studies in Honour of T. P. Wiseman*, Exeter, 295–319.

Chaniotis, Angelos (1997), "Theatricality Beyond the Theater: Staging Public Life in the Hellenistic World", in: Brigitte Le Guen (ed.) (1997), *De la scène aux gradins: théâtre et représentations dramatiques après Alexandre le Grand* (= *Pallas* 47), Toulouse, 219–59.

Charlton, H. B. (1946), *The Senecan Tradition in Renaissance Tragedy*, Folcroft.

Chiasson, Charles (2003), "Herodotus' Use of Attic Tragedy in the Lydian logos", in: *ClAnt* 22, 5–36.

Cohen, Walter (1997), "*Troilus and Cressida*: Introduction", in Stephen Greenblatt / Walter Cohen / Jean E. Howard / Katharine Eisaman Maus (eds.), *The Norton Shakespeare*, New York and London, 1823–32.

Conte, Gian Biago (1994), *Genre and Readers. Lucretius, Love Elegy, Plinius Encyclopedia*, Baltimore.

Cowan, Bob (2005), "Review of M. Erasmo, Roman Tragedy: Theatre to Theatricality, Austin 2004", in: *BMCR* 2005.07.53.

Cribiore, Raffaella (1996), *Writing, Teachers and Students in Graeco-Roman Egypt*, Atlanta.

—— (2001), "The Grammarian's Choice: the Popularity of Euripides' *Phoenissae* in Hellenistic and Roman Education", in: Y. L. Too (ed.), *Education in Greek and Roman Antiquity*, Leiden/ Boston/ Cologne, 241–59.

Csapo, Eric (2010), *Actors and Icons of the Ancient Theatre*, Oxford.

Dangel, Jacqueline (1995), *Accius: Oeuvres (Fragments)*, Paris.

Daube, David (1996), "Reflections on Job and Greek Tragedy", in: *SCI* 15, 72–81.

Decreus, Freddy / Kolk, Mieke (eds.) (2004), *Rereading Classics in East and West: Post-Colonial Perspectives on the Tragic*, Gent.

Dormeyer, Detlev (2005), "Bakchos in der Apostelgeschichte", in: Raban von Haehling (ed.), *Griechische Mythologie und frühes Christentum*, Darmstadt, 153–72.

Dox, Donnalee (2002), "*De tragoediis* and the Redemption of Classical Theater", in: *Viator* 33, 43–53.

—— (2004), *The Idea of the Theater in Latin Christian Thought: Augustine to the Fourteenth Century*, Ann Arbor.

Drakakis, John / Conn Liebler, Naomi (eds.) (1998), *Tragedy*, New York.

Eagleton, Terry (2003), *Sweet Violence: the Idea of the Tragic*, Oxford.

—— (2008), "Commentary", in: Rita Felski (ed.), *Rethinking Tragedy*, Baltimore, 337–46.

Easterling, Patricia E. (1993), "The End of an Era? Tragedy in the Early Fourth Century", in: Alan Sommerstein et al. (eds.), *Tragedy, Comedy and the Polis*, Bari, 559–69.

—— (ed.) (1997a), *The Cambridge Companion to Greek Tragedy*, Cambridge.

—— (1997b), "From Repertoire to Canon", in: Easterling (1997a), 211–27.

—— (2005), "*Agamemnon* for the Ancients", in: Fiona Macintosh et al. (eds.) (2005), 23–36.

—— (2006) "Sophocles: the First Thousand Years", in: John Davidson et al. (eds.), *Greek Drama III: Essays in Honour of Kevin Lee*, London, 1–15.

Easterling, P. E. / Hall, Edith (eds.) (2002), *Greek and Roman Actors: Aspects of an Ancient Profession*, Cambridge.

Edwards, Catharine (1993), *The Politics of Immorality in Ancient Rome*, Cambridge.

Elm von der Osten, Dorothee (2004), "Martyrdom Performed: on the Interrelation of Roman Comedy and Christian Martyrdom", in: Friederike Pannewick (ed.), *Martyrdom in Literature: Visions of Death and Meaningful Suffering in Europe and the Middle East from Antiquity to Modernity* (= Literaturen im Kontext 17), Wiesbaden, 77–89.

—— (2005), "Konkurrenz der Aufführungen: christliche Taufe auf römischen Bühnen. Überlegungen zu einer spätantiken Märtyrerlegende", in: Vasilios Makrides / Jörg Rüpke (eds.), *Religionen im Konflikt: vom Bürgerkrieg über Ökogewalt bis zur Gewalterinnerung im Ritual*, Münster, 73–83.

—— (2006), "Mimes into Martyrs: Conversion on Stage", in: Ian H. Henderson / Gerbern S. Oegema (eds.), *The Changing Face of Judaism, Christianity, and Other Greco-Roman Religions in Antiquity* (= Jüdische Schriften aus hellenistisch-römischer Zeit, Studien 2), Gütersloh, 87–100.

Enders, Jody (1992), *Rhetoric and the Origin of Medieval Drama*, Ithaca.

—— (1999), *The Medieval Theater of Cruelty: Rhetoric, Memory, Violence*, Ithaca.

Etman, Ahmed (1981), "Cleopatra and Antony: a Study in the Art of Plutarch, Shakespeare and Ahmed Shawky", in: *Athena* 78, 97–107.

—— (2004), "The Greek Concept of Tragedy in the Arab Culture: How to Deal with an Islamic Oedipus?", in: Freddy Decreus / Mieke Kolk (eds.), 281–99.

Falkner, Thomas (2002), "Scholars Versus Actors: Text and Performance in the Greek Tragic *scholia*", in: Easterling / Hall (eds.), 342–61.

Fantham, Elaine (1989), "The Growth of Literature and Criticism at Rome", in: George A. Kennedy (ed.), *The Cambridge History of Literary Criticism, volume 1: Classical Criticism*, Cambridge, 220–44.

—— (2002), "*Orator* and/*et Actor*", in: Easterling / Hall (eds.), 362–76.

Fantuzzi, Marco / Hunter, Richard (2004), *Tradition and Innovation in Hellenistic Poetry*, Cambridge.

Feickert, Arne (2005), *Euripidis Rhesus: Einleitung, Übersetzung, Kommentar*, Frankfurt a. M.

Felski, Rita (ed.) (2008), *Rethinking Tragedy*, Baltimore.

Flaig, Egon (2003), *Ritualisierte Politik: Zeichen, Gesten und Herrschaft im Alten Rom*, Göttingen.

Flashar, Helmut (^{2}2009), *Inszenierung der Antike. Das griechische Drama auf der Bühne. Von der frühen Neuzeit bis zur Gegenwart*, Munich (first edition published in 1991).

Flower, Harriet (1996), *Ancestor Masks and Aristocratic Power in Roman Culture*, Oxford 1996.

Foucault, Michel (1977), "Nietzsche, Genealogy, History", in: *Language, Counter-Memory, Practice: Selected Essays and Interviews*, edited, with an introduction, by D. F. Bouchard, Ithaca/ NY, 139–64.

Fraenkel, Eduard (1965), "Review of Ritchie (1964)", in: *Gnomon* 37, 228–41.

Garland, Richard (2004), *Surviving Greek Tragedy*, London.

Geertz, Clifford (1980), *Negara: The Theatre State in Nineteenth-Century Bali*, Princeton.

Gentili, Bruno (1979), *Theatrical Performances in the Ancient World: Hellenistic and Early Roman Theatre*, London.

Gildenhard, Ingo / Zissos, Andrew (1999), "'Somatic Economies': Tragic Bodies and Poetic Design in Ovid's *Metamorphoses*", in: Philip Hardie / Alessandro Barchiesi / Stephen Hinds (eds.), *Ovidian Transformations: Essays on Ovid's Metamorphoses and its Reception*, Cambridge, 162–81.

—— (2007), "Barbarian Variations: Tereus, Procne and Philomela in Ovid (*Met.* 6.412–674) and Beyond", in: *Dictynna* 4, 1–25.

Goff, Barbara / Simpson, Michael (2007), *Crossroads in the Black Aegean: Oedipus, Antigone, and Dramas of the African Diaspora*, Oxford.

Goldberg, Sander (2007), "Research Report: Reading Roman Tragedy", in: *IJCT* 13, 571–84.

Goldhill, Simon (1990), "The Great Dionysia and Civic Ideology", in: Jack Winkler / Froma Zeitlin (eds.), 97–129.

—— (1990), "Character and Action, Representation and Reading: Greek Tragedy and its Critics", in: Christopher Pelling, *Characterization and Individuality in Greek Literature*, Oxford, 100–27.

—— (2004), *Love, Sex & Tragedy: How the Ancient World Shapes Our Lives*, London.

—— (2007), *How to Stage Greek Tragedy Today*, Chicago.

—— (2008a), "Review of C. W. Kallendorf (ed.) *A Companion to the Classical Tradition*, Oxford 2006", in: *CR* 58, 290–93.

—— (2008b), "Generalizing about Tragedy", in: Rita Felski (ed.), *Rethinking Tragedy*, Baltimore, 45–65.

Graziosi, Barbara / Greenwood, Emily (eds.) (2007), *Homer in the Twentieth Century: Between World Literature and the Western Canon*, Oxford.

Gregory, Justina (ed.) (2005), *A Companion to Greek Tragedy*, Oxford.

Griffin, Jasper (1998), "The Social Function of Attic Tragedy", in: *CQ* 48, 39–61.

Habermehl, Peter (2004), *Perpetua und der Ägypter oder Bilder des Bösen im frühen afrikanischen Christentum*, 2nd ed., Berlin.

Hall, Edith (2004), "Towards a Theory of Performance Reception", in: *Arion* 12, 51–89.

—— (2007), "Greek Tragedy 430–380 BC", in: Robin Osborne (ed.), 264–87.

—— (2010), *Greek Tragedy. Suffering under the Sun*, Oxford.

Hall, Edith / Macintosh, Fiona / Wrigley, Amanda (eds.) (2004), *Dionysus Since 69: Greek Tragedy at the Dawn of the Third Millennium*, Oxford.

Hall, Edith / Macintosh, Fiona (2005), *Greek Tragedy and the British Theatre 1660–1914*, Oxford.

Hall, Edith / Macintosh, Fiona / Taplin, Oliver (eds.) (2000), *Medea in Performance 1500–2000*, Oxford.

Hall, Edith / Wyles, Rosie (eds.) (2008), *New Directions in Ancient Pantomine*, Oxford.
Halliwell, Stephen (1998), *Aristotle's Poetics*, 2ⁿᵈ ed., London.
Hanink, Johanna (2007), "Review of O. Vox, *Memoria di testi teatrali antichi*, Lecce 2006", in: *BMCR* 2007.11.23.
Hardie, Philip (1990), "Ovid's Theban History: The First Anti-*Aeneid*?", in: *CQ* 40, 224–35.
—— (1997), "Virgil and Tragedy", in: Charles Martindale (ed.), *The Cambridge Companion to Virgil*, Cambridge, 312–26.
Hardison, O. B. (1965), *Christian Rite and Christian Drama in the Middle Ages: Essays in the Origin and Early History of Modern Drama*, Baltimore.
Hardwick, Lorna (2000), *Translating Words, Translating Cultures*, London.
—— (2003), *Reception Studies*, Oxford.
—— (2007), "Decolonising the Mind? Controversial Productions of Greek Drama in Post-Colonial England, Scotland and Ireland", in: Christopher Stray (ed.), 89–106.
—— (2009), "Editorial", in: *Classical Receptions Journal* 1, 1–3.
Hardwick, Lorna / Gillespie, Carol (eds.) (2007), *Classics in Post-Colonial Worlds*, Oxford.
Hardwick, Lorna / Stray, Christopher (eds.) (2008), *A Companion to Classical Receptions*, Oxford.
Harrison, Stephen (2007), *Generic Enrichment in Vergil and Horace*, Oxford.
Holub, Robert (1984), *Reception Theory: A Critical Introduction*, London/NY.
Hutcheon, Linda (2006), *A Theory of Adaptation*, New York and London.
Jacobson, Howard (1972), "Augustine and Dido", in: *Harvard Theological Review* 65, 296–7.
—— (1983), *The Exagoge of Ezekiel*, Cambridge.
Jocelyn , H. D. (1967), *The Tragedies of Ennius*, Cambridge.
Kannicht, Richard (1991), *Musa Tragica: die griechische Tragödie von Thespis bis Ezechiel, unter Mitwirkung von R. Kannicht bearbeitet von einer Arbeitsgruppe des philologischen Seminars der Universität Tübingen* (= Studienhefte zur Altertumswissenschaft 16), Göttingen.
Karanasiou, Argyri (2002), *Die Rezeption der lyrischen Partien der attischen Tragödie in der griechischen Literatur* (= Palingenesia 78), Stuttgart.
Kelly, Henry Ansgar (1993), *Ideas and Forms of Tragedy from Aristotle to the Middle Ages*, Cambridge.
Kolb, Frank (1981), *Agora und Theater, Volks- und Festversammlung*, Berlin.
Lada-Richards, Ismene (2007), *Silent Eloquence: Lucian and Pantomime Dancing*, London.
Laird, Andrew (ed.) (2006), *Ancient Literary Criticism (Oxford Readings in Classical Studies)*, Oxford.
Lambropoulos, Vassillis (2006), *The Tragic Idea*, London.
Lape, Susan (2003), *Reproducing Athens: Menander's Comedy, Democratic Culture, and the Hellenistic City*, Princeton.
Latacz, Joachim (1995), *Achilleus. Wandlungen eines europäischen Heldenbildes* (= Lectio Teubneriana III), Stuttgart and Leipzig.
Lefèvre, Eckhard (ed.) (1978), *Der Einfluß Senecas auf das europäische Drama*, Darmstadt.
Le Guen, Brigitte (1995), "Théâtre et cités à l'époque hellénistique", in: *REG* 108, 59–90.
Leigh, Matthew (2006), "Review of M. Erasmo, Roman Tragedy: Theatre to Theatricality, Austin 2004", in: *AJP* 127, 149–52.

Lennartz, Klaus (1994), *Non verba sed vim: kritisch-exegetische Untersuchungen zu den Fragmenten archaischer römischer Tragiker*, Stuttgart.

Letoublon, Françoise (1990), "Sophocle entre Homère et Héliodore", in: *IL* 43, 3–6.

Lim, Richard (2003), "Converting the Unchristianizable: The Baptism of Stage Performers in Late Antiquity", in: Kenneth Mills / Anthony Grafton (eds.), *Conversion in Late Antiquity and the Early Middle Ages: Seeing and Believing*, Rochester, 84–126.

Lyne, Raphael (2000), "Ovid, Golding, and the 'Rough Magic' of *The Tempest*", in: A.B. Taylor (ed.), *Shakespeare's Ovid. The Metamorphoses in the Plays and Poems*, Cambridge, 150–64.

MacCormack, Sabine (1998), *The Shadows of Poetry: Vergil in the Mind of Augustine*, Berkeley, Los Angeles and London.

Macintosh, Fiona (2009), *Oedipus Tyrannus*, Cambridge.

Macintosh, Fiona / Michelakis, Pantelis / Hall, Edith / Taplin, Oliver (2005) (eds.), *Agamemnon in Performance 458 BC to 2004 AD*, Oxford.

Malinowski, Bronislaw (1931), "Culture", in: *Encyclopaedia of Social Sciences*, vol. 4, rpr. New York 1948, 621–45.

Manuwald, Gesine (2004), "Römische Tragödien und Praetexten republikanischer Zeit: 1964–2002", in: *Lustrum* 43, 11–237.

Martina, Antonio (ed.) (2003), *Teatro greco postclassico e teatro latino: teorie e prassi drammatica: atti del convengno internazionale, Roma 18–18 ottobre 2001*, Rome.

May, Regine (2006), *Apuleius and Drama: The Ass on Stage*, Oxford.

Mayer, Wendy / Allen, Pauline (2000), *John Chrysostom*, London.

Melas, Natalie (2007), *All the Difference in the World. Post-Coloniality and the Ends of Comparison*, Stanford.

Michelakis, Pantelis (2008), "Performance Reception: Canonization and Periodization", in: Lorna Hardwick / Christopher Stray (eds.), 219–28.

Miola, Robert S. (2000), *Shakespeare's Reading*, Oxford.

Morgan, Theresa (1998), *Literate Education in the Hellenistic and Roman Worlds*, Cambridge.

Nervegna, Sebastiana (2008), "Staging Scenes or Plays? Theatrical Revivals of 'Old' Drama in Antiquity", in: *ZPE* 162, 14–42.

Osborne, Robin (ed.) (2007), *Debating the Athenian Cultural Revolution. Art, Literature, Philosophy and Politics, 430–380 BC*, Cambridge.

Pace, Giovanna (2003), "Le parti della tragedia in Giovanni Tzetze *Peri tragikes poieseos*", in: Antonio Martina (ed.), 229–63.

Panayotakis, Costas (1997), "Baptism and Crucifixion on the Mimic Stage", in: *Mnemosyne* 50, 302–19.

Pattoni, Maria Pia (2005), *Longo Sofista: Dafni e Cloe*, Milan.

Parker, Robert (1983), *Miasma: Pollution and Purification in Early Greek Religion*, Oxford.

Paulsen, Thomas (1992), *Inszenierung des Schicksals: Tragödie und Komödie im Roman des Heliodor*, Trier.

Petzl, Georg / Schwertheim, Elmar (2006), *Hadrian und die dionysischen Künstler: drei in der Alexandria Troas neugefundene Briefe des Kaisers an die Künstler-Vereinigung*, Bonn.

Pollmann, Karla (1997), "Jesus Christus and Bacchus", in: *Jahrbuch für Österreichische Byzantinistik* 47, 87–106.

Poole, Adrian (2005), *Tragedy: a Very Short Introduction*, Oxford.

Potter, David (1993), "Martyrdom as Spectacle", in: Ruth Scodel (ed.) *Theater and Society in the Classical World*, Ann Arbor, 53–88.

Regenbogen, Otto (1930), "Schmerz und Tod in den Tragödien Senecas", in: *Vorträge der Bibliothek Warburg* 7, 167–218.

Rehm, Rush (2003), *Radical Greek Theatre: Greek Tragedy and the Modern World*, London.

Reid, Jane Davidson (1993), *The Oxford Guide to Classical Mythology in the Arts, 1300–1990s*, Oxford.

Revermann, Martin (1999/2000), "Tragedy and Macedon: Some Conditions of Reception", in: Martin Cropp / Kevin Lee / David Sansone (eds.), *Euripides and Tragic Theatre in the Late Fifth Century* (= Illinois Classical Studies 24–5), 451–67.

—— (2006), *Comic Business: Theatricality, Dramatic Technique, and Performance Contexts of Aristophanic Comedy*, Oxford.

—— (2008), "Reception Studies of Greek Drama", in: *JHS* 128,175–8.

Revermann, Martin / Wilson, Peter (eds.) (2008), *Performance, Iconography, Reception: Studies in Honour of Oliver Taplin*, Oxford.

Reynolds, Leighton D. / Wilson, Nigel G. (1991), *Scribes and Scholars: a Guide to the Transmission of Greek and Latin Literature*, 3rd ed., Oxford.

Rhodes, Peter (2003), "Nothing to do with Democracy: Athenian Drama and the 'Polis'", in: *JHS* 123, 104–19.

Ripoll, François (2004), "L'inspiration tragique au chant VII des Argonautiques de Valérius Flaccus", in: *RÉL* 82, 187–208.

Ritchie, William (1964), *The Authenticity of the Rhesus of Euripides*, Cambridge.

Rüpke, Jörg (2006), "Triumphator and Ancestor Rituals: between Symbolic Anthropology and Magic", in: *Numen* 53, 251–289.

Schechner, Richard (1985), *Between Theater and Anthropology*, Philadelphia.

Schierl, Petra (2006), *Die Tragödien des Pacuvius: ein Kommentar zu den Fragmenten mit Einleitung, Text und Übersetzung*, Berlin and New York.

Schiesaro, Alessandro (2003), *The Passions in Play: Thyestes and the Dynamics of Senecan Drama*, Cambridge.

—— (2005), "Roman Tragedy", in: Bushnell (ed.), 269–86.

Shirley, Frances (ed.) (2005), *Shakespeare: Troilus and Cressida (Shakespeare in Production)*, Cambridge.

Schmidt, Peter Lebrecht (1978), "Rezeption und Überlieferung der Tragödien Senecas bis zum Ausgang des Mittelalters", in: Eckhard Lefèvre (ed.), 12–73.

Schmitz, Thomas (2007), *Modern Literary Theory and Ancient Texts: an Introduction*, Oxford.

Schumacher, Claude (ed.) (2004), *Artaud on Theatre*, 2nd revised edition, Chicago.

Seidensticker, Bernt (1982), *Palintonos harmonia: Studien zu komischen Elementen in der griechischen Tragödie*, Göttingen.

Sifakis, Gregory (1967), *Studies in the History of Hellenistic Drama*, London.

Silk, Michael S. (1996), "The Greek Tragedians and Shakespeare", in: id. (ed.) *Tragedy and the Tragic: Greek Theatre and Beyond*, Oxford, 458–96.

—— (2000), *Aristophanes and the Definition of Comedy*, Oxford.

—— (2004), "Shakespeare and Greek Tragedy: Strange Relationship", in: Charles Martindale / Albert B. Taylor (eds.), *Shakespeare and the Classics*, Cambridge, 241–60.

Silk, Michael S. / Stern, Joseph Peter (1981), *Nietzsche on Tragedy*, Cambridge.

Simon, Eckehard (ed.) (1991), *The Theatre of Medieval Europe: New Research in Early Drama*, Cambridge.

Sista, M. A. (2003), "Scene di ispirazione tragica, forme vascolari, contesti tombali", in: Antonio Martina (ed.), 135–46.

34   Ingo Gildenhard and Martin Revermann

Slater, William J. (1995), "The Theatricality of Justice", in: *CB* 71, 143–57.
Small, Jocelyn Penny (2003), *The Parallel Worlds of Classical Art and Text*, Cambridge.
Staley, Gregory (2009), *Seneca and the Idea of Tragedy*, Oxford.
Steiner, George (1961), *The Death of Tragedy*, London.
— (1996), "Tragedy, Pure and Simple", in: Michael S. Silk (ed.), *Tragedy and the Tragic: Greek Theatre and Beyond*, Oxford, 534–46.
— (2008), " 'Tragedy,' Reconsidered", in: Rita Felski (ed.), 29–44.
Stray, Christopher (ed.) (2007), *Remaking the Classics: Literature, Genre and Media in Britain 1800–2000*, London.
Stroh, Wilfried (2007), *Latein ist tot, es lebe Latein! Kleine Geschichte einer grossen Sprache*, Berlin.
Suerbaum, Werner (ed.) (2002), *Handbuch der lateinischen Literatur der Antike, erster Band*, Munich.
Süss, Wilhelm (1911), *Aristophanes und die Nachwelt*, Leipzig.
Swift, Laura (2010), *The Hidden Chorus. Echoes of Genre in Tragic Lyric*, Oxford.
Taplin, Oliver (2006), "Aeschylus' *Persai* – the Entry of Tragedy into the Celebratory Culture of the 470s?", in: Douglas Cairns / Vayos Liapis (eds.), 1–10.
— (2007), *Pots & Plays: Interactions Between Tragedy and Greek Vase-Painting of the Fourth Century B.C.*, Los Angeles.
Tarrant, Richard J. (1978), "Senecan Drama and its Antecedents", in: *HSCP* 82, 213–63.
Thum, Tobias (2005), "Der *Rhesos* und die Tragödie des 4. Jahrhunderts", in: *Philologus* 149, 209–32.
Turner, Victor (1974), *Dramas, Fields, and Metaphors: Symbolic Action in Human Society*, Ithaca-London.
Valentin, Jean-Marie (2001), *Les jésuites et le théâtre (1554–1680)*, Paris.
von Haehling, Raban (2005), "Voraussehung und Willensfreiheit: die geistige Auseinandersetzung der frühen Christen mit dem Erzählgut der griechischen Tragödie", in: id. (ed.) *Griechische Mythologie und frühes Christentum*, Darmstadt, 339–58.
Versnel, Henk S. (1970), *Triumphus: An Enquiry into the Origin, Development, and Meaning of the Roman Triumph*, Leiden.
Vox, Onofrio (ed.) (2006), *Memoria di test teatrali antichi*, Lecce.
Walbank, Frank W. (1955), "Tragic History: a Reconsideration", in: *BICS* 2, 4–14.
— (1960), "History and Tragedy", in: *Historia* 9, 216–34.
Walton, J. Michael (2006), *Found in Translation: Greek Drama in English*, Cambridge.
Webb, Ruth (2005), "The Protean Performer: Mimesis and Identity in Late Antique Discussions of the Theater", in: Luisa Del Guidice and Nancy Van Deusen (eds.) *Performing Ecstasies: Music, Dance, and Ritual in the Mediterranean*, Ottawa, 3–11.
— (2008), "Basil of Caesarea and Greek Tragedy", in: Lorna Hardwick / Christopher Stray (eds.), 62–71.
Weismann, Werner (1972), *Kirche und Schauspiele. Die Schauspiele im Urteil der lateinischen Kirchenväter unter besonderer Berücksichtigung von Augustin*, Würzburg.
West, Martin L. (1987), *Euripides: Orestes*, edited with translation and commentary, Warminster.
— (2007), "A New Musical Papyrus: Carcinus, *Medea*", in: *ZPE.* 161, 1–10.
Wiles, David (2007), *Mask and Performance in Greek Tragedy: from Ancient Festival to Modern Experimentation*, Cambridge.

Wilson, Peter (1996), "Tragic Rhetoric: the Use of Tragedy and the Tragic in the Fourth Century", in: Michael S. Silk (ed.) *Tragedy and the Tragic: Greek Theatre and Beyond*, Oxford, 310–331.

—— (ed.) (2007), *The Greek Theatre and Festivals: Documentary Studies*, Oxford.

—— (2008), "Costing the Dionysia", in: Martin Revermann / Peter Wilson (eds.), 88–127.

Winkler, Jack / Zeitlin, Froma (eds.) (1992), *Nothing to Do with Dionysus? Athenian Drama in its Social Context,* Princeton.

Xanthakis-Karamanos, Georga (1980), *Studies in Fourth Century Tragedy*, Athens.

A. Getting the Show on the Road

The Classical Tragedians,
from Athenian Idols to Wandering Poets

JOHANNA HANINK

In recent years scholars of Athenian tragedy have been drawing ever more attention to the need to look more carefully into the circumstances that attended tragedy's enormously successful spread outside of Athens, throughout the Hellenic (and Hellenized) world.[1] The last decade or so has seen a great deal of research devoted to the question of to what extent tragedy, and certain tragedies in particular, may have been composed with non- (or at least not exclusively) Athenian audiences in mind;[2] studies such as these and others of ancient Greek theater have examined literary, epigraphical, and visual evidence in attempts to sketch maps and fix chronologies of the form's early diffusion in the fifth-fourth centuries BCE.[3] Here, however, I wish to consider the genre's *fortuna* from a different angle, by mining a body of evidence whose potential to contribute to our understanding of Attic tragedy's early reception stands largely under-exploited. This corpus consists in the testimonia for the reception of the tragedians themselves, rather than in the evidence for the 'afterlives' of the plays that constituted their creative output.[4]

While any reappraisal of Aeschylus, Sophocles and Euripides will necessarily operate within the framework of scholarship on tragedy (that is, the

*   I owe many thanks to the editors of this volume for reading and commenting upon earlier versions of this chapter; on the same count I owe debts of gratitude to Richard Buxton, James Diggle, Marco Fantuzzi, Richard Hunter, and Lucia Prauscello. I am also very grateful to Peter Bing and Paola Ceccarelli for allowing me to see unpublished versions of their work.
1   For a sampling see Allan 2001, esp. 66, Revermann 1999–2000, esp. 465–67, and Taplin 1999, esp. 33–34 and 55–57; see also Ceccarelli's reflections in this volume on the importance of considering how tragedy adapted itself to new local settings.
2   Important examples include Kowalzig 2008, Carter 2004, Rhodes 2003, Taplin 1999, Easterling 1997 and 1994, Hall 1996 and 1989, 160–65.
3   See Revermann 1999–2000, Dearden 1999 and Taplin 1992.
4   Palomar Pérez 1998 currently represents the largest comparative survey of the testimonia for the lives of Aeschylus, Sophocles and Euripides; it however is not explicitly a study in reception.

tragic poetry itself), this chapter takes fundamental cues from another area that has lately also seen increased interest and significant advances, namely the study of ancient literary biography.[5] In fact it is Barbara Graziosi's account of the value of the Homeric biographical traditions that has most strongly informed the approach adopted here. In her book *Inventing Homer* she argued:

> Precisely because they are fictional, early speculations about the author of the Homeric poems must ultimately derive from an encounter between the poems and their ancient audiences. For this reason they constitute evidence concerning the reception of the Homeric poems at a time in which their reputation was still in the making.[6]

Although the tragedians admittedly present fewer basic problems to the student of ancient literary biography than does the unique case of Homer (it is beyond reasonable doubt, for example, that Aeschylus, Sophocles and Euripides were individuals who actually existed and composed original tragedies for the Athenian stage), here I intend to show that the testimonia constituting the biographies of the tragedians also make for important case-studies in how, again in Graziosi's words, "authors can themselves be objects of creative processes".[7]

The specific question that I consider is that of how the tragedians' biographical traditions,[8] largely as represented by the 'Lives' (the *Vitae*) that have been transmitted in certain manuscripts containing their plays,[9] served to forge links between these poets and certain places – places that in two out of three cases (those of Aeschylus and Euripides) prove a far cry from democratic Athens. While the *Vitae* that survive from antiquity tend to rep-

---

5   On biographies of the poets see Fairweather 1974, Lefkowitz 1981 (on the concept of biographical *topoi* and the inferences made about poets' biographies on the basis of their poetry) and most recently Compton 2006 (on the notion of the poet as scapegoat). On hero-cults of poets in the *polis* see Clay 2004. Graziosi's monograph of 2002 on the biographical tradition for Homer represents a fundamental contribution to this area, especially in its methodologies. While Kris and Kurz 1979 (the English translation of the original 1935 German volume) may now be dated, the book provides a fascinating and hugely insightful comparative overview of themes and tropes in Western biographies of artists – but has been essentially overlooked by classicists writing in this area.

6   Graziosi 2002, 3. For Graziosi's programmatic statement of overall approach and the reasoning behind the scope of the work see pages 2–10.

7   Graziosi 2002, 8.

8   Lefkowitz 2007 has recently maintained that "ancient literary biographies tell us little or nothing about the poets they purport to describe", but that "they are worth studying as mythology" (n.pag.). Using the popular story of Euripides' Macedonian "exile" as a test-case, I have elsewhere argued, in the wake of Graziosi 2002, that these biographies also have the potential to tell us something about the cultural contexts within which they developed and circulated (Hanink 2008).

9   I will be using the following abbreviations: *VA* = *Vita Aeschyli*, *VE* = *Vita Euripidis* and *VS* = *Vita Sophoclis*.

resent the messy end-products of centuries of ancient and Byzantine textual accretion, abridgment and rewriting, their basic narratives do seem to have begun to coalesce relatively early on in the history of drama's reception, in the same period in which Arnaldo Momigliano first located the concrete beginnings of ancient biography as a literary form.[10] We know, for example, that many of the sources cited in these *Vitae* (e.g. Hieronymus of Rhodes, Hermippus of Smyrna, Ister and Philochorus) were at work in the third century BC. Peter Bing has also demonstrated that there were a number of ways in which the fourth and third centuries BCE witnessed a flourishing of interest in poets' biographies in particular, and he has further linked this interest with a broader 'cultural phenomenon,' an 'intense antiquarian interest in poets who are dead and gone, in the literary greats of the distant past.'[11] In the pages that follow, then, I will be exploring some of the ways in which this ancient (yet already to some extent antiquarian) biographical interest manifested itself in connection with the three giants of Attic tragedy, a literary triad effectively canonized at least as early as Aristophanes' *Frogs*.

In order to argue that certain moments and trends in antiquity's reception of tragedy may be illuminated by the evidence for the reception of the tragedians themselves, I begin by looking at the very different ways in which Lycurgus of Athens and Dionysius I of Syracuse each set a high premium on the inheritance and even "ownership" of the Attic tragedians' legacies. I then investigate the patronage narratives found in the tragedians' *Vitae*, where yet a different presentation of tragedy's "politics" serves rather to foreground the positive potential of a tragedian's association with a foreign royal patron. On this count the biographical traditions cast each of the members of the Lycurgan canon – Sophocles surprisingly included – as a kind of praise poet. By the time (and in the place) that the biographies apparently crystallized, a new way of imagining the tragedians' 'geographies' seems to have gained considerable currency, and this was a way that did much to suppress the role of Athens in these poets' life stories.

1

Modern studies of actors, interpolation and the transmission of tragic texts often invoke and interpret a passage from pseudo-Plutarch's biography of the Athenian statesman Lycurgus. This passage records how one of the new laws that Lycurgus introduced to Athens dictated

---

10   1971, 12f.
11   1993, 620.

that bronze statues of the poets Aeschylus, Sophocles and Euripides be erected and
that their tragedies be written down and conserved in a public archive, and that the
city's secretary read them out to those acting in them for the purpose of comparison.
For it was not allowed for these plays to be performed out of accordance with the
official texts. (*Decem oratorum vitae* 841f)[12]

The law, probably passed in the late 330s BC, also dates to about the time that
Aristotle would have been compiling the *didascaliae* (the tragic victory records) on the basis of the results of dramatic competitions kept on stone by the
Athenian archons.[13] Both Lycurgus' law and Aristotle's compilations might be
viewed as attempts with antiquarian motivation to take stock of, restore, establish and preserve the texts that documented the artistic (and civic) achievement
of the prior century's tragedy. But while pseudo-Plutarch's passage has raised
many questions about texts and the theater in fourth century Athens (questions regarding e.g. the role of actors, the phenomenon of re-performance, the
developing notion of a classical canon,[14] the *demos*' "policing" of cultural life,
etc.), what tends to be overlooked is how it witnesses to a wider fourth-century
phenomenon concerning the tragedians themselves, namely the consideration
and use of their names and images as sources of cultural capital. Before examining ways in which these poets were remembered and how their legacies
were appropriated abroad, it is therefore worth first developing this point of
reference for their early reception in Athens.

Tragedy played a significant role in rhetorical constructions of civic identity during Lycurgus' own era. For example, the single surviving oration by
Lycurgus himself, *Against Leocrates* (330 BCE)[15] serves as an important testament to discourses that assumed tragedy as a crucial and authoritative piece
of the city's cultural patrimony. In the *Against Leocrates*, Lycurgus accuses
Leocrates, an Athenian citizen, of violating emergency measures that had been
passed in the wake of Athens' defeat by Macedon at the Battle of Chaeronea
in September 338. Even though one of these measures effectively forbade citi-

12 On the text of the passage see esp. Prauscello 2006, 69–83. Scodel 2007 discusses
    the "social meaning of establishing a public text". On the notion of literary "ar-
    chiving" in Athens see Whitmarsh 2004, 106–21. On visual representations of the
    tragedians see *EAA s.v.* 'Eschilo', 'Sofocle' and 'Euripide'. Pausanias mentions see-
    ing Euripides and Sophocles' statues in the Theater of Dionysus (along with those of
    other playwrights) at *Periegesis* 1.21.1–2.
13 For fragments of didascalic records see *IG* II² 2318 (the dramatic "Fasti") and
    2319–23; on what the Fasti would have looked like and how they would have been
    preserved see Sickinger 1999, 41–47; on Aristotle's project of collecting them see
    Pfeiffer 1968, 82, Pickard-Cambridge 1988, 71 and West 1989.
14 On canons and classicism see especially Easterling 1997 and Porter 2006.
15 See Ober 2006 and Allen 2000 for recent interpretations of the oration, with biblio-
    graphy.

zens from leaving Attica,[16] Leocrates sailed away with his family to Rhodes and on to Megara, where he took up residence as a metic. Upon his return to Athens eight years later, he faced prosecution for having abandoned the city in its time of crisis. At one point in the oration, Lycurgus appears to have quoted fifty-five continuous lines of Euripides' *Erechtheus*,[17] a play now lost, but of whose plot we have a basic idea thanks to Lycurgus' speech[18] and a summary in pseudo-Apollodorus' *Library*:[19] when Athens was at war with the Thracians, the Delphic oracle told King Erechtheus that the only way for his city to triumph was for him to sacrifice one of his daughters.[20]

The passage that Lycurgus quotes constitutes an entire speech made by Erechtheus' wife, Praxithea, in which she explains – in rousing patriotic terms – why she has agreed to let her daughter be sacrificed for the sake of the *polis*. Commenting on the lines, Lycurgus commends not only the historical exemplum of Praxithea's decision, but also the tragedian himself for his good judgment in choosing to memorialize it in his play: "Euripides deserves our praise", he says,

> because, in addition to his other poetic virtues, he chose to make a tragedy out of this story, believing that their deeds would serve as an example that citizens could look to and study and thus acquire in their hearts the habit of loving their country. (*In Leocratem* 100, transl. Harris)

Fourth-century orators in general had a habit of appealing to the authority of fifth-century tragic poets as fonts of "implicit authority, and a storehouse of edifying moral and political models",[21] and this practice bears witness to a certain discursive substitution occurring in Athens at that time which emphasized the city's cultural prestige over its waning political might:[22] as Peter Wilson puts it, tragedy had "become for a later generation what the power of the *polis* itself was ideally for the citizens of 'Periklean' Athens – an edifying object of contemplation that will seduce its viewers, turning them into lovers."[23] This conclusion might be reinforced by other evidence from another genre entirely: we know of two fourth-century comedies called *The Euripides Lover* (Φιλευριπίδης) – a Middle Comedy by Axionicus and

---

16 *In Leocratem* 16.
17 *In Leocratem* 100 = Kannicht *TrGF* 5.1 F 360.
18 *In Leocratem* 99.
19 *Bibliotheca* 3.15.4.
20 On variants of the myth and the mythographical influence of Euripides' version see Falappone 2006, 68–74.
21 Wilson 1996, 315.
22 In the words of Glenn Most, "Athens's decline in political importance [...] was compensated by an inflationary generalization of the *topos* of its role as cultural teacher" (2006, 385).
23 Wilson 1996, 314.

a New Comedy by Philippides[24] – as well as this remarkable fragment by Philemon, quoted in the Euripidean *Vita*:

εἰ ταῖς ἀληθείαισιν οἱ τεθνηκότες
αἴσθησιν εἶχον, ἄνδρες, ὥς φασίν τινες,
ἀπηγξάμην ἄν, ὥστ' ἰδεῖν Εὐριπίδην.
(*VE* § 31 = fr. 118 Kassel-Austin)

If it were really true as some people say, men,
That the dead still had feeling,
I would have hanged myself so as to see Euripides.

Philemon's lines straightway recall not only the basic premise of Aristophanes' *Frogs*, but indeed the very spark that sets that celebrated (and first-prize winning) piece of Old Comedy into motion: in the *Frogs* Dionysus describes how, while reading Euripides' *Andromeda*, he became overwhelmed with a sudden longing (πόθος) – not to see the play performed but to see its author, Euripides, himself (52–54): "Don't make fun of me", he warns Heracles, "I'm really doing badly, such is the passion that is driving me crazy [τοιοῦτος ἵμερός με διαλυμαίνεται]" (58–9). Part of the appeal of the *Frogs*, as James Porter has persuasively shown, is that with this play "going to the theater is like going to a museum."[25] Philemon's character, too, seeks fulfillment of this "fantasy of classicism",[26] the kind of fulfillment with which Aristophanes tantalized his own spectators by putting the great tragedians onstage and back into the city's sight.

While fragments of comedy attest to a kind of nostalgic adoration of the deceased tragedians themselves,[27] the serendipitous survival of evidence for both Lycurgus' forensic and cultural activity allows an idea of how tragedy was not only invoked before the juries of Athens (and longed for on the stages), but was also becoming enshrined by the city both in textual form and bronze:[28] as the tragedians' scripts were going into the state archive, their statues were being erected in a culturally significant civic space, right outside the Theater of Dionysus.[29] And while the tragic texts, now in the form of state-

---

24   See Axionicus F 3–4 and Philippides F 22–24 Kassel-Austin.

25   2006, 302.

26   2006, 302.

27   For an account of how Old Comedy itself was largely responsible for generating the celebrity of certain tragedians, especially Euripides, see Rosen 2006. Far more testimonia exist for the reception and popularity of Euripides, antiquity's second most popular author after Homer, than for any other tragedian: see Bing 2006.

28   Lycurgus was also responsible for expanding the Theater of Dionysus and rebuilding it in stone: for the ancient testimony see Pickard-Cambridge 1946, 137; on Lycurgus' building programs more generally Habicht 1997, 16–18 and 22–30. Wilson 2000, 265–66 in particular points out that the significant ideological motivations behind this part of the Lycurgan building program.

29   *Vit. dec. or.* 841f; cf. Zanker 1995, 43.

sanctioned (even state–mandated) 'editions', were to serve as the city's memory of tragedy's words, the Lycurgan statues would have encouraged citizens to remember and to revere the very men who had authored them.[30] Aeschylus, in another passage of Aristophanes' *Frogs*, asserts that "[my] poetry did not die with me" (ἡ πόησις οὐχὶ συντέθνηκέ μοι, 868)[31], and in a sense Lycurgus' law represents a move to ensure that a certain idealized image of tragedy and its poets remained vividly alive in his city's collective memory.

2

In his studies of Hellenistic poetry, Peter Bing has shown how stories of literature's transmission to Ptolemaic Alexandria are sometimes coded as stories of the movement of objects that somehow represent or embody that literature.[32] One example of such a "transmission narrative" recounts what is perhaps now the most famous incident in the life of the tragic scripts, a sort of sequel to the tale of the Lycurgan editions.[33] Galen, in his commentary on Book III of the *Epidemics*,[34] tells of how Ptolemy (III 'Euergetes', reigned 246–222 BC) ordered any books found on ships weighing anchor at Alexandria to be seized and copied, allowing only the copies to be returned to the owners. "No small evidence" of Ptolemy III's bibliophilia, Galen goes on, was his deception of the Athenians into believing that they were only loaning "the books of Sophocles and Euripides and Aeschylus" by putting down a fifteen-talent "deposit". It was thus the Alexandrian library, and not the Athenian archive, which in the end could boast of these texts in its collection.

---

30 Zanker 1995, 43–57 shows how each of the three statues would have cast its subject as the "type" of an ideal Athenian citizen (Sophocles, the "politically active citizen"; Aeschylus, the "Athenian everyman"; Euripides, "the wise old man").

31 Plays by Aeschylus were apparently re-performed already in Aristophanes' lifetime: cf. Ar. *Ach.* 9–12 (with the *scholion* to line 10). The *Frogs* was described in antiquity as φιλόλογος ("philological"): see Porter 2006, 304 with n.6. In Aeschylus' next breath he complains that Euripides' poetry, however, did die with him – and so Euripides will have the advantage of having it to hand for recitation in Hades. Rosen argues that the passage "shows Aristophanes having great fun with contemporary notions of classicism and fan-dom" (2006, 45–46).

32 For stories relating specifically to Euripides see Bing 2006; see also Bing 2005, 127–31 on the "movement" of Arion's lyre to Alexandria in a Posidippan epigram (on which cf. also Stephens 2004, 173).

33 This is the way in which the story is regarded by e.g. Pfeiffer 1968, 82, through I subscribe to the skepticism voiced by Prauscello 2006, 74–76 in her more detailed consideration of the anecdote's context in Galen's commentary.

34 *Comm. in Hipp. epidem.* III (12 a 606–7; *CMG* V 10, 2, 1 p. 70).

There are, however, other narratives that illustrate a monarch's less deceptive (though still remarkable) contrivances to acquire the physical artifacts of tragedy. The protagonist of two of these is Dionysius I of Syracuse, the infamous tyrant of Sicily who died in 367 BC. The first story comes from a fragment ascribed to the third-century BC biographer Hermippus of Smyrna,[35] and is preserved in the *Vita Euripidis*.[36] Hermippus explains how

> following Euripides' death, Dionysius the tyrant of Sicily sent a talent to Euripides' heirs to purchase his lyre and writing-tablet and pen. And he ordered the people who procured them for him to dedicate [ἀναθεῖναι] them in the temple of the Muses, having had them inscribed with both his and Euripides' names. (*VE* § 27 = Hermippus fr. 84 Bollansée)

For this reason, Hermippus concludes, Euripides was ξενοφιλώτατος, "immensely loved by foreigners".[37] In his piece on the early reception of Euripides, Bing incisively zeroes in on how this fragment, a vivid illustration of Euripides' celebrity abroad, "goes to the heart of [Euripides'] poet's reception". Below I will return to Euripides' fame and popularity outside Athens as a crucial aspect of his reception, but for the moment I wish to linger on ancient perceptions of Dionysius' own particular and peculiar relationship with tragedy and the Athenian tragedians.

A notoriously hostile ancient historiographical tradition[38] portrayed Dionysius I of Sicily as a cruel despot and a terrible amateur poet.[39] Apart from the historical texts, it is also possible that some of the more humorous stories about Dionysius' behavior derive ultimately, like so much of the material found in biographies of poets,[40] from comic portrayals of him on the Athenian stage: a *Dionysius*, for example, is ascribed to Eubulus, a fourth-century BC poet of Middle Comedy,[41] and it may even be the case that Euripides himself featured among the *dramatis personae* of this play.[42] On the other hand Lucian's *Ignorant Book Collector* (second

---

35   Called "the Callimachean" in Athenaeus' *Deipnosophistae* (at 58f, 213f and 696f). On Hermippus' biographies of the tragedians see Bollansée (1999, 98–100).
36   H, Q and V; *Vita Euripidis* = Kannicht *TrGF* 5.1 T 1 (the 'Γένος καὶ βίος Εὐριπίδου').
37   Bing 2006.
38   For a summary and reevaluation of which see Sanders 1987, 1–40. This tradition is ascribed largely to the historian Timaeus; on Polybius and Diodorus Siculus' criticisms of Timaeus see Brown 1958, 91–108.
39   Though Dionysius did supposedly win a festival victory at the Lenaea of 367 BC with a Ἕκτορος Λύτρα (*Ransom of Hector*), Diod. Sic. 15.74.1. Dionysius' excessive joy at his victory was, in one tradition, the cause of his death: cf. Pliny *NH* 7.180 = Snell *TrGF* 1 Dionysius T 8. On Dionysius' activity as a tragedian see esp. Hunter 1983, 116–17 and Sanders 1987, 1–5.
40   This is a central thesis of Lefkowitz 1981.
41   For which see the edition of Hunter 1983.
42   See Hunter 1983, 117: "If fr. 27 [= K.A. fr. 26] is spoken by Euripides […], then it is tempting to imagine a scenario in which he came back from Hades to protest that

century AD) preserves an anecdote that similarly to Hermippus' depicts Dionysius as desperate to acquire the Athenian tragedians' possessions.[43] Lucian suggests that this zeal was motivated by the tyrant's own poetic failures:[44]

> When Dionysius finally figured out that everyone was laughing at him [because of his terrible tragedies], he went to great lengths to get his hands on Aeschylus' wax-tablets, thinking that through the tablets he too would be divinely inspired [ἔνθεος]. Nevertheless, when he wrote upon it he composed things far more ridiculous [μακρῷ γελοιότερα]...[45] (*Adversus Indoctum* 15)

Dionysius, then, was apparently remembered in antiquity not only for his attempts to link his name with that of Euripides (as in Hermippus' account), but for appealing to what he considered the talismanic powers of the physical artifacts surviving from the creative processes of the classical tragedians. Taken together, Hermippus and Lucian's stories portray a Dionysius who believed that ownership of the poets' writing materials could make him heir to the poetic geniuses and legacies of their former owners. This notion that Dionysius hoped, by using Aeschylus' tablets, to become similarly ἔνθεος also nods to an ancient tradition that considered the works of the classical tragedians as having been divinely inspired.[46] But while Aeschylus, Sophocles and Euripides may have had the Muses to aid their art, in Lucian's account we see the epigonal and untalented Dionysius looking to the earlier poets themselves – and specifically to their relics – for his own source of *enthousiasmos*.[47]

The narrated tragic relic-collecting of Dionysius thus reveals certain beliefs (whether held by Dionysius himself or exaggerated by the many authors

---

such a λωβητὴς τέχνης as Dionysius had enjoyed the dramatic success which he himself had notoriously failed to win."

43   The two anecdotes may represent variant versions of the same story.

44   Bing 2006 cites the Aeschylean story at n.2. On Dionysius' reputation for incompetence as a poet see esp. Cicero *Tusculan Disputations* 5.22 (=Snell *TrGF* 1 Dionysius T 6).

45   Cf. Karavas 2005, 217.

46   Cf. e.g. Athenaeus 1.19e, where we hear that the Athenians allowed the marionetteer Potheinus to use the same stage as that which had been used by Euripides and his contemporaries for their "divinely-inspired plays" (ἀφ᾽ ἧς ἐνθουσίων οἱ περὶ Εὐριπίδην) (= Kannicht *TrGF* 5.1 T 224).

47   The idea that poets performed under the influence of the god is articulated by Socrates in Plato's *Ion* (for the "presupposti culturali" of Socrates' arguments see Velardi 1989, 95–113; cf. also Plato *Apology* 22b – which is even cited in the *scholia* to Aeschylus' *Seven Against Thebes*, *ad* 593–4). On Aeschylus and Sophocles' divine "initiations" see Palomar Pérez 1998, 66–68. For another way in which the tragedians were Muse-like see Lada-Richards 2002, 71, who argues that in dramatic performances the Muse's "pivotal mediating function has now become amalgamated with the role of the *poeta creator* himself: the dramatist 'plays Muse' to this stage-actor, the professional performer who will bring his creations into being".

who lampooned him) about what means were available for the transmission and appropriation of literary heritage. In fervently acquiring the personal effects of tragedians, Dionysius is represented as seeking to come into possession on the one hand of their artistic talent (or divine inspiration), but on the other of the patrimony for which these physical objects stood and which itself held the power to legitimize his own attempts at tragic composition. His case thus represents another instance illustrating the commodification of the legacies of the tragedians themselves, again an important element in processes of tragedy's reception: while in Lycurgus' Athens the city's bid for this inheritance manifested itself in part through the public display of portrait statues, in Sicily we see Dionysius hopefully considering his private ownership of Aeschylus and Euripides' pens, tablets and lyres as the key to following in their poetic footsteps.

3

In the second part of the fourth century certain rhetoricians praised the tragedians for having used their art to stage Athenian patriotism. In the first half of the century, however, Plato appears to have taken a less idealistic view of the same poets' civic virtues and value when he portrayed Socrates as condemning the tragedians (and explicitly Euripides) for their tendency to glorify tyrants. In *Republic* 8, for example, Glaucon (an older brother of Plato's) agrees with Socrates that tragedy is a wise thing and that tyrants are wise for keeping company with tragedians (568a-b). He observes that Euripides

> sings the praises [ἐγκωμιάζει] of tyranny as something godlike and says many other such things – both Euripides and the other poets do this.

Socrates is of the same mind, and responds to Glaucon with a conclusion about the relationship between tragedians and the ideal society that looks wholly contradictory to Lycurgus' appraisal of tragedy's value later in the century:

> Since, then, they are wise [σοφοὶ ὄντες], the poets of tragedy will forgive us and those who have governments similar to ours, for not welcoming them into our state [πολιτείαν], lauding [ὑμνητάς] tyranny as they do. (8.568b)

After all, for the Socrates of the *Republic* mimetic poetry in general is capable of effecting degradation from the philosophical to the tyrannical soul,[48] and its poet should be barred from the well-ordered (εὐνομεῖσθαι) city, since he fosters (τρέφει) a part of the soul other than that which is the best (βέλτιστον, 10.605b).

---

48   Ferrari 1989, 139, comparing in particular *Republic* 10.606d and 9.578b.

At this point, however, I wish to pursue a third interpretation of tragedy's (or really the tragedians') politics, the evidence for which comes from
two of the ancient biographies. The *Vitae* of Aeschylus and Euripides foreground narratives of each poet's visit to places far from Athens; both poets
are said to have worked and died at the court of a magnanimous foreign king
– Aeschylus in Sicily at the court of King Hieron of Syracuse (reigned 478–
467 BC), and Euripides in Pella at the court of King Archelaus of Macedon
(reigned 413–399 BC).[49] In these *Vitae* the relationship between "tyranny"
and the tragedian is, as it is for Plato's Socrates, certainly explicit, but here
the relationship is cast as a positive and productive one. From these texts
we hear of how the two tragedians were received far more warmly by the
monarchs who hosted them than by their fellow countrymen. In fact, the
"exiles" of both poets from their common native city are explained in both
Vitae by some injustice or calamity that they suffered at the hands of the
Athenians.[50] Importantly, moreover (see further below), the two biographies
each name one drama which the poet composed in honor of his royal patron: when Hieron was founding the colony of Aetna, Aeschylus – whom
Macrobius would later call *vir utique Siculus*[51] – produced the *Aetnaeae* to
augur a good life for the city's synoecists;[52] half a century later, Euripides is
supposed to have written his *Archelaus* (about the mythical Archelaus, first
king of Macedon) for his patron and friend the Macedonian king.[53] Both
narratives thus seem to reflect traditions about tragedy characterized by a de-

---

49 On patronage and the tragedians see Bremer 1991. For Aeschylus in Sicily see esp.
    Cataudella 1963, Herington 1967 and Griffith 1978; on Euripides in Macedon see
    esp. Revermann 1999–2000, and Scullion 2003 (from whose view I depart, see
    Hanink 2008).

50 Aeschylus' *Vita* cites three explanations for his departure (1) his defeat by a young
    Sophocles (cf. Plutarch *Vita Cimonis* 8.483f) or (2) Simonides, and (3) the terrify-
    ing appearance of the chorus in the *Eumenides* (infants died and pregnant women
    miscarried) (§ 8–9). Euripides' *Vita* explains that when the comic poets ridiculed
    him (because of their jealousy, φθόνος; see esp. Stevens 1956), he disdained their
    abuse (ὑπεριδὼν δὲ πάντα) and left to live in Macedon until his death (*VE* § 35).
    See Compton 2006, 139 for a reading of Euripides as a *pharmakos* forced to leave
    his city. We also hear that Plato, e.g., was relentlessly mocked in comedy (Diogenes
    Laertius 3.22).

51 *Saturnalia* 5.19.17 = Radt *TrGF* 3 T 91. The phrase is usually cited in discussions
    of Aeschylus' "Sicilianisms" (cf. Athenaeus 9.376c = Radt *TrGF* 3 T 92a, Herington
    1967, 78–79, Griffith 1978).

52 *VA* § 9: ἐπεδείξατο τὰς Αἴτνας οἰωνιζόμενος βίον ἀγαθὸν τοῖς συνοικίζουσι τὴν
    πόλιν. Dougherty discusses the poetry created for the founding of Aetna, where "Ae-
    schylus, Simonides [*PMG* F 552] and Pindar [*Pythian* 1] all celebrated the colonial
    moment in choral song" (1993, 88).

53 *VE* § 11: χαριζόμενος αὐτῷ δρᾶμα ὁμονύμως ἔγραψε. On the play see esp. the edi-
    tion and commentary of Harder 1987. Bremer 1991, 39–44 summarizes the *Aet-
    naeae* and *Archelaus* with short juxtaposed analyses; see also Taplin 1999, 41–42.

gree of "de-Athenianization": effectively extracting two of the genre's most important authors from their (and tragedy's) native city, the stories depict the foreign kings and communities who welcomed them as far better judges of their poetry's worth.

If fourth-century Athenian orators connected tragedy and the tragedians closely with Athens, and particularly with certain ideals of Athenian citizenship, it is then perhaps surprising that two members of Lycurgus' tragic canon should in their *Vitae* be so directly and successfully associated with foreign monarchs. In post-classical antiquity, however, both Aeschylus and Euripides were considered to have been paradigmatic participants in what were perceived as the "ancient" systems of literary patronage.[54] For example, in the second century CE Pausanias tells of seeing the cenotaph of Euripides and tomb of Menander among the monuments lining the road that led from Athens to the Peiraeus. When Pausanias explains that the actual tomb of Euripides is in Macedon because he died there while a guest of Archelaus, he reflects on how "even back then" (καὶ τότε) kings played hosts to poets. In a short list of other, earlier examples of poets and patrons, he then also mentions the names of Aeschylus and Hieron:[55]

> Even then poets went to the courts of kings, and still earlier Anacreon went to the court of Polycrates, tyrant of Samos, and Aeschylus and Simonides traveled to Hieron in Syracuse. (*Periegesis* 1.2.3)

Likewise Plutarch in his *De Exilio* (an early second-century essay of consolation to an exiled friend) mentions the travels and patronage of Aeschylus and Euripides in the same breath, although he glosses over any suggestion that problems in Athens were what lay behind their departure.[56] He also claims that few of the wisest and most sensible men are buried in their native countries, and that most of those who died abroad left their homelands "forced by no one" (μηδενὸς ἀναγκάζοντος, 604d). Quoting nine verses by Euripides in praise of Athens (from two different passages, one of which is from the *Erechtheus* and contains lines also quoted by Lycurgus[57]), he asks who else has ever produced such an encomium of his native land (τῆς ἑαυτοῦ πατρίδος ἐγκώμιον) yet reminds us that Euripides left that land to live at the court of Archelaus.[58] Like Pausanias, Plutarch presses on with

---

54   For an overview of these see Hunter-Rutherford 2009, 9–13 and Bremer 1991.

55   For a survey of royal patronage of poets from archaic to Hellenistic times see Hunter 2003, 24–45; on patronage and the poetics of praise in the archaic period see esp. Goldhill (1991, 116–28).

56   This idea contradicts Plutarch's account in the *Life of Cimon* of how Aeschylus left for Sicily out of anger (δι' ὀργήν) after being defeated by Sophocles (483f).

57   Kannicht *TrGF* 5.1 360.7–10 (*Erechtheus*) and 5.2 981 (*adespoton*).

58   604e.

other examples of poets who did the same: Aeschylus, Simonides, Herodotus and Homer.[59]

What may then be even more surprising about the biographies than the very prominence of the foreign narratives is how favorably the royal patrons are characterized within those narratives – here for example we find no trace of the tyrannical ruler with a penchant, as Dionysius I notoriously had, for banishing court poets to the quarries.[60] Rather we hear that Aeschylus was "exceedingly honored" by Hieron and the Geloans[61] and that Euripides was likewise "very successful" at Archelaus' court (so much so that he was put in charge of the royal finances).[62] And yet it seems unlikely that the Athenians – at least Athenians of Lycurgus' (and Demosthenes') political leanings – would have been well-disposed toward seeing any Macedonian king in the flattering light cast on Archelaus, not just in Euripides' *Vita*, but throughout his biographical tradition.[63] It had been the Macedonians, led by King Philip, who slaughtered the Athenian and Theban forces at Chaeronea in 338, and thus it was the threat of Macedonian invasion that triggered the emergency measures Lycurgus sought to uphold in his *Against Leocrates*, in part by invoking Euripides' name and poetry. The two years following Philip's death in 336 had then seen two Athenian rebellions against expanding Macedonian power,[64] and the decade came to a close with Demosthenes impassionedly reprising, in his speech *On the Crown*, the rhetorical barrage against Macedon that had marked his *Olynthiacs* and *Philippics* in more or less the previous decade.[65] The existence of a vigorous anti-Macedonian discourse in the mid-

---

59 On this passage see Herington 1967, 77–78. He maintains that Pausanias and Plutarch had the same source: "One might surmise that a handbook of *exempla*, containing a chapter on 'Famous Literary Exiles', underlies both lists" (p. 78 n.23).

60 A popular ancient story told of how Dionysius sent the dithyrambic poet Philoxenus of Cythera to the Syracusan quarries after he expressed a negative opinion about some of Dionysius' poetry (Cicero *Ad Atticum* 4.6.2; Plu. *De tran. an.* 471e-d; Lucian *Ind.* 15; Aelian *VH* 13.44). Hieron himself is said by Diodorus to have been exceedingly cruel, especially in relation to his well-liked brother Gelon (whom he succeeded) (11.67.4–5).

61 *VA* § 10 (cf. § 11): σφόδρα ...τιμηθείς.

62 *VE* § 11: μάλα <εὖ> ἔπραττε παρ᾽αὐτῷ [i.e. Archelaus] ὥστε καὶ ἐπὶ τῶν διοικήσεων ἐγένετο. On details of Archelaus' supposed generosity see [Euripides] *Epistle* 5.

63 The perception of a good, close relationship between Euripides and Archelaus reflected in Satyrus Fr. 6 fr. 39 XVIII, Aulus Gellius *N.A.* 15.20.9 (*Is* [sc. Euripides] *cum in Macedonia apud Archelaum regem esset utereturque eo rex familiariter, ...*), Plutarch *Regum et imper. Apothegm.* 177a, [Euripides] *Epistles*.

64 In 336, when the Macedonian army proclaimed Alexander King (see Bosworth 1988, 188) – Alexander had promised to continue his father's policies: Diod. Sic. 17.2, Justin 11.1.7–10 – and in 335 BC, when false reports of Alexander's death reached Athens and Thebes (see Habicht 1997, 14–15).

65 "The outcome of the trial represented a political triumph for Demosthenes; it also

fourth century, coupled with the orators' habit of invoking classical tragedy to illustrate Athenian democratic ideals, makes it difficult to accept that a vision of Archelaus' cultured magnanimity belonged to contemporary Athenian lore. Likewise, it is doubtful that the representation of Aeschylus' warm Sicilian welcome at the court of Hieron (contrasted with the maltreatment by his countrymen) represented a popular Athenian version of events: in both Aeschylus' and Euripides' cases we should be highly wary of assuming that these narratives took their essential, final shape in democratic Athens.

Instead, it is more plausible that the stories surrounding Aeschylus and Euripides' patronage reflect one of the mechanisms by which tragedy's spread through the Greek world achieved a certain discursive justification: namely through the molding of the tragedians' biographies.[66] Elsewhere I have argued that, regardless of the real truth of the story, Euripides' stay in Macedon became so emphasized in his biography because the tradition for it was largely a product of a time and place (third-century BC Alexandria) whose rulers (the Ptolemies) wanted to present themselves as the legitimate heirs to the legacy of Euripides' – and by extension tragedy's – patronage.[67] And while it is impossible to pinpoint the chronological or geographical provenances of the testimonia for these biographical traditions, their overriding dissonance with our idea of Athens' own sense of its cultural primacy and patrimony, at least in the fourth century BC, makes it reasonable to suspect that they are products of a different context. It is also worth noting that Aeschylus' and Euripides' patronage narratives are effectively distributed between the two places in the Greek world outside of Athens, namely Magna Graecia and Macedon, where evidence for tragedy's early popularity is most abundant. The primary speaker in Satyrus' biography of Euripides (late third or early second century BC[68]) even remarks that the Athenians only ever learned to love Euripides because of the example set for them by precisely these two groups of foreigners:

> It is not worthwhile to mention [the taste] of the Athenians, since they at any rate learned later what a great poet [Euripides] was, from the Macedonians and Sicilians.[69] (Fr. 6 fr. 39 XIX Schorn)

---

    indicated clearly that popular opposition to Macedonia was still widespread, and that Macedonia was indeed the prime target of Athenian national sentiment" (Habicht 1997, 28).

66   The study of Kowalzig 2008, however, historicizes the evidence for Aeschylus' time in Sicily and makes an important case for the political and economic importance and implications of tragedy's early arrival on the island.

67   Hanink 2008.

68   The standard edition of Satyrus is Schorn 2004, though Arrighetti 1964, an edition only of the βίος of Euripides, remains useful for its introduction and notes. On the dates of Satyrus see West 1974, who argues he was a peripatetic of Aristotle's school in Athens – not an Alexandrian scholar.

69   Euripides seems to have been sympathetic to others in the same situation: he suppos-

As we shall see, the speaker in Satyrus' dialogue is in fact participating in a larger discussion about where memory of Aeschylus and Euripides was most legitimately located, whether in their native Athens or in the foreign lands where they were buried and whose people had better appreciated them.

4

In the light of the stories of the tragedians' deaths abroad, it is not particularly surprising that threads of the debate over "ownership" of their legacies run strong in sepulchral epigram, where a persistent theme in the epitaphs for both Aeschylus and Euripides is the fact of the foreign gravesite. An epitaph by Antipater of Thessalonica, for example, describes Aeschylus as "doing honor to Trinacria [i.e. Sicily] with his tomb" (4)[70] – even though Aeschylus' *Vita* suggests that the honor flowed primarily in the opposite direction, since it was the Geloans who honored him with burial in their city cemetery (§ 11).[71] In another epigram, ascribed to Diodorus of Sardis, the tombstone informs passersby that Aeschylus lies "by the white waters of Gela in Sicily, far from the Cecropian [i.e. Athenian] land".[72] An epitaph ascribed to Ion of Chios calls Euripides the "glory of Athens" (κόσμον Ἀθηνῶν), and rationalizes that his tomb is in Pella since, as a servant of the Muses, he desired to dwell near Pieria.[73]

Other epitaphs for Euripides not only underscore the strangeness of his final resting place, but account for it by engaging their poetics in longstanding discourses about memory's localization. The poem supposedly inscribed on Euripides' cenotaph (the same monument mentioned by Pausanias), attributed in Euripides' *Vita* to either Thucydides or Timotheus, declares that in reality it is "all Hellas" that serves as Euripides' funeral monument (μνῆμα):

Μνῆμα μὲν Ἑλλὰς ἅπασ' Εὐριπίδου· ὀστέα δ' ἴσχει
γῆ Μακεδών, τῇ γὰρ δέξατο τέρμα βίου.

---

edly consoled and encouraged Timotheus when he was criticized by the Greeks for his musical innovation (καινοτομία): Satyrus Fr. 6 fr. 39 XXII Schorn, Plutarch *An seni* 795d.

70   Antipater XIII Gow-Page = *AP* 7.39

71   See Wilson 2007, esp. 356–57.

72   Diodorus XIII Gow-Page = *AP* 7.40. The epigram goes on to bewail the φθόνος that plagues the "descendents of Theseus." On the epitaph Aeschylus supposedly composed for himself (Athenaeus 14.627c, Pausanias 1.14.5; cf.*Vita Aeschyli* § 11) see Sommerstein 1995–96.

73   Ion of Chios 8 Diehl = *AP* 7.44: ὡς ἂν ὁ λάτρις | Πιερίδων ναίης ἀγχόθι Πιερίης (lines 5–6; cf. *AP* 7.43 – also ascribed to Ion of Chios – lines 1–2). The attribution of the epigrams to Ion is considered spurious (see most recently Leurini 2000, 84).

πατρὶς δ' Ἑλλάδος Ἑλλάς, Ἀθῆναι. πολλὰ δὲ μούσαις
τέρψας ἐκ πολλῶν καὶ τὸν ἔπαινον ἔχει. (*VE* § 14 = *AP* 7.45)

All Hellas is the funeral monument of Euripides; yet the Macedonian ground holds his bones, since there he met with the end of his life. But his fatherland was the Hellas of Hellas, Athens. Since he often delighted others with the Muses, he has the praise of many.

The phrase "all Hellas" (ἅπασα Ἑλλάς) also appears in Thucydides' *Histories*,[74] and in other respects the epigram echoes ideology expressed in the Thucydidean account of Pericles' funeral oration – regardless of the truth of the attribution to Thucydides, the epigram would seem to engage with his work. For example, while the author of the epitaph calls Athens the "Hellas of Hellas", in the second book of the *Histories* Pericles claims that the whole of Athens is "the school of Hellas": λέγω τήν τε πᾶσαν πόλιν τῆς Ἑλλάδος παίδευσιν εἶναι (2.41.1).[75] Even more striking are the ideological points of contact with Pericles' identification of the *epitaphios logos* itself as a kind of sepulcher (τάφος). The Athenian dead, he says, have won unaging praise (ἀγήρων ἔπαινον; cf. line 4 of *AP* 7.45 above) and the most distinguished of all tombs (τὸν τάφον ἐπισημότατον), which is

> not the one in which they lie, but the one in which their glory survives in everlasting remembrance, celebrated on every occasion which gives rise to word of eulogy or deed of emulation. (2.41.2, transl. Smith)

Thucydides' Pericles goes on to explain:

> For the whole world is the sepulcher [τάφος] of famous men, and it is not the epitaph upon monuments set up in their own land that alone commemorates them, but also in lands not their own there abides in each breast an unwritten memorial [ἄγραφος μνήμη] of them, planted in the heart rather than graven on stone. (2.41.3, transl. Smith)

The author of the epitaph of Euripides however adjusts the "Periclean" model of memory to discount the significance of the presence of Euripides' grave in a foreign land, just as Pericles suggests that *logos* (μνήμη) has the power to surmount the geographical restriction of a fixed *ergon* (the τάφος itself).[76] Many praise Euripides, just as many will always praise the Athenian dead.

---

74 *Hist.* 1.123, 1.143, 2.8, 6.92. Note that in one of the *Epistles* of [Euripides] Euripides writes a letter of condolence to Sophocles for a shipwreck on the way to Chios. Apparently some of Sophocles' plays were lost, and 'Euripides' calls this misfortune a loss precisely to all Greece, 'ἅπασα Ἑλλάς': ἦν τίς οὐχὶ κοινὴν ἁπάσης Ἑλλάδος νομίσειεν ἄν; (2.1).

75 A comparison recognized also by Gomme 1956 *ad loc.*, who paraphrases Hippias of Elis' claim in *Protagoras* 337d: "all men of science and learning are by nature akin and fellow citizens, and here in Athens they were συνεληλυθότας τῆς Ἑλλάδος εἰς αὐτὸ τὸ πρυτανεῖον τῆς σοφίας." On the *topos* of Athens as the "school of Greece" see Most 2006.

76 Cf. Loraux 1986, 78: "after proclaiming the superiority of ergon over logos, [Peri-

This conceptual slippage, between τάφος as "tomb" and τάφος as the "repository of memory", also appears in another sepulchral epigram for Euripides, supposedly by Adaeus of Mytilene.[77] Although conceding that Euripides' body lies in Macedon (where it is "honored by the companionship of Archelaus", ἑταιρείῃ τίμιος Ἀρχέλεω), Adaeus rhetorically dispels the idea that this is the site of his true τάφος:

σοὶ δ᾽ οὐ τοῦτον ἐγὼ τίθεμαι τάφον, ἀλλὰ τὰ βάκχου
βήματα καὶ σκηνὰς ἐμβάδι σειομένας.[78]
(3.15–16 G-P = *AP* 7.51.5–6)

However, I do not consider this your tomb, but rather the stages of and scene-paintings of Bacchus that quake with the step of buskins.

Yet while what remains of a tradition of sepulchral epigram for Euripides attempts to disassociate him from the land of his body's final resting place, an anecdote from Aulus Gellius' *Attic Nights* intimates that the Macedonians themselves held very dear the fact that the location of his grave was in their country: not only did they firmly deny a request from an Athenian delegation to send Euripides' remains back to Athens,[79] they also eagerly and faithfully tended the tomb:

The Macedonians regarded his tomb and his memory with such honor that as a kind of boast they would declare "never, Euripides, shall your tomb perish" [οὔποτε σὸν μνῆμα, Εὐριπίδης, ὄλοιτό που], because an exceptional poet had died and was buried in their land. (*N.A.* 15.20.10)

Here the μνῆμα that the Macedonians declare will never be destroyed does the double work, just as the word τάφος does in Thucydides and Adaeus, of signifying not only the grave monument itself but also the community's memory of the poet, who was now apparently honored by the Macedonians as a *de facto* "local" one.[80]

5

The manuscript-transmitted *Vitae* of Aeschylus and Euripides, in addition to other testimonia found elsewhere (e.g. in Pausanias and Plutarch), serve to normalize the travels of the two poets as well as to portray them as having been best appreciated outside of Athens, in foreign lands. Yet we have now

---

cles' speech] reverses the order of values by substituting for the soldiers' real grave, initially exalted as ergon, a purely symbolic monument (*taphos*)."

77 Adaeus 3 G-P = *AP* 7.51.

78 Hartung: πειθομένας codd.

79 *N.A.* 15.20.9: *maximo consensu Macedones in ea re deneganda perstiterunt.* Cf. Hanink 2008 on the Macedonian appropriation of Euripides.

80 The *Suda* reports that Euripides died when he was 75, whereupon Archelaus "moved his bones to Pella".

also seen that in certain sepulchral epigrams it is possible to trace an argument that seeks to "repatriate" to Athens the memory of Euripides (since attempts at recuperating his remains evidently proved unsuccessful), or to locate his memory in "all Hellas" and on every stage. In these epigrams, the battle for a tragedian becomes a battle for ownership of the literary past: thus while some people may have desired to possess images and artifacts (and even physical remains!) of these poets, the authors of the epigrams rely rather on the power of their epitaphic rhetoric so as to construct certain "sites" of literary memory.

But what of the near-wholesale absence of Sophocles from this sketch of the tragedians' celebrity and "internationalization"? In stark contrast with Aeschylus and Euripides, the *Vita* of Sophocles suggests that this tragedian closely resembled Socrates in his preference to remain at home in Athens.[81] Because Sophocles loved his city so much, apart from his military service he never left it:

> Such a lover of Athens (φιλαθηναιότατος) was he that, even with many kings sending for him, he never wanted to leave his fatherland (τὴν πατρίδα) behind. (*VS* § 10)

This part of Sophocles' story reflects one aspect of the difference that sets his biographical tradition apart from the other two canonical tragedians: wherever Aeschylus and Euripides failed personally and professionally, Sophocles seems to have succeeded and so to have exemplified what has been described as "the Pindaric line of development in poetic *vitae*, the positive life".[82] Whereas, for example, the characters and plots of Euripides' plays earned him a notorious reputation for impiety,[83] Sophocles' biography quotes the historian Hieronymus of Rhodes[84] (fr. 43a White) in claiming that Sophocles loved the gods as no one else.[85] He was remembered as an ac-

---

81   Cf. Plato *Crito* 52b, where Socrates, speaking to himself as the "Laws", says: "Socrates, we have great proofs of these things, namely that both we [i.e. the laws] and the city have pleased you. For you would have never stayed home in [the city] more than all other Athenians unless it pleased you more than them." It was also a popular story that Menander rejected invitations from Ptolemy I Soter to work at his court in Alexandria: cf. Alciphron *Epistles* 18 and 19 Avezzù-Longo and Pliny *N.H.* 7. 30.31.

82   Compton 2006, 130.

83   Sophocles' *Vita* (§ 11) says he held the priesthood of Halon (ἡ τοῦ Ἅλωνος ἱερωσύνη) According to Satyrus (F 6 fr. 39 X Schorn) Euripides was accused of ἀσεβεία by Cleon. *P. Oxy* 2400 (3rd c. AD) contains a list of subjects for rhetorical exercises; in one the orator must address the charge of Euripides' impiety: Εὐρειπίδης [sic] Ἡρακλέα μαινόμενον ἐν Διονυσίοις ποιήσας ἐν δράματι κρίνεται ἀσεβείας.

84   Hieronymus was a member of Aristotle's school, active in the first half of the third c. BC. He wrote a Περὶ ποιητῶν in four or more books: see T 40 in Matelli 2006, 289–314.

85   θεοφιλὴς ὁ Σοφοκλῆς ὡς οὐκ ἄλλος, *VS* § 12. On Sophocles and Asclepius see Radt *TrGF* 4 T 67–73 (pages 57–58). For skepticism that Sophocles was heroized as Dexion, the "receiver" of Asclepius, see first Lefkowitz 1981, 84, whose doubts

complished, devout and loyal citizen, chosen to serve as both *hellenotamias* and *proboulos*; he is also said to have led the paean at the sacrifices celebrating the Athenian victory at the Battle of Salamis (*VS* § 3) and to have been elected general during the Samian War (440–439 BC) (*VS* § 9). Euripides, on the other hand, lived a life antithetical to what we now think of as the fifth-century Athenian civic ideal of political engagement,[86] since he supposedly passed his days thinking and writing in a cave on Salamis, "shunning the crowd" (*VE* § 21). The *Vita Euripidis* offers this grim general appraisal of his character:

> he came off as sullen and anxious and severe, a hater of laughter and a hater of women (*VE* § 22)[87]

And while Aeschylus' *Vita* gives few indications as to his personal qualities, Sophocles' biography sketches a portrait of an all-around affable individual, whose personality was entirely the opposite of Euripides':

> Put simply, [Sophocles] had such a charming disposition (τοσαύτη τοῦ ἤθους αὐτῷ γέγονε χάρις) that everyone everywhere loved him.[88] (*VS* § 7)

The contrast between Sophocles and Euripides' character emerges even more explicitly if we consider the use of the adjective φιλαθηναιότατος for Sophocles (*VS* § 10, quoted above) in the light of the epithet that Hermippus of Smyrna had claimed was often used of Euripides. Earlier I mentioned that Hermippus cites the story about Dionysius of Syracuse's purchase of Euripides' harp, tablet and stylus as an illustration of why Euripides was said to be extremely beloved by foreigners (ξενοφιλώτατος):

> And so they say he was ξενοφιλώτατος, since he was so loved by foreigners, for he was victim of the Athenians' jealousy. (*VE* § 27 = Hermippus fr. 84 Bollansée)

Hermippus claims this was a word used particularly of Euripides (it is attested nowhere else in the superlative), and φιλαθηναιότατος[89] is also extremely rare and elsewhere applied with sincerity only to Socrates (Demosthenes

---

are elaborated by Connolly 1998. Sophocles' piety was proverbial, cf. Libanius *Ep.* 390.9. The most extensive recent treatment of the supposed (private) cult of Sophocles-Dexion is Clay 2004, 78–79.

86 Cf. for example the passage in Thucydides where, during the funeral oration, Pericles remarks that Athenians do not consider the politically disengaged man to be unengaged, but useless (οὐκ ἀπράγμονα, ἀλλ' ἀχρεῖον, 2.40).

87 Cf. Satyrus Fr. 6 fr. 39 IX Schorn: 'everyone hated him' (ἀπήχθοντ' αὐτῶι πάντες), men because of his anti-socialness (δυσομιλία), women because of how he portrayed them in his plays.

88 See Pelling 1990, 235–44, on the "integrated personalities" presented in Plutarch, for an account of the relatively simplistic descriptions of individual character generally found in ancient biography.

89 Libanius *Declamation* 2.1.33; Libanius also uses it of an undefined 'someone' (τις) in *Declamation* 14.1.14.

uses it sarcastically of King Philip II of Macedon[90]). In both cases, then, an extraordinary word describes an extraordinary trait: if Euripides was a poet exceptionally loved by foreigners, Sophocles was a poet who loved Athens to an exceptional extent.[91]

It has been argued that the ancient biographers concocted the "tradition of an embittered Euripides abandoning the Athens that treated him with contempt" precisely in order to create a contrast with portrayals of Sophocles in his "standard role as model of happy success and patriotism, beloved of his people".[92] The biographers would, then, have been able to invent Euripides' Macedonian 'exile' on the basis of the existence of the *Archelaus*, which traced the line of Macedonian kings back to Heracles and which the *Vita Euripidis* says he wrote as a favor to his patron.[93] Yet there is no way of knowing that one of the two biographies developed first, nor even whether the characterizations of the poets had some roots in reality or simply reflected the fantasies and exaggerations of oral and anecdotal traditions, comedy, and the biographers themselves. What is demonstrable, however, is that the recurrence of certain themes and keywords in each of the tragedians' *Vitae* implies that at some point the three biographical traditions were read, interpreted and elaborated upon in relation to each other.[94] Furthermore, it is possible, if we look carefully at these texts and other sources of ancient scholarship, to recognize that the story of Sophocles the "lover of Athens" is itself crafted according to the same template that shapes the patronage narratives found in the biographies of his two counterparts.

---

90   Demosthenes *De falsa legatione* 308.2.
91   See crucially Bing 2006: the word ξενοφιλώτατος "is a pointed and witty inversion of the convention virtually embodied in the more common *philoxeinos*. For while *philoxeinos* reflects the idealized attitude of a host toward any given stranger, *xenophilos* regards the anomalous quality of a stranger beloved abroad by every imaginable host – even as he is unappreciated in his native land."
92   Scullion 2003, 39.
93   Scullion 2003, 39.
94   Here for the sake of comparison we might mention the two editions (1550 and 1568) of Giorgio Vasari's *Lives of the Artists*. Maginnis 1993 convincingly demonstrates that the *prima parte* of Vasari's work (which included biographies of the thirteenth-century artists Cimabue, Giotto, Simone Martini, and Duccio) underwent the most extensive revision for the second edition. For example, in the later edition the theme of a "fraternity of art" linking various pairs of master artists and apprentices is much more developed and has clearly been embellished. In the cases of both the ancient *Vitae* of tragedians and Part I of Vasari, it seems that once the biographies had been set down in an initial form the process of later revision was marked by the temptation to draw out or to "infer" (or even to dream up) connections and parallels between the lives of (roughly) contemporary authors/ artists.

Between Aeschylus and Euripides' *Vitae* a neat pattern emerges in the representation of the poet-patron relationships. Whereas we hear that *Archelaus* was written for Euripides' Macedonian patron, Aeschylus is said to have composed the *Aetnaeae* so as to augur a good life for the synoecists of the city his own patron, Hieron, had just founded (*VA* § 10). In both of these biographies, the patronage relationship is constructed as operating according to an economy of "favor", χάρις and "honor", τιμή: Euripides wrote the *Archelaus* "to please" or "as a favor" to the king (χαριζόμενος αὐτῷ δρᾶμα ὁμονύμως ἔγραψε, *VE* § 11), while Aeschylus' own poetic activity in Sicily made him "exceedingly honored" by the tyrant Hieron and the Geloans (σφόδρα ... τιμηθείς, *VA* § 10).[95] And although it may seem that this framework, which links tragedians via their plays with patrons and royal geographies, allows no room for the "Athens-loving" Sophocles, the tragic *scholia* contain evidence that there was indeed one tragedy which was read in a way that allowed Sophocles to be absorbed into the general model of tragedian patronage.

The *scholia*[96] to *Oedipus at Colonus* (a play that even in antiquity was viewed as Sophocles' swansong for his homeland[97]) also interpret certain lines of the play as having been written as a sort of favor, a χάρις. This time however the favor is not one for any foreign monarch, but rather for the Athenians, Athens and Colonus itself (Sophocles' native *deme*). For example, when Oedipus first arrives in Colonus and makes a prayer to the Eumenides (*OC* 84–110), he tells of an oracle from Apollo which had promised that, when he arrived at the final site of his wanderings,

> there I will make the last turn in the course of my wretched life bringing advantages by the fact of my settlement to those who receive me, but ruin to the ones who had sent me away, who had driven me out. (Lines 91–3)

In two of the manuscripts, a *scholion* to line 92 explains:

> the poet says this to please the Athenians [χαριζόμενος Ἀθηναίοις]. For it appears that at that time the Boeotians and the Athenians were at odds with each other. (*LM*)

---

95   Cf. also *VA* § 10: when Aeschylus died, they honored him greatly (ἐτίμησαν μεγαλοπρεπῶς).

96   I use the edition of de Marco 1952. For a survey of some of the literary critical issues raised by the Sophoclean scholia see esp. Easterling 2006 and Dickey 2007, 34–35.

97   See Valerius Maximus 8.7 ext. 12 = Nauck *TrGF* 4 T 168: *Prope enim centesimum annum attigit, sub ipsum transitum ad mortem Oedipode* ἐπὶ Κολωνῷ *scripto, qua sola fabula omnium eiusdem studi poetarum praeripere gloriam potuit.* The play is also often read as closely connected to Sophocles' own biographical tradition: See esp. the Appendix of Edmunds 1996, "Life of Sophocles and reception of *Oedipus at Colonus*" (163–8), Lefkowitz 1981, 84–5 and Palomar Pérez 1998, 96–8. On Sophocles' reading from the play in defence of himself at a trial for neglecting family affairs see Nauck *TrGF* 4 T 81–84a (the story appears with little variation in Cicero, Plutarch, Apuleius, [Lucian], and Pausanias).

The *scholia* offer a similar exegesis of line 457, when Oedipus is promising the chorus that, if they receive him, he will prove a savior of the city and a bane to their enemies[98] because an oracle once prophesied that if his tomb were in Athenian soil it would protect the city from Theban siege. Again the *scholia* see the lines as an attempt at glorifying Athens:[99]

> ταῦτα δὲ εἰκὸς ποιητικώτερον ὑπὸ τοῦ Σοφοκλέους πεπλάσθαι ἐπὶ θεραπείᾳ τῶν Ἀθηναίων· (*LRM*)

> It is likely that these things are a poetic invention[100] of Sophocles', for the sake of showing favor to the Athenians.[101]

When the chorus sings a hymn to Poseidon praising the god's invention in Colonus of the horse-bridle, the *scholia* again explain that Sophocles included this passage, too, as a kind of homage to his native land (ἐπὶ θεραπείᾳ... τῆς οἰκείας).[102] In fact, the first of the hypotheses transmitted with the *Oedipus at Colonus* indicates that it was not merely single passages that were regarded as Sophocles' "favors" to the Athenians and his *deme*, but rather the play as a whole which was understood as having been composed with encomiastic intent:

> Τὸ δὲ δρᾶμα τῶν θαυμαστῶν· ὃ καὶ ἤδη γεγηρακὼς ὁ Σοφοκλῆς ἐποίησε, χαριζόμενος οὐ μόνον τῇ πατρίδι, ἀλλὰ καὶ τῷ ἑαυτοῦ δήμῳ· ἦν γὰρ Κολωνῆθεν· (lines 12–13) (*LARM*)

> The drama is one of the admired ones. Sophocles wrote it when he was already old, to delight not only his own fatherland, but even his own *deme* – for he was from Colonus.

For both Sophocles and Euripides, then, ancient scholars used the verb χαρίζεσθαι (here "to delight" or "to do as favor to"), to describe the motivations for the praise of a specific locale in one particular play: while for Euripides this play was the *Archelaus*, for Sophocles it was his celebrated *Oedipus at Colonus*. In Sophocles' case, however, the recipient of the χάρις is not a foreign king, but rather his homeland (πατρίς), the Athenians, and his very own *deme*.

---

98   *OC* 459–60.
99   Easterling 2006, 32–36 surveys the *scholia* on the *OC*, and observes that the similarly skeptical author of at least the note on line 388 "seems to reflect concern for the existence of an attested source" for the oracle (32).
100 On the use of the word πλάσμα ('fiction, invention') in the *scholia* see Papadopoulou 1998–1999; Easterling nicely renders ποιητικώτερον as "with a degree of licence" 2006, 33.
101 This *scholion* goes on to say that "Tragedians often write words of praise like this about their homelands" (πολλαχοῦ δὲ οἱ τραγικοὶ χαρίζονται ταῖς πατρίσιν ἔνια). Is the "scholiast" here thinking along the lines of the Eurpidean praise of Athens cited by Lycurgus *et al.*, or does he have later tragedians in mind, too?
102 Σ in *OC* 712 (*LRM*).

Elsewhere, especially in *scholia* to the poetry of Pindar, the verb χαρίζεσθαι is used to describe what a poet does when he extols certain people(s) or places. For example, a *scholion* to Pindar's tenth *Nemean* ode (on the occasion of Theaios of Argos' wrestling victory) explains that, since the ode was to be performed in Argos, Pindar especially praises or flatters (χαρίζεσθαι) the Argives.[103] And a *scholion* to *Olympian* 10, an ode in which Pindar calls Epizephyrian Locri "dear to Calliope", explains that Pindar is aware the Locrians will "show favors in return" (ἀντιχαρίζεσθαι) for his encomium of their city.[104] The use of χαρίζεσθαι for a poet's (usually compensated) work for a patron hearkens to an ideology of aristocratic gift exchange to whose "rules" Pindar himself alludes in, for example, these lines for Hippocleas of Thessaly' victory in the boys' *diadromos*:

I trust in the *xenia* of Thorax, who labouring for *charis*
Yoked this, my four-wheeled chariot of the Pierian Muses,
Loving one who loves him, leading one who gladly leads. (*Pythian* 10.64–66)

When the *scholia* use the verb χαρίζεσθαι to express what Sophocles does for his countrymen and *deme* in *Oedipus at Colonus*, they therefore effectively assimilate Sophocles' own "gift-exchange" with Athens – where the "gift" is the play, and the compensation might be the festival prize or the citizens' favor – to a model of poetic patronage.[105]

Thus it is the case that even in the Sophoclean *scholia* we are able to recognize traces of a template perhaps more familiar from ancient constructions of the "wandering" poet (one thinks of Simonides, Pindar, Bacchylides, Archilochus ... even of Homer), whose job it was to spread the *kleos* of a place through poetry.[106] For the Hellenistic period – the period in which we have located the consolidation of these biographical traditions – we also know of a number of poets who did indeed receive official honors from a city (such as *proxenia*, exemption from tax, or land grants) in return for praising and commemorating that city's history.[107] In one of these inscriptions, for example,

---

103 Σ in *Nemean* 10 49b.
104 Σ in *Olympian* 17c, 17g *bis*.
105 On the poet-patron relationship as one of aristocratic gift-exchange see especially Kurke 1991, 85–107; on "social *charis*" see also MacLachlan 1993, 73–86, who writes: "The visible form [Pindar's gift in the exchange] took was no doubt that of financial remuneration, but Pindar's description of his patron relationship as one of *xenia* or *philia* as well as *charis* suggests that it provided mutual benefit. His patrons he calls *xeinoi* (guest-friends); he is their *philos* (friend)" (104). On the poet's *charis* ("both his graceful song and his grateful recompense") see also Martin 2009, 85 and 88–89.
106 See esp. Hunter and Rutherford 2009 on the importance of this conceit "in both the reality and the *imaginaire* of Greek poetry" (1); also Martin 2009, 86.
107 On these kinds of honors for poets see Hunter 2003, 26. On specific Hellenistic *poeti vaganti* and the honors they received see Guarducci 1926, who prints a corpus of in-

the Delians honor Amphiklos of Chios for writing poems that "made illustrious" (κεκόσμηκεν) both themselves and a Delian temple. It therefore may be the result of this more typically Hellenistic practice that, for example, the *Vita Euripidis* informs us that Euripides was awarded precisely *proxenia* (in addition to *ateleia*) when he moved to Magnesia (§ 9) – could this be because the biographers believed (or presumed) that, while there, he wrote plays that brought luster to the Magnesians?[108]

Finally, according to the *Vita* each of the three tragedians was elevated after his death to "cult" status in precisely the land praised by the particularly encomiastic play (i.e. Aeschylus' *Aetnaeae,* Sophocles' *Oedipus at Colonus,* Euripides' *Archelaus*).[109] Sophocles alone was honored by the Athenians; not with anything like *proxenia,* but rather with annual sacrifices. Quoting the fourth-century Atthidographer Ister, his *Vita* tells us that

> Because of the man's *arete*, the Athenians voted to make sacrifices to him [αὐτῷ θύειν] each year. (*VS* § 17 = FGr Hist 334 F 38)

It is then Gellius who informs us that the Macedonians dutifully honored Euripides' tomb (*N.A.* 15.20.10, quoted above), while the *Vita Aeschyli* records that, after Aeschylus' death,

> everyone who worked in the business of tragedy frequented his tomb (τὸ μνῆμα) and performed their dramas there. (§ 11)

Thus while Aeschylus and Euripides' *Vitae* may furnish much more clearly cut cases of "patronage narratives", the evidence of the *scholia* imply that Sophocles' story, too, was absorbed by ancient scholars and biographers into the model. His narrative does, however, remain an exceptional one, given that the site of his work as a "court poet" was his own democratic polis, with his "patron" configured as the entire body of the Athenian citizenry.

Conclusion

It is perhaps a similar fantasy of the tragedians as traveling poets of local praise that Hermesianax captures in (the very textually corrupt) "Catalogue of Loves", from his lost elegiac work the *Leontion*.[110] In this fragment,

---

scriptions that witness to these (648–57); cf. also Hunter-Rutherford 2009, 3–6. See Martin 2009, esp. 84, for the importance of praising place to what he calls "planetic poetics".

108 On this episode in the *VE* see esp. Easterling 1994, 76, also Taplin 1999, 42.
109 On ancient cults of poets see Clay 2004; on the "divinity" that the biographical stories seem to attribute to the tragedians (divinity nevertheless mitigated by certain defects of theirs) see Palomar Pérez 1998, 84–94.
110 Hermesianax fr. 7 Powell.

Hermesianax recounts the loves, requited or not, of famous poets, and the travels which these poets undertook on account of their infatuations. Here Sophocles appears as the "Attic bee" who wandered away from many-hilled Colonus (57) to sing of his loves in tragic choruses. And, the poem goes on, "even Euripides", that misanthropist, was himself struck by Cupid's bow and so roamed the streets of Aegae (the Macedonian capital) by night, tortured by his love for one of the King's servants (61–68). In this Hellenistic "Catalogue", then, these two tragedians are quite naturally fitted into the same paradigm within which Hermesianax inscribes other, perhaps more archetypically "wandering" poets such as Homer, Sappho and Archilochus.[111]

In their introduction to the volume *Wandering Poets in Ancient Greek Culture*, Richard Hunter and Ian Rutherford describe how, in Greek antiquity, "The itineracy, both real and imagined, of poets is intimately tied to the ambitions of and for their poetry to enjoy fame and reception all over the world".[112] Here as a kind of corollary to this statement I have argued that the "international" fame of certain poetry – Athenian tragedy – might have also found a degree of justification precisely in discourses which emphasized the itineracy of its best-loved poets. As Paola Ceccarelli points out in the next chapter of this volume, tragedy outside of Athens adjusted itself to specific local contexts, and as we have now seen this "adjustment" also left palpable traces in the tragedians' biographical traditions: regardless of the truth of the testimonia placing Aeschylus in Sicily and Euripides in Macedon, these stories certainly captured the popular imagination for centuries after their deaths:[113] what is more, the malleability of the *Vitae* traditions meant that biography itself could serve as a battleground for the assertion of stakes in poetic legacies, a "site" on which to lay claim to literary patrimony. Thus if ancient tales of the tragedians' travels may be read as allegories for the travel of tragedy,[114] then already in antiquity Athens itself represented only one of a number of geographies that were crucial to the story (and imagination) of the Athenian genre par excellence.

---

111 On the biographical and literary allusions in Sophocles and Euripides' portions of the poem see Caspers 2006, 29–35, on Euripides in Hermesianax fr. 6 see Matthews 2003.

112 2009, 7.

113 A few examples: the Archaeological Museum of Thessaloniki hosts an exhibit that focuses on Euripides' time as court poet in Macedon (Hanink 2008, 131), while the modern theatre on the island of Salamis (where Euripides supposedly spent time in isolation in a cave) is called the *Euripideion*. See also Kowalzig's discussion of the "Eschilo d'Oro", the "annual prize awarded by the Istituto Nazionale del drama Antico (INDA) at Syracuse during the institute's summer festival" (2008, 128).

114 Kowalzig has described Aeschylus' arrival in Sicily as "Athenian tragedy's disembarkation on the island" (2008, 142).

Bibliography

Allan, William (2001), "Euripides in Megale Hellas: Some Aspects of the Early Reception of Tragedy", in: *G&R* 48, 67–86.

Allen, Danielle (2000), "Changing the Authoritative Voice: Lycurgus' *Against Leocrates*", in: *ClAnt* 19.1, 5–33.

Arrighetti, Graziano (1974), *Satiro: Vita di Euripide*, Pisa.

Avezzù, Elisa and Longo, Oddone (1985), *Alciphron: Lettere di parassiti e di cortigiane*, Venice.

Bing, Peter (2006), "Image and Hypothesis in the Hellenistic Reception of Euripides", (paper delivered at the conference "Euripides: The first Hellenistic poet? Problems in periodization, poetics and reception", University of Chicago, November 11–12, 2006).

—— (2005), "The Politics and Poetics of Geography in the Milan Posidippus, Section One: On Stone (P.Mil.Vogl. VIII 309, Col. I–IV 6)", in: Kathryn Gutzwiller (ed.), *The New Posidippus: A Hellenistic Poetry Book*, Oxford, 119–140.

—— (1993), "The *Bios*-Tradition and Poets' Lives in Hellenistic poetry", in: Ralph Rosen and Joseph Farrell (eds.), *Nomodeiktes. Greek Studies in Honor of Martin Ostwald*, Ann Arbor, 619–631.

Bollansée, Jan (1999), *Hermippos of Smyrna and his Biographical Writings: A Reappraisal*, Leuven.

Bosworth, Albert Brian (1988), *Conquest and Empire: The Reign of Alexander the Great*, Cambridge.

Bremer, Jan (1991), "Poets and their Patrons", in: Annette Harder and Heinz Hoffman (eds.), *Fragmenta Dramatica*, Göttingen, 39–60.

Brown, Truesdell S. (1958), *Timaeus of Tauromenium*, Berkeley, Calif.

Carter, David (2004), "Was Attic Tragedy Democratic?", in: *Polis* 21.1–2, 1–25.

Caspers, Christiaan L. (2006), "The Loves of the Poets: Allusions in Hermesianax fr. 7 Powell", in: Annette Harder / R.F. Regtuit / G.C. Wakker (eds.), *Beyond the Canon: Hellenistica Groningana 11*, Leuven, 21–42.

Cataudella, Quintino (1963), "Eschilo in Sicilia", in: *Dioniso* 37, 5–24.

Clay, Diskin (2004), *Archilochus Heros: The Cult of Poets in the Greek Polis*, Cambridge, Mass.

Compton, Todd (2006), *Victim of the Muses: Poet as Scapegoat, Warrior, and Hero in Greco-Roman and Indo-European Myth and History*, Washington, DC.

Connolly, Andrew (1998), "Was Sophocles Heroised as Dexion?", in: *JHS* 118, 1–21.

Dearden, Chris (1999), "Plays for Export", in: *Phoenix* 53, 222–48.

de Marco, Vittorio (1952), *Scholia in Sophoclis Oedipum Coloneum*, Rome.

Dickey, Eleanor (2007), *Ancient Greek Scholarship*, Oxford.

Dougherty, Carol (1993), *The Poetics of Colonization: From City to Text in Archaic Greece*, New York.

Easterling, Patricia E. (2006), "Notes on Notes: The Ancient Scholia on Sophocles", in: Sten Eklund (ed.), *Συγχάρματα: Studies in Honour of Jan Fredrik Kindstrand*, Uppsala, 21–36.

—— (1997), "From Repertoire to Canon", in: Patricia E. Easterling (ed.), *The Cambridge Companion to Greek Tragedy*, Cambridge, 211–27.

—— (1994), "Euripides outside Athens", in: *ICS* 19, 73–80.

Edmunds, Lowell (1996), *Theatrical Space and Historical Place in Sophocles' Oedipus at Colonus*, Lanham, MD.

Fairweather, Janet (1974), "Fiction in the Biographies of Ancient Writers", in: *AncSoc* 5, 231–75.

Falappone, Maria (2006), "Citazioni della tragedia antica nelle *archaiologiai*",
     in: Onofrio Vox (ed.), *Memoria di Testi Teatrali Antichi*, Lecce, 67–104.
Ferrari, G.R.F. (1989), "Plato and Poetry", in: George Alexander Kennedy (ed.),
     The Cambridge History of Literary Criticism Vol. 1, Cambridge, 92–148.
Fraser, Peter Marshall (1972), *Ptolemaic Alexandria*, Oxford.
Goldhill, Simon (1991), *The Poet's Voice: Essays on Poetics and Greek Literature*,
     Cambridge.
Gomme, Arnold W. (1956), *A Historical Commentary on Thucydides: Vol. 2,
     Books II–III*, Oxford.
Gow, Andrew S. F. and Page, Denys Lionel (1968), *The Greek Anthology: The Garland
     of Philip and Some Contemporary Epigrams*, Cambridge.
Graziosi, Barbara (2002), *Inventing Homer: The Early Reception of Epic*, Cambridge.
Griffith, Mark (1978), "Aeschylus, Sicily and Prometheus", in: Roger D. Dawe /
     James Diggle / Patricia E. Easterling (eds.), *Dionysiaca. Nine Studies in Greek
     Poetry by Former Pupils, Presented to Denys Page on His Seventieth Birthday*,
     Cambridge, 105–39.
Guarducci, Margherita (1929), "Poeti vaganti e conferenzieri nell'età ellenistica",
     in: *Memorie dell'Accademia dei Lincei* 6, 629–65.
Habicht, Christian (1997), *Athens from Alexander to Anthony*, trans. D.L. Schneider; origi-
     nally published as *Athen in hellenistischer Zeit* (Munich, 1994), Cambridge, Mass.
Hall, Edith (1996), "Is there a *Polis* in Aristotle's *Poetics*?", in: Michael Silk (ed.),
     Tragedy and the Tragic: Greek Theatre and Beyond, Oxford, 294–309.
—— (1989), *Inventing the Barbarian: Greek Self Definition Through Tragedy*, Oxford.
Hanink, Johanna (2008), "Literary Politics and the Euripidean *Vita*", in: *CCJ* 54, 115–35.
Harder, M. Annette (1985), *Euripides' Kresphontes and Archelaos: Introduction, Text
     and Commentary*, Leiden.
Herington, C.J. (1967), "Aeschylus in Sicily", in: *JHS* 87, 74–85.
Hunter, Richard (2003), *Encomium of Ptolemy Philadelphus*, Berkeley, Calif.
—— (1983), *Eubulus: The Fragments, Edited with Commentary*, Cambridge.
Hunter, Richard, and Rutherford, Ian (2009), "Introduction", in: Richard Hunter /
     Ian Rutherford (eds.), *Wandering Poets in Ancient Greek Culture: Travel, Locality and
     Pan-Hellenism*, Oxford, 1–22.
Karavas, Orestis (2005), *Lucien et la Tragédie*, New York and Berlin.
Kassel, Rudolf and Austin, Colin (1983), *Poetae Comici Graeci*, Berlin.
Kris, Ernst and Kurz, Otto (1979), *Legend, Myth and Magic in the Image of the Artist:
     A Historical Experiment*, trans. Alastair Laing (originally published as *Die Legen-
     de vom Künstler: Ein historischer Versuch*, Vienna, 1934), New Haven, Conn.
Kowalzig, Barbara (2008), "Nothing to Do with Demeter? Something to Do with
     Sicily! Theatre and Society in the Early Fifth-Century West",
     in: Martin Revermann / Peter Wilson (eds.), *Performance, Iconography,
     Reception: Studies in Honour of Oliver Taplin*, Oxford, 128–157.
Kurke, Leslie (1991), *The Traffic in Praise: Pindar and the Poetics of Social Economy*,
     Ithaca, NY.
Lada-Richards, Ismene (2002), "Reinscribing the Muse: Greek Drama and the Discourse
     of Inspired Creativity", in: Efrossini Spentzou / Don Fowler (eds.), *Cultivating the
     Muse: Struggles for Power and Inspiration in Classical Literature*, Oxford, 69–91.
Leurini, Luigi (2000), *Testimonia et fragmenta: Ionis Chii*, Amsterdam.
Lefkowitz, Mary (2007), Review of *Victim of the Muses: Poet as Scapegoat, Warrior
     and Hero in Greco-Roman And Indo-European Myth and History*, by T. Compton,
     in: *BMCR* 2007.02.09.
—— (1981), *Lives of the Greek Poets*, Baltimore, Md.

Loraux, Nicole (1986), *The Invention of Athens: The Funeral Oration in the Classical City*, trans. Alan Sheridan; originally published as *L'invention d'Athènes: histoire de l'oraison funèbre dans la 'cité classique'* (Paris, 1981), London.

Maginnis, H.B.J. (1993), "Giotto's World through Vasari's Eyes", in: *Zeitschrift für Kunstgeschichte* 56, 385–408.

Martin, Richard (2009), "Read on Arrival", in: Richard Hunter / Ian Rutherford (eds.), *Wandering Poets in Ancient Greek Culture: Travel, Locality and Pan-Hellenism*, Oxford, 80–104.

Matelli, Elisabetta (2006), "Hieronymus in Athens and Rhodes", in: William Fortenbaugh / Stephen White (eds.), *Lyco of Troas and Hieronymus of Rhodes*, New Brunswick, NJ, 289–314.

Matthews, Victor J. (2003), "Interpreting the Euripides Narrative of Hermesianax", in: *Des géants à Dionysos. Mélanges de mythologie et de poésie grecques offerts à Francis Vian*, ed. Domenico Accorinti and Pierre Chuvin, Alessandria, 281–6.

MacLachlan, Bonnie (1993), *The Age of Grace: Charis in Early Greek Poetry*, Princeton.

Momigliano, Arnaldo (1971), *The Development of Greek Biography*, Cambridge, Mass.

Most, Glenn W. (2006), "Athens as the School of Greece", in: James I. Porter (ed.): *Classical Pasts*, Princeton, 377–88.

Ober, Josiah (2006), "From Epistemic Diversity to Common Knowledge: Rational Rituals and Cooperation in Democratic Athens", *Episteme* 3, 214–33.

Palomar Pérez, Natalia (1998), "La figure du poète tragique dans la Grèce ancienne", in: Nicole Loreaux / Carol Miralles (eds.), *Figures de l'intellectuel en Grèce ancienne*, Berlin 65–106.

Papadopoulou, Thalia (1998–1999), "Literary Theory and Terminology in the Greek Scholia: The Case of *Plasma*", in: *BICS* 43, 203–10.

Pelling, Christopher (1990), "Childhood and Personality in Greek Biography", in: Christopher Pelling (ed.), *Characterisation and Individuality in Greek Literature*, Oxford, 213–44.

Pfeiffer, Rudolf (1968), *History of Classical Scholarship from the Beginnings to the End of the Hellenistic Age*, Oxford.

Pickard-Cambridge, Sir Arthur Wallace (1988), *The Dramatic Festivals of Athens* (2nd ed.), London.

—— (1946), *The Theatre of Dionysus in Athens*, Oxford.

Porter, James I. (2006), "Feeling Classical: Classicism and Ancient Literary Criticism", in: James I. Porter (ed.), *Classical Pasts*, Princeton, 301–52.

Powell, John U. (1925), *Collectanea Alexandrina: Reliquiae minores poetarum Graecorum aetatis Ptolemaicae 323–146 A.C.*, Oxford.

Prauscello, Lucia (2006), *Singing Alexandria: Music between Practice and Textual Transmission*, Leiden.

Revermann, Martin (1999–2000), "Tragedy and Macedon: Some Conditions of Reception", in: Martin Cropp / Kevin Lee / David Sansone (eds.), *Euripides and Tragic Theatre in the Late Fifth Century*, ICS 24/25, 451–67.

Rhodes, Peter J. (2003), "Nothing to Do with Democracy? Athenian Drama and the *Polis*", in: *JHS* 123, 104–19.

Rosen, Ralph (2006), "Aristophanes, Fandom and the Classicizing of Greek Tragedy", in Lynn Kozak / John Rich (eds.), *Playing Around Aristophanes: Essays in Celebration of the Completion of the Edition of Comedies of Aristophanes by Alan Sommerstein*, Oxford, 27–47.

Sanders, Lionel Jehuda (1987), *Dionysius I of Syracuse and Greek Tyranny*, London.

Schorn, Stefan (2004), *Satyros aus Kallatis: Sammlung der Fragmente mit Kommentar*, Basel.

Scodel, Ruth (2007), "Lycurgus and the State Text of Tragedy", in: Craig Cooper (ed.), *Politics of Orality (Orality and Literacy in Ancient Greece Vol. 6)*, Leiden, 129–54.

Scullion, Scott (2003), "Euripides and Macedon, or the Silence of the *Frogs*", in: *CQ* 53, 389–400.

Sickinger, James P. (1999), *Public Records and Archives in Classical Athens*, Chapel Hill.

Sommerstein, Alan, (1995–1996) "Aeschylus' Epitaph", in: *Museum Criticum* 30–31, 111–17.

Stephens, Susan (2003) "For You, Arsinoe", in: Benjamin Acosta-Hughes / Elizabeth Kosmetatou / Manuel Baumbach (eds.), *Labored in Papyrus Leaves: Perspectives on an Epigram Collection Attributed to Posidippus (P.Mil.Vogl. VIII 309)*, Washington, DC, 161–76.

Stevens, P.T. (1956), "Euripides and the Athenians", in: *JHS* 76, 87–94.

Taplin, Oliver (1999), "Spreading the Word through Performance", in: Simon Goldhill / Robin Osborne (eds.), *Performance Culture and Athenian Democracy*, Cambridge, 33–57.

—— (1993), *Comic Angels and Other Approaches to Greek Drama through Vase Paintings*, Oxford.

Velardi, Roberto (1989), *Enthousiasmòs: Possessione rituale e teoria della comunicazione poetica in Platone*, Rome.

West, Martin L. (1989), "The Early Chronology of Attic Tragedy", in: *CQ* 39, 251–4.

West, Stephanie (1974), "Satyrus: Peripatetic or Alexandrian?", in: *GRBS* 15, 279–87.

Whitmarsh, Tim (2004), *Ancient Greek Literature*, Cambridge.

Wilson, Peter J. (1996), "Tragic Rhetoric: The Use of Tragedy and the Tragic in the Fourth Century", in: Michael Silk (ed.) *Tragedy and the Tragic: Greek Theatre and Beyond*, Oxford, 310–31.

—— (2000), *The Athenian Institution of the Khoregia: The Chorus, the City and the Stage*, Cambridge.

—— (2007), "Sicilian Choruses", in: Peter Wilson (ed.), *The Greek Theatre and Festivals: Documentary Studies*, Oxford, 351–377.

Zanker, Paul (1995), *The Mask of Socrates: the Image of the Intellectual in Antiquity*, trans. A. Shapiro; originally published as *Die Maske des Sokrates: das Bild des Intellektuellen in der antiken Kunst* (Munich, 1995), Berkeley.

Situating the Gaze of the Recipient(s): Theatre-Related Vase Paintings and their Contexts of Reception

Martin Revermann

The very process of reception implies the existence of points of contact where connections between the recipient and the received are being estab- lished. This, in turn, implies a variety not only of intersections but also of modalities: there are different ways of making contact in the first place. The point of contact I wish to explore in this paper is visual and mediated. When I describe its modality as the 'gaze', I do not intend to conjure up associations with Lacanian psycho-analysis (from which the term derives its continued popularity). Rather, it is deployed because the term insinu- ates that the viewer does not "view" or, even worse, "watch" but has an ac- tive and central, indeed indispensable, share in the construction of mean- ing (a phenomenon which Gombrich memorably termed the "beholder's share"[1]). So while the ostensible, or at least initial, focus of this paper is on the analysis of the pictorial programmes of theatre-related vase paintings, what is at stake here, really, is thinking through contexts of their reception. The 'gaze' I will be examining is both that of the individual and that of the collective, each taken in isolation but also scrutinized as interacting with each other. And while I will be primarily concerned with one single vessel, the 'gaze' I will be examining is, if you will, generic: I am interested in the kind(s) of response(s) which, I submit, viewers of this type of vessel would characteristically develop, and which this type of vessel conditions or even cues them to develop.

'Situating the gaze' in this way requires confronting head-on the prob- lem of reception contexts for theatre-related vase paintings. In the second part of this paper, therefore, the notion of 'context' itself is being scrutinized briefly. This leads to the distinction between primary and secondary (or even tertiary) contexts which happily co-exist, as well as to the argument that for

---

*   An earlier and significantly shorter version of this paper appeared in *Theatre Re- search International* 30 (2005) 3–18.
1   The title of chapter 3 of *Art and Illusion* (Gombrich 1960).

theatre-related vase paintings such non-exclusive, yet often hierarchically structured, multi-contexts provide the most plausible model for situating the relationship between the vessels and their viewers. In the current state of research, however, eminent scholars working on those theatre-related vessels have strongly and exclusively favoured one context, the (public) funerary, over another, the (private) symposium. This paper, then, attempts to shift the balance of the current discussion towards accepting multi-contexts and at the same time emphasizing the (private) household context of use and display, in particular during the symposium as part of which, I argue, many theatre-related vessels – not least the *Cleveland Medea*, the showpiece item of this paper – make excellent sense and for which many of them were primarily intended.

This second part of the paper is preceded by an analysis of that magnificent *Cleveland Medea* calyx crater [figs. 1, 2 and 3]. The length of the analysis and its level of detail are, I hope, justified on the grounds that we need to understand in some depth how exactly the painter attempts to shape the gaze of the recipient(s) in the first place by his iconographical choices, especially in those instances where he departs from the play as we have it. These strategies of visual defamiliarization, I argue, not only challenge the onlooking recipient(s) but in fact *enrich* and *deepen* the experience of reception itself. They are the product of continued artistic reflection "beyond the fifth century", on tragedy itself as a classic and a cultural icon, as well as on the modes of coming to terms with it as artists and human beings.

1   An introductory case study

Exciting things are currently happening in the study of ancient Greek drama. This is because the field boasts of a huge asset, steadily growing in quantity, which is unique in theatre history: household pottery painted with motifs which are inspired by the theatre, *i.e.* masks, Dionysus (with or without company) and, most intriguing of all, scenes from individual plays. This remarkable cultural phenomenon peaked only for a comparatively brief period of time (essentially the late fifth and fourth century BCE). Most of the evidence does not, as one would expect, come from the homeland of classical drama, Athens and Attica, but from Southern Italy, an area colonized by Greek settlers and hence referred to as "Greater Greece" (*Megale Hellas*). Many of these vases have been known for a while, although some of the most important ones are fairly recent additions to the tally. In total, there are currently ca. 400 vessels known which can be related to tragedy with various degrees of confidence, while ca. 100 can plausibly be connected with come-

Fig. 1–3: Lucanian calyx crater, ca. 400 BCE (=*LIMC* VI (1992) 391 no. 36).

dy. And it is telling that of the 104 vases discussed in Taplin's *Pots and Plays* (published in 2007) nearly half (48) have only been known since 1970.[2]

Their study has traditionally been regarded as a somewhat dubious exercise, belittled by archaeologists for the vessels' alleged inferior artistic quality and treated with caution by text-focused students of ancient literature who question the value of South–Italian vase-painting for literature in general and Athenian drama in particular. Only recently have the vases gained new authority. This is because the iconography of a number of South Italian objects could beyond reasonable doubt be shown to be inspired by plays first

2   Taplin 1993, 32–6 and 2007, 15–17.

performed in Athens several decades earlier. The crucial link between Attic drama of the fifth century and fourth-century South Italian pottery had been established. Much else now continues to fall into place.

But rather than rehash in detail the story of this revival of interest over (roughly) the past 15 years and provide an introduction to this type of evidence at large – a job well done by a number of fine contributions[3] – I wish to concentrate on a magnificently beautiful and particularly thought-provoking single artifact, the *Cleveland Medea* vase.

The vessel is unique among the currently known theatre-related vases: it is the only vase on which not just one but both sides of the vessel are scene-specific representations of tragedy. In addition, these two sides are linked by one common theme (infanticide), and both sides are inspired by the same playwright, Euripides.

Yet beyond its function as an introductory case study this paper serves a more ambitious purpose. By taking the vessel for what it is, a document of creative appropriation, I wish to sketch the relevance of the *Cleveland Medea* and its peers for the cultural history of Greek tragedy in antiquity. While recent work on these vases has focused mainly on trying to connect the visual evidence from South Italy with Athenian drama and, more recently, on trying to identify patterns of regional differentiation within the whole corpus. I, on the other hand, will concentrate on putting this sort of evidence firmly into its social, aesthetic and intellectual context. Two questions will be of particular interest:

How and to what effect does the painter re-configure a theatre-inspired topic in his medium in order to (re)-tell the story "*his* way"?

Can the vessel's context of use be specified with any degree of certainty, and if so how is the artifact itself designed to perform and interact with its target viewers, thus shaping the gaze of its recipient(s)?

---

3   Green 1991, Taplin 1993 (on comedy-related vases), 1997 and 2007 (on tragedy-related vases, superbly illustrated and with an important introduction), Csapo 2001, 2010, 1–82 and forthcoming, Förtsch 1994, Lissarrague 2008, Osborne 2008 (on the painters' motivation for iconographic choices) and Walsh 2009, 74–9. See also Seeberg 2002–03 for a historical survey of this particular field. Mitchell 2009 has brief sections on comedy-related vases (150–6) and on the social contexts for painted pottery in general (20–2). Keuls 1997 contains a series of stimulating pieces on theatre-related iconography from various stages of her career. The iconocentric (or, using the author's word, "skeptical") manifesto in Small 2003, 37–78 is vivid but poorly argued and one-sided. Its compressed version is Small 2005 (106–9 on the *Cleveland Medea* crater).

Telephus

One of the most spectacular recent finds of theatre-related vase-paintings, published in 1983 and now in the Cleveland Museum of Art[4], is a splendid calyx crater (50cm high) dated to c. 400 by Arthur Dale Trendall, the late doyen of South Italian vase-paintings. He attributed the vase to a painter near the Policoro Painter. Initial private reservations about authenticity became obsolete once Trendall had been given the chance to examine the vase.[5] The position of the handles on a calyx crater makes for an unobstructed visual field, which in this case is entirely devoted to two memorable scenes. Of these the less spectacular one [fig. 3] is best to start with. At an altar a naked bearded man with a sword has captured a young boy. In his despair the boy stretches out his hands for help from the central figure, another naked bearded man. Full of anxiety he is about to draw his sword, while a tall woman tries to prevent him from doing just this in order to protect the boy.

Why should this scene have anything to do with the theatre? No name tags facilitate the identification of any of the individuals, and a viewer who brings no advance knowledge to the vase will hardly get more out of it than that this is some form of hostage scene and that the central male figure and the upset woman are close relatives of the boy. There are no overt signals of theatricality like masks or costumes. Nonetheless, there can be no doubt that many ancient viewers of this vessel instantly deciphered the puzzle and immediately made sense of it in theatrical terms.

How so? It is the pictorial narrative itself which provides the necessary clues for competent viewers to activate their knowledge. Euripides had famously adapted the myth of Telephus, king of barbarian Mysia (in Asia Minor, the West of modern Turkey) but of Greek descent, for a play first performed in Athens in 438 BCE (it came second in the competition after Sophocles' entry). When warding off a Greek assault on Troy Telephus is wounded by Achilles. As the wound will not heal and with an oracle indicating that only "the wounder" can cure it, he leaves for Argos where the Greeks have gathered in preparation of a second attack, and ultimately manages to be liberated from his pains by "the wounder", Achilles' spear, as it turns out. We know of other dramatic versions of the myth by Aeschylus and Sophocles[6] but Euripides' play caused the biggest repercussions. Here

---

4   Cody 1983, 76–9. Discussions of the vase are Sourvinou-Inwood 1997, Dearden 2002, 189f. and 193f., Taplin 2007, 122f.

5   Hardwick 1999, 179 n.1: "(...) I. McPhee has informed me that Trendall was himself intially in doubt about the authenticity of the vase, but his final verdict, after he saw the vase, was that it is genuine."

6   Preiser 2000, 41–63, also see the other commentaries on the fragments of this play in Collard/Cropp/Lee 1995 and Jouan/van Looy 2002.

it is in the disguise of a beggar that the Mysian king manages to sneak into the Greek assembly. Upon disclosure of his true identity Telephus snatches the young Orestes, Agamemnon's son, flees to an altar with his hostage and threatens to kill him. Both these features, disguise and lethal threat, are typical of Euripides' penchant for paradox and climactic stagings. They are extensively parodied in comedies of the 420s and 410s which explicitly connect them with Euripides' version of the myth. Hence there is every reason to regard them as Euripidean innovations.

The Cleveland vase, in keeping with the iconography of more than a dozen other representations of this tragic scene on South Italian artifacts[7], captures the emotional intensity and theatrical pace of this key-scene while making no hint at Telephus' disguise as a beggar, a crucial and highly significant element of Euripides' version. If there is nonetheless near-certainty that the play which inspired this painting is Euripides' and not someone else's, this is because of Euripides' enormous popularity in the fourth century in general[8] and the large impact which the altar-scene of his *Telephus* had in particular.

But not only is there no disguise. While the woman is wearing an ornate dress with a crown-like headgear, the male figures are naked, with only the faintest of hints at garments (the central male figure is wearing shoes and has a small robe draped about his left arm to indicate the swiftness of his movements at this very moment). Male nakedness (or half-nakedness) too is common in the standard iconography of this scene, and any explanation of it has to be derived not from the performance which inspired the vase painting but the artistic conventions governing its representation.

The background story here is, in a nutshell, the following. There is, on a general level, a marked distinction between the vase paintings inspired by tragedy and those inspired by comedy. Put simply, the latter tend to signal much more explicitly the fact that they are inspired by the theatre. Markers of theatricality on comedy-inspired vases typically include at least two of the following: a (raised) stage; characters with comic mask and costume (snub nose, protruding jaws, fat bottom and a dangling leather phallus); comic masks (unrelated to the specific scene) to fill the visual field; name tags or even blurbs with dramatic dialogue.

Tragedy-inspired vases like the *Cleveland Medea* crater, on the other hand, are characteristically much more reticent about giving away their theatrical connections: faces are faces and not masks; characters are not presented as wearing costume, and may even be naked or half-naked; usually there is no indication of a stage; name tags are rare, and no vase currently

7   *LIMC* vol. VII (1994) 866–8 (M. Strauss).
8   Revermann 1999–2000.

known shows a play-title. As a consequence, it becomes methodologically much more difficult to connect some vase paintings with particular tragedies. In the minimalist scenario the cues to make the case for linking a vase painting with a play are the following: a scene to match in the preserved textual evidence; high theatricality as conveyed through gesture and proxemics ("blocking"); and reason to believe that the scene depicted is a "signature scene", memorable, flamboyant and climactic enough to function as a tag for the tragedy as a whole.

With this background story in mind, the male nakedness of the Telephus scene on the *Cleveland Medea* crater starts to become less puzzling. The painter has captured the tension, high pace and emotionality of the traditional tale as manifested in its Euripidean theatrical instantiation. At the same time, he tells the story "*his* way", which includes both painter- and genre-specific modes of representation like the suppression of tragic masks or a stage. The nakedness of the male characters has to be seen along these lines: as the woman's beauty, height, dress and headgear signal her aristocratic status to an ancient viewer, so the nakedness of the flawless and beautiful male bodies is the painter's (or, in this case, the painters') means of elevating them to the heroic sphere.

A comparison with the Euripidean treatment of the scene which provoked the vase painting quickly reveals a difference of some importance: the key notions associated with Euripides' famous "ragged hero" theme (which "Telephus in beggar's disguise" is a variation of) have become totally obliterated on the vase. Enough of the fragmentary Euripidean *Telephus* survives to be certain that the power of deception and the discrepancy between appearance and reality, words and actions, true and apparent social status were central concerns and strongly articulated in theatrical terms.

Vase paintings inspired by this tragedy, however, will have none of this when telling the story "*their* way". The process of appropriating Euripides results in losing depth by smoothening the play's visual complexity and the forces driving it. On the other hand, the vase representation gains intensity by giving more linear emphasis to tension inherent in the situation, the male opponents' equality of heroic status and the lethal threat posed to a royal heir. Whether this smoothening is in any way to be connected ideologically with the self-perception of the vessel's intended viewers – male aristocrats gathering with their peers at a drinking party – is an issue that must presently be postponed until the concluding paragraphs of this paper.

Telling it "his way", again: Medea and the notion of perverted sacrifice

Intricate as the Telephus-scene may be, it is the splendid other side of the
vase [fig. 1 and 2] which instantly captures any viewer's attention. No one
with some background in classical Greek culture will fail to connect the
iconography quickly with the Medea-myth, in particular its most famous
and forceful instantiation, the tragedy by Euripides. But, again, why regard
the painting as inspired by theatre rather than myth-telling or, very generally
speaking, the Greek cultural imaginary? In other words, many of the methodological problems discussed in the previous paragraph re-surface. They
can be pinpointed to the following features of the vase painting:

(1) No masks or name tags.
(2) No hint that the characters' attire is theatrical costume. In particular, the
     bottom-left male character is half-naked.
(3) No indication of a stage house or a raised stage.

In the light of what I just said about the Telephus-scene and the vase iconography of tragedy in general, none of these three items is particularly
problematic. In fact, this sort of non-theatricality is the rule, and not the
exception, with vase paintings inspired by tragedy. The reasons for linking
this scene with tragedy are the same as in the Telephus-scene, and of similar
strength: a scene from preserved tragedy to match – Euripides' *Medea*; a
"signature scene" of particular importance and theatrical flamboyance – the
spectacular ending of this play; a high degree of theatricality as far as gesture and proxemics are concerned; and, as an aggravating factor, the fact that
the scene-to-match is by Euripides, who is known to have been particular
popular on fourth-century stages all over the Greek cultural continuum.

So far so easy. Things become particularly interesting, and difficult,
as soon as the painting is compared in detail to the preserved performance
script. A (long) series of (substantial) discrepancies emerges. I will list them
first before engaging with them:

(4) No indication of other theatrical devices, although a crane was certainly
     used for staging Medea's spectacular in-flight final exit.
(5) The large halo-like sun with rays which encircle Medea on her chariot –
     unstageable, it would seem, in any fifth- or fourth-century Greek theatre.
(6) Snakes are drawing the chariot. Only the latter is mentioned in our pre-
     served performance script, at lines 1320f. Snakes, however, become a
     standard iconographic feature from 400 onwards[9] and are mentioned in

---

9   *LIMC* VI (1992) 391–3 (M. Schmidt).

a (probably Hellenistic) summary (ὑπόθεσις) of the play (hypothesis (a) in Diggle (1984) 88, lines 8–11).

(7) Two figures, male and female. They are clearly the children's nurse and their paedagogue, both of whom are *dramatis personae* but are highly unlikely to have appeared on stage in the final moments of the play as we have it.

(8) The slaughtered children are not on the chariot, as the preserved performance-script by Euripides clearly requires (1317–22), but on an altar.

(9) Two props (a sheep and a hydria) which are certain not to have featured in the performance of the preserved Euripidean *Medea*. And whether or not a permanent altar was a feature of the Athenian theatre and others[10], in the play it was not associated in any way with the infanticide (which happened offstage) or its aftermath.

(10) Two winged old female figures who frame the scene.

The absence of theatre equipment in action (4) is to be expected, *a fortiori* as it were, on the grounds that tragedy-related vase paintings tend to hide, as a matter of principle, most forms of theatricality (see (2) above). In fact none of the theatre-inspired vases currently known – be they influenced by tragedy, satyr-play or comedy – shows technical theatre equipment. This is somewhat of a surprise (and disappointment) in so far as overt theatricalism is standard on scene-specific vases inspired by comedy, of which *ca.* 100 are known to-date.[11] It is crucial to note at this point that in none of these scene-specific representations of comic theatre the use of the crane or the *eccyclema* in the underlying comic scene is at all likely. There is, in other words, no means of saying whether vase painters suppressed a technical feature or not. At any rate, the reasons for the current silence of the vases is this particular respect are likely to be manifold. Luck of the draw must be one of then. Also, the technically most elaborate scenes need not be the "signature scenes" of a play, hence painters (or their commissioners) did not choose them. In addition, theatre equipment is not easy to represent and may have been considered dispensable by vase painters as it would crowd the narrow visual field of vases. Last but not least, in fifth- and most of all fourth-century comedy the crane and the eccyclema may not have been used as often as is assumed by some.[12]

The testimony of the vases is badly needed in this area: some notorious technical questions about staging, the design and shape of the infamous *eccyclema* for instance, cannot be settled unless visual evidence of some

---

10 Rehm 1988, Wiles 1997, 70–2.
11 Taplin 1993, 32–6 conveniently classifies the evidence.
12 Notoriously so by Dearden 1976.

description presents itself. My personal guess is that, before long, a comedy-related vase which shows theatre equipment being deployed *will* crop up: the art market has produced many surprises in the recent past, and will continue to do so.

It is discrepancies (5) to (10) which lead to less technical issues. Closer examination of the forces which drive these deviations will show not only how the medium affects representation, but also how the painter (and/or the commissioner of the vase) appropriates and engages with the scene in thoughtful, creative and intellectually stimulating ways. (Re)-telling it *"his way"*, then, implies that the vase painting becomes much more than a representation: it is a document of reception, an important witness of the early cultural history of classical Greek tragedy in *Megale Hellas* around 400 BCE.

Discrepancy (5), the halo-like sun which encircles Medea, is a case in point. The motif derives from the fact, rather casually mentioned in the final scene (1321f.), that *Helios*, the sun-god, is Medea's paternal grandfather.[13] The painter develops this theme into the spectacular and eye-catching highlight of the vessel. Defamiliarizing, unexpected and dominating the visual field the halo articulates a complex set of key-notions: Medea's semi-divine and super-natural status; the protagonist's uncanny stature through her connection with an elementary natural force; the power, nature and impact of her magical powers (note that Creon's daughter burns to death, and that Medea's final exit is through the sun's domain); danger and unleashed aggressiveness (this notion in particular is supported by the fact that Medea's costume is clearly marked as oriental); and a sense of detachment and elusiveness.

Auxiliary to all these notions, especially Medea's connection with magic and poison, are the snakes which pull the chariot. Erring on the side of caution, I listed them as discrepancy (6) in the list above, although it is not at all clear whether there is in fact a difference between vase iconography and theatrical practice. As I just pointed out, the snake-drawn chariot becomes a standard feature of the scene (developing Medea's traditional association with snakes.[14] Above all, the mention in one of the (probably Hellenistic) summaries (*hypotheseis*) of the play may well be influenced by stage practice, be it contemporary or earlier.

---

13   It is entirely possible that in productions the audience, or parts of it, would be invited to make a connection between the chariot of *Helios* and the real sun. In an environmental theatre the association is an easy way to make for the audience. It can conveniently be reinforced by actors' deixis. Also note that the majority of known Greek theatres (including the Athenian one) has the audience face south, see Ashby 1999, 97–117.

14   Sourvinou-Inwood 1997, Nussbaum 1997, 234–40.

One is on safer ground with discrepancy (7). The nurse and the paedagogue, who both have speaking parts in Euripides, are highly unlikely to
have been on stage in the final scene (the paedagogue left with the children
at line 1020). Not only is there no reference in the performance script but,
more importantly, there would be little point to either one's presence: Jason's helpless isolation should be echoed by the stage configuration.

Why did the painter add at two figures in his rendering of the final scene?
The main reason, surely, is an increased emphasis on suffering and loss:
adding to the tableau those who principally nurtured and raised Medea's
children heightens the intensity of the scene's pathos. In addition, the sheer
crowdedness of the visual field creates a sense of some closural "wrap-up".
The painter thus adopts a technique commonly used by dramatists, including ancient Greek ones, who re-introduce a large number of characters in the
grand finale to strengthen the sense of closure. Interestingly enough, this sort
of crowded closure, while common in comic stage practice and, it appears,
satyr play, is very rare in Greek tragedy with its interest in an individual's
response to catastrophe (the joyful procession at the end of Aeschylus' *Eumenides* being the most notorious exception). In other words, the painter's
agenda to increase pathos (and fill the visual field) overrides concerns that
were dominant in the play's theatrical instantiation. Ultimately, however, the
presence of the nurse and the paedagogue is rooted in the biggest, and most
significant, discrepancy of all: the fact that the children lie slaughtered on
the altar (8).

This, we know, is profoundly at odds with the Euripidean script which is
unambiguous in this respect. Here Medea takes the children, who had been
killed off-stage, with her on the chariot for burial not in Athens, where she is
headed, but at the temple of Hera in Corinth. Denying the corpses to Jason is
Medea's final act of revenge and humiliation (aggravated by the fact that the
children are male and not female). Again, it is the forces which drive devia-
tion that command interest.

Not the least important of these must be the organization of the visual
field: the corpses would detract from, and seem incompatible with, the lavishness and detailing of Medea and her accessories. But by means of the
altar, the peculiar shape of which marks the scene as set in Corinth[15], the
vase painter crucially picks up on and develops a notion which is central to
the play (and many other tragedies[16]): sacrifice, or rather its perversion. He
does so, I wish to argue, by adding visual markers (discrepancies (9) and
(10) above) which *evaluate* the deed: the infanticide is visually highlighted

---

15 Hardwick 1999, *passim*.
16 Burkert 1966, Foley 1985, Krummen 1998, Blome 1998.

as a perverted form of sacrifice, the distortion of a religious frame and of ritual practice.

Associations with perverted sacrifice are clearly evoked by the altar on which the slaughtered children lie (and might the sheep[17] and the hydria point to sacrifice as well, bloody and bloodless respectively?). The point of discrepancy no. 10, the two winged females who frame the upper visual field, appears to be similar in kind. Confronted with a scene centred around the shedding of kindred blood an ancient viewer, I believe, cannot but decode such winged creatures as the revenge-deities *Erinyes*.[18] In the Euripidean performance script Jason wishes that "the *Erinys* of the children and deadly justice" (1389f., cf. the chorus at 1258–60) may punish Medea for her crime. But this rhetoric was certainly not reflected in the staging as envisaged by Euripides[19], nor do one or two visible *Erinyes* make sense as a theatrical gimmick added by some ancient producer. Rather, it is, once again, the painter who capitalizes on the internal logic of the scene (and, perhaps, on Jason's rhetoric). As elsewhere on this vase, the pressure of the medium, iconographic tradition and individual appropriation combine to make for a distinct statement not found elsewhere in the currently known iconography of the scene: the doubling of *Erinys*-figure, their position and not least their ugliness all call for special attention.

While symmetrical framing must be one function of the doubling[20], it should be mentioned that the two *Erinyes* can be regarded as the revenge deities for each child respectively (also note Jason's phrasing in the passage just mentioned (1389f.), although he of course uses the singular). The position of the *Erinyes* combines notions of being stationary and potentially mobile: seated on (or leaning against) rocks and gazing on the scene of horror below they seem ready to pursue Medea any time and anywhere. Sour-

---

17   The animal is a sheep and not a dog: only sheep hold their feet in this way – in a pastoral economy a detail more than well-known to anyone.

18   *Pace* Schmidt (n. 9) and Taplin 2007, 123 who regard them more generally as ugly demons.

19   Had Euripides wanted them to appear, there *would* be a comment of some sort in the text. This is not a question of philological narrow-mindedness but of theatrical dyamics. *Erinyes* were manifestly very rare on the stage (which is quite surprising given the nature of tragic crimes). Aeschylus' *Eumenides* and Cratinus' comedy of the same name (probably a parody of the former) are the only known (or likely) cases in the complete and fragmentary plays of Attic drama. The actual physical appearance of one or several *Erinyes* would therefore be totally unexpected, exciting, provocative – in a word: worthy, even in need of, some comment by the chorus or another character.

20   As is the representation of Eros and Aphrodite on a Lucanian hydria contemporary with the *Cleveland Medea* (Taplin 1993, fig. 2.103). See also the symmetrical framing on the mosaic in Clarke 1991, pl. 15.

vinou-Inwood may well be right to argue that the presence of the *Erinyes* is designed to instill in the viewer a sense that the crime "will or ought to be punished" and that Medea will, or at least may, not get away with it.[21] In a sense, then, by introducing the deities of (possible or prospective) revenge the vase denies closure to the action in a way Euripides' play does not.

The ugliness of the *Erinyes*, finally, is a neglected but important peculiarity of this vase. In the standard iconography *Erinyes* are scary because of their snake-infested dishevelled hair (or snakes in their hands) – but are also young and beautiful[22], a fact which tends to be overlooked in an almost uncanny way.[23] Youth and beauty crucially underline their status as goddesses who deserve respect and reverence (a point of great importance for Aeschylus' *Eumenides*, esp. its ending). I know of only no other ugly *Erinys*, the closest runner-up being an older *Erinys* on the fragment of an Apulian vessel dated to 375–350 BCE and now in the Cahn Colllection.[24] On the Cleveland *Medea* crater their age and ugliness are stressed not just by the face but also the saggy breasts. Snakes are absent, perhaps since this would have interfered with the snakes that draw Medea's chariot. The bird-features of the ugly avengers include not only the wings but also the arms and legs. This, like the ugliness, is untypical of standard Greek iconography. My suspicion is that the Lucanian painter may have been influenced by the iconography of Etruscan underworld deities (like Vanth and Tuchulcha) who are portrayed as bird-like with wings and feathers but also beaks or claws, even if the female deity Vanth is neither old nor, in the human sense, ugly. The usual way of looking at the phenomenon is to assume a transfer from Greek to Etruscan. Thus Vanth, for instance, would not be ugly precisely because it is assumed that her iconography is influenced by the Greek *Erinyes*.[25] But

---

21 Sourvinou-Inwood 1997, 271f.

22 *LIMC* III (1986) 824–43 (H. Sarian).

23 Thus, for instance, Giuliani 2003, 248–58 has good and interesting things to say about the interface between the *Erinyes*-iconography and their role in Aeschylus' *Oresteia*, but fails to notice that on the vases he discusses the Erinyes are invariably young and beautiful (*e.g.* figs. 51f. and 54f. in Giuliani) whereas the Aeschylean text seems to suggest, and is universally taken to imply, that they are old, even monstrous (as they indeed are in most modern productions of the *Oresteia*). There are, in other words, two options: either Aeschylus' production featured old and ugly Erinyes, which would be at variance with the standard iconography of these deities; or the Erinyes were as young and beautiful on stage as they are on the vases, in which case our text of the play has either been corrupted in the process of transmission or needs to be understood differently, namely as emphasizing the Erinyes' never-ceasing vigour and vitality. On this last point, and the significance in the *Eumenides* of integrating polarities (such as young/old) in general, see Revermann (2008).

24 *LIMC* III (1986) 832 no. 48 (H. Sarian), picture and discussion in Cambitoglou/ Chamay 1997, 164f.

25 Krauskopf 1987, 83f.

there is no reason at all not to assume transfer in the other direction as well as liberal conflation of iconographies in the rich and diverse melting pot of the Italian peninsula in the fifth and fourth centuries BCE. The ugly *Erinyes* on the *Cleveland Medea* may be precisely such a case.

Whatever the origins of the peculiar iconography, its function on the vase is perfectly obvious. Again, the painter evaluates, and the physicality of the *Erinyes* mirrors the horror and appalling nature of the crime which made them appear in the first place. If anything, the *Erinyes* illustrate the complex dynamics that exist between the three driving forces: the play, the iconographic tradition and the painter's eagerness of telling the story "*his* way".

Excursus: Déjà vu or Déjà lu? South Italian performances? Euripides?

At this point I wish to take a brief side-step and address, in a very compressed manner, three further problems, two very general and one more specific, put on the agenda by the *Cleveland Medea* crater. First, if a play underlies the iconography of the vase, in which format was the painter (and/or commissioner) of the vase exposed to it, as a performance or as a text?

Both hypotheses have found their adherents[26], and both are respectable arguments. Greek cultural life surely continues to be very much performance–oriented with an infrastructure to match, while texts, including dramatic ones, become demonstrably more common in the late fifth and early fourth century. Three points, I believe, need to be made in this context. One is that, wherever painters got their inspirations from, they clearly listened, watched or read carefully – and then, as I have been arguing throughout this article, went on to do their own thing. Secondly, the opposition of "performance-inspired" *vs.* "text-inspired" is not an exclusive one. I see no reason whatsoever why painters as well as their patrons should not have been exposed to both on a regular basis. Thirdly, given the obvious importance of the visual dimension for their artistic products, I find it incredible to assume that painters should have been totally unaffected by contemporary performances of plays, whether they saw them themselves or whether they heard about them from others.

If the case for a theatrical performance as *a* or the inspiration (of some sort) for theatre-related iconography is a sound one, what format did these performances take? local performances in Lucania? other places in *Megale Hellas*? mainland Greece? Again, we will never be in a position to answer a question of this kind with confidence. Iconographies travel, as do the vessels

---

26 Giuliani 2003, 243–5 with further lit., Thomas 1992 chapters 6 and 7 Taplin 2007, 26–8.

which manifest them: the *Pronomos Vase*, probably the most famous the-atre-related vessel[27], was fabricated in Attica and somehow, at some point, made it to Southern Italy where it was found. On the other hand, the bigger cities in *Megale Hellas* like Syracuse or Taras had the infrastructure, esp. venues and expert manpower needed for staffing dramatic choruses, in order to satisfy demand for fully-fledged theatrical entertainment. Local perfor-mances in smaller places, finally, must have been common too: troupes of travelling actors were mobile and willing enough to perform (perhaps using makeshift stages), although finding a sufficient number of chorus-men might have posed somewhat of an obstacle to mounting plays full-scale.[28]

The third problem I briefly wish to touch on is the following. We know that other dramatic versions of the Medea-story existed, so how can we be sure that the deviations from the Euripidean script which are found on the *Cleveland Medea* are not to be explained by assuming that one of these other versions underlies the iconography? Thus our sources provide us with information about a Medea-play by Neophron which, it seems, bore close resemblance to the Euripidean tragedy. Whether Neophron's version pre- or post-dates the Euripidean one continues to be a matter of dispute.[29] Perhaps more worryingly a new (yet unpublished) papyrus from Oxyrhynchus con-tains mention of a Medea-play with an onstage-infanticide which Euripides is said to have corrected.[30] The infanticide motif itself was demonstrably subject to experimentation: we now know that in Carcinus' *Medea*, a fourth-century tragedy, Medea at one point said that she had not killed her children, and it is at least possible that this in fact turned out to be true later in the play.[31]

Lastly, an Apulian volute-crater from the 320s (so produced roughly 75 years after the *Cleveland Medea*) is inspired by a Medea-tragedy which, it would seem, introduced the ghost of Aeetes, Medea's father, as a *dramatis persona* and had one child escape from Medea's assault.[32] We have no idea whether the play which underlies this vase pre- or post-dates the Euripidean one, but whatever its age it is clearly very different from Euripides' treat-ment of the story.

---

27 See, for instance, Csapo/Slater 1995, 69f. and Wilson 2000, 78.

28 On travelling actors and their logistics see Hughes 1996, Pöhlmann 1997, Wilson 2002, 64f., Lightfoot 2002.

29 A circumspect discussion (including the fragments and testimonia) can be found in Mastronarde 2002, 57–64, who leans towards a post-Euripidean date. For the frag-ments of a possible Euripidean satyr play *Medea* see Kannicht 2004, 1137–42.

30 Mentioned in Mastronarde 2002, 57 n. 94.

31 This is based on a papyrus first published in 2004, discussed in detail by West 2007.

32 Taplin 1997, 80.

I do not wish to downplay the difficulties posed by the existence of other versions. Nonetheless, the case for arguing that the Euripidean script we have underlies the *Cleveland Medea* crater remains an extremely strong one, and one that I endorse without unease: the Telephus-scene on the other side of the vessel surely *is* Euripidean, and picking another play by the same author would seem natural, not least in view of the increasingly pre-eminent position in Greek cultural life which Euripides started acquiring by the final quarter of the fifth century. Also note the *Cleveland Medea* was painted just about 30 years after the first Athenian performance of Euripides' play which is a small gap, comparatively speaking. Last but certainly not least I would bring to bear what I have been trying to argue in the preceding paragraph: that all aspects of the vessel's peculiar iconography invariably make excellent sense if seen as the result of the painter and/or commissioner(s) using the vase as a platform for serious intellectual engagement with the Euripidean play.

2   The Gaze of the Recipient(s) and its Context(s)

The problem of context(s)

The task of establishing contexts (socio-political, performative, aesthetic, and so forth) for just about any cultural commodity of antiquity – be it part of literature or art – is a notoriously difficult one. Contexts are often insufficiently attested. When, on the other hand, a context happens to be comparatively well-documented, it may be the case that we know very little in detail about the cultural commodity that is to be contextualized. Moreover, the allocation of a cultural commodity to a specific context may be highly uncertain. Or the case for any allocation may, as it often does, rest solely on internal indicators which tend to be 'soft' and usually somewhat inconclusive. Last but not least, scholarly discussion of possible contexts is almost invariably characterized by a distinct tendency towards binaries: either "public" or "private", "civic" or "ritual", "solo" or "chorus", "funerary" or "symposiastic" and so forth – binaries, one often discovers fairly quickly, that may be doing serious injustice to social reality.

The painted clay vessels that are the object of this paper are, fundamentally, household vessels. Even if they accompany their owner to the grave, which those that are preserved self-evidently did, they carry with them an air of domesticity, personal identity and human intimacy (even if all of the above may be "on display", for others to see and notice). While the funerary context was the final one for the preserved vessels, it may itself be part of a chain of contexts: everyday use and storage, ornamental display (if only to signal the owner's wealth or sophistication and cultural competence) or use as part of a symposium are contexts which may well co-exist as a chain, even if one context may stand out as dominant and primary.

Sometimes, to be sure, hard evidence precludes certain contexts and favours, or even dictates, others. Thus, as I will discuss in a moment, some of the theatre-related vessels have an unglazed base (or even a hole in the base), which renders them unusable for any function that involves actual storage such as symposiastic or menial domestic use. This, in conjunction with the shape of those vessels, makes their use in a funerary context a certainty. But in the vast majority of cases no such "knock-out" criterion exists, and the search for context(s) becomes more of an exercise in matching a vessel's shape, size and iconography with various possible scenarios that have to be thought through and evaluated individually. Here, certainty gives way to degrees of plausibility. It is to this kind of contextualization that I now turn.

Contextualizing the *Cleveland Medea* and other theatre-related vessels

The *Cleveland Medea* crater, like most of its peers, owes its survival to being part of tomb. As with so many vases, the specific provenance is irrecoverable, because the vessel was not found as part of a systematic excavation and eventually cropped up on the art market. But the generic context, a Greek funeral in South Italy in the fourth century BCE, is less opaque. In two of the most stimulating contributions to have appeared on the subject, Luca Giuliani[33] contextualized a particular sub-set of often large and elaborate tragedy-inspired vases within funerary ritual. These big vases, painted in Apulia (a region neighbouring onto Lucania where the *Cleveland Medea* was produced) in the late fifth and fourth century, were display vases. Never intended for practical use – they have, among other things, an unglazed, hence permeable base – they were deployed exclusively for funerary ritual. The iconography of these vessels, Giuliani argues, explores and interacts with the key-themes of the funeral (death, suffering, the human condition, praise of the deceased). Functioning both as narratives and allegories, these vases have a consolatory effect by presenting *a fortiori* tragic examples of human suffering. As such, some of them might have featured as cues for someone delivering a funeral speech.

Is the *Cleveland Medea* to be contextualized along similar lines? Quite certainly not, since it is difficult to see which role it could possible have fulfilled in the funeral celebration held in honour of the deceased. The theme common to both sides of the vessel is infanticide, threatened (Telephus) and accomplished (Medea). What cues could this iconographic programme pos-

---

33   Giuliani 1996 and 2001.

sibly provide in a funeral context which calls for praise and/or consolation? That evil deeds will be punished by the will of the gods (represented by the two ugly Erinyes)? That women are dangerous, especially those of the barbarian-and-magician variety? Given the infanticide theme invoked by the vase I can think of only one vaguely plausible funeral context to function as a cue: the burial of a child. But this is very far-fetched, and what would the point be? "Medea's children also died young"? "Young Orestes was nearly killed by Telephus"?

The underlying general problem is not that this kind of "morale of the story" is so clearly reductionist, not to say simplistic, and insufficient to do justice to the complexity and sophistication with which tragic playwrights tackle issues of, for instance, gender or divine justice. Quite the contrary: there is very good reason to believe that throughout antiquity such "moralist" reduction and simplification is, embarrassingly enough to a modern mind, the standard level of appropriating tragedy in a variety of intellectual and social discourses, especially education.[34] Why should funerary contexts be an exception? Also note that "moralizing" of this sort tends to be intrinsically simplistic, in any situation. Thus Giuliani, speaking of the Apulian funerary display vases, insists that "triviality is a frequent, perhaps even necessary characteristic of allegorical meaning" and that extracting allegorical meaning from these vessels is meant to be easy for the viewer.[35]

Rather, the problem is that extracting a "morale" and *exempla* from a tragic plot often makes little or no sense in the context of a funeral oration. Medea is a case in point. But even those tragic plots which might be considered suitable for consolation or praise are either not at all or only sparsely represented in the vase evidence we currently have. Sophocles' *Oedipus*, Euripides' *Heracles* or the self-sacrificing women of several Euripidean plays (like *Phoenissae*, *Erechtheus* or *Alcestis*), for instance, one might imagine in a funeral oration as *a fortiori* exemplars of endurance, courage, faithfulness and patriotism. But of the tragedies just mentioned only one (Sophocles' *Oedipus*) left its mark in the vase evidence we currently have – on perhaps as little as one single vessel.[36] An important separate yet related point – and one which requires fuller discussion than can be offered here – is that the scenes found on theatre-related vases are often (though certainly not always) not particularly eschatological, which would involve showing a tragic hero

---

34 Suffice it, in this context, to point to Lycurgus' use of Euripides *Erechtheus*, or to the widespread practice of collecting *sententiae* from playwrights like Menander and Euripides.

35 Giuliani 2001, 26f.

36 *LIMC* VII (1994) 9 (I. Krauskopf) no. 83. Nos. 82 and 84 are dubious, no. 85 may well be inspired by the Euripidean *Oedipus* (where Oedipus is blinded by Laius' slaves).

or heroine in a situation confronting or reflecting on "last things". The emphasis, it seems to me, is usually on action, tension and visible conflict rather than reflection. The mood, in other words, is often exterior and flamboyant (even to the point of being flashy) rather than inward-looking.

To be clear, I would not want to rule out in principle the possibility that tragedy-inspired vases other than the Apulian ones considered by Giuliani could feature prominently in a funeral context as consolatory cues of some sort.[37] There is, I guess, no limit to what a simpleton funeral orator can do to a tragedy, and to what his audience will tolerate. It is also crucial to note, as Junker has done, that there is a distinction between 'grave offerings' (to be deposited in the tomb) and 'funerary vases' (to be used in the funeral).[38] Junker notes that the latter function can, in principle, be served by any vase, and the two functions may also overlap (as they do in Giuliani's scenario). In the absence of a 'hard' indicator of context (or non-context) such as permeable bases or even holes in the vessel's interior, the only way, for us, to distinguish, or prioritize rather, between various context options is to look at the iconography of any individual vessel (the 'soft' indicator) and think through how it interacts best, and most plausibly, within the eligible contexts of use. In addition to the funeral, these eligible contexts are sheer display of the vase, as a marker of status and cultural competence, in the home of the owner or the specific use of the vessel at the symposium (again, these two functions are not mutually exclusive – as, of course, funerary and sympotic context do not preclude each other either).

It is surely significant to note that most theatre-related vessels we have (esp. those related to comedy) have shapes designed for the consumption or storage of wine. While it is impossible to prove that every single theatre-related drinking vessel was in fact used at a symposium, the likelihood is very high. Unless a crater, for instance, is produced only for a funeral and instantly becomes a tomb-accessory, putting it to use in the cheerful context of a drinking party is the natural option. This, however, is not common currency in the field right now. Taplin, like Giuliani one of the finest interpreters of theatre-related vases around, follows Giuliani and zooms in on the funeral context.[39] That said, Taplin at least acknowledges the existence of the symposium context when stating that tragedy-related vases were "made primarily for display at funerals and for the tomb, even if some were first given practical use at the symposium."[40] But once the existence of the symposium

---

37 For the grotesque antics of vases inspired by comedy or even satyr-play I do not see any place in a funeral context at all.

38 Junker 2002.

39 Taplin 2007, 43–6.

40 Taplin 2007, 44.

context is accepted, not regarding it as the primary context of use strikes me as utterly counter-intuitive.

Vessels performing at the symposium

Little attention (if any) has, then, been devoted to thinking through the roles which theatre-inspired vessels played at the symposium. As Junker noted, for us it all boils down to situating individual iconographies within plausible social contexts. And it is in the symposium context, I wish to argue, that the iconographic choices made by the painters of most theatre-related vessels, be they inspired by tragedy, comedy or satyr-play, make perfect sense (which does not, of course, preclude subsequent re-contextualizations of any of these vessels in any kind of funerary context – if only signal the connoisseurship of the deceased).

The *Cleveland Medea* is an excellent example for illustrating how a theatre-related vessel might itself be considered to perform at the symposium. Because of its shape, it naturally occupies the centre stage: the mixing vessel is both the spatial and conceptual focal point of the party. The men, reclining on their couches, are grouped around the crater. The "leader of the symposium" (*symposiarchos* or *symposiarches*) determines the ratio with which wine is to be mixed with water in it, hence setting the pace and level of inebriation for the hours to come. The height of the *Cleveland Medea* (50 cm) is sufficient to move it into the field of vision of the reclining men even if the vase is standing on the ground. But tables were commonly used[41] so that the crater was probably even more exposed to the group of men who may suitable be called the vessel's "audience". Also note that the crater would be re-visited on a regular basis in order to re-fill the cups, and that it might itself be re-filled several times in the course of a symposium (unless a new full crater was being brought in).[42] The latter occasion naturally focuses attention on the crater again, and we know that each re-fill could be linked to a theme (this practice underlies the humour of Eubulus *fr.* 93).

Visual and literary sources (including a whole genre of writings which choose the symposium as a setting) provide us with an unusually good idea of what happened during symposia.[43] A "play space"[44] informed by an atmosphere which combined relaxed and intimate festivity with a characteristi-

---

41   See, for instance, Napoli 1970, fig. 33.
42   For some pertinent symposium scenes see Lissarrague 1990, figs. 20, 24 and 77–80.
43   On the symposium and (often competitive) symposiastic activities see Murray 1990, Murray-Tecusan 1995, Slater 1991, Davidson 2000, Neer 2002 chapter 1, Collins 2004, 63–163 and Halliwell 2008 chapter 3 (esp. 100–127).
44   Kurke 2000, 66.

cally Greek spirit of overt competitiveness the symposium would feature banter, games (of both physical and intellectual nature, riddles being especially popular), political and philosophical discussions, hetero- and homosexual activity and, not least, performance of poetry. Much of preserved Greek lyric poetry was composed for solo song or recitation at the symposium (which is often referred to in the songs we have), and this codification, of course, reflects a much wider social practice. Depending on the host's wealth and the prestige factor of the occasion, more sumptuous and theatrical entertainment could be provided: mime and pantomime are well-attested for the late fifth century BCE onwards.[45] We have particularly rich evidence for the symposiastic antics of the Roman imperial aristocracy.[46] There can, in sum, be no doubt that the symposium is a fixture in ancient cultural, social and intellectual life, esp. that of the elite who had the time and the money.

The role which vase iconography performed within the "play space" of the symposium has left no traces in paintings illustrating the symposium or in the textual record – not a huge surprise given the little attention which our literary sources tend to pay to visual culture in general and the lowly genre of household pottery in particular. Rather, it is the combination of shape, iconography and symposium context which, intrinsically as it were, suggests certain modes of usage. Thus Lissarrague[47] famously inferred a quasi-theatrical use of the so-called "eye cups" in the symposium context: as symposiasts were holding these cups in front of their faces the vessels would appear to their peers like masks.

Similar strategies of interpretation can be deployed in order to make sense of theatre-inspired vessels like the *Cleveland Medea* crater at the symposium. Like the temporary impersonation associated with the "eye cups", the theatrical theme fits naturally within the ideology of a gathering in honour of Dionysus. The advent of theatre-related vessels at the symposium, which must date back at least to the beginning of the fifth century if not earlier[48], invites forms of interaction which both capitalize on and at the same time expand established symposium practice, esp. riddles, speeches and the performance of lyric poetry.

---

45   See Csapo/Slater 1995 chapter 5. Of particular interest is the erotic ballet-mime which concludes Xenophon's *Symposium* (9,2–7) (with Huss 1999, 440ff., Davidson 2000, 49–51, Gilula 2002 and Wohl 2004, 354–60). The performance celebrates the union of Dionysus and Ariadne – as does, among other things, the Pronomos vase. It is easy to imagine how in this case symposium performance and vase iconography might interact.

46   Jones 1991, Dunbabin 2004.

47   Lissarrague 1990, 140–3.

48   See Csapo 2001 on the earliest preserved vessels.

In this environment the unique characteristics of the *Cleveland Medea* fully "play out": its unity of theme (infanticide), genre (tragedy) and, not least, author (Euripides). The spatial configuration of the symposium implies that there is no way of any participant being able to escape the horror, theatricality and fascination of Euripidean tragedy. The vessel, like many cultural commodities, is more than a household utensil. It is a means of social differentiation, of inclusion and exclusion: any viewer who is unfamiliar with the vase's nature and themes is automatically debarred from seeing anything more in it than a flamboyant storage vessel. For those "in the know" the vase, far from being an object solely to be used for menial tasks or to be gazed at, becomes an invitation, incentive and challenge. It creates a matrix of competition, between symposiast(s) and the vessel as well as the symposiasts among each other. The iconographic puzzle of the vase (note, again, the lack of a play-title or labels for individual characters) can easily be construed as the cue for songs from the play and speeches from or about it. It also seems to be ideally suited to function as a "thematic crater" (a symposiastic practice implied by Eubulus *fr*. 93), with a great variety of possible themes to explore for the willing and creative symposiast: toasts, topics and trivia can be derived from the genre, the author, the infanticide-topic, the specific plays, the presentation of women, barbarian otherness, magic and so forth.

The vessel asks for, even pre-supposes, intimate familiarity with Euripides from its target audience[49], and failure to relate, or to relate well, may imply social exclusion (if only partial and temporary) or a competitive disadvantage within the peer group. Note, however, that the ideology underlying the symposium is fundamentally one of inclusion and creating cohesion within the group. In other words: this vessel would not have been produced for this context if failure to relate to its iconography had been the predominant response of its target audience. The number of "those in the know" at the symposium which featured the *Cleveland Medea* must have been substantial.

It becomes obvious at this point that the symposium context of the vessel provides a brief but fascinating glimpse at an area we would like to know much more about: the sociology of reception of ancient drama. As a cultural institution, the symposium is very much a favourite past time of the leisurely elite. These aristocratic connotations do not preclude in principle the possibility of downward mobility in social practice. It has, for instance, been argued that symposium culture became increasingly democratized in

---

49   Against this backdrop something like Plutarch's famous anecdote (*Nicias* 29) about Athenian POWs reciting Euripides to their tragedy-friendly Sicilian captors starts to make sense.

fifth-century Athens. But the case is much disputed: the evidence for private dining of the sub-elite is extremely tenuous, and the much better attested instances of public dining (where the elite would mingle with the sub-elite) in the spatial context of the expressly egalitarian Athenian agora seem to suggest that those occasions tended to *replicate*, or at least imitate, key-features of the private aristocratic symposium, especially (sexual) banter and, most significantly, the ethos of (differentiating) competitiveness instead of egalitarianism.[50] In general, there can be no doubt that while the Athenian democracy may have tried to appropriate the institution of the elite symposium, it certainly did not obliterate it as an aristocratic social practice.[51] On the contrary: democratic attempts at appropriation may well have encouraged the aristocracy to subscribe even more to the importance of the elite symposium, and to emphasize even more clearly its differentiating features such as monetary expense and the sheer lavishness of the entertainment provided – or, indeed, the cultural competence of its participants: the 'real thing', in other words. This, at any rate, is precisely what happens in Plato's and Xenophon's *Symposium*, two fourth-century Athenian texts.

Whether and how such appropriations played out in fourth-century Southern Italy we have no idea. Most of all, however, there can be no question that within the Greek cultural continuum the symposium never ceases to be what it always had been: a central part of aristocratic bonding, net-working, representation and self-definition of an economically and ideologically homogeneous group of men (*hetairoi*) who perceive themselves as members of a 'club' (*hetairia*). Chances that the commissioners, purchasers and intended viewers of as flamboyant and no doubt comparatively expensive a vessel as the *Cleveland Medea* crater came from precisely this stratum of society in fourth-century Lucania are, to say the least, extremely high.

How would male aristocrats respond to the vessel? This questions brings us back to some of its iconographic peculiarities. Is Jason, the social ancestor of those male symposiasts, to be pitied and Medea, the cruel barbarian murderess, to be punished – hence the ugly Erinyes? And, regardless of their flaws and shortcomings, are the heroes of old who feature in tragedy to be represented on the symposium vases as youthful, honourable, straight and without deceit, strong and beautiful – hence the suppression of disguise in the Telephus-scene and the delight in displaying the naked bodies of men in their prime and of Agamemnon's royal heir?

---

50 See Steiner 2002, who discusses the ceramic finds of a dining space (*syssition*) in the Athenian agora in the context of other public dining venues on that very site, *i.e.* the *prytaneion* and the *tholos* (where diners were probably sitting instead of reclining, see Cooper/Morris 1991).

51 On the sociology of the symposium see Cooper/Morris 1991, 77–81 (excellent), Bowie 1997, 1–4, Neer 2002 *passim*, esp. 87–93.

Some further thoughts

I wish to conclude by making two general points. First, I propose a new solution (or part of such) to an old problem by linking the symposium context,
for which most theatre-related vessels from South Italy were produced, with
the funeral context to which they owe their survival. The old problem is the
fact that, while we have a fairly large amount of theatre-inspired vessels
from Southern Italy (especially, but not exclusively, from the fourth century)
there are very few indeed from Athens and Attica in mainland Greece, the
birthplace and hotspot of drama. Why this surprising paradox? Did the Athenians, who so much enjoyed watching tragedy take its catastrophic course,
positively avoid putting it onto their household vessels because they felt it
was too "political", hence somewhat uncanny and dangerous in a domestic
context? Is for Athenians humble pottery too low a medium for representing
tragedy? Or is the contrast between Athens and South Italy less stark and a
question of representational modes, with Athenians being more interested in
dramatic referents than theatrical signs, hence reluctant to represent theatre-
inspired scenes as scenes in performance?[52]

The solution I propose is based on the assumption that theatre-related
vessels made it into the tombs not just to illustrate the wealth of the deceased but, more importantly, to serve as equipment at cheerful symposia in
the anticipated blissful after-life. There appear to be pronounced differences
between Greek and Etruscan symposia[53]: the latter feature food in addition
to wine, making the occasion more like a (festive) replica of ordinary life;
upper-class, respectable (non-naked) women are shown to be in attendance;
and there seems to be a higher symbolic value to the crater, which is often
shown in central position. Crucially, however, there is a significant divide
of religious practice: the notion of the after-life symposium is not attested
for mainland Greece but common in South Italy, among both Greeks and
Etruscans from whom it may originate.[54] Much of Etruscan tomb-painting is
symposiastic in theme, illustrating what the deceased is to expect and creating a symposiastic environment already. Symposium-related funeral gifts,
including left-over food, serve the same purpose. The Greeks who started to
colonize Southern Italy from the eighth century BCE onwards adopted the
notion of the after-life symposium – and, unlike Greeks on the mainland,
started to provide their dead too with the necessary equipment for the good
life in the form of symposium vessels. Athenians, on the hypothesis I wish

---

52   See Taplin 1996, 89f. and Csapo 2001, 36f. respectively.
53   Dunababin 2004, 24f.
54   Napoli (1970), Camporeale (2000) 144–7 and Barker/Rasmussen (1998) 248–51
     with further lit.

to propose, adorned their household vessels with theatre-related scenes as well – but lacking the notion of the after-life symposium they would not normally include them in tombs which is why so very few of them survived.

Secondly, I would like to hint at what, keeping the big picture in mind, are perhaps the two greatest give-aways of the *Cleveland Medea* crater and theatre-related pottery in general. Both points concern, broadly speaking, the interface of theatre and people's lives. The first one is that by the fourth century BCE tragedy has become the main vehicle for telling mythical stories. Theatre-related vase-paintings are but one indicator of the ways in which not epic or lyric poetry but the versions of traditional tale as put on stage by the great dramatists start to dominate cultural discourse in all its ramifications.[55] My second general observation concerns a cultural phenomenon of arguably even greater importance and repercussions. I wish to call it the "privatization" of the Greek theatrical experience. A big and exciting story awaits to be told about the shift from whole-length, public, outdoor presentation of drama in front of a heterogeneous crowd of spectators to the fragmented re-contextualization (mostly) indoors by individuals or troupes to small homogeneous groups with strong socio-economic and ideological bonds.[56] This shift, which seems to gain considerable momentum in the fourth century BCE, is a gradual one, and it appears that for centuries neither mode of consumption becomes dominant at the total exclusion of the other. The theatre-related vases are among our first and best witnesses for these cultural dynamics. It is in keeping with the nature of Greek theatre iconography in general to say that here as elsewhere the *Cleveland Medea* crater, much to its credit, raises more questions than it answers.

Bibliography

Ashby, Clifford (1999), *Classical Greek Theatre: New Views of an Old Subject*, Iowa.
Barker,Graeme / Rasmussen,Tom (1998), *The Etruscans*, Oxford.
Barsby, John (2002), *Greek and Roman Drama: Translation and Performance*, Stuttgart.

---

55 Wilson (1996) (on political discourse becoming "tragedic") and Taplin (1998) (on vase paintings as prime communicators of traditional tale) articulate first thoughts on this monumental subject.

56 "Privatization", in other words, is not (or not necessarily) to be equated with "individualization", nor does it preclude the possibility of a public element. The symposium, for instance, is "private" in the sense that it is an indoor gathering of a small group. It also has an aspect of public exposure, because at the end of the party the group continues to have a good time out on the streets (in the so-called κῶμος). But, thus qualified, "private" continues to be a proper tag, the point being that the cohesion and self-presentation of the peer group never stop dictating the patterns of behaviour. An initial account of "privatization" is Csapo 2010, 168–204 (esp. 170–8).

Blome, Peter (1998), "Das Schreckliche im Bild", in: Graf (ed.) 72–95.

Bowie, Angus (1997), "Thinking with Drinking: Wine and the Symposium in Aristophanes", in: *Journal of Hellenic Studies* 117, 1–21.

Burkert, Walter (1966), "Greek Tragedy and Sacrificial Ritual", in: *Greek, Roman and Byzantine Studies* 7, 87–121.

Cambitoglou, Alexandre and Chamay, Jacques (1997), *Céramique de Grande Grèce. La collection de fragments Herbert A. Cahn*, Zurich.

Camporeale, Giovannangelo (2000), *Gli etruschi. Storia e civiltà*, Firenze.

Clarke, John (1991), *The Houses of Roman Italy, 100 B.C.-A.D. 250: Ritual, Space, and Decoration*, Berkeley.

Clauss, James / Johnston, Sarah (eds.) (1997), Medea. Essays on Medea in Myth, Literature, Philosophy, and Art, Princeton.

Cody, Jane (1983), *Wealth of the Ancient World: The Nelson Bunker Hunt and William Herbert Hunt Collections*. Kimbell Art Museum, Fort Worth.

Collard, Christopher / Cropp, Martin / Lee, Kevin (1995), *Euripides: Selected Fragmentary Plays*. Vol. 1 ,Warminster.

Collins, Derek (2004), *Master of the Game: Competition and Performance in Greek Poetry*, Washington DC/Cambridge, Mass.

Cornell, Tim (1995), *The Beginnings of Rome. Italy and Rome from the Bronze Age to the Punic Wars (c. 1000–264 BC)*, London/NY.

Cropp, Martin / Lee, Kevin / Sansone, David (eds.) (1999–2000), *Euripides and Tragic Theatre in the Late Fifth Century* (= *Illinois Classical Studies* 24–25), Urbana.

Cooper, F./Morris, S. 1990, "Dining in Round Buildings", in: Murray (ed.) 66–85.

Csapo, Eric / Slater, William (1995), *The Context of Drama*, Ann Arbor.

Csapo, Eric (2001), "The First Artistic Representations of Theatre: Dramatic Illusion and Dramatic Performance in Attic and South Italian Art", in: Katz/Golini/Pietropaolo (eds.) 17–38.

—— (2010), *Actors and Icons of the Ancient Theatre*, Oxford.

—— (forthcoming): "The Iconography of Comedy", in: Revermann (forthcoming).

Davidson, James (2000), "Gnesippus paigniagraphos: the Comic Poets and Erotic Mime", in: Harvey/Wilkins (eds.) 41–64.

Dearden, Christopher (1976), *The Stage of Aristophanes*, London.

—— (2002), "From Athens to Magna Graecia: Dramatic Vision", in: Barsby (ed.) 183–96.

Diggle, James (1984), *Euripidis fabulae*. vol. 1, Oxford.

Dunbabin, Katherine (2004), *The Roman Banquet. Images of Conviviality*, Cambridge.

Easterling, Patricia (1997) (ed.), *The Cambridge Companion to Greek Tragedy*, Cambridge.

Förtsch, Reinhard (1997), "Die Nichtdarstellung des Spektakulären. Griechische Bildkunst und griechisches Drama im 5. und frühen 4. Jahrhundert v. Chr.", in: *Hephaistos* 15, 47–68.

Foley, Helene (1985), *Ritual Irony: Poetry and Sacrifice in Euripides*, Cornell.

Gombrich, Ernst (1960), *Art and Illusion: A Study in the Psychology of Pictorial Representation*, London.

Gilula, Dowra (2002), "Entertainment at Xenophon's *Symposium*", in: Athenaeum 90, 207–13.

Giuliani, Luca (1996), "Rhesus between Dream and Death: on the Relation of Image to Literature in Apulian Vase-Painting", in: *Bulletin of the Institute of Classical Studies* 41, 71–86.

—— (2001), "Sleeping Furies: Allegory, Narration and the Impact of Texts in Apulian Vase-Painting", in: *Scripta Classica Israelica* 20, 17–38.

—— (2003), *Bild und Mythos. Geschiche der Bildererzählung in der griechischen Kunst*, Munich.

Graf, Fritz (ed.) (1998), *Ansichten griechischer Rituale (Festschrift* Burkert), Stuttgart/ Leipzig.

Green, Richard (1991), "On Seeing and Depicting the Theatre in Classical Athens", in: *Greece, Roman and Byzantine Studies* 32, 15–52.

Gregory, Justina (ed.) (2005), *A Companion to Greek Tragedy*, Oxford.

Hall, Edith / Easterling, Patricia (eds.) (2002), *Greek and Roman Actors. Aspects of an Ancient Profession*, Cambridge.

Halliwell, Stephen (2008), *Greek Laughter. A Study of Cultural Psychology from Homer to Early Christianity*, Cambridge.

Hardwick, Nicholas (1999), "A Triglyph Altar of Corinthian Type in a Scene of Medea on a Lucanian Calyx crater in Cleveland", in: *Quaderni Ticinesi* 28, 179–201.

Harvey, David and Wilkins, John (2000), *The Rivals of Aristophanes. Studies in Athenian Old Comedy*, London.

Hughes, Alan (1996), "Comic Stages in *Magna Graecia*: the Evidence of the Vases", in: *Theatre Research International* 21, 95–107.

Hunter, Richard (1983), *Eubulus: the Fragments*, Cambridge.

Huss, Bernhard (1999), *Xenophons Symposion: ein Kommentar*, Stuttgart/Leipzig.

Jones, Christopher (1991), *Dinner Theatre*, in: Slater (ed.) 185–198.

Jouan, François/van Looy, Herman (2002), *Euripide: Tragédies*, vol. 8.3 (=Fragments part 3), Paris.

Junker, Klaus (2002), "Symposiongeschirr oder Totengefässe? Überlegungen zur Funktion attischer Vasen des 6. und 5. Jahrhunderts v. Chr. ", in: *Antike Kunst* 45, 3–26.

Kannicht, Richard (2004), *Tragicorum Graecorum fragmenta*, vol. 5 (Euripides), Göttingen.

Katz, Giuliana, Golini, Vera and Pietropaolo, Domenico (eds.) (2001), *Theatre and the Visual Arts*, NY/Ottawa/Toronto.

Keuls, Eva (1997), *Painter and Poet in Ancient Greece. Iconography and the Literary Arts*, Stuttgart/Leipzig.

Krauskopf, Ingrid (1987), *Todesdämonen und Todesgötter im vorhellenistischen Etrurien. Kontinuität und Wandel* (Biblioteca di studi etruschi 16), Florence.

Krummen, Eveline (1998), "Ritual und Katastrophe. Rituelle Handlung und Bildersprache bei Sophokles und Euripides", in: Graf (ed.) 296–325.

Kurke, Leslie (2000), "The Strangeness of 'Song Culture': Archaic Greek Poetry', in: Taplin (2000) 58–87.

LeGuen, Brigitte (ed.) (1997), *De la scène aux gradins: théâtre et représentations dramatiques après Alexandre le Grand* (=*Pallas* vol. 47), Toulouse.

—— (2001), *Les associations de technites dionysiaques à l'époque hellénistique*, Nancy.

Lightfoot, Jane (2002), "Nothing to Do with the *technitai* of Dionysus?", in: Hall/Easterling (eds.) 209–24.

LIMC: Lexicon Iconographicum Mythologiae Classicae. 8 vols. (+ indices), Zurich/Munich/Düsseldorf 1981–1999.

Lippolis, Enzo (*et al.*) (eds.) (1995), *Taranto. Culti greci in occidente*, vol. 1, Taranto.

Lissarrague, François (1990), *The Aesthetics of the Greek Banquet* (Princeton, French original Paris 1987).

—— (2008), "Image and Representation in the Pottery of Magna Graecia", in: Revermann/Wilson (eds.), 439–49.

Mastronarde, Donald (2002), *Euripides Medea*, Cambridge.

Mitchell, Alexandre (2009), *Greek Vase-Painting and the Origins of Visual Humour*, Cambridge.

Murray, Oswyn (ed.) (1990), *Sympotica. A Symposium on the Symposion*, Oxford.

Murray, Oswyn / Tecusan, Manuela (1995), *In vino veritas*, London.

Murray, Penelope / Wilson, Peter (eds.) (2004), *Music and the Muses. The Culture of 'Mousike' in the Classical Athenian City*, Oxford.

Napoli, Mario (1970), *La tomba del tuffatore. La scoperta della grande pittura greca*, Bari.

Neer, Richard (2002), *Style and Politics in Athenian Vase-Painting. The Craft of Democracy, ca. 530–460 BCE*, Cambridge.

Nussbaum, Martha (1997), "Serpents of the Soul: A Reading of Seneca's *Medea*", in: Clauss/Johnston (eds.) 219–49.

Osborne, Robin (2008), "Putting Performance into Focus", in: Revermann/Wilson (eds.) 395–418.

Pöhlmann, Ernst (1997), "La scène ambulante des Technites", in: Le Guen (ed.) 3–12.

Preiser, Claudia (2000), *Euripides: Telephos. Einleitung, Text, Kommentar*, Hildesheim/Zurich/NY.

Rehm, Rush (1988), "The Staging of Suppliant Plays", in: *Greek, Roman and Byzantine Studies* 29: 263–307.

Revermann, Martin (1999–2000), "Euripides, Tragedy and Macedon: Some Conditions of Reception", in: Cropp/Lee/Sansone (eds.) 451–67.

—— (2008), "Aeschylus' *Eumenides*, Chronotopes, and the 'Aetiological Mode'", in: Revermann/Wilson (eds.) 237–61.

—— (ed.) (forthcoming), *The Cambridge Companion to Greek Comedy*, Cambridge.

Revermann, Martin / Wilson, Peter (eds.) (2008), *Performance, Iconography, Reception: Studies in Honour of Oliver Taplin*, Oxford.

Seeberg, Axel (2002–03), "Tragedy and Archaeology: Forty Years After", in: *Bulletin of the Institute of Classical Studies* 46, 43–75.

Silk, Michael (1996), *Tragedy and the Tragic. Greek Tragedy and Beyond*, Oxford.

Slater, William (ed.) (1991), *Dining in a Classical Context*, Ann Arbor.

Small, Joyce Penny (2003), *The Parallel Worlds of Classical Art and Text*, Cambridge.

—— (2005), "Pictures of Tragedy? ", in: Gregory (ed.) 103–18.

Sourvinou-Inwood, Christine (1997), "Medea at a Shifting Distance: Images and Euripidean Tragedy", in: Clauss / Iles Johnston (eds.), 253–96.

Steiner, Ann (2002), "Private and Public: Links between *Symposion* and *Syssition* in Fifth-Century Athens", in: *Classical Antiquity* 21, 347–80.

Taplin, Oliver (1993), *Comic Angels and Other Approaches to Greek Drama through Vase-Painting*, Oxford.

—— (1997), "The Pictorial Record", in: Easterling (ed.) 69–90.

—— (1998), "Narrative Variation in Vase-Painting and Tragedy: the Example of Dirke", in: *Antike Kunst* 41, 33–9.

—— (ed.) (2000), *Literature in the Greek and Roman Worlds. A New Perspective*, Oxford.

—— (2007), *Pots and Plays. Interactions between Tragedy and Greek Vase-Paintings of the Fourth Century*, Los Angeles.

Thomas, Rosalind (1992), *Literacy and Orality in Ancient Greece*, Cambridge.

Walsh, David (2009), *Distorted Ideals in Greek Vase-Painting: The World of Mythological Burlesque*, Cambridge.

West, Martin (2007), "A New Musical Papyrus: Carcinus, *Medea*", in: *Zeitschrift für Papyrologie und Epigraphik* 161, 1–10.

Wiles, David (1997), *Tragedy in Athens. Performance Space and Theatrical Meaning*, Cambridge.

Wilson, Peter (1996), "Tragic Rhetoric: the Use of Tragedy and the Tragic in the Fourth Century", in: Silk (ed.) 310–31.
—— (2000), *The Athenian Institution of the Khoregia. The Chorus, the City and the Stage*, Cambridge.
—— (2002), "The Musicians among the Actors.", in: Hall/Easterling (eds.) 39–68.
Wohl, Victoria (2004), "Dirty Dancing: Xenophon's *Symposium*", in: Murray/Wilson (eds.) 337–63.

Changing Contexts:
Tragedy in the Civic and Cultural Life of Hellenistic City-States

Paola Ceccarelli

Tragedy and the honorific decree belong among the enduring legacies of fifth-century Athens. And at least in the fifth and fourth centuries, both constituted integral and distinctive components of the larger civic culture, even though scholars continue to dispute the "politics of Athenian tragedy", including both the significance of the tragic festivals and the message of tragic scripts.[1] Still, our evidence leaves no doubt that the composition and the staging of tragedies in fifth-century Athens was a profoundly civic form of art, a medium in which the polis "came together", sharing, reflecting, and negotiating its identity as a community, just as, in the honorific decree, it came together in speaking in a single voice. In terms of both quality and quantity, the Athenian data are far superior to the evidence we have of the performance culture of any other Greek city-state in any period, and this in itself tends to exercise an implicit tyranny over historical scholarship: simply because we have the means of knowing a lot about fifth-century Athens, it is tempting to assume that matters were alike, or at least not too dissimilar, in other locations and in other historical periods for which our evidence is far less rich and extensive. I would like to challenge this assumption, by way of investigating the meaning and function of tragic performances in the political culture of cities elsewhere in Greece, in particular during the Hellenistic period. And, as we shall see, an important aspect of this enquiry is the honorific decree.

Already in the early fifth century, tragedy began to spread beyond the confines of Attica. Thus, tradition closely associates Aeschylus and Sicily: besides the performance of his *Women of Aetna* at Gela (possibly in 471/70, to celebrate the founding of the city by Hieron in 476/5), the *Life*

---

1   While scholars seem to concur on the civic importance of tragedy (if only because of the importance of the *choregia*: Wilson 2000), positions diverge as to its precise political significance: Goldhill 1987; Griffin 1998; Rhodes 2003; Carter 2004; Wilson 2009 (with literature).

of Aeschylus attests a reperformance of the *Persians* on the island; and legend has it that the tragedian was buried in Gela.[2] Towards the end of the fifth century, tragedy also arrived at the Macedonian court, which saw visits by both Euripides and Agathon.[3] And many other Greek cities will have had theatrical performances.[4] Even though the surviving evidence is slim, the story of the dissemination of Attic drama throughout the Greek world has been studied repeatedly.[5] What has received far less attention is the question of how tragedy fitted into the various local settings. Needless to say, tragedy abroad became part of contexts that differed from each other just as much as the various traditions, cults, rituals, and political and administrative cultures of the individual *poleis* did – and changes in context surely also influenced how the genre was perceived (and performed).

A first step towards appreciating the contexts of tragedy outside Athens is to look at the types of festivals that featured tragedies. In his collection of 'Fasten-ähnliche Texte', which mention dramatic performances in various contexts, Mette lists some fourteen festivals, comprising the *Soteria* of Delphi (III century BC), the *Mouseia* of Thespiai (with a scenic festival already in place in the second half of the third century BC), the *Heraia* (mid-second century BC) and *Dionysia* of Samos (mid-third century to second century BC), the *Dionysia* of Teos, the *Ptolemaia* of Delos (II century BC), the *Rhomaia* of Magnesia (II–I century BC), the *Sarapieia* of Tanagra (90–80 BC), the *Charitesia* and *Homoloia* of Orchomenos (I century BC), the *Amphiaraia/Rhomaia* of Oropos (I century BC), the *Soteria* of Akraiphia

---

2   See respectively *TrGF* 3 T A 1, 33–4 and F 6–11 (*Aitnaiai*); T Gd 56ab, T A1, 68, and F 285 (*Persai*); and T A 1, 35–9, T A 2, and T M 96–9 (death). Csapo / Slater 1994, 3 and 14; Taplin 1999, 41; and, on early Sicilian choruses, Wilson 2007b.

3   Hanink, this volume; Csapo / Slater 1994, 3 and 14–15; Taplin 1999, 42–3; Revermann 1999/2000; but note the sceptical stance on the story of the death of Euripides taken by Scullion 2003.

4   Cf. again Csapo / Slater 1994, 3 and 15–17; Heath 2009, 472–3. The *scholion* to Eur. *Andromache* 445, if it can be trusted, affirms that the *Andromache* (produced in the 420s) was not produced in Athens, and thus implies the possibility of new productions, rather than simply reperformances, outside Athens; see, however, Allan 2000, 149–60.

5   Dissemination of tragedy: Taplin 1993 and 1999; Dearden 1999; Wilson 2000, 279–302 (on whether and in what measure the Athenian system of *choregia* was exported) Allan 2001. Changes in outlook and performance: Easterling 1993 and 1997; Jones 1993; Xanthakis-Karamanos 1993 (a comprehensive, but sweeping and at times imprecise survey); Le Guen 1995, 2001, 2003, and, especially, 2007; Csapo 2004, 208–16; Hunter / Fantuzzi 2004, 432–37 (a convenient synthesis); Hall 2007, 271–2; Nervegna 2007; Rehm 2007.

(I century BC), the *Kaisareia* of the Isthmus of Korinth (127 AD), and an *agon* in Thessalonike (252–253 AD).[6]

The list, though far from complete, suffices to establish two important points: it allows us to gauge the diffusion and the vitality of dramatic performances all over the Greek world; and it makes instantly apparent that dramatic performances were not exclusively associated with the *Dionysia*: various other types of festivals featured dramatic shows. Moreover, at times dramatic festivals had no civic context at all, as when tragedy was performed on the initiative of kings. Thus Philip seems to have held games to celebrate his destruction of Olynthus in 348 BC (Demosth. 19.192–5), while Alexander staged dramatic competitions in honour of the Muses and Zeus at Dion to celebrate his sack of Thebes in 335 BC (Diod. 17. 16, 3–4).

But the list in itself does not allow us to gauge the relative importance of the dramatic performances within the political culture of the community that sponsored them. To make progress here, various options present themselves. One can, for instance, consider the prizes awarded in each of the competitions; unfortunately, though, the information we have about such prizes tends to be both sporadic and relatively late.[7] Another means of ap-

---

6   Mette 1977, 46–72. See also Csapo / Slater 1994, 186–206; Larmour 1999, 171–92 (the first three appendices list evidence for festivals with athletic and dramatic *agones*; festivals with athletic and musical *agones*; and festivals with musical and/or dramatic *agones*); Le Guen 1995, 64–5; Vial 2003; Nervegna 2007, 19–24. Parker 2004 gives an extremely useful survey of the status (and change thereof) of a number of festivals, irrespective of whether they included drama. The letters by Hadrian to the Dionysiac *technitai* recently published (Petzl and Schwertheim 2006) provide important new evidence about the (re)arrangement of the "circuit" of dramatic festivals, and reflect the continued buoyancy of this international business.

7   The list of prizes for the *Panathenaia* IG II² 2311 (Shear 2003) is not helpful, because drama does not seem to have been part of the festival in the fourth century (dramatic performaces were, however, part of the festival from the second century BC to the first century AD: Jones 1993, 45; Shear 2001, 369–71). In a catalogue of victors and their prizes from the *Sarapieia* of Tanagra, dated to ca. 85 BC (Mette 1977, 53; SEG 19,335, cf. Csapo / Slater 1994, 193–6; Le Guen 1995, 73; Nervegna 2007, 20), the three categories which receive the highest prizes are the *auletes*, the *kitharodos*, and the actor of old tragedy (168 dr. each); the poet of tragedies (135 dr.) won, however, the epinician (overall?) crown as well (168 dr.), so that his final prize is the highest. Other prize lists, such as those from Aphrodisias or the one concerning the institution of the *Demostheneia* in Oinoanda (SEG 38,1462B) are later than the time span here considered (respectively, 100/200 AD and 124 AD; ample discussion of the organization of the festivals of this period in Wörrle 1988, 227–58); interestingly, at Aphrodisias the prizes for athletic events are higher than those for drama, while at Oinoanda singing to the lyre is more highly recompensed than acting (see Csapo / Slater 1994, 187–92). Throughout the Hellenistic period, in the musical/dramatic categories the citharodes are the best paid, followed by the *aulos*-players: see Le Guen 2001a, II 71–4.

praising the prestige of a festival (and of the performances it comprised) is to look at the type of prize awarded: in some festivals it was a crown (whence the name *stephanites*), in others a sum of money.[8] Here, however, I want to pursue a third possibility of assessing the civic and religious importance of tragedy abroad, namely the venue a specific *polis* chose to announce the award of civic honours. I submit that consideration of the sites where honorific decrees were publicly announced allows us to evaluate (a) the relative importance of tragedy (whatever 'tragedy' at any given moment may have meant) *vis-à-vis* other genres of performance; and (b) the relative importance of festivals involving the performance of tragedies *vis-à-vis* other types of festivals. For besides the various privileges given by a *polis* to a benefactor (such as *ateleia*, i.e. exemption from taxes, *enktesis*, i.e. the right to buy land in the territory of the city, or *prohedria*, i.e. the right to a front seat in the theatre), honorific decrees sometimes include a clause stating that the honours conferred (and in particular, the conferment of a crown) should be announced in public, by a herald or by specific magistrates, at some particularly important ceremony.[9] The reason is publicity, as is shown by the frequently added further clause "so that everyone may know that the *polis* is thankful towards those who serve her well", and by the very fact of the inscription of the decree on stone.[10] It thus seems reasonable to assume as a working hypothesis that the moment chosen for the announcement would be among those the *polis* and the honorand considered the most important.

---

8 Definition of the various categories of festivals, and their impact: Pollux III 153 (τοὺς μὲν οὖν καλουμένους ἱεροὺς ἀγῶνας, ὧν τὰ ἆθλα ἐν στεφάνῳ μόνῳ, στεφανίτας ἐκάλεσαν καὶ φυλλίνας, τοὺς δ' ὀνομαζομένους θεματικοὺς ἀργυρίτας); Nachtergael 1977, 299–300 and 339; Csapo / Slater 1994, 187; Le Guen 2001, 266 and 286; Robert 1984, 36–7 and 1989, 20; Vial 2003; Parker 2004, stressing continuity between the classical and the Hellenistic period. Especially in the Hellenistic period, the fact that a festival is *stephanites* does not imply the absence of an economic reward; on the complex mechanics of this, see the important study by Slater / Summa 2006.

9 As pointed out by Henry 1983, 28, at least in Athens provisions for the proclamation of crowns were not automatic. The inclusion of a motion to have a crown proclaimed thus probably reflected a greater desire on the part of the Athenians to honour and gratify the recipient. For Delphi see Nachtergael 1977, 370: "C'était sans doute un honneur supplémentaire, conféré à des personnes de premier plan, puisque d'autres décrets qui décernent les mêmes distinctions ne prévoyent pas de proclamation". More general discussion of this practice in Osborne 1999, 354–6, who, however, also points out, in a different connection, that the wording of the inscriptions cannot be trusted to reproduce exactly the decisions taken – i.e. a proclamation might have taken place even though the inscription did not record it.

10 On the inscription as an honour in itself, see Lambert 2006, 116; on the status of honorific decrees as "monumentalised diplomacy", see (besides Gauthier 1985) Lambert 2006, 116–17, and Liddel 2007, 172–4; on publicity through inscriptions and oral announcements, Migeotte 2002.

The occasion of choice was almost always some kind of agonistic festival, which turns the conferment of honours and their public announcement into an articulation of the agonistic mentality of the Greeks: from the point of view of the city, its benefactors participated in a permanent competition for honours and the winners received public acknowledgement via the award of a honorific decree, its public announcement, and its permanent preservation and display on stone.[11] This practice reflects common values shared across the entire Greek world: for the honours conferred to be meaningful, they needed to be appreciated equally by giver and recipient.[12]

Generally speaking, this economy applied to all honorific decrees, both those for citizens and those for foreigners. But the politics involved in the conferment of honours appear in a clearer light in those honorific decrees awarded to a foreign entity, such as a king or royal emissary, another *polis*, or individuals from another *polis*, such as judges, *presbeis,* or doctors. In those cases, the decree conferring the honours often includes a clause which specifies that ambassadors are to be sent to the other *polis*/entity to ask that the decree be also proclaimed at some public event there. The conferment of an honour thereby not only rewarded the recipient, but also served the honoring *polis* to advertise its presence at another location in the wider Greek world.[13] When the honorand is a member of the civic community, honorific decrees tend, as a rule, to be specific about the moment of the announcement; but they usually leave greater leeway concerning the announcement to be made in another *polis*. A third century decree of Thasos for Coan judges, for instance, asks the Coans to proclaim the honours "in those *agones* in which it is prescribed for them to do this kind of announcements".[14] This hardly surprises: while each *polis* would know exactly when it wanted to

---

11 Gauthier 1985, 12, who aptly quotes, among other texts, Aeschin. 3.180; Liddel 2007, 165–70. See also for the honours ὡς ἀθλητής Blech 1982, 113 and n. 20, 124, and 162; and Osborne 1999, 354–6, who sees in this a form of political neutralization, of "de-politicization" of the honours.

12 Gauthier 1985, 11. In quite a few parts of the Greek world, however, the awarding of a crown is not attested, as, for instance, at Oropos: Habicht 2002, 20–1.

13 This parallels how cities recompensed athletic victories in agreed *stephanitai* ag-ones: a nice instance is *I.Ephesos* 1415 (II BC). See Slater / Summa 2006, esp. 281 for a statement of the question and 297–8 for discussion of the inscription; further below 130.

14 SEG 49, 1108, ll. 10–12. See also the example cited below, n. 99. In numerous cases the specific occasion is not indicated even when it concerns the city issuing the decree: thus a honorific decree for an Herodotos, passed by the Coan deme of Halasarna around 300–250 BC, specifies only that the honours have to be announced at the next *agon* that the people will dedicate to Dionysos (*SEG* 48, 1094.24–26: [κα] λεσεῦντι τὸς πολ[ίτας --- | ..ΟΛΕΙ ἐν τῶι ἀγῶνι [τῶι πράτωι, ὃν συν]-| [τελ]εῖται ὁ δᾶμος τ[ῶι Διονύσωι - -). Note, however, that Wörrle (as cited by the first editors) suggested to restore [ἀναγορεῦσαι ---ἐν τᾶι π]όλει ἐν τῶι ἀγῶνι τ[ῶι χορικῶι].

proclaim honours, it might have been less clear as to the most prestigious moment (or simply the preferred one) in another *polis*. As a result, there is considerable variation in local practice across the Greek world.

A range of practical reasons may have influenced the choice of venue, such as the necessity to spread the announcements over more than just one day or event, depending on their number;[15] there are also instances in which the choice appears to have been influenced by the specific activities of the person the *polis* wanted to honour. But as a general rule we may assume that in most cases the venue chosen for the proclamation will have been the one considered the most prestigious. The sites specified in honorific decrees for the announcement of public honours thus afford insight into the perceived importance of tragic, and more generally dramatic, festivals, in comparison to other public festivals of a musical or athletic nature, and should contribute to our appreciation of variations in local practice and of changes over time, from the classical to the Hellenistic period. This is not a new idea: Brigitte Le Guen, in attacking the notion that the Hellenistic period saw a decline in the importance of theatrical performances, a notion fostered, in her opinion, by the similarly misguided notion of the "mort de la cité", has repeatedly pointed to the testimony of the public proclamations of honours for asserting the continued importance of theatrical performances.[16] While her main points stand, and while neither the city nor the theatre died, I will argue that in quite a few cases the focus of the city's identity, in religious and civic terms, or at any rate the moment considered the most appropriate for public proclamations, either never were dramatic festivals or moved from the dramatic (tragic) performances to choral or gymnic competitions. While it is thus most certainly wrong to talk of a decline in dramatic activity, the status and function of this activity within the civic life of the *polis* shows considerable variation and may have declined over time.[17]

---

15 So Chaniotis 2007, 57, who interprets all variations in the choice of venue thus.

16 Le Guen 1995, 73–4 and 80 (an influential article: Taplin 1999, 54); 2001, 265–6. Le Guen sees a remarkable continuity between the role of the theatre, and in particular of drama, in fifth-century Athens, and in later periods or other parts of the Greek world. But her analysis of the public proclamation of honours is restricted to an excessively small sample, and leaves out (as does Wilson 2009) those instances in which honours are announced in contexts other than tragedy. On rituals in the theatre, as attested by the "crowning formulae" in honorific decrees, see also Chaniotis 2007.

17 Easterling 1997 stresses the development of tragedy towards "cosmopolitanism"; for Hall 1996, 305, the absence of the *polis* from Aristotle's *Poetics* has to do with the fact that "tragedy was about to lodge a petition for divorce from the Athenian democratic city". The criticisms made by Le Guen 2007 are not convincing; but see now Heath 2009 for a different explanation of the absence of the *polis* (Athens) from the *Poetics*.

Before approaching the primary evidence, however, some qualifications are in order. To begin with, what precisely is "tragedy"? For us, it is exceedingly difficult to ascertain what exactly the performance of a tragedy or, to use the idiom frequently found in our sources, "tragic choruses", entailed at any given moment in time or place after the fifth century. Several factors complicate the issue: with the possible exception of the *Rhesus*, no play from the fourth and later centuries has survived; there were considerable changes in production, linked, not least, to the rise of professional actors; and new ways of organizing programmes and awarding prizes emerged.[18] Variations in the choice of venue for the announcement of honours are thus but one element within a wider history.[19] It is therefore vital to try to understand, through close attention to the exact wording of the documents, what kind of tragedy (old or new, with a chorus or without) was performed at any given moment – even though the lack of precision of honorific decrees in this respect means that in many cases we may not be able to reach definitive conclusions.

Secondly, a word is needed about the corpus of documents taken into account. Among Greek decrees, those preserving some kind of honorific award are the most numerous; I have not attempted a comprehensive analysis of all of them, but have chosen a representative sample of areas and *poleis*.[20] Even so, in almost no case – with the exception of Athens – is there enough material to allow for a complete, diachronic picture; what one gets, in lucky instances, are a few reliable synchronic 'snapshots'. It is even more difficult to move from local contexts to general synthesis, though the shared values that underwrote the granting of honours in the Greek world may facilitate generalization from specific instances.

Since what follows will involve the detailed, and at times inconclusive, engagement with a wide range of rather thorny pieces of data, it may be useful to anticipate the results of the investigation here, almost as a set of working hypotheses, to be tested against the evidence: (i) the theatre is one of the most common venues for the proclamation of honours (in quite a few documents honours are to be proclaimed simply "in the theatre", with-

---

18   The latest survey of the evidence concerning plays is Le Guen 2007. For the rise of professional actors see Csapo 2004b; 2010,83–116.

19   A story perceptively sketched in its main lines by Easterling 1997; see also Hall 2007. Nervegna 2007, even for late antiquity, assumes continuity with the classical period in the staging of complete plays, rather than, as is usually assumed, pantomimic solo-pieces. Le Guen 2007 sensibly opts for temporal and geographical variation in the type of spectacle.

20   I here follow Habicht 2002. The lists in Larfeld 1898–1907, 1, 513–16 (for the Greek world in general) and 2.2, 774–5 and 838–9 (for Athenian state decrees, and for decrees of *phylai*, cleruchs, and other corporations respectively) are still very useful; see also his synthesis at 2.2, 810–11.

out further precision); (ii) in classical Athens, the moment preceding tragic performances was clearly the preferred one for the public announcement of honours[21] – as part of the so-called "preplay ceremonies", i.e. religious and civic ceremonies, that also included the libations offered by the generals, the parade of the war orphans, and, at the time of the Delian league, the presentation by the allies of their annual tribute;[22] (iii) but in many other parts of the Greek world dramatic performances were not the preferred moment for honorific announcements; (iv) even in those localities where this seems to have been the case at some point, the evidence testifies to a trend away from dramatic performances as the venue for prestigious public announcements to choral or gymnic ones instead; while the reasons for this may be discussed, the trend itself seems clear.

1   Contexts for the announcement of honours in Athens

Athens offers the natural point of departure for our enquiry: it is the *polis* that invented both tragedy and the practice of the honorific decree; it is also the city for which we have the most ample documentation of the practice of publicly announcing honours.[23] A passage from Aeschines' speech *Against*

---

21   Conversely, Lambert 2006, 117 singles out the theatre, together with the main-
     tenance of diplomatic relations with Macedon and the securing of grain supply,
     as one of the three main concerns of Athenian honorific decrees. Wilson 2009
     makes a strong case for the connection of theatre with proclamation of honours
     and ultimately democracy.

22   Cf. e.g. Isocr. *De Pace* 82; Pickard-Cambridge 1988, 59, 67. For the significance
     of the inclusion of these civic ceremonies in the theatre contrast Goldhill 1987
     and Griffin 1998, 47, further Guettel-Cole 1993, 29, 34 and Rhodes 2003, Carter
     2004; and Wilson 2009. Henderson 2007, 182–3 sensibly stresses that the *Dio-
     nysia*, a festival celebrated in late spring, when communications between *poleis*
     where good, attracted a uniquely large and international audience; this still does
     not explain the choice of a specific moment within the festival. Timetabling may
     have been an issue (some days were more charged than others); it should also be
     noted that the order of the events at the Great *Dionysia* is disputed, and that this
     is the case for most of the festivals we shall discuss. On the probable order of
     events at the *Dionysia* see the possibilities sketched in Csapo / Slater 1994, 107–
     8 (9 Elaphebolion: *eisagoge*, religious ceremonies; 10 Elaphebolion: beginning
     of the *Dionysia* proper, with *pompe*, and in the afternoon dithyrambic contest;
     and then four or five days devoted to dramatic competitions, which opened with a
     number of ceremonies); and the alternative proposal of Pickard-Cambridge 1988,
     65–7.

23   Guettel-Cole 1993, 29 states that the *Dionysia* and honorific decrees were exported
     together from Athens, and adds that "it is by the wide appearance in Greek cities of
     decrees of formal praise that the spread of the *Dionysia* can be measured". For the
     influence of the Athenian decrees on those of other *poleis* see Larfeld 1898–1907,

Ctesiphon includes, as part of a polemic against the crown that his archrival Demosthenes had been awarded by the people, a more general depiction of how such proclamations took place:

> First, however, I will tell the reason why the laws governing the proclamations in the theater were enacted (ἕνεκα οἱ νόμοι ἐτέθησαν οἱ περὶ τῶν ἐν τῷ θεάτρῳ κηρυγμάτων). It frequently happened that at the performance of the tragedies in the city proclamations were made without authorization of the people, now that this or that man was crowned by his tribe, now that others were crowned by the men of their deme, while other men by the voice of the herald manumitted their household slaves, and made all Hellas their witness (γιγνομένων γὰρ τῶν ἐν ἄστει τραγῳδῶν ἀνεκήρυττόν τινες, οὐ πείσαντες τὸν δῆμον, οἱ μὲν ὅτι στεφανοῦνται ὑπὸ τῶν φυλετῶν, ἕτεροι δ' ὅτι ὑπὸ τῶν δημοτῶν· ἄλλοι δέ τινες ὑποκηρυξάμενοι τοὺς αὐτῶν οἰκέτας ἀφίεσαν ἐλευθέρους, μάρτυρας τοὺς Ἕλληνας ποιούμενοι); [42] and, most invidious of all, certain men who had secured positions as agents of foreign states managed to have proclaimed that they were crowned – it might be by the people of Rhodes, or of Chios, or of some other state – in recognition of their merit and uprightness (διεπράττοντο ἀναγορεύεσθαι ὅτι στεφανοῖ αὐτοὺς ὁ δῆμος, εἰ οὕτω τύχοι, ὁ τῶν Ῥοδίων ἢ Χίων ἢ καί τινος ἄλλης πόλεως, ἀρετῆς ἕνεκα καὶ ἀνδραγαθίας). And this they did, not like those who were crowned by your senate or by the people, by first obtaining your consent and by your decree, and after establishing large claims upon your gratitude, but themselves reaching out after the honour with no authorization from you. [43] The result of this practice was that the spectators, the choregi, and the actors alike were discommoded, and that those who were crowned in the theater received greater honours than those whom the people crowned (τοὺς δὲ ἀνακηρυττομένους ἐν τῷ θεάτρῳ μείζοσι τιμαῖς τιμᾶσθαι τῶν ὑπὸ τοῦ δήμου στεφανουμένων). For the latter had a place prescribed where they must receive their crown, the assembly of the people, and proclamation "anywhere else" was forbidden; but the others were proclaimed in the presence of all the Hellenes; the one class with your consent, by your decree; the other, without decree. (Aeschin. 3, 41–43; transl. Ch.D. Adams, Cambridge-London 1919).

Aeschines clearly has his own case to peddle, but the passage shows well the key issue at the root of honorific decrees: the public conferment of prestige, for both the *polis* and the individual. From what we can piece together of the arguments brought by Aeschines against the crowning of Demosthenes in the theatre, it would appear that in Athens various possibilities for the proclamation of crowns existed. Thus, a crown conferred by the *boule* had to be announced in the *bouleuterion*, while one given by the *demos* would normally have been announced in the *ekklesia*, "and nowhere else".[24] Other

---

1, 487–8; Rhodes and Lewis 1997, 550–56. Only state decrees will be taken into account here; for deme decrees see Whitehead 1986, 257 and n. 8 and Wilson and Hartwig 2009, 20; for decrees by various other groups, see Larfeld 1898–1907, 2.2, 838–9; Lawton 1995, 4–8. Liddel 2007, 160–209 offers an excellent description of the overall working of Athenian honorific decrees.

24   Aeschin. 3.32–4. This kind of precision compares neatly with the frequent indications on the same documents of where to put a stele or a statue. For iconographical

venues might also be chosen: Isocrates attests the proclamation of a crown for an Athenian citizen in the *agora*, close by the monument of the Eponymous Heroes, probably for the year 404;[25] a fragmentary inscription honouring an Aristomenes and dated to 357/6 BC specifies that the crown is to be announced "when the *demos* will deem it appropriate".[26] But Aeschines concedes the existence of a law concerning the *Dionysia* that allows a crown conferred by the *demos* to be announced in the theatre, at the moment of the tragedies; on this, Aeschines anticipates, Demosthenes will try to build his defence.[27]

Whatever the validity of Aeschines' case against Demosthenes, the epigraphical evidence shows that honorific decrees were usually content to praise someone (*epainesai*) – and in such cases the praise will have resonated wherever the decision to praise was taken: in the *boule* or in the *ekklesia*. Yet in quite a few cases, in addition to the praise (*epainos*), the conferment of a crown is attested – as well as the further honour of a proclamation of this award in the theatre, or at any rate at a festival. There are, however, some variations to this basic scheme, and it is on these that we shall now concentrate.[28] As we shall see, the evidence dovetails neatly with what is otherwise known of the changes in Athenian theatrical life.

---

evidence of awards by the *boule* and the *demos* see Blech 1982, 175–6, and more generally the artifacts listed in his catalogue L20.

25 Isocr. *Against Callimachos* (18) 61.

26 *Agora* 16 54, 10–11: ἀνειπεῖν] ὅταν τῶι δή[μωι δοκῆ]-| [ι, where Woodhead notes that the formula is otherwise unparalleled, and thus the restoration open to doubt.

27 Aeschin. 3, 36: ἕτερον δ᾽εἶναι νόμον ... ἐναντίον τούτῳ, τὸν δεδωκότα ἐξουσίαν ποιεῖσθαι τὴν ἀνάρρησιν τοῦ στεφάνου τραγῳδοῖς ἐν τῷ θεάτρῳ, ἐὰν ψηφίσηται ὁ δῆμος. Demosthenes does briefly refer to this at 18.120–1; a crown for him had been announced in the theatre in 340 BC (Dem. 18.83; Yunis 2001, 157). According to Aeschines, the Dionysiac law permitted only crowns awarded by foreign *poleis* to Athenian citizens to be proclaimed in the theatre; the orator even quotes a further regulation specifying that the crowns would then be dedicated to Athena (Aeschin. 3.47–48). On the affair see Gwatkin 1957, 135–41; Yunis 2001, 157, 179; Harris 1994, 141–8; 1995, 142–5, pointing out the relative weakness of Aeschines' case; and Carey 2000, 160–1. On the widespread tensions concerning honouring in the second part of the fourth century, and on their reasons, see more generally Liddel 2007, 161–4.

28 The list of proclamations given by Mette 1977, III A 4a, 94–100, is in need of updating – and it anyway refers only to the *Dionysia*. Also focused only on the *Dionysia* are the important contributions of Wilson 2009 and Wilson and Hartwig 2009 (the latter offering at p. 22f. a chronological list of the literary and epigraphical evidence for the announcement of honours at the Athenian City Dionysia with explicit reference to tragedy). A good entry into the world of Athenian honorific decrees is Henry 1983 (who does not, however, try to be comprehensive); discussion of the venues for the proclamation of honours *ibid.*, 28–36. See also Lawton 1995, *passim*, and, specifically on crowns, Blech 1982, 153–61. Osborne 1999 has remarks on the content

In Athens, the proclamation of crowns is attested for foreigners from the end of the fifth century onwards; the recipients are kings, states, or distinguished individuals, who in most cases are simultaneously made citizens. (The proclamation of crowns for actual citizens is epigraphically attested only for much later, from the second half of the fourth century onwards.) The oldest surviving instance is for Thrasyboulos of Kalydon in 410/9, for his role in the assassination of the oligarch Phrynichos.[29] The text is fragmentary, but on the basis of later evidence all editors supply the *agon* of the *Dionysia* as the place of proclamation.[30] The second is a decree in honour of a Cyrenaean, Epikerdes, dated to 405/4: it is heavily restored, but the provision seems to refer to a proclamation "at the imminent next *agon* in the city", and *en astei* always refers to the *Dionysia*.[31] A third decree, dated to the end of the fifth / beginning of the fourth century, may have been more precise, for it seems to stipulate that the honours should be announced by the herald "at the *Dionysia*, in the contest of the tragedies".[32] The next document, a de-

---

of the proclamation, on its limited relationship with what had been discussed in the assembly, and on the "neutralizing" effect of keeping the formulations as generic as they appear to have been.

29   See Osborne 1999, 354–5; Henry 1983, 29–30; Blech 1982, 153–61. As underlined by Blech 1982, 156, the fact that crowns for citizens are attested only later cannot simply be an accident in the transmission of documents but must reflect the political feelings of the Athenians. Lambert 2004, 86–87 points out that the practice of conferring high honours on citizens was not entirely new in the 340s, and that it is only the regular inscribing of the decrees by the *polis* that is new, and part of the developing culture of the written word. But concerning proclamations (which are arguably close to inscriptions, because of the publicity they imply), he too agrees that until 322/1 BC the proclamation of crowns occurs occasionally for foreigners, but normally not for Athenians (Lambert 2004, 107 n. 75). See however the instance given above, n. 25.

30   IG I³ 102.12–13: καὶ [ἀνειπ]-| [ἐν τὸν κέρυκα Διονυσίον ἐν τõι] ἀγõνι hõν hέν-| [εκα αὐτὸν ho δῆμος ἐστεφάνοσ]ε. For the momentous character of this proclamation see Wilson 2009; Wilson and Hartwig 2009 canvass restorations that bring the tragic *agon* into the text (e.g. καὶ [ἀνειπ]-| [ἐν Διονυσίον τραγωιδῶν ἐν τõι] ἀγõνι). Earlier crowns for non-Athenians are known: the document relief from the Akropolis, IG I³ 65, Blech 1982, 156 and 435 L 20, 4 (= Lawton 1995, n° 65), dated to 427/26, shows Athena crowning Apollophanes of Kolophon (the text of the *stephanosis* is, however, lost).

31   IG I³ 125.23–26 (= Lawton 1995, n° 10): the herald had been instructed to proclaim an earlier crown as well as the new one: ἀνειπῖν [δὲ καὶ τὸν κήρυκα π]-| [ρ]οσκηρύξαντα ἐ[ν τῶι ἀγῶνι τῶι αὐτί]-| 25 κα μάλα ἐν ἄστει [ὅτι πρότερον Ἐπικέ]-| ρδης... On the temporal clause αὐτίκα μάλα see Wilson 2009, 14–15; note the additional specification of what exactly the herald is to announce in this text – a rare instance, which Osborne 1999, 355 deems unique – but cf. for example the later (post-236) IG II² 1299.32–37, discussed below, n. 61.

32   IG II² 2b (honours for Arist... son of Simon, Boiotian and proxenos), ll. 10–12: [ἀνειπῖν δὲ τὸν] | [κήρ]υκα Δ[ιονυσίοις ὅταν] | [ἦι ὁ] ἀγὼ[ν τῶν τραγωιδῶν]. For

cree dating to 393/2 and honouring king Euagoras of Salamis, is also fairly lacunose; but according to the commonly accepted restoration, the herald should proclaim the honours at the contest of the tragedians.[33]

Despite the textual difficulties, these four documents clearly show the absence of an established formular.[34] This offers welcome confirmation of the fact that the habit of proclaiming the crowns (or at any rate of recording their proclamation epigraphically) was a relatively recent one, and that the absence of documents from earlier periods is not simply due to accident. A large chronological gap separates this group, which comprises exclusively foreign honorands (Thrasyboulos was granted citizenship in a rider to the decree honouring him), from the next. From the late fourth century onwards a number of texts (all in all, seven decrees, ranging from ca. 319 BC to ca. 280 BC) specify, with a fairly consistent formular, that the crown has to be announced in the theatre, at the agon of the *Dionysia*, during the contest of the tragedians.[35] To these seven documents, the evidence from the invento-

---

doubts on Wilhelm's restorations see however Henry 1983, 31 and n. 67; the date is uncertain as well (SEG 32, 38). Wilson and Hartwig 2009, 23–26 propose now to restore at ll.10–12 [ἀνειπεῖν δὲ τὸν] | [κήρ]υκα Δ[ιονυσίων ἐν τοῖ] | [ς τρ]αγωι [δοῖς], and offer a good discussion of the date.

33   SEG 29, 86 (IG II² 20 +) = Rhodes / Osborne 2003, 11c, 29–30: ὁ δὲ κῆ[ρυξ - - - -]| [- - - -]Ι ὅταν οἱ τρα[γωιδοὶ - - -].

34   So also Wilson 2009, 20–21 (for the early group). Even a later document, such as IG II² 575, 323/2, prescribing honours for Euphron, son of Adeus of Sikyon, and for Sikyon (the first case of honours for states: Osborne 1999, 355), destroyed in the aftermath of the Lamian war and reinscribed as IG II² 448 (cf. Lambert 2006, 122 and n. 24), has the vague formulation καὶ ἀνειπεῖν αὐτὸν Διονυσίων μεγάλων τῶι ἀγῶνι (Summa 2009, 490 n. 24 erroneously states a proclamation at the tragic agon); and the same vague formulation has been plausibly restored in SEG 21, 357.2–3 (honours for hipparchs, 286–261 BC).

35   The following recurrent formulae may be identified: a) ἀνειπεῖν τὸν στέφανον Διονυσίων τῶν μεγάλων τραγωιδῶν τῶι ἀγῶνι: IG II² 555, 307/6–304/3 BC, for Asklepiades of Byzantion; IG II² 654, 285/4 BC, for Audoleon king of the Paionians; IG II² 657, 283/2 BC, for the comic poet Philippides, son of Philokles, from Kephale. b) ἀνειπεῖν τὸν στέφανον Διονυσίων τῶν μεγάλων τραγωιδοῖς ἐν τῶι ἀγῶνι: IG II² 653, 284 BC, for Spartokos, son of Eumelos, from Bosporos. c) ἀνειπεῖν τὸν στέφανον Διονυσίων τῶν ἐν ἄστει τραγωιδῶν τῶι ἀγῶνι: IG II² 646, 295/4 BC, for Herodoros, son of Ph-; SEG 45, 101, ll. 41–3, 293/2 BC (=IG II² 649+, discussed also below, n. 45); IG II² 693 (very fragmentary, various restorations possible), mid-third century BC or slightly later (Tracy 2003, 149), for the *demos* of Priene. A case apart is the very fragmentary IG II² 385, 319/8 BC (cf. SEG 21, 341), honours for Aristonikos, son of Aristomedes, from Karystos, where Dow proposed to restore at l. 10–11 [..ἀνειπεῖν Διονυσίων τῶν με]-| γάλ[ων] τοῖς [τραγωιδῶν ἀγῶσιν...]; see Wilson and Hartwig 2009, 22 n. 37. I do not consider IG II² 354 (Schwenk 54, 328/7 BC), honouring the priest of Asklepios Androkles, a case of public proclamation: the formula at ll. 16–19 οἱ λαχ-| όντες ἐπιμελητ[α]ὶ τῆς εὐκοσμίας τῆς περ[ὶ] |τὸ θέατρον ἀπέφη[να]ν αὐτὸν ἐν τῶι δήμω[ι χρ]-| ἥσιμον γεγονέναι [αὐτ]οῖς περὶ τὴν ἐπ[ιμέλ]-|

ries of the treasurers of Athena and the Other Gods may be added: besides the very fragmentary inventory of the year 321/0 BC (IG II² 1468, 12–13, mentioning crowns, probably proclaimed at the tragic contests of the *Dionysia*, two years earlier), three more inventories refer back to the proclamation of crowns at the *Dionysia*, during the contests of the tragedians, in 321/0 or 318/17 BC, in 307/6, and in 304/3.[36] This group is followed by two tantalisingly fragmentary inscriptions, which seem to imply proclamation of a crown "at the *Dionysia*, in the new competition of tragedies" (Διονυσίων τραγωιδῶν τῶι καινῶι ἀγῶνι);[37] this is certainly what is prescribed in another, slightly later (270/69) inscription, the decree for Kallias of Sphettos,

---

εϊαν τοῦ θεάτρου is too vague for this (differently, Liddel 2007, 172). For announcements at the *Dionysia* and other festivals see below; Summa 2008, 490, as well as Wilson and Hartwig 2009, rather misleadingly lump together both the decrees that prescribe proclamation at the *Dionysia* only and those that, besides the *Dionysia*, include other festivals.

36 Respectively IG II² 1479.8–11, dated to ca. 312/1 BC (heavily restored: στέφανος χρυσοῦς ὁ] | [ἀνακηρυχ]θεὶς Διο[ν]υσ[ίων τῶν μεγάλων τραγωιδοῖς,|10 [ὧι ἐσ] τεφάνωσεν ὁ δῆμ[ος ὁ Ἀθηναίων τοὺς ἱππάρχους]| [τοὺς ἐπὶ] Ἀρχίππου ἄρχον[τος); at l. 18–20 of this same document a crown proclaimed for Konon son of Timotheus at the gymnic agon of the *Panathenaia* is also mentioned; IG II² 1491.10–13; and SEG 38, 143, B col. 2.3–18: (στ[ε]φᾳ[ν]ου [ς το]-| ὺς ἀνακηρ[υχθέντας Διο]-|5 νυσίων τῶν τ [ραγωιδῶν] | τῶι ἀγῶνι, οὓς ἀ[νεκήρυξε]-| ν Φίλιππος Νικ[ίου Ἀχαρ]-| νεὺς ὁ ἐπὶ τ [ῆ]ι [διοικήσε]-| ι κατὰ τὸ ψ[ή]φ[ισμα τοῦ δή]-| 10 μου, ὃ ἔγ[ρ] αψε [Φίλιππος] |Νικίου Ἀχαρν[εύς, ταμίαις] | τοῖς ἐπὶ Λεωσ [τ]ρά[του ἄρχοντος] | (vac.) οἵδε ἀνεκηρύχ[θησαν] | στέφανοι (vac.) |15 ὁ δῆμος Ἀντίγον[ον] ἀπὸ : [Χ(?)] | ὁ δῆμος Δημήτ[ρ]ιο[ν] ἀπὸ : [Χ(?)] | ὁ δῆμος | Ἀντίγονον καὶ Δημήτριο[ν] | (vac.). The crowns that follow these were awarded in previous years, and we do not know whether there was a repeated proclamation or not. Chaniotis 2007, 55–6 speaks of proclamation of twelve crowns, but see *contra* Koumanoudes / Miller 1971, 455–7: the crowns from ll. 19 onwards are in a different category, as shown by the vacats, and by recoupments with other inscriptions. Arguably the elaborate mention of the proclamation, with the name of the proponent, in what is after all an inventory, is evidence that these proclamations were relatively exceptional. Most inventories mention crowns but not their proclamation (for instance IG II² 1485, 1486 and 1487 all refer to crowns awarded under Anaxikrates, without speaking of a proclamation, although IG II² 1491, when these crowns were first awarded, mentions the proclamation).

37 IG II² 692, honours for the *strategoi,* post 303/2 BC (and not later than 283 BC, see Tracy 1995, 157, who considers this the work of the cutter of IG II² 650, whose activity he dates 318–7/283/2); and IG II² 708, honours for the *demos* of the Erythraioi, beginning of the third century. In the first document, ἀνειπεῖν τὸν [στέφανον Διονυσίων τραγωιδῶν τῶι καινῶι ἀγῶ]-[νι] fits exactly the *stoichoi* at disposal; as for the second –non *stoichedon*– text, the restoration proposed ([καὶ ἀνειπεῖν τὸν στέφανον Δι]-| ονυσίοις τραγωιδ[ῶν τῶι καινῶι ἀγῶνι) seems in the overall context convincing.

which requires the crown to be proclaimed at the great *Dionysia*, "in the new *agon* of the tragedies".[38]

The meaning of τραγωιδῶν τῶι ἀγῶνι τῶι καινῶι is unclear. Because some later documents prescribe announcements τραγωιδοῖς καινοῖς, which certainly means "at the moment of the performance of new tragedies", it has been suggested that τραγωιδῶν τῶι ἀγῶνι τῶι καινῶι refers to a contest of new tragedies (as opposed to a competition of old dramas).[39] This, however, would seem to strain the Greek since τραγωιδῶν τῶι ἀγῶνι τῶι καινῶι means, literally, "at the newly instituted *agon* of tragedies" – with many scholars assuming that this newly instituted agon must have been an *agon* of *old* tragedies.[40] In this case, however, we would have to explain why the Athenians at some point shifted the announcement of honours from the newly created *agon* of old tragedies to the *agon* of new tragedies, as documented by the later inscriptions. Not only that: the two expressions τραγωιδῶν τῶι ἀγῶνι τῶι καινῶι and τραγωιδοῖς καινοῖς appear to be interchangeable in a number of later documents.[41] I would hence favour a different solution and take the expression τραγωιδῶν τῶι ἀγῶνι τῶι καινῶι to refer to a global reorganization of the dramatic *agones* of the *Dionysia*, within which the "new" *agon* would have been the *agon* of new plays. The literary evidence is in this respect not helpful: the decrees transmitted in Demosthenes' speech *On the crown*, according to which honours would have been announced in the theatre at the moment of the contest of new tragedies (and which constitute Mette's main evidence for the existence of a the contest of new tragedies in the 340s), are not original documents, but late – at the earliest, first century BC – creations, while Aeschines in his *Against Ctesiphon* refers to procla-

---

38 SEG 28, 60.91–3: καὶ ἀ-| νειπεῖν τὸν στέφανον Διονυσίων τῶν μεγάλων τραγωιδῶ[ν] | τῶι ἀγῶνι τῶι καινῶι.

39 Instances of the new formulation are discussed below (some are listed by Mikalson 1998, 117 n. 35: IG II² 956.33–4, 957.19, and 958.29–30, dated respectively to 161/60, 157/6, and 153/2 BC). In favour of interpreting the expression as "contests of new tragedies" are Mette 1977, 94–100 (who trusting the documents quoted by Demosthenes in his speech *On the crown* pushes back the formulation to the 340s); Pickard-Cambridge 1988, 361–2; Perrin 1997, 205–6; Wilson 2000, 316 n. 58; Nervegna 2007, 18 and n. 27.

40 Thus Peppas-Delmousou 1984, followed by Mikalson 1998, 116–17 and Summa 2003, 299; Summa 2008, 491.

41 Most glaringly in IG II² 1011 (106/5 BC), prescribing at l. 26 the proclamation of the crown awarded to the ephebes Διονυσίων τε τῶν ἐν [ἄστ]ει καινοῖς τραγωιδοῖς καὶ Παναθηναίων καὶ Ἐλευσι<νί>ων τοῖς γυμνικοῖς ἀγῶσιν, and at l. 48–49 the proclamation of the crown awarded to the kosmetes of the ephebes Διονυσίων τ]ε τῶν ἐν ἄστει τραγωιδῶν τῷ καινῷ ἀγῶνι καὶ Παναθηναίων καὶ Ἐλευσινί-|ων τοῖς γυμνικοῖς ἀγῶσιν. See Perrin 1997, 205–6 and footnotes 23–4; Summa 2008, 491.

mation in the theatre, at the moment of tragedies, without further qualifications.[42]

Whatever the exact meaning of the expression, it at any rate presupposes a distinction between old and new plays. Some other evidence does indeed point to the existence of contests of old tragedies at the *Dionysia* in the third century BC. We know from the *Fasti* that in the archonship of Theodotos, in 387/6, an old tragedy had been performed, as an addition, at the *Dionysia*; a fragment of the *Didaskaliai* listing victories in (new) tragedy at the *Dionysia* mentions performances of old tragedies for the years 341, 340 and 339, in what seems to be a fairly standardised form.[43] These performances were probably offered outside the contest; but an inscription listing ancient comedies, satyrplays and tragedies that placed first, second and third in the years 256 to 254 shows that an agon of old dramas indeed existed, although it is unclear from the inscription whether this happened at the *Dionysia*.[44] And of course the institution of a regular competition of old plays at the *Dionysia* would have made it necessary to distinguish between

---

42 On Demosthenes, see Yunis 2001, 29–31, with bibliography. Summa 2008, 490 appears to accept the testimony of the decrees of the *On the Crown* (Dem. 18. 54, 55, 84, 115, 116, and 118) concerning new tragedies, but then proceeds to interpret the expression 'new tragedies' as equivalent to 'tragedies' *tout court*. As for Aeschines, in the *Against Ctesiphon* he uses expressions such as τραγῳδοῖς ἐν τῷ θεάτρῳ (36), the simple τραγῳδοῖς (45; 176), γιγνομένων τραγῳδῶν (41), μελλόντων... τῶν τραγῳδῶν γίγνεσθαι (154) and μελλόντων τραγῳδῶν εἰσιέναι (204). τραγῳδῶν γιγνομένων καινῶν at Aeschin. 3.34 is the text of Blass, accepted by V. Martin and G. Budé (and Dilts, and Summa 2008, 490): but the tradition is here divided, with k (the Parisinus 2998, one of the msscr. considered most reliable by Martin and Budé) giving the simple τραγῳδῶν γιγνομένων, while other mss. have τραγῳδῶν ἀγωνιζομένων καινῶν.

43 Respectively, IG II² 2318.201–3 for the first reperformance of an old tragedy, and IG II² 2320.1–2, 18–19, and 32–3 for regular performances of old tragedy at the *Dionysia*. See Pickard-Cambridge 1988, 105 and 109, with a chronological summary at 124, and the addenda, 361–2; Nervegna 2007, 15–18; Summa 2003, and 2008, 486–8. Good discussion of the broader implications of the fragment from the *Didaskaliai* in Easterling 1997. Both Easterling 1997 and Hall 2007, 279 state that the revival of old tragedy at the Dionysia begun as a permanent feature in 387 BC: this may not have been the case (cf. e.g. Wilson 2000, 23; Summa 2008, 486–8; Revermann 2006, 73).

44 *Hesperia* 7, 1938, 116–18 (Meritt). Meritt thought of the *Lenaia*, but see Pickard-Cambridge 1988, 123, and 361–2 for the likelihood of this festival being the *Dionysia*. The inscription is thoroughly discussed in Summa 2003, 297–8 (who reprints the text, and compares it to the fragments published by Peppas-Delmouzou, "Zu den Urkunden dramatischer Aufführungen II", *Athenische Mitteilungen* 93, 1978, 109–18), and Summa 2008 (arguments for the *Dionysia* are listed at 488–9). See also Csapo and Slater 1994, 42.

the two types of tragic *agones*, and to indicate specifically at which of the two the announcement should be made.

Overall, the most likely moment for such a change are the years immediately following the departure of Demetrios Poliorketes (287/6) from Athens. The decree honouring Philippides son of Philokles with a crown to be proclaimed Διονυσίων τῶν μεγάλων τραγωιδῶν τῶι ἀγ-| ῶνι (IG II² 657.62–3) shows that in 283/2 no need was felt of the further precision "new", while the decree for Kallias of Sphettos, prescribing proclamation at the "new" *agon* of tragedies, gives a *terminus ante* in 270 BC. If we are to trust the restorations and the date proposed for IG II² 692 (and IG II² 708), the change would have taken place early within this frame, by ca. 282 BC. The *Didaskaliai*, too, were probably incised in 279/8 BC, and the decision to inscribe them implies a "taking stock" of Athenian dramatic activity, which is more easily explained in the wake of innovations. Moreover, one important change is well documented: during the years of Demetrios' stay in Athens, the organisation of the *Dionysia* must have undergone some alteration, as the festival took on the name of *Dionysia kai Demetrieia*, a label attested by literary sources and by the decree honouring a Philippides son of Philomelos, of the deme Paiania, passed in 293/2 BC.[45] This is the only document mentioning proclamation at the *Dionysia kai Demetrieia*: after the departure of Demetrios, the festival went back to its old name.[46] Part of the process whereby Demetrian elements were removed from the Athenian scene will have involved a reorganization of the *Dionysia*, and the creation of a new *agon* might have been part of this.[47]

Five more decrees, covering the time span between the mid-third century and 187/6 BC, and most of them heavily restored, attest to the continued practice of proclaiming the honours at the moment of "the new contest of tragedies" (the first two), or of "the contest of new tragedies" (the remaining three).[48] To these documents others may be added, which specify that the

45 The decree: SEG 45, 101.41–44 (= IG II² 649+): κ]αὶ [ἀ]νειπεῖν τὸν στέφ[α]- | [νον Διονυσίων τῶν ἐν ἄστ]ει καὶ Δημητριε[ί]ων τρ[α]-| [γωιδῶν τῶι ἀγῶνι· τῆς δ' ἀν] αγορεύσεως ἐπιμεληθ[ῆ]-| [ναι τὸν ἀγωνοθέτην. Literary sources: Plutarch *Dem.* 12.2. On Demetrios' impact on Athenian theatrical (and religious) life see Mikalson 1998, 75–104 (general) and 116–20 (theatre); Ceccarelli 2004.
46 Mikalson 1998, 116–17; Summa 2003.
47 Summa 2008, 491–496 proposes to see in the victory on the Galatians in 279 BC the impulse for a reorganization of the festival, and for the inscription of the *Didaskaliai* (IG II² 2319–2323) and *Catalogi victorum* (IG II² 2325); she does not mention IG II² 692, but it might be possible to extend the activity of that cutter for three more years. On the whole, events internal to Athens seem to explain the change well enough.
48 Honours for king Antigonos, after 255 BC, IG II² 793. 5–6 (cf. SEG 38, 96): [— ἀναγ]ορευσάτωσαν δὲ καὶ Ἀθη-| [ναῖοι τραγωιδῶν τῶι καινῶι ἀγῶνι ἐν τ]ῶι θεάτρωι κατὰ ταὐτά; honours to the *demos* of Ephesos, ca. 200 BC, *Agora* 16 238.8–9:

announcement be made in more than just one venue; they indicate that the practice of announcing honours at the moment of the performance of new tragedies went on at least until ca. 38 BC.

This brings us to another change that also took place in this period: honours are now often announced at more than one festival. The first document to require multiple announcement is a decree honouring Phaidros of Sphettos, dated to the mid-third century: it prescribes that the honours be announced at the great *Dionysia*, in the competition of new tragedies, but also during the gymnic agon of the Greater *Panathenaia*; two slightly later documents feature a similar clause.[49] Starting with the last quarter of the third century, honours are regularly proclaimed at three or even four festivals, the *Dionysia*, the *Panathenaia*, the *Eleusinia* and the *Ptolemaia*, in the latter three festivals at the moment of the gymnic competitions.[50] Gymnic

---

ἀνειπε]ῖν τὸν στέφανον τοῦτον Δι-| [ονυσίων τῶν ἐν ἄστει τραγωιδῶν τῶι καιν]ῶι ἀγῶνι; honours to the *polis* of Lamia who sent judges, end of the third century BC, IG II² 861.19–20: ἀνειπεῖν τὸν στέφα]νον Διονυσί-|20 [ων τραγωιδοῖς καινοῖς; honours for a familiar of king Seleukos helpful to Athens, 187/6 BC, *Agora* 16 266 (b.1-3 = IG II² 925); honours for Straton of Argos, 200–150 BC, *Hesperia* 40, 1972, 197/98 n. 51, to be announced Διονυσίων τε [τῶν ἐν ἄστει καινοῖς] |15 τραγωιδοῖς. In this last case it has been argued on the basis of the τε that the scribe may have omitted one entire line, and that the honours may have been announced at more than just one venue.

49   Decree for Phaidros, post 261 (251?) BC, IG II² 682.75–78: καὶ ἀναγορεῦσαι τὸν στέφανον Δι-| ονυσίων τῶν μεγάλων τραγωιδῶν τῶι ἀγῶνι τῶι | καινῶι ν καὶ Παναθηναίων τῶν μεγάλων τῶι γυ-| μνικῶι ἀγῶνι; *Agora* 16 208, IG II² 778, SEG 50, 146 (praise for the city of Lamia, 251/50 BC); and *Agora* 16 224, IG XII Suppl. 200,2, SEG 25, 106.36–38 (honours for Prytanis of Karystos, 226/5 BC): ἀνειπεῖν τὸν στέφανον τοῦ-| τον Διονυσίων τῶν ἐν ἄστει τραγωιδοῖ[ς] τῶι | καινῶι ἀγῶνι καὶ Παναθηναίων τῶι γυμνικῶι. As Woodhead notes, the *Ptolemaia* had not yet been instituted, but already in 224/3 we find announcements there as well (see next footnote). Overall discussion of announcements at these festivals: Shear 2001, 415–22 and 428–432.

50   Proclamation at *Dionysia*, *Panathenaia* and *Ptolemaia*: honours for Antioch of the Chrysaoreis in c. 203 BC (SEG 28, 75, *Agora* 16 255J, 15–17: [καὶ ἀναγορεῦσαι τὸν] στέφανο[ν Διονυσίων] | [τῶν ἐ]ν ἄστει καινοῖς [τραγωιδοῖς τῶι ἀγῶνι κ]αινῶι ν καὶ Παναθηνα[ί]-| [ων] καὶ Πτολεμ[α]ίων τ[οῖς γυμνικοῖς ἀ]γῶσιν; the text is however problematic, as there is an overkill in terms of newness of the tragic agon). Proclamation at *Dionysia*, *Panathenaia*, and *Eleusinia*: IG II² 836, slightly later than 229 BC, honours for Phraseas son of Aetos from Phlious: καὶ ἀνε[ιπεῖν τὸν στέφανον Διονυσίων τε τῶν ἐν ἄστε<ι> και[νοῖς τραγωιδοῖς καὶ Παναθη]-|[ναίων καὶ Ἐ]λευσιν[ίω]ν τοῖς [γυμνικοῖς ἀγῶσι?; IG II² 851, ante 224/3 BC, for an unknown; *Agora* 16 249, III/II BC, very fragmentary, for an unknown. From the late third century (SEG 26, 98) until ca. 38/7 BC (IG II² 1043), the ephebes seem to be honoured at these festivals (ca. 10 documents; the formulation presents some variants, e.g. ἀνειπεῖν τὸν στέφανον Διονυσίων [τῶν μεγά]λων τῶι καινῶ[ι ἀγῶνι] καὶ Παναθηναίων καὶ Ἐ-| λευσινίων τοῖς γυμνικοῖς ἀγῶσιν, IG II² 1039.62–63, 83–78

agones have by now become the central – possibly the most important, at any rate, the most conspicuous – element in the group; and the decision to announce honours at other venues clearly implies that, if the *Dionysia* are still important, they are not anymore *the* main venue. This is particularly clear in some instances such as that of the honours for Prytanis of Karystos, decreed in 226/5, not long after the greater *Panathenaia* of that year: even though his honours could (and would, according to the text of the decree) be announced at the next *Dionysia*, and notwithstanding the necessity of waiting for four years for the next greater *Panathenaia*, proclamation at the latter festival was considered important enough to be stipulated in the decree.[51]

But this shift had begun much earlier: for almost one century the *Panathenaia*, the other festival with an international appeal in Athens, had rivaled the *Dionysia* as a potential venue for the proclamation of honours. The specific historical situation, the status of the honorands, and the date at which the honorific decrees were passed may all help to explain the choice of the *Panathenaia* over the *Dionysia*. The first document is a fairly early one, as it reports the decision to honour Spartokos and Pairisades, the joint rulers of Bosporos, in 347/6 BC: the award and announcement of the crown are to be repeated every four years, at the greater *Panathenaia*.[52] The wording of the decree (that the crowns be made according to the decree voted for Leukon) opens the pos-

---

BC). Proclamation at *Dionysia*, *Panathenaia*, *Eleusinia*, and *Ptolemaia*: praise of the demos of Ephesos, 224/3–222/1 BC, Agora 16 225, SEG 25, 108.10–11: Διονυσίων τῶν ἐν ἄστει καινοῖς τραγωιδοῖς καὶ Πανα[θη]-| ναί[ω]ν καὶ Ἐλευσινίων καὶ Πτολεμαίων τοῖς γυμνικοῖς ἀγῶσιν; honours to Kephisodoros, 196/5 BC, Agora 16 261[1], SEG 25, 112 and 41, 59; IG II² 891. 14–15, c. 188/7 BC, honours to an Alexandros for services rendered in connection with kings (καὶ ἀνειπεῖν τὸν στέφα] νον Διονυσίων τε τῶν ἐν ἄστει τραγωιδῶν τῶι και-|[νῶι ἀγῶνι καὶ Παναθηναίων καὶ Ἐ]λευσινίων καὶ Πτολεμ[αί]ων τοῖς γυμνικοῖς ἀγῶσιν); IG II² 900, 185/4 BC; SEG 21, 435, 187/6 BC, honours for an unknown hipparch; *I.Delos* 1479bis, honours to king Pharnakes of Pontus and queen Nysa, 160–59 BC; IG II² 966.21–22, 159–133 BC, very fragmentary; IG II² 983, mid II BC, for Ptolemy VI Philometor son of Ptolemy; IG II² 963, ca. 140 BC. Moreover, in four inscriptions dated from 161/60 to c. 140 the crowns for the *agonothetai* of the *Theseia* are announced at these festivals; from 185 BC (SEG 32, 129) to ca. 94/3 (IG II² 1030), the ephebes are honoured at these festivals.

51 Decree for Prytanis: *Agora* 16 224 (SEG 25, 106.36–38), with Shear 2001, 418 and 430–31; see also above, n. 49. The greater *Panathenaia* involved, besides gymnic events, also musical and, starting at any rate from 160 BC, dramatic events (see on the evolution of the festival Shear 2001); the *Eleusinia* had musical, gymnic and equestrian contests (at any rate in 329/8 BC: IG II² 1672.258–61; cf. Parker 2005, 201–2; Larmour 1999, 180), so there was choice.

52 IG II² 212 = Rhodes and Osborne 2003, 64.24–32, who note that the award of crowns regularly, rather than on a single occasion, is an unusual and expensive honour (323). One wonders whether the choice of the *Panathenaia* over the *Dionysia* may not have been due also to the desire of avoiding a yearly repetition of the award.

sibility that their father Leukon may have been also honoured in the same way. Already as early as the mid-fourth century, the *Panathenaia* may have appeared as the best venue in which to honour these individuals, by giving them virtually the same status as athletic victors.[53] The second instance is preserved in an inventory of the treasurers of Athena and the Other Gods, recording the award and announcement of a crown to Conon (III) son of Timotheos (II) at the gymnastic games of the greater *Panathenaia*, probably in 318/7 BC.[54] Three more decrees (for the Kolophonians, for an unknown state, and for an Apollonides son of Charops from the Piraeus), prescribing the announcement of the crown at the gymnastic games of the *Panathenaia*, fall into the years 307/6 to 302/1.[55] Here, too, besides the date at which the decrees were passed, there may have been specific reasons for the choice of this venue rather than another; in the last document in which the gymnic games of the *Panathenaia* are chosen as the only place for the proclamation (a decree dated after 270 BC), it is clearly because the honorand, Herakleitos son of Asklepiades from Athmonon, restored the stadion for the festival.[56] One further inscription, a decree of the Athenians in Delos dated to 160–150 BC honouring Euboulos son of Demetrios of Marathon for having managed that the Athenians in Delos be crowned and their crown announced at the *Panathenaia*, in the theatre, implies proclamation at a music/dramatic *agon*, rather than at the gymnic one (at this date, a contest of tragedies is a possible option).[57] As gymnic *agones* were always a possibility at the *Panathenaia*, this document implies a choice; but to evaluate this choice correctly more data would be needed.

As for other venues: we do not have a single instance of honours announced at the comic contests of the city *Dionysia*. This is in keeping with the Greek world at large; the only exception is the Attic deme of Aixone, where announcements of honours took place at the local *Dionysia* during

---

53 On the parallelism between victors and honorands in this specific instance see Osborne 1999, 355–6. Shear 2001, 415 and 429–31 suggests that the date at which the decree was passed may have conditioned the choice of the festival for the announcement; but she also makes the important point that this does not account for the lack of repetition at the future *Dionysia*.

54 IG II 1479.18–21. Cf. Shear 2001, 415–6.

55 Respectively, IG II² 456, 307/6, fr.b ll. 3–8: τὸν δὲ κή[ρυκα ἀνειπε]-| ῖν Παναθηναίων τῶι γυμνικῶι ἀγῶνι ἐν τ[ῶι σταδίωι] |5 ὅτι ὁ δῆμος ὁ Κολοφωνίων ἀνατίθησι [τόνδε τὸν στέφ]-| ανον καὶ τὴν πανοπλίαν ἀριστεῖον τεῖ Ἀθ[ηνᾶι ὑπὲρ] | τοῦ δήμου τοῦ Ἀθηναίων καὶ τοῦ δήμου τοῦ [Κολοφωνί]-| ων; IG II² 557; and IG II² 492, 302/1 BC.

56 IG II² 677; for the date, see Tracy 2003, 96.

57 I.Delos 1498.8–14: τό τε πρῶτον Παναθηναίοις ἐποίησεν τὸν | δῆμον τὸν Ἀθηναίων τῶν ἐν Δήλωι τιμηθῆ-| ναι χρυσῶι στεφάνωι ἀν<η>γορευμένοι ἐν | τῶι ἐν ἄστει θεάτρωι. For dramatic contexts at the *Panathenaia*, from the second century BC until at least the first century AD, including also new tragedies (cf. IG II² 3157) see Shear 2001, 369–71.

the contest of comedy – but then, Aixone may have had a particularly strong comic tradition.[58] The cyclic choruses also appear not to have been a favourite venue for public announcements in Athens: the only instance of a proclamation at a choral contest is a decree appended to a *traditio* of the *epimeletai* of the dockyards, dated to 325/4 BC. The document prescribes that gold crowns of 500, 300 and 200 drachmas respectively be offered to efficient trierachs and the awards be publicly proclaimed at the *Thargelia*.[59] It is worth noting that this is the first epigraphical instance of such honours being awarded to citizens, even though the literary evidence shows that it was already possible to announce honours for citizens, at the *Dionysia* and elsewhere. The choice may have been motivated by practical considerations, as the festival was celebrated in the month following the moment in which the ships had to be ready.[60]

To summarise: the *Dionysia*, and the contest of tragedy in particular, remained throughout Athenian history the main venue for the proclamation of crowns, even though other festivals took on increasing importance. The fact that honours were proclaimed at the moment of the contest in new tragedies allows us to infer – as observed by Mette – that drama must have been alive and in good health;[61] it is worth noting that the venue chosen for the announcements – by definition a prestigious one, linked closely with civic life – is not the moment reserved for old tragedy, which harked back to the great period of Athenian theatre, but the contest of

---

58 IG II² 1202, ἀνειπεῖν δὲ καὶ Διονυσίων τοῖς κωμῳδοῖς τοῖς Αἰξωνῆσιν ἐν τῶι θεάτρωι, and *Athen. Mitt.* 66, 1941, 218, 1, respectively dated to 340/39 and 313/2 BC. Csapo and Slater 1994, 128 tersely comment: "In demes where honorific decrees call for proclamations 'at the comic contest', it seems a reasonable assumption that no tragedy was performed".

59 IG II² 1629 = Rhodes and Osborne 2003, 100.190–9, but in particular 196–9: καὶ ἀναγορευσά-| [τω ὁ κῆ]ρυξ τῆς βουλῆς Θαρ-| [γηλίων] τῶι ἀγῶνι τοὺς στε-| φάνους.

60 See Wilson 2000, 48–9, who further suggests the lower level of agonistic prestige to be derived from financing the navy as a possible reason for the choice. This would imply a conscious decision of announcing the honours at the *Thargelia*, in order to make them less conspicuous. Wilson 2007, 164 assumes that these honours were not occasional, but were proclaimed yearly; this does not seem to be borne out by the text.

61 According to Mette 1977, 100, there were no *Dionysia* in the archonships of Symmachos (188/87 BC) and Theoxenos (187/6 BC), nor in those of Anthesterios (157/6 BC) and Kallistratos (156/5 BC); the decree honouring the strategos Aristophanes, dated to 236/5 (IG II² 1299.28–32: ν ἀνειπεῖν δὲ τὸν στέφαν[ον] | [κα]ὶ τὴν ἀνάθεσιν τῆς εἰκόνος Ἁλώιων τε τῶι πατρίωι ἀγῶνι καὶ ἐμ Πανάκτω[ι Ἀπα]-|30 [το]υρίων τῆι θυσίαι καὶ ἐπὶ Φυλεῖ ὅταν γίνηται ἡ θυσία τῆι Ἀρτέμιδι τῆι [Ἀγροτέ]-| [ρα]ι καὶ Διονυσίων τῶν ἐν ἄστει τραγωιδῶν τῶι καινῶι ἀγῶνι ὅταν πρῶτο[ν ὁ δῆμος] | [συ]ντελεῖ τὰ Διονύσια) is the only document which seems explicitly to allow for the possibility that there may not be *Dionysia* in the following year.

new tragedies.[62] The reperformance of old tragedies may have been felt as mainly an affair of actors, something spectacular, but fairly distant from contemporary civic life; as no "new" plays have survived, it is difficult to assess their potential meaning for the audiences.[63] The instances in which crowns were proclaimed only at other festivals, and not also at the *Dionysia*, are very rare and can be explained with reference to the nature of the action that the city wished to reward, the specific historical circumstances, or considerations to do with the honorand. Yet while the tradition of proclaiming crowns at the *Dionysia* survived, there was a visible trend towards proclamation at more than one venue. One reason for this may have been the fact that access to the *Dionysia* was subordinated to the payment of a fee. In other terms, at the *Dionysia* the audience was international, and thus suited for the proclamation of honours for foreigners; but that festival may have been felt as less suited for the proclamation of honours for citizens – with the first epigraphically attested proclamation at the *Dionysia* for a citizen being that for the comic poet Philippides son of Philokles in 283/2 BCE. (This incidentally highlights, to return to our starting point, the extraordinary character of the honour granted to Demosthenes.)[64] Later, proclamation of honours began to be repeated across festivals, reaching thus both internal and external audiences. But in the other festivals (*Panathenaia, Eleusinia, Ptolemaia*) the proclamations were made in the context of gymnic competitions.

---

62 In Ar. *Ach.* 9–12 Dicaeopolis remembers how he suffered when, waiting for a play by Aeschylus (a reperformance obviously) the herald announced Theognis. Should we put this down to Aristophanes' comic verve, and assume that new performances notwithstanding were eagerly awaited? On the implications of the fact that since the fifth century we are dealing with a "reperformance culture" see Revermann 2006, 66–87, and 72 on the passage from *Acharnians*.

63 See however Le Guen 2007. For tragedy in the fourth century and after, see Easterling 1993; Hall 1996, stressing the absence of the *polis* in Aristotle's discussion of tragedy in *Poetics*; Mikalson 1998, 118–9, arguing for an overall dissociation.

64 Payment for access: Sommerstein 1997, 66–7; Csapo 2007, 96–115 (but see Rhodes 2003, 100–11, for the uncertainties surrounding the date of introduction of the fee). Wilson 2009 ignores this point – as well as the fact that other venues for the proclamation of honours for citizens existed and were made use of. More specifically, if entrance to the theatre followed on the payment of a fee, the oath of Demophantos (Andoc. 1.96–98) cannot have been sworn by all Athenians in the theatre "just before the *Dionysia*", as part of the pre-play ceremonies (Wilson 2009, 23–27). Shear 2007, 153–8 must be right in suggesting the agora as the location, in a moment shortly "before the start of the festival of the *Dionysia*".

2   The announcement of honours outside Athens:
mainland Greece and the islands.

What about the rest of the Greek world? It is generally agreed that Athenian habits strongly influenced the form of Greek decrees (and in particular that of honorific decrees) elsewhere. Moreover, it has been suggested that the very spread of the honorific decree throughout the Greek world should be linked to the spread of tragedy, and of the *Dionysia*, organised along the Athenian model (with civic ceremonies preceding the tragic plays).[65] In the Hellenistic period, tragic performances were a frequent occurrence in the festive life of the Greek cities, on the mainland, on the islands, and in Asia Minor – as has been shown with abundance of details by Le Guen. But was tragedy felt to be sufficiently important to impose itself everywhere as the natural occasion for the public announcement of honours? To answer this question, I shall concentrate on a few representative places: Delphi; some of the islands (in particular Euboea, Chios, Samos, Delos, Cos, and Rhodes); and some cities of Asia Minor (Ephesos, Iasos, Priene, Kolophon).[66]

2.1   Delphi

Drama was not part of the cult of Dionysos in Delphi; it was rather associated with Apollo. While we do not know with certainty when plays were first performed at Delphi, it seems likely that dramatic performances in Delphi took place from the first part of the fourth century onwards. But apart from the stone theatre itself, the earliest concrete evidence comes from documents pertaining to the festival of the *Soteria*, instituted in 279/8, to commemorate the defeat of the Gauls.[67] A number of decrees by the Amphictiony and the city of Delphi offer instances of proclamation of honours that allow us to gain a sense of the status of these dramatic performances.[68] Irrespective of the hon-

---

65   Guettel-Cole 1993, 29 and above n. 23.
66   Dramatic activity on the islands is discussed in Le Guen 2001, who specifically remarks on the interest of honorific decrees (265), but does not distinguish between choral and dramatic performances, and uses "theatre" as an all-inclusive category. Le Guen 2003 discusses dramatic activity in Asia Minor (again lumping together choral and dramatic performances); Vial 2003 offers a very nuanced discussion of musical and theatrical activity in the Hellenistic period.
67   Sifakis 1967, 61–3.
68   The present survey does not claim completeness; but the number of instances examined is sufficiently high to be representative. Habicht 2002, 21–6 discusses the documents from Delphi connected with grants of proxeny (thus, only *polis* decrees);

ouring entity, it seems fairly clear that the chosen venues for announcements were, during the period of Aetolian control in Delphi, either the *Soteria* or the *Pythia*, while after 190 BC honours are proclaimed at both the *Soteria* and the *Pythia*.[69] In most cases the specific occasion, when the detail is given, is that of the gymnic *agones*.[70] There are however two exceptions: in two honorific decrees of the *polis* of Delphi, one for a Milesian proxenos, dated to 258/6 or 255/4, and another one for judges from Thespiai, of the second half of the second century BC, the chosen venue is the *agon* of the *auletai* (the name of the festival is lost in the lacuna). On this basis, Nachtergael maintained that honours could be proclaimed indifferently on the occasion of the musical agones or of the gymnic ones, in either one of the two main festivals, and that whenever only the indication "at the *Pythia*" or "at the *Soteria*" occurs, both possibilities should be left open.[71] Strictly speaking, this is correct. Yet, if we

---

Bouvier 1978 offers a systematic analysis of the changes in the local system of honours and rewards. I will take into account here both the decrees of the *polis* and those of the Amphictiony. For a general analysis of the various types of Amphictionic decrees, see Lefèvre 1998, 223–36. Fifteen decrees, eight of the Amphictiony and seven of the *polis* of Delphi, requesting a proclamation at the *Soteria* are conveniently printed in Nachtergael 1977, 465–74; see ibid. 368–71 for a discussion.

69　16 Amphictionic decrees prescribe the proclamation of honours: CID 4, 33, 263 BC, honours announced at *agon* of (depending on the restoration) either *Pythia* or *Soteria*; CID 4, 49, 255/4 or 252/1 BC, at *Soteria* (and in Athens at the *Dionysia* in the theatre); CID 4, 65, 237/30, at *Pythia*; CID 4, 86, 207/6 BC, at gymnic *agon* of either *Soteria* or *Pythia*; same for CID 4, 87, 206/5 BC; CID 4, 88, III/II BC, at gymnic *agon* of *Pythia*; CID 4, 89, III /II BC, at gymnic *agon* of either *Soteria* or *Pythia*; CID 4, 95, 206/203 BC, at *Soteria*; CID 4, 96, 206/203 BC, at gymnic agon of *Soteria*; CID 4, 99, 201/200 BC, at *Pythia*; CID 4, 102, III/II BC, at either *Pythia* or *Soteria*; CID 4, 100, 194/3 BC, from Magnesia, at gymnic *agon* of *Soteria*; CID 4, 106, 184/3 BC, at gymnic *agon* of the first *Pythia*; CID 4, 107, 182/1 BC, at both *Pythia* and *Soteria*; CID 4, 117, 118/7 or 117/6, at gymnic *agon* of *Pythia*; CID 4, 130, 48 BC, at gymnic *agon* of *Pythia*. As for the decrees of the *polis*, the following nine prescribe a proclamation: FD III 2:88, 258/7 or 255/4 (see Nachtergael 1977, 369) at either *Soteria* or *Pythia*, agon of the *auletai*; FD III 3:224 = Nachtergael n° 48, III/II BC, gymnic *agon* of *Pythia*?; FD III 1:458 = Nachtergael n° 51, second half of second century BC, at either *Soteria* or *Pythia*, agon of the *auletai*; FD III 4:52 = Nachtergael n° 52, dated between 121 and 108 BC, at both *Pythia* and *Soteria*; FD III 4:49 = Nachtergael n° 53, 106/5 BC, at gymnic *agon* of both *Pythia* and *Soteria*; FD III 4:50 = Nachtergael n° 54, also 106/5 BC, as above; FD III 2:49 = Nachtergael n° 55, 106/5 BC, as above; FD III 4:77, 102/1 BC, at *Pythia*; FD III 2:48 = Nachtergael n° 56, 98/87 BC, at gymnic *agon* of both *Pythia* and *Soteria*.

70　Nachtergael 1977, 371. On the *Pythia* and the *Soteria,* Lefèvre 1998, 236–40, with further bibliography (in particular, for the *Pythia* Amandry 1990; for the *Soteria*, Knoepfler 1995, 154, defending the thesis that the Amphictionic festival was trieteric and not annual; the Aetolian *Soteria* became penteteric after ca. 246 BC.

71　Nachtergael 1977, 368–9. The inscriptions are FD III 2:88 (on which see also Habicht 2002, 24 n. 48), and FD III 1:458 = Nachtergael n° 51.

look at the texts, there would seem to be a clear preference for the gymnic *agones*. In the group of the Amphictionic decrees, they are explicitly mentioned nine times out of a total of sixteen announcements; the remaining ones leave the issue open and indicate only the name of the main festival. As for the city decrees, besides the two cases of announcement during the *agon* of the *auletai* already mentioned, we have nine proclamations during gymnic contests, and three where only the festival is specified, but not the contest. (NB: The instances in which a decree prescribes announcements at both *Pythia* and *Soteria* have been counted twice.) The musical part of the *Soteria* comprised instrumental and singing contests, competitions for choruses and aulos players, and dramatic contests; yet the announcements, when they were made here and not in the gymnic *agon*, did not take place at the moment of the dramatic contests, but rather before the contest of the *auletai*.

A group of Amphictionic decrees for *hieromnamones* from Chios, to which may be added one decree of the *polis* of Delphi for one of the honoured *hieromnamones*, features a request of proclamation in both Delphi and Chios: it is thus possible to compare the choice of venues in each location. Strikingly, in Chios this choice is always the competition of the choruses of *paides* at the *Dionysia*, while in Delphi, when the occasion is specified, it is the gymnic *agon*; tragedy is never mentioned.[72]

2.2   Euboea

The cities of Euboea offer some instances of conferment of honours, but very few of them include also their proclamation. The one early inscription that contains such a clause, a decree from Eretria dating to the end of the fourth century BC, specifies that the honours awarded to the Macedonian Timotheos, son of Lysanias, shall be proclaimed by the *probouloi* at the *Dionysia*, during the competition of the cyclic choruses.[73] Compared with the situation

---

72   CID 4, 65, dated in the 230s BC: *Pythia* in Delphi and *Dionysia*, in the theatre, for Chios; CID 4, 86 (dated, as the following documents, to end III BC) = Nachtergael n° 44: gymnic *agon* of *Pythia* or *Soteria* in Delphi, and *Dionysia* in Chios, in the theatre, ἐπεί κα τῶν πα-|45 [ἴδων χοροὶ μέλλωντι ἀ]γωνίζε[σθ]αι; CID 4, 87 = Nachtergael n° 43: same as the preceding; CID 4, 88, same as the preceding; CID 4, 89 = Nachtergael n° 42, slightly different formular: the choruses of *paides* seem absent (but the text is very fragmentary); CID 4, 102, again extremely fragmentary, ca. 190 BC; and a decree of Delphi for the same man, Hermokles, FD III 3:224 = Nachtergael n° 48, which indicates the choruses of *paides* at the *Dionysia* as chosen venue in Chios. On these documents, and more generally on Chios and Delphi in the second half of the third century BC, Amandry 1986, 218–23; Lefèvre 1998, 232–3.

73   IG XII 9 196.15–17: ἀνακηρῦξαι | τοὺς προβούλους τοῖς Διονυσίοις | ἐν τῶι ἀγῶνι τῶν κυκλίων χορῶν. Detailed commentary in Knoepfler 2001, 175–77 and n. 433,

in Athens, the choice of the venue is striking. Two later decrees, also from Eretria, specify that the honours for Theopompos, son of Archedemos, and for Hipposthenes, son of Aischylos, have to be proclaimed yearly, at the *Dionysia*, at the moment of the *pompe*, and during the *Artemisia*, during the *agon* of the *pyrrhiche*.[74] Drama does not appear as a possibility at all – *prima facie* a rather surprising fact: it is true that Euboea (and in particular Chalkis) had an ancient and important choral tradition (the *Marmor Parium* records Hypodikos of Chalkis as the first victor in the dithyrambic contests at Athens in 509 BC; another famous poet, Tynnichos, singled out by Plato as the author of the best paean ever, hailed from the same city); but drama was also from early on rooted in Euboea. Thus, Chalkis is the home of one of the best-known among early actors, Mynniskos; the important tragic poet Achaios, a contemporary of Sophocles and Euripides, came from Eretria.[75] Moreover, the Euboean cities have preserved for us the very first law regulating the organisation of the *Dionysia* (and *Demetrieia*), with many details on the hire of the various artists, including tragic actors.[76] At the end of the fourth century, dramatic business in the Euboean cities was regulated by this common theatrical law; still, in Chalkis, in the second century BC, the venues chosen for the annual announcement of the honours conferred on Archenous son of Charikles are the gymnic *agon* of the *Rhomaia* organized by the Euboean *koinon* and the *pompe* and sacrifice of the *Dionysia*.[77] Similarly, the one known honorific decree of Histiaea, published in Delos, prescribes that the

---

74   IG XII 9 236.44–47 (ἀναγορεύεσθαί τε τὰς τιμὰς Διονυσίοις τε, ἐν ᾗ |45 συντελεῖται τοῦ Διονύσου ἡ πομπή, καὶ Ἀρτεμισίων | τῷ ἀγῶνι τῆς πυρρίχης, τοῦ δὲ κηρύγματος ἐπιμε-| λεῖσθαι τοὺς προβούλους τοὺς ἀεὶ ἐν ἀρχῇ ὄντας), c. 100 BC (second copy of the decree: IG XII suppl. 553.28–30 – these honours have to be proclaimed each year); and IG XII 9 237.21–23, 100–95 BC (IG XII 9 910 is a decree of the Dionysiac *technitai* from Chalkis, and as such is not pertinent; at any rate, the honours for Mnasaigos son of Charidemos have to be announced yearly at the moment of the sacrifice).

75   Hypodikos: *FGrHist* 239 F A 46; Tynnichos: Plato *Ion* 534 D (cf. Page *PMG* 707); Mynniskos: Stephanis 1988, n° 1757; Achaios: *TrGF* 1 20. On the Euboean *Dionysia*, and more generally Euboean choral culture, see Wilson 2000, 283–4, who ascribes an important role to Athenian influence.

76   IG XII 9 207 and *Add.* 176; IG XII Suppl. p. 178; Pickard-Cambridge 1988, 281–2 and 306–8; Wilson 2000, 292–3; and most recently Le Guen 2001a, I 41–56 for text, French translation and commentary. The law regulates the *Dionysia* at Karystos, Eretria, Chalkis, and Oreos, the *Demetrieia* at Oreos, and the *Aristonikeia* (Aristonikos was a companion of Alexander the Great) at Karystos: these festivals are more or less on the same level.

77   IG XII 9, 899.B11–13 and C1–3.

---

crown conferred on Athenodoros of Rhodes be announced at the *pompe* of the *Antigoneia*, by the care of the *agonothetes*.[78] Geographical closeness and the early intertwining of traditions strongly suggest Athenian influence; but the Euboean cities seem to have distanced themselves from common Athenian practice in the choice of the venue for the announcement of honours.

2.3   Chios, Samos.

Chios has already been mentioned: there, proclamation of honours took place at the *Dionysia*, on the occasion of the choruses of *paides*.[79] As for Samos, the island was an important member of the Delian league and remained fairly close to Athens through most of its history. It seceded from the league in 440 BC, but was forced to capitulate, and stayed loyal to Athens until the end of the Peloponnesian war. An Athenian cleruchy was installed on the island in 365 BC, which lasted until Alexander's exile decree; it thus does not surprise to find that announcements were made at the moment of tragic performances.

The overall number of Samian honorific decrees is 146.[80] The oldest is a decree of the Athenian cleruchs in Samos, dated to ca. 350 BC, honouring the Athenian Diotimos, son of Nikostratos, with a crown, and prescribing

---

78   IG XII p. 169, 107–8 (=IG XI 4, 1055), dated to ca. 230–220 BC. Clearly the Histiaeans want to publicise these honours, since they ask the Delians for the permission of erecting a stele close to the temple of Apollo in Delos; yet they choose the *Antigoneia*. Nothing else is known of the Histiaean *Antigoneia* (the choice of venue by the Histiaeans may have been influenced by the existence of Delian *Antigoneia*); but this should be weighed against the fact that no festival from Histiaea is recorded at all, while there certainly must have been festivals: a good instance of how very lacunose our information is.

79   To the Amphictionic and city decrees from Delphi mentioned above, n. 72, add the decree of the Chians granting citizenship to the Aetolians and honouring them: Moretti, *ISE* 78.23–24, dated to 247/6, and McCabe, *Chios* 13.13–15. Otherwise, if honours are at all to be announced, it is at the *Dionysia*, without further specifications.

80   IG XII 6, 9–154; of these, eight are for Samians (nn. 9–16); twenty-five are for foreigners who helped Samians during their exile (17–41); ninety are for foreigners (42–131); and two more are decrees of collegia (132–133). To this group, we have to add the excessively fragmentary decrees (133–40), decrees by foreign cities (140–8) that conferred honours on Samian citizens and then decided to ask the Samians to proclaim these honours in their local festivals as well, and Samian decrees found outside Samos (149–54). General discussion in Habicht 2002, 26, who takes into account only 122 decrees, because he considers only those for foreigners. The ratio between overall numbers and instances of proclamation is interesting: here as in Athens, proclamations do not reach 10% of the decrees. On Samian practice concerning *choregia* see Wilson 2000, 286.

that the crown be announced at the *Dionysia* (in Samos) on the occasion of the tragedies.[81] Here we see Athenian practice at work. The series of inscriptions that falls into the period of Samian independence begins at the end of the fourth century and peters out towards the end of the second century BC. A number of these decrees are so fragmentary as to make it impossible to know for certain whether or not the document included a clause conferring a crown and specifying its public proclamation. Out of the c. hundred decrees, of which we can ascertain the content with some measure of likelihood, only twelve grant a crown to the honorand; of these, ten, falling in between the end of the fourth and the end of the second century, require the announcement to be made at the *Dionysia*, and more specifically at the moment of the tragic contests, Διονυσίων τραγωιδοῖς.[82]

Two of these documents, a (probably) Samian decree from Thasos honouring Thasian judges and a Samian decree from Magnesia on the Maeander honouring a Magnesian, deserve special mention. Both specify that the proclamation is to be done by the *agonothetes* "when the polis will offer the first χοροί to the god" (first document, l. 13–14, entirely restored) and "at the tragic *agon* of the Dionysia, when the *polis* will offer the first χοροί to the god" (second document, ll. 26–27, repeated at 31–32, which makes for reasonably reliable restorations).[83] This formulation shows that still in the

---

81 IG XII 6, 253 (cf. Rhodes with Lewis 1997, 276 n. 9).

82 IG XII 6, 11.56, honours for the Samian Boulagoras son of Alexis, post 243/2 (the only crown for a citizen); 56.29, honours for the actor Polos of Aigina, slightly after 306 BC; 95.25, honours for judges from Myndos, ca. 280 BC; 141, a decree from Eresos, with honours to be announced in Eresos Διονυσίοισι τοῖς ἀγώνεσσι τοῖς τραγώι]δοισι (l. 16–17; the text is however very fragmentary, the restoration Διονυσίων τοῖς κιθαρώι]δοις has also been proposed; at l. 31 a χοροστάτας appears), and in Samos too, ll. 32–34, but the text does not allow any precisions; 150.3, from Cos, honours for Coan judges, end of the fourth century BC (here, the announcement is to be made Διονυσίων τραγωιδοῖς ἐν τῶι θεάτρωι); 151.29, from Cos, honours for the Coan doctor Philistos, after 241 BC; 152.9 and 21, from Thasos, honours for judges and a secretary sent by Thasos, II century BC; 153.8 and 12–14, also from Thasos; 154.27 and [31], from Magnesia on the Maeander, honours for Telestratos of Magnesia; and 156.15, a decree for Ptolemy III, dated ca. 245/4 BC, prescribing crowning in the theatre at the tragic *agones* of the *Dionysia*, and announcement, presumably on the same occasion. To these documents should be added the very fragmentary IG XII 6, 129.14–19 (II century BC): a gold crown is to be announced [--], in the day in which [--]... A mention of *Dionysia* has also been restored at the end of a decree, as potentially being the place for the proclamation of an alliance with Antiochia on the Maeander, in a text dated slightly later than 167 BC, IG XII 6, 6.34.

83 IG XII 6, 153.12–14, from Thasos, first half of the II century BC: [καὶ στεφανῶσαι αὐτὸν θαλλοῦ] στεφ[ά]νωι Διονυσίων τραγῳ[δοῖς, τῆς δὲ ἀναγγε]-| [λίας τοῦ στεφάνου ἐπιμεληθῆναι] τὸν ἀγωνοθέτην, ὅ[ταν τοὺς πρώτους χοροὺς] | [ἡ πόλις τῶι θεῶι συντελῆι]; and *I.Magnesia* 103 = IG XII 6, 154.26–28: [...στεφανωθῆι χρυσῶι

second century BC dramatic performances might be referred to in terms that foreground the choruses (a point to which I shall return in section 4 below).

In another troubled moment in the history of the island, the Samians experimented with a different occasion for the announcement of honours: the (unfortunately fairly fragmentary) decree honouring Antileon and Leontinos of Chalkis specifies that Antileon is to be awarded a gold crown, "when we organise the *agon* for the kings" (IG XII 6, 42. 61–65). (The kings in question are most likely Philip Arrhidaios and Alexander IV, hence the proposal to date the inscription to 321–19 BC.)

Thus, with this one exception linked to a specific historical situation, we may say that the *Dionysia*, and in particular the tragic contests, remained the main venue for announcements in Samos. The *Heraia*, which according to the catalogues of victors seems to have been at least as important as the *Dionysia* – it did, at any rate, attract competitors from the wider Greek world – does not seem to have been chosen for announcements.[84]

2.4   The Cyclades

A similar continuity is attested for Siphnos and Tenos. In the first island, five decrees prescribe the announcement of honours at the tragic competitions of the *Dionysia*.[85] No other Siphnian festivals are known – the only further

---

στεφάνωι]| Διονυσίων τραγωιδ[οῖς, ὅταν τοὺς πρώτους χοροὺς ἡ πόλις τῶι θεῶι συν]-| τελῆι, and 31–32: καὶ στεφανῶσα[ι χρυσῶι στεφάνωι Διονυσίων τραγωιδοῖς, ὅταν τοὺς]| πρώτους χοροὺς ἡ [πόλις τῶι θεῶι συντελῆι, τῆς δὲ ἀναγγελίας...]. The τῆι θεῶι printed throughout in the IG, in both inscriptions, is surely wrong. Hallof refers to L. Robert's restoration of *I.Magnesia* 103 = IG XII 6, 154, our second document; but Robert (*BCH* 1926 = *OMS* II, 962–965) restored a male god, obviously Dionysos. Hera would be a possibility in Samos, but not when *Dionysia* are mentioned.

84   Three catalogues of *Dionysia* (IG XII 6 176, 177, and 178, spanning the time from the mid third to the second century BC) give lists of *choregoi*. The verb *enika* appears only in the first two documents, not in the (later) third; moreover, of the two *choregoi* for tragedy and comedy, one "wins" for comedy, the other for tragedy – i.e. it seems likely that at least in IG XII 6 177 these are performances and not competitions. Besides names of magistrate and *choregoi*, the only other individual named is, in the older document, the *auletes*; unluckily, the lacunae do not allow us to determine wether he was a foreigner, and of what standing. For the *Heraia*, see IG XII 6 173 (first half of second century BC), 174, and 175 (late second/early first century BC).

85   IG XII 5 481 (*Add.* p. 317, IG XII *Suppl.* 111, *BE* 1965.6, *BE* 1969.85, and *BE* 1971.498), for an *auletes*, 274/270 BC; IG XII 5 482, *Add.* p. 318, for a *kitharodos*, third/second century BC; IG XII 5, 471 (with SEG 33, 680, not from Oliaros), two honorific decrees for secretaries, II century BC; Daux, *Klio* 52, 1970, 70 (*BE* 1971.497), third century.

piece of information on festival activity in the island comes from Isocrates' *Aiginetikos*, written for a Siphnian exile at the beginning of the fourth century BC: in it, the Siphnian defendant affirms that his ancestors served brilliantly as choregoi and discharged a number of litourgies: thus, a choregic system was functioning on the island.

As for Tenos, two decrees of the third century BC, IG XII 5, 798 and 800, attest to the practice of proclaiming the honours at the tragic *agon* of the *Dionysia* (although other decrees confer crowns without explicitly mentioning a proclamation); the honorands are foreigners. But a decree of ca. 300 BC (SEG 40, 688) attests to a proclamation of honours for a citizen at the *agon* of the *Posideia*, in the theatre; and from the third century onwards (IG XII 5, 802), the inscriptions in most instances prescribe proclamation of honours in the sanctuary of Poseidon and Amphitrite, when the *polis* celebrates the *thusia* and the *panegyris*, and in the theatre when the *polis* organizes the tragic *agones* of the *Posideia* and the *Dionysia*.[86]

Other places in which the tragic competition of the *Dionysia* seems to have been the main venue, although the scarcity of material does not allow us to trace any changes in time, include Andros, Karthaia and Ioulis in the island of Keos,[87] Ios, Siros, Paros (where *Megala Dionysia* of unknown frequency took place), Naxos, and Aigiale in the island of Amorgos.[88] Howev-

---

86 Some twenty instances (not including extremely fragmentary documents), covering the period from the end of the third century to the first century BC: IG XII 5, 813, 820, 822, 823, 825, 828, 830, 831, 832, 833, 835, 836, 839, 840, 841, 843, 849, 850, 851, IG XII *Suppl.* 307, and SEG 40, 697.

87 Andros: SEG 44, 699 (IG XII 5, 714, IG XII Suppl. p. 119), dated to 275–225 BC, ll. 10–11: ἀναγγεῖλαι τόνδε τὸν στέφαν[ον] |[Διο]γ υσίοις τραγωιδῶν τῶι ἀγῶνι; later, the announcement is to be made 'in those *agones* organised by the *polis*', cf. IG XII 5 719 (SEG 53, 2191), early first century AD?; see also the very fragmentary IG XII Suppl. 248. Karthaia: IG XII 5, 531/1063 and 529/1064, third century BC; IG XII 5, 1061 (second part of third century BC); SEG 48, 1130 (two decrees, ca. 194–192 BC); and IG XII 5, 1070 (entirely, and not very reliably, restored). To these should be added the decrees that designate simply the *Dionysia* as the place for the announcement: IG XII 5, 535, 536, and 538. Ioulis: IG XII 5, 599, II BC (interestingly, the announcement is to be repeated every year); IG XII 5, 604 (almost entirely restored). For Keos see Wilson 2000, 286.

88 Ios: IG XII 5, 1010, III BC; and the completely restored 1011. Syros: IG XII 5, 653, I BC, proclamation to be made at the *Dionysia* during the tragic competitions, in the pompe of the *Heracleia*, and at the *lampas* of the *Demetrieia*. Paros: Rigsby *Asylia* 100, 41–2 = *I. Magnesia* 50; IG XII 5, 129.33–5 (*megala Dionysia*) and 37–8 ("when we will first celebrate the *Great Dionysia*"), second century BC. Naxos: SEG 49, 1106.b16–17, ca. 280 BC (ἐν τῶι θεάτρωι Διονυσίων | τῶ[ν μεγά]λων τραγωιδοῖς). Aigiale: IG XII 7, 387, third century BC, with a fairly generic provision, ll. 9–12: τοὺς δὲ ἀγωνοθέτας καὶ τοὺς [πρυτά]-| [νεις καὶ] τοὺς χορηγοὺς τοὺς ἀεὶ καθισταμέν[ους] | [ἐν τοῖς ἀ]γῶσιν τοῖς θεατρικοῖς προστάττ[ειν τῶι] | [κήρυκι ἀνα]γορεύειν, ὅτι...; but IG XII 7, 386 (SEG 53, 2191), second century BC, is

er, the Euboean preference for announcing honours on the occasion of cyclic choruses is not isolated. Delos offers a good example. 508 more or less complete honorific decrees for foreigners remain from the period of independence (314–167 BC); of these, a relatively small number confer crowns on recipients, who either have already received the proxeny or are receiving it in the same decree.[89] The majority of the decrees that award a crown include its proclamation among the honours specified. The occasion for the public announcement is sometimes given simply as the *Apollonia*,[90] but whenever the phrasing is more precise (and this is usually the case), then the reference is to the choruses of *paides*, with a very consistent and uniform formular.[91]

more specific: the honours should be announced Διονυσίοις ἐν τῶι ἀγῶνι τῶν τ|[ρ] αγωιδῶν, ll.35–36 (for both see SEG 44, 1736).

89   Numbers from Habicht 2002, 14–15, according to whom only twenty-four decrees confer crowns (he lists the decrees mentioned in *BCH* 111 (1987) 229, n. 108, and IG XI 4,542, 600, 664, 666, 680, 682, 687, 744, 749, 782, 820, 843 and 844); I list below a few more, without claiming completeness. As Habicht points out, the numerous fragmentary decrees will not have been different in their content and organisation. There are no decrees honouring Delians, even though from statue dedications we know that they received honours; but these were not inscribed.

90   Thus for instance IG XI 4, 514, honours for Telesinos of Athens, beginning of the third century BC; IG XI 4, 542, honours for Damaratos son of Gorgion, of Lacedaimon, beginning of the third century BC; IG XI 4, 559, ca. 280 BC, honours for the king of Sidon Philokles; IG XI 4, 565, ca. 260 BC, honours for Hermias of Halicarnassos.

91   IG XI 4, 572.7–8 (honours for Amphiklos son of Kallistratos of Chios, ca. 260 BC): στεφανῶσαι αὐτὸν δάφνης | στεφάνωι ἐν τῶι ἀγῶνι <τῶι> μουσικῶι τοῖς | Ἀπολλωνίοις καὶ ἀναγορεῦσαι κτλ.; IG XI 4, 600.8–13 (honours for Artemidoros of Antioch of the Chrysaoreis, 300–250 BC, with 'transitional' formulation: στεφανῶσαι αὐτὸν δάφνη[ς]|[στ]εφάνωι τοῖς Ἀπολλωνίοις |10 [ὅ]ταν ἦι τῶν παίδων ἀγὼν κα[ὶ]|[ἀν]αγορεῦσαι τὸν ἱερο[κ]ήρυκα |[ἐν] τῶι θεάτρωι); IG XI 4, 649.10–11 (honours for Sosibios of Alexandria, mid-third century: καὶ ἀναγορεῦσαι τὸν ἱε[ρ] οκήρυκ[α τοῖς Ἀ]-|[π]ολλω[νίοι]ς ἐν τῶι ἀγῶνι τῶμ πα[ίδων]; IG XI 4, 664. 8–12 (honours for Admetos the Macedonian, 240–230 BC: ἀναγορεῦσαι τὸν ἱεροκήρυκα ἐν τῶι θεάτρωι | τοῖς Ἀπολλωνίοις, ὅταν ἀγωνίζωνται οἱ χοροὶ τῶν | παίδων); IG XI 4, 666 (honours for Aristoboulos of Thessalonike, ca. 239–210 BC); IG XI 4, 680 (honours for Autokles, son of Ainesidemos of Chalkis, 239–229 BC); IG XI 4, 682 (honours for Autokles, son of Autokles of Chalkis, ca. 230); IG XI 4, 687, honours for Leon of Massalia, end of the third century; IG XI 4, 744, honours for Onomarchos of Knidos, beginning of II BC; IG XI 4, 749, honours for Charmantidas of Melos, beginning II century; probably the much restored IG XI 4, 753; IG XI 4, 755, honours for Anaxidikos of Rhodes; IG XI 4, 764, honours for Mantineus of Tenos, beginning of second century BC; IG XI 4, 766, honours for Demetrios of Pergamon, beginning of II century BC; IG XI 4, 771 (fragmentary, beginning second century BC); IG XI 4, 774, honours for Herakleitos of Seleucia, beginning of II century BC; IG XI 4, 780, honours for Theon of Byzantion, beginning of II century BC (here however the name of the festival does not appear, and the choruses are specified as sacred: ἀναγορεῦσαι τὸν |5 ἱεροκήρυκα ἐν τῶι θεάτρωι, ὅταν οἱ ἱεροὶ χ[ο]-| ροὶ τῶν

The Delians' policy of announcing honours at the *Apollonia*, which did not comprise dramatic performances, instead of at the *Dionysia*, may have been dictated by a conscious desire of differentiating themselves from Athens. Tellingly, when the island fell again under Athenian control, the announcement of honours was transferred to the *Dionysia*.[92]

2.5   Other islands: Nisyros, Cos, Rhodes

Two honorific decrees of the third century BC show that on the small island of Nisyros the honours were announced at the *Dionysia*, during the first day of the *kyklia*, the choral performances.[93] For Cos, recent new evidence has considerably enriched our knowledge of the local *Dionysia*. At least in the third/second century BC the festival could comprise a *pompe*, *agones* of pyrrhic dance, tragedy, and comedy, contested among the three Dorians tribes (Hylleis, Pamphiloi, and Dymanes), under the leadership of a *choragos* for *pompe*, pyrrhic dance, and tragedy, and of an *epimeletas* for comedy. The inscriptions show that foreign artists could be called in for the tragic and comic competitions: the actor who won in drama, be it tragedy or comedy, is almost always mentioned, and in the documents we have he is never from Cos.[94] But the most prestigious competition – or at any rate, the one which is hardly ever missing from such records as we have – is the choral *agon*, and it would seem that honours were announced during choral performances. The earliest document is a proxeny decree from the end of the fourth century BC for a Sinopean, Dionysios: the crown awarded to him was to be

---

παίδων ἀγωνίζωνται, τόδε τὸ κή-|[ρ]υγμα); IG XI 4, 782, honours for Androkles of Polyrrhenia, beginning of second century BC, also sacred choruses of *paides*; IG XI 4, 784, honours for Chaireas the Macedonian, beginning II BC, normal choruses; IG XI 4, 809, beginning of the second century BC, honours for Marcus son of Publius, Roman; IG XI 4, 820, beginning of the second century BC, honours for Ktesippos of Chios; possibly also the extremely fragmentary IG XI 4, 836; IG XI 4, 843; IG XI 4, 844. Slightly different is IG XI 4, 1022, first half of the third century: here the Chians ask the Delians to be allowed to honour the Delian Teleson son of Autokles, and are granted permission to do this in Delos, at the *Apollonia* during the choruses of the *paides*.

92   Sifakis 1967, 14, with references.

93   Schwyzer *ad* 271 = Ἀρχ. Ἐφ. 1913, 7 n.1, ll. 12–13: ἀναγορεῦσαι δὲ τὸν στέφανον ἐν τῶι | ἀ[γ]ῶνι τῶν Διονυσίων τᾶι πράται ἀμέραι τῶν κυκλίων; W. Peek, *Inschriften von den dorischen Inseln*, Berlin, 1969 (Abh. Sächs. Akad. der Wiss. in Leipzig, Philol.-hist. Kl. 62, 1) 27, n° 63 (c.300–250 BC): δεδό[χ]θαι τῶι δάμωι ἐπαινέσαι Πείσιογ κ [α]ὶ στε[φανῶσαι χρυσέωι] | στεφάνωι ἐν τῶι ἀγῶνι τῶν Διονυσίων τᾶι πράται ἀμέραι τ[ῶν] | κυκλίων ἀρετᾶς ἔνεκα καὶ εὐνοίας...

94   Segre *ED* 52 and *ED* 234, with Ceccarelli 1995.

proclaimed when the *polis* first celebrated a choral *agon*.[95] The specification recurs in some further documents;[96] the other possibility for the announcement of honours in the context of the *Dionysia* festival seems to be just after the libations, the *spondai*, as in five decrees all dated to the second century BC.[97] Otherwise, reference is made simply to an announcement at the next *Dionysia* or *Asclepieia*.[98] For what concerns us, it is enough to remark that the decrees either give no specifications, or prescribe moments for the announcement different from the dramatic performances.

---

95 Segre *ED* 20.8–10: ἀναγγεῖλαι τὸν σ[τέφανον] | [ἐ]ν τῶι χορικῶι ἀγῶνι ὅκκα πρᾶτ[α συντελῆι ὁ δᾶ]-| μος (cf. SEG 48, 1091). See also SEG 48, 1094 (cited *supra* n. 14).

96 Segre *ED* 67, second century BC, an unknown *polis* requires that the honours granted may be announced also in Cos, at the choral *agon*; SEG 53, 846, decree of the Theangeleis of ca. 300–250 BC, requiring that the honours granted be announced in Cos at the choral *agon* of the *Dionysia* (ll. 30–31, but this part is entirely restored); *Tit. Calymnii* Test XIV, mid-third century BC, decree in which Calymna requires that the honours granted to Praxilas be announced at the choral *agon* of the Dionysia as well as at the gymnic *agon* of the great Asklepieia; SEG 48, 1099, honorific decree of a Coan deme (?) for the doctor Praxianax, second half of the third century BC, requiring the honours to be announced in Cos (ll. 18–20: ἐν τῶι χορι-| κῶι ἀγῶνι τῶν Διονυσίων καὶ ἐν τῶι γυμνι-| κῶι τῶμ μεγάλων Ἀσκλαπιείων). Libation in the *chorikoi agones* is also mentioned as one of the privileges/duties of the priest of the Kyrbantes, *ED* 177.9, end of third century BC; same for the first century BC regulation for the priesthood of Herakles Kallinikos, *ED* 180.20–21.

97 The decrees SEG 49, 1110; 49, 1112; 53, 860, 861 and 862, all fragmentary, and all dating to the II century BC, contain a reference to *spondai* in what seems to be an almost standard formulation: ὅπως ἀ[ν]αγορευθῆι ὁ στέ[φανος Διο]-|[νυσ]ίων τε τῶι π[ρ]ώτωι ἀγῶνι μετὰ τ[ὰς σ]-|[πο]νδὰς καὶ ἐν τῶι γυμνικῶι τῶν κατὰ | πενταετηρίδα Ἀσκλαπιείων (SEG 53, 862.6–9).

98 The wording of Segre *ED* 132 B.16–17 (a second century decree of Halicarnassos for the Coan doctor Hermias, cf. SEG 49, 1109, *BE* 1995, 448, SEG 53, 2191) does not imply the existence of two *Dionysia* in Kos, as supposed by Sherwin-White: rather, the honours have to be announced when the city will first celebrate the *Dionysia*, while in the case of the *Asklapieia* the city will wait until the *megala Asklapieia*. SEG 48, 1097, a honorific decree of Sinope for Dionnos of Cos, ca. 220 B.C, requiring the announcement to be made in Cos (ll. 25–27) is similar: Διονυσίων τε τῶι πρώτωι ἀγῶν]-| [ι καὶ τοῖς Μεγάλοι]ς Ἀσκληπιείοις ἐν τῶι γυμν[ικῶι] | [ἀγῶνι. The Sinopeans may have deliberately left open the occasion of the announcement at the next *Dionysia*, in order to allow the Coans a free decision as to the choice of the specific *agon*. So also SEG 48, 1108, decree of Halicarnassos for a Coan, III/II BC; SEG 53, 863.45–48, a decree of Chalkis for Coan judges (the *demos* of Chalkis requests that the honours they have given be announced at the next *Dionysia*, as well as at the great *Asklapieia* and *Rhomaia* in the gymnic *agones*), ca. 150 BC; SEG 49, 1107 = *Chiron* 29, 1999, 275–6, mid-second century BC, with a clause requesting the announcement of crowns – but the text is too fragmentary for it to be possible to say anything else. A third century decree of Thasos for Coan judges, SEG 49, 1108 (above, n. 14) asks the Coans to announce the honours "in those *agones* in which it is prescribed for them to do this kind of announcements", ll. 10–12.

In Rhodes, too, choral contests seem to have been considered as a particularly appropriate venue for proclamations. A very fragmentary decree of the first half of the third century BC prescribes that the *agonothetai* of the *Dionysia* and *Seleukeia* announce the honours in the theatre (IG XII 1 6). In an Argive decree for the Rhodians dated to ca. 300 BC, the honours have to be announced by the *agonothetes* at Argos at the gymnic *agon* of the *Hekatomboia*, in Nemea again during the gymnic *agon*, and at Rhodes at the *Dionysia*, on the first day of the *agon* of cyclic choruses (Διονυσίοις ἐν τῶι ἀγῶνι τῶν κυκλίων | [χ]ορῶν τᾶι πράται ἁμέραι): clearly, the Rhodian ambassadors gave detailed indications as to the best occasion for the announcement in Rhodes.[99] On the other hand, a honorific decree of Camiros for Panaitios, son of Simos, dated to the third century BC, shows that the *polis* had the choice among various venues: the *demos* decides that the *agonothetes* will announce the honours conferred onto Panaitios at the *Dionysia*, on the first day of the *agon* of the cyclic choruses (Διονυσίοις ἐν τῶι ἀγῶνι τῶν κυκλί-| ων τᾶι πράται ἁμέραι, l. 6–7); but the text goes on to add that the next *damiourgos* should also crown Panaitios at the gymnic *agon* of the *Panathenaia* (l. 14–15). In another, slightly later (second century BC) honorific decree from Camiros, the *agonothetes* chosen for the following year will have to make the announcement of the honours at the *agon* of the *Panathenaia* (l. ll. 55–6); the *Dionysia* have altogether disappeared.[100] In the mid-third century, another venue for the announcements of honours was the *agon* of the *Helieia*; unfortunately, no details as to the exact moment are given.[101] Decrees by *demes* could also prescribe proclamation of honours: thus the honours conferred by the Brykountioi on a Samian doctor, Menokritos, son of Menodotos, will be – fittingly – announced at the *agon* of the *Asklapieia* (IG XII 1 1032, second/first century BC, with SEG 44, 683). At Lindos, a possibility seems to have been to announce the honours in a *syllogos*.[102] Other documents content themselves with stipulating that the honours will have to be announced, forever, with a very simple formulation.[103] This later

---

99   SEG 19, 317.19–21 and 25–26; cf. SEG 30, 358.
100 M. Segre, G. Pugliese Carratelli, *Tituli Camirenses* (*ASAA* XXVII–XXIX, 1949–51), respectively 106 and 110.
101 IG XII 5 8/1009, IG XII Suppl. p. 96, a decree of Ios dated to ca. 257 BC renewing friendship with the Rhodians.
102 IG XII 1 890, 129 BC: οἱ ἐπισ[τά]-15 ται καὶ οἱ κ[άρυκες ἐπιμ]ελη θέντω τᾶς | στεφανώσ[ιος καὶ ἀναγο]ρεύσιος ἐν τῶι ἔπε[ι]-| [τ]α συλλόγωι; and IG XII 1 922, ca. 160–150 BC (on both, SEG 44, 683).
103 Basically, δεδώκαντι δὲ αὐτῶι καὶ ἀναγόρευσιν τάνδε τᾶν τιμᾶν εἰς τὸν ἀεὶ χρόνον, which is found in IG XII 1 734, from Ialysos; IG XII 1 847, 848, 851, and Maiuri *Nuova silloge epigrafica* 24, from Lindos, late second century BC; *Lindos* II 281, ca. 100 BC, and the following II 297, 305, 330, 333, 389, 404, 407, spanning the entire century and specifying announcement of the *timai* forever (this continues into

formulation is much simpler, and may have developed out of the unwilling-
ness or the impossibility to decide in advance on some specific occasion.

To summarise: the picture from the islands is far from uniform. If in
Samos, Paros, Siphnos or Ceos the honours seem to have been announced at
the *Dionysia*, at the moment of the tragic competitions, just as was the case
in Athens, in a remarkably high number of places, such as Euboea, Delos,
Chios, Rhodes, and Cos, choral contests were the venue of choice.

3   The announcement of honours outside Athens (2): Asia Minor.

In Asia Minor, too, the possibilities for the announcement of honours vary.
The tragic *agones* at the *Dionysia* feature frequently. In a unique instance,
the exact day of tragic performances is specified, implying that these lasted
several days: this must have been the case in many other places (including
Athens), though few if any found it crucial to distinguish among the days.
At any rate, in a decree of an unknown city – not necessarily located in Asia
Minor – which honours judges sent by Iasos, the crowns are to be given on
the first day of the tragedies, which are themselves part of a music *agon*.[104]
In many other instances the only thing we can say is that at a specific moment in time honours were proclaimed on the occasion of choral dances:
this is the case of the honours decreed for the Tenians and their envoys by
the Trallianeis, at the end of the second century BC: the honours are to be
announced in Tralleis during the *Dionysia*, on the first day of the *kyklia*, and
in Tenos on the occasion when announcements are usually made.[105] We thus
know that Tralleis celebrated *Dionysia*, which included performances of cyclic choruses, and that these lasted at least two days; but everything else is

---

the first century AD, with Lindos II 415); Camiros too presents this possibility, in
a decree of the first century BC, *Tit.Cam.* 86. On the bodies emanating decrees in
Rhodes, see Gabrielsen 1994.

104 *I.Iasos* 83.19–22: χρυσέωι στεφάνωι ἐν τοῖς Διονυσί-|20 [οις τῆ]ι πρώτηι ἡμέραι
[τ] ῶν τραγωιδῶν, τῆς δὲ | [ἀναγγε]λίας τῶν στ[ε]φάνων τοὺς ἀγωνοθέτας | [τοῦ
μου]σικοῦ τὴν ἐπιμέλειαν ποιήσασθαι. The inscription is undated; for the use of the
short formula *agonothetai tou mousikou*, now attested for three cities (Magnesia,
and two other documents of unknown origin), see *BE* 1974, 545.

105 IG XII 5, 869[1], 59–64 = *I. Tralleis* 24: ἡ ἀ-| [ναγόρευσις γένηται τῶ]ν τιμῶν καὶ
τῶν στεφάνων παρ' ἡμῖν μὲν Διο-| [νυσίοις κυκλίων τῆι πρ]ώτηι ἡμέραι, ἐπιμελὲς
γενέσθαι τῶι ἐσο-| [μένωι γραμματεῖ ἐν τῶι ἐχομέ]νωι ἔτει, ἐν Τήνωι δὲ προνοηθέντων
| [οἱ ἄρχοντες(?) τοῦ γενέσθαι τὴ]ν στεφάνωσιν αὐτ[ῶ]ν καὶ ἀναγορευ-| [σιν, ὅταν
καὶ οἱ ὑπὸ Τηνίων ἐπ[ηνημένοι ἀναγορεύονται. For the choice left to the Tenians,
see above, 99 and n. 14.

uncertain, beginning with the question of what else was part of the *Dionysia* (tragedy and comedy? old or/and new?).[106]

A few unattributed decrees show that an unknown city chose choral performances for announcements. Thus a long text originating from an unknown city (Magnesia on the Maeander being one possibility), confers, at a date around ca. 100 BC, honours on Assos and the judges it sent. In the city issuing the decree, the crowns will be conferred at the first *Dionysia*, on the first day of the *auletai*, and the announcement will be made by the *agonothetai* of the *mousikos agon*; at Assos, the local *agonothetes* of the musical *agon* is asked to do the same.[107] On the basis of this text, a similar context for announcements has been restored in a decree of a Ionian city for the Coan *demos* and the judges it sent, dated ca. 150–100 BC.[108]

Another type of difficulty is presented by a situation such as the one found in Ephesos. This city, thanks to a fairly high number of early Hellenistic honorific decrees for foreigners (ca. 100), might be thought to allow for a reasonably reliable analysis.[109] But crowns, and even more so proclamations of crowns, are comparatively rare; moreover, the decrees mostly do not give any details as to the occasion when the announcement is to be made, apart from specifying that this should happen at the *Dionysia*, in the theatre.[110] There are, however, some exceptions to this rule: for instance, a Hellenistic inscription honouring Skythes son of Archidamos (an Ephesian) prescribes that he be crowned, and the honour announced, at the next *Dionysia*, "in the contest of men" (ἐν τῶι ἀγῶνι τῶν ἀνδρῶν).[111] How are we to evaluate this

---

106 In an inscription from Didyma dated to ca. 299 BC, Antiochos, the son of Seleukos, is offered the *prohedria* at the *Dionysia* in Miletos and at the *Didymeia* in Didyma ἐν | τοῖς κυκλίοις ἀγῶσιν, *Didyma II. Die Inschriften*, 479.38. There is no proclamation here, but obviously the king will have been offered what was best; one wonders about the reason for the specification "in the cyclic *agones*": front seating might have been desirable throughout the festival, one hardly imagines the king being asked to change place once cyclic choruses are over and tragedy begins. On the other hand, if there was no drama, why the addition?

107 *I.Assos* 7, possibly from Magnesia, as suggested already by Wilhelm, cf. *I. Magnesia* 102.13; but see above n. 104, and *BE* 1974, 545.

108 SEG 53. 864.8–10: στεφα]-| [νῶσαι αὐτὸν ἐν τοῖς π]ρώτοις Διονυσ[ίοις αὐλητῶν] | [τῆι πρώτηι ἡμέραι, and ll. 20-22: [τήν τε ἀναγ]-| [γελίαν τῶν στ]εφάνων ποιήσασθ[αι τοὺς ἀγωνοθέτας τοῦ] | [μουσικοῦ] ἀγῶνος.

109 Ephesian proxeny decrees are discussed in Habicht 2002.

110 At *Dionysia*, in the theatre: *I.Ephesos* 1452, 302 BC ca.; *I.Ephesos* 1405, III BC; *I.Ephesos* 1408; *I.Ephesos* 1411; *I.Ephesos* 1440, 306/294 BC; *Suppl. Ephes.* 126, 2 and 126, 3, both early Hellenistic (the announcement in the second is completely restored); *I.Ephesos* 2003, ca. 300. Uniquely, at the *Epheseia*, in the theatre: *I.Ephesos* 1453.10 (ca. 300 BC): [καὶ ἀ]ναγγεῖλαι τοῖς [Εφε]σείοις ἐν τῶι θεάτρωι.

111 *I.Ephesos* 1390.5–7: σ[τεφα]-| [νῶσαι αὐ]τὸν χρυσῶι στεφάνωι ἐν τοῖς Διονυσίοις

one specific stipulation against all the others where the text simply says "in the theatre"? That the sound of the *aulos* was appreciated in Ephesos appears clearly from a decree, dated to the beginning of the third century, honouring the Boeotian *aulos*-player]on, son of Ismenodoros (*I.Ephesos* 1470); it would have been interesting to know in what context his crown was to be announced, but the stone breaks off just at that moment. However, honours for an *aulos*-player, in the early third century, are not enough to make a case for the overall importance of choral performances. Another document from Ephesos – a decree giving citizenship to a victorious young athlete, who gave Ephesos as his origin at the moment of his victory at Nemea, thus conferring glory on the city – complicates the situation yet further: the city proclaims that he will be Ephesian, as was proclaimed at Nemea; that he will receive the honours which the laws prescribe for those who win at the *Nemea* in his category; and "that he be announced in the *agora*, as all other victors are announced".[112] This is the only instance of what must have been a fairly frequent occurrence, and it shows how insufficient our evidence is.

Nonetheless, there are cases where it is possible to go into some detail. Thus, for instance, for Iasos: we are fairly well informed of the theatrical life of the city thanks to its subscription lists.[113] These make clear that theatrical performances were deemed important enough for the *polis* to resort to the subscription system to guarantee their survival; the first series also allow us to see that besides citharodes and aulodes, the Iasians regularly hired tragedians.

So what of the announcement of honours? In an inscription from Calymna dated to ca. 270–260, the honours decreed to the *polis* of Iasos and to its judges will be announced by the *agonothetes* in Iasos at the *Dionysia*, on the first day of the *kyklia*.[114] Similarly in another (undated) decree the honours for Hermophantos, son of Noumenios, are to be announced during the Dionysiac *agon*, in the theatre, when the city first will organise chorus-

---

τοῖς μετὰ Βαδρόμιον πρύτανιν ἐν τῶι ἀγῶνι τῶν ἀνδρῶν γενομέν[ης ἀν]-|
[αγγε]<λί>ας τῆσ<δε>,…

112 *I.Ephesos* 1415.12–13 (for Athenodoros son of Semon, probably Hellenistic): καὶ ἀναγγεῖλαι αὐτὸν ἐν τῆι ἀγορᾶι καθ[ά]-| περ οἱ ἄλλοι νικῶντες ἀναγγέλλονται (mentioned *supra*, n. 13). See on this text Slater / Summa 2006.

113 See most recently Crowther 2007, with earlier bibliography. To date, 56 lists of contributors are known, falling in two groups, a first series of seven lists, covering the period from the end of the third century to the early 180s BC, in which the citizens offer specific spectacles; and a second, later series, in which the citizens make uniform payments of 200 drachmas (the *metoikoi* 100).

114 M. Segre, *Tituli Calymnii*, p19, XVI, A, 19–21= *I. Iasos* 82.18–20: τὸν μὲν αγωνο-| θέτην ἀναγγεῖλαι τὸν τῆς πόλεως στέφανον καὶ τὸν | [τ]ῶν δικαστῶν κυκλίων τῆι πρώτηι. That this happens in the context of the *Dionysia* is specified in the request of the Calymnians, 17–18.

es.[115] A different venue is chosen in a decree of the Iasians honouring a Coan citizen, Teleutias: the *agonothetes* will announce the crown at the first next *Dionysia*, after the *pompe*.[116] While more data (and specific dates for the texts!) would help, it is striking that although there were theatrical performances *stricto sensu* at Iasos, the inscriptions never mention tragic *agones*, and prefer to indicate choral performances, or the *pompe*, as the venue for the announcement of honours. On the other hand, a decree of the Koinon of the Dionysiac *technitai* of Ionia and the Hellespont shows that the term "choruses" may include tragedy and comedy: it allocates anually two *aulos*-players, two tragedians, two comedians, a *kitharodos,* a *kitharistes*, and their *hyperesiai* so that the Iasians may be able to celebrate every year choruses for the god according to their traditions.[117]

In some other instances it is possible to notice an evolution. At Priene, the earliest honorific decrees (328 to 270 BC) prescribe that the honours be announced at the *Dionysia*, during the contests of tragedy.[118] In two more cases the occasion is not specified beyond "in the theatre, at the *Dionysia*". But later documents show a shift in the preferred venue: announcements during the tragic competitions are no more to be found. This change may be adumbrated in the wording of a Prienean third century decree for three *sitophylakes*: their crowns must be announced in the theatre, at the first *Dionysia*, during the musical *agon* – though what exactly is meant with musical *agon* is left unspecified.[119] The first certain example of the new trend is

---

115 *I.Iasos* 43.4–7: στεφανῶσαι αὐτὸν χρυσῶι στε[φάνωι τῶι ἐκ τοῦ]‖5 νόμου ἐν τῶι θεάτρωι τῶι Διονυ[σιακῶι ἀγῶνι,] | καὶ ἀναγγεῖλαι τὸν κήρυκα, ὅτα [ν ἡ πόλις πρῶτον] | χοροὺς ἄγηι.

116 *I.Iasos* 51.31–34 (Segre ED 133, from Cos): τὸν δὲ ἀγωνοθέτην ἐπιμελὲς πο[ιή]-| σασθαι ὅπως ἀναγγελῇ ὁ στέφανος ὧι τετίμη[ται] | Τελευτίας, τῆς ἀναγγελίας γινομένης ἐν | τοῖς πρώτοις Διονυσίοις μετὰ τὴν πομπήν.

117 *I.Iasos* 152.15–16 (mid second century BC): αὐλητὰς δύο, τραγῳδοὺς δύο, κωμῳδοὺς δύο, κιθαρῳδόν, κιθαριστήν, ὅπως | ἄγωσιν τῶι θεῶι τοὺς [χ]ορούς κατὰ τὰς πατρίους αὐτῶν διαγραφάς. Cf. Crowther 2007, 309–10.

118 So in a decree for judges from Phokaia, another unknown city, and Astypalaia, dated to 328 BC, *I. Priene* 8, 32–33, the *agonothetes* will announce the crown τοῖς πρώτ[οι]ς Διονυσίοις τραγωιδῶ[ν τ]ῶ[ι αγῶνι, δη]-|[λ]οῦντα διὰ τῆς ἀναγγελίας τὰς αἰτίας...; moreover, ambassadors will be sent to each of the three *poleis*, asking that the honours may be announced there too Διο[νυ]σίοις ἐν τῶι αγ[ῶ]νι τῶν τραγωιδ[ῶ]ν,| καθότι καὶ Πριηνεῖς παρ' αὐτοῖς ἐψηφισμένοι εἰσίν (52–53). Similarly, *I. Priene* 23, 14–15, a decree for the *phrourarchos* Bias dated to the III century BCE, stipulates for the proclamation to happen in the theatre Διο]νυσίων τραγωιδῶν τῶι ἀ-| γῶνι; this is also the case of *I. Priene* 18, 8–9, a decree for Larichos of ca. 270–262 BC (crown to be announced Διονυσίοις τραγωιδῶ[ν] | [τ]ῶι πρώτωι ἀγῶνι). The third decree honouring Nymphon too stipulates that the honours will be announced at the first *Dionysia*, during the tragic competitions: *I.Priene* 22, 16.

119 *I. Priene* 81.13–16: καὶ ἀναγγεῖλαι αὐτῶν τοὺς σ[τεφάνους]‖ ἐν τῶι θεάτρωι τοῖς πρώτοις Διονυσίοις ἐ[ν ἀγῶνι]‖15 τῶι μουσικῶι, δηλοῦντας διὰ τ[ῆ]ς ἀναγγ[ελίας

a honorific decree of the Prieneans for their *phrourarchos* Nymphon, dated
to ca. 270–262 BC (*I. Priene* 21.19–20): the *agonothetes* will announce the
crown at the next *Dionysia*, during the first *agon* of the *auletai* (i.e, of the
choruses accompanied by the aulos, τοῖς πρώτοις Διονυσίοις αὐλητῶ[ν] |
τῶι πρώτωι ἀγῶνι). Similarly, a honorific decree of the garrison in Telonea
for their commander Helikon, dated around 250 BC (*I. Priene* 19.53–54),
prescribes that the honours will be announced "at the next *Dionysia*, at the
choral *agon* of the children accompanied by aulos-music" (ἐν τοῖς πρώτοις
| [Δ]ιονυσίοις αὐλητῶν τῶ[ι] ἀγῶνι τῶι παιδικῶ[ι·]). Exactly the same for-
mulation appears in two Prienean inscriptions of the second century BC:
the choral competitions of the *paides* seem to have gained in prestige at
the cost of the tragic ones.[120] A further development, which may give some
indications as to the reason for the change, happens in the latter part of the
second century BC: now the proclamation is to be made by the *agonothetes*
just before the choral dances of the *paides* at the *Dionysia*, when the *demos*
proceeds to the ancestral libations to Dionysos: this is what happens in the
case of the decree honouring Moschion, son of Kydimos, dated to after 129
BC;[121] very similar is the slightly later decree for Herakleitos son of Thedo-
ros.[122] The choral dances of the *paides* occupy a privileged position; and the
civic status of the occasion receives considerable stress, through the mention
of the libations and common sacrifices.

An evolution similar to that argued for in the case of Priene can be pos-
ited for Kolophon. A recently published decree of Aigai for Kolophonian
judges, of the first half of the third century, has the Kolophonians agree to
the request of proclamation of honours made by the people of Aigai, and
stipulate that the proclamation will be made at the next celebration of *agones*
by their city, at the *great Klaria* by the *agonothetai*, and at the *Dionysia* by
the *prytanis*.[123] In a honorific decree of the second half of the third century

---

τὰς] | αἰτίας δι' ἃς στεφανοῦνται. A similarly open formulation in a decree of the
Parianoi for the Prieneans of ca. 200 BC, (*I.Priene* 63.15–17)= *I.Parion* 1.15–17
(restorations by Louis Robert) : παρακαλέ]σει Πριηνεῖς ἀναγγεῖλαι τὸν [στέφ]ανον
το[ῦ δήμου] | [καὶ παρ' αὐτοῖς ἐν τῶι θεάτ]ρωι ἐν τῶι ἀγῶνι τῶν Διονυσίω[ν] ὅτ[α]ν
[ἡ πόλις πρῶτον] |[συντελῆι τοὺς χοροὺς, ὅτι...

120 *I. Priene* 53 (34, 59 and 70), and *I. Priene* 54 (31, 54 and 65), two very similar
     honorific decrees of the Iasians for judges from Priene, with the acceptance of the
     honours by the Prieneans.

121 *I. Priene* 108, VIII 332: ἐν τῶι θεάτρωι Διονυσίων αὐλητῶν | τῶι ἀγῶνι τῶι
     παιδικῶ[ι, ὅταν ὁ δῆμος τὰς] | πατρίους σπονδὰς συντ[ελῆι...

122 *I. Priene,* 117. 68–69 (dated to the I century BC): Διονυσίοις αὐλ[ητῶν τῶι ἀγῶνι
     τῶι παιδικῶι,] ὅταν ὁ δῆμος τὰς πατρί-| [ους θυσία]ς τῷ Διονύσωι ἐπιτελῆ...

123 Gauthier 1999 (SEG 49, 1502), ll. 44–46. For the request of the Aigeans, see ll.14–
     16, and ll.30–32 and 42–43, where it is cited by the Kolophonians. The specification
     'great' does not here imply an *agon stephanites*, but local competitions, trieteric or

for foreign judges from Lampsakos, the crown has to be announced at the *Dionysia*, at the *Klaria megala* and at the *Antiocheia*, when the *polis* first will present the *agones*, respectively by the *prytanis* and the *agonothetai*, without further precisions.[124] In another third century honorific decree for Prienean ambassadors, the announcement will be made by the *prytanis* at the *Dionysia*, when the *polis* first (lacuna) presents the choruses to the god, and in the *Klaria* and *Antiocheia* in the gymnic *agones*.[125] This is a little more precise, although it would be nice to know exactly what kind of choruses are meant. Finally, in two honorific decrees of the last quarter of the second century BC, the choruses have disappeared; the announcement is still to be made at the *Dionysia* and the *Klaria*, but in the pyrrhic contest and in the gymnic *agones*, forever.[126] So here too, while proclamation at the *Dionysia* remains a feature, the specific context of the proclamation changes: in the third century, the decrees mention proclamation at "*agones*", or when the *polis* presents choruses to the god; by the end of the second century, the proclamation is made at the moment of the pyrrhic contest. It is unclear how far back we may project this: can the unspecified choruses of the early third century have been pyrrhic choruses? More generally, in these and other documents, what exactly does the reference to choric competition imply? Could it have included tragedy?

Two further instances of announcements at the moment of choruses comes from Halicarnassos: a possibly fourth century honorific decree points to "the [...] day when choruses perform"; in the second century BC a more elaborate formula is used for the same purpose.[127] A similar wording is found in a decree of the *demos* of Teos honouring a citizen of Magnesia on the Maeander, probably to be dated to the first half of the second century BC: the crown is to be given in Teos, at the *Dionysia*, when the city offers

---

pentateric, more important than the yearly ones; even so, the *Klaria*, a gymnic festival, seem to have been more important. Comparing *Klaria* and *Dionysia*, Gauthier remarks that the *Dionysia*, "a rather banal festival in all of Greece, with the exception of Teos, remained, irrespective of whether we mean greater or smaller *Dionysia*, a local agon".

124 *I. Lampsakos* 33, ll. 18–23.

125 *I. Priene* 57, with the restorations proposed by P. Frisch, *ZPE* 13, 1974, 112–116 (cf. *BE* 1974, 457, 483, 546; Robert 1989, 52–53), ll. 3–6: τῆς δὲ ἀναγγελ[ίας / [τῶν στεφάνων τὴ]ν ἐπιμέλειαν ποιήσασθαι τοῖς μὲν Διονυσίοις τὸν πρύτανιν ἐν τῷ ἀ[γω- / [νι ...... ὅταν] ἡ πόλις πρῶτον τοὺς χοροὺς συντελῆι τῶι θεῶι, τοῖς δὲ Κλαρίοις τοῖ[ς / [μεγάλοις καὶ τοῖς Ἀντ]ιοχείοις τοὺς ἀγωνοθέτας ἐν τῶι ἀγῶνι τῶι γυμνικῶι.

126 *SEG* 39, 1243 (130–110 BC), col. V 30–37 and *SEG* 39, 1244 (post 120/119 BC), col. III 23–28; ample commentary in J. and L. Robert 1989, 57–59 and 102–103; on the pyrrhic at Kolophon, Ceccarelli 1995, 298, and Ceccarelli 1998, 132–4.

127 GIBM 890, McCabe Halikarnassos 5.2 (Robert 1937, 150): [— ἡ]μέραι ὅτα[ν οἱ χοροὶ συντελῶνται; and *SEG* 29, 1072,1–2 (McCabe Halikarnassos 11): [ἐν τῶι θεάτρωι ἐν τῶι ἀγῶνι τῶι] | [μου]σικῶι, ἐπὰν ὁ δῆμος χοροὺς ἄγη[ι.

the choruses to Dionysos; the *timouchoi* will take care of the announcement.[128]

4   References to choruses in epigraphic texts:
how to interpret them?

We have seen that if some formulations are rather vague, in at least one
case, the definition "choral competition" includes tragedy: two Samian honorific decrees made it clear – if the restorations are to be trusted – that the
announcement of honours was to be done during the tragic *agones* of the
Dionysia, when the city would first present choruses to the god. The decree
of the *Koinon* of the Dionysiac *technitai* of Ionia and the Hellespont for
the Iasians also included tragedy and comedy under the term "choruses".
Another very fragmentary (and undated) decree of the Samians in Minoa
on the island of Amorgos, dated to the second/first century BC, has a very
similar formulation: the crown is to be conferred at the *Dionysia*, during the
tragic performances, when the city offers the first choruses to the god.[129] If
the restorations are correct, "choruses" here means "tragic performances".
Of course, dramatic performances were "*choroi* for Dionysos": the *tragodoi*
are initially the members of the tragic chorus, although the term later was
used also for the actors.[130] But should we think of dramatic choruses in all of
the instances where choruses only are mentioned? The changes in terminology between the fifth century and the late Hellenistic period should not be
underestimated, nor should the conservatism and the variations in practice
from one place to the other.

   The epigraphical evidence, at any rate, suggests that matters were rather
complex. A number of documents attests, in a more or less secure way, the
persistence of a tragic chorus in Hellenistic times.[131] These comprise the

---

128 I.*Magnesia* 97.34–38: ἐπαινέσαι Γ[λαῦκον]|35 [Ἀδμ]ήτου Μάγνητα ὄντα εὐεργέτην
    τοῦ δ[ήμου] | [στε]φανῶσαι δὲ αὐτὸν ἐν τοῖς Διονυσ[ίοις] | [ὅταν] τοὺς χοροὺς
    συντελῶμεν τῶι Διονύ[σωι] | [στεφ]άνωι χρυσῶι; and again at line 45.
129 Resp. *supra*, 125–6 and n. 83; 135 and n. 117; and IG XII 7, 231, ll. 34–36:
    [στεφ]ανοῦσ[θαι δ]ὲ αὐτὸν καὶ / [θαλλοῦ(?)] στεφάνωι Διο[ν]υσίων τρ[αγωι]δοῖς
    ὅταν τοὺς / [πρώτου]ς χοροὺς [ἡ πόλις] τῶι θεῶι συ[ν]τελ.[ῆι]· (see also IG XII,7
    Corr. p. 127; L. Robert, *RA* 1924, 180; and SEG 53, 2191).
130 Wilson 2000, 6 and 312 n. 19–21: a poet asked for a chorus; the archon granted a
    chorus; the festival judges judged the *choroi*; tragedy and comedy are respectively
    the "*choroi* of the tragedians" and "of the comedians"; the use of *choregos* for the
    citizen appointed to fund a tragic chorus fits this pattern. However, it must be noted
    that the Athenians could distinguish quite well between the various types of *choroi*.
131 Sifakis 1967, 116–26. I omit from the documents he cites the inscriptions concern-
    ing the *Soteria* at Delphi: Sifakis' hypothesis that the members of the dithyrambic

already discussed decree passed by Chalcis, Eretria, Karystos and Oreos in the early third century concerning the organization of the *Dionysia* and *Demetria* in Euboea, which mentions, in a very discussed passage, both choruses of men and boys, and choruses of tragedians;[132] a decree of the Dionysiac artists of Ptolemais in Egypt, dated around 246 BC, where the names of a tragic actor, six comedians, four supporting actors of tragedy and a *chorodidaskalos* are followed, after a few illegible lines, by the name of a tragic *aulos*-player: as Sifakis comments, the inference that the *chorodidaskalos* mentioned in such a contest was an intructor of tragic choruses is hardly avoidable.[133] *Chorodidaskaloi* (one comic, three tragic) are also among the Dionysiac artists who performed in honour of Apollo at Delphi in the second Athenian *Pythais*, in 127 BC. Dramatic choruses are not recorded, but they might have been formed out of the chorus who sang the paean for Apollo.[134] Sifakis rounds up his list with an inscription from Argos, dated to the beginning of the first century BC, recording a very large number of Athenian *tragikoi chorodidaskaloi*; and with an inscription of the same period from Tanagra, detailing the expenses incurred for the celebration of the *Sarapieia*: *chorodidaskaloi* are again mentioned, possibly also choruses (this part is fragmentary), and since there are no cyclic choruses, these should be interpreted as tragic choruses, performing in the contest of new tragedy.[135]

To these documents others can be added. A particularly interesting case is that of the city of Eresos on Lesbos: three decrees, spanning the period from the third to the second century BC, and covering various possibilities in terms of honorands, concur in making it clear that honours are announced (also) at the *Dionysia*, on the occasion of the tragic competition, by a magistrate bearing the name of *chorostatas* (the other favoured venues being the gymnic competitions of the *Herakleia* and of the *Ptolemaia*). The first

---

choruses might also have served as tragic dancers, is not supported by the evidence: cf. Nachtergael 1977, 313; Slater 1993, 195.

132 Euboean law: IG XII 9.207, l. 31 τοὺς χοροὺς τῶν ἀνδρῶν τραγικῶν; the reading of this line is however debated (see the comments of Slater 1993). Text and commentary in Pickard-Cambridge 1988, 306–8; Csapo / Slater 1994, 196–200; Le Guen 2001a, I 41–56. See Sifakis 1967, 116; Wilson 2000, 292–3; Nervegna 2007, 28.

133 Sifakis 1967, 117; see now for the document Le Guen 2001a, I 296–300.

134 FD III 2 47, Sifakis 1967, 117. As noted *ibid.* by Sifakis, the presence of trainers of dramatic choruses among members of the Athenian *technitai* serves also as evidence for performances in Athens.

135 Argos: Sifakis 1967, 117–19 and 143–4 (SEG 33, 290). Tanagra: Sifakis 1967, 117–18; Slater 1993, 191–7 rightly points out that it is nowhere question in this document of a chorus for the old tragedy; but he admits to the presence of a comic, a (new) tragic and a satyric chorus.

document honours a citizen, Damon, son of Polyarchos;[136] the other two are
in one instance a request of the Parianoi to proclaim in Eresos the honours
which they have voted for the demos of Eresos and the judges it sent; and
a honorific decree of Eresos for judges from Miletos, dated to the first half
of the second century.[137] In all of these cases, the *chorostatas* takes care of
the proclamation during the tragic *agones* of the *Dionysia*, while the gymna-
siarch takes care of that at the *Herakleia* and *Ptolemaia*. Proclamation by a
chorostatas thus does not exclude tragic *agones*; it seems, however, highly
significant that the person responsible for the proclamation (and thus most
likely for the organisation of the performances, dramatic and otherwise)
bears the name of *chorostatas*. Evidently, if these were tragic performances,
the chorus retained at least some of its importance. A *chorostatas* is also in
charge of proclaiming honours in small Nesos, but here the document does
not specify in what *agon*.[138] A few more documents may be added to these
intriguing pieces of evidence for dramatic choruses in the Hellenistic period:
thus, two documents from Cyrene, both dating to the last third of the fourth
century, mention choruses of tragedians (*choroi tragikoi* in one, *tragoidik-
ous chorous* in the other inscription, both dated to the 330s BC) alongside
dithyrambic choruses;[139] much later, a list of victors in the *Lysimacheia* of
the second century AD mentions a victorious tragic chorus;[140] the invention,
in the imperial period, of the term *mesochorus* also points to the continued
importance of the chorus.[141]

---

136 IG XII 2, 527. ll. 24–26 (but see the text offered in IG XII suppl. p. 33: [στεφ]ά[νωσα]ι
     δὲ αὗτον ἔν τε τοῖς Διονυσίοισι [τῶ ἄγωνι τῶν τραγώδων καὶ] / ἐν τοῖς γυμνίκοισι
     ἀγώνεσσι οἷς συντέλ[ει ἁ πόλις τῶ τε Ἡράκλει καὶ τῶ] /[β]ασίλει Πτολεμαίω· , and
     τᾶς δὲ ἀγ[αγγελίας ἐπιμέλεσ]-/[θαι ἐμ μ]ὲν τοῖς Διονυσίοισι τὸγ χοροστάταον, ἐ[ν δὲ
     τοῖς Πτολεμαέ]-/[οισι] τὸγ γυμνασίαρχον ἄι τὸν ἐνεστάκοντα. The editor provides no
     date, but the decree may reasonably be put somewhere in the III–II century BC.
137 IG XII *Suppl.* 121 (= *I. Parion* 2), ll. 30–35: ἀναγόρευσαι δὲ καὶ τοῖς [σ]τεφάνοις,/
     [κ]αθάπερ ἀξίαισι Παρίανοι, ἔν τε τοῖς Ἡρακλέοισι τῶ / [ἄ]γωνι τῶ γυμνίκω καὶ ἐν
     τοῖς Διονυσίοισ[ι] τῶ ἄγωνι / [τ]ῶν τραγώιδων· τᾶς δὲ ἀναγορεύσι[ος] ἐπιμέλεια[ν]
     / [π]ρήσασθαι ἐμ μ[ὲν] τοῖς Ἡρακλέοισι [τ]ὸν γυμνασίαρχο[ν], / 35[ἐν] δὲ τοῖς
     Διονυσί[οισι] τὸν χορ[οσ]τάταον; and *I.Milet* I 3 152C.76–78, 82–83, and 88–89.
     The proclamation is to be repeated yearly.
138 IG XII 2 645 = *OGIS* 4 = *I. Adramytteion* 34, ll. 36–39 (dated to 319–317 BC):
     [στε]φανώτω δὲ αὗτον ὁ χοροστάτας ἄι ὁ ἐν[έ]-/ ων] ἐν τῶ ἄγωνι καὶ ὀγκαρυσσέτω
     ἀνδραγ[α]-/ [θί]ας ἔνεκα καὶ εὐνοίας τᾶς πρὸς τὸν δᾶ-/[μον].
139 SEG 9, 13 and SEG 48, 2052; discussion in Ceccarelli and Milanezi 2007.
140 *MAMA* VIII 420; Wilson 2000, 308; Nervegna 2007, 28.
141 Discussion in Robert 1938, 96–7. References include: Sidon. Apoll. 1 2.9; schol. Ju-
     venal 11 72; *FD* III 1,219. Slater 1993, 199 and n. 35, adds some references from lit-
     erary texts to *tragodoi* with a chorus: Lucillius, *Anth. Pal.* 11.11; Epict. *Diss.* 3.14.1;
     Plut. *Mor.* 63a, and suggests that these choruses pertained only to new tragedies. Le
     Guen 2007 infers the existence of tragic choruses from the continued existence of
     titles of tragedies in the plural.

Thus, in themselves references to choruses in honorific decrees may be taken to include tragic choruses (possibly only of new drama, following a hypothesis advanced by Slater);[142] but in the great majority of the instances, it is quite clear (for instance through the use of the term "cyclic") that we have to do with choral and not with dramatic performances.[143]

Were these hired choruses? Some – probably most – certainly were (so the Euboean ones); but I would submit that not all of them were; we should, at any rate, seriously consider the possibility of citizen participation. Claros offers a striking example of the persistence of local (citizen) choruses, choruses of *paides* and *parthenoi*, for the gods: Louis Robert has published a number of lists, mainly of the second century AD, recording the visit of delegations (of *theoroi*, as is specified in a few cases) from cities of Asia Minor sent to consult the oracle. Among the cities who sent choruses are nearby cities from Asia Minor, such as Tabai, Heraklea on the Salbake, Laodikeia on the Lycos, Aizanoi, Aphrodisias, Bargasa; but also Amaseia in Pontos, Phocea, Chios, Corinth, Hierapytna, Lappa. The delegations are usually composed of a *theopropos* or *prophetes*, of a *hiereus*, and of a chorus of *paides* or, less frequently, *eitheoi*; some cities, such as Chios, sent mixed choruses, of *paides / eitheoi* and *parthenoi*.[144] The choruses sent by Tabai number usually seven members, those of Heraclea nine: as pointed out by Robert, the regularity in number shows that to be a member of this special, yearly chorus was a great honour. The singers are accompanied by various dignitaries, whose function seems to have been the same (the name varies depending on the local habit): sometimes a *didaskalos* joins the group; in other instances, *choregoi* (Heraklea) are mentioned; alternatively, one finds a *chorodidaskalos* or *hymnodidaskalos* (the same man, a kitharist sent from Lappa); Hierapytna sends along an *hymnodarches*.[145] Against the theory ad-

---

142 Slater 1993. If this were the case, then maybe the continued existence of the chorus might have played a role in the decision of the Athenians to proclaim honours at the moment of the contest of *new* tragedies.

143 Reisch 1899, 2431–2 maintained that *chorikoi agones* refers, from the Hellenistic period onwards, to competitions, or sometimes only performances, of cyclic choruses, considered as distinct from the dramatic *agones*.

144 For Chios, cf. SEG 37, 973.8, 974.5: ἤϊθεοι παρεγένοντο καὶ παρθένοι οἱ ὑμνήσαντες τὸν θεόν.

145 Ten documents from Tabai, n° 24 to 31, 33, 192, and 193 (discussion in Robert 1954, 115–18); eighteen from Heraklea on the Salbake, n° 132 to 146, and 194, 195, 196 (discussion in Robert 1954, 203–16). I reproduce here the list 192, one of the most extensive (it comprises a *didaskalos* as well): Ταβηνῶν.| ἐπὶ πρυτάνεως Ἀπόλλωνος | τὸ π´, ἱερέως Κλ(αυδίου) Ῥούφου, θεσπι-| ῳδοῦντος Γναί(ου) Ἰου(λίου) Ῥηγί(νου) Ἀλε-|5 ξάνδρου, προφητεύοντος | Κάρπου τοῦ Ἀττάλου, γραμματεύ-| οντος Ἀλεξάνδρου τοῦ Μηνοφίλου·| οἱ ὑμνήσαντες τὸν θεόν | *vac* παῖδες · ἱερεοὺς |10 Τ(ίτος) Φλ(άβιος) Φλ(αβίου) Μιθριδάτου υἱὸς Παπίας, | Πυλάδης Ὀρθρίου, Ὄρθριος Πυλάδου,| Μαρσύας β´ Σαμου, Ζήνων καὶ Ἀνδρέ-| ας οἱ Ἀνδρέου,

vanced by Haussoullier, according to whom the choruses were recruited in Colophon, it is clear now, as conclusively shown by Louis Robert, that the various choruses were composed of citizens, just like the rest of the personnel. Very often, moreover, the author of the poem sung was a citizen of the *polis* that was sending a chorus: we must reckon with a relatively rich, if extremely local, tradition of songs.

The documents from Claros may be fruitfully compared with a record of bringing decorations to Artemis by listed *paides* and *parthenoi,* dated by *prytanis,* found at Ephesos.[146] Another fascinating document is a decree of the *boule* of Stratonikeia concerning the appointment and training of *hymnodoi.* The Stratonikeis vote to choose thirty well-born *paides,* whom every day the *paidonomos,* together with the public *paidophylakes,* will bring, dressed in white and crowned, to the *bouleuterion*; the *paides,* accompanied by a citharist and herald as well, will sing a hymn, which the *grammateus* Sosandros, son of Diomedes, will compose. This is followed by exemption clauses and restrictions or punishments if the boys fail to do as prescribed.[147]

Bowie has made the important point that these groups are not called *choroi,* possibly because of a reluctance to use *choros* for a group attached to a temple cult; this would imply lack of continuity with the earlier, classical tradition. The issue of continuity remains a moot point; but all of this suggests the possibility, not to say the likelihood, of citizen participation in choruses (cyclic or dramatic), or at least of joint choruses formed by a few professionals reinforced by local dancers.[148] And if the choruses were at least

---

Μενεκλῆς Καλλικλέο[υς]·| θεοπρόποι Θεαγένης Διονυσίου καὶ Ἀλ[έ]-|15 ξανδρος Θεαγένους· διδάσκαλος Τ(ίτος) Φλ(άβιος) | Σωτᾶς παράδοξος. A number of other lists in *SEG* 37 961–980. See also the discussion in Bowie 2006, 90–2.

146 JÖAI 55, 142–143, no. 4369; SEG 34, 1124.

147 *I.Stratonikeia* 1101, probably end of the second century AD (discussion in Robert 1937, 516–23; see also Bowie 2006, 90–1): ἔδοξε τῇ βουλῇ, α[ἱρεῖσθαι] νῦν ἐκ τῶν εὖ γεγονότων παῖδας τριάκον-| τα, οὕστινας καθ' ἑκάστην ἡμέραν μετὰ τῶν δημοσίων παιδοφυλάκων ἄ[ξετ]αι ὁ παιδονό[μος ἰς τὸ β]ουλευτήριον λευχιμονοῦντας καὶ ἐστε-| φανωμένους θαλλοῦ, ἔχοντας δὲ μετὰ χῖρας ὁμοίως θαλλούς, οἵτινες συνπαρόν[των κα]ὶ κιθαριστοῦ καὶ κήρυκος ᾄσονται ὕμνον, ὃν |10 ἂν συντάξῃ Σώσανδρος Διομήδους ὁ γραμματεούς. See also the decree of Stratonicea in Caria for Assos, mid II century BC, Michel 477: crowns to be announced by the *agonothetai* in the musical *agon* for Rome (ἐν τῶι ἀγῶνι τῶι μουσικῶι τῶι συντελουμένωι τῆι Ῥώμηι).

148 Bowie 2006, 92. The possibility of civic choruses in the Hellenistic period, both tragic and cyclic, is strongly argued for e.g. by Wilson 2000, 278–302; see also Wilson 2003, 166, who sees cyclic choruses (which he qualifies as dithyrambic – but that is not inevitable) as "tenaciously epichoric in character", unlike tragedy, which was more and more the preserve of travelling professional actors.

in part formed by locals, that would explain the choice of choral performances as the venue for announcements.[149]

5 Tragedy and the city: the end of symbiosis?

It is time to attempt some conclusions. At the beginning, I suggested that one could address the question of the change in the civic import of tragedy by looking at the occasion chosen for the proclamation of civic honours. In particular, I wanted to test the assumption of a continued civic importance of dramatic performances, and also more generally of their prestige, vis-à-vis other forms of choral and gymnic performance.

From the collection of documents we have just examined the following main points emerge:

First, the range of festivals at which drama was performed shows that the strong connection between tragic performances and Dionysiac festival, which is such a distinctive feature of fifth-century Athens, did not apply everywhere. Even in Athens, tragedy entered into the frame of other, non-Dionysiac festivals, such as the *Panathenaia*. Moreover, from the fourth century onwards, dramatic performances were often added to pre-existing athletic and musical competitions. Nonetheless, a link with Dionysos remained, inasmuch as the associations of *technitai* called upon to participate in the various festivals chose to stress, in their very name (*hoi peri ton Dionyson technitai*), their link with Dionysos.[150]

Secondly, the record of prizes assigned to winners in the various specialties, dramatic, musical, and gymnic, is too sketchy to allow any definitive conclusions. Still, it seems to have been the case that not infrequently gymnic victories could fetch higher prizes than those in drama; and similarly, that citharodes and *aulos*-players were better rewarded than actors. Some caution is, however, needed in interpreting the evidence from prize lists: not only are they few, they are also late, and we have to reckon with changes. Moreover, the artists were also paid, in order to guarantee their participation

---

149 Further evidence for civic choruses has been collected by Wörrle in his discussion of the festival instituted by C. Iulius Demosthenes in the 120s AD at Oinoanda; particularly striking is the existence of a *choros politikos* in a third century list of victors of the *Mouseia* of Thespiai, IG VII 1776, post 212 AD; the winner is – as expected – a Thespian, while for the other musical categories the winners have come from all over the ancient world. See Wörrle 1988, 227–9; Bowie 2006, 90.

150 All of this is fairly uncontroversial: for the early divorce from the Dionysiac frame, cf. Scullion 2002 (who actually argues for the non-existence of a Dionysiac frame), *passim*. For the addition of drama to gymnic or musical festivals, see Csapo / Slater 1994, 186, for the *technitai*, Ceccarelli 2004.

in a festival; but of the prices agreed usually no record survives.[151] Yet on the whole it seems fairly uncontroversial to say that at least in the fifth and fourth centuries BC a famous dithyrambist would hardly have been considered a lesser poet than a tragic playwright; in that same period, the same would have applied to top performers in acting, *aulos* playing or *kithara* playing. Matters seem to have changed in the Hellenistic period, with *aulos*-players and *kithara*-players becoming the real stars, who could easily travel – actors needed a troupe and group rehearsals, and whenever we find decrees honouring playwrights, they are honoured because they wrote plays on local themes.[152]

Thirdly, the analysis of the proclamation of honours shows that there is no uniformity across the Greek world. The category of the *agon* (local versus *stephanites*, for instance) may have made a difference in the choice of the venue for the announcement, just as the status of the honorand may have dictated the type of venue selected; but on the whole, it seems clear that these were not the main elements in the decision.[153] Repeated announcements at more than one festival, such as are found almost systematically in late Hellenistic Athenian decrees, are rarer elsewhere: but they exist, as the cases of Delphi, Tenos, Rhodes and Mylasa show, and announcements may be distributed between a gymnic and a music *agon*.[154] As for the specific moment of the announcement, in the context of a music festival: is it the moment of the tragic competitions, as in the "model", Athens? Did tragic competitions, from this point of view, continue to be important for the civic life of the *polis*? In Athens, this probably holds true. And the Athenians may have chosen the tragic *agones* for public announcements (rather than, for instance, the moment preceding the dithyrambic competitions) because of the civic value of the performance to follow. Compared to the dithyramb, which features an inter-tribal competition, tragedy is the outcome of, and puts on display, a collective civic endeavour. But in other parts of the Greek world, the state of the documentation is such that one cannot really tell whether tragedy ever was the central moment; what

---

151　See Slater 1993.

152　See, for instance, Dymas from Iasos, with discussion and some further instances in Rutherford 2007; but this is a widespread phenomenon, touching also historiographers etc.

153　This is in line with the argument made by Parker 2004.

154　Delphi and Tenos: see above. Mylasa: cf. the Hellenistic honorary decree for Ouliades, *I.Mylasa* 101.60–63, prescribing the announcement of the crown to be made in the gymnic *agon* for Zeus, and in the musical one, when the *demos* offers choruses to Dionysos: τ<ὴ>ν δὲ ἀ-|60 [ν]αγγελί[αν] τοῦ στεφάνου ποιήσαν[τος τοῦ] γραμμ[ατέως τοῦ δήμου —]ΙΣ <κ>α[τὰ] | τὸν νόμο[ν —] ἐν τῶι γυμνικῶι ἀγῶνι τῶι συντελουμένωι [τῶι Διὶ καὶ ἐν τ]ῶι μου-| σικῶι ἐπὰ[ν] ὁ δῆμος [χ]ο[ροὺς ἄγηι] τῶι Διονύσωι. Exactly the same wording is found in the (heavily restored) *I.Mylasa* 149, of the same period.

is at any rate clear is that choral and gymnic performances assumed more and more importance in the overall economy of distributing honours. Just as Mette could say for Athens that there must always have been new tragedies, so we can affirm, on a minimal interpretation of the assembled evidence, that most of the *poleis* of the islands and Asia Minor continued with choral (non-tragic) performances – possibly for the simple reason that they were less expensive. In this case, we would not be facing a choice between dramatic and choral performances, but rather an issue of what any given *polis* could afford at any given moment.

However, this cannot be the only answer: for we know of cases where the festival chosen for the announcement comprised both choral and dramatic performances, but the choral ones were chosen. In at least some cases, the choral performances may have been felt to be the more prestigious ones; and in others, they may have been more closely linked to the civic community. We do not know with certainty who formed the choruses which performed in the *chorikoi agones* (in most cases, either *andres* or *paides*); the choruses of *paides* tend to be preferred for the announcement of honours (thus we find expressions such as ἐν τοῖς χοροῖς τῶν παίδων, ὅταν ἦι τῶν παίδων ἀγών, ὅταν ἀγωνίζωνται οἱ χοροὶ τῶν παίδων, attested in Delos, Chios, Minoa and Arkesine in the island of Amorgos).[155] Were they professional or recruited locally? As so often, there is no clear-cut answer. *Paides choreutai* were members of the associations of Dionysiac *technitai*, as we see from the lists of the *Soteria* at Delphi;[156] but the hypothesis, often advanced, of a mixed composition, with a professional *auletes* leading a chorus formed by locals and a few professional dancers makes a lot of sense. What is, at any rate, clear is that the world of choral performance maintained its importance.[157]

---

155 IG XII 7, 221b.15–17, from Minoa in Amorgos, ca. 250–200 BC (crown to be announced in the theatre, during the *agon* of the *auletai*, at the *Hekatonbioia*; IG XII 7, 225 honours to be announced in Minoa at *Dionysia* and *Heraia* (no mention of the precise moment) in the III century BC (with Robert 1938, 113 for the story of the expansion of Samos in the neighbouring islands in the Hellenistic period); IG XII 7, 228, 6–8, dated to the II century BC (οἱ δὲ χορηγοὶ [κ]αθ᾽ ἕκαστον [ἐν] ιαυτόν, | ὅταν οἱ χοροὶ τῶν παίδων ἄγωνται ἐν τῶι | θεάτρῳ, ἀναγορευέτωσαν διὰ τοῦ ἱεροκή-| ρυκος ὅτι ὁ δῆμος ὁ Ἀμουργίων τῶν κατοι-| κούντων Μινώιαν ἐπαινεῖ καὶ στεφανοῖ...); IG XII 7, 231 (first or second century BC), 34–36. See also IG XII 7, 49.23–25, a decree of Arkesine for the euergete Theodosia, undated but certainly fairly late: ἀνακηρυσσέσθω δὲ | [ὁ στέφανος] ἐν τοῖς ἐπιτελουμένοις χο-|25[ρικοῖς ἀγ]ῶσιν ἐν τῷ θεάτρῳ.

156 Nachtergael 1977, 257–60. Cf. also Hug 1956, and Jory 1967.

157 Bowie 2006 assembles much important evidence but then oddly argues that his collected references to *choroi* do not refer to contemporary life. I would dispute this conclusion. See in this direction also Wilson 2003, 165–7.

Tragedy definitely did not die; quite a few aspects of it changed, how-ever. Easterling has identified one of the factors for the change in "a new kind of cosmopolitan sensibility deeply influenced by, and interacting with, the classical repertoire"; this internal change corresponded with a change in the conditions of production, and with the accrued importance of the ac-tors, and of the acting guilds.[158] As a result of all this, the "cité" and tragedy went their own independent ways: tragedy as a form could adjust to changed circumstances, and indeed, already in the mid fourth century BC, Aristotle noted that contemporary tragedians wrote their speeches *rhetorikos* rather than *politikos* (*Poetics* 1450b7).[159]

My warmest thanks to Peter Rhodes and the editors for comments and corrections on various draft versions of this paper.

Bibliography

Allan, William (2000), *The* Andromache *and Euripidean Tragedy*, Oxford.
—— (2001), "Euripides in Megale Hellas: Some Aspects of the Early Reception of Trag-edy", *Greece and Rome* 48, 67–86.
Amandry, Pierre (1986), "Chios and Delphi", in: John Boardman / C. E. Vaphopolou – Richardson (eds.), *Chios. A Conference at the Homereion in Chios, 1984*, Oxford, 205–32.
—— (1990), "La fête des Pythia", in: *Praktika tes Akademias Athinon* 65, 279–317.
Blech, Michael (1982), *Studien zum Kranz bei den Griechen*, Berlin – New York.
Bouvier, H. (1978), "Honneurs et récompenses à Delphes", in: *ZPE* 30, 101–18.
Bowie, Ewen (2006), "Choral Performances", in: Suzanne Saïd / David Konstan (eds.), *Greeks on Greekness. Viewing the Greek Past in the Roman Empire*, Cambridge, 61–92.
Carey, Chris (2000), *Aeschines*, Austin.
Carter, David M. (2004), "Was Attic Tragedy Democratic?", in: *Polis* 21, 1–25.
Ceccarelli, Paola (1995), "Le dithyrambe et la pyrrhique. A propos de la nouvelle liste de vainqueurs aux Dionysies de Cos (Segre, *Iscrizioni di Cos*, ED 234)", in: *ZPE* 108, 287–305.
—— (1998), *La pirrica nell'antichità greco-romana. Studi sulla danza armata*, Pisa – Roma.
—— (2004), "'Autour de Dionysos': remarques sur la dénomination des artistes diony-siaques", in: Christophe Hugoniot / Frederic Hurlet / Silvia Milanezi (eds.), *Le statut de l'acteur dans l'antiquité grecque et romaine*, Tours, 109–42.

---

158 Easterling 1993, 569; see also Hall 2007, 265.
159 See also *Rhet.* 1403b31–35; and Xanthakis-Karamanos 1979. Rehm 2007, 191–2, however, goes too far when he argues that from the third century onwards, the *tech-nitai* of Dionysos dominated the Greek theatre, receiving massive support from the Hellenistic kings and rulers and the festivals ceased to represent "the community to itself": the community did find a way of expressing itself in the festivals, but the place for doing so may not have been the moment of the dramatic performances.

Ceccarelli, Paola and Milanezi, Silvia (2007), "Dithyramb, Tragedy – and Cyrene", in: Peter Wilson (ed.), *The Greek Theatre and Festivals. Documentary Studies*, Oxford, 185–214.

Chaniotis, Angelos (2007), "Theatre Rituals", in: Peter Wilson (ed.), *The Greek Theatre and Festivals. Documentary Studies*, Oxford, 48–66.

Csapo, Eric (2004), "The Politics of the New Music", in: Penny Murray / Peter Wilson (eds.), *Music and the Muses. The Culture of Mousike in the Classical Athenian City*, Oxford, 207–48.

—— (2004b), "The Rise of Acting. Some Social and Economic Conditions behind the Rise of the Acting Profession in the Fifth and Fourth Centuries BC", in: Christophe Hugoniot / Frédéric Hurlet / Silvia Milanezi (eds.), *Le statut de l'acteur dans l'antiquité grecque et romaine*, Tours, 53–76.

—— (2007), "The Men Who Built the Theatres: *Theatropolai, Theatronai*, and *Architektones*", in: Peter Wilson (ed.), *The Greek Theatre and Festivals. Documentary Studies*, Oxford, 87–115.

—— (2010), *Actors and Icons of the Ancient Theatre*, Oxford.

Csapo, Eric / Slater, William J. (1994), *The Context of Ancient Drama*, Ann Arbor.

Crowther, Charles (2007), "The *Dionysia* at Iasos: its Artists, Patrons, and Audience", in: Peter Wilson (ed.), *The Greek Theatre and Festivals. Documentary Studies*, Oxford, 294–334.

Dearden, Chris (1999), "Plays for Export", in: *Phoenix* 53, 222–248.

Easterling, Patricia E. (1993), "Continuity and Change in Greek Tragedy under Postclassical Conditions", in: Alan Sommerstein *et al.* (eds.), *Tragedy, Comedy, and the Polis*, Bari, 545–58.

—— (1997), "From Repertoire to Canon", in: Patricia E. Easterling (ed.), *The Cambridge Companion to Greek Tragedy*, Cambridge, 211–27.

Fantuzzi, Marco / Hunter, Richard (2004), *Tradition and Innovation in Hellenistic Poetry*, Cambridge.

Gauthier, Philippe (1985), *Les cités grecques et leurs bienfaiteurs*, BCH suppl. 12, Paris.

—— (1999), "Nouvelles inscriptions de Claros", in: *REG* 112, 1–17.

Gabrielsen, Vincent (1994), "Subdivisions of the State and Their Decrees in Hellenistic Rhodes", in: *Classica & Mediaevalia* 45, 117–35.

Goldhill, Simon (1987), "The Great Dionysia and Civic Ideology", in: *JHS* 107, 58–76.

Griffin, Jasper (1998), "The Social Function of Attic Tragedy", in: *CQ* 48, 39–61.

Guettel-Cole, Susan (1993), "Procession and Celebration at the *Dionysia*", in: Ruth Scodel (ed.), *Theater and Society in the Classical World*, Ann Arbor, 25–38.

Gwatkin, William E. Jr. (1957), "The Legal Arguments in Aischines' *Against Ktesiphon* and Demosthenes' *On the Crown*", in: *Hesperia* 26, 129–41.

Habicht, Christian (2002), "Die Ehren der Proxenoi. Ein Vergleich", in: *MH* 59, 13–30.

Hall, Edith (1996), "Is there a *Polis* in Aristotle's *Poetics*?" in: Michael Silk (ed.), *Tragedy and the Tragic. Greek Theatre and Beyond*, Oxford, 295–309.

—— (2007), "Greek Tragedy 430–380 BC", in: Robin Osborne (ed.), *Debating the Athenian Cultural Revolution. Art, Literature, Philosophy and Politics 430–380 BC*, Cambridge, 264–87.

Harris, Edward M. (1994), "Law and Oratory", in: Ian Worthington (ed.), *Persuasion: Greek Rhetoric in Action*, London, 130–51.

—— (1995), *Aeschines and Athenian Politics*, New York and Oxford.

Heath, Malcolm (2009), "Should there have been a *polis* in Aristotle's *Poetics*?", in: *CQ* 59, 468–85.

148 Paola Ceccarelli

Henderson, Jeffrey (2007), "Drama and Democracy", in: Loren J. Samons II (ed.), *The Cambridge Companion to the Age of Pericles*, Cambridge, 179–95.

Henry, Alan S. (1983), *Honours and Privileges in Athenian Decrees*, Hildesheim.

Hug, Aug. (1956), *"paides"*, in: *RE* Suppl. 8, cols. 375–400.

Jones, C. P. (1993), "Greek Drama in the Roman Empire", in: Ruth Scodel (ed.), *Theater and Society in the Classical World*, Ann Arbor, 39–52.

Jory, E. J. (1967), "A *pais komoidos* and the *dia panton*. Some Problems of Festival Competitions", in: *BICS* 14, 84–90.

Knoepfler, Denis (1995), "Les relations des cités eubéennes avec Antigone Gonatas et la chronologie delphique au début de l'époque étolienne", in: *BCH* 119, 137–159.

—— (1996), "La réorganisation du concours des *Mouseia* à l'époque hellénistique: esquisse d'une solution nouvelle", in A. Hurst and A. Schachter (eds.), *La Montagne des Muses*, Genève, 141–67.

—— (2001), *Eretria fouilles et recherches XI. Décrets érétriens de proxénie et de citoyenneté*, Lausanne.

Koumanoudes, S. N. / Miller, Stephen (1971), "IG II² 1477 and 3046 Rediscovered", in: *Hesperia* 40, 448–58.

Lambert, Stephen D. (2004), "Athenian State Laws and Decrees, 352/1–322/1: I. Decrees Honouring Athenians", in: *ZPE* 150, 85–120.

—— (2006), "Athenian State Laws and Decrees, 352/1–322/1: III. Decrees Honouring Foreigners A. Citizenship, Proxeny and Euergesy", in: *ZPE* 158, 115–158.

Larfeld, Wilhelm (1898–1907), *Handbuch der griechischen Epigraphik* 1–2.2, Leipzig.

Larmour, David H. J. (1999), *Stage and Stadium: Drama and Athletics in Ancient Greece, Nikephoros Beihefte* 4, Hildesheim.

Lawton, Carol L. (1995), *Attic Document Reliefs. Art and Politics in Ancient Athens*, Oxford.

Lefèvre, François (1998), *L'amphictionie pyléo-delphique: histoire et institutions*, Paris.

Le Guen, Brigitte (1995), "Théâtre et cités à l'époque hellénistique – Mort de la cité – mort du théâtre?", in: *REG* 108, 59–90.

—— (2001), "L'activité dramatique dans les îles grecques à l'époque hellénistique", in: *REA* 103, 261–298.

—— (2001a), *Les associations de technites dionysiaques à l'époque hellénistique*, I – II, Nancy.

—— (2003), "Théâtre, cités et royaumes en Anatolie et au Proche-Orient de la mort d'Alexandre le Grand aux conquêtes de Pompée", in: Francis Prost (ed.), *L'Orient méditerranéen de la mort d'Alexandre aux campagnes de Pompée*, Rennes, 329–55.

—— (2007), "'Décadence' d'un genre? Les auteurs de tragédie et leurs oeuvres à la période hellénistique", in: Brigitte Le Guen (ed.), *A chacun sa tragédie? Retour sur la tragédie grecque*, Rennes, 85–139.

Liddel, Peter (2007), *Civic Obligation and Individual Liberty in Ancient Athens*, Oxford.

Mette, Hans-Joachim (1977), *Urkunden dramatischer Aufführungen in Griechenland*, Berlin – New York.

Migeotte, Léopold (2002), "Information et vie politique dans la cité grecque", in: J. Andreau / C. Virlouvet (eds.), *L'information et la mer dans le monde antique*, Rome.

Mikalson, Jon D. (1998), *Religion in Hellenistic Athens*, Berkeley – Los Angeles – London.

Moretti, Luigi (1967–75), *Iscrizioni storiche ellenistiche*, I–II, Firenze.

Nachtergael, Georges (1977), *Les Galates en Grèce et les Sôtéria de Delphes*, Bruxelles.

Nervegna, Sebastiana (2007), "Staging Scenes or Plays? Theatrical Revivals of 'Old' Greek Drama in Antiquity", in: *ZPE* 162, 14–42.

Osborne, Robin (1999), "Inscribing Performance", in: Simon Goldhill / Robin Osborne (eds.), *Performance Culture and Athenian Democracy*, Cambridge, 341–58.

Parker, Robert (2004), "New 'Panhellenic' Festivals in Hellenistic Greece", in: Renate Schlesier and Ulrike Zellmann (eds.), *Mobility and Travel in the Mediterranean from Antiquity to the Middle Ages*, Münster, 9–22.

—— (2005), *Polytheism and Society at Athens*, Oxford.

Petzl, Georg / Schwertheim, Elmar (2006), *Hadrian und die dionysischen Künstler. Drei in Alexandria Troas neugefundene Briefe des Kaisers an die Künstler-Vereinigung*, Bonn.

Peppas-Delmousou, Dina (1984), "Le théâtre attique dans le monde hellénistique", *Actes du VIIIe Congrès international d'épigraphie grecque et latine,* Athènes 1984, 62–8.

Perrin, Eric (1997), "Propagande et culture théatrales à Athènes à l'époque hellénistique", in: Brigitte Le Guen (ed.), *De la scène aux gradins*, Pallas 47, 201–18.

Pickard-Cambridge, Arthur (1988), *The Dramatic Festivals of Athens*, second edition, revised by John Gould and David M. Lewis, Oxford.

Reisch, Emil (1899), "Chorikoi agones", in: *RE* III 2, 2431–8.

Rehm, Rush (2007), "Festivals and Audiences in Athens and Rome", in: Marianne McDonald / Michael Walton, *The Cambridge Companion to Greek and Roman Theatre*, Cambridge, 184–201.

Revermann, Martin (1999/2000), "Euripides, Tragedy and Macedon: Some Conditions of Reception", in: M. Cropp/K. Lee/D. Sansone (eds.), *Euripides and Tragic Theatre in the Late Fifth Century. Illinois Classical Studies* 24/25, 451–67.

—— (2006), *Comic Business: Theatricality, Dramatic Technique, and Performance Contexts of Aristophanic Comedy*, Oxford.

Rhodes, Peter J. (2003), "Nothing to Do with Democracy: Athenian Drama and the *Polis*", in: *JHS* 123, 104–19.

Rhodes, Peter J. with Lewis, David M. (1997), *The Decrees of the Greek States*, Oxford.

Rhodes, Peter J. / Osborne, Robin (2003), *Greek Historical Inscriptions 404–323 BC*, Oxford.

Robert, Louis (1937), *Etudes anatoliennes. Recherches sur les inscriptions grecques de l'Asie Mineure*, Paris.

—— (1938), *Etudes épigraphiques et philologiques*, Paris.

—— (1940), "Deux inscriptions d'Aptera", *Hellenica* I, 116–18.

—— (1984), "Discours d'ouverture", *Actes du VIIIe congrès international d'épigraphie grecque et latine à Athènes* (Athènes 1982), Athens, 35–45 = *OMS* VI, Amsterdam 1989, 709–19.

Robert, Louis and Jeanne, (1954), *La Carie II: Le plateau de Tabai et ses environs*, Paris.

—— (1989), *Claros* I, Paris.

Rutherford, Ian (2007), "Theoria and Theatre at Samothrace: The *Dardanos* by Dymas of Iasos", in: Peter Wilson (ed.), *The Greek Theatre and Festivals. Documentary Studies*, Oxford, 279–93.

Scullion, Scott (2002), "'Nothing to do with Dionysos': Tragedy Misconceived as Ritual", in: *CQ* 52, 102–37.

—— (2003), "Euripides and Macedon, or the Silence of the *Frogs*", in: *CQ* 53, 389–400.

Shear, Julia Louise (2001), *Polis and Panathenaia: the History and Development of Athena's Festival*, Diss., University of Pennsylvania.
—— (2003), "Prizes from Athens: the List of Panathenaic Prizes and the Sacred Oil", in: *ZPE* 142, 87–108.
—— (2007), "The Oath of Demophantos and the Politics of Athenian Identity", in: Alan A. Sommerstein / Judith Fletcher (eds.), *Horkos: the Oath in Greek Society*, Exeter, 148–60.
Sifakis, Gregory M. (1967), *Studies in the History of Hellenistic Drama*, London.
Slater, William J. (1993), "Three Problems in the History of Drama", in: *Phoenix* 47, 189–212.
—— (2007), "Deconstructing Festivals", in: P. Wilson (ed.), *The Greek Theatre and Festivals. Documentary Studies*, Oxford, 21–47.
Slater, William J. / Summa, Daniela (2006), "Crowns at Magnesia", in: *GRBS* 46, 275–299.
Summa, Daniela (2003), "Le Didascalie e il teatro postclassico", in: Antonio Martina (ed.), *Teatro greco postclassico e teatro latino. Teorie e prassi drammatica*, Roma, 293–303.
—— (2008), "Un concours de drames «anciens» à Athènes", in: *REG* 121, 497–514.
Taplin, Oliver (1993), *Comic Angels and other Approaches to Greek Drama through Vase-Painting*, Oxford.
—— (1999), "Spreading the Word Through Performance", in: Simon Goldhill / Robin Osborne (eds.), *Performance Culture and Athenian Democracy*, Cambridge, 33–57.
Tracy, Stephen V. (1995), *Athenian Democracy in Transition. Attic Letter-Cutters of 340 to 290 B.C.*, Berkeley / Los Angeles / Oxford.
—— (2003), *Athens and Macedon: Attic Letter-Cutters of 300 to 229 B.C.*, Berkeley – Los Angeles – Oxford.
Tracy, Stephen V. / Habicht, Christian (1991), "New and Old Panathenaic Victor Lists", in: *Hesperia* 60, 189–236.
Vial, Claude (2003), "A propos des concours de l'Orient méditerranéen à l'époque hellénistique", in: Francis Prost (ed.), *L'Orient Méditerranéen de la mort d'Alexandre aux campagnes de Pompée*, Rennes, 321–8.
Whitehead, David (1986), *The Demes of Attica 508/7 – ca 250 BC: A Political and Social Study*, Princeton.
Wilson, Peter (2000), *The Athenian Institution of Choregia*, Cambridge.
—— (2003), "The Politics of Dance: Dithyrambic Contest and Social Order in Ancient Greece", in: David Phillips / David Pritchard (eds.), *Sport and Festival in the Ancient World*, Swansea, 163–96.
—— (2007), "Performance in the *Pythion*: the Athenian *Thargelia*", in: Peter Wilson (ed.), *The Greek Theatre and Festivals. Documentary Studies*, Oxford, 150–182.
—— (2007b), "Sicilian Choruses", in: Peter Wilson (ed.), *The Greek Theatre and Festivals. Documentary Studies*, Oxford, 351–77.
—— (2009), "Tragic Honours and Democracy: Neglected Evidence for the Politics of the Athenian Dionysia", in: *CQ* 59, 8–29.
Wilson, Peter and Hartwig, Andrew (2009), "IG I 102 and the Tradition of Proclaiming Honours at the Tragic *Agon* of the Athenian City Dionysia", in: *ZPE* 169, 17–27.
Wörrle, Michael (1988), *Stadt und Fest im kaiserzitlichen Kleinasien: Studien zu eine agonistische Stiftung aus Oinoanda*, München.
Xanthakis – Karamanos, Georgia (1979), "The Influence of Rhetoric on Fourth-Century Tragedy", in: *CQ* 29, 66–76.
—— (1993), "Hellenistic Drama: Developments in Form and Performance", in: *Platon* 45, 117–33.
Yunis, Harvey (2001), *Demosthenes. On the Crown*, Cambridge.

B. From Greece to Rome

Buskins & SPQR:
Roman Receptions of Greek Tragedy

INGO GILDENHARD

1 Introduction

Roman republican tragedy has all but disappeared. No single play has come down to us in its entirety. All we have are meager fragments, in modern editions often littered with *cruces*, amounting to some two-thousand lines of text; the names of c. twenty playwrights; and the titles of about a hundred of their plays – in all, nothing more than tattered remnants of "a vanished totality".[1] They suffice to suggest something of the vitality of the genre at the time; but they do not yield the same range of meanings that one can milk from (or plausibly ascribe to) texts transmitted by and large intact. Yet, as Anthony Grafton puts it, "fragments provoke".[2] And this holds true especially in a discipline like classics, which, from Friedrich August Wolf onwards, has systematically substituted scientific comprehensiveness for canonical selectivity.[3] "Everything, everything belongs to philology", intones Wilamowitz, "since it belongs to the object that she [sc. *Philologia*] wishes to understand: she cannot miss even one"[4] – not even, that is, the tragic fragments from republican Rome, although Wilamowitz himself once curtly dismissed Livius and his successors as "barbarians".

More than half a millennium of intense study has shown that the bits and pieces can indeed sustain a wide range of scholarly interests, from

---

*   I have had the opportunity to present earlier versions of this chapter at Oxford and Zurich and am grateful to Fiachra McGowrain, Stephen Harrison and Ulrich Eigler for the invitations and to both audiences for probing discussions. First thoughts on the subject date back to a joint presentation with Ulrich Gotter entitled "Die früh-römische Tragödie: politisch oder politisierbar?" at the symposium "Identität und Alterität in der frührömischen Tragödie", Freiburg i. Br. 1999, which initiated an ongoing dialogue on the topic that informs the argument presented here as well.

1   A formulation used by Gumbrecht 1985 with respect to literary history.
2   Grafton 1997, 124.
3   Gildenhard 2003.
4   Wilamowitz 1892/1902, 105: "… alles, alles gehört zur Philologie, denn es gehört zu dem Objekte, das sie verstehen will, auch nicht eines kann sie missen."

detailed and minute philology to sweeping musings about the origins and profile of Western culture.[5] For centuries, the topmost priorities of scholars have been the collection of fragments and the reconstruction of individual plays from the remaining debris[6] – but there are signs that this approach has hit the point of diminishing returns: the nature of the evidence is such that most plot-reconstructions remain too speculative to serve as sound basis for further argumentation.[7] Issues of production have been high on the agenda as well, with a focus on the playwrights, in particular their social status and degree of creativity as translators or original dramatists, but also their specific aesthetic preferences and sensibilities.[8] A related area of enquiry concerns the (intended) meaning and message of the plays (what speech-act theorists call illocution), ranging from the political allegories that Bilinski thought could be detected in certain of the plays to the identity politics that have dominated discussion of this aspect in more recent scholarship.[9] Its flip-side, i.e. perlocution, or what the plays meant to (changing) audiences has received rather less critical attention, though a vast body of scholarship exists on the wider performance context and the Roman theater. Much – and often controversially – discussed aspects include the history of dramatic performances at Rome; reasons for, and consequences of, the "Greek turn" round about 240; the relationship of plays based on Greek models to "pre-literary" drama; modes of interaction between stage and *cavea*; the organization of the *ludi publici* (and their history); the social status of actors; as well as, more specifically, potential matches between subject matter of a tragic play and the occasion of its original performance.[10] One type of secondary reception that has received

---

5   E.g. Weber 2000, 140: "Mit der Übernahme der griechischen – nicht nur der tro-
     janischen – Sagenstoffe hat sich auch die römische Tragödie eingegliedert in die
     universelle kulturgeschichtliche Identität der Menschheit – bis heute." For the state
     of scholarship see Manuwald 2004 (a bibliographical survey) and Goldberg 2007 (a
     research report).
6   These efforts have culminated in three major recent editions with commentary of
     Ennius (Jocelyn 1967), Accius (Dangel 1995), and Pacuvius (Schierl 2006).
7   Already Jocelyn, in his 1967 edition of Ennius, took the radical and programmatic
     step of printing the fragments of each individual play in the chronological order of
     the authors who preserve them, instead of attempting to arrange them in the order of
     a possible plot.
8   See e.g. Manuwald 2003 (a study of Pacuvius) and Seele 1995 (on the archaic Latin
     poets as translators).
9   See e.g. Bilinski 1960, 1962 and many of the papers collected in Manuwald 2000.
10   For the larger historical context, see e.g. Bernstein 1998. While it is still possible to
     identify specific occasions for *fabulae praetextae* (Flower 1996), the same is not the
     case for the overwhelming majority of Greek mythological tragedies. An exception
     is Ennius' *Thyestes*, which was performed at the *Ludi Apollinares* of 169. See Leigh
     2000, 298–9, who points to the fact that this play, unusually, dramatized the events

a lot of exposure in recent years are the re-performances of archaic trag-edies in the late republic since the record of the audience-behaviour at some of these events yields interesting insights into the terms of interac-tion between the senate and the Roman people.[11] What still lacks a sys-tematic treatment (though individual case studies of course exist) are the secondary receptions of tragedy at Rome outside the theatre – in rhetorical education, public oratory, and political discourse more generally; in the realm of allusive dialogue, from Plautus' *para-tragoedia* to Catullus 64 to Virgil, Ovid, and beyond; and in philosophical discourse, in particular the literature of consolation.[12] Some scholars have attempted to write the literary history of Roman tragedy *tout court*.[13] But, again, rather little sys-tematic work has been done on the significance of the Roman reception of Greek tragedy within larger cultural configurations – such as the role of translation from the Greek in the evolution of Latin as a literary language; the development of a literary culture (not to be confused with literacy) at Rome;[14] and, more generally, tragedy's contribution to the (seismic) re-percussions of the large-scale import of Greek cultural goods on Roman society in the last three centuries BCE.

Within this vast and varied field, this paper will (re-)consider some of the ways in which the tragic plays relate to their wider cultural context. It starts with some remarks on the beginnings, i.e. 240 (2), proceeds to chal-lenge some prominent political interpretations of Roman republican tragedy (3), before looking at some examples of how the semantics of tragic scripts interact with the nomological knowledge of Roman society (4). The final section considers the correlation between the Roman import of Greek trag-edy and Rome's societal evolution over the last centuries of the republic (5).

---

after the gruesome feast, which involved the oracle of Apollo to Thyestes, and thus argues for a "a felicitous harmony between festive context and dramatic context".

11   See e.g. Flaig 1995.

12   See e.g. Gildenhard and Zissos 1999 for the status of tragedy in "new formalist" criticism of the Augustan poets and Gildenhard 2007a for Cicero's use of tragic figures of thought in his invective writings.

13   See e.g. Erasmo 2004 who plots its history as a development from theater to theatri-cality – in not always compelling fashion: Cowan 2005, Leigh 2006. Contrast Boyle 2006, who balances literary history and cultural poetics in a rather more sophisti-cated way.

14   A partial exception is Goldberg 2005.

2   *240 BCE* (or thereabouts)[15]

Over the last decade or so, the age-old debate over the beginnings of Latin
literature has experienced a determined reinvigoration. Much that had been
taken for granted has become again controversial, and the scholarship is
very much in flux, as new vistas and models are put into circulation and their
plausibility tested (at times to destruction). Quite a few scholars have emphasized that Livius Andronicus' supposed translation of a Greek drama at
the *Ludi Romani* of 240 ought not to be considered a *creatio e nihilo*; rather,
it needs to be appreciated as a contribution to an indigenous performance
culture, which featured a wide range of dramatic genres and themes and
formed part of a long tradition of dialogue with other cultures (especially the
Etruscans).[16] Conversely, other scholars have issued a note of caution against
downplaying the extraordinary nature of what happened in the middle of the
third century BCE, and continue to see Rome's embrace of Greek literary
culture as the big bang, or at least archetype, of the classical tradition. As
Feeney puts it, the creation of "a national literature in the vernacular on the
model of another national literature" is "an undertaking which no one in the
Mediterranean had ever contemplated before, but which became a paradigm
for later literary history."[17] Intriguingly, each camp has accused the other
of Hellenocentrism: the former argues that privileging Livius' translation
elevates Greek cultural production into a trans-historical standard and in-
sidiously devalues indigenous Roman traditions; the latter maintains that using Greek models to reconstruct the performance culture of pre-literary (not
pre-literate!) Rome by means of analogy with what we know about archaic
Greece constitutes a fraudulent and crypto-normative assimilation of Rome
to Greece that obfuscates cultural distinctiveness.[18]

It is, of course, quite unproblematic to posit the existence of a vibrant
culture of dramatic performances in mid-republican Rome (of whatever
type) and still to recognize Livius' act of translation (whenever it happened)
as a historical watershed – or, to use a formulation that avoids over-em-
phasizing a singular event, as epitomizing a period of remarkable innovation and change. A century later, at any rate, a significant portion of Rome's
dramatic repertory consisted of plays translated from the Greek. In fact, the
more we are inclined to take on board the reconstructions of Roman the-

---

15   The ancient sources are by no means unanimous in dating Livius' first drama to
     240. Even if one sets aside Accius' alternative chronology, in which Livius arrived
     in Rome in 209, Cassiodorus dates the first performance of a tragedy and a comedy
     from the pen of Livius to 239 (chron. II 128 M).
16   See e.g. Habinek 1998, Suerbaum 2002, and Wiseman 1995, 1998.
17   Feeney 1998, 51.
18   Contrast Habinek 1998, 34–6 and Feeney 2005.

atre before Livius that Wiseman and others have proposed, the more curious Rome's "Greek turn" from the middle of the third century onwards becomes. While it is easy to grasp, at least intuitively, why a cultural vacuum of sorts should have been filled, it is more difficult to understand why foreign imports should have overpowered – or at least stolen significant stage time from – indigenous traditions of performance that were (one is asked to assume) intimately related to Rome's larger civic culture, including hot-button issues in the field of power. Jocelyn has put his finger on the problem: "it is hard to see how such performances [sc. of Greek mythological tragedies] could have been thought more pleasing to the Roman gods than those which preceded them, and doubtlessly still continued, or what pleasure they could have given to the mass of the Roman citizenry."[19]

The puzzle increases if one juxtaposes the dramas derived from Greek mythology to plays that revolved around figures from Roman history and legend. What survives of such so-called *fabulae praetextae* tends to be even more pitiful than the remnants of tragedies adapted from the Greek.[20] But two crucial facts are more or less certain: such plays were, comparatively speaking, rather rare; and they carried a partisan (and hence often controversial) message. If Flower is right in arguing that the two facts are to some extent related, insofar as the politically controversial nature of these plays may help to account for their relatively small number, then this would seem to imply that the comparatively large number of Greek mythological tragedies performed at Rome was at least in part due to their presentation of subject matter that was considered to be politically less explosive, if not simply uncontroversial.[21] From this point of view, the switch from plays about, say, Romulus and Remus or Camillus, which put on stage issues of relevance to domestic politics, to stage-time for Greek figures whose significance for Roman history and politics was tangential at best, would seem to imply a large-scale transformation in the political semantics of "ordinary" dramatic performances at Rome – punctured by plays on topical, contested issues, such as the legacy of Marcellus or whether or not Fulvius Nobilior's victory over Ambrakia entailed the right to celebrate a triumph.[22] Even if the *occa-*

---

19   Jocelyn 2000, 327.
20   Manuwald 2001.
21   Flower 1996.
22   The allusions are, respectively, to the *fabulae praetextae Clastidium* by Naevius (see Flower 2003 for the larger picture) and *Ambrakia* by Ennius. Gruen's interpretation of the plays as celebrating national victories (1990, 93–4 and 113–7) would have pleased the playwrights and their patrons: this is exactly how they will have spun the events. But see Flower 2003 for the larger picture on Marcellus; and in the case of Nobilior, the senators who argued against granting him a triumph would have dismissed as partisan propaganda his claims about the sack of the city – as well as Ennius' drama, which indeed is likely to have promoted Nobilior's arguably fraudu-

sion and the *context* of the performance remained politically charged – not least as a public arena of interaction between the elite (or members thereof) and the wider populace – , the semantics and personnel of the plays (stories about Greek heroes rather than contentious figures from Roman history or legend) arguably diminished in political relevance. Instead of the domestic tussles, conflicts between the elite and the populace, and aggressive aristocratic self-promotion that (perhaps) featured in Rome's pre-literary drama and certainly constituted an important aspect of *fabulae praetextae*, the political dimension of Greek mythological tragedy arguably went little beyond exploring in somewhat vague terms the place of Rome within the wider Mediterranean *oikoumene* – a topical concern, to be sure, but rather less explosive than other subject matter.

It is, of course, hardly coincidental that this "international" reorientation in preferred dramatic *sujets* happened at the time when Rome began to assert itself as a military juggernaut, not just in Italy and Magna Graecia but also beyond, and imperial expansion was surely one of the enabling conditions for the changes in Rome's dramatic repertory that started to acquire momentum in the second half of the third century. But an enabling condition is not quite the same as an explanation of what is, again, a peculiar phenomenon, i.e. one culture starting to base a significant portion of its dramatic portfolio on that of another. And thus, Rome's interest in Greek drama has often been ascribed to the inherent value and superiority of Greek culture *tout court* and Greek tragedy in particular. In this view, Rome's Greek turn was well-nigh inevitable once Rome and Greece started to interact more intensely after the creation of a "contact zone" in Southern Italy, defined as much by military encounters as cultural exchange[23] – the natural outcome, as it were, of a natural desire on the part of the Romans to become a genuine and enlightened civilization. We can call this explanatory model the "Horatian paradigm", with reference to his famous statement in the *Letter to Augustus* that "captured Greece captured her savage conqueror and invaded Latium with her arts".[24] Yet the plausibility of the implicit assumptions that sustain this model, which carried much appeal for the bourgeois scholar and his investment in "high culture", especially of Greek provenance, has crumbled under the impact of social theory and historical anthropology.[25] In contrast, others have argued that the Roman take-over of Greek cultural goods belongs squarely into the context of imperial growth, national pride, and international

---

lent achievement as an articulation of national interest and patriotism. See already Sall. *Cat.* 38.3.

23 Feeney 1998.
24 *Ep.* 2.1.156–7.
25 Flaig 1999.

self-promotion.[26] We may call this the "Ciceronian paradigm", on the basis of such passages as *Tusculans* 2.5, where Cicero exhorts his countrymen to rip out the cultural riches from Greece and transfer them to Italy, in an act of conquest that extends to literature. A third school of thought argues that "the invention of literature at Rome", including the importation of Greek tragic drama, was designed to maintain an organic society: "Virtually every scrap of information that we have pertaining to Latin literature in the third century B.C.E. can be related to the preservation of social cohesion at Rome."[27]

While these models, or motivating factors, differ radically in outlook and degree of theoretical sophistication, they all share the striking tendency to ascribe key collective agency to an elite group or, indeed, state apparatus that had its center in the senate and is believed to have pursued a deliberate policy of cultural enhancement or cohesion. Gruen's formulations in this respect are particularly blunt: "it was the judgment of the senate", he claims, "to entrust so visible a public function [*sc.* that of preparing a drama for staging at the *Ludi Romani* in 240] to a Greek writer and dramatist." And he generalizes: "Rome's officialdom embraced the Hellenic artistic tradition and utilized it in the expression of their own national achievement."[28] Others see central planning at work in the Roman desire to be like the Greeks: "No myths, no literature; no literature, no culture", says Feeney, "and the Roman elite, for some unfathomable complex of reasons, did want an equivalent to the culture of the Greeks."[29] These explanatory schemes appeal insofar as they produce a neat and tidy historical plot, with a collective agent, a clear intention concerning neatly reified objectives ("culture", "literature", "promotion of the national interest", "social cohesion"), its realization in practice, and a well-defined outcome; but upon inspection, they rest on very little (if any) evidence and raise all sorts of methodological scruples.

Moreover, they strikingly ignore one of main factors – aristocratic competition and self-promotion – that fuelled the creative sponsorship of games and the introduction of innovative cultural material from Greece in the much better documented second and first centuries BCE. One should of course beware of projecting the state of affairs that applied in later periods back

---

26 Gruen 1990, esp. 79–123.
27 Habinek 1998, 39.
28 Gruen 1990, 83 and 84; see also 82 ("Rome's officialdom made the decision, shaped the event, and selected its man") and 83 n. 17 where Livius becomes "a cultural servant of the state".
29 Feeney 1998, 66. He here comes close to endorsing the discredited notion of culture as tantamount to "high culture", as if the Romans did not have a culture before they came into intensified contact with the Greeks in the course of their imperial expansion. Suerbaum 2002, 97 seems to endorse a similar position when he calls Livius' drama "eine bildungspolitische Neuerung römischer Aristokraten". (The precise meaning of "bildungspolitisch" remains obscure.)

into the third century. But the *possibility* of continuity at least raises the question why we need an intervention of the senate as a collective into the dramatic repertory of games of which individual magistrates were in charge. And likewise: do we have to assume a deliberate programme of cultural and educational policy that smacks more of league tables and nation states in the age of PISA than mid-republican Rome, when the reason may have been that a tragedy based on a Greek script performed by professional actors would have made the occasion so much more spectacular and memorable – and thus more useful for the sponsors in the context of inner-aristocratic competition for recognition and prestige? These are, of course, rhetorical questions: we do not have the evidence to render the hypothesis empirically plausible that the first Roman plays based on Greek models constituted, at least in part, experiments in aristocratic self-promotion. But at the very least, they ought to introduce an element of contingency (and creativity) into the well-oiled wheels of "state planning" that dominates scholarly orthodoxy and to draw attention to the fact that the sponsorship of cultural activities in republican Rome was usually one of the means by which individual Roman aristocrats tried to get an edge over their peers – rather than the outcome of what the senate as a collective deemed best. This does not mean that one should disregard the aspects of national self-promotion or a widespread aristocratic appreciation for Greek culture altogether – but in or around 240, they may have been among the enabling factors, rather than having constituted the primary causes or strategic reasons, for the staging of the first Greek tragedy in a Latin translation.

3   The politics of Roman republican tragedy

Greek mythological tragedy most likely appealed to a Roman audience for a wide variety of reasons: Eastern witches stimulated ethnographic curiosity; the problems of societies at war (including failures of leadership) cannot have helped to resonate strongly; outrageous tyrants and their cannibalistic instincts catered to voyeuristic fascination with the uncanny and prohibited; the sensational staging of *nefas*, lethal clashes among family, kin-groups, and aristocratic peers, societal breakdown, and metaphysical chaos are all bound to have captivated the imagination. We cannot tell what degree of topical relevance Roman audiences granted to the events they saw displayed on stage, i.e. to what extent they watched these plays as belonging to a foreign, and inherently dysfunctional culture, increasingly under Roman rule, or to what extent they saw themselves and their own societal problems negotiated in the medium of tragedy. Both are distinct possibilities and not necessarily mutually exclusive, and may have varied significantly among the spectators.

Positing thematic correlations between the contents of Greek mythological tragedies and political issues that would have preoccupied the Roman audience is, at any rate, methodologically rather unproblematic.[30]

Rather more questionable, however, are the search for (and identification of) a coherent political meaning and message and a precise social function within the semantics of Roman republican tragedy. In the previous section, we already had occasion to comment on the fact that Greek mythological tragedy seems to have been rather less explosive than *fabulae praetextae*. Nevertheless, a long and distinguished tradition of exegesis exists that endows the plays with a powerful (and primary) political meaning and message. Thus one very influential school of thought has it that the Romans began to stage Greek mythological tragedies as a new form of identity politics, rooted in Rome's supposedly Trojan past and its desire to establish a place for itself in the Greek *oikoumene* via mythic genealogies:[31]

> einerseits entnahmen sie [sc. die Dichter] ihre Stoffe der für Rom besonders wichtigen Troia-Sage, zum anderen wählten sie aus dem griechischen Mythos mit Vorliebe solche Helden aus, die in irgendeiner Beziehung zu Italien, meist Latium oder gar Rom, gestanden hatten. Man darf in den historischen und aitiologischen Tendenzen der frührömischen Tragödie den Grund für ihre Entstehung in Rom überhaupt vermuten.

There is some textual evidence that playwrights did indeed make use of the creative freedom afforded by the medium of myth to suggest links between their tragic personnel and Roman history. Danae, Philoctetes and others were heroes with a connection to Italy, a fact that plays about them might well have underscored.[32] Likewise, in his *Atreus*, so Servius informs us, Accius endorsed a genealogy that rendered the Romans distant kin of the Atreidae:[33]

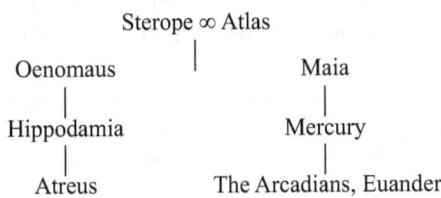

Sterope ∞ Atlas

Oenomaus   Maia

Hippodamia   Mercury

Atreus   The Arcadians, Euander

---

30 It is the approach that Leigh 2004 advocates as most promising for comedy.

31 Lefèvre 1978, 8 ("On the one hand, the playwrights took their material from the Trojan legend, which was particularly important for Rome; on the other they liked to choose heroes who had some connection to Italy, most frequently Latium or even Rome. One is allowed to suspect that the historical and etiological tendencies of early Roman tragedy were the reason for its emergence in Rome in the first place.")

32 See Lefèvre 2000 for Danae and 1999 for Philoctetes.

33 Serv. auct. *ad Virg. Aen.* 8.130 (*quod Accius in Atreo plenius refert*).

Playwrights, then, explored the possibilities of mythic kinship between the Romans, other parts of Italy, and the wider Greek *oikoumene*. This should not come as a surprise: after all, genealogies and etiologies were common discursive practices of the Greek literary imagination (as well as everyday politics). It is, however, by no means certain what these links were supposed to signify (and actually signified) to a Roman audience. In the case of Accius' *Atreus*, Dangel argues that the family connection between Atreus and Euander, via the giant Atlas, was meant to suggest that the Romans, too, were liable to outbursts of hubristic violence and grotesque savagery.[34] But the opposite could also have been the case: why do we need to assume that Accius thought the Arcadians and Euander to manifest the same genetic faults that wreaked havoc in the house of Atreus? Could he not equally well have wanted to highlight the difference between the Greek butchers and the superior Roman stock, where violence is tempered with shrewdness and justice? The Italic lineage, after all, includes genetic contributions from the Olympian deities Jupiter and Mercury. More generally speaking, how can we be sure that the genealogical connection should be regarded as a major and privileged element within the overall economy of meaning, to the point that the Roman audience watched the events unfolding on stage in the awareness that "*de nobis fabula narratur*"? Could Accius' elaborate genealogies not have been little more than learned ornaments, resonating, perhaps, with some erudite members in the audience, but without impacting on the larger significance of the plot and its message?

Similar questions arise when one considers the perhaps strongest link between the Western hemisphere and the world of Greek myth, i.e. Rome's supposedly Trojan roots. Superficially, the argument that Lefèvre and others have advanced looks attractive: if the Romans thought of themselves in any profound way as latter-day Trojans, then plays that thematized the events at Troy would have been, in a very real sense, part of Roman history. And quite a few scholars, among them Alföldi, Bickerman, Gruen, and Momigliano, have viewed the legend of Rome's Trojan origins as a key aspect of Roman identity from the middle or even early republic onwards. But the argument that Roman tragedy constituted an important medium of identity politics by way of broadcasting Rome as Troy re-founded becomes less attractive the more one subjects it to scrutiny. To begin with, an emphasis on Rome's Trojan heritage is very difficult to pinpoint in our evidence. In the absence of any fragments that explicate the link, scholars have started to count the number of plays to do with Troy as the basis for their argument – a somewhat problematic procedure, as Jocelyn points out, since the distribution

---

34   Dangel 1995, 46.

may be accounted for in any number of ways.[35] But even if we were to grant, despite the lack of evidence, that imaginative dramatists played up Rome's Trojan past in their plays, this does not say anything about the impact on and importance of such allusions for a Roman audience. In fact, several considerations suggest that any appeal to a common Roman identity as "latter-day Trojans" would have resonated only feebly, if at all, with the vast majority of the body politic in attendance.

Quite apart from the fact that it seems quite a stretch to turn plays about the conflict between Achilles and Agamemnon or Odysseus and Ajax into part of Roman history via the story of Aeneas, none of the scholars cited above has bothered to enquire about the cultural standing of mythic genealogies in Roman public discourse. Until recently, the view prevailed that the Romans, just like the Greeks, placed a premium on divine and heroic descent. Thus in 1974 Wiseman asked, rhetorically, "with a god in the family tree, who needed consuls?"[36] But now Hölkeskamp has shown, on the basis of recent research on Roman republican memorial culture, that the emphasis needs to be reversed: "Mit mehr als zwei Dutzend Consuln, diversen Dictatoren und Censoren im Stammbaum, wer brauchte da einen Gott?" He explains, with reference to the tight nexus of historical memory and political competition in republican Rome: "Einem *nobilis* nutzte ein Gott zunächst und vor allem allein überhaupt nichts – dazu mußte man Consuln im Stammbaum und als verräucherte und halb zerfallene Ahnenbilder im Atrium haben."[37] In other words, in Rome legendary origins constituted, comparatively speaking, a rather feeble type of symbolic capital, with little or no persuasive force in the competition for *honores*, imperial

---

35 Jocelyn 2000. His paper is a wholesale, and by and large compelling attack on the premises that inform many of the other papers in Manuwald (2000). See also Stärk (2000), who in the same volume also takes apart key tenets of the Lefèvre-school about the alleged civic ideology and significance of Roman republican tragedy; he concludes: "Die Athener 'brauchten' die Tragödie beim Abarbeiten des Schwierigen und Bedrohlichen, in das sie die Volksherrschaft geführt hatte. ... Die Römer hingegen 'brauchten' die Tragödie im großen und ganzen nicht" (131).

36 Wiseman 1974/1987, 164. His view still has considerable currency.

37 Hölkeskamp 1999/2004. The quotations are, respectively, from pages 20 and 19. (Note, though, that the emphasis on "vor allem allein" is infelicitous: those families who had the real (historical) goods did not need to rely on supplementary prestige, though often did, whereas those that did not, or not to the same extent, will have preferred an emphasis on divine and legendary lineage as a freely available resource. In other words, gods and consuls ideally go together, but do not have to. The best example of someone branching out into myth to make up for lack of historical capital is, of course, Caesar who, in the *laudatio funebris* for his aunt (itself an innovation), boasted descent from gods and kings. See Gildenhard 2007b, 100–2 on how Virgil undertook to turn this marginal voice in the discourse of Roman memory into epic orthodoxy for the Roman people.

commands, and *gloria*; not coincidentally, those who brought them into play were often political losers whose family had little historical attainment to advertise.[38] Legendary genealogies are thus one of those areas where the evolved and evolving nomological knowledge of Greece and Rome differed in important respects, where, in other words, Rome was precisely *not* like Greece.[39] This does not mean that individual families did not broadcast descent from those Trojans who arrived in Italy with Aeneas, as a supplementary form of self-promotion.[40] But this should neither obfuscate basic differences in the symbolic and persuasive value that Greeks and Romans assigned to various types of lineage nor encourage the assumption that anything to do with Troy (and be it the shenanigans of Greek heroes in their camp) had by definition "national" importance at Rome.

Overall, these considerations suggest that we may wish to reckon with a possible disjunction between illocution and perlocution: portions of the plays that have not survived may well have shown that mythic genealogies were important to the playwrights, steeped as they were in Greek ways of thinking about the past; but *even if* such genealogies featured prominently (though, it is worth repeating, we have hardly any evidence that they did), they may still have resonated only feebly with the wider Roman audience, which, arguably, did not ascribe particular political significance to the mythic figures and events that appeared on the tragic stage – unlike (again) to the Roman personnel that populated the *fabulae praetextae*.

To make headway with the vexed question of the overarching political significance of tragic plays in mid-republican Rome, it is anyway a methodological prerequisite to shift the heuristic focus from the text to the recipient, or, more generally, the wider cultural parameters of reception. Current scholarship has a distinct tendency to view Roman republican tragedy as a civic occasion on the model of fifth-century Athens, at which the citizen community came together to watch dramatic spectacles of immediate rel-

---

38　Erskine 2001 argues that while the legend of Rome's Trojan origins was indeed known in Italy from early on, it did not acquire particular importance until the age of Augustus – though he may be overstating his case.

39　This difference also shaped inter-cultural communication: appeals to *sungeneia* were an important aspect in Greek inter-state diplomacy, yet more or less irrelevant in Rome – even though Greek states tried to win Roman support through claims of kinship and savvy Romans used legendary lineage to promote themselves within the Greek world, most notably, perhaps, Flamininus (Plut. *Titus Quinctius Flamininus* 12.11–12). On kinship diplomacy in the ancient world (including the differences between Greece and Rome) see e.g. Curty 1995, Erskine 2002, Jones 1999, Lucke 2000, and Weber 1972, 2000.

40　The ancient evidence in collected by Jocelyn (2000) 334–5 n. 85.

evance to their communal identity.[41] But doubts to the applicability of this model are again in order. If one compares and contrasts tragic performances in fifth-century Athens and mid-republican Rome some significant differences emerge:

	Fifth-century Athens	Mid-republican Rome
Social status of playwrights	Fully enfranchised upper-class citizens	Outsiders: non citizens, or foreigners granted citizenship, but with no voice, let alone *auctoritas* in the public sphere
Social status of actors	Members of the civic community	Professionals who carried a social stigma
Occasion	Religious festivals: Greater Dionysia, Lenaia, local performances in the *demes*	Religious festivals: *ludi* (public games + games sponsored by individuals, such as triumphal celebration or funeral games)
Sponsors	Rich citizens (*choregoi*) + state contributions from public funds	Public funds, subject or client states, supporters of individual statesmen + subsidies by the presiding magistrate
Performance context	Competition among (usually) three playwrights for a civic honour	Hired entertainment (competition with previous organizers regarding display and spectacle)
Seating arrangement	Special seats for officials and honorands; probably seating by tribes	From 194 BCE: social stratification of the citizen body
Staged material	Myth and (legendary) history, at times of explicit etiological relevance to the *polis* (Areopagus and *Oresteia*, Salamis and *Ajax*, the theatre and Dionysus), always of (implicit) thematic relevance for the political culture of democratic Athens	Foreign subject matter domesticated via translation and adaptation
(Political) message of occasion	Self-promotion of the *polis* in front of a pan-Hellenic audience; religious festival	Self-promotion of the magistrate in charge of the games; maintenance of the *pax deorum*; civic celebration
(Political) message of the plays	Medium of reflection and commentary on issues of central concern to the community; *Laudes Atheniensium*: safe-haven of exiles; Displaced confrontation with dysfunctional possibilities ('tragic Thebes'); Parainetic warning against the pitfalls of hubris; Emotional impact via 'anthropological' or 'civic' empathy (pity/ fear)	?

---

41   Even for fifth-century Athenian tragedy, it is of course much easier to determine the civic importance of the performance context than of the performances. The political dimension of the plays remains controversial and should perhaps not be overemphasized – or at least understood in relation to other aspects.

This table, which is, to be sure, overly schematic, points up a significant problem for any attempt to identify a coherent political, civic, or national message for tragic performances in mid-republican Rome. Unlike in fifth-century Athens, tragedy was by no means a wholesale civic enterprise, i.e. written and staged by citizens for citizens. The enabling conditions of the genre in the Roman republic rather resemble those that applied in cities across the Hellenistic *oikoumene*, where tragedy played an important role in the entertainment culture, but only possessed a marginal political relevance.[42] In fact, if at all, the ideological demarcation that separated the world of the *cavea* from the world on stage was deeper at Rome, where the acting profession carried a significant social stigma, than in an ordinary Greek city.

Arguably, the ideological matrix in which tragic performances in republican Rome played themselves out opened up different modes of interaction and engagement. The information that Cicero provides at *de Officiis* 1.97–8 on how Roman spectators reacted to a staging of Accius' *Atreus* is in this respect rather suggestive:

> sed tum servare illud poetas, quod deceat, dicimus, cum id quod quaque persona dignum est, et fit et dicitur, ut si Aeacus aut Minos diceret "oderint dum metuant" aut "natis sepulchro ipse est parens" indecorum videretur, quod eos fuisse iustos accepimus; at Atreo dicente plausus excitantur, est enim digna persona oratio. sed poetae quid quemque deceat, ex persona iudicabunt, nobis autem personam imposuit ipsa natura magna cum excellentia praestantiaque animantium reliquarum; (98) quocirca poetae in magna varietate personarum etiam vitiosis quid conveniat et quid deceat videbunt...

> [We say that poets observe decorum when the speech and action of a character befit his role so that it would seem indecorous if Aeacus or Minos were to say "May they hate me as long as they fear me" or "The father himself is the tomb of his sons" since myth has it that they were just. But when Atreus says these things, it generates applause since in that case speech conforms to role. Poets will judge decorum according to the requirements of each *dramatis persona*; in real life, nature itself has imposed on us a distinction and excellence that outdo those of all the other creatures; (98) given the wide range of roles, the poets will therefore also see to applying the protocols of decorum to the representation of the morally depraved.]

Cicero here argues that the entertainment value of tragedy depended in part on the skillful depiction of ethical failure: the most appalling aphorisms, if uttered by the greatest villains, elicited resounding applause from the spectators since they were relished as masterful and supremely fitting instances of ethopoiea, a brilliant enactment of character in speech. Such a response is at variance with both a moral-political reaction to the events on stage and a disposition of aesthetic distance that grants the dramatic events a reality and authenticity designed to move and affect. Instead, the response seems

---

42   See Ceccarelli in this volume.

rooted in the keen appreciation of rhetorical spectacle and verbal ingenu-
ity in the portrayal of character. How may we account for this behaviour?
Two interrelated aspects seem crucial: first, it is quite clear that the Roman
audience knew how to distinguish fiction from reality. If, in fifth-century
Athens, the world of myth remained firmly rooted in the historical presence,
partly because the Athenians used myth as a medium to rehearse and negotiate issues of civic relevance, the same seems not (always) to have been the
case with Greek stories in late-republican Rome. And secondly, it is patent
that the degree of existential identification and emotional bonding between
the dramatic protagonists and the spectators must have been low.[43] Nobody
watching the *Atreus* under the impression *"de me fabula narratur"* would
have cheered on the tyrant and his cannibal brother. The Roman habit of role
differentiation (*personae*), which also informs Cicero's discussion of the
persona-concept in *de Officiis*, most likely furthered the reception of Greek
tragedy as a realm of, above all, fiction, rhetoric, and spectacle.

   In short, at least in this Ciceronian passage the reception of Roman
tragedy based on Greek material took the form of dramatic (and rhetorical)
entertainment provided by a fictional spectacle (nothing more and nothing
less). It bears emphasizing that the absence of any overt civic or political
dimension in this form of tragic reception is not necessarily a loss; on the
contrary, the irrelevance of moral and political concerns arguably allowed
the playwrights to explore a new aesthetics of the gruesome, in which wit
and brutality merge in a novel exploration of genuine evil – via Seneca in
particular, but also Virgil and Ovid, the momentary tragic monsters that orig-
inated in Roman republican tragedy, especially the theatre of Accius, are still
haunting our imagination. From the point of view of method, it is, of course,
highly suspect to build too much on one isolated piece of evidence from the
late republic; but what Cicero reports chimes with the larger parameters of
dramatic performances that applied also in earlier centuries, and we perhaps
should reckon with the possibility that from early on Greek mythological
material had "fictional" rather than "historical" status for a Roman audience.

   If the political message of the plays thus remains dubious or debat-
able, there can be little doubt that the performance context was politically
charged, and for various reasons. To begin with, the divide that separated the
personnel on stage, marked as it was by a social stigma, from the audience
assembled in the *cavea*, arranged or dressed up in such a way, especially
from 194 onwards, as to reflect the different strata of Roman society, must
have generated some sense of civic identity – whatever type of drama played
itself out on stage. Secondly, the dramatic festivals were implicated in the

---

43 Fiction does not necessarily entail emotional distance, but it makes it easier. Cic.
    Marc. 9 illustrates both points.

competitive emulation that defined aristocratic self-promotion throughout the last three centuries of the republic. The desire to do or stage something spectacular and to go beyond the standards set by predecessors or rivals underwrote innovations and experiments in virtually all cultural domains, but in particular games and triumphal celebrations. Livy, for instance, chronicles the escalation of expenditure at aristocratic funerals. For 216, he records three days of gladiatorial combat involving twenty-two pairs (23.30.15); for 200 four days involving twenty-five (31.50.4); and for 183, three days involving a hundred and twenty gladiators, in addition to a *visceratio* and an *epulum* (39.46.2). And in the triumphal celebrations, Romans freely enacted the Homeric dictum always to be the best and outshine all others – to the point of arguably bringing down the commonwealth.[44] This dynamic played itself out whether or not lavishly funded public entertainment proved a decisive factor in furthering careers.[45]

While there is virtually no evidence at all that playwrights were hired to write *mythological* tragedies with a specific political message, actors, audiences, and sponsors were able to turn dramatic performances into enacting such a message, over and against whatever the plays were designed to signify by the dramatists. During the shows that celebrated his victory over the Illyrians in 167, the propraeter L. Anicius Gallus seems to have stage-managed (and man-handled) a group of tragic actors he had brought over from Greece for the occasion in particularly grotesque fashion – Polybius, at least, pointedly remarks that he will have to pass over the event because his readers would simply not believe what happened.[46] And for the late re-

---

44 Flaig 2003, 40–8.
45 *Pace* Gruen 1994, 188–97, who takes the absence of a correlation between expenditure and political advancement to show that investment in games was not politically motivated. But the fact that some who invested did not get the hoped-for returns, and others who did not invest still had a splendid career does not mean that the sponsorship of games did not constitute an arena for competitive emulation at Rome; it only shows that it was one of secondary importance: while investment in it was not a requirement and the benefits dubious, it offered one way of leaving a mark on one's term in office. Cicero, at any rate, remarks on the pressure that aediles were under to mark their term in office by memorable displays, which could include spectacular games, fueled by the desire to meet or, ideally, outdo the high standards set by previous incumbents (*Off.* 2.57). See Jocelyn 2000, 326–7 for a reassertion of the orthodox view. At the same time, Gruen is absolutely correct in stressing that the financial expenditure on games and spectacles does not mean that Roman magistrates were financially or symbolically invested in dramatic scripts; in fact, it seems to have been the case that this aspect of the festivals was usually hired out to contractors, again indicating that the plays themselves were not usually designed or regarded as an obvious means or medium of political communication or advancement – even though they could be *turned into* such a medium.
46 Plb. 30.22.1; Gruen 1994, 216.

public, we have evidence for how the plays themselves could be integrated into the dynamic of emulation and aristocratic self-promotion by resourceful organizers or their advisers.[47] The most notorious instance is the festival that Pompey celebrated in 55, to inaugurate his new stone theatre, the first such fixture in the cityscape. In "the most lavish and magnificent games", as Cicero refers to the celebrations, the general opted for a dramatic repertory designed to underscore his affinities with the king of kings in Greek myth, Agamemnon (Cic. *Fam.* 7.1.2 = 24 SB):

> omnino, si quaeris, ludi apparatissimi, sed non tui stomachi; coniecturam enim facio de meo ... quid enim delectationis habent sescenti muli in 'Clytemestra' aut in 'Equo Troiano' creterrarum tria milia aut armatura varia peditatus et equitatus in aliqua pugna? quae popularem admirationem habuerunt, delectationem tibi nullam attulissent.

> [In all, in case you wonder, the games were most lavish, but not to your taste (to judge by my own). ... For what pleasure is to be had from six hundred mules in a *Clytemnestra* or, in a *Trojan Horse*, three thousand mixing bowls or diverse weaponry of infantry and cavalry in some battle or other? They elicited admiration from the populace, but would not have brought you any enjoyment.]

As Beacham and Champlin emphasize, the theatre-temple complex was designed as a monument to Pompey's Eastern victories and a lasting reminder of the lavish triumph he celebrated in 61.[48] The thematically and geographically topical *Clytemnestra* (by Accius) and the *Trojan Horse* (by Naevius) were thus ideally suited to establish an elective affinity between Pompey and another *triumphator* over Eastern foes, Agamemnon, and Pompey turned the plays into triumphal showpieces: the former play featured, so Cicero claims perhaps hyperbolically, a procession of 600 mules in advance of Agamemnon's entry and the latter displayed 3,000 bowls as symbolic representation of the booty that the Greeks captured in the sack of Troy – and of Pompey's own Eastern triumph celebrated six years previously.

Four aspects of this remarkable episode are particularly pertinent for our concerns. First, it bears noting as a postscript to the previous discussion that Pompey clearly thought nothing of identifying himself with the Greek general who vanquished the supposedly proto-Roman Trojans and sacked their city – an irony that the adherents of those who like to highlight the Trojan roots, or even identity, of the Romans tend to pass over in silence, though it is difficult to imagine that he would have done so if many in the audience thought of themselves as latter-day Trojans. Secondly, Pompey's choice of mythic analogies rested on a rather superficial interpretation of the tragic plots. Naevius' play most likely focused, rather innocuously, on the sack of the city; but Accius' seems to have thematized the fatal homecom-

---

47   The most recent discussion of the relevant evidence is Boyle 2006, 149–52.
48   Beacham 1999, 62–77; Champlin 2003, 298, with reference to Beacham.

ing. It will have featured Agamemnon's triumphal entry into Argos, but, as the title suggests, also his murder at the hands of his wife. By turning Accius' *Clytemnestra* into a *pompa triumphalis* and casting himself as a latter-day Agamemnon, Pompey (or his advisors) took over the heroism, but left out the tragedy.[49] It seems that Pompey did not fully think through the implications of casting himself as a latter-day Agamemnon – and history caught up with him.[50] Thirdly, the episode illustrates the potential for the political instrumentalization of Greek mythological tragedy *extraneous* to the play itself. The contemporary political message of the performance derived not from the plot (or any authorial intent), but from the staging, and reflected the special interests of the organizer and patron. The fourth and final point to note is the emphasis on spectacle rather than dramatic art.

To be sure, we are here again dealing with a special case from the late republic. Pompey was able to choose his plays from a large dramatic repertory built up over centuries, and he had the means and resources at his disposal to make a spectacle of himself. The way scholars have dealt with this and similar evidence is to say that tragedy had lost its bearings as an art form in the dying years of the republic. Essentially, this is the story Horace tells in his *Letter to Augustus* (*Ep.* 2.1.189–93):

> quattuor aut plures aulaea premuntur in horas,
> dum fugiunt equitum turmae peditumque catervae;
> mox trahitur manibus regum fortuna retortis,
> esseda festinant, pilenta, petorrita, naves,
> captivum portatur ebur, captiva Corinthus.

> [For four or more hours the curtain is kept down, while formations of cavalry and hordes of foot soldiers sweep past; in due course ill-fortuned kings are dragged on stage with their hands tied behind their backs, chariots and coaches, vehicles and ships rush across, captured ivories and captured Corinthian treasures are carried along in triumph.]

Just before the verses quoted, Horace laments a change in emphasis from dramatic eloquence to visual spectacle, even among the more educated members of the audience (187–8: *verum equitis quoque iam migravit ab aure voluptas/ omnis ad incertos oculos et gaudia vana*) and, afterwards, notes with contempt that the contemporary performances (not necessarily Greek mythological tragedies), must have been designed for a deaf ass with

---

49 The tragedy at the games was provided by the elephants (and their slaughter in the arena). See Cic. *Fam.* 7.1.3: *extremus elephantorum dies fuit. in quo admiratio magna vulgi atque turbae, delectatio nulla exstitit, quin etiam misericordia quaedam consecuta est atque opinio eius modi, esse quandam illi beluae cum genere humano societatem.*

50 As Boyle 2006, 157 remarks wryly, "Rome's tragic repertoire was not something to be played – or played with – lightly".

their insufferable din (199–200). In his account, the decline seems to have set in recently, and scholars have been happy to retell the tale: "With mimes, pantomimes, and other public spectacles on the rise, tragedy began losing its popular audience."[51] That may well be the case, though to put "tragedy", however implicitly, in contradistinction to "public spectacles" seems misguided: "public spectacle" is clearly the common denominator across the entire range of dramatic genres (tragedy included). Indeed, as suggested above, one ought to reckon with the possibility that the mass appeal of spectacular staging was a key factor in the Roman appropriation of Greek mythological tragedy from the beginning, and it is tempting to identify the urge to increase the grandeur and sophistication of spectacle as one of the factors that made it such a success. Whatever drama could be seen on Rome's stages before 240 BCE, it is difficult to imagine that it could rival the sheer semiotic impact of a full-scale tragedy rehearsed and staged by professional actors. Once the step had been taken, there was no way back. Hence, while we should not rashly suppose that most, if any, of the tragic performances in previous centuries resembled Pompey's shows, the spirit that informed his spectacles may have had a history.

Finally, it is worth concluding this section by recalling that at least during the late republic tragic performances also functioned as an indirect medium of political communication between the ruling elite and the people. This communication could take various forms, such as the choice of an "oldie" that promised to resonate in a contemporary key (witness Pompey), the instruction of actors to deliver certain lines in such a way as to render them topical (see, for instance, Cicero's *pro Sestio*), or the use of claques. Put differently, in the late republic it seems to have been a frequent occurrence that individuals or groups of Rome's civic community endowed tragic scripts with allegorical political meaning when and if the occasion arose. The secondary literature on this peculiarly Roman phenomenon is by now significant, and there is no need to rehearse the details.[52] Suffice it to say that the manipulation and reception of specific lines within a tragic performance as a form of commentary on current political affairs devalues the play *as play*, i.e. as an artistic artifact designed to provide some form of aesthetic experience in its own right and convey a certain message, political or otherwise. As Flaig puts it:[53]

---

51 Goldberg 1996, 272.
52 See especially Flaig 1995, 118–24 (with further bibliography) and Stärk 2000.
53 Flaig 1995, 122–3 ("[By reading current political matters into tragic performances] the Romans negated that aesthetic distance, which theatrical performances in Greece required. They grouped the dramatic patterns around new semantic centers. Indeed, they treated the dramatic texts as a huge dump of potential signs, which were to be activated and given contemporary relevance according to the specific political situ-

Damit negierten die Römer jene ästhetische Distanz, die hellenische Theateraufführ-
rungen erforderten; sie gruppierten die Sequenzen des Dramas um neue semantische
Zentren; ja sie behandelten den dramatischen Text als eine riesige Halde von poten-
tiellen Zeichen, die man je nach der spezifischen politischen Situation der Aufführ-
rung zu aktivieren und zu aktualisieren hatte. Das Schauspiel dergestalt politisieren
heisst es entästhetisieren.

Again, it is impossible to know whether, and to what extent, we ought to
backdate this form of political communication to earlier decades or centuries. But the late republican sources clearly demonstrate that individuals and
groups knew the principles and protocols of this mode of engagement with
tragedy well – it formed part of the cultural knowledge that sustained interactions in the field of power. As such it most likely evolved over the course
of time – or constituted an option from the very beginning, was, perhaps,
even a feature that the Romans retained from their pre-literary period of
dramatic performances.

4   Translations between identity and alterity

However we conceive of the working methods of Roman playwrights,
whether they translated, adapted, or freely created in producing their scripts,
they rendered foreign subject matter into Latin.[54] Texts that are translated or
adapted from another culture are by definition curious hybrids that defy easy
categorization. A Greek tragic plot presented in Latin is a *tertium quid* as it
were, which *nec utrumque et utrumque videtur*.[55] Greek figures, plot-pat-
terns, and ideas here jostle with the views of the world that are built into the
concepts and the vocabulary of the Latin language. Translation thus renders
both the foreign familiar and the familiar foreign, generating an interesting oscillation between moments of perceived identity and moments of perceived alterity. Such oscillation takes place within larger cultural frames:[56]

---

ation at the time of the performance. To politicise theater in such a way means to
de-aestheticize it.")

54   The precise classification of the archaic Roman playwrights was, until recently, hotly
contested, partly since "translator" long carried the stigma of (at best) "secondary"
and "unoriginal". I here leave this particular arena of ideological combat to one side
because the precise mode of engagement on the part of the Roman dramatists with
Greek material does not affect the argument of this section – apart from the fact that
the recent rehabilitation of translation as a creative activity in its own right seems to
have shifted the terms of the debate.
55   To speak with Ovid. The quotation comes from the assessment of Hermaphrodite's gender after his merging with the nymph Salmacis at *Met.* 4.379: it seemed both and neither.
56   Bassnett and Lefevere 1995, 6.

> Translation is … a rewriting of an original text. All rewritings, whatever their inten-
> tion, reflect a certain ideology and a poetics and as such manipulate literature to
> function in a given society in a given way. Rewriting is manipulation, undertaken
> in the service of power, and in its positive aspects can help in the evolution of a
> literature and a society. … the history of translation is the history also of literary
> innovation, of the shaping power of one culture upon another.

There is, to be sure, much in this passage that annoys: it is too sweeping, too dogmatic, and too reductive in its emphasis on power. With their dollop of abstractions, the authors fudge issues of agency and import; and their grand generalizations (*all* rewritings, *whatever* their intention), while getting at something important, are, ultimately, unwarranted or outright counterproductive: manipulation may well be ubiquitous, but, surely, there are differences in degree – to be detected only, at the appropriate level of nuance, if one asks some rather traditional questions about (say) authorial intention and the semantic equivalence between source and target text.[57] At the same time, the passage delineates a heuristic agenda for the investigation of the inter-cultural poetics of translation and its socio-political consequences that is ideally suited for placing Roman translations (or adaptations) of Greek tragic scripts within wider contexts.

Unfortunately, only in rare instances do we still possess the source text and some of the target fragments. But where that is the case, it is possible to study how the playwrights themselves introduced shifts in cultural ideology in the translation from Greek to Latin, not least to enhance the intelligibility and resonance of the foreign material. The fragments of Ennius' *Medea*, based as it is on Euripides' play, offer some interesting examples of this phenomenon, starting with the opening lines. If Euripides' heroes sail on a boat made of pinewood, Ennius' crew mans a fir-wood ship. As Jocelyn points out: "A fir-wood Argo suggested to Ennius' audience a military expedition whereas a pine-wood one would have suggested commercial enterprise."[58] Put differently, Ennius wished to foreground from the start the aggressive nature of the undertaking. He continues in the same vein when he opts for not reproducing Euripides' famous *hysteron – proteron* (first the image of the Argo flying over the sea; then the reference to the felling of the trees from which she is build) in his translation; instead, he sticks to the chronological order, a rearrangement that both facilitates understanding and introduces a shift in ideology: if in the Greek text, the first image is one of

---

57   The passage also seems to presuppose that translation necessarily happens between
     two specific cultures; but this is not always the case, as the multi-lingual environ-
     ment of early modern Europe and the translations from classical languages into the
     vernacular *within* a specific culture show.

58   Jocelyn 1967, 353. See also 351.

cultural achievement (sea-faring), in Ennius' version the focus is on "das Gewaltsame, Destruktive des Akts" (wood-cutting).[59]

Elsewhere, Ennius can be shown to adjust the imagery of the Greek original to achieve a better fit with the cultural knowledge of his Roman audience. A good example is his translation of one of the most famous utterances in all of Greek drama, Medea's exclamation that she would rather stand three times in the line of battle than bear one child. Here is the passage from Euripides (Diggle's edition) and the Ennian fragment as transmitted by Varro (*Med.* 248–51):

> λέγουσι δ' ἡμᾶς ὡς ἀκίνδυνον βίον
> ζῶμεν κατ' οἴκους, οἱ δὲ μάρνανται δορί,
> κακῶς φρονοῦντες· ὡς τρὶς ἂν παρ' ἀσπίδα
> στῆναι θέλοιμ' ἂν μᾶλλον ἢ τεκεῖν ἅπαξ.

> [And they say of us that we live a life free from danger at home while they fight wars, fools that they are. How I would rather stand three times in the line of battle than bear one child!]

> nam ter sub armis malim vitam cernere
> quam semel modo parere.
> (Ennius, fr. 232–3 Jocelyn)

Ennius translated the italicized part of the Euripidean passage virtually verbatim:[60]

> ὡς τρὶς ~ [*nam*] *ter*
> θέλοιμ' ἂν μᾶλλον ~ *malim*
> ἢ τεκεῖν ἅπαξ ~ *quam semel modo parere*

Yet he renders the phrase παρ' ἀσπίδα στῆναι rather freely with *sub armis vitam cernere*. This departure from his Greek model is best explained with reference to the different military cultures of fifth-century Athens and second-century Rome. The Greek hoplite fought in close-formation, and it was absolutely vital that he kept rank (which is what παρ' ἀσπίδα στῆναι essentially means), since his shield protected both himself and the man fighting on his left. The Roman legionary, on the other hand, equipped as he was with the *gladius*, the short sword, needed room to maneuver; Roman military encounters normally involved man-to-man combat, i.e. situations in which the individual soldier was effectively on his own, fighting for his

---

59 Vogt-Spira 2000, 269–70. He discusses further instances, including the change in Medea's status, from *despoina* in Euripides to a disenfranchised *concubina* in Ennius (270–1). The opening lines also show Ennius' concern with glossing, explaining, and commentary, in short a concerted attempt to explain the myth to his audience.

60 The *nam*, a particle with causal force, can be accounted for if we assume that Ennius read the Euripidean text with an imaginary full stop after δορί, and a comma after φρονοῦντες, taking ὡς as a causal conjunction ('because'), instead of an exclamation ('how').

life. Given these differences in warfare, a literal translation of the Euripidean phrase, such as *ad clipeum stare*, would have been all but pointless for Ennius' audience. He therefore substituted for the Greek phrase with its culturally specific hoplite-ideology an expression that would resonate at Rome. In effect, to put it in Cicero's terminology, he lost the *verba* but kept the *vis*, the emotive force, of Medea's outcry.

Similar shifts in ideology and meaning can also be identified in fragments for which the source text has not survived, simply by considering the effects of expressing Greek plot patterns in Latin. A closer look at a single line from Ennius' *Achilles* will illustrate the point:

fr. 1 R^2 (= 8 Jocelyn): *Serva cives, defende hostes cum potes defendere!*

[Save the citizens, ward off the enemy, while you are able to ward them off!]

As Jocelyn plausibly argues, this line from Ennius' *Achilles* is part of an entreaty to the sulking Achilles to resume fighting.[61] The immediate background of the appeal can be reconstructed in various ways. One could imagine it as part of the famous embassy scene portrayed in *Iliad* 9; or, as is more likely, given that the plea in the *cum*-clause intimates a more specific situational force of the utterance, as coming from a renewed exhortation to Achilles at a more advanced stage of the battle of the ships (the situation recounted in *Iliad* 15 and 16). Be that as it may, this Latin entreaty of the Greek Achilles engenders an interesting cross-cultural discontent. The emotive force of the Latin phrase *serva cives, defende hostes* derives from three key notions of Roman public ideology: the concept of the Roman citizen (*civis*); a defensively minded disposition which wards off danger from the community of citizens (*hostes defendere*); and the belief in the welfare and ultimate salvation of the Roman state through its socio-political arrangements and its religious support (*servare*). Overall, the line recalls the tight fabric of normative bonds, which tie together the Roman citizenry into a cohesive and mutually committed collectivity, clearly demarcating the boundaries of Roman identity against outside foes. Let us take a closer look at each of these elements in turn.

The notion of the *civis Romanus* is the common denominator in Roman society, and reinforcement of a basic solidarity among all members of the citizen community surfaces in almost every aspect of public discourse and practice. The simple term *patres* by which senators were addressed defines the ruling elite in the idiom of family affiliations, signaling the obligation of persons in authority to take care of the welfare of the people, just as they would of members of their own *domus*. While the ideology of the civic community as one large family underscores the interdependence of leaders and

---

61   Jocelyn 1967, 173.

the people, the concept of citizen ultimately applied to the members of the ruling class as well.[62] One of the most prominent outgrowths of this civic identity was the practice of awarding a crown of oak-leaves, the *corona civica,* for saving the life of a citizen on the battlefield. What this achievement meant in Roman terms is best summed up by a passage from Pliny where he specifies the conditions required for receiving the award (he calls them *leges artae et ideo superbae*) (*Nat.* 16.12–4):[63]

> civem servare, hostem occidere, utque eum locum in quo sit actum hostis optineat eo die, ut servatus fateatur – alias testes nihil prosunt – ut civis fuerit: auxilia quamvis rege servato decus non dant. nec crescit honos idem imperatore conservato, quoniam conditores in quocumque cive summum esse voluere. accepta licet uti perpetuo; ludis ineunti semper adsurgi etiam ab senatu in more est, sedendi ius in proximo senatui; vacatio munerum omnium ipsi patrique et avo paterno. ... o mores aeternos qui tanta opera honore solo donaverint et, cum reliquas coronas auro commendarent, salutem civis in pretio esse noluerint, clare professi ne servari quidem hominem fas esse lucri causa!

> [to save the life of a fellow-citizen, to kill an enemy; that the enemy occupied the area where the deed took place on the same day; that he who was saved acknowledges it – other witnesses do not count; that he was a Roman citizen: auxiliary forces even if the saved person is a king do not bestow this distinction. The same honor does not increase if the rescued person is a general since the founders wished it to be highest in the case of any citizen. Once the crown has been awarded, he may wear it for the rest of his life; at his entrance at the games, it is custom that even the senate always rises; he has the right to sit next to the senate; he himself and his father and his paternal grandfather are exempt from all public obligations ... O everlasting customs that reward such deeds with honor alone and, whereas they make attractive the other crowns with gold, they refused to set a price for the rescue of a citizen, clearly stating it is unlawful even to save the life of a human being for the sake of profit!]

For obvious reasons, this award bears immediate relevance for our fragment. It is not unlikely that the line when performed on the Roman stage would have evoked the very institution of honouring those who had saved the life of a fellow-citizen.[64] The passage from Pliny illustrates the ideological force of the Latin utterance, not least the sharp distinction between the Roman community and the outside world. Not only is the antithesis between *civem servare* and *hostem occidere* extraordinarily marked; even among those who fight on the Roman side a clear-cut line is drawn between Roman citizen-soldiers and auxiliary troops. Likewise, the life of any member of the civic community ranks higher in importance than that of any king who might have supported the Roman military effort. And among the Roman citizens, hierarchies are leveled in the ritual of the award: *imperator* and common soldier

---

62   See e.g. Cic. *Mur.* 36; *Cael.* 77; *Mil.* 3.
63   See also Gel. 5.6.13; cf. Maxfield 1981, 70–74 (with a picture on p.73).
64   Jocelyn 1972, 48.

have the same value – or, rather, each Roman life is priceless. The senate, the *patres rei publicae*, acknowledge and honour the achievement of saving the life of a fellow-citizen during public occasions, the games, in which the civic community replenishes itself and renews its contract with the gods; specifically, the rise of the senators and the proximity in seating visually assimilate the deed of preserving the life of a citizen to the purpose and function of the senate as a group, namely to provide and care for the wellbeing and protection of the civic community. While the crown itself is only of symbolic value, financial advantages are granted to the entire family of the Roman hero, reinforcing the integration of family unit and public service.[65]

Concern for one's fellow soldiers was of course not an inborn Roman quality. The Pliny passage already indicates the great advantages that accrue from successfully performing such a deed. Whereas the Homeric Achilles gains immortal glory at least in part by defying the needs of his community, Romans achieved standing and fame within their culture only through actions of solidarity with the overall interest of the commonwealth. The heroic world of Greece and the Roman republic rewarded very different types of actions and chose different ways to express public appreciation. The military decorations displayed on the houses of Roman battle heroes, which elicited the admiration of Polybius, are functionally equivalent to heroic song in archaic Greece.[66] Given this cultural context, it is unsurprising that annalistic legends should attribute the repeated award of the civic crown to select figures among the *patres*, such as Manlius Torquatus or Lucius Sicinius (or Siccius) Dentatus, the winner of fourteen and, ironically, called "Roman Achilles" on account of his martial prowess.[67]

---

65 For the importance of the civic crown, cf. also *HA Pius* 9.10 (*ut Scipionis sententiam frequentarit ... malle se unum civem servare quam mille hostes occidere*) and V. Max. 5.2.6.

66 Plb. 6.39.8–10.

67 Liv. 6.20.8; Plin. *Nat.*, 16.14; Gel. 2.11 (*... nomenque ei factum ob ingentem fortitudinem appelllatumque esse Achillem Romanum*). Gellius ends his entry, which details Dentatus' astonishing accomplishments on the battlefield, by noting that Dentatus, a tribune of the plebs, partook in nine triumphs with his generals (*triumphavit cum imperatoribus suis triumphos novem*): the syntax hints at the possibility of a Homeric scenario (who triumphs? the general in charge or his best warrior? Gellius' choice of Dentatus as the subject of *triumphavit* leaves the issue perfectly ambiguous), but the overall image is one of joint efforts on behalf of the commonwealth – though in Gellius Dentatus certainly occludes the fame and the names of the generals under whom he served. Within a hermeneutics of suspicion, one could entertain the possibility that initially the designation of Dentatus as "Roman Achilles" not only recognized his military prowess, but also his special and uncomfortable status, if not dysfunctional conduct, within the socio-political hierarchies in the Roman field of power or on military campaign – an aspect then silenced in our annalistic and antiquarian sources.

In the light of this larger cultural background, the Ennius-fragment acquires its special complexion. Its Roman vocabulary is particularly pointed at the precise moment when the invading Greeks face a decisive defensive struggle at their ships. The mentality of going out for plunder, of sacking cities and capturing spoil, which was prevalent in the Greek camp before the fall-out between Agamemnon and Achilles, has been replaced with an immediate concern for basic safety. Whoever turns to Achilles for deliverance employs a vocabulary that recalls the centuries-old history of the Roman struggle to maintain civic identity and independence throughout continual warfare and outside threats.[68] From this point of view, the full ambiguity of the figure of Achilles in a tragic context begins to emerge. Already the playwrights of fifth-century Athens staged the incompatibility of Homer's Achilles with the needs and values of a civic community at war, turning the hero into a despicable traitor of the common cause.[69] And Pleusicles in Plautus' *Miles Gloriosus* pithily summarizes what must have struck a Roman first and foremost about the Greek warrior: *occidi Achilles civis passus est* (1289).[70] Within the universe of Homer, the conduct of Achilles was at least intelligible; due to a very specific societal topography and normative order, his actions, if hardly praiseworthy, still make sense. Yet the antagonistic clash of aristocratic egos to the point that one of them, quite openly, schemes about the defeat of the larger community was already considered intolerable in fifth-century Athens. Casting these Greek plot elements in the Latin language further heightens the social inexplicability of his behaviour and causes an awkward disjunction between the political values and convictions built into the Latin vocabulary and Achilles' actions. Horace gives the advice that anybody depicting an Achilles may portray him as someone who defies that laws exist for him (*iura neget sibi nata, A. P.* 122). And this statement sums up an overall truth about tragic protagonists – whether feuding aristocrats or tyrants lusting after power, such as Atreus: in their presence the tight fabric of *iura* and *mores* that regulates social intercourse at Rome tears asunder.[71]

---

68 For *civis* in opposition to *hostis* see *TLL* 1228.71–84.
69 See esp. Aeschylus, *Myrmidones*, fr. 132 Radt. The attribution to Aeschylus, however, remains controversial. In *Iliad* 9, Odysseus tries to sway Achilles also by evoking the undeserved sufferings of his fellow Greeks – an argument pointedly ignored by Achilles in his response. Plato's discussion of the Homeric Achilles and the consequences of his actions in *Republic* 386c–91c focuses on such topics as attitudes to death (speech in Hades, comment on the shade of Patroclus, *Il.* 23.103f.), display of grief, insubordination, irreverence, and cruelty.
70 Horace makes the more general point that at Troy the common soldiers suffered for the foolishness of their leaders (*Ep.* 1.2.14: *quidquid delirant reges plectuntur Achivi*).
71 See below on Caesar.

In short, the *concordia discors* produced by the translation of Greek tragedies into Latin raises complex questions about the effects this phenomenon had on the semantics of the Latin lexicon.[72] Given that societies construct their realities in and through language and that the meaning of words is in turn grounded in social practice, the emergence of Latin tragedies could not help but disjoin and complicate the correlation of "language" and "society" at Rome.[73] This effect was amplified further by the fact that these tragedies were "preserved communication", i.e. remained accessible beyond their initial performance in the theater. Texts – in the sense of "consolidated semantics" that can be stored and transmitted (whether orally or in writing) – introduce inevitable disjunctions between discourse and practice (especially if the texts have their origins in a foreign culture) and thereby expand the scope of what becomes conceivable in a given society.

5   Correlations

Greek tragedy had a noticeable presence in the middle and late Roman republic also outside the theatre. Simultaneous changes in Roman primary and secondary schooling ensured that the dissemination of tragic thought did not remain restricted to performances in the theater. Following Hellenistic precedents, upper-class Romans of this period began to practice novel forms of instruction that employed epic and dramatic texts in both languages to develop facility in the oral and written use of Greek and Latin and to hone rhetorical and argumentative skills. The beginning of the formal teaching of rhetoric at Rome is conventionally dated to 167 BC, with the arrival and stay (extended, so myth has it, by a broken leg) of Crates of Mallos in the city; but the practice of using poetry in school exercises must have started decades earlier. Significantly, our sources consistently link archaic Roman poets, mostly outsiders of low social standing, with educational settings in the homes of powerful *nobiles*. By the end of the second century, handbooks began to circulate that referred to the works of Roman playwrights – among

---

72 An effect reinforced by the playwrights themselves, who persistently explore the semantic range of individual words and potential synonyms. Cf. the excellent discussion in Dangel 1995.

73 Translation therefore significantly complicates the traditional language and culture debate, as summed up by Hymes 1964, 167: "If language were an exact mirror of culture…, so that entries in a complete dictionary and the contents of a complete ethnography were in one-to-one relationship, ethnography, indeed, might dispense with linguistic work, since the results of the latter would be isomorphic…. If, on the other hand, language were a perfect and inseparable symbolism of culture, … then ethnography might be reduced to a branch of linguistics."

the tragedians in particular Ennius, Pacuvius, and Accius – to illustrate the principles and techniques of persuasive argumentation, quite frequently by pointing out cases of flawed reasoning and logical loopiness in the dramatic corpus. The detailed attention to specific texts and the large amount of required memorisation involved in the process of acquiring, as Quintilian puts it, *recte loquendi scientiam et poetarum enarrationem* meant that, by the end of the Republic, a speaker in the law courts could presuppose that his audience knew certain plays, or at least passages thereof, intimately.[74] This period also saw the re-staging of "classic" crowd-pleasers from the previous centuries during the public festivals. Briefly put, for the last generations of the Roman republic, Greek mythological tragedy (as well as the Roman *praetexta*) were integral components of Rome's theatrical repertory and played a significant role in preparing members of Rome's elite for their public career as *oratores*. In fact, some aristocrats started to write tragic plays themselves, in a process that Goldberg has termed "gentrification".[75]

This raises the question as to whether this extensive exposure to tragic thought had any repercussions in the field of power, in particular public speech. Some references to tragic myths in Cicero's orations points to widespread familiarity with the basic tragic personnel. Just as Pompey could assimilate himself to Agamemnon in a positive way, so the figures of Greek myth provided welcome opportunities for invective identifications. A notorious example is the series of mythic *femmes fatales* to which Cicero compares Clodia in the *pro Caelio*. In speeches to the people allusions to Greek myths are rarer, but they do occur: in the *pro lege Manilia*, for instance, Cicero compares Mithridates' retreat to Medea's flight, the point of comparison being how Eastern potentate and Eastern witch delayed their pursuers, one scattering money, the other her brother.[76] But beyond such learned allusions for rhetorical amplification one ought to enquire further to what extent the importation of tragedy actually influenced Roman habits of thought and practice. Put differently, what role (if any) did tragic discourse play in the overall evolution of Rome's societal order and its "imaginary spaces" – or, more specifically, the breakdown of republican consensus that coincided with the rise of Roman tragedy?[77] Accius' *oeuvre* in particular, Jacqueline

---

74 Quintilian, 1.4.2; cf. Morgan 1998, 161.
75 See Goldberg 1996, 270–1 for the evidence.
76 *Man.* 22. For the dramatic dimension of Cicero's oratory see Klodt 2003, with further bibliography; Gildenhard 2007a, 2010.
77 Gotter 1994, 495 identifies the issue at stake as follows: "Überzeugend ist zwar, dass die römische Aristokratie mit bestem Wissen und Gewissen die geistigen und materiellen Importe aus Griechenland zu steuern gemeint hat. Nur: War dies überhaupt möglich? Übernahm man nicht mit dem vermeintlich Nützlichen auch ästhetische Hypotheken, unbewusste Denkfiguren und implizite Wahrnehmungsmuster, die im

Dangel maintains, manifests a profound engagement with the internal and external turmoil of the decades during which he was active as a playwright – among other things, he witnessed the onset of assassination as a continuation of internal politics by violent means, outright civil war, and Rome's military expansion, especially in the Greek East, with its domestic repercussions; in particular, she detects reflections on the baneful change in the mentality of Roman generals that gradually set in during this period:[78]

> Géographiquement et thématiquement, rien n'est vraiment étranger au théâtre accien. Mieux encore: à l'example de ce même théâtre, s'introduit subrepticement, mais inéluctablement, dans l'esprit des généraux romains, trop longtemps au contact des terres orientales et trop souvent reconduits dans des fonctions exceptionnelles, une réelle séduction pour les monarchies orientales de droit divin et pour un pouvoir despotique.

Dangel prudently abstains from positing a direct causality between the Roman reception of Greek tragedy (and its dysfunctional semantics) and the disintegration of elite consensus, preferring to situate both phenomena within the wider context of Rome's contact with the Greek East. For Cicero, though, Greek tragedy had left the stage and become a real presence in Roman society. He drew on tragic figures of thought throughout his career as public orator, not least in the *de Haruspicum Responso*, in which he casts Clodius as a tragic fiend who threatens to destroy Roman society on account of his divinely inspired insanity.[79] In his first letter to Atticus after Caesar crossed the Rubicon, he turns the warlord into a Greek tragic monster lusting for absolute power by means of a quotation from Euripides' *Phoenissae*.[80] And in his *de Officiis* a programmatic series of quotations from Greek and Roman tragedy aids his efforts to conceptualize the decline and fall of the *res publica libera* and to develop a new ethics for Rome's political elite.[81] From Cicero's point of view, by the end of the republic, Greek literature had turned into Roman life.

Gegensatz zum römischen Wertesystem standen und deshalb eine die Ordnung gefährdende Eigengesetzlichkeit entfalten mussten?"

78 Dangel 1995, 19–20. ("In terms of geography and thematics, there is nothing foreign to the theatre of Accius. What is more, just as in his theatre, a real attraction to oriental, divinely sanctioned monarchies and despotic power surreptitiously, yet inevitably, entered the outlook of Roman generals, because of their excessively long contact with the East and their exceptional functions.")

79 Gildenhard 2007a.

80 Cic. *Att.* 7.11.1; Gildenhard 2006, 197–9.

81 Gildenhard 2007a. See esp. *Off.* 3. 82, where Cicero maintains that Caesar, very much like Achilles, dismissed *ius* in his strife for power and prestige – and justified doing so with a quotation from Euripides' *Phoenissae*.

Bibliography

Bassnett, Susan and Lefevere, Andrew (1995), "General Editors' Preface" in: Lawrence Venuti, *The Translator's Invisibility: a History of Translation*, London and New York, vii–viii.

Bernstein, Frank (1998), *Ludi publici: Untersuchungen zur Entstehung und Entwicklung der öffentlichen Spiele im republikanischen Rom*, Stuttgart.

Bilinski, Bronislaw (1960), "Dulorestes de Pacuvius et les guerres serviles en Sicile", in: *Hommages à L. Herrmann*, Brussels, 160–70.

—— (1962), *Contrastanti ideali di cultura sulla scena di Pacuvio* (= Accademia Polacca di Scienze e Lettere, Biblioteca di Roma, Conferenze, Fasc. 16), Rome.

Carter, David M. (2007), *The Politics of Greek Tragedy*, Exeter.

Champlin, Edward (2003), "Agamemnon at Rome: Roman Dynasts and Greek Heroes", in: David Braund / Christopher Gill (eds.), *Myth, History and Culture in Republican Rome: Studies in Honour of T. P. Wiseman*, Exeter, 295–319.

Cowan, Bob (2005), "Review of M. Erasmo, *Roman tragedy: theater to theatricality*, Austin 2004", in: *BMCR* 2005.07.53

Curty, O. (1995), *Les parentés légendaires entre cité grecque*, Geneva.

Dangel, Jacqueline (1995), *Accius: Oeuvres (fragments)*, Paris

Easterling, Patricia E. (ed.) (1997), *The Cambridge Companion to Greek Tragedy*, Cambridge.

Erasmo, Mario (2004), *Roman Tragedy: Theater to Theatricality*, Austin.

Erskine, Andrew (2001), *Troy Between Greece and Rome: Local Tradition and Imperial Power*, Oxford.

—— (2002), "O brother where art though? Tales of Kinship and Diplomacy", in: Daniel Ogden (ed.), *The Hellenistic World: new Perspectives*, London.

Farrell, Joseph (2003), "Classical Genre in Theory and Practice", in: *New Literary History* 34, 383–408.

Feeney, Denis C. (1998), *Literature and Religion at Rome: Culture, Contexts, and Beliefs*, Cambridge.

—— (2005), "Review of Suerbaum (2002)", in: *JRS* 95, 226–40.

Flaig, Egon (1995), "Entscheidung und Konsens: zu den Feldern der politischen Kommunikation zwischen Aristokratie und Plebs", in: M. Jehne (ed.), *Demokratie in Rom? Die Rolle des Volkes in der Politik der römischen Republik*, Stuttgart, 77–127.

—— (1999), "Über die Grenzen der Akkulturation: wider die Verdinglichung des Kulturbegriffs", in: Gregor Vogt-Spira / Bettina Rommel (eds.), *Rezeption und Identität: die kulturelle Auseinandersetzung Roms mit Griechenland als europäisches Paradigma*, Stuttgart, 81–112.

—— (2003), *Ritualisierte Politik: Zeichen, Gesten und Herrschaft im alten Rom*, Göttingen.

Flower, Harriet (1996), "*Fabulae Praetextae* in context: when were plays on contemporary subjects performed in Republican Rome?", in: *CQ* 45, 170–90.

—— (2003), "'Memories' of Marcellus: History and Memory in Roman Republican Culture", in: Ulrich Eigler / Ulrich Gotter / Nino Luraghi / Uwe Walter (eds.), *Formen römischer Geschichtsschreibung von den Anfängen bis Livius*, Darmstadt, 39–52.

Gildenhard, Ingo (2003), "*Philologia perennis*? Classical Scholarship and Functional Differentiation", in: id. / Martin Ruehl (eds.), *Out of Arcadia: Classics and Politics in Germany in the Age of Burckhardt, Nietzsche and Wilamowitz*, London, 161–203.

—— (2006), "Reckoning with Tyranny: Greek Thoughts on Caesar in Cicero's *Letters to Atticus* in early 49", in: Sian Lewis (ed.), *Ancient Tyranny*, Edinburgh, 197–209.

—— (2007a), "Greek Auxiliaries: Tragedy and Philosophy in Ciceronian Invective", in: J. Booth (ed.), *Cicero on the Attack: Invective and Subversion in the Orations and beyond*, Swansea, 149–82.

—— (2007b), "Virgil vs. Ennius, or: The Undoing of the Annalist", in: Emily Gowers / William Fitzgerald (eds.), *Ennius perennis: the Annals and Beyond*, Cambridge, 73–102.

—— (2010), *Creative Eloquence: the Construction of Reality in Cicero's Speeches*, Oxford.

Gildenhard, Ingo / Zissos, Andrew (1999), "'Somatic Economies' – Tragic Bodies and Poetic Design in Ovid's *Metamorphoses*", in: Philip Hardie / Alessandro Barchiesi / Stephen Hinds (eds.), *Ovidian Transformations. Essays on Ovid's Metamorphoses and its Reception*, Cambridge, 162–81.

Goldberg, Sander (1996), "The Fall and Rise of Roman Tragedy", *TAPA* 126, 265–86.

—— (2005), *Constructing Literature in the Roman Republic: Poetry and its Reception*, Cambridge.

—— (2007), "Research Report: Reading Roman tragedy", in: *IJCT* 13 (4) 571–84.

Goldhill, Simon (2000), "Civic Ideology and the Problem of Difference: the Politics of Aeschylean Tragedy, Once Again", in: *JHS* 120, 34–56.

Gotter, Ulrich (1994), "Review of Gruen 1992", in: *Klio* 76, 494–5.

—— (2008), "Cultural Differences and Cross-cultural Contact: Greek and Roman Concepts of 'Power'", in: *HSCP* 104, 179–230.

Grafton, Anthony (1997), "Fragmenta historicorum Graecorum: Fragments of Some Lost Enterprise", in: Glenn Most (ed.), *Collecting fragments – Fragmente sammeln*, Göttingen, 124–43.

Griffin, Jasper (1998), "The Social Function of Attic Tragedy", in: *CQ* 48, 39–61.

Gruen, Erich S. (1990), *Studies in Greek Culture and Roman Policy*, Berkeley, Los Angeles, London.

—— (1992), *Culture and National Identity in Republican Rome*, Ithaca.

Gumbrecht, Hans Ulrich (1985), "History of Literature – Fragment of a Vanished Totality", in: *New Literary History* 16.3, 467–79.

—— (1997), "Eat your Fragment! About Imagination and the Restitution of Texts", in: Glenn Most (ed.), *Collecting fragments – Fragmente sammeln*, Göttingen, 315–27.

Habinek, Thomas (1998), *The Politics of Latin Literature: Writing, Identity, and Empire in Ancient Rome*, Princeton.

Hölkeskamp, Karl-Joachim (1999), "Römische *gentes* und griechische Genealogien", in: Gregor Vogt-Spira / Bettina Rommel (eds.), *Rezeption und Identität: die kulturelle Auseinandersetzung Roms mit Griechenland als europäisches Paradigma*, Stuttgart, 3–21 [reprinted, with bibliographical update, in: *Senatus Populusque Romanus: die politische Kultur der Republik – Dimensionen und Deutungen*, Stuttgart 2004, 199–217].

Hunter, Richard (1985), *The New Comedy of Greece and Rome*, Cambridge.

Hymes, Dell (1964), *Language in Culture and Society: a Reader in Linguistics and Anthropology*, New York and London.

Jocelyn, Henry D. (1967), *The Tragedies of Ennius: the Fragments edited with an Introduction and Commentary*, Cambridge.

—— (1972), "Ennius as a Dramatic Poet", in: O. Skutsch (ed.) *Ennius* (= Fondation Hardt 17), Geneva, 41–95.

—— (2000), "Accius' *Aeneadae aut Decius*: Romans and the Gallic Other", in: Gesine Manuwald (ed.), *Identität und Alterität in der frührömischen Tragödie*, Würzburg, 325–61.

Jones, Christopher P. (1999), *Kinship Diplomacy in the Ancient World*, Cambridge/ M.A. and London.

Klodt, Claudia (2003), "Prozessparteien und politische Gegner als dramatis personae: Charakterstilisierung in Ciceros Reden", in: Bianca-Jeanette and Jens-Peter Schröder (eds.), *Studium declamatorium: Untersuchungen zu Schulübungen und Prunkreden von der Antike bis zur Neuzeit*, Munich and Leipzig, 35–106.

Lefèvre, Eckard (1978), "Versuch einer Typologie des römischen Dramas", in: id. (ed.) *Das römische Drama*, Darmstadt, 1–90.

— (1999), "Die Politisierung der griechischen Tragödie durch die Römer im 3. und 2. Jahrhundert v. Chr. Eine geographische und literarische Grenzüberschreitung", in: Monika Fludernik / Hans-Joachim Gehrke (eds.), *Grenzgänger zwischen Kulturen*, Würzburg, 367–78.

— (2000), "Aitiologisch-politische Implikationen in Naevius' *Danae*", in: Gesine Manuwald (ed.), *Identität und Alterität in der frührömischen Tragödie*, Würzburg, 175–84.

Leigh, Matthew (1996), "Varius Rufus, Thyestes and the Appetites of Antony", in: *PCPS* 42, 171–97.

— (2000), "Primitivism and Power: The Beginnings of Latin Literature" in: O. Taplin (ed.), *Literature in the Greek and Roman World: A New Perspective*, Oxford, 288–310.

— (2004), *Comedy and the Rise of Rome*, Oxford.

— (2006), "Review of M. Erasmo, *Roman Tragedy: Theater to Theatricality*, Austin 2004", in: *AJP* 127, 149–52.

Lennartz, Klaus (1994) *Non verba sed vim: kritisch-exegetische Untersuchungen zu den Fragmenten archaischer römischer Tragiker*, Stuttgart.

Lücke, Stephan (2000), *Syngeneia: epigraphisch-historische Studien zu einem Phänomen der antiken griechischen Diplomatie*, Frankfurt.

Manuwald, Gesine (ed.) (2000), *Identität und Alterität in der frührömischen Tragödie*, Würzburg.

— (2001), *Fabulae praetextae: Spuren einer literarischen Gattung der Römer* (= Zetemata 108), Munich.

— (2003), *Pacuvius summus tragicus poeta: zum dramatischen Profil seiner Tragödien*, Munich and Leipzig.

— (2004), "Römische Tragödien und Praetexten republikanischer Zeit: 1964–2002", in: *Lustrum* 43 [2001], 11–237.

Maxfield, Valerie A. (1981), *The Military Decorations of the Roman Army*, London.

Meier, Christian (1993), *The Political Art of Greek Tragedy*, Cambridge.

Rau, Peter (1967), *Paratragodia: Untersuchung einer komischen Form des Aristophanes*, Munich.

Rhodes, Peter J. (2003), "Nothing to Do with Democracy: Athenian Drama and the *polis*", in: *JHS* 123, 104–19.

Schechner, Richard (2002), *Performance Studies: an Introduction*, London.

Schierl, Petra (2006), *Die Tragödien des Pacuvius: ein Kommentar zu den Fragmenten mit Einleitung, Text und Übersetzung*, Berlin and New York.

Seaford, Richard (1984), *Euripides, Cyclops, with Introduction and Commentary*, Oxford.

Seele, Astrid (1995), *Römische Übersetzer: Nöte, Freiheiten, Absichten*, Darmstadt.

Sommerstein, Alan (ed.) (1993), *Tragedy, Comedy and the Polis: Papers from the Greek Drama Conference, Nottingham, 18–20 July*, Bari.

Stärk, E. (2000), "Politische Anspielungen in der römischen Tragödie und der Einfluß der Schauspieler", in: Gesine Manuwald (ed.), *Identität und Alterität in der frührömischen Tragödie*, Würzburg, 123–33.

Suerbaum, Werner (ed.) (2002), *Handbuch der lateinischen Literature der Antike, erster Band*, Munich.

Thomas, Richard (1982), "Catullus and the Polemics of Poetic Reference (poem 64.1–18)", in: *AJP* 103, 144–64.

Vogt-Spira, Gregor (2000), "Ennius, *Medea*: eine Fremde in Rom", in: Gesine Manuwald (ed.), *Identität und Alterität in der frührömischen Tragödie*, Würzburg, 265–75.

Weber, Ekkehard (1972), "Die trojanische Abstammung der Römer als politisches Argument", in: *WS* 86, 213–25.

—— (2000), "Die ältere Tragödie in Rom und die Legende von der trojanischen Abstammung", in: Gesine Manuwald (ed.), *Identität und Alterität in der frührömischen Tragödie*, Würzburg, 135–41.

Wilamowitz-Moellendorff, Ulrich von (1892/1902), "Philologie und Schulreform: Prorektoratsrede, gehalten zur akademischen Preisverleihung am 1. Juni 1892", in: *Reden und Vorträge*, 2nd edn, Berlin, 96–119.

Wiles, David (1999), *Tragedy in Athens: Performance Space and Theatrical Meaning*, Cambridge.

Winkler, John J. / Zeitlin, Froma (eds.) (1990), *Nothing to Do with Dionysos? Athenian Drama in its Social Context*, Princeton.

Wiseman, Timothy P. (1974), "Legendary Genealogies in Late Republican Rome", in: *Greece & Rome* 21, 153–64 [reprinted in *Roman Studies, Literary and Historical*, Liverpool 1987, 207–18].

—— (1995), *Remus: a Roman Myth*, Cambridge.

—— (1998), *Roman Drama and Roman History*, Exeter.

Dionysiac Theme and Dramatic Allusion in Ovid's *Metamorphoses* 4

Alison Keith

This study explores the tragic themes and imagery of Ovid's "Theban History," with a particular focus on the episode of the daughters of Minyas that opens the fourth book of Ovid's *Metamorphoses* – the stories the three sisters tell as they spurn the worship of the new god Bacchus and their subsequent transformation into bats by the scorned god (4.1–415). Scholarship on the episode falls into three broad categories: one approach has been to consider the sources and models for one of the sisters' narratives, usually in isolation from the others;[1] a second approach has been to analyze the Minyads' narrative artistry in narratological or poetological terms without detailed discussion of the relations between the stories;[2] the third, which might be broadly described as liberal-feminist, has been to focus on rape narratives in the poem (there are two in the Minyads' tales), again without regard to narrative context.[3] Almost without exception, the scholarly literature on the Minyads and their tales has not sought to integrate detailed discussion of the framing tale, concerning the sisters' transformation into bats, with the stories they tell one another as they spin, let alone to integrate the episode as a whole into the larger context of Ovid's Theban narrative that spans books three and four of the *Metamorphoses* (3.1–4.603); but then neither has the scholarship on Ovid's so-called "Thebaid" included discussion of the Minyad episode.[4] This integration is the project of this chapter. I begin with a discussion of

* I am grateful to my colleague Martin Revermann for the invitation to participate in the workshop on 'Points of Contact: Greek Tragedy in the Western Tradition up to the 17th Century' in July 2005; to my colleague Ingo Gildenhard and my husband Stephen Rupp for their acute comments on an earlier version of this paper; and to my research assistant Jessica Westerhold for her editorial assistance with the final version. All remaining errors are my own.
1 Duke 1971; Rohrer 1980; Perraud 1983–84; Holzberg 1988; Knox 1989; Castellani 1980; Labate 1993; Robinson 1999.
2 Leach 1974, 107–11; Rosati 1999.
3 Curran 1978, 221, 224, 227; Janan 1994; Nugent 1990; Richlin 1992, 165–6.
4 Notable exceptions are Perdrizet 1932; Newlands 1986; and Schmitzer 1992, 533; cf. Rosati 1999, 241.

the sources and themes of Ovid's "Thebaid" in its entirety, as preface to my discussion of the Minyads' transformation, and the relationship of their stories both to their own transformation and to the larger context of Ovid's "Thebaid."

1

The point of departure for my sketch of the sources and themes of Ovid's "Thebaid" is the brilliant 1990 paper by Philip Hardie, entitled "Ovid's The-ban Narrative: The First 'Anti-*Aeneid*'?" In this article, Hardie discusses Ovid's narrative of the House of Cadmus at Thebes as an example of *ktisis* or "foundation" poetry, a popular subject of Hellenistic Greek epic. Noting that "the story of Cadmus and his family forms a self-contained unit"[5] that "tells of a *ktisis* that goes wrong,"[6] Hardie argues that Ovid's "Thebaid" is con-structed with constant reference to the great epic of Rome, Vergil's *Aeneid*. He builds on Ernst Bernbeck's stylistic analysis of Ovid's rupture of the epic texture of his Vergilian models in the Ino-episode (*Met.* 4.416–564),[7] to offer a thematic and structural analysis of the "inversions"[8] that Ovid performs on the models of the *Aeneid*. Hardie identifies several themes that unify the diverse tales of Ovid's Theban narrative, not all of which concern Cadmus and his relatives (summary in Figure 1): a contrast between city and country; man and beast; the related themes of exile and wandering in the wilds; "the repeated intervention of a vengeful god as a way of structur-ing the narrative";[9] spectacle, recognition and reversal. This final thematic complex points to what Hardie calls "the pervasive presence of the themes of Attic tragedy in Ovid's Theban tales,"[10] and alerts us to Ovid's ongoing engagement with the genre of tragedy in this section of the *Metamorphoses* (synopses in Figure 1).[11]

   Many scholars have thought that "the πάθη of Dionysus, the patron god of the drama [as Ovid knew, *Am.* 3.15], may well be the oldest of all dramatic

---

5   Hardie 1990, 224.
6   Hardie 1990, 225.
7   Hardie 1990, 224 n.1 acknowledges the relation of his study to that of Bernbeck 1967.
8   Hardie 1990, 224 n.1.
9   Hardie 1990, 226.
10   Hardie 1990, 229; cf. Hardie 1990, 224–6, 229–30.
11   On tragedy in the *Metamorphoses* see Hardie 1990; Curley 1999; Gildenhard and Zis-sos 1999, 170–6; Keith 2002. For plays on Dionysiac themes, see Dodds 1960, xxviii–xxxiii; Seaford 1996, 26 nn. 8–9; Flower 2000, 27 n. 27. I note in addition Aeschylus' *Toxotides* (on Actaeon), *Athamas*; Sophocles' *Athamas* A and B; Euripides' *Ino*.

subjects,"[12] and Froma Zeitlin has recently argued that Thebes, as the birth-place of Dionysus, is the site *par excellence* of Athenian tragedy.[13] Certainly the eponymous founder of the drama, Thespis himself, is credited with a *Pentheus*. We possess only one extant tragedy from an Aeschylean trilogy on a Theban theme: the *Septem contra Thebas* which followed a *Laius* and an *Oedipus*, with satyr play *Sphinx*. But we hear in addition of two trilogies on specifically Dionysian subjects, from which little or nothing survives. The scholiast on Aristophanes' *Thesmophoriazousai* mentions an Aeschylean *Lycurgeia*, consisting of an *Edonoi* ("Edonians"), *Bassarides* ("Bacchants"), *Neaniskoi* ("Youths"), and the satyr play *Lycurgus* (schol. *ad* Ar. *Thesm.* 134), and "a second Dionysiac trilogy, including a *Semele* and *Pentheus* is highly probable."[14] Other incontrovertibly Theban or Dionysiac titles attributed to Aeschylus include an *Athamas*, *Bacchae*, "Nurses of Dionysus" (*Dionysou trophoi*, possibly a satyr play), and "Wool-carders" (*Xantriai*, a play to which I shall return). Sophocles' Theban repertoire is more restricted: in addition to the surviving Theban plays (*Antigone*, *Oedipus Tyrannus*, *Oedipus at Colonus*), we hear of two other plays likely set at Thebes (*Amphitryon*, *Epigoni*) and three on presumably Dionysiac subjects (two plays entitled *Athamas*, and a satyr play, *Dionysiscus*, "Little Dionysus"). Euripides' Theban total is eight (*Bacchae*, *Phoenissae*, *Supplices*, *Ino*, *Cadmus*, *Oedipus*, *Antigone*, *Antiope*), of which his posthumously produced *Bacchae* articulates most fully and most self-consciously the Dionysian origins of the genre. The Roman adaptors of Attic tragedy also wrote on specifically Dionysiac subjects: Naevius a *Lycurgus*; Ennius an *Athamas*; Pacuvius, an *Antiopa* and a *Pentheus*; and Accius, an *Epigoni*, a *Bacchae*, a *Phoenissae*, an *Amphitryo*, an *Athamas*, a *Stasiastae* or *Tropaeum liberi*, and a *Thebais*.

This survey of the Athenian and Roman production of plays that centre either on Thebes or Dionysus (or both) lays bare Ovid's thematic debt to tragic models in his Theban narrative. Within the two-book compass of his "Thebaid," Ovid narrates at length the tales of some seven Theban charac-ters, most of them well represented in the Attic (and later Roman) tragic canon: Cadmus (*Met.* 3.3–136, 4.563–603), Actaeon (3.137–252), Semele (3.253–315), Pentheus (3.511–733), the Minyads (4.1–415), Athamas and Ino (4.416–562). In addition, Ovid makes pointed allusion in these books to Lycurgus (4.22–23), himself a popular subject of the Greek dramatists and their Roman heirs,[15] and the poet also pays considerable attention to Teire-sias, the blind seer who features prominently in many a Theban tragedy.

---

12   Dodds 1960, xxviii.
13   Zeitlin 1990, 130–67.
14   Winnington-Ingram 1989, 30 n. 4.
15   Plays about Acrisius are attributed to Naevius (*Danae*); about Lycurgus, to Naevius (*Lycurgus*) and to Accius (*Stasiastae*, or *Tropaeum Liberi*).

Summary of Ovid's "Thebaid" (*Met.* 3.1–4.603)

3.1–137:   Cadmus
              Themes: exile (3.4–8); city-foundation (3.8–13, 129–32); man
              vs. beast (3.26–98); spectacle; recognition and reversal
              (*dum spatium uictor uicti considerat hostis,* | *uox subito audita*
              est … |*… 'quid, Agenore nate, peremptum* | *serpentem spectas?*
              et tu spectabere serpens,' 3.95–8)

3.138–252   Actaeon
              Themes: city vs. country (3.204–5); man vs. beast (3.143–54;
              206–50); wandering (3.142, 146–7, 174–6); the encounter with
              Artemis (3.155–98); spectacle/voyeurism; reversal
              (hunter ⟶ hunted)

3.253–315   Semele
              Themes: city (3.273–309, esp. 274, 305–6); the vengeance of Juno
              (3.273–88);the encounter with Juno (3.253–72); the encounter
              with Jupiter (3.288–309); recognition and reversal
              (hybris, 3.279 ⟶ nemesis, 3.308–9)

3.316–38   Teiresias
              Themes: wandering in woods (3.324–5); gender reversal
              (3.326–31); voy eurism the vengeance of Juno (3.333–5);
              blindness and insight (3.336–8)

3.339–510   Echo and Narcissus
              Echo
                        Themes: woods (3.393–4, 400–1); vengeance of Juno
                        (3.361–9); reversal (protector of lovers,
                        3.361–4 ⟶ consumed by love, 3.370–401)

              Narcissus
                        Themes: wandering in the woods (3.370); man vs. beast;
                        reversals: hunter (3.356, 378) – hunted (3.371–2; beloved
                        – lover; the intervention of Nemesis (3.402–6);
                        the encounter at the pool (3.407–510)

3.511–733   Pentheus
              Themes: city vs. country (3.531–61, 582–700 vs. 3.702–10);
              blindness and insight (3.514–25); spectacle/voyeurism; the
              encounter with the god's devotées (*sparagmos*, 3.519–23, 715–31)

4.1–415   Minyeides
                 Themes: city vs. country (4.32–5, 389–414); the encounter with
                 Bacchus (4.389–415; rejected, 4.31–5, 272–3)

    4.55–388 Tales of the Minyeides

              4.55–166   *Pyramus et Thisbe*
                          Themes: city foundation (4.57–8); city
                          (4.55–92) vs. country (4.93–166); man vs. beast

              4.169–270   *Solis amores* (Leuconoe)
                          Themes: city (Venus and Mars, 4.174–86;
                          Leuco thoe, 4.212-33) vs. country (Leucothoe,
                          4.239–40; Clytie, 4.256–70); the vengeance of
                          Venus (4.190–203); the encounter with the
                          divine (4.218–33, 241–55); spectacle and
                          voyeurism; reversals (watcher ⟶ watched,
                          4.264–70; lover ⟶ beloved, 4.234–5, 270)

              4.276–388   *Salmacis* (Alcithoe)
                          Themes: city vs. country (4.294–7); wandering
                          (4.292–8); the encounter with the nymph
                          (4.356–79); spectacle/ voyeurism ephebe –
                          puer ~ *semiuir* (4.292, 316, 320, 329, 380–6)

4.416–562   Athamas and Ino-Leucothoe
             Themes: city (4.416, 437–45, 449–50, 453, 484, 486–90, 510–12)
             vs. country (4.513–30); man vs. beast (4.513–30); the vengeance
             of Juno (4.420–80, 547–62); the encounter with Tisiphone
             (4.481–509)

4.563–603   Cadmus
             Themes: exil (4.564–8); city vs. country (4.567–603); man vs.
             beast; the vengeance of the gods (4.571–5); reversal
             (snake-killer, 3.95, 4.571–3, ⟶ snake, 4.576–98)

Even the final episode of Book Four, the rescue of Andromeda by Perseus – which stands, strictly speaking, as a coda to the book and outside of the "Thebaid" proper (4.663–803) – contributes to the dramatic colour of this section of the *Metamorphoses*, for it too was a common subject of tragedy.[16]

As befits such popular subjects of tragic drama, these tales exemplify the themes of Athenian tragedy. The first of the disasters to come upon the House of Cadmus, for example, Actaeon's fatal fascination with the hunt, recalls the hunts of the Athenian stage, both literal (the Eumenides' tracking of Orestes at the outset of the final play of the *Oresteia*) and metaphorical (Oedipus' energetic hunt for Laius' killer in Sophocles' *Oedipus Tyrannus*). The series of fatal encounters with the divine – Actaeon with Artemis, Semele and Teiresias with Juno and Jupiter, Pentheus and the Minyads with Dionysus, Athamas and Ino with Juno – repeatedly dramatize the conflict between man and god that structures so many tragedies (*Bacchae*, *Hippolytus*, *Eumenides*, *Ajax*, among others). The quintessential tragic theme of blindness and insight – literalised to gruesome effect in Sophocles' *Oedipus Tyrannus* – informs every tale in the Ovidian sequence, from Actaeon and Semele to Teiresias and Pentheus, including even the otherwise anomalous Narcissus episode. Finally, recognition and reversal, which so often instantiate the tragic themes of blindness and insight, structure each episode in the sequence starting with the framing tale of Cadmus himself, who kills a serpent to found the city of Thebes but ends up becoming a serpent and going into exile.

Ovid's concentrated focus on the Dionysian themes and primal subjects of Greek drama in this section of the *Metamorphoses* emerges still more clearly from comparison with the conventional treatment of Thebes in ancient epic.[17] Theban epos seems traditionally to have avoided material associated with the arch anti-Apollonian Dionysus himself in favour of the more martial themes of the Seven against Thebes and the Epigoni, and Propertius' allusions to the *Thebaid* of Ponticus (1.7.1–2, 17–18) suggest that contemporary Augustan epic shared this bias. Ovid, by contrast, saturates his Theban narrative with tales drawn from the tragic repertoire and specifically

---

16 Euripides' production of 412 was the most popular, but plays of this title are also ascribed to Sophocles, Phrynichus and Lycophron among the Greek tragedians, while Roman plays with this title are attributed to Livius, Ennius, and Accius.

17 The archaic Theban cycle consisted of an *Oedipodea*, *Thebaid* (apparently treating the Seven against Thebes), and *Epigoni*: see Lesky 1966, 80–1. In the classical period, Antimachus narrated the story of Oedipus and the Seven against Thebes in Homeric style: see Wyss 1974[1936] and Lombardi 1993. In the Flavian period, Statius' Latin epic *Thebaid* seems to have enjoyed critical and popular success at Rome: see Juv. 7.82–7 and cf. Stat. *Theb.* 12.812–15.

associated with Dionysus, the patron god of the theatre, while he carefully avoids the martial themes associated with Theban epic.[18]

As Hardie shows, Ovid reworks the opening of the *Aeneid* particularly closely in his portrait of the exiled Cadmus wandering the Mediterranean before consulting the oracle at Delphi to learn where to settle (*Met.* 3.6–9), on the model of the exiled Aeneas consulting the oracle of Apollo at Delos (*Aen.* 3.84–9).[19] But Ovid follows even more closely Euripides' account of Cadmus' foundation of Thebes in the *Phoenissae* (638–75),[20] and he explicitly signals his engagement with tragedy soon after when Cadmus, having killed the snake of Mars that attacked his men, hears a disembodied voice prophesy his own transformation into a snake (*Met.* 3.97–8): "*quid, Agenore nate, peremptum | serpentem spectas? et tu spectabere serpens*" ("Why, son of Agenor, do you stare at the dead snake? You too will be seen in the form of a snake").[21] This prophecy echoes that given to Cadmus at the conclusion of Euripides' *Bacchae* by Dionysus as *deus ex machina* (*Ba.* 1330): δράκων γενήσῃ μεταβαλών ("undergoing a metamorphosis, you will become a snake").

A famous simile in the following episode confirms the generic significance of the allusion here. Like Vergil, who marks an important debt to tragedy in the Dido episode by comparing her to characters from the tragic stage (*Aen.* 4.469–73),[22] Ovid signals the importance of tragic conventions in his "Thebaid" in a famous simile that compares the birth of the Spartoi, the Sown Men who emerge from the earth after Cadmus sows the slain serpent's teeth, to the figures represented on the stage curtain which rise from the ground when the curtain is raised (*Met.* 3.111–14):

> sic, ubi tolluntur festis aulaea theatris,
> surgere signa solent primumque ostendere uultus,
> cetera paulatim, placidoque educta tenore
> tota patent imoque pedes in margine ponunt.

> [Thus, when the curtains are raised in the theatres on holidays, the figures are accustomed to rise and show first their faces, and the rest little by little, until drawn up with steady motion, whole figures lie revealed and place their feet on the very edge of the curtain.]

---

18 On Dionysiac myth as the original subject of the drama, see Dodds 1960, xxviii–xxxiii and Seaford 1996, 26–52. Hardie (1990, 226) has recently emphasized the crucial importance of tragic models in the whole of Ovid's "Thebaid."

19 Hardie 1990, 226–7; cf. Ovid's reprise of the motif in Pentheus' speech, *profugos posuistis ... penates* (*Met.* 3.539).

20 Accius adapted Euripides' play for the Roman stage.

21 I quote the text of Ovid's *Metamorphoses* from Tarrant 2004; translations are adapted from Miller [rev. Goold] 1977.

22 Hardie 1990, 226 n.14.

Ovid thereby "glosses," as Alessandro Barchiesi puts it, his literary "operations outside the epic code."[23]

Ovid comments on the specifically Dionysiac origins of the drama[24] in the
Pentheus episode (itself heavily indebted to tragic models as D'Anna and others have shown), by implicitly inscribing a literary contest between the genres
of epic and tragedy in the confrontation between Pentheus and Dionysus. Pentheus overvalues his descent from Echion (3.513, 531, 701), one of the Spartoi
sprung from the teeth of the serpent of Mars, and repeatedly contrasts his
martial ancestry and morals with Dionysus' softness and effeminacy (3.531–7,
540, 553–6). When Pentheus goes to Cithaeron to spy on the rites of the god,
he is compared to a horse fired to battle by the war trumpet (3.704–7):

> ut fremit acer equus, cum bellicus aere canoro
> signa dedit tubicen, pugnaeque adsumit amorem,
> Penthea sic ictus longis ululatibus aether
> mouit et audito clamore recanduit ira.

> [As a keen horse rages, when the war-trumpet of sonorous bronze sounds the signal,
> and he is fired by love of battle, so was Pentheus stirred by the long-drawn cries
> ringing in the ether, and his anger kindled at the sound of the clash.]

The simile is drawn from martial epic,[25] and stamps Pentheus as a heroic
figure, especially in conjunction with the anger that traditionally motivates
epic action (3.577, 693). Pentheus, however, is unable to sustain the role
of epic hero to which he aspires, for on Mount Cithaeron he finds himself
in the theatre not of war but of Dionysus (3.708–9): *monte fere medio est,
cingentibus ultima siluis, | purus ab arboribus spectabilis undique campus*
("nearly in the middle of the mountain was a field, its edges girt with woods,
but itself free of trees and visible from every side"). Ovid's emphasis on the
visibility of the setting of Pentheus' demise, continued in the following lines
where the watching Pentheus is himself the object of others' gaze (*hic oculis
illum cernentem sacra profanis | prima uidet*, 3.710–11; cf. 3.725), cannot
fail to evoke the Greek θέατρον, literally "place for seeing" (*Schauplatz*),
the setting in which the drama was staged.[26]

In the rest of the Theban narrative, however, spectacle tends to take the
form not of the staged action familiar from theatrical performance in the
ancient world, but rather of voyeurism. Pentheus' "staged" demise is itself
the reversal and result of his voyeurism already in Euripides' play, as in
Ovid's version of the myth. But voyeurism is also an important theme in the

---

23   Barchiesi 1993, 353.
24   Ovid alludes to Dionysus' patronage of tragedy already in his earliest poetry collec-
     tion: see *Am.* 3.15.
25   Hom. *Il.* 6.506–11, 15.263–8; Ap. Rhod. 3.1259–62; Enn. *Ann.* 535–9 Sk; Verg. *Aen.*
     11.492–7.
26   For a different analysis of spectacle in the episode, see Feldherr 1997.

"Thebaid" as a whole, for it occurs in the Actaeon, Teiresias, and Echo and Narcissus episodes, as well as in the tales of the Minyads in book four to which I now turn.

2

Hardie does not discuss the relationship of the episode of the daughters of Minyas or their tales to the Theban narrative in which it is set, but as the longest single episode in the sequence it would seem to constitute an important test-case for the validity of his thesis. The episode has traditionally been felt to constitute a digression from the overarching narrative of the foundation and precipitate decline of Thebes, for the tale concerns a family unrelated to the House of Cadmus at Thebes and it is set at some distance from Thebes in Bœotian Orchomenus. Ovid, however, insists on its relevance to the Theban context (4.416), and the following episode of Athamas and Ino, which concerns Cadmus' daughter, son-in-law and grandsons, is itself set in Orchomenos, where Athamas was king. The Minyads' transgression and punishment, moreover, rehearse those of Pentheus, whose tale immediately precedes the episode. Furthermore, Greek versions of the Pentheus story include among those who spurn the new god – and who are accordingly punished by him – Semele's sisters Agave (Pentheus' mother), Autonoe (Actaeon's mother), and Ino (Eur. *Ba.* 26–42).[27] Ovid does not include this part of the Pentheus myth in book three, but he retains the motif of a trio of sisters who spurn the god in his account of the much less well-known myth of the daughters of Minyas. In its structure too the Minyad sequence mimics the gross imbalance between frame and infill that Hardie identifies in the Theban narrative as a whole, speaking of its "typically Ovidian imbalance between the frame, which tells ... the ... foundation legend, and the infill with its proliferation of wilderness settings."[28] This imbalance of frame narrative to inner narrative is also striking in the episode of the daughters of Minyas, whose tales occupy over two hundred and thirty lines while the poet devotes only about fifty to the sisters' impiety and transformation (*Met.* 4.1–4, 31–54, 389–415).

The sisters are otherwise known only from three Greek writers of imperial date, although we know that the story was treated by Nicander in his *Transformations* (Nic. *apud* Ant. Lib. 10).[29] The mythographers relate that

27 Cf. *Ba.* 811–15, 829, 838, 912–16, 955–6, 981, 1047–50, 158–62, 1075.
28 Hardie 1990, 224.
29 Ant. Lib. *Met.* 10, following Corinna and Nicander *Het.* 4; Plut. *Quaes. Gr.* 38; Ael. *Var. Hist.* 3.42.

the three daughters of Minyas were excessively devoted to woolworking and its patroness, Athena, and reviled the other women of Orchomenos for abandoning the city and going off to the mountains to celebrate the rites of Dionysus; the tale thus constitutes a feminine doublet of the story of Pentheus, who in Ovid's version (as in Euripides) reviles his citizens for the same reason (*Met.* 3.531–61). As in the case of Pentheus, the spurned god grows angry and causes the sisters to go mad, appearing to them successively as maiden, bull, lion, and leopard, all standard features of the god's iconography.[30] At the same time their looms begin to drip with milk and wine. In their madness the sisters draw lots to contribute a sacrifice to the god, and when the lot falls to Leucippe, they tear her son Hippasus to pieces, then rush off to join the maenads in the mountains, where Hermes finally transforms the sisters into birds (a bat, an owl, and another nocturnal bird which has not been identified). Tales of divinity spurned are frequent in Greek literature, of course, but are particularly characteristic of the mythic material associated with Dionysus and purveyed to the audiences of Greek tragedy; it has therefore been suggested that Aeschylus' lost Dionysiac tragedy *Xantriai* ("Wool-carders") dealt with the daughters of Minyas.[31]

Ovid opens his account with a scene indebted to hymnic invocations of the god in Roman tragedy, contrasting the Minyads' impious rejection of Bacchus at the outset of Book 4 with the piety of the Theban women, who invoke the god in lengthy recitation of his titles (4.11–17):

> turaque dant Bacchumque vocant Bromiumque Lyaeumque
> ignigenamque satumque iterum solumque bimatrem;
> additur his Nyseus indetonsusque Thyoneus
> et cum Lenaeo genialis consitor uuae
> Nycteliusque Eleleusque parens et Iacchus et Euhan
> et quae praeterea per Graias plurima gentes
> nomina, Liber, habes …

> [They bring incense, and invoke the god by his titles 'Bacchus,' 'Thunderer,' and 'Loosener,' calling him fire-born and twice-born, who alone has two mothers; to these titles are added god 'of Nysa,' unshorn son of Thyone (Semele), along with god 'of the wine-vat' and sower of the cheering grape, god 'of nocturnal rites,' father Eleleus, Iacchus and Euhan, and the very many names you hold in addition, Liber, throughout the Greek nations.]

The poet here assimilates the Theban women worshipping the new god Bacchus to tragic choruses of Bacchantes hymning the god of drama (αἰεὶ |

---

30 Bull: Aesch. fr. 23, Soph. fr. 959; Eur. *Ba.* 100, 920–2, 1017, 1159; Plut. *Mor.* 299b; and see further *LIMC* III.1.435–6 s.v. "Dionysos tauromorphos," *ibid.* 440–1; and Frenkel 1978. Lion: *h.Hom.* 7.44, Eur. *Ba.* 1019, Philostr. *Imag.* 1.18. Panther: *LIMC* III.1.430–4, 457–8, 554. Maiden: *LIMC* III.2. fig. 50.
31 Seaford 1996, 26 nn. 6, 8, 9, and 37 n. 49.

Διόνυσον ὑμνήσω, Eur. *Ba.* 71), for they invoke the god in the hymnic style and ritual language familiar from tragedy. A fragment of Ennius' *Athamas* furnishes a model for Ovid's diction here (*trag.* LII 120–4 Jocelyn):[32]

> His erat in ore Bromius, his Bacchus pater,
> illis Lyaeus uitis inuentor sacrae.
> Tum pariter †euhan euhium†[33]
> ignotus iuuenum coetus alterna uice
> inibat alacris Bacchico insultans modo.
>
> [On their lips were the titles of the god, 'Bromius,' 'Father Bacchus,' 'Loosener,' 'discoverer of the sacred vine.' Then an unknown band of youths in their turn entered swiftly, uttering the god's ritual cries and calling him by the titles 'Euhan' and 'Euhium,' dancing a Bacchic reel.]

Even the context of the Ennian lines is relevant, for they are attributed to the tragedy *Athamas*, whose hero is the subject of the episode immediately following the Minyads' transformation. A line from Accius' *Bacchae*, for which there is no model in Euripides' play of the same name, may also influence the Ovidian hymn (Accius *trag.* 204–5 W): *O Dionyse | pater optime uitisator Semela genitus, Euhie!* ("O Dionysus, father, best, vine-sower, born of Semele, Euhius!").[34]

Despite the conspicuous display of tragic diction with which the episode opens, Ovid has drastically curtailed the prominence of tragic themes in the Minyad-episode, although he naturally retains the metamorphosis: the sisters do not draw lots, they have no children, and they indulge in no Bacchic rending of flesh. Nonetheless, the sisters' impious rejection of Bacchus' rites, expressed in their refusal to leave the confines of the house and abandon their domestic labours (*Met.* 4.32–5), brings upon them the god's vengeance. Since they will not participate in his worship (as even Pentheus does, albeit inadvertently, at the end of Book 3), the god brings his rites to them (4.389–404):

> Finis erat dictis, et adhuc Minyeia proles
> urget opus spernitque deum festumque profanat,   390
> tympana cum subito non apparentia raucis
> obstrepuere sonis et adunco tibia cornu
> tinnulaque aera sonant; redolent murraeque crocique,
> resque fide maior, coepere uirescere telae
> inque hederae faciem pendens frondescere uestis;   395

---

32 Quoted by Charisius, G.L. I, 241, 3ff. K.

33 On the text, see Jocelyn 1967 ad loc.

34 Like the Ennian passage, which reports the worship of Dionysus by his followers, the Accian fragment comes from an invocation of the god and includes reference not only to Dionysus' patronage of the grape, but also to his birth from Semele. Like the Ennian and Ovidian hymns, the Accius fragment concludes with a cult-title of the god derived from the ritual cry "euhoe."

pars abit in uites et, quae modo fila fuerunt,
palmite mutantur; de stamine pampinus exit;
purpura fulgorem pictis accommodat uuis.
iamque dies exactus erat tempusque subibat
quod tu nec tenebras nec possis dicere lucem,   400
sed cum luce tamen dubiae confinia noctis;
tecta repente quati pinguesque ardere uidentur
lampades et rutilis conlucere ignibus aedes
falsaque saeuarum simulacra ululare ferarum.

[Alcithoe finished speaking, and still the daughters of Minyas plied their task, spurn-
ing the god and profaning the holiday, when suddenly unseen tambourines sounded
harshly, and the flute of curved horn and the clanging bronze cymbals rang out;
myrrh and saffron scented the air, and past all belief, the loom began to grow green
and the cloth hanging on it to turn into the foliage of ivy; part became grape-vines,
and what had just now been threads were transformed into vine-shoots; from the
warp came forth vine foliage; purple matched its gleam to the depicted grapes. The
day was already finished, and the time was coming on which you could call neither
shadows nor light, but nonetheless the boundaries of hesitant night with day: suddenly the halls seemed to shake, the oil lamps to blaze, the house to be lit with red
flames, and false images of wild beasts to howl.]

The music and rhythm of the sacred cult objects, the fragrances associated
with Dionysiac worship, and the ivy, emblematic plant of the god which
twines about the Minyads' tapestries, all imply Bacchic epiphany, as do the
strange half-light and lights in the house (4.399–403),[35] and the howling of
phantom-beasts which terrifies the sisters (404). These Dionysian symbols
can all be paralleled from the god's earlier appearances in the Theban narrative, and are especially prominent in his epiphany to the Tyrrhenian sailors
in Book Three (3.658–69), and the hymn to the god at the beginning of Book
Four (4.11–30).[36]

The epiphany of the god culminates in the sisters' transformation into
bats as punishment for their impiety (4.405–15):

fumida iamdudum latitant per tecta sorores   405
diuersaeque locis ignes ac lumina uitant;
dumque petunt tenebras, paruos membrana per artus
porrigitur tenuique includit bracchia penna.
nec qua perdiderint ueterem ratione figuram
scire sinunt tenebrae. non illas pluma leuauit,   410
sustinuere tamen se perlucentibus alis.
conataeque loqui minimam et pro corpore uocem
emittunt peraguntque leues stridore querellas;

---

35   For this as a sign of epiphany, cf. Hinds 1988, 9 and Seaford 1996, 202 on Eur. *Ba.*
     630–1: "The mystic light appearing in the darkness was identified with deity."
36   Cf. 3.528, 532–7, 542, 555–6, 706–7, 732.

tectaque, non siluas celebrant lucemque perosae
nocte uolant seroque tenent a uespere nomen.   415

[While the sisters hide in the smoking halls they avoid the fires and lights in different places, and while they seek the shadows, a membrane stretches over their
slender limbs and covers their arms in thin wings; nor did the shadows allow them
to understand how they lost their former shape: feathers do not lift them, yet they
hold themselves aloft on translucent wings, and when they try to speak they produce
the slightest of sounds, in proportion to their bodies, and utter shrill complaints in a
squeak. They frequent houses, not woods, and hating the daylight, they fly by night
and take their name from the late evening.]

Their metamorphosis has often been interpreted as a final index of the sisters'
continuing hostility towards Bacchus and rejection of his cult, since in their
avian form they continue to shun the wilderness setting of the god's rites.
Their new form, however, takes its name from a new feature of their character as bats (the Latin word for which was *uespertiliones*), their avoidance
of daylight (*seroque tenent a uespere nomen*, 4.415). The association of bats
with night, stressed by Ovid here (4.415) is still more evident in the Greek
word for bat, νυκτερός ("night-squeaker"), derived from νύξ ("night") and
τρίζω ("make a shrill sound"), which Ovid glosses by his use of the Latin
cognates *nocte* (4.415) and *stridore* (4.413). In fact, the sisters' avoidance
of the daylight seems compatible with at least one aspect of Dionysiac cult,
namely its association with night celebration, an association alluded to by
Ovid in his uses of the god's title Nyctelius, "whose rites are accomplished
by night" (4.15).[37] Moreover, their afterlife as bats may assimilate them to
Dionysus' worshippers in a second way. Aristotle called the bat a night-ani-
mal, recognising that the bat is not exactly a bird; but throughout antiquity,
from Homer to the elder Pliny, bats are popularly described as birds,[38] and
Antoninus Liberalis, summarising Nicander's version in which the sisters
are turned into a bat and two different kinds of night owl, simply states
that all three were transformed into birds (εἰς ὄρνιθας, Ant. Lib. *Met.* 10.4).
Euripides refers in the *Bacchae* to Maenads imitating birds (*Ba.* 748ff.),[39]
and there is some evidence for a connection between birds and Maenads in

---

37   The epithet is derived from the celebration of Dionysus' rites at night; cf. Eur. *Ba.*
     425, 486, 862; Paus. 1.40.6; Plut. *de E Delph* 9.389A; O. *Ars* 1.567, *Met.* 6.588–90;
     Liv. 39.8.6, 36.13.9, 36.13.10; for night festivals, cf. Plut. *Mor.* 364f, 672a, etc.; for
     the title Nyctelius, cf. Plut. *Mor.* 389a, etc. At *Ars* 1.567 O. supplies an etymologi-
     cal gloss: *Nycteliumque patrem nocturnaque sacra* (i.e., Gk. τέλη). The nocturnal
     celebration of the god's rites was a continuing cause for concern among the Roman
     ruling classes, who passed the *Senatus consultum de Bacchanalibus* in 186 BCE to
     control an outbreak of violence associated with the celebration of the cult in south-
     ern Italy: see *CIL* 8.196 [= *ILS* 18], Livy 39.8–18, and cf. V. *Aen.* 7.376–407.
38   Cf. Hom. *Od.* 24.6; Plin. *NH* 10.168, 11.164, 232; Isid. *Orig.* 12.7.36.
39   *Ba.* 748, 957, 1365.

Roman tragedy as well (Naevius, *Lycurgus* fr. 30–2W): *alii | sublime in altos saltus inlicite … | ubi bipedes uolucres lino linquant lumina*, "Go, others of you, lure them up on high | To the lofty glades, … wherein these hopping birds | In flaxen toils may leave the light of day"). Brief, then, though Ovid's version of the tale of the Minyads' impiety and punishment is, the narrative itself seems to be constructed with constant reference not to the *Aeneid* but rather to tragic models and Dionysiac themes.

3

As I noted earlier, however, Ovid shifts the focus of the myth away from the Minyads themselves to the stories they tell one another as they weave. Their impious rejection of Bacchus thereby becomes a pretext for a sequence of amatory tales set in the fabled East: Pyramus and Thisbe in Babylon (*Met.* 4.55–166), the loves of the Sun in Persia (4.169–270), and Salmacis and Hermaphroditus in Caria (4.285–388). The Eastern geography of the Minyads' tales is particularly ironic in the light of the Theban women's celebration of Bacchus' Eastern victories, to which the poet refers in the hymn that opens Book Four (4.20–1); we may compare, in particular, the first sister's *Oriens* in the opening line of her Pyramus et Thisbe (4.56). Indeed we shall see that Dionysiac themes and imagery saturate the Minyads' amatory tales, and constitute throughout an unsettling reminder of the god's peculiar powers of intoxication.

The tale of Pyramus and Thisbe, narrated by the first (unnamed) sister, is usually discussed in relation to the generic conventions of the ancient romance, but I think we can adduce some evidence to bolster Hardie's thesis of the centrality of foundation narrative to Ovid's Theban tales, as well as to support his observation of the pervasive use of tragic themes in the sequence (4.55–8):

> Pyramus et Thisbe, iuuenum pulcherrimus alter,
> altera, quas Oriens habuit, praelata puellis,
> contiguas tenuere domos, ubi dicitur altam
> coctilibus muris cinxisse Semiramis urbem.

> [Pyramus and Thisbe, the one the most beautiful of youths, the other the loveliest of all the maidens of the East, lived in houses side by side, where Semiramis is said to have encircled a lofty city with brick walls.]

Ovid's internal narrator opens her tale by emphasizing its metropolitan setting: the Minyad's reference to Semiramis' foundation of Babylon gestures towards the narrative context of the tale in Ovid's "Thebaid," briefly recapitulating the episode's frame in *ktistic* epic, although she will highlight elegiac,[40] comic,[41] and especially novelistic conventions against this urban backdrop.[42] Conventional features of the ancient romance in the episode include the opening conjunction of the names of the young lovers,[43] their superlative beauty,[44] the fabulous Eastern setting,[45] and the reference to Semiramis (legendary queen of Babylon and heroine of the Ninos-romance), but the tale also displays considerable thematic and imagistic overlap with the sphere of Dionysus.[46]

An early and apparently harmless example is the superlative beauty of the pair of adolescent lovers described at the outset (4.55–6). The Minyad's description here is clearly indebted to the conventions of romance, but at the opening of Book Four it is Bacchus whose superlative youthful beauty is hymned, in terms applicable to both sexes (4.17–20):[47]

> … tibi enim inconsumpta iuuenta est,
> tu puer aeternus, tu formosissmus alto
> conspiceris caelo; tibi, cum sine cornibus adstas,
> uirgineum caput est …

> [For to you belongs everlasting boyhood, you are an eternal youth, you are admired as the most lovely in the lofty sky; your face is maidenly, when you stand before us without horns …]

The Theban women's praise of Bacchus' feminine beauty here recalls the description of the god's maidenly beauty by his devoté in the preceding book (*uirginea puerum ducit per litora forma*, 3.607), and can be paralleled in ancient literature and art from the late fifth century B.C.E. on.[48] Thus although the first Minyad rejects the adolescent beauty of the dangerous god of the theatre to tell the tale of a beautiful pair of adolescent lovers drawn from elegy and romance, the ominous presence of Dionysus lurks in the background to her narrative and constrains it increasingly forcefully as she proceeds.

Pyramus and Thisbe decide to elude their parents and meet by night under a mulberry tree near the tomb of Ninos outside the city (4.84–92, 99, 111). Nocturnal action is another staple of the romance genre, but the night

---

40 Perraud 1983–84; Knox 1986, 35–7; cf. Due 1974, 126–7.
41 Holzberg 1988.
42 Due 1974, 126–7; Newlands 1986.
43 Cf. *Chaereas and Callirhoe*; *Parthenope and Metiochus*; *Daphnis and Chloe*; *Leucippe and Clitophon*.
44 Cf. *Chaereas and Callirhoe* 1.1, Ach. Tat. *Leucippe* 1.4, [Long.] *Daphnis and Chloe* 1.7, Hel. *Aeth.* 1.2, etc.
45 Cf. the Ninos-romance; the Sesonchosis-romance; Xenophon's *Ephesiaca*; *Leucippe and Clitophon* 1.1; Iamblichus' *Babyloniaca*; Heliodorus' *Aethiopica;* etc.
46 Curley 1999, 217–20 shows "how fundamental tragic coding is to the episode."
47 Cf. *uirginea puerum ducit per litora forma* (*Met.* 3.607).
48 Cf. *Met.* 3.555–6; Eur. *Ba.* 235–6, 353, 453–9; Aesch. *Edonians* (fr. 61), Ar. *Thesm.* 134–40, Aesch. *Theoroi* fr. 78a68; cf. Liv. 39.15.9.

setting is also a prominent feature of Dionysiac worship to which Ovid alludes at the outset of the book with the god's epithet Nyctelius. When the young lovers abandon the urban setting of Babylon for the world of untamed nature beyond the city walls, their love takes a decidedly tragic turn. Outside the comparative safety of the city and their parents' guardianship, the youngsters encounter the terrors of untamed nature, a more obviously Dionysiac theme, in the form of a lioness which comes from the kill to slake her thirst at a nearby spring (4.96–8):

> … uenit ecce recenti
> caede leaena boum spumantes oblita rictus
> depositura sitim uicini fontis in unda

> [Look, a lioness comes, her foaming jaws smeared with recently slaughtered cattle, to slake her thirst at the water of a near-by spring.]

Bacchus is associated with wild cats both in the preceding book (3.668–9) and in the hymn that opens the fourth (4.25), and as early as the Homeric Hymn to Dionysus the god himself is represented as taking the form of a lion to threaten the sailors who have kidnapped him (*h. Hom.* 7.44–8).[49] Moreover the "sure traces of a wild beast" (*uestigia certa ferae*, 4.105–6) Pyramus sees when he arrives at the rendezvous anticipate the "phantoms of savage beasts" (*saeuarum simulacra ferarum*, 4.404) whose howling terrorises the Minyads just before the god transforms them into bats; and they also recall the *simulacraque inania lyncum* which surround Dionysus when he reveals himself to the Tyrrhenian sailors before their transformation (3.668).[50]

More Dionysiac still is the suggestion of dismemberment (σπαραγμός) and the eating of raw flesh (ὠμωφαγία) in Thisbe's torn and bloodied cloak (4.103–4, 107–8), and Pyramus' despairing invitation to the lions to rend and devour his body (4.112–14): *nostrum diuellite corpus | et scelerata fero consumite uiscera morsu, | o quicumque sub hac habitatis rupe leones!* Gruesome descriptions of blood and intimations of mangled flesh recur throughout the episode, from the bloody mouth of the lioness to the blood-spattered tree under which Pyramus kills himself (4.125–7, 160–1), and Thisbe's death by a sword still warm from Pyramus' blood (4.163). The most spectacularly bloody scene, however, is the graphic description of Pyramus' self-inflicted death (4.118–24):

> "accipe nunc" inquit "nostri quoque sanguinis haustus."
> quoque erat accinctus, demisit in ilia ferrum;
> nec mora, feruenti moriens e uulnere traxit.

---

49 For Dionysus' association with the lion, see Dodds 1960, xviii and cf. n. 31 above.
50 Cf. Athamas' Erinys-inspired delusion (*Met.* 4.514–19): '*hic modo cum gemina uisa est mihi prole leaena*', | *utque ferae sequitur uestigia coniugis amens | deque sinu matris ridentem et parua Learchum | bracchia tendentem rapit et bis terque per auras | more rotat fundae rigidoque infantia saxo | discutit ora ferox.*

ut iacuit resupinus humo, cruor emicat alte,
non aliter quam cum uitiato fistula plumbo
scinditur et tenues stridente foramine longe
eiaculatur aquas atque ictibus aera rumpit.[51]

["Now," he said, "drink my blood too!" And he plunged the sword which he wore
into his groin, and without delay, dying, drew it from the warm wound. As he lay
on his back on the ground, his blood spurts high, just as when a pipe with a crack in
the lead is split, and spurts slender streams of water far and wide through the hissing
opening, and strikes the air with its jets.]

If Thisbe's apparent death lies fully within the generic parameters of the ancient novel, Pyramus' real death breaks sharply with novelistic conventions
to introduce a familiar motif of tragedy, the suicide of a protagonist.[52] What
is generally taken to be a characteristically Ovidian excess in the simile has
an intriguing parallel in Ennius' description of the suicide of Ajax in his
tragedy of the same name (Ennius, *trag.* XII 14 Jocelyn): *misso sanguine
tepido tullii efflantes uolant* ("with gushing warm blood the spouting jets
fly"). Moreover, the Minyad's use of the phrase *tenues stridente foramine
longe ... aquas* (*Met.* 4.123–4) anticipates the shrill sound she and her sisters
will emit as bats (cf. *stridore*, 4.413), while it also recalls the poet's description of the boxwood flute among the paraphernalia of Dionysiac worship
(*longoque foramine buxus*, 4.30).[53] So too she remarks that Thisbe grows
"paler than boxwood" at the sight of her mortally wounded lover (4.133–5):
*tremebunda uidet pulsare cruentum | membra solum retroque pedem tulit
oraque buxo | pallidiora gerens* ("she sees his trembling limbs writhe on the
bloody ground, and takes a step back, her face paler than boxwood"). The
Minyad thus applies to the description of Pyramus' death throes a simile
that recalls the materials of Dionysiac worship and foreshadows her own
transformation.

Finally, we may consider the relation of the first sister's (carefully
thought-out) choice of story to the larger narrative context of Ovid's "Thebaid." Having passed in review three obscure Babylonian tales out of a Callimachean preference for an unfamiliar story (4.43–51),[54] she finally selects
that of the mulberry, an aetiological tale that explains the dark colour of the

---

51   On the Lucretian overtones of this simile, see Newlands 1986 and Schmitzer 1992,
     529, 532, 535.
52   Katsouris 1976; Seidensticker 1982; Zeitlin 1996, 350–2.
53   Cf. *ubi curua choros indixit tibia Bacchi*, V. *Aen.* 11.737.
54   On the Babylonian tales, see Perdrizet 1932 and Duke 1971. They share a number
     of thematic affinities with the tale of Pyramus and Thisbe. Semiramis was the leg-
     endary founder of Babylon, where Pyramus and Thisbe dwell, and her story, like
     theirs, shares close affinities with the genres of romance and elegy, while Semiramis,
     Dercetis and the Naiad are all celebrated in Greek mythology for their clandestine
     affairs.

fruit of an unnamed tree as coloured by the blood of the lovers' suicides beneath it (*cogitat et dubia est ... an, quae poma alba ferebat, | ut nunc nigra ferat contactu sanguinis arbor*, 44, 51–2). In the *Deipnosophistai*, Athenaeus preserves the information that the second century BCE. grammarian Demetrius Ixion derived μόρα, a Greek loan word into Latin, from αἱμόροα, flowing blood.[55] Vergil clearly alludes to this etymology in the one reference he makes to the mulberry, where he glosses the noun with an etymologically significant adjective (*sanguineis ... moris, Buc.* 6.22), and Ovid follows Vergil by signalling the Greek etymology at the outset and conclusion of the first sister's tale (*contactu sanguinis arbor*, 4.52; *at tu ... arbor ... | semper habe fetus, gemini monimenta cruoris*, 4.158, 161).[56]

Even the context of the Vergilian reference to the blood-coloured mulberry is of interest to us in the context of our investigation into Dionysiac themes in the Pyramus and Thisbe episode. Ulrich Schmitzer observes:

> According to modern interpretation, the red paint [on Silenus' face] identifies him (along with Bacchus, to whose retinue he belongs) as belonging to the class of rustic fertility gods. Servius comments (on *Buc.* 6.22) that Vergil expresses himself in this way "because the red colour is characteristic of gods: for that reason too generals celebrating a triumph paint their faces red." Since Bacchus is closely related to the triumph, the ancient and modern explanations complement one another. Above all, it shows that Bacchus and his triumphal procession through Thebes not only dominates the framework of the Minyad episode, but also that the god is present in her very tale through the explanation of the colour of the fruit associated with him.[57]

Thus the first Minyad's tale is devoted to an explanation of the origins of a fruit whose colorful berries the literary tradition suggests themselves have Bacchic associations. It should therefore come as no surprise that verbal details evocative of the rites of Bacchic worship and the larger themes of Dionysiac myth repeatedly intrude into the first sister's tale. All combine to suggest the god's diffuse penetration of the Minyads' household long before the decisive revelation of his godhead at the end of the episode.

Leuconoe, the second Minyad, takes up the theme of unhappy love, set in play by the first sister's "Pyramus et Thisbe," in her tale of the loves of the Sun. The first of Leuconoe's tales explains Venus' persecution of the Sun

---

55 Δημήτριος δὲ ὁ Ἰξίων τὰ αὐτὰ συκάμινα καὶ μόρα οἷον αἱμόροα καὶ σύκων ἀμείνω ("Demetrius Ixion says that *sycamina* and *mora*, which are the same, are derived from *sycôn ameina* ['better than figs'] and *haimoroa* ['flowing blood'],"Ath. *Deipn.* 2.51f): see Keith 2001.

56 On Greek etymological learning in Rome, see Maltby 1993, and O'Hara 1996a and 1996b. On Ovidian use of Greek etymological learning, see especially André 1975; Porte 1985, 197–264; and Tissol 1997, 172–6. On the single adjective gloss of a noun in Vergilian etymological wordplay, see O'Hara 1996a, 64–5, who does not, however, note the etymology in his catalogue.

57 Schmitzer 1992, 533.

(and the devastation his passion wreaks) as revenge for his part in revealing her affair with Mars to Vulcan. The story was a frequent subject of stage performance in mime and pantomime in early imperial Rome, and may even have been the subject of dramatic performance in classical Greece.[58] If so, Leuconoe may make punning reference in the conclusion of her tale to the popularity of the myth in the theatre (*diuque | haec fuit in toto notissima fabula caelo*, 4.188–9), since fabula is both a "scandalous piece of gossip," and a "play."[59] Theatricality is, indeed, a striking feature of the tale, for the trick by which Vulcan traps his wife and her lover is revealed to an invited company of divine spectators when the outraged husband opens the doors of his palace (4.185–8):

> Lemnius extemplo ualuas patefecit eburnas
> immisitque deos. illi iacuere ligati
> turpiter, atque aliquis de dis non tristibus optat
> sic fieri turpis; superi risere ...

> [The Lemnian god immediately opened the ivory doors and sent in the gods: the two of them lay there, shamefully bound, and one of the not unhappy gods wishes to be disgraced in this way: the gods laughed ...]

Ovid's phrasing here characterizes Vulcan more as a showman or master of ceremonies than a wronged husband, while the spectators laugh like the satisfied audience at a comedy.

In fact Leuconoe's story-sequence invites interpretation as a meditation on spectacle as voyeurism, for it is voyeurism that motivates each step of the action. Its point of departure is the Sun's visual discovery of the affair of Venus and Mars (4.169–72):

> 'hunc quoque, siderea qui temperat omnia luce,
> cepit amor Solem; Solis referemus amores.
> primus adulterium Veneris cum Marte putatur
> hic uidisse deus; uidet hic deus omnia primus.

> ["This god too, who governs all things with heavenly light, the Sun was also seized by love; we shall relate 'the Sun's amours.' This god is thought to have been the first to have seen Venus' adulterous affair with Mars; this god sees all things first."]

The Sun's report prompts Vulcan's decision to construct a trap to deceive the eyes (*quae lumina fallere possent*, 4.177) in which to display the lovers to the other gods (4.185–6). Venus' humiliation in this tableau prompts her to

---

58 Cf. Achaios of Eretria's satyr-play, *Hephaistos* (apud Philod. *piet.* 127 Gomperz), and the mime version mentioned by Lucian (*de salt.* 62–63). On the performance of Ovid's elegies as mime or pantomime, see *Tr.* 2.519–20. On Roman mime generally, see Fantham 1989, McKeown 1979, and Reynolds 1946; and on pantomime see Zanobi in this volume.

59 Cf. Var. *ling. lat.* 6.55: *ab eodem uerbo fari fabulae, ut tragoediae et comoediae, dictae.*

punish the Sun so that he has eyes only for the Persian princess Leucothoe (4.195–7). Clytie's resulting jealousy (*inuidit Clytie*, 4.234),[60] prompts her to inform Leucothoe's father of his daughter's transgression, for which he punishes her by burying her alive. The sun god scorns Clytie (expressed with a compounded form of *specto*: *despecta*, 4.206), and her grief leads to her transformation into the heliotrope, a flower that never takes its eyes from the Sun (4.264–5).

Leuconoe's emphasis on sight in her story offers ironic comment not only on the actions and main characters of her story-sequence but also on her own activity as story-teller, since she herself bears a name that means "Light-perceiving."[61] There is some confusion in the textual transmission of her name, but the manuscripts' "Leucothoe" (at 4.168) is corrected to "Leuconoe" by most editors on the basis of Planudes' Greek version of the Ovidian tale and ps. Lactantius *fab. Ov.* 4.12, where one of the Minyads is called by this name.[62] If we can trust this evidence, Ovid has adapted his sources to give his Minyad a significant name (*redender Name*), for while the mythographers offer variants for the two other sisters' names (Arsippe-Arsinoe, Alkathoe-Alkithoe), all three concur in naming the third sister Leukippe.[63] The manuscript confusion also points to a second significant result of Ovid's adaptation of his sources, the near homonomy of the names of the story-teller, Leuconoe, and her character Leucothoe (4.196, 208, 220), whose name means "light-quick."[64] The Persian princess' name, moreover, has a close analogue in the larger context of the Theban narrative with that of a character in the story of Athamas and Ino, the episode that follows the Minyad-sequence, for Ovid concludes that episode with the metamorphosis of Ino into the Homeric sea-goddess Leucothea (*Od.* 5.333–4). There is more manuscript confusion concerning the correct spelling of her name, but it does not call into question the close similarity of the three characters' names; on the contrary, it confirms it. Further play with proper names in this section of the narrative may lie in Ovid's application of the name Orchamus to the father of the Persian princess (*Met.* 4.212), a name that recalls the traditional setting of the Minyads in the Boeotian city of Orchomenos.[65]

---

60 Davis 1969, 28; Keith 1992, 125–7.
61 Leuconoe's name is composed of λευκός, "light, bright, brilliant" of sunlight, and νοέω, "perceive by the eyes, observe, notice."
62 See Slater 1927 ad *Met.* 4.168 for the reading of Leucothoe in ps. Planudes, and cf. Castiglioni 1910.
63 Leukippe, Arsippe, and Alkathoe (Ant. Lib. *Met.* 10, following Corinna and Nicander *Het.* 4); Leukippe, Arsinoe, and Alkathoe (Plut. *Quaes. Gr.* 38); and Leukippe, Arsippe, and Alkithoe (Ael. *Var. Hist.* 3.42).
64 composed of λευκός, "light, bright, brilliant" of sunlight, and θόος, "quick, nimble."
65 Cf. Bömer 1976, 75–6 on Symmikta *uel sim.*

The play on names is typical of Ovidian poetic technique,[66] but the proliferation of such plays in Leuconoe's tale is particularly dizzying and lends something of a *mîse-en-abyme* effect to the narrative, especially when we consider the similarity of the context in which Leuconoe narrates her story to the setting of Leucothoe's rape. Ovid contrasts the Theban women's worship of Dionysus out of doors (4.4–10, 31–5; cf. 3.528–30, 701–33), with the housebound daughters of Minyas in their devotion to woolworking (4.31–40, 54, 275, 389–98)[67] despite Teiresias' injunction to the Thebans to take the day off (4.4–5), which is obeyed by the other Theban woman (4.9–10). Leuconoe locates the Sun's approach to Leucothoe in a similar setting for, disguised as her mother, he finds her in her chamber, weaving in the company of twelve maidservants (4.218–21; cf. 4.225):

> noxque uicem peragit, thalamos deus intrat amatos
> uersus in Eurynomes faciem genetricis et inter
> bis sex Leucothoen famulas ad lumina cernit
> leuia uersato ducentem stamina fuso.

> [Night came on in turn and the god entered his beloved's bed-chamber, transformed to look like her mother Eurynome, and by the light he saw Leucothoe amid her twelve maid-servants turning the spindle and spinning the slender threads.]

As Gianpiero Rosati has observed, Ovid thus "keeps active a semantic relationship between the framing scene (the hostility towards the cult of Bacchus [expressed in the Minyads' woolworking]) and the stories that are framed within it."[68]

A final manifestation of this relationship between frame and inset tale can be seen in the Sun's metamorphosis of his dead beloved into frankincense when he cannot revivify her (4.249–55):

> sed quoniam tantis fatum conatibus obstat,
> nectare odorato sparsit corpusque locumque,
> multaque praequestus "tanges tamen aethera" dixit.
> protinus imbutum caelesti nectare corpus
> delicuit terramque suo madefecit odore,
> uirgaque per glaebas sensim radicibus actis
> turea surrexit tumulumque cacumine rupit.

> [But since destiny blocked such attempts, he sprinkled both her body and the place with scented nectar, and lamenting greatly, said "nonetheless, you will touch the ether." Immediately her body, smeared with heavenly nectar, began to liquify, and stained the earth with a scent, and through the clods of earth little by little a frankincense shrub rose, its roots driven deep, and split the tomb with its head.]

---

66   Cf. Keith 1992; O'Hara 1996a and 1996b; Tissol 1997,11–88.
67   Cf. Rosati 1999.
68   Rosati 1999, 241.

Leuconoe calls Persia the land of perfumes early in her narrative (*gentis odoriferae*, 4.209), and her tale documents the origin of one of the most famous of these oriental fragrances. Bömer notes a curious connection between Helios and frankincense among the Sabaeans, reported by Theophrastus in his *Enquiry into Plants*: "myrrh and frankincense were brought from all parts [of the region] into the temple of the sun, and … this temple was the most sacred thing which the Sabaeans of that region possessed."[69] Ovid himself, however, emphasises the use of frankincense (and myrrh for that matter; cf. 3.555; 4.393) in the worship of Bacchus, in the aftermath of the Pentheus episode at the end of Book Three, and again at the beginning of Book Four (3.733, 4.11).[70] Although frankincense and myrrh were burnt for many gods on different occasions in Greco-Roman religion, Dionysus' association with the East lent him an especially close connection with the spice trade in Hellenistic literature and society,[71] a connection that seems to be reflected in Ovid's narrative here. Thus like her sister's tale of Pyramus and Thisbe, Leuconoe's story of the Sun's loves offers an explanation for the origin of a feature of Bacchic cult, in this case the very incense that the Theban women offer to the god she and her sisters scorn.[72]

Alcithoe, the third sister, considers and rejects five stories before embarking on the tale of Salmacis and Hermaphroditus (4.276–84):

> "uulgatos taceo" dixit "pastoris amores
> Daphnidis Idaei, quem nymphe paelicis ira
> contulit in saxum; tantus dolor urit amantes,
> nec loquor ut quondam naturae iure nouato
> ambiguus fuerit modo uir, modo femina Sithon.   280
> te quoque, nunc adamas, quondam fidissime paruo,
> Celmi, Ioui largoque satos Curetas ab imbri
> et Crocon in paruos uersum cum Smilace flores
> praetereo dulcique animos nouitate tenebo.

> [I pass in silence over the well-known loves of Daphnis, the shepherd of Ida, whom a nymph turned into a rock out of anger over a rival: too great is the pain that burns lovers; nor am I going to tell how ambiguously-gendered Sithon once became now

---

69 ἔλεγον δ' οὗτοι καὶ τόδε καὶ ἔφασαν ἀκούειν, ὅτι συνάγεται πανταχόθεν ἡ σμύρνα καὶ ὁ λιβανωτὸς εἰς τὸ ἱερὸν τὸ τοῦ ἡλίου· τοῦτο δ' εἶναι μὲν τῶν Σαβαίων ἁγιώτατον κτλ. (Theophr. *Hist. Plant.* 9.4.5).

70 Cf. Men. *Dysk.* 443–53, cited by Ath. *Deipn.* 4.146 e-f.

71 Rice 1983.

72 Cf. Ath. *Deipn.* 1.273–28a, which reports a poem by Hermippus on the special products of each city which Dionysus brought to men since the time he sailed over the wine-dark sea, including frankincense and myrrh from Syria; *Deipn.* 5.201a, on spices in the procession of Dionysus' return from India in the Grand Procession of Philadelphus; and 14.626f, on incense burned at the tragic festivals of Dionysus. For the association of Syrian frankincense with Dionysus already in the fifth century, cf. Eur. *Ba.* 144–5.

a man, now a woman, with the law of nature renewed. You too Celmis, now steel, once most faithful to little baby Jove, I pass by, and the Curetes, sprung from abundant rain, and Crocus turned along with Smilax into small flowers; instead I shall hold your attention with a sweet novelty.]

None of these stories is well known (despite Alcithoe's disparaging reference to the "much-publicised" story of Daphnis' loves, *uulgatos ... amores*, 4.276), but many of them can be shown to have parallels with parts of Dionysiac myth, and it is presumably for this reason that Alcithoe rejects them. The first tale she passes over is that of Daphnis, transformed into a rock by a nymph whom he has scorned, a pastoral "paradigm of unhappy love," as E. J. Kenney has called it.[73] Richard Hunter has recently demonstrated Theocritus' extensive debt to tragedy in *Idyll* 1, where "the sufferings of Daphnis" are most famously narrated.[74] The story shares thematic parallels with the tale that Alcithoe eventually chooses to narrate, that of Salmacis and Hermaphroditus, which concerns another lustful nymph scorned by a beautiful youth, and it also resonates with the larger Dionysiac context of divinity scorned in the Theban narrative. In this regard, it is particularly interesting that Wojaczek has characterised Daphnis as "the prototype of Dionysus' initiates."[75]

The story of Sithon's shifting gender, unattested elsewhere, likewise displays tantalising parallels both to the tale Alcithoe finally tells and to the frame narrative of Dionysiac worship. Salmacis' rape of Hermaphroditus, after all, results in their fusion into a single hermaphroditic being (i.e., another ambiguously gendered creature, albeit in a different way), while Bacchus is represented in classical art and literature from the fifth century B.C.E. on as a youth of "womanly appearance" (θηλύμορφον, Eur. *Ba.* 353), who combines in his person the beauty of both male and female (cf. Ov. *Met.* 4.17–20; 3.607). Celmis was one of the Idaean Dactyls, dwarfish metal-workers who invented iron and are associated with the eastern cult of the mother of the gods (itself closely associated with Dionysus' rites). Sophocles mentioned them in his Satyr play entitled ΚΩΦΟΙ ("The Dumb Ones") and located them near Mt. Ida in the Troad. Zenobius (4.80) reports a proverb from this play, Κέλμις ἐν σιδέρωι, to which Ovid here alludes in the phrase *nunc adamas* (4.281), and Zenobius explains that the play included Celmis' punishment for having insulted Rhea (identified with the mother of the gods). The eastern setting of the tale, its provenance in a Sophoclean satyr play, and the Dactyl's punishment by the goddess all link this tale to the larger tragic thematics of the Theban narrative, and suggest that Alcithoe

---

73   Kenney 1959, 252.
74   Hunter 1999, 61–2.
75   Wojaczek 1969, 5.

passes over it here in accordance with her hostility towards the new god Bacchus. In close association with Celmis and his faithful service to the infant Jupiter, Alcithoe mentions the Curetes, who protected the infant god from discovery by drowning out his cries with dancing and tambourine-playing. The myth is a doublet of the concealment of the infant Dionysus in the cave of the numphs of Nysa, which Ovid mentions in Book Three (*Met.* 3.313–15), and is associated with the aitiology of Dionysus' cult object, the *tympanum* (cf. 4.29, 391), in the parados of Euripides' *Bacchae* (120–34).

Lastly, Alcithoe passes over the myth of Crocus and Smilax, two plants closely identified with Bacchic ritual. Dionysus and his followers are characteristically clothed in saffron-coloured robes,[76] while the fragrance is closely associated with Dionysus' worship and presages his epiphany to the sisters (4.393). Even more closely associated with the god is the plant bryony, *smilax aspera* (a kind of bindweed).[77] Euripides' chorus of Bacchants mentions this plant together with ivy and several other of the god's attributes in the parados of the *Bacchae* (105–19, at 108), and later in the play a Messenger reports to Pentheus that he saw the Theban Maenads wearing crowns of ivy, bryony and oak (*Ba.* 703). The Elder Pliny deprecates the use of bryony wreathes, which he says is common because the plant resembles ivy, and he preserves a fuller version of the tale of Crocus and Smilax (Plin. *NH* 16.153):

> Similis est hederae e Cilicia quidem primum profecta sed in Graecia frequentior quam uocant smilacem … fert racemos labruscae modo, non hederae, colore rubro, conplexa acinis maioribus nucleos ternos, minoribus singulos, nigros durosque, infausta omnibus sacris et coronis, quoniam sit lugubris uirgine eius nominis propter amorem iuuenis Croci mutata in hunc fruticem. id uolgus ignorans plerumque festa sua polluit hederam existimando, sicut in poetis aut Libero patre aut Sileno, quis omnino scit quibus coronentur?[78]

> [Resembling ivy is the plant called *smilax*, which first came from Cilicia, but is now more common in Greece … It bears clusters of berries like those of the wild vine, not of the ivy; they are red in colour, and the larger ones enclose three hard black stones but the smaller a single stone. This plant is unlucky to use at all sacred rites and for wreaths, because it has a mournful association, a maiden named Smilax having been turned into a smilax shrub because of her love for a youth named Crocus. The common people, not knowing this, usually pollute their festivals with it because they think it is ivy; just as in the case of the poets or Father Liber or Silenus, who wear wreathes made of who in the world knows what.]

---

76 Cf. Ar. *Frogs* 46; Kratinos fr. 40; Naevius, *Lycurgus* fr. 39W, *pallis patagiis crocotis malacis mortualibus*; and see further *RE* s.v. "Saffran."

77 Frequent references in fifth-century BCE tragedy and comedy: Eur. *Ba.* 108, 703; Ar. *Nu.* 1007; Eup. 14.3; cf. Ar. *Av.* 216.

78 Cf. *NH* 21.52, 24.82.

Pliny's discussion of the plant suggests two reasons for Alcithoe's avoidance of it here: the unhappy love of Smilax and Crocus bears a certain resemblance to her sister Leuconoe's tale of the origin of the frankincense shrub, while the plant's close association with Dionysus' emblem, the ivy, and the festivals of his Roman counterpart, Father Liber, make it an unpalatable theme for the Minyads in the context of their disavowal of his godhead.

In every case, then, we can see that the narratives Alcithoe passes over have a close thematic relationship to the myth of the new god Bacchus and/or his cult objects and emblems. But although she rejects this Dionysiac material, the god and his emblems cannot be so easily ignored, and the tale that she finally decides to tell, the origin of the enervating powers of the Carian spring Salmacis, itself features Dionysiac themes and imagery. We may note, in addition, the similarity of the names of the last-mentioned character whose story Alcithoe passes over, Smilax (especially since it appears in an oblique case, *Smilace*, at 4.283), and the main character of the narrative she chooses to tell, Salmacis (*Met.* 4.285–7): '*unde sit infamis, quare male fortibus undis | Salmacis eneruet tactosque remolliat artus, | discite. causa latet, uis est notissima fontis*' ("Learn where the bad reputation of Salmacis comes from, how the spring emasculates with its powerful waters and softens the limbs it touches. The cause lies hidden, but the force of the power is very well known"). Alcithoe insists upon Salmacis' power to soften any limbs she touches both at the opening of her narrative, here, and at its close, where Hermaphroditus asks that all men who enter the spring may emerge, like himself, as *semiuiri* (4.380–8):

> 'ergo ubi se liquidas, quo uir descenderat, undas
> semimarem fecisse uidet mollitaque in illis
> membra, manus tendens, sed iam non uoce uirili
> Hermaphroditus ait: "nato date munera uestro,
> et pater et genetrix, amborum nomen habenti:
> quisquis in hos fontes uir uenerit, exeat inde
> semiuir et tactis subito mollescat in undis."
> motus uterque parens nati rata uerba biformis
> fecit et incesto fontem medicamine tinxit.'

> [And so when Hermaphroditus saw that the liquid waves into which he had descended as a man had made him half-man and softened his limbs, he held out his hands and said in a voice no longer manly: "Grant a gift to your son whose name derives from both of you, father and mother: whoever enters this spring as a man, let him go forth a half-man, let him suddenly be emasculated at the touch of the waters!" His parents, moved by his plea, ratified the words of their bi-gendered son, and touched the spring with an impure drug.]

With this uncanny power of the spring (and its nymph, Salmacis), we may compare the transformation effected in the population of Thebes by Dionysus, as Pentheus reports it (3.540–7):

[mirer] ... uosne, acrior aetas,
o iuuenes, propiorque meae, quos arma tenere,
non thyrsos, galeaque tegi, non fronde decebat?
este, precor, memores, qua sitis stirpe creati,
illiusque animos, qui multos perdidit unus,
sumite serpentis. pro fontibus ille lacuque
interiit; at uos pro fama uincite uestra.
ille dedit leto fortes, uos pellite molles
et patrium retinete decus.

[Should I admire you, young men, a more energetic age and nearer my own, whom it befits to bear arms, not the thyrsus, and to be sheltered with war-helmets, not with foliage. Remember, I beg you, from what stock you are descended, and take on the courage of that snake who killed many a foe alone. He perished for his spring and water: but you, conquer for your reputation! He gave brave men to death: you drive out soft men and retain your ancestral glory.]

Indeed Pentheus characterizes the followers of Bacchus simply as *molles* (3.547–8), and disdainfully dismisses their leader because, like a woman, his hair is drenched with myrrh, he wears soft garlands and a rich cloak of gold and purple (3.555–6): *madidus murra crinis mollesque coronae* | *purpuraque et pictis intextum uestibus aurum.*[79] Thus Salmacis' power to enervate all those who enter her spring is similar in its effects to Dionysus' impact on devoté and non-devoté alike.

Alcithoe's Salmacis turns herself out in similarly luxurious style (4.311–15):

saepe Cytoriaco deducit pectine crines
et quid se deceat spectatas consulit undas;[80]
nunc perlucenti circumdata corpus amictu
mollibus aut foliis aut mollibus incubat herbis;
saepe legit flores.

[Often she combs her hair with a boxwood comb, and checks her spring to see what becomes her; now dressed in a translucent gown she reclines on soft leaves or soft grasses; often she gathers flowers ...]

Salmacis' delight in the pleasures of the flesh aligns her with the god Bacchus whose sensuality so inflames Pentheus, and Alcithoe's similes imply further connections. In response to Salmacis' bold speech of proposition, Hermaphroditus blushes as becomingly as ripening apples on the tree grow red, or stained ivory, or the moon tinged with crimson when bronze cymbals clash in vain (4.329–33):

... pueri rubor ora notauit
(nescit enim quid amor), sed et erubuisse decebat.
hic color aprica pendentibus arbore pomis

---

79 Cf. Naevius, *Lycurgus* fr. 39W, quoted above n. 77.
80 On the use of mirrors in Dionysiac ritual, see Seaford 1987.

aut ebori tincto est aut sub candore rubenti,
cum frustra resonant aera auxiliaria, lunae.

[A blush marked the boy's face; for he does not know what love is, but it became him
to blush. This is the color of fruit hanging in a sunny orchard or of painted ivory, or
of the moon, growing red beneath her white glow, when the cymbals clash in vain
to assist her.]

The clash of the cymbals was popularly supposed to conjure up aid for the
moon during an eclipse, but it is still more familiar from its prominent cult
use in Bacchic ritual,[81] in which it is on display throughout the Dionysiac
episodes of Ovid's "Thebaid" (4.393; cf. 3.532–3, 4.30). Alcithoe's simile
dramatizes her rejection of Dionysus' godhead by attributing his instruments
of worship to the moon, but at the conclusion of her tale the cymbals ring out
in honour of Bacchus during the god's epiphany.

Other Dionysiac images intrude into Alcithoe's tale in the course of a
second series of similes. After Hermaphroditus rebuffs the amorous advances of the nymph, Salmacis pretends to abandon her spring to the youth, but
instead withdraws only far enough so that she can spy on him secretly as he
dives into her pool and disports himself (another instance of voyeurism in
the Theban narrative). Inflamed with desire at the sight, the nymph launches
herself at him, embracing him and overcoming all his efforts at resistance,
like a serpent clinging to an eagle, or ivy to a tree, or an octopus to its prey
(4.361–7):

denique nitentem contra elabique uolentem
implicat; ut serpens, quam regia sustinet ales
sublimemque rapit (pendens caput illa pedesque
adligat et cauda spatiantes inplicat alas),
utue solent hederae longos intexere truncos,
utque sub aequoribus deprensum polypus hostem
continet ex omni dimissis parte flagellis.

[Finally she entwined herself around him as he struggled against her, wishing to escape, like a snake, which an eagle snatches up and carries off; but the hanging snake
binds the bird's head and feet, and embraces the spreading wings with her tail; or
like ivy, which is accustomed to embrace tall trees; or like an octopus which holds its
prey caught beneath the sea, its tentacles embracing him on every side.]

In Euripides' *Bacchae*, the god is "crowned with crowns of snakes" (*Ba.*
101–2) and invoked by the chorus as "a many-headed snake" (*Ba.* 1017–
18),[82] but ivy is an even more pervasive feature of Dionysiac iconography.
In the third book of the *Metamorphoses*, the god reveals himself wreathed
in ivy to the Tyrrhenian sailors, and causes the proliferation of ivy over their

---

81   Cf. Lucr. 2.619; Cat. 64.262; Tib. 1.3.24; O. *Ars* 1.537, *Fasti* 4.213, *Met.* 3.532–3,
     4.393, 6.589, 9.777.
82   On snakes in Bacchic cult, see Seaford 1996, 160 on 101–3, with further bibliography.

oars and sails (3.663–7). Moreover the appearance of the god's ivy on the Minyads' loom is the final element in Bacchus' preparations for epiphany, an epiphany that is the prelude to the sisters' transformation into bats (4.394–8, quoted above). After resolutely spinning and story-telling in the seclusion of their quarters all day long, the daughters of Minyas must finally confront the god whose rites they have ignored and whose godhead they have spurned. The climactic encounter underscores both the Minyads' impiety and the overwhelming power of Dionysus, the dangerous god of intoxication whose shadowy presence has exerted constant pressure on the sisters' tales. The god's ruthless suppression of the Minyads' voices brings to a close the sisters' narrative parade of borrowed Bacchic themes and imagery with truly poetic justice.

Bibliography

André, Jacques (1975), "Ovide helléniste et linguiste", in: *Revue Philologique* 49, 191–5.

Barchiesi, Alessandro (1993), "Future Reflexive: two Modes of Allusion and Ovid's *Heroides*", in: *Harvard Studies in Classical Philology* 95, 333–65.

Beare, William (1964), *The Roman* Stage,[3] London.

Bernbeck, E.J. (1967), *Beobachtungen zur Darstellungsart in Ovids Metamorphosen*, Munich.

Bömer, Franz (ed.) (1969), *P. Ovidius Naso Metamorphosen. Kommentar Buch I–III*, Heidelberg.

Bömer, Franz (ed.) (1976), *P. Ovidius Naso Metamorphosen. Kommentar Buch IV–V*, Heidelberg.

Castellani, Victor (1980), "Two Divine Scandals: Ovid Met. 2.680ff. and 4.171ff. and his Sources", in: *Transactions of the American Philological Association* 110, 37–50.

Castiglioni, Aloysius (1910), "Analecta Planudea ab Ovidi Metamorphoses Spectantia", in: *SIFC* 18, 189–283.

Curley, Daniel (1999), *Metatheater: Heroines and Ephebes in Ovid's Metamorphoses*, Ph.D. Diss., University of Washington, Seattle.

Curran, Leo C. (1978), "Rape and Rape Victims in the Metamorphoses", in: *Arethusa* 11, 213–41.

Currie, Hugh MacLeod (1981), "Ovid and the Roman Stage", in: *Aufstieg und Niedergang der römischen Welt* 2.31.4, 2701–42.

D'Anna, Giovanni (1959) "La Tragedia Latina Arcaica nelle 'Metamorfosi'", in: *Atti del Convegno Internazionale Ovidiano* II.217–34, Roma.

Davis, N. Gregson G. (1969), *Studies in the Narrative Economy of Ovid's Metamorphoses*, Ph.D. Diss. University of California, Berkeley.

Dodds, E.R. (ed.) (1960), *Euripides, Bacchae, edited with introduction and commentary*,[2] Oxford.

Due, Otto Steen (1974) *Changing Forms*, Copenhagen.

Duke, T.T. (1971), "Ovid's Pyramus and Thisbe", in: *Classical Journal* 66, 320–7.

Erren, Manfred (1979), "Die Metamorphose des Maulbeerbaums. Ein Mimus bei Ovid", in: *AU* 22, 87–91.

Fantham, R. Elaine (1989), "Mime: The Missing Link in Roman Literary History",
    in: *Classical World* 82.3, 153–63.
Feeney, Denis (1991), "The Slippery Stuff of Epic", review of J.B. Hainsworth,
    The Idea of Epic (Berkeley 1991), *Times Literary Supplement* 2.7.91.
Feldherr, Andrew (1997), "Metamorphosis and Sacrifice in Ovid's Theban Narrative",
    in: *Materiali e Discussioni* 38, 25–55.
Flower, Harriet (2000), "*Fabula de Bacchanalibus*: the Bacchanalian Cult of the
    Second Century BC and Roman Drama", in: Gesine Manuwald (ed.), *Identität und
    Alterität in der frührömischen Tragödie*, Würzburg, 23–35.
Frenkel, V. (1978), "ΦΑΝΗΘΙ ΤΑΥΡΟΣ: Un elemento arcaico nel Dioniso delle
    Baccanti", in: *Acme* 31, 93–105.
Gasparri, Carlo (1986a), "Dionysos", in: *Lexicon Iconographicum Mythologiae
    Classicae* III.1, Zürich and München, 414–514.
Gasparri, Carlo (1986b), "Dionysos/Bacchus", in: *Lexicon Iconographicum
    Mythologiae Classicae* III.1, Zürich and München, 540–66.
Gildenhard, Ingo / Zissos, Andrew (1999), "'Somatic Economies': Tragic Bodies and Po-
    etic Design in Ovid's Metamorphoses," in: Hardie / Barchiesi / Hinds (eds.), 162–81.
Gildenhard, Ingo / Zissos, Andrew (2000), "Ovid's Narcissus: Echoes of Oedipus",
    in: *American Journal of Philology* 121, 129–47.
Hardie, Philip (1990), "Ovid's Theban History: the First 'Anti-Aeneid'?",
    in: *Classical Quarterly* 40, 224–35.
Hardie, Philip / Barchiesi, Aessandro / Hinds, Stephen (eds.) (1999), *Ovidian
    Transformations: Essays on Ovid's Metamorphoses and its Reception*, Cambridge.
Hinds, Stephen (1988), "Generalizing about Ovid", in: *Ramus* 16, 4–31.
Holzberg, Niklas (1988), "Ovids Babyloniaka", in: *Wiener Studien* 101, 265–77.
Hunter, Richard (ed.) (1999), *Theocritus: A Selection*, Cambridge.
Janan, Micaela (1994), "'There Beneath the Roman Ruin Where the Purple Flowers
    Grow': Ovid's Minyads and the Feminine Imagination", *American Journal of
    Philology* 115, 427–48.
Jocelyn, Henry D. (ed.) (1967), *The Tragedies of Ennius*, Cambridge.
Katsouris, Andreas G. (1976), "The Suicide Motif in Ancient Drama",
    in: *Dionysio* 47, 5–36.
Keith, Alison M. (1992), *The Play of Fictions: Studies in Ovid's Metamorphoses,
    Book 2*, Ann Arbor.
—— (2001), "Etymological Wordplay in Ovid's 'Pyramus and Thisbe'
    (*Met.* 4.55–166)", in: *Classical Quarterly* 51, 309–12.
—— (2002), "Sources and Genres in Ovid's *Metamorphoses* 1–5", in: Barbara Weiden
    Boyd (ed.), *A Companion to the Study of Ovid*, Leiden, 235–69.
Kenney, E. J. (1959), "Notes on Ovid II", in: *Classical Quarterly* 9, 240–60.
Knox, Peter (1986), *Ovid's Metamorphoses and the Traditions of Augustan Poetry*.
    Cambridge.
—— (1989), "Pyramus and Thisbe in Cyprus", in: *Harvard Studies in Classical Philol-
    ogy* 92, 315–28.
Labate, Mario (1993), "Storie di instabilità: l'episodio di Ermafrodito nelle
    Metamorfosi di Ovidio", in: *Materiali e Discussioni* 30, 49–62.
Lateiner, Donald (1984), "Mythic and Non-mythic Artists in Ovid's *Metamorphoses*",
    in: *Ramus* 13, 1–30.
Leach, Eleanor Winsor (1974), "Ekphrasis and the Theme of Artistic Failure in Ovid's
    Metamorphoses", in: *Ramus* 3, 102–41.
Lesky, Albin (1966), *A History of Greek Literature*, translated by J. Willis and
    C. de Heer, New York.

Lombardi, Michela (1993), *Antimaco di Colofone: la poesia epica*, Rome.
Loraux, Nicole (1987) *Tragic Ways of Killing a Woman*, Cambridge MA.
Maltby, Robert (1993), "Varro's Attitude to Latin Derivations from Greek",
     in: *Papers of the Leeds Latin Seminar* 7, 47–60.
McKeown, James (1979), "Augustan Elegy and Mime", in: *Proceedings of the
     Cambridge Philological Society* 205, 71–84.
Miller, John F. (ed.) (1977), [rev. G.P. Goold] *Ovid, Metamorphoses.*[2] 2 vols.
     Cambridge MA.
Myers, K. Sara (1994), *Ovid's Causes*, Ann Arbor.
Newlands, Carole (1986), "The Simile of the Fractured Pipe in Ovid's *Metamorphoses*
     4", in: *Ramus* 15, 143–53.
Nugent, S. Georgia (1990) "This Sex Which Is Not One: De-Constructing Ovid's
     Hermaphrodite", in: *differences* 2.1, 160–85.
O'Hara, James J. (1996a), *True Names: Vergil and the Alexandrian Tradition of
     Etymological Wordplay*, Ann Arbor.
—— (1996b), "Vergil's Best Reader? Ovidian Commentary on Vergilian Etymological
     Wordplay", in: *Classical Journal* 91, 255–76.
Parry, Hugh (1964), "Ovid's *Metamorphoses*: Violence in a Pastoral Landscape",
     in: *Transactions of the American Philological Association* 95, 268–82.
Perdrizet, Paul (1932), "Légendes babyloniennes dans les Métamorphoses d'Ovid",
     in: *Revue d'Histoire et Religion* 105, 192–228.
Perraud, Louis (1983–84), "*Amatores Exclusi*: Apostrophe and Separation in the
     Pyramus and Thisbe Episode", in: *Classical Journal* 79, 135–9.
Porte, Danielle (1985), *L'étiologie religieuse dans les Fastes d'Ovide*, Paris.
Reynolds, Robert W. (1946), "The Adultery Mime", in: *Classical Quarterly* 40, 77–84.
Rice, Ellen E. (1983), *The Grand Procession of Ptolemy Philadelphus*, Oxford.
Richlin, Amy (1992), "Reading Ovid's Rapes", in: Amy Richlin (ed.), *Pornography and
     Representation in Greece and Rome*, Oxford, 158–79.
Robinson, Matthew (1999), "Salmacis and Hermaphroditus: When Two Become One
     (Ovid, *Met.* 4.285–388)", in: *Classical Quarterly* 49, 212–23.
Rhorer, Catherine C. (1980), "Red and White in Ovid's *Metamorphoses*: the Mulberry
     Tree in the Tale of Pyramus and Thisbe", in: *Ramus* 9, 79–88
Rosati, Gianpiero (1999), "Form in Motion: Weaving the Text in the *Metamorphoses*",
     in: Hardie / Barchiesi / Hinds (eds.), 240–53.
Schmitzer, Ulrich (1992), "Meeresstille und Wasserrohrbruch", in: *Gymnasium* 99,
     519–45.
Seaford, Richard (1987), "Pentheus' Vision: *Bacchae* 918–22", in: *Classical Quarterly*
     37, 76–8.
Seaford, Richard (1996), *Euripides, Bacchae*, Warminster.
Segal, Charles (1969), *Landscape in Ovid's Metamorphoses*, Wiesbaden.
Seidensticker, Bernd (1982), "Die Wahl des Todes bei Sophokles", in: *Fondation Hardt
     Entretiens* 29, 108–44.
Slater, David A. (1927), *Towards a Text of the Metamorphoses of Ovid*, Oxford.
Tarrant, Richard (ed.) (2004), *P. Ovidi Nasonis Metamorphoses*, Oxford.
Tissol, Garth (1997), *The Face of Nature*, Princeton.
Winnington-Ingram, Reginald P. (1989), "Aeschylus", in: *Cambridge History of
     Classical Literature* I.2, Cambridge, 1–6.
Wojaczek, Günter (1969), *Daphnis: Untersuchungen zur griechischen Bukolik*,
     Meisenheim am Glan.
Wyss, Bernhard (1974), *Antimachi Colophonii Reliquiae*, repr. Hildesheim. [Originally
     published in Berlin, 1936]

Zeitlin, Froma I. (1990), "Thebes: Theater of Self and Society in Athenian Drama",
    in: John J. Winkler / Froma I. Zeitlin (eds.), *Nothing to do with Dionysos?*,
    Princeton, 130–67.
Zeitlin, Froma I. (1996), "Playing the Other", in: Froma I. Zeitlin (ed.), *Playing the
    Other*, Chicago, 341–74.

"I'm A Celebrity, Get Me Out of Here": the Reception of *Euripides' Iphigenia among the Taurians* in Ovid's Exile Poetry

JENNIFER INGLEHEART

The importance of Greek tragedy for Ovid's exile poetry is often overlooked by scholars, who treat it as part of Ovid's more general exilic engagement with myth,[1] but it is extensive, complex, and repays careful attention: the poet frequently draws suggestive parallels between himself (and others involved in his exile) and characters most familiar from tragedies, and paints the circumstances surrounding his exile along the lines of tragic plots. For example, Ovid's identification of himself and the circumstances of his exile with Actaeon, who destroyed himself and his *domus* by an unwitting *error* of sight (*Tristia* 2.103–110), recalls the tragic figure of Actaeon in Aeschylus' fragmentary *Toxotides* and Euripides' *Bacchae*;[2] the actions and words of the

---

*   I would like to thank Edith Hall for her encouragement to write on this topic for a seminar on the *I. T.*, held at Durham University in early 2006, and her helpful criticism; and Ingo Gildenhard for inviting me to deliver a version of this paper at a Reception of Greek Tragedy workshop at Durham University in March 2007, and his useful comments on various drafts. Thanks are also due to all those present on these occasions for their stimulating comments. All errors which remain are my responsibility, and all translations are my own.

1   See for example Broege 1972, 42, who notes after cataloguing Ovid's use of myth in exile that these mythological parallels are "drawn exclusively from tragedy and epic", but does not explore Ovid's engagement with Greek tragedy in any meaningful way. Davisson 1993 does not treat Ovid's exilic use of myths drawn from tragedy in her selective exploration of Ovid's use of mythological *exempla*; Claassen 2001 provides an overly mechanical survey of myth in the exile poems, noting only cases where mythological characters are named.

2   Ovid's engagement with Greek tragedy here is more wide-ranging than simple use of a character most familiar from that genre: the parallel with Actaeon gains for Ovid some of the pathos felt for Greek tragic characters (cf. Drucker 1977, 149 ff.); Ovid directs the reader to revisit his earlier, tragic version of the myth of Actaeon at *Met.* 3.138–255; the evocation of Ovid's destroyed *domus* (*Tr.* 2.110) recalls the centrality of the tragic δῶμα/ -τα (cf. Drucker 1977, 150–1); and *error* (*Tr.* 2.109) should perhaps be read as equivalent to ἁμαρτία (cf. Fairweather 1987, 185, on *Tr.* 4.10.90 and

tragic Philoctetes are simultaneously evoked at *Tristia* 5.1.59–62, as Ovid offers precedents for his continual complaints;[3] and when he addresses his wife at *Tristia* 3.3.65–8, Ovid raises the possibility that she may have to act the part of Antigone, with himself as Polynices, and Augustus as a potential Creon to be defied:

> ossa tamen facito parua referantur in urna:
> > sic ego non etiam mortuus exul ero.
> non uetat hoc quisquam: fratrem Thebana peremptum
> > supposuit tumulo rege uetante soror.

> But make sure my bones are carried back in a small urn;
> > so I shall not still be an exile even in death.
> Nobody forbids this: the Theban sister placed her dead brother
> > in a tomb, even though the king forbade it.

Ovid frequently deploys tragedy via such brief references to tragic characters and the myths surrounding them, often without detailed allusion to specific tragedies, and the myth of the rescue of Iphigenia from the Black Sea region by Orestes and Pylades, most famous from Euripides' *Iphigenia among the Taurians*, features briefly at *Tristia* 1.5.21–2, 1.9.27–8, and *Pont.* 1.2.78.[4] In these short references, Ovid alludes to Orestes' and Pylades' mission to the Black Sea region, stressing the devoted friendship of the young men,[5] as well as the geographical proximity of such events to his own place

---

tragic colouring in Ovid's poetic autobiography more generally). On Ovid's exilic uses of the Actaeon myth, see further Ingleheart 2006, 69–76.

3   Cf. in particular 61–2 (*hoc erat, in gelido quare Poeantius antro/ uoce fatigaret Lemnia saxa sua* = "This was why in the chill cave the son of Poeas/ wore out the Lemnian rocks with his voice") with Soph. *Phil.* 1081–2 (Philoctetes: ὦ κοίλας πέτρας γύαλον/ θερμὸν καὶ παγετῶδες = "O my cave of hollow rock, hot and ice-cold"). Accius' *Philoctetes* also seems to have influenced Ovid: Cic. *Fin.* 2.94 comments ... *sed 'saxum illud Lemnium' clamore Philocteteo funestare* before introducing a direct quotation from Accius' *Philoctetes* (fr. 11 Ribbeck): (Philoctetes) [*iaceo in tecto humido*] *quod eiulatu, questu, gemitu, fremitibus/ resonando mutum flebiles uoces refert* (= "I lie in a moist house, which mutely with wailing, complaints, groans, and growls echoes tearful utterances"). Philoctetes features at 5.1.59–62 as part of a catalogue of figures who were able to express their pain (the mythological Priam, Niobe, Procne, Halcyone, and Perillus, victim of the historical tyrant Phalaris; see 5.1.53–62). The catalogue owes much to the genre of *consolatio* (on which, see Kassel 1958) and philosophical debates about suffering (in which Phalaris frequently makes an appearance: Cicero, for instance, attributes an interest in this tale to Epicurus: cf. *Tusc.* 2.17, 5.73, and *Fin.* 2.88). In this example, therefore, Ovid's use of tragic *exempla* is mediated through consolation literature and philosophy.

4   Other allusions to the friendship between Orestes and Pylades do not make links with their visit to the Black Sea region explicit: cf. *Tr.* 5.4.25, 5.6.23–8, *Pont.* 2.3.45–6, and 2.6.25.

5   The main point to Ovid's use of the myth at *Tr.* 1.5.21–2 (note too that Orestes is here identified with the exiled Ovid through the description of him as *tristis* – evoking

of exile.[6] However, in a break from his usual more limited exilic engagement with tragedy, Ovid provides his readers with clear and detailed reception of a specific Greek tragedy by narrating the plot of Euripides' *Iphigenia among the Taurians*, together with detailed verbal reminiscences of this tragedy, in two poems, *Tristia* 4.4 and *Ex Ponto* 3.2.[7]

Ovid does, however, diverge from Euripides in some important details, and it is perhaps this that led Elaine Fantham, in an article from 1992 which provides many valuable insights into these poems,[8] to downplay the extent to which Ovid's versions of this myth are dependent upon Euripides' trage- dy: she singles out some details from Ovid which echo Euripides, but claims that "these are not details that would depend on close memory or reading of the Euripidean text" (Fantham 1992, 272). In fact, as this chapter demon- strates, Ovid reacts to Euripides' *Iphigenia among the Taurians* in a detailed and multi-faceted way, and the differences that can be observed between his narrative of the tragic plot and Euripides' play are an important part of his complex reception of Greek tragedy. In the first section of this chapter, I demonstrate, through exploration of numerous verbal parallels and allu- sions, how Ovid responds to specific elements of Euripides' tragedy in first *Tristia* 4.4. and then *Ex Ponto* 3.2; I then examine some features common to both Ovidian versions, and their implications for his exile poetry and wider use of tragedy.

Ovid's earliest extended exilic use of the *I. T.* is comparatively simple: in a letter to an anonymous friend, to be identified with M. Valerius Mes- salla Messallinus, the elder son of the literary patron Messalla Corvinus,[9] Ovid considers the possibility that his banishment might one day be ended by the emperor Augustus, and talks about his current circumstances, playing

---

the very title of the *Tristia* – and as suffering from madness; see further below) and 1.9.27–8. In the latter, the information that the king of the Taurians, Thoas, approved of the devotion of Pylades to Orestes has no textual authority in Euripides' *I. T.* (*con- tra* Fantham 1992, 271, who notes Thoas' forgiveness of Iphigenia and Orestes at *I. T.* 1477–8, but not the fact that Thoas does not mention *Pylades* at this juncture).

6   Cf. *Pont.* 1.2.78, where Augustus is presented as being unaware of what is happen- ing in the region to which Ovid has been relegated; this may subtly align Augustus with Thoas, given that Thoas is a leader unaware of what is happening in this region in the *I. T.*, and only becomes aware of the escape plot after the fact, at *I. T.* 1307 ff.

7   The closest parallel in the exile poetry for the lengthy narration of a myth with strong tragic *and* local connections is Ovid's version of the myth of Medea's killing of her brother Absyrtus (which provides an *aetion* for the name of Tomi, Ovid's place of exile) at *Tr.* 3.9.

8   Such as connections between the two Ovidian poems, the paradigm of devoted friendship provided by Orestes and Pylades, post-Euripidean versions of the myth in literature and the visual arts, and Ovidian self-presentation.

9   Cf. Syme 1978, 122, and Hollis 1996, 26.

up the danger and barbarity of his place of exile by linking it to the myth of Iphigenia; I give below lines 55–85 (the close of the poem):

frigida me cohibent Euxini litora Ponti: 55
    dictus ab antiquis Axenus ille fuit.
nam neque iactantur moderatis aequora ventis,
    nec placidos portus hospita navis adit.
sunt circa gentes, quae praedam sanguine quaerunt;
    nec minus infida terra timetur aqua.   60
illi, quos audis hominum gaudere cruore,
    paene sub eiusdem sideris axe iacent,
nec procul a nobis locus est, ubi Taurica dira
    caede pharetratae spargitur ara deae.
haec prius, ut memorant, non invidiosa nefandis   65
    nec cupienda bonis regna Thoantis erant.
hic pro supposita virgo Pelopeia cerva
    sacra deae coluit qualiacumque suae.
quo postquam, dubium pius an sceleratus, Orestes
    exactus Furiis venerat ipse suis,   70
et comes exemplum veri Phoceus amoris,
    qui duo corporibus mentibus unus erant.
protinus evincti tristem ducuntur ad aram,
    quae stabat geminas ante cruenta fores.
nec tamen hunc sua mors, nec mors sua terruit illum;   75
    alter ob alterius funera maestus erat.
et iam constiterat stricto mucrone sacerdos,
    cinxerat et Graias barbara vitta comas,
cum vice sermonis fratrem cognovit, et illi
    pro nece complexus Iphigenia dedit.   80
laeta deae signum crudelia sacra perosae
    transtulit ex illis in meliora locis.
haec igitur regio, magni paene ultima mundi,
    quam fugere homines dique, propinqua mihi est;
aeque mea terra prope sunt funebria sacra,   85
    si modo Nasoni barbara terra sua est.
o utinam venti, quibus est ablatus Orestes,
    placato referant et mea vela deo!

The cold shores of Pontus Euxinus check me;   55
    it was called A-xenus by men of old.
For neither are its waters tossed by moderate winds,
    nor does a visiting ship approach calm harbours.
There are tribes round about who seek booty through bloodshed;
    the land is as fearful as the treacherous sea   60
They who are reported to rejoice in men's blood
    live almost under the same constellation,
nor far from us is where the Taurian altar
    of the quivered goddess is spattered by terrible slaughter.
In past times, men say, this was Thoas' kingdom,
    not envied by the wicked nor desired by the good.   65

Here the Pelopian maiden, for whom a deer was substituted,
    cared for the rites of whatever kind of her goddess.
Here afterwards Orestes came, either pious or wicked,
    driven by his own Furies,
and his Phocean comrade, a model of true love,   70
    who were one mind in two bodies.
Straightaway bound they are led to the grim altar,
    which stood, blood-stained, before the twin doors.
His own death scared neither man;
    both were sad at the other's end.   75
And the priestess was already standing, sword drawn,
    barbarian bands binding her Greek locks,
when in their talk she recognised her brother, and
    instead of death, Iphigenia gave him embraces.
Happily she carried off from there to better places   80
    the statue of the goddess who hated cruel rites.
So this is the region, almost the edge of the entire world,
    which men and gods fled, which is next to me;
near my land are rites of death,
    if only a barbarian land can be Ovid's own land.   85
Would that the winds which carried Orestes away
    might carry home my sails too, with the god appeased.

The plot of Euripides' tragedy is narrated at 63–82 but there are potential allusions to the *I. T.* before this narrative section. The description of the Black Sea (Euxine) as *dictus ab antiquis Axenus* (= "called A-xenus [in-hospitable] by men of old", 55) may at first glance appear simply to draw attention to the inappropriateness of the Greek name for this sea, Εὔ-ξεινος ("kindly to strangers", "hospitable"), as elsewhere in the exile poems.[10] But there may be other undercurrents: for *Axenus* is found here alone in Ovid's poetry, and this, coupled with the fact that Ovid specifies the antiquity of those who used to call the sea by this name, may point to an allusion to the long literary pedigree of punning on the name of the Euxine Sea: such puns are already found, for example, in Orestes' description of the land of the Taurians as ἄξενον (= "unfriendly", *I. T.* 94).[11] Again, line 58 could be interpreted as a reference both to the locale's lack of decent harbours and calm weather and also to the small number of ships visiting the Black Sea region; if read as the latter, as well as eliciting sympathy for the exiled cosmopolitan poet, it may nod towards *I. T.* 267–8, where the majority of the local cowherds mistake the new arrivals Orestes and Pylades for deities, suggesting (as well as the heroism of the young men) that there are not many visitors to this region.

---

10 Cf. e.g. *Tr.* 2.197 (*Euxini ... sinistri* = "the ill-omened/ on the left-hand side Euxine"),
    3.13.27–8 (*Pontus,/ Euxinus falso nomine dictus* = "the Pontus Euxinus, called by a
    false name"), and 5.10.13 (*Euxini mendax cognomine* = "the false-named Euxine").
11 See also *I. T.* 218, 258, and 341.

Reference to the tribes round about Tomi who seek "booty with bloodshed" (*praedam sanguine*, 59) provides a fairly precise allusion to the practices of the bloodthirsty natives of Euripides' tragedy, who hang spoils taken from sacrificed Greeks from the bloody temple of Artemis, as Orestes and Pylades nervously note at *I. T.* 72–5:[12]

Ορ.	καὶ βωμός, Ἕλλην οὖ καταστάζει φόνος;
Πυ.	ἐξ αἱμάτων γοῦν ξάνθ' ἔχει θριγκώματα.
Ορ.	θριγκοῖς δ' ὑπ' αὐτοῖς σκῦλ' ὁρᾷς ἠρτημένα;
Πυ.	τῶν κατθανόντων γ' ἀκροθίνια ξένων.

Orestes:	And is this the altar, where Greek blood drips down?
Pylades:	It is; at any rate, it has copings brown from blood.
Orestes:	And under those copings do you see hanging spoils?
Pylades:	To be sure, the first fruits of dead strangers.

Ovid stresses the relevance of the myth to his own exilic situation, pointing out on no fewer than four occasions that all of this happened nearby (*paene*, 62, *nec procul*, 63, *propinqua*, 84, *prope*, 85). Such strong emphasis on the geographical relevance of the *I. T.* is necessary because, in actuality, the Crimea (the location of the Taurians) is on the other side of the Black Sea to Tomi, Ovid's place of exile. Ovid's slightly spurious claiming of this as a 'local' myth can be paralleled elsewhere in the exile *corpus*: for example, he includes the Colchians in a list of tribes who threaten Tomi at *Tristia* 2.191–2, thereby evoking the barbarity of another tragic figure, Medea, even though Colchis was a substantial distance away. The Crimea's 'local' appeal is undoubtedly one reason why Ovid devotes so much attention to this myth, and Ovid's geographical imprecision may serve to highlight for readers safe in Rome that the periphery of the Roman empire is blurred and confusing, a place of frightening tribes and monstrous events.[13]

Reception of Euripidean material begins in earnest at 61, with reference to *hearing* about the Taurian people who rejoice in human sacrifice, alluding to the role played by oral tradition in the other major ancient account for this local practice, a major source for Euripides himself: Herodotus 4.103.[14] *ut*

---

12 For more general comments on the violent nature of the Taurians, cf. e.g. *I. T.* 38–9 (Iphigenia notes the practice of sacrificing Greeks to Artemis before her arrival), 279–80 (the herdsmen decide to hunt down Orestes and Pylades for sacrifice), 389–90 (Iphigenia declares that the natives, being murderous, ascribe their practice of human sacrifice to Artemis), and 1325–6 (Thoas plans to forcibly recapture the fleeing Greeks).

13 I am grateful to Ingo Gildenhard for this point. Compare *Tr.* 2.187 ff. for Ovid's portrayal of his plight in Tomi, on the very edge of the civilized world.

14 Although Kyriakou 2006, 21, and Wright 2005, 175 ff., note differences in details in Herodotus' and Euripides' accounts of Taurian human sacrifices, it cannot seriously be doubted that Euripides' "debt to Herodotus was considerable" (Hall 1989, 111).

memorant (65) then acts as an Alexandrian footnote, signalling Ovid's debt to his sources.

The description of Iphigenia as *uirgo Pelopeia* (67) evokes Πέλοψ (*I. T.* 1), the first word of Euripides' play, where Iphigenia herself traces her ancestry from Pelops; furthermore, *uirgo* may allude to one of Iphigenia's earliest speeches in the play, *I. T.* 203–35, where she bewails the fact that she has never married (cf. *I. T.* 208, 216, 220). Ovid's roundabout phrase *qualiacumque* (68) for the sacrifices Iphigenia carries out for the goddess echoes Iphigenia's own reluctance to describe her rôle in the rite at *I. T.* 35 ff.:[15]

[Iphigenia:] ὅθεν νόμοισιν οἷσιν ἥδεται θεὰ
Ἄρτεμις ἑορτῆς, τοὔνομ' ἧς καλὸν μόνον -
τὰ δ' ἄλλα σιγῶ τὴν θεὸν φοβουμένη
θύω γὰρ ὄντος τοῦ νόμου καὶ πρὶν πόλει,   38
ὅς ἂν κατέλθη τήνδε γῆν Ἕλλην ἀνήρ.

And so by the laws of the festival which please the goddess
Artemis, a festival which has only a beautiful name –
but the rest I am silent about, fearing the goddess;[16]
for, it being the city's law even before [sc. I arrived], I sacrifice
every Greek man who comes to this land here.

Similarly, the description of Orestes (69–70) draws on the words of the Euripidean Orestes: διαδοχαῖς δ' Ἐρινύων/ ἠλαυνόμεσθα φυγάδες ἔξεδροι χθονός (= "the Erinyes' [Lat. Furies'] repeated attacks were driving me into exile from the land", *I. T.* 79–80),[17] and Ovid's doubt as to whether Orestes is *pius an sceleratus* (69) recalls Iphigenia's paradoxical reaction to the news that Orestes avenged his father's murder by killing his mother: ὡς εὖ κακὸν δίκαιον ἐξεπράξετο (= "How well he performed a just evil", *I. T.*

---

15 *postquam* (69) then sets up the events of the *I. T.*, in Euripidean manner, as the aftermath of the terrible events in Aulis: cf. e.g. Iphigenia's first speech (particularly *I. T.* 6 ff.), where she dwells on the attempted sacrifice, years after the event and half a world away, or her acknowledgement at 361 that she is unable to forget Aulis and events there.

16 Given Ovid's identification with Iphigenia, these lines provide an interesting parallel with Ovid's exilic poetry, where he stresses the need for his own silence about his *error* through fear of offending the god (Augustus) who caused his banishment: cf. Ingleheart 2006, 63 n. 2.

17 Note that, in Euripides, although we are told that the Erinyes drive Orestes out of Argos, it is also revealed that Apollo orders him to come to Ταυρικῆς ... ὄρους χθονός (= "the borders of the Tauric land", *I. T.* 85) in order to steal the statue of Artemis and give it to the Athenians. Ovid emphasises that Orestes is *driven* abroad rather than his Apollo-inspired mission to the Black Sea region, but knowledge of this divine mission may provide some explanation for Ovid's doubt as to whether Orestes is *pius an sceleratus*: the former in obeying Apollo's command, the latter in stealing a religious artefact (for which Orestes asks Artemis' forgiveness at *I. T.* 1400).

559).[18] 69–70 are also suggestive of Ovid's own exilic fate: whereas Iphigenia's arrival in the region can be seen as a form of sanctuary granted to her, rescuing her from sacrifice at home,[19] Ovid in exile is closer to Orestes, whom some believe to be wicked, just like the poet himself.[20] In addition, Ovid describes himself as driven to the region,[21] and his exilic downfall is frequently presented as a case of Ovid having been destroyed by his own books;[22] it might be more accurate to describe the Erinyes that drive Orestes in Euripides' tragedy as those of his *mother*,[23] but Ovid's description of them as Orestes' *own* furies evokes Ovid's downfall more clearly.[24] Ovid spells out the relevance of Orestes as a suggestive parallel for his own case at the end of this letter, when he wishes in the final couplet that the winds which carried Orestes back to Greece would take him home too.[25]

---

18 *dubium pius an sceleratus* (69) also reflects Ovid's more general recognition of the paradoxical blurring of straightforward moral categories in the tragic universe: cf. e.g. *Met.* 3.4–5 (Cadmus' father, in exiling him for failing to find his sister, Europa, is *facto pius et sceleratus eodem*), 6.635 (Procne says *scelus est pietas in conuige Tereo*), and 8.477 ([Althaea] *impietate pia est*), and Gildenhard / Zissos 1999, 164–70.

19 She is thus like Ovid in being parted from her homeland but not being an exile; for Ovid's stress in the exile poetry that he is technically *relegatus* and not *exul*, cf. *Tr.* 2.137, 5.2.61, and 5.11.21–2.

20 Although Ovid emphasizes that what led to his exile should not be called a crime: cf. e.g. *Tr.* 1.2.99–100 (*si me malus abstulit error,/ stultaque mens nobis, non scelerata fuit* = "If a bad mistake carried me away,/ and my mind was stupid, not wicked"), 1.3.37–8 (*caelestique uiro, quis me deceperit error,/ dicite, pro culpa ne scelus esse putet* = "tell the divine man what error deceived me so that he may not think a fault to be a crime"), 4.10.89–90 (*scite, precor, causam . . ./ errorem iussae, non scelus, esse fugae* = "you know, I pray, that the cause of my ordered flight was a mistake, not a crime").

21 Cf. e.g. *Tr.* 4.10.109–110: *tacta mihi tandem longis erroribus acto/ iuncta pharetratis Sarmatis ora Getis* (= "At last driven through long wanderings I touched the shore that joins the Sarmatians with the quiver-bearing Getae").

22 Ovid attributes his exilic downfall to his books at e.g. *Tr.* 2.1–12, 4.1.27–36, 5.7.31–2, and *Ibis* 6 (*artificis periit cum caput Arte sua* = "when the life of the artificer perished because of his own *Ars* [sc. the *Ars amatoria*]").

23 Cf. *I. T.* 285–291, where one of the Erinyes which Orestes alone sees holds a stone effigy of Orestes' mother in her arms.

24 Ovid even provides a verbal parallel: the emphatic juxtaposition at the end of 68 *exactus Furiis ... ipse suis* recalls the description of Actaeon (an explicit parallel for Ovid) as *praeda fuit canibus non minus ille suis* (= "no less was he the prey for his own dogs", *Tr.* 2.106).

25 4.4.87–8 are closely based on *I. T.* 1487, where Athena says ἴτ', ὦ πνοαί, ναυσθλοῦσθε τὸν Ἀγαμέμνονος / παῖδ' εἰς Ἀθήνας (= 'Go, winds, give passage for Agamemnon's son to Athens'), mentioning the escape of *Orestes* alone. Roman tragedy perhaps intervenes as an additional influence on these lines: Naevius' *Iphigenia* fr. 21 may record the words of Orestes: *passo uelo uicinum, Aquilo, me hinc in portum fer foras* (= 'North wind, with sails spread full out, carry me from here to a neighbouring harbour').

Ovid's longer treatment of the myth in the later *Pont.* 3.2 is more complex than that of *Tristia* 4.4, suggesting that he has now fully realized the potential of Euripides' escape tragedy as a suggestive parallel for his own circumstances, as a writer of exilic letters marooned in the Black Sea region.

The letter opens with Ovid saying that his addressee Cotta, named in the first line,[26] is a good friend and stood by him after his exile when others deserted, afraid of the anger of the gods (1–18; see in particular 18: *aduersos extimuere deos* = "they feared hostile gods"), recalling the words of Orestes at *I .T.* 947–8 on his reception at Athens: ἐλθὼν δ' ἐκεῖσε, πρῶτα μέν μ' οὐδεὶς ξένων/ ἑκὼν ἐδέξαθ', ὡς θεοῖς στυγούμενον (= "When I went there, at first none of my guest-friends/ was willing to receive me, as a man hated by the gods"). There is therefore already a hint in the opening lines of Ovid's letter at the devoted friendship of Pylades for Orestes, a man shunned by others; this impression is strengthened by knowledge of the nautical metaphor which the Euripidean Orestes uses for the friendship, echoed here in Ovid's description of his relationship with Cotta: compare *Pont.* 3.2.5–6 with Orestes' words at *I. T.* 599–600:

> cumque labent aliqui iactataque uela relinquant,
>   tu lacerae remanes ancora sola rati.

> When others slip away and leave behind the tossed about sails,
>   you remain the sole anchor of my shattered ship.

> [Orestes:] ὁ ναυστολῶν γάρ εἰμ' ἐγὼ τὰς συμφοράς
> οὗτος δὲ συμπλεῖ τῶν ἐμῶν μόχθων χάριν.

> For I am the sea-farer of these misfortunes,
> but this man sails with me because of my toils.

Ovid frequently uses nautical metaphors when talking of the disaster of his exile,[27] but the *positive* use of such a metaphor, here indicating the support of a friend, is, given the context, almost certainly an allusion to the *I. T.*[28]

At 33–4, Ovid begins to spell out the implicit connections between this letter and the mythological narrative that follows, by saying that Cotta and the few other friends who did not desert Ovid,[29] will have an immortal repu-

---

26 M. Aurelius Cotta Maximus Messalinus, the youngest son of the literary patron Messalla Corvinus: see Syme 1986, 217–26.

27 Ovid often refers to himself as shipwrecked: see e.g. La Penna 1957 on *Ib.* 17–18.

28 The only other positive examples of nautical metaphors in the letters from exile are *Tr.* 1.5.35–6, 4.5.5–6 and 19–20, 5.6.1–2 (but note 7 and 46), 5.9.17–19, *Pont.* 1.10.39–40, 2.3.57–60 (also addressed to Cotta), 2.6.12–16, 2.7.83–4, 2.8.68, 2.9.9 ff., and 4.12.41–2.

29 Cf. 25–32, where Ovid addresses the *pauci* who did not reject him after his exile, and says that they will gain an immortal reputation through his poetry: *uestri* (27), *uos* (35, 37), *uestra* (36, 39) are thus genuine plurals, addressed to this entire group.

tation after Ovid's death, as did Pylades, who accompanied Orestes: *occidit et Theseus et qui comitauit Oresten:/ sed tamen in laudes uiuit uterque suas* (= "Theseus died, as did he who was companion to Orestes:/ yet all the same either lives in the praise he receives"). There is witty play with *I. T.* here in the failure to name Pylades, which recalls the naming of Pylades early in the *I. T.* (249), and the concealment of *Orestes'* identity for the purposes of the plot.[30]

Ovid moves from promises that Cotta will gain immortal fame from Ovid's writings (35–6) to state that Cotta already has a good reputation among the local barbarians because of Ovid (37–8). Introducing the mythological narrative proper, Ovid says that when he was praising Cotta and his other friends, a certain old man, *quidam senex* (41) told him the plot of the *I. T.* as an illustration of his claim that barbarians recognize friendship (43–4). I give below lines 39–102 with translation:

> cumque ego de uestra nuper probitate referrem
>   – nam didici Getice Sarmaticeque loqui –   40
> forte senex quidam, coetu cum staret in illo,
>   reddidit ad nostros talia uerba sonos:
> "nos quoque amicitiae nomen, bone, nouimus, hospes,
>   quos procul a uobis Pontus et Hister habet.
> est locus in Scythia – Tauros dixere priores –   45
>   qui Getica longe non ita distat humo.
> hac ego sum terra – patriae nec paenitet – ortus.
>   consortem Phoebi gens colit illa deam.
> templa manent hodie uastis innixa columnis
>   perque quater denos itur in illa gradus.   50
> fama refert illic signum caeleste fuisse,
>   quoque minus dubites, stat basis orba dea
> araque, quae fuerat natura candida saxi,
>   decolor adfuso sanguine tincta rubet.
> femina sacra facit taedae non nota iugali,   55
>   quae superat Scythicas nobilitate nurus.
> sacrifici genus est, sic instituere parentes,
>   aduena uirgineo caesus ut ense cadat.
> regna Thoas habuit Maeotide clarus in ora,
>   nec fuit Euxinis notior alter aquis.   60
> sceptra tenente illo liquidas fecisse per auras

Ovid thereby undermines the paradigm of Pylades and Orestes as a pair of devoted friends; an interesting and independent twist on a view of Pylades and Orestes that is rather hackneyed by the time Ovid writes (see below).

30 Cf. *I. T.* 250–1 and 499–504 for Euripidean teasing about the possibility that Orestes' name will be revealed prematurely, thus ruining the recognition scene; Orestes' identity is finally revealed by Pylades at 791–2 (although Iphigenia does not at first accept that the Greek who embraces her is in fact Orestes, only naming him as such at 829).

nescio quam dicunt Iphigenian iter,
    quam leuibus uentis sub nube per aequora uectam
        creditur his Phoebe deposuisse locis.
praefuerat templo multos ea rite per annos,   65
    inuita peragens tristia sacra manu,
cum duo uelifera iuuenes uenere carina
    presseruntque suo litora nostra pede.
par fuit his aetas et amor, quorum alter Orestes,
    ast Pylades alter: nomina fama tenet.   70
protinus inmitem Triuiae ducuntur ad aram,
    euincti geminas ad sua terga manus.
spargit aqua captos lustrali Graia sacerdos,
    ambiat ut fuluas infula longa comas,
dumque parat sacrum, dum uelat tempora uittis   75
    dum tardae causas inuenit ipsa morae:
'non ego crudelis, iuuenes, ignoscite,' dixit,
    'sacra suo facio barbariora loco.
ritus is est gentis. qua uos tamen urbe uenitis
    quodue parum fausta puppe petistis iter?'   80
dixit et audito patriae pia nomine uirgo
    consortes urbis comperit esse suae:
'alter ut e uobis,' inquit, 'cadat hostia sacris,
    ad patrias sedes nuntius alter eat.'
ire iubet Pylades carum periturus Orestem;   85
    hic negat inque uices pugnat uterque mori.
extitit hoc unum quo non conuenerit illis:
    cetera par concors et sine lite fuit.
dum peragunt iuuenes pulchri certamen amoris,
    ad fratrem scriptas exarat illa notas.   90
ad fratrem mandata dabat, cuique illa dabantur,
    – humanos casus aspice! – frater erat.
nec mora, de templo rapiunt simulacra Dianae
    clamque per inmensas puppe feruntur aquas.
mirus amor iuuenum; quamuis abiere tot anni,   95
    in Scythia magnum nunc quoque nomen habent."
fabula narrata est postquam uulgaris ab illo,
    laudarunt omnes facta piamque fidem.
scilicet hac etiam, qua nulla ferocior ora est,
    nomen amicitiae barbara corda mouet.   100
quid facere Ausonia geniti debetis in urbe,
    cum tangant duros talia facta Getas?

When I was recently talking about your probity
    – for I have learned to speak Getic and Sarmatian –   40
by chance a certain old man, standing in that circle,
    replied such words to my sounds:
"We also know the name of friendship, you good stranger,
    who are kept from Rome by the Pontus and Hister.
There is a place in Scythia – men before us called it Tauri –   45
    which is not far distant from the Getic land.

I come from that land – I do not regret my fatherland.
    That tribe worships Apollo's companion goddess.
A temple remains there today resting on huge columns
    which is entered through four score steps.   50
Rumour reports that there was a heavenly statue there,
    and to prove it, the pedestal stands bereft of the
goddess and the altar, which was of naturally white stone,
    is discoloured, stained red from the blood spilled.
A woman who has not known marriage tends the rites,   55
    who surpasses the Scythian women in nobility.
The nature of the sacrifice, as our parents ordained,
    is that a newcomer falls killed by the virgin's sword.
Thoas, famous in the Maeotic region, ruled the kingdom,
    nor was anyone more famous in the Euxine waters.   60
While he held the sceptre, men say that some Iphigenia
    made a journey through the clear skies,
and, carried over the waters in a cloud by gentle winds,
    Phoebe is believed to have deposited her there.
She had duly presided over the temple for many years   65
    fulfilling grim rites with her unwilling hand,
when two young men arrived in a sail-bearing ship
    and disembarked on our shores with their feet.
They were equals in age and love, one named Orestes,
    and the other Pylades; report retains their names.   70
Straightaway they are led to the harsh altar of Trivia,
    their twin hands bound behind their backs.
The Greek priestess scattered the captives with lustral water
    so a long fillet might encircle their blond locks.
While she prepared the rite, while she covered their heads with bands, 75
    and while she herself found reasons for slow delay:
'I am not cruel, young men, forgive me,' she said,
    'I make sacrifices more barbarous than this place.
This is the rite of the tribe. But what city do you come from
    and why did you seek a journey on an unlucky ship?'   80
The pious maiden spoke and when she heard the name of
    the fatherland, she discovered they shared her own city.
'One of you,' she said, 'must fall a victim in the rites,
    and the other go as a messenger to his ancestral home.'
Pylades, ready to die, ordered his dear Orestes to go;   85
    he refused and in turn each fought to die.
This was the one thing on which they did not agree:
    everything else was harmonious and quarrel-free.
While the beautiful young men strove in a contest of love
    she marked out written signs to her brother.   90
She was sending orders to her brother, and the man she gave
    the orders to – tragic reversal! – was her brother.
There's no delay: they snatch the statue of Diana from the
    temple and slip off by ship over huge waters.
The love of the young men was amazing; many years   95

have passed, but they still have a great name in Scythia."
After the famous tale was told by that man,
    everyone praised deeds of pious devotion.
Evidently here too, the most savage shore of all,
    the name of friendship moves barbarian hearts.   100
What should you do, who were born in the Italian city,
    when such deeds touch the hard-hearted Getae?

The old man's rôle as the narrator of this myth is an Ovidian innovation,[31] and it is worth exploring why this narrative comes from a third party rather than Ovid himself. First, Ovid's choice of narrator provides variation from his earlier version; the old man identifies himself as a native Taurian, so Ovid fittingly gives this local myth to a local narrator.[32] This adds much to Ovid's narrative: such as the faux naïve touch of the old man describing Iphigenia as "a certain Iphigenia", *nescio quam … Iphigenian* (62),[33] as well as the more important point for Ovid's exilic circumstances that he can claim that if even barbarians are moved by this story of friendship, Romans should be moved; a clear pointer to his friends in Rome to help him in his exilic circumstances, spelled out in the final lines I quote above.

 Imprecision about the identity of the native "certain old man" (*senex quidam*, 41) is also worth probing, not least because Ovid may thereby comment on a device typical of Euripidean tragedy, where minor characters who hasten along his plots are left unnamed and their identity vague and open to speculation. One such example occurs within the *I. T.* itself, at 275, where, according to the cowherd/ messenger ἄλλος δέ τις μάταιος, ἀνομίαι θρασύς (= "Some other man, a fool, bold in his irreverence") persuades the Taurian cowherds that Orestes and Pylades are not in fact gods but are shipwrecked sailors, who can be hunted down and sacrificed to Artemis; another example is the mysterious τις πλάνης κατ' ἄστυ καὶ τρίβων λόγων (= "Some wanderer from the city, slick in his use of words", *Bacchae* 717),[34] who persuades another set of herdsmen to hunt down the Bacchants. These parallels might lead us to think more deeply about the identity and rôle of the old man in Ovid's version of the myth, and a number of options seem worth exploring.

---

31   Fantham 1992, 276, notes "Ovid's bold imaginative device of telling the Greek legend from a Taurian, or shall we say Getic, point of view."

32   Fantham 1992, 276, already notes the "local angle" of Ovid's focalisation through a native Taurian.

33   A sign that the exiled Ovid is capable of viewing Greco-Roman myth from a standpoint which is not Romano-centric, contra Habinek's comments about Ovid's nationalistic, Roman construction of his identity in the exile poetry (see Habinek 1998, 151 ff.).

34   Perhaps to be identified with Dionysus, who elsewhere stage-manages the plot of the *Bacchae* in fine detail?

Stephen Harrison has suggested that the old man gives a tragic messenger speech here, in reporting tragic action that takes place "off stage";[35] an interesting idea, but the old man is perhaps presented rather as speaking from a tragic *chorus*, given that we are told that he stands in a *coetus* (41), which can have the sense of 'circle' (*OLD* 4) or 'assembly' of persons.[36] This would revisit and rewrite Euripides by giving the chorus of the play not to captive Greek girls, who share Iphigenia's displacement from their homeland,[37] and in whom Iphigenia can confide,[38] but to a local aged man, a more appropriate narrator in the context of Ovid's exile corpus, where he is keen to stress his complete isolation.[39] In contrast to Iphigenia, who converses freely with her fellow countrywomen, Ovid has been forced by his isolation to learn the native languages – or so he claims in the lines that precede the old man's narration of the myth, parenthetically explaining his ability to tell the natives about Cotta (*nam didici Getice Sarmaticeque loqui* = "for I have learned to speak Getic and Sarmatian", *Pont.* 3.2.40).[40]

Again, it is possible that in the figure of the *senex* we should recognize Euripides: this would not fit with the detail that the old man was a native Taurian, but the role of storyteller would be appropriate for the dramatic poet, whose priority in telling this myth, and literary stature, would thus be signalled by the label *senex*.[41] A further possibility is that the storytelling

---

35 In a paper on *Ex Ponto* 3.2 (as yet unpublished) delivered as part of the faculty reading classes led by Stephen Harrison and the late Oliver Lyne on *Ex Ponto* 3 at Oxford in 2001.

36 See Jocelyn 1967 on Enn. *Scaen.* 123.

37 Cf. e.g. *I. T.* 132–5 (where the chorus lament that they have left their homes in Greece behind), 447–55 (where they lament their sufferings as slaves and wish to dream of their homes), 647–8 (where they call Pylades blessed for returning to his homeland), and 1089–1152 (where they lament leaving Greece and being sold into slavery in barbarous regions, and envy Iphigenia's escape to Greece). Ovid may also draw on Roman tragedy for his reassignment of the rôle of the chorus in this tragic narrative, given that Ennius' *Iphigenia in Aulis* (which is based on Euripides' play) had substituted a chorus of male soldiers for Euripides' female chorus: see Jocelyn 1967, 334–7. I am grateful to Ingo Gildenhard for pointing out this parallel.

38 Cf. e.g. *I. T.* 1056 ff., where Iphigenia appeals to the chorus to keep her escape attempt a secret from the natives.

39 Cf. e.g. *Tr.* 1.9.6, 5.7.41, *Pont.* 4.2.39–40.

40 A claim that is hard to take entirely seriously (cf. e.g. Casali 1997, 92–6); this parenthesis is a humorous afterthought which attempts to account for the unlikely information which comes before it, very much in the Ovidian manner (cf. Hollis 1970 on *Met.* 8.860). Furthermore, as one of the participants at the Oxford reading classes on this poem observed, there does not seem to be much point to learning the native languages, since Ovid hears a tale already well known from Euripides!

41 Cf. e.g. *Tr.* 2.364: *lyrici Teia Musa senis* (= "the Teian Muse of the lyric old man" = Anacreon), Virgil *Ecl.* 6.70: *Ascraeo .. seni* (= "the Ascraean old man" = Hesiod; see with Clausen 1994, who notes the parallel of Call. *Hymn* 4.304, where Λυκίοιο

senex, a traveller outside his homeland, should be identified with Euripides' source for the *mores* of the Taurians, Herodotus.

The *senex* also has a number of suggestive affinities with Ovid himself, who is after all the primary narrator of this embedded narrative; has left his homeland; and consistently presents himself as a *senex* in the exile poetry.[42] Given the unlikelihood of Ovid having learned Getic and Sarmatian, and so being able to hear this tale, and the unbelievable scenario that the people of Tomi would stand around to listen to Ovid talking about Cotta's probity (since they regularly have to defend themselves against attacking hordes in Ovid's exile poetry),[43] the parallels between the *senex* and Ovid himself may be a case of the author tipping a wink to his readers that he himself is pulling all the strings in this narrative.

Let us turn now to the narrative itself. The old man's grounding of the tale in fact through the evidence of the temple of Artemis which still exists in his native country (*manent hodie*, 49) at the start of his narrative, its pedestal now bereft of the statue of Artemis it once held (51–2), and its altar stained from human sacrifice (53–4), nods to Euripides in several ways.[44] Most obviously, "the story goes" (*fama refert*, 51) alludes to Ovid's tragic source; however, this Alexandrian footnote should be read with the description of the statue as *caeleste* (51; 'divine' or 'of the sky') as an allusion to *I. T.* 87–88, where Orestes reports that men say (φασιν, 87) that the statue of Artemis which he has come to steal fell from heaven (οὐρανοῦ … ἄπο, 88). *fama refert* therefore alludes to Orestes' own claim that he is relying on others for this fantastic story. The perfect tense of *fuisse* (51), together with *orba dea* (52), points to Orestes' theft of the statue in the *I. T.* Furthermore, the old man's proof of the myth through the contemporary existence of the temple is surely a witty reference to Euripides' characteristic fondness for providing *aetia* for contemporary cult;[45] in the *I. T.*, for example, Athene

---

γέροντος seems to refer to the prehistoric poet Olen), and *Pont.* 4.14.32: *agricolae Musa … senis* (= Hesiod).

42 Cf. e.g. *Tr.* 2.544, 4.1.73 (Ovid, now *senior*, is forced to take up arms in Tomi), 4.8 (*passim*) and *Pont.* 1.4.20.

43 See e.g. *Tr.* 4.1.65–86, 5.2.69–72, and 5.10.15–28 and 44 (where Ovid notes that wounds are often inflicted in the forum – presumably the venue for this story-telling).

44 Fantham 1992, 276, describes *Pont.* 3.2.45 (*est locus in Scythia*) as an "ecphrasis … in the best epic style" and the detail of the empty pedestal as "a rhetorical *tekmerion* or source of a Callimachean *aition*"; fair points, but she misses Ovid's play with a feature characteristic of Euripidean tragedy (see above).

45 On which, see e.g. Dunn 1996, 46–50. Ovid also slightly reverses Euripides' usual placement of *aetia* (almost always at the *end* of a play: Dunn 1996, 48–9) by giving his *aetion* at the start of his account.

instructs Orestes to build a temple at Halai and set up the stolen statue of Artemis there as Artemis the Tauropolian (1453 ff.).

The old man's account of the human sacrifices offered in this temple responds in several ways to Euripides' tragedy. First, let us examine the claims of the *senex* that the woman who presides over these rites is unmarried and surpasses the local women in nobility (55–6). The Euripidean Iphigenia bewails the fact that she has never been able to marry at *I. T.* 220 and 856, but the old man's description of the class qualification for holding the priesthood is unparalleled in Euripides, and suggests strongly that the priestess is a native rather than an outsider. Ovid must purport to reflect the Taurian point of view through the old man here:[46] present tenses describe the rôle of the native priestess not only for vividness, but also because the sacrifices presumably still go on, presided over by a native noblewoman. The version of the practices given in Ovid points out that the foreigner Iphigenia was a one-off as priestess, just as she herself notes at *I. T.* 38–9 that human sacrifice was a local custom long before her arrival: θύω γὰρ νόμου καὶ πρὶν πόλει/ ὃς ἄν κατέλθη τήνδε γῆν Έλλην ἀνήρ (= "For the law being in place for the city even before, I sacrifice whichever Greek men come to this land"). With lines 55–6, Ovid thus highlights a disturbing and easily overlooked element of the closure of Euripides' tragedy: although Athena, the *deus ex machina* who arrives at *I. T.* 1435, prevents violence by ordering Thoas to stop his pursuit of the escaping Greeks (1437) and by telling Orestes that honours to Artemis the Tauropolian should stop short of human sacrifice (1458–61), there is no mention in the play of any orders to Thoas to end the Taurian practice of human sacrifice.[47] Ovid's hint that human sacrifice still goes on thus draws attention to the fact that barbarians are not necessarily civilised through their contact with the Greek world, which looks particularly pointed given that he is writing from Tomi, founded as a Greek colony.[48]

---

46   Ovid also reflects *Roman* religious practices: the virgin surpassing others in nobility surely alludes to the Vestal Virgins, demonstrating Roman cultural imperialism in understanding others' religious rites in the light of Roman practices (compare the old man's claim that the custom of human sacrifice is *mos maiorum* at 57; a very Roman way of looking at things, as Fantham 1992, 276 n. 25 already notes).

47   Cf. Kyriakou 2006, 415 ff. It is possible that there is a lacuna at 1469 and that such orders were included in it; however, this is unlikely, and the detail of the bloodless sacrifices in *Greece* would draw attention to the absence of similar orders for the native Taurians.

48   Ovid stresses the Greek origin of Tomi at *Tr.* 1.10.41 (*Miletida ... urbem* = "the Milesian city") and 3.9.1–4; at 5.7.51–2, Ovid notes that a few locals retain some Greek speech but that Getic accents have made it barbarous, and at 5.10.33–4 that those of Greek descent wear Persian trousers.

Secondly, the old man's description of the *aduena* (= 'incomer', 58) falling in the sacrifice *uirgineo ... ense* (= "by a virgin's sword") picks up on two ambiguities in Euripides. First, the *I. T.* sometimes specifies that Iphigenia's victims are Greeks, and sometimes simply refers to the slaughter of strangers.[49] Ovid's focus upon the neutral *aduena* rather than Greeks as victims stresses that, as an exile in these parts, who might end up subjected to such barbaric behaviour, it is not the Greek aspect of this myth that interests him. Secondly, the old man's description of the instrument of death being the sword of a maiden neatly echoes the squeamishness of the tragedy about Iphigenia's exact rôle in human sacrifices,[50] since *uirgineo ... ense* is open to interpretation. On the most obvious reading, this phrase attributes responsibility for the sacrifices to the virgin priestess of line 55, but Ovid's failure to specify *which* virgin's sword carries out the ritual may suggest that *another* virgin's sword is the instrument of death,[51] hinting at the *I. T.*'s ambiguity about the rôle played by Iphigenia in these practices.

Iphigenia's rôle in barbaric sacrifices has particular resonance for Ovid writing from the Black Sea: her complicity (and the fact that the sacrifices

---

49   For Iphigenia's sacrifice of *Greeks*, see *I. T.* 39, 72, 241–7 (the herdsman reports the capture of Orestes and Pylades and that these Greeks should be prepared for sacrifice), and 459–60; for the sacrifice of *strangers*, cf. e.g. *I. T.* 53, 75, 226, 278 ff. (a herdsman says that Orestes and Pylades will have heard about sacrifices of strangers, and the herdsmen then decide to hunt them down as victims, without knowing whether they are Greek), and 776; cf. also the particularly ambiguous passages 336–9 (the herdsman tells Iphigenia to pray to have strangers like this to sacrifice, but then says that if she sacrifices them, *Hellas* will make amends for her 'sacrifice' at Aulis), and 344–7 (Iphigenia says that she has always been compassionate towards strangers – whenever Greeks have fallen into her hands). Euripidean ambiguity here fits with Herodotus 4.103, who says that shipwrecked sailors *and* captured Greeks were sacrificed in this way.

50   Cf. *I. T.* 38–9 (where Iphigenia says that she sacrifices Greeks), 444–5 (where the chorus hope that Helen might come to this land, so that she can die in a sacrificial ritual "by the throat-cutting hand of my mistress": i.e. Iphigenia), the following exchange between Iphigenia and Orestes at 621–4: Or. αὐτὴ ξίφει κτείνουσα θῆλυς ἄρσενας; / Iph. οὔκ, ἀλλὰ χαίτην ἀμφὶ σὴν χερνίψομαι/ Or. ὁ δὲ σφαγεὺς τίς, εἰ τάδ' ἱστορεῖν με χρή; / Iph. ἔσω δόμων τῶνδ' εἰσὶν οἷς μέλει τάδε = "Or: Will you yourself, a female, kill me, a male, with a sword?/ Iph: No, but I will sprinkle your head with holy water/ Or: Who will be my slaughterer, if I can ask this?/ Iph: Inside the temple are those who care for such things"), and 870–2.

51   *Which* virgin does the sword belong to, if not Iphigenia? Perhaps the virgin goddess Artemis, in whose name the human sacrifices are carried out; her virginity is under-emphasised within the *I. T.* (the only definite mention of it comes at 1230), but Ovid had a Latin model in Lucr. 1.84–7, who stresses the virgin status of *both* Artemis and Iphigenia (in the context of the sacrifice at Aulis). If we understand *uirgineo ... ense* in this way, the goddess would play an appropriately threatening rôle for Ovid's exile poetry (see further above).

do not end after the Greeks depart) plays up an important contrast between civilisation and barbarity, showing that even innocent Greek maidens can be brutalised once they are transferred to the borders of the civilised world. Hence Ovid's deployment of this myth issues a self-reflexive challenge for the exile poet: will Ovid become like Iphigenia, and adjust to the barbarous practices of his new surroundings?[52]

Having laid out the specifics of the practice of human sacrifice in his native land, the old man then grounds the plot of the *I.T.* in 'local history' at 59 ff., explaining how Iphigenia came to be in the land. Ovid stresses affinities between himself and Iphigenia in the lines which follow in a variety of ways: first, the emphasis on her having presided over the temple in this barbarian land for many years (65) recalls the many references in the later exilic books to the length of Ovid's exile.[53] Furthermore, the description of Iphigenia carrying out *tristia* sacrifices with her *inuita* hand (66), acts as a *mise en abyme* which evokes Ovid's own situation, reluctantly forced by his exile into writing a collection entitled *Tristia*.[54] Ovid plays the rôle of heroines elsewhere in his exile poetry,[55] but nowhere do the circumstances of a heroine so neatly fit Ovid's own exilic lot.

Pont. 3.2 is by far Ovid's longest version of this myth, but having set up the tragic plot, he fast-forwards at dizzying pace. Immediately we are told at 67–70 of the arrival of the youthful Orestes and Pylades and the crucial detail of their mutual love (which is, after all, the peg on which this lengthy narrative hangs; for more on the very Roman aspect of their love, see below), Ovid hurries them to the altar with *protinus* (71),[56] cutting out a lengthy Euripidean scene, where they hide themselves and have to be captured by the natives (*I.T.* 104–339). Just after we are told that Iphigenia realizes the identity of her brother via the letter, Ovid says that there is no

---

52   I am grateful to Ingo Gildenhard for clarifying this point.

53   Cf. e.g. *Tr.* 5.10.1–2 (Ovid has spent three winters in exile), *Pont.* 1.1.1 (Ovid is *non nouus incola* in Tomi), 1.2.26 (the fourth winter in Tomi tires Ovid), and 4.6.5–6 (Ovid has already passed five years in 'Scythia'). The third book of the *Epistulae Ex Ponto* was probably written in AD 13 (cf. Syme 1978, 42), by which time Ovid had been in the area for around four years.

54   Cf. with *Pont.* 1.5.10 (*scribimus inuita uixque coacta manu*). For puns on the title of the collection and Ovid's own sorry exilic circumstances, see *Pont.* 1.1.15–16 (*inuenies, quamuis non est miserabilis index,/ non minus hoc illo triste, quod ante dedi*), and cf. e.g. *Tr.* 2.493–4, 3.1.9–10 (where the book says *inspice quid portem: nihil hic nisi triste uidebis,/ carmine temporibus conueniente suis*), 4.10.112 (*tristia, quo possum, carmine fata leuo*), 5.1.47 (*interea nostri quid agant, nisi triste, libelli?*), and *Pont.* 3.9.35 (*laeta fere laetus cecini, cano tristia tristis*).

55   Cf. Rosenmeyer 1997 *passim* on the way in which Ovid re-enacts the rôles of the heroines of his own *Heroides* in his exile poetry.

56   Also at *Tristia* 4.4.73, immediately after Ovid tells us that the pair arrived in the area.

delay, they snatch the statue from the temple and flee (93–4), thereby removing Euripidean hindrances to the action such as Iphigenia's questions about Electra and what has brought Orestes to the Black Sea after she learns of his identity (*I. T.* 912–78; Pylades even tells the siblings to face the problem of how to escape at 905–6, acknowledging the delay), and the issue of how the theft of the statue and escape are going to be brought off (debated at length at *I. T.* 1017 ff.). This abbreviation of the action of the tragedy is a notable feature of *both* of Ovid's versions of the myth: *Tristia* 4.4.79 provides an even more radically slimmed down version of Euripides' plot by cutting out the letter recognition-scene with the information that Iphigenia recognized her brother in conversation.

Pont. 3.2 is a little more suspenseful and dramatic than this: Ovid has Iphigenia make the preparations for sacrifice at 73–5, hinting that he is giving an expanded version of the myth in comparison with his earlier narration in the *Tristia* when he says that Iphigenia finds causes for delay (76), and he even allows Iphigenia two examples of direct speech within the old man's narration (77–80, 83–4), acknowledging the dramatic form of his model, and perhaps playing on the speech-within-a-speech Iphigenia herself gives in her account of the sacrifice at Aulis (*I. T.* 364–71). It is hard not to see all of this as Ovid having fun at the expense of the expansive nature of Euripides' play, whose plot could be extremely simple: if Orestes were to reveal his identity straightaway, this would speed things up immensely, and the audience would be deprived of the planned sacrifice, as well as the tragic recognition scene and tender reunion of brother and sister. Ovid may tease the reader with the possibility that Iphigenia will recognize Orestes and so bypass much of the Euripidean plot with his description of the *fuluas ... comas* (= "golden locks", 74) of the captive Orestes and Pylades; there is stress on Orestes' golden hair at *I. T.* 51–52, and this could easily have been used by Euripides to hasten along the recognition scene, given that Iphigenia has the same hair colour at *I. T.* 174, and the rôle which hair plays in other tragic recognition scenes between these siblings.[57] If we cannot be sure of the tone within the scenes leading up to the recognition in Euripides, it seems fairly certain that here Ovid is playing the tragic for laughs.

Euripidean material persists. Iphigenia's first speech draws upon Euripides quite closely: her claim at 77–8 that it is not her but the customs of the place that are cruel should be compared with *I.T.* 380 ff., where she deplores human sacrifice and says that the locals have invented Artemis' cruelty for their own ends. Iphigenia's speech in Euripides ends with her stating that she does not believe that any deity is evil (391); she makes no explicit statement

---

57   Cf. Aeschylus *Choephoroi* 183 ff. and Euripides *Electra* 513 ff.

to this effect in Ovid's version of the myth in this poem,[58] but if we look back to *Tristia* 4.4.81, we are told that Artemis hates the cruel rites carried out in her name, which seems to confirm Iphigenia's statement.

Iphigenia's next speech in *Pont.* 3.2 (83–4) informs the young men that one of them can go home as a messenger – *nuntius* (84) acknowledges the importance of messenger scenes in ancient tragedy in general and the *I. T.* in particular, where there are (unusually) two lengthy messenger speeches –[59] and one must be sacrificed. This elegiac couplet on the future of the pair echoes well the balanced but different fates spelled out by Iphigenia at *I. T.* 582–96. The message to be carried home here must be the same as that in Euripides: that Iphigenia is alive and well and living in Tauris, and that her brother Orestes should come and take her home (*I. T.* 770–76). Ovid, however, only makes this clear when he stresses that she writes a letter to her *brother* (90 ff.).

The contest to die between Orestes and Pylades at 85–9 is worth considering in the light of Ovid's reception of Euripides. In the *I. T.*, the young men are told by Iphigenia at 577–96 that one of them has to fall as a victim in the sacrifices and that one should carry her letter home. Orestes immediately volunteers to die (599 ff.). At 674 ff., Pylades states that it would be shameful for him to live on after Orestes' death, and, citing his fear for his reputation in Greece if he were to return alone, says that he should die together with Orestes (684–6). Orestes refuses this offer and tells Pylades that he should return home with the letter (687 ff.), a plan which Pylades appears to accept. Note the subtle differences in Ovid's version: Pylades is set on death and orders Orestes to go (85), Orestes refuses, and they fight to die (86). Ovid thereby removes Pylades' self-centred motivation for agreeing to be sacrificed, while at the same time stressing his heroism in presenting him as the first one prepared to die. The overall effect of Ovid's changes to Euripides, however, is to emphasise the mutual love of the young heroes, and this is an element which owes much to *Roman* tragedy. Cicero records at *de Amicitia* 24, *de Finibus* 2.79, and 5.63 a popular theatrical scene in which Orestes and Pylades compete to die: I give the relevant passages below:

> (Laelius, praising friendship:) qui clamores tota cauea nuper in hospitis et amici mei M. Pacuui noua fabula cum ignorante rege uter Orestes esset, Pylades Oresten se diceret, ut pro illo necaretur, Orestes autem, ita ut erat, Oresten se esse perseuerat. stantes plaudebant in re ficta … (Cic. *Am.* 24)

> What cries there were recently in the whole theatre for the new play of my guest-friend Marcus Pacuvius, when, the king being ignorant as to which of the pair was

---

58   Perhaps there are good reasons for Ovid, exiled by the divine Augustus, not to have his Iphigenia say such a thing here; see below for more on the gods in this poem.

59   *I. T.* 236–391 and 1327–1419.

Orestes, Pylades said that he was Orestes in order to die for him, but Orestes, telling it as it was, maintained that *he* was the real Orestes. The spectators were applauding this made-up material.

... aut Pylades cum sis, dices te esse Oresten ut moriare pro amico, aut si esses Orestes, Pyladen refelleres, te indicares, et si id non probares, quo minus ambo una necaremini non precare (Cic. *Fin*. 2.79)

... Or when you might be Pylades, you would say that you are Orestes in order to die for your friend, or if you might be Orestes, you would say Pylades is a liar, point yourself out, and if you were not to prove the fact, not to appeal against dying both together.

qui clamores uulgi atque imperitorum excitantur in theatris, cum illa dicuntur:
    Ego sum Orestes,
contraque ab altero:
    Immo enimuero ego sum, inquam, Orestes!
cum autem etiam exitus ab utroque datur conturbato errantique regi:
    ambo ergo una necarier precamur.
quotiens hoc agitur, ecquandone nisi admirationibus maximis?

                      (Cic. *Fin*. 5.63)

What cries of the people and of the educated are aroused in the theatres, when these lines are said:
    I am Orestes,
and, contrariwise by the other man:
    No, indeed, I am, I say, Orestes!
As often as this is acted, is it ever without the greatest admiration?

These passages seem to refer to Pacuvius' *Chryses*, in which Orestes and Pylades are tracked down by Thoas after their escape from the land of the Taurians, and Thoas attempts to kill the man who has spirited the statue and priestess of Artemis away. Ovid is here playing to popular tastes and a specifically Roman and not Greek gallery by alluding to a scene in a rapturously received Roman tragedy which seems to have appealed to the value Romans of all classes placed on friendship.[60]

Ovid next further emphasises the affinities between himself and Iphigenia: the information that she is writing a letter home at 90 ff. should be compared with the first couplet of the poem, where Ovid stresses that he is writing a letter to be sent to Cotta: *Quam legis a nobis missam tibi, Cotta, salutem,/ missa sit ut uere perueniatque precor* (= "The good health which is sent by me to you, Cotta,/ I pray that it might be sent in fact and get through to you"). Ovid's depiction of Iphigenia herself writing a letter is in strong contrast with the *I. T.*, where Iphigenia claims that a *prisoner* she later sacri-

---

60 Compare Gildenhard / Zissos 1999, 178–180 on the "change in cultural outlook" from Greek tragedy to the Roman world in Ovid's version of the myth of Hippolytus / Virbius in *Met*. 15.

ficed physically wrote this letter for her (*I. T.* 584–5).[61] By this change from his Euripidean model, Ovid makes a very Roman and generic point: women are frequently writers of letters in Latin poetry and love elegy in particular (for example, in *Amores* 1.11 and 12, Ovid's beloved replies to his request for a rendezvous in the negative, and the entire premise of Ovid's *Heroides* is that various heroines of myth write letters to their distant lovers); Iphigenia is therefore aligned with other female writers in Ovid's corpus, showing continuity within his oeuvre.[62] In terms of Ovid's reception of Euripides, Iphigenia's writing of the letter comments on and cuts out an inconsistency in the Euripidean plot, whereby she appears to read out to the young men the contents of the letter in case the letter as physical object is lost by Pylades on the voyage home (*I. T.* 770 ff.); another delaying tactic in Euripides which finally leads to the recognition scene proper.

Ovid further reduces the complexity of the Euripidean plot by having Iphigenia give the letter to her brother at 91–2 and not to Pylades (as at *I. T.* 744 ff.). Ovid's potted and simple version of the plot of the *I. T.* arguably again flags up the implausibility and long-winded nature of the Euripidean plot. Ovid further abbreviates the Euripidean plot by omitting the attempted opposition of Thoas to the escape-plot (*I. T.* 1284 ff.), and the divine help Athena provides to ensure that the Greeks escape (*I. T.* 1435 ff.). Ovid had already alluded to the *deus ex machina* who can effect escapes from such barbarous regions at *Tristia* 4.4.45 ff., where Augustus is a god who can end Ovid's sojourn in this region. Reasons for the absence of Thoas from Ovid's version in *Pont.* 3.2 will be further considered below.

I wish now to take a broader overview of these Ovidian versions of Euripides' *Iphigenia among the Taurians* in his exile corpus, and the wider implications for his exile poetry that can be uncovered from examining his reception of this particular tragedy.

Ovid's decision to reproduce the plot of Euripides' tragic *I. T.* (with certain significant divergences, as noted above) within *Tr.* 4.4 and *Pont.* 3.2 has generic significance. His recasting of plot of the *I. T.* as elegiac narrative provides a commentary upon the origins, development, and uses of elegy: Ovid returns elegy to its roots by using it as a vehicle for mythological narrative, recalling and reasserting the importance of mythological narrative in early elegiac poetry, an element which seems gradually to have become subordinated to subjective concerns in Hellenistic and then Roman erotic

---

61   Strongly implying that Iphigenia cannot write, a surprising piece of information, which is surely dictated by Euripides' plot: see Cropp 2000, 214.

62   In particular, Iphigenia is aligned with Penelope in *Heroides* 1, who also unwittingly gives a letter to its intended addressee: cf. Kennedy 1984, 416. It is notable that the letter here leads to tragic *anagnorisis*, but this will be delayed in Ovid's version of the end of the *Odyssey*.

elegy.[63] Such interest in the origins of elegy is characteristic of the exile poems, where Ovid explores a number of possibilities for the uses to which elegy can be put, frequently stressing the supposed origins of elegy in funeral lament as he presents himself mourning his elegiac 'death'.[64] *Pont.* 3.2 adds a further commentary on the development of elegy by introducing an interlocutor who relates this tragic narrative to Ovid, thereby recalling Callimachus' elegiac *Aetia*, which frequently presents the elegiac poet as being instructed by those with greater knowledge. More specifically, the scenario of an aged narrator relaying information about the religious practices of his homeland to an elegiac poet who speaks *in propria persona* and includes his interlocutor's narrative within a wider frame, while both men are abroad, owes much to *Aetia* fr. 178 (Pfeiffer), where Callimachus is at a banquet in Egypt, and talks with an Ician guest about his homeland and why his countrymen worship Peleus. Thus Ovid's versions of the *I. T.* not only show the poet of the tragic *Medea* as capable of appropriating Greek tragedy for elegy, but also stress the very *elegiac* nature of Ovid's versions of tragedy.

Ovid's use of this particular tragedy emphasizes that this work contains important parallels for his own situation. Most immediately, it provides a paradigmatic tale of return home from the barbarous Black Sea area, which is highly relevant to Ovid's own circumstances, particularly given that the exiled Ovid does not have many such positive paradigms. The only examples in the letters from exile where a return to Rome is envisaged are *Tristia* 1.1, 3.1, 5.4, *Pont.* 4.5 and 4.9 (Ovid's exile poems go to Rome), 3.3.65–6 (Ovid instructs his wife to bring his bones to Rome in the event of his death), 3.8.1 ff. (Ovid wishes for the chariot of Triptolemus, Medea's winged dragons when she escaped from Corinth, and the wings of Perseus or Daedalus, to return to his *patria*, before concluding that prayers must be addressed to Augustus), 4.2.57 ff. and *Pont.* 1.2.47 ff., 1.7.31 ff., 2.1, 4.4.15 ff. (Ovid 'returns' in memory or through dreams or reports), 4.3 (in which Ovid imagines the Greater and Lesser Bear going from the far North – his current location – to Rome to view his wife), *Pont.* 2.8.9 ff. (where the Augustan coins Ovid receives 'return' him to Rome). Such scenes are, additionally, often compromised by their emphasis on the fact that Ovid cannot go back in person. That the *I. T.* offers a plot of escape from the dangers of the Black Sea region as well as Iphigenia's rescue by a fellow countryman will be seen to be further relevant to Ovid's circumstances; see below.

---

63   See Cairns 1979, 214–28, Butrica 1996, and Lightfoot 1999, 71–6. For extended mythological narratives in Latin love elegy, cf. e.g. Prop. 1.20, 3.15, and Ovid's own *Amores* 3.6.45–82.

64   See e.g. *Tr.* 2.2 with Luck 1977 *ad loc.*, 5.1.5–6 and 47–8, and Nagle 1980, 22–32.

Reception of this Euripidean tragedy also has another important consequence. In the exile poetry, Ovid frequently uses characters from myth
to stress similarity or dissimilarity between their fates and his exilic situation, encouraging us to consider how well their circumstances map on to his
own,[65] and Ovid's choice of the *I. T.* as a mythological model is particularly
appropriate, given that identity is an important theme of Euripides' play.[66]
Ovid's use of the *I. T.* thus encourages us, even more strongly than is usually the case with the mythological material in the *Tristia* and *Ex Ponto*, to
think about identity and identification, and possible affinities between Ovid's situation and the characters involved in the Euripidean plot as narrated.
I have already explored briefly some identifications readers are encouraged
to make: Iphigenia stuck in the Black Sea region for years by the will of the
gods and engineering her return through a letter is a clear parallel for Ovid,
exiled to Tomi by the will of the divine Augustus, writing letters he hopes
will earn him a reprieve.[67] Ovid can also be seen to have strong affinities
with Orestes, a hero who committed terrible acts in the past, was driven in-
sane, and finally reprieved by a journey to the Black Sea, partly through the
friendship of a devoted friend.

Given that Ovid draws clear parallels between himself and Orestes, it is
tempting to map the Pylades rôle together with the paradigm of a devoted
male friend who comes to the Black Sea region and rescues a fellow countryman, on to Ovid's addressees in these poems, the brothers Messallinus
and Cotta.[68] Syme 1978, 127 has already suggested that *sospes* (*Pont.* 3.2.3)
would be 'suitable if Cotta was in the field or on a journey' at the time of the
letter's composition; perhaps it is pushing his point too far to suggest that
Cotta's travels as a major figure in Roman politics at this time may have
brought him to the Roman province of Moesia, where Ovid was incarcer-

---

65   See e.g. the early *Tr.* 1.5.57 ff., where Ovid stresses the differences between Odys-
     seus' wanderings away from his homeland and his own exile, which sets the tone for
     much of Ovid's later use of myth; see too Davisson 1993, 224–37.
66   See for example, Euripides' opening word, which reveals Iphigenia's identity as the
     descendant of Pelops (and hence heir to the unusually violent – one might even say
     barbaric – family dynamics of that dynasty, in that she is both victim of her father,
     and potential killer of her own brother) as well as the more obvious play with the
     revelation of the identities of Iphigenia (as sister of the man she is about to kill), Py-
     lades, and Orestes (for which, see above). The tragedy also plays with the question
     of whether identities remain the same when characters are transposed to a different
     geographical area.
67   See e.g. *Tr.* 2.183–6, where Augustus is presented as a divinity who can remove
     Ovid from the Black Sea.
68   Given the importance of 'brotherly' love between Orestes and Pylades in many ver-
     sions of this myth, it is highly appropriate that the two letters which narrate this myth
     are addressed to a pair of brothers, whose love is compared with that of mythological
     brothers at *Pont.* 1.7.31–32.

ated, but this – admittedly speculative – possibility would certainly add an extra dimension to Ovid's choice of addressee in the later epistle.

What about Thoas, an important figure in Euripides? Ovid cuts out in both of his versions of the plot the king's opposition to the return of the Greeks; in practical terms, Thoas' desire to keep Iphigenia in his country does not fit Ovid's purposes, since nobody locally was opposed to Ovid's escape from the region. In fact, only one person fits this description within Ovid's exile corpus: Augustus, who had exiled Ovid to Tomi and keeps him there. Augustus already appears in the rôle of Thoas at *Tristia* 1.9.27–28, where he approves of Pylades' devotion to Orestes, in a passage on Augustus' leniency towards those friends who may continue to support the exiled Ovid: *De comite Argolici postquam cognouit Orestae,/ narratur Pyladen ipse probasse Thoas* (= "After he heard of the companion of Argive Orestes,/ Even Thoas is said to have approved of Pylades."). It therefore might have been better for Ovid's cause to omit Thoas altogether from his accounts of the myth, but he does feature in both versions, albeit briefly, at *Tristia* 4.4.65–6 and *Pont.* 3.2.59–60. Simply by mentioning him, Ovid may therefore evoke the idea of opposition to return to civilisation from a barbarian region and hence the figure of Augustus.

Given parallels between the plot of the *I. T.* and Ovid's exilic circumstances, it is also worth considering Ovid's focus on the statue of Artemis taken away by the escaping Greeks at the end of both of his versions. It may at first glance appear surprising that, in using this myth as a paradigm of escape from barbarism and return to civilisation, Ovid finally concentrates not upon the human actors who provide various parallels with his own situation, but this cult statue. However, mention of the rescue of the statue is partly down to the use of the plot of *I. T.* where Orestes reveals from the start that Apollo has sent him to rescue the statue of Artemis (*I. T.* 85 ff.); if Ovid were not to include this element in the story, he would give no reason for Orestes and Pylades to come to the region. Furthermore, Stephen Harrison has plausibly suggested that Ovid's focus on this statue presents the poet as an artefact to be rescued;[69] this is lent additional support by Ovid's hints at *Pont.* 3.2.27–30 that he will ultimately become his works (*legar*, 3.2.30), which will live on as physical object after his death:[70]

> tunc igitur meriti morietur gratia uestri,
>   cum cinis absumpto corpore factus ero.
> fallor, et illa meae superabit tempora uitae,
>   si tamen a memori posteritate legar.

---

69 See Harrison (forthcoming).
70 Revisiting similar statements earlier in his *corpus*: cf. *Am.* 1.15.31–42 and *Met.* 15.871–9.

So my thanks for what you have done for me will die then,
    when I will be made ash with my body used up.
I am mistaken, and my thanks will surpass the limits of my life,
    if however I am read by posterity, which remembers.

Furthermore, Ovid's concentration in these poems on the statue appears diplomatic: if he were to focus rather on the escaping Orestes, Pylades and Iphigenia, this would bring up the opposition of Thoas to their escape; not a comfortable parallel given the equation between Augustus and Thoas outlined above. If, on the other hand, Ovid is to be identified with the statue, he plays a more passive rôle: not leaving the region in defiance of anyone's wishes, but rather being rescued by those who, like Messallinus and Cotta, want him (or his poetry) back.

Athena's rôle in Euripides as a *deus ex machina* (*I. T.* 1435 ff.), elided from Ovid's versions of the myth, is also worth consideration here. Several reasons for, and effects of, the Ovidian omission of the goddess present themselves. Ovid thereby focuses on the human drama laid out by Euripides, and since Ovid is not actually writing a tragedy in either account, but elegiac narratives of a tragic plot, he simply does not have to follow tragic convention and end his narrative in this way. Another consideration is political: Augustus is presented throughout Ovid's exile poetry as a divinity who has banished Ovid to the Black Sea region, and Ovid may reflect this by removing the god who steps in to save the day from the equation. But there is perhaps another, more interesting aspect to Ovid's omission of the goddess who turns up at the last minute to save the day in Euripides: Ovid *does* provide his readers with a divine epiphany, but in *Pont.* 3.3, the poem which follows Ovid's lengthiest version of the myth. In this poem, Cupid appears to the poet in a nocturnal vision, which may be real or may be a dream (*Pont.* 3.3.1–5, 13):

Si uacat exiguum profugo dare tempus amico,
    o sidus Fabiae, Maxime, gentis, ades,
dum tibi quae uidi refero, seu corporis umbra
    seu ueri species seu fuit ille sopor.
nox erat …
stabat Amor, uultu non quo prius esse solebat

If you have leisure to give a little time to an exiled friend,
    Maximus, star of the Fabian family, pay attention,
while I tell you what I saw, whether it was the shadow of a body
    or the appearance of reality or a dream.
It was night …
Cupid was standing there, not with the face he used to have …

It is very tempting to compare this with Iphigenia's dream at the start of the *I. T.* (42 ff.), which heralds her return to Greece. In Ovid's poem, Cupid goes on to stress his connection with the region, and Ovid, and to predict that the wrath of Augustus will be softened (*Pont.* 3.3.79–84):

> haec loca tum primum uidi, cum matre rogante
>> Phasias est telis fixa puella meis.
> quae nunc cur iterum post saecula longa reuisam,
>> tu facis, o castris miles amice meis.
> pone metus igitur: mitescet Caesaris ira,
>> et ueniet uotis mollior aura tuis.

> I saw these regions for the first time when, at my mother's request,
>> the Phasian girl [i.e. Medea] was transfixed with my weapons.
> Why now again after long ages I see them again
>> is your doing, o friendly soldier from my camp.
> Therefore place aside your fear: the anger of Caesar will grow gentle,
>> and a breeze that is softer will come in answer to your prayers.

Given his detailed engagement with Euripides' *Iphigenia among the Taurians* in the previous poem, Ovid may thereby comment upon the dream scene at the start of Euripides' tragedy, but in fact his dream proves to be misleading (just as Iphigenia's interpretation of her own dream was incorrect), since the anger of the divine Augustus never lessened: Ovid, unlike Iphigenia, never made it back from the Black Sea. Tragedy, even when closely read, cannot provide an exact fit for Ovid's exilic circumstances, however much he tries to cast himself in the tragic mould.

Bibliography

Broege, Valerie (1972), "Ovid's Autobiographical Use of Mythology in the *Tristia* and *Epistulae ex Ponto*", in: *EMC* 16, 37–42.

Butrica, James L. (1996), "Hellenistic Erotic Elegy: the Evidence of the Papyri", in: *PLLS* 9, 297–33.

Cairns, Francis (1979), *Tibullus: a Hellenistic Poet at Rome*, Cambridge.

Casali, Sergio (1997), "*Quaerenti plura legendum*: On the Necessity of 'Reading More' in Ovid's Exile Poetry", in: *Ramus* 26, 80–112.

Claassen, Jo-Marie (2001), "The Singular Myth: Ovid's Use of Myth in the Exilic Poetry", in: *Hermathena* 170, 11–64.

Clausen, Wendell (1994), *Virgil, Eclogues*, Oxford.

Cropp, M. J. (2000), *Iphigenia in Tauris*, Warminster.

Davisson, Mary H. T. (1993), "*Quid moror exemplis?:* Mythological *exempla* in Ovid's Pre-exilic Poems and the Elegies from Exile", in: *Phoenix* 47, 213–37.

Drucker, Michael (1977), *Der verbannte Dichter und der Kaiser-Gott: Studien zu Ovids späten Elegien*, Leipzig.

Dunn, Francis M. (1996), *Tragedy's End: Closure and Innovation in Euripidean Drama*, NY/ Oxford.

Fairweather, Jane (1987), "Ovid's Autobiographical Poem, *Tristia* 4.10",
     in: *CQ*, n.s. 37, 181–96.
Fantham, Elaine (1992), "Ovidius in Tauris: Ovid *Tr.* 4.4 and *Ex Pont.* 3.2",
     in: R. M. Wilhelm / H. Jones (eds.), *The Two Worlds of the Poet: New Perspectives
     on Virgil*, Detroit, 268–80.
Gildenhard, Ingo / Zissos, Andrew (1999), "Somatic Economies: Tragic Bodies and
     Poetic Design in Ovid's *Metamorphoses*", in: Philip Hardie / Alessandro
     Barchiesi / Stephen Hinds (eds.), *Ovidian Transformations: Essays on Ovid's
     Metamorphoses and its* reception, Cambridge (= *PCPhS* Suppl. 23), 162–81.
Habinek, Thomas (1998), *The Politics of Latin Literature*, Princeton.
Hall, Edith M. (1989), *Inventing the Barbarian*, Oxford.
Harrison, Stephen (forthcoming), Unpublished paper on *Ex Ponto* 3.2 delivered in the
     Faculty Reading Classes on *Epistulae Ex Ponto* 3 at Oxford University,
     Michaelmas 2001.
Hollis, Adrian (1970), *Ovid:* Metamorphoses *Book VIII*, Oxford.
—— (1996), "*Ovidius Exulans*" (= Review of G. Williams, *Banished Voices*),
     in: *CR* 46, 26–7.
Ingleheart, Jennifer (2006), "What the Poet Saw: Ovid, the *error* and the Theme of
     Sight in *Tristia* 2", in: *MD* 56, 63–86.
Jocelyn, Harry D. (1967), *The Tragedies of Ennius*, Cambridge.
Kassel, Rudolf (1958), *Untersuchungen zur griechischen und römischen
     Konsolationsliteratur* (= *Zetemata* 18), Munich.
Kennedy, Duncan F. (1984), "The Epistolary Mode and the First of Ovid's *Heroides*",
     in: *CQ* 34, 413–22.
Kyriakou, Poulheria (2006), *A Commentary on Euripides' Iphigenia in Tauris*, Berlin/NY.
La Penna, Antonio (1957), *Ibis*, Florence.
Lightfoot, Jane (1999), *Parthenius of Nicaea*, Oxford.
Luck, Georg (1977), *P. Ovidius Naso: Tristia Band II: Kommentar*, Heidelberg.
Nagle, Betty Rose (1980), *The Poetics of Exile: Program and Polemic in the Tristia and
     Epistulae ex Ponto of Ovid*, Brussels (= *Collection Latomus* 170).
Rosenmeyer, Patricia A. (1997), *"Ovid's Heroides and Tristia"*, in: *Ramus* 26, 29–56.
Syme, Ronald (1978), *History in Ovid*, Oxford.
Syme, Ronald (1986), *The Augustan Aristocracy*, Oxford.
Wright, Matthew (2005), *Euripides' Escape-Tragedies: a Study of Helen, Andromeda,
     and Iphigenia among the Taurians*, Oxford.

C. The Roman Empire

Drama and Epic Narrative:
The Test Case of Messenger Speech
in Seneca's *Agamemnon*

ANNETTE M. BAERTSCHI

The messenger is a familiar figure on the Greek tragic stage. He appears in more than three quarters of the surviving tragedies, very often in pivotal moments, and reports important action that has occurred offstage.[1] It is through a messenger that we learn, for instance, about the suicide of Jocasta and the self-blinding of Oedipus in Sophocles' *Oedipus Tyrannus,* or the sacrifice of Polyxena, the madness of Heracles, and the death of Hippolytus in the works of Euripides.[2]

Similarly, in Senecan tragedy long, graphic messenger speeches are repeatedly included at the very centre of the dramatic action. For example, at the core of the *Oedipus* stands Creo's detailed description of the necromancy performed by the seer Tiresias and his daughter Manto in order to identify the murderer of Laius (*Oed.* 530–658). In the *Agamemnon* Eurybates' report of the great storm that destroyed the Greek fleet on the return voyage from Troy takes up almost the entire third act (*Ag.* 421–578), while in the *Thyestes* the messenger's eloquent recounting of the site where Atreus slaughters his brother's sons is the gruesome climax of the play (*Thy.* 634–788). But in contrast to his Greek predecessors Seneca has often been censored for incorporating large amounts of description into his tragedies, as this was felt to be detrimental to the structure and coherence of his plays. Eurybates' *rhesis* in the *Agamemnon* in particular, the longest messenger speech in Seneca's dramatic oeuvre, has provoked criticism, since scholars pointed out that the messenger relates much more than he actually could have seen, thus illustrating the poet's predilection for rhetorical elaboration at the expense of theatrical plausibility.

By making use of recent studies on the narratives of tragic messengers and comparing the report in the *Agamemnon* with that given by the Per-

---

1   This calculation is based on the criteria of de Jong 1991, vii, n. 5, and 179–80, and Barrett 2002, 20, n. 33.

2   Cf. S. *OT* 1223–96, E. *Hec.* 484–582, *HF* 909–1015, *Hipp.* 1153–1254.

sian runner in Aeschylus' *Persians*, itself constituting the longest messenger scene in extant Greek tragedy (*Pers*. 249–514), I want to demonstrate, however, that Seneca adopts the same strategies to establish his messenger's authority as narrator that we can find in Greek drama. I shall argue that the Roman author – like his Greek model – endows his messenger with a decidedly epic narrative voice in order to allay any doubts about the credibility of the latter's account. Furthermore, I wish to suggest in the second part of this paper that Seneca actually takes this tendency to 'epicize' the messenger's report a step further and, in doing so, enhances the pathos and dramatic impact of the scene. By examining Seneca's appropriation of practices that can be traced as far back as to Aeschylus' *Persians*, our oldest surviving play, it is thus possible not only to shed light on the intertextual dimension of Seneca's tragedies and his sustained engagement with the literary tradition, but also to acquit him of the charge of merely showing off his rhetorical talent and revelling too much in 'Baroque' décor.

The tragic messenger usually manages to leave a distinctive mark on the audience's memory despite his limited presence onstage, because he most often reports terrible disasters or abominable crimes that contribute in no small way to the development of the plot. More importantly, his speech is different from that of other characters in that he typically can claim to possess a secure form of knowledge, having been an eyewitness to the events he is narrating. Being an eyewitness is, of course, "the messenger's very theatrical *raison d'être*".[3] He is the one who happens to have seen certain things that the other characters onstage (and the audience in the theatre) have not, and his role is to recount them. Many messengers in ancient tragedy refer explicitly or implicitly to their activity as eyewitnesses, emphasizing in particular the greater reliability of their information in comparison with that gained only by hearsay.[4]

The messenger's stressing of the veracity of his account is all the more important in ancient tragedy, where the spectator is confronted with a multitude of voices that all lay claim to truth and authority. The absence of a single, authoritative narrator, who orders, interprets, or comments on what is being said, "renders all speech onstage equally [reliable] or suspect, equally bound by its status as a rhetorical creation".[5] Given this context, the mes-

---

3   de Jong 1991, 8.
4   Cf., e.g., A. *Pers*. 266–67 and S. *Tr*. 746–48. An example for an indirect reference to the messenger's presence at the events he is relating is E. *Hipp*. 1215–16, cf. de Jong 1991, 10. – The topos that autopsy is a more reliable source of information than hearsay is, of course, traditional and goes back to Homer and Herodotus, cf., e.g., Hom. *Il*. 2.484–87 and *Od*. 8.487–91, and Hdt. 2.44, 75, 106, 148, and *passim*. Cf. also de Jong, 1991, 11 with n. 24 for further references.
5   Barrett 2002, xvi.

senger's claim to autopsy not only establishes his credentials as narrator and legitimizes his report, but also helps the spectator to navigate his way in the ensemble of voices to which he is exposed. Moreover, the apparent impartiality of the messenger's speech, who seems solely concerned with narrating mere "facts", undistorted by personal interests or loyalties, encourages the viewer to accept his account as objective and truthful.

In his capacity to recreate for the audience an otherwise irretrievable scene and to do so with a reliability and disengagement unavailable to other characters, the messenger thus is an important tool of the tragic poet for incorporating offstage events. However, as has been objected by Irene de Jong, no speech is ever fully neutral and inseparable from its speaker, since also a messenger is a focalizer and as such shapes and manipulates his narrative.[6] Furthermore, there is a fundamental tension in the messenger's status as eyewitness, for as a stage character – and human being – he can only recount what he has seen depending on where he found himself at the time of the action. The natural limitations of his perspective stir doubts as to whether he really is able to give an account that is accurate as well as comprehensive or whether it lacks essential information.[7] This is especially true when the location of the events that the messenger claims to have witnessed is large, for instance an enormous battle-field. Here skepticism about the very feasibility of one person perceiving everything that has happened is almost inevitable.

As Irene de Jong has emphasized in her seminal study on tragic *angeliai*, Euripides in such cases takes care either to locate the messenger on a high vantage point, or to guarantee him an "ambulant position".[8] In the *Suppliants*, for example, the messenger is a prisoner of war (*Supp.* 635–37), who, finding himself at Thebes, watches the battle from a tower near the Electran gate (*Supp.* 651–52). In the *Phoenissae*, the tragedian makes the messenger a shield-bearer of Eteocles (*Ph.* 1073–74), who takes round the password and follows his master all over the battle-field (*Ph.* 1139–40, 1164, 1170–71). In both plays Euripides is therefore intent on overcoming the restrictions of the messenger's vision and stifling potential reservations about the credibility of his report. For the authenticity of the messenger's narrative is vital, as the tragic messenger is a messenger precisely because he has been present at events that nobody else has seen and "to limit him too much in this respect would run counter to his theatrical function as 'stand-in' spectator".[9]

Another strategy of establishing the messenger's authority onstage and creating the illusion of him giving a "rational account of objective fact" is

---

6   Cf. de Jong 1991, 65 and 74.
7   Cf. Barrett 2002, 40.
8   de Jong 1991, 13.
9   *Ibid.*

adopted by Aeschylus in the *Persians* (*Pers*. 249–514).[10] As James Barrett has demonstrated, in his relaying the Persians' defeat in the sea-battle of Salamis the messenger describes the events taking place in a way that suggests both an "enormous scope [...] of his visual field" and a close proximity to the action.[11] In his portrayal of the Greeks' attack, for example, he relates that the numerous Persian ships in the strait "struck each other with their bronze-mouthed beaks, and shattered all the rowing equipment" (*Pers*. 415–16), thus making it easy for the Greeks to encircle them and turn them upside down (*Pers*. 417–19).[12] This seems to imply a privileged position of the messenger during the battle, similar to that of Xerxes, whom he locates on a nearby hill, whence he could look down on the struggle below (*Pers*. 466–67). Likewise, the messenger's stressing that the sea could no longer be seen because of the many shipwrecks and corpses and that the rocky coasts also filled up with dead bodies indicates a broad sweep of vision (*Pers*. 419–21).

Conversely, the messenger's description of the end of the Persian leader Matallos in a sort of close-up within a long catalogue of dead (*Pers*. 314–17) – he minutely reports how Matallos' full, thick, tawny beard turns dark as it is dipped into the bloody water (*Pers*. 316–17) – signals a much narrower scope, for a detail like the beard of Matallos would certainly not have been visible from afar. The messenger in Aeschylus' *Persians* thus "places himself alternately at a distance from and very close to the scene".[13] He combines two entirely different perspectives, resulting in a point of view that equals omnipresence.

At the same time, as Barrett further shows, the messenger in his account of the naval battle tends to minimize his own participation in the events he is relating and to fade into the background.[14] Most of his speech is dominated by third-person predicates and impersonal constructions. Furthermore, there are only very few instances of self-reference.[15] The messenger's self-effacement is even so complete that those who listen to his report may easily forget about who is narrating the story. Rather, the events presented seem independent from the observer, and the narrative appears to "tell itself".[16]

In his (implicit) claim to both omnipresence and non-presence, so Barrett's conclusion, the messenger's narrative voice closely resembles that of epic. For the epic poet, too, moves freely within the location he is describ-

---

10 Barlow 1971, 61.
11 Barrett 2002, 32–33.
12 All translations of Aeschylus' *Persians* are taken from Hall 1996.
13 Barrett 2002, 34.
14 *Ibid*., 34–40.
15 Line 502 (*ēmōn*) is the exception that confirms the rule. For the four occurrences of first-person plural forms from line 485 to the end cf. Barrett 2002, 37, n. 24.
16 Barrett 2002, xvii, quoting Benveniste 1971, 208.

ing, and yet appears nowhere in the (fictional) scene. On the tragic stage the voice of the messenger differs considerably from that of the other *dramatis personae*. "While there is, on the whole, a strong identification of speaker and speech in tragedy, the messenger, in sharp distinction, offers a narrative that in general is conspicuously disassociated from any particular point of view."[17] By assuming the voice of the epic poet the messenger thus liberates his account from the partiality that defines the speech of the other characters onstage. Simultaneously, the affiliation with epic enhances his credibility, establishing his voice – as is essential for his role – as authoritative in the many competing claims to truthfulness. "Tragedy [therefore] shows itself to be indebted to epic not only for its characters and plots, but also for its successful functioning as theater."[18]

I have summarized the results of de Jong's and Barrett's analysis of the role of the messenger in Greek tragedy and the narrative practices to overcome the limitations inherent in his status as eyewitness in some detail, because their approach can also be fruitfully applied to the messenger scene in Seneca's *Agamemnon*. As mentioned, Eurybates' report has been criticized not only for being disproportionally long, but also for lacking all probability, thus running counter to the very function of the tragic messenger. However, I want to show in the following that Seneca employs the same strategies to forge Eurybates' narrative authority that we find in Euripides and Aeschylus. I shall argue that the Roman dramatist also creates a scenario as realistic as possible and additionally endows his messenger with a distinctly epic voice, having him assume a variety of perspectives which suggest omnipresence, while simultaneously obscuring his involvement in the events that he is recounting.

Ironically, it was precisely the comparison with the messenger speech in another play by Aeschylus, his *Agamemnon*, that was responsible for the highly unfavourable assessment of Seneca's version. In the Greek tragedy, the herald after reporting the arrival of Agamemnon at Argos (*A.* 503–37) and recapitulating the many discomforts the Greek army had to endure at Troy before its late victory (*A.* 551–82), ends his speech with a description of the storm that overtook the Greeks by night on their return voyage (*A.* 620–80). He first describes the storm itself and the destruction it caused (*A.* 650–60), then relates the escape of Agamemnon's ship on which he himself was sailing (*A.* 661–67), and finally speculates about the fate of the fleet's other ships (*A.* 668–79), especially that of Menelaus, about whom the chorus had asked him in its introductory question (*A.* 616–18). All this is told in no more than thirty lines.

---

17 Barrett 2002, xvii.
18 *Ibid.* xviii.

The content and structure of Eurybates' narrative in Seneca's *Agamemnon* is markedly different.[19] Of the three main topics covered by the Aeschylean herald, the last two are dealt with in the preceding dialogue between Eurybates and Clytemnestra (*Ag.* 395a–401, 410a–13), *i.e.* are not part of the messenger's speech proper. The storm, on the other hand, is portrayed in exhaustive detail (*Ag.* 470–556), taking up almost one-hundred lines in contrast to only ten in Aeschylus. The report includes not only a minute description of the turmoil of the winds (*Ag.* 474–84), the heavy rain and absolute darkness (*Ag.* 485–97a), the damage done to the ships (*Ag.* 497b–506), and the despair of all men present (*Ag.* 507–27), but also of the death of Ajax (Oileus) at the hands of Athena and Neptune (*Ag.* 528–56). In addition, Seneca further enlarges Eurybates' *rhesis* by integrating at the beginning an extensive description of the Greeks' departure from Troy and initial period of calm sailing (*Ag.* 421–55) and by concluding it with an account of the treachery of Nauplius, who lured the Greeks' ships onto the Capherean rocks by lighting beacons at the top (*Ag.* 557–76). In contrast to Aeschylus, Seneca thus concentrates his attention in the messenger speech of the *Agamemnon* exclusively on the voyage and the destruction of the fleet,[20] whereas the Greek tragedian makes this only the theme of the last section of the herald's report.

Previous scholarship has taken some pains to identify the (tragic) sources that Seneca used for his detailed, graphic storm description, especially with regard to his combination of the death of Ajax and the deceit of Nauplius with the wrecking of the Greek ships on their way home. To sum up: the first known accounts to contain all three incidents come from the Hellenistic period. A late successor of Seneca is Quintus Smyrnaeus, who in the last book of his *Posthomerica* likewise reports the destruction of the Greek fleet in conjunction with the drowning of Ajax and the revenge of Nauplius.[21] However, since most dramatic poetry between the fifth century BCE and the first CE is lost, all attempts to determine Seneca's specific models must remain highly speculative.

Besides, it is not the connection of the three episodes that mainly evoked criticism, even though many a reader may have felt that, by doing so, Seneca made the already overly long speech of Eurybates even longer. Rather, it has been objected that Eurybates relates much more than a person on board of one of the ships could have seen, given that the location was very large and, more importantly, that it was so dark during the storm – a fact that is high-

---

19 For an outline of the speech cf. Tarrant 1976, 249.
20 Cf. Stackmann 1949, 211.
21 For the general similarity of the accounts including verbal parallels and the consequences that may be drawn from this, *i.e.* the hypothesis of a common source, cf. Tarrant 1976, 22–23; cf. also Heinze [4]1957, 77–78 and Liedloff 1902, 13 with n. 53.

lighted several times – that one could simply not see anything at all.[22] By having Eurybates recount events that he could not have observed himself, so critics claimed, Seneca disregards the messenger's conventional status as eyewitness and undermines his narrative credibility. His report can thus not create the illusion of being a "transparent window upon the truth" like the herald's speech in Aeschylus' *Agamemnon*, but has to be interpreted as the product of the poet who wanted to contribute to the literary tradition of storm descriptions and secure himself a prominent position.[23]

Admittedly, it cannot be denied that Eurybates in his speech repeatedly emphasizes the pitch darkness of the night of the storm. Before the storm arises, for instance, he points out that the moon and the stars suddenly disappeared and that the night was additionally darkened by dense clouds (*Ag.* 470, 472–74):

> cum subito luna conditur, stellae latent.
> nec una nox est: densa tenebras obruit
> caligo et omni luce subducta fretum
> caelumque miscet.

> Suddenly the moon was hidden, the stars invisible.
> Night was redoubled: a dense gloom smothered
> the darkness, stole every trace of light and
> confounded sea and sky.[24]

Once the storm rages at full speed, it gets even darker, in fact, as dark as in the underworld,[25] making the men's fate worse because they are unable to recognize what destroys them (*Ag.* 491–94):

> nec hoc levamen denique aerumnis datur,
> videre saltem et nosse quo pereant malo
> premunt tenebrae lumina et dirae Stygis
> inferna nox est.

> The sufferers were not even granted the relief of
> at least seeing and knowing the disaster that destroyed them.
> Darkness weighed on their eyes, the infernal
> night of terrible Styx.

---

22 Cf. Schindler 2000, 138: "[…] auch lässt Seneca ihn [*sc.* Eurybates] viel mehr berichten, als er in finsterer Nacht, die seinen eigenen Angaben nach während des Seesturms herrscht, beobachten konnte". Similarly already Stackmann 1949, 210: "Aber wenn einmal festgestellt ist, dass während der Katastrophe rabenschwarze Nacht herrscht, sodass man die Hand vor Augen nicht sieht, dann kann einer, der die Katastrophe miterlebt hat, am Tag darauf höchstens das berichten, was sich an Bord des eigenen Schiffes zugetragen hat." – The vastness of the Greek fleet is repeatedly emphasized, cf., e.g., Ag. 434.

23 Michelini 1982, 75.

24 All translations of Seneca's *Agamemnon* are taken from Fitch 2004.

25 Cf. also *Ag.* 486–87: ... *crederes* ... *atrum rebus induci chaos.*

However, as clearly as Eurybates stresses the thick darkness of the night, just so clearly does he refer to the fact that some light nevertheless illuminated the scenery. After describing the infernal gloom he goes on to report that occasionally flashes of lightning break through the *dirae Stygis nox* (*Ag.* 494–95):

> excidunt ignes tamen
> et nube dirum fulmen elisa micat.

> Yet fires did fall,
> and terrible lightning flashed from shattered clouds.

Tamen in line 494 unambiguously indicates that despite the overwhelming darkness there is some light. It may not be good or much light (cf. *Ag.* 496: *lucis … malae*),[26] but it is enough for Eurybates to see (and estimate) the damage done to the fleet, which he recounts in the following lines (*Ag.* 497–506).

Even more carefully Seneca makes sure to explain how and why the death of Ajax could be perceived by the other Greeks, prompting the audience's visual imagination at the beginning of the scene with *ecce alia clades*! (*Ag.* 528). When Athena's lightning-bolts strike Ajax's ship, it is torn apart, carrying away on one half its helmsman (*Ag.* 537–38). Although surrounded by blazing flames (*Ag.* 540: *ambustus*), Ajax sails on, "standing out from the saltwater like a lofty crag" (*Ag.* 539–40) – a spectacle that, of course, *can* be seen because the burning shipwreck provides the necessary light. Finally, as the Greek hero holds on to his ship more tightly, he catches fire himself and becomes a living torch, before he is eventually drowned by Neptune (*Ag.* 541–43):

> et navem manu
> complexus ignes traxit et caeco mari
> conlucet Aiax; omne resplendet fretum.

> As he grasped his ship tightly,
> he caught fire from it, and in that blind sea
> Ajax was a source of light; the whole strait was illuminated.

It is thus not true that Eurybates cannot know anything of the death of Ajax, because it was too dark, as Stackmann and others have claimed.[27] On the contrary: Ajax dies in full spot-light, visible for everybody present.

But Seneca's efforts to enhance the authenticity and plausibility of Eurybates' speech in the *Agamemnon* are not limited to questions of darkness and light. Rather, it can be demonstrated that the Roman author adopts the very same narrative strategies to establish his messenger's authority that we also find in Aeschylus' *Persians*. For Eurybates, too, is able to see from a

---

26 I retain here (*pace* Fitch) the transmitted text. For the difficulties of *malae* and the textual revisions suggested to solve them cf. Tarrant 1976, 269–70.

27 Stackmann 1949, 210.

number of perspectives amounting to virtual omnipresence, and at the same time plays down his own participation in the events he is relating. Thus, like the Persian runner in Aeschylus' *Persians* he is endowed with an authoritative narrative voice that is comparable to that of the epic poet. Strangely, though, the messenger speech in the *Persians* has never been considered as a potential model for Eurybates' *rhesis*, even though both reports describe the destruction of a large fleet.

Exactly like his Greek counterpart, Eurybates sees on a scale both large and small. His description of the collision and mutual obstruction of the ships during the storm, for instance, and the various damages caused by this, not only underlines the vastness of the fleet, but also stresses his all-encompassing vision (*Ag.* 497–506):[28]

> ipsa se classis premit
> et prora prorae nocuit et lateri latus.
> illam dehiscens pontus in praeceps rapit
> hauritque et alto[29] redditam revomit mari;
> haec onere sidit, illa convulsum latus
> summittit undis, fluctus hanc decimus tegit;
> haec lacera et omni decore populato levis
> fluitat, nec illi vela tonsae manent
> nec rectus altas malus antemnas ferens,
> sed trunca toto puppis Ionio natat.

> The fleet did damage to itself,
> prow crashing on prow and side on side.
> One ship was pulled down headlong by the yawning sea,
> swallowed and then spewed up again from the depths;
> this one foundered under its burden, that one dipped its shattered side
> under the flood, this one was smothered by a tenth wave.
> Another, battered and despoiled of all its finery, drifts lightly
> to and fro; with neither sails nor oars remaining,
> nor the upright mast with its lofty sailyards,
> it floats as a mutilated hulk all over the Ionian Sea.

Conversely, a detail like that of Ajax "straining on the ropes to shorten sail" (*Ag.* 533–534), when he is struck by the first of Athena's lightning bolts, signals a close proximity to the action and thus a much narrower scope.

Furthermore, Eurybates excludes himself – just as the messenger in Aeschlyus' *Persians* – as much as possible from the events he is narrating. In fact, his minimizing of his own presence is so effective that "often enough he seems to be missing altogether".[30] Eurybates' entire speech, more

---

28   The same applies *mutatis mutandis* to Eurybates' portrayal of the wrecking of the
     ships at the Capherean rocks as a result of Nauplius' treachery (cf. *Ag.* 571–76).

29   For another reading cf. Tarrant 1976, 270.

30   Barrett 2002, 34.

than 150 lines long, consists exclusively of third-person predicates, coupled with numerous impersonal constructions. When the Greeks prepare for their departure, he simply speaks of *miles* (*Ag.* 423, cf. also *Ag.* 444), in no way indicating that he was among the soldiers. Similarly, when the fleet already sails on the sea, he points out that *omnis iuventus* (*Ag.* 437) was eager "to flex the oars and assist the winds", again leaving it up to the audience whether he is to be included in this group or not (*Ag.* 438). He also often uses the passive, fading out the person(s) who perform an action.[31] Thus the "oars are fitted to the soldiers' hand" (*Ag.* 425: *ad militares remus aptatur manus*) or "the ship is trusted to the wind" (*Ag.* 443: *credita est vento ratis*). Finally, even when talking about emotions and feelings, Eurybates chooses impersonal expressions such as *iuvat*, referring to the Greeks' joy at leaving Troy (*Ag.* 435–36):

> iuvat videre nuda Troiae litora,
> iuvat relicti sola Sigei loca.

> What a pleasure to see the empty shores of Troy,
> to see the lonely terrain of deserted Sigeum![32]

Eurybates' self-effacement is further illustrated by his description of his fellow-sailors' reaction to the destructive force of the storm. They are completely helpless and drop their equipment, paralysed by fear and terror (*Ag.* 507–9):

> nil ratio et usus audet, ars cessit malis;
> tenet horror artus, omnis officio stupet
> navita relicto, remus effugit manus.

> Neither reason nor experience gave courage; skill surrendered to the disaster.
> Gripped and stupified by terror,
> the sailors all abandoned their duties, and let the oars slip from their hands.[33]

So overwhelming is their despair that all men still afloat, Greeks and Trojans alike, resort to praying to the gods (*Ag.* 510–11). Eurybates relates their invocations in direct speech (*Ag.* 517–26) – I will come back to this passage – which implies that he must have been close enough to hear it. One could even infer that he prayed along. Yet, tellingly, he suppresses all reference to his specific location, thus sheltering himself from danger. For when a torrent of water washes away the praying men, abruptly cutting off their supplications (*Ag.* 527: *nec plura possunt: occupat vocem mare*), he alone escapes the disaster.

---

31 Cf. also that things and not men initiate action, e.g., *signum* (*Ag.* 427), *tuba* (*Ag.* 428), *aurata … prora* (*Ag.* 429), *aura … lenis* (*Ag.* 431), etc.

32 Moreover, there is only one self-reference in the entire speech (*Ag.* 557: *nos*) – exactly as in Aeschylus' *Persians*.

33 Cf. again the impersonal construction in *Ag.* 509: *remus effugit manus*.

Eurybates' invulnerability as well as his "freedom of movement within the scene he describes" clearly suggest that he – like the epic poet – "stands outside of his narrative".[34] His affiliation with epic becomes even more evident in the lines that immediately precede the aforementioned prayer. When Eurybates reports the distress of the men caught in the storm, he points out that many of them call those fortunate who fell at Troy and received a proper burial.[35] So, for instance, Pyrrhus envies his father, Ulysses Ajax (the Greater), Menelaus Hector and Agamemnon Priam (*Ag.* 512–14).[36] Considering that the four Greek leaders certainly did not all sail on one ship, Eurybates' knowledge of their lament once again reflects his specific point of view that equals omnipresence. Moreover, in relating that Ulysses, Menelaus and Agamemnon "envied" the victims of the Trojan war, even Hector and Priam who met a particularly cruel death or the unhappy Ajax, he truly speaks with the authority of an epic, that is omniscient, narrator, who interprets for his audience the protagonists' thoughts and feelings.

So far I have tried to show that Seneca endows Eurybates in the *Agamemnon* with an epic narrative voice in order to overcome the messenger's visual restrictions, since he, although claiming to have been an eye-witness to the events he is recounting, *qua* his status as a character can only report what he has seen from a particular point of view. The sustained engagement with epic displayed in the *rhesis* of Eurybates, however, is just one example of a broader phenomenon, as it has long been recognized that Seneca's messenger scenes in general bear a strong resemblance to epic. Apart from the fact that they share the quality of lengthy narration, critics have pointed out that typical epic features like the *ecphrasis topou* or the simile, in conjunction with markedly epic diction, occur regularly in the messenger speeches of Senecan drama.[37] In addition, the high incidence of direct speech in the reports of Seneca's messengers further assimilates them to epic.

The epic nature of messenger speeches has also been highlighted with regard to Greek tragedy, even though there has been some debate among scholars what this exactly means. Especially the question as to whether there are any specific "epicisms" in Greek tragic *angeliai* and, if so, whether this is the result of the poet's intention to create a messenger that is clearly marked

---

34 Barrett 2002, 43–44.
35 This is, of course, a topical element in storm descriptions.
36 Shelton 1983, 173 points to the irony of Agamemnon lamenting that "death at sea was much less honourable than death in war", since for him "there awaits the most humiliating of deaths, and he will find that his ancestral home is more dangerous than war or the sea. He sailed the open sea (and the metaphorical use must be seen here as well) and he survived the storm, but he will not escape the stormy turmoil at home."
37 Cf., e.g., Tietze (Larson) 1994, 65–66.

as epic or simply a coincidence, based on formal similarities or technical, that is metrical, constraints, is highly disputed. More recently, the skeptics concerning definite "epicisms" have gained the upper hand.[38] But even if one were a supporter of the opposite view, one would have to admit that the messenger speeches of Greek drama are not half as "epicized" as Seneca's.

The pervasive presence of epic elements in Seneca's messenger scenes, both in terms of topics[39] and narrative practices, has always had an unfavourable effect on the assessment of the poet as dramatist. Critics have claimed that Seneca by incorporating long descriptive passages into his messenger speeches, e.g. by means of an *ecphrasis*, makes them "resemble self-contained episodes of stories and destroys the dramatic credibility of the messenger and the situation in which the speech is recounted".[40] It is thus not surprising that the advocates of the view that Seneca's tragedies were not written for stage representation but for recitation often cite(d) the messenger speeches as proof for their argument.[41]

The messenger speech of the *Agamemnon* is a particular case in point, since Eurybates' report fills almost the entire third act, which very often in Senecan tragedy is devoted to a crucial confrontation of the main protagonists. Moreover, the events related seem of secondary importance to the plot. This is not to say that Eurybates' speech is without any connection to the story presented and the tragedy's overall message. On the contrary, as Jo-Ann Shelton has emphasized the messenger's report is "essential to the thematic development of the play", which is chiefly concerned with the "instability and mutability of human life".[42] To put it simply: "[T]he Greeks returning from Troy, happy because of their victory, were made unhappy by the storm; the fortunate survivors of the war met with misfortune at sea".[43] Furthermore, so Shelton, "the storm must be viewed [...] as nature's response to violations of order" or unnatural acts on the human level, themselves provoked by inner turmoil and conflicting emotions.[44] The Greeks, especially Agamemnon and Ajax, were responsible for various sacrileges

---

38 Cf. Barrett 2002, 46.
39 As mentioned, Eurybates' *rhesis* is not unique in adapting a typical epic set-piece, a storm description, but we find similar treatments of conventional epic motifs also in the messenger speeches of other tragedies, e.g., the portrayal of Hercules' catabasis including a long description of the underworld in the *Hercules furens* or the report of the necromancy carried out by Tiresias and his daughter Manto in the *Oedipus*.
40 Tietze 1989, 297–98.
41 Cf., e.g., Zwierlein 1966, 113, n. 3 regarding the *Agamemnon*: "So fremd solche Prunkerzählungen dem echten Dramatiker sind, so gross ist Senecas Vorliebe für sie." Cf. also Stackmann 1949, 209.
42 Shelton 1983, 168–69 (quotation on p. 168).
43 *Ibid.*, 168.
44 *Ibid.*, 169.

– Agamemnon had murdered his daughter in order to get the Greek expedition under way and take revenge on Troy, Ajax had raped Cassandra at the altar of Athena once the city was taken – and the universe reacts to these transgressions of cosmic or natural law by producing a storm of cosmic dimensions.[45] That said, a concluding judgement like that of Richard Tarrant's may still resonate with many today: "The inflation of picturesque or horrific messenger-speeches into centrally-situated scenes may be another sign of Seneca's freedom from and lack of interest in the theatrical focus of Greek tragedy."[46]

This claim notwithstanding, I would like to suggest another interpretation in the remaining part of my paper. I do not deny that Eurybates' speech in the *Agamemnon* is a long and highly "epicized" passage. In fact, I shall argue that Seneca not only "epicizes", but actually "hyper-epicizes" Eurybates' *rhesis* and, in doing so, enhances the dramatic impact of his report.[47] For the (over-)extensive use of epic narrative strategies adds heightened pathos and suspense in the specific dramatic situation of the messenger speech, where the audience knows that important (and authentic) news is delivered, which will have a particular bearing on those to whom it is delivered. I shall thus claim that the prominence of (epic) narration in the middle act of the *Agamemnon* does not shatter the empathy of the spectator, but rather increases it. Besides, by reading Seneca's tragic narrative against epic texts, especially Homer's *Odyssey* and Vergil's *Aeneid*, I hope not only to bring to light some allusive moments, but also to demonstrate how tragedy adapts as well as further develops and intensifies the literary techniques of epic.

Eurybates begins his narrative of the destruction of the Greek fleet with a prolonged account of the Greeks' preparations for departure and the subsequent period of favourable sailing (*Ag.* 421–55). He first describes the general hurry of the Greeks to make their ships ready for casting off (*Ag.* 421–30)[48] and then portrays in great detail the excellent conditions they encounter at sea and the joyous atmosphere that dominates the situation. The weather is fair, the waters are calm, a gentle breeze billows the sails, and everybody is happy to leave Troy behind (*Ag.* 431–36):

> hinc aura primo lenis impellit rates
> adlapsa velis; unda vix actu levi

---

45 For the cosmic dimension of Senecan tragedy in general cf. Schmitz 1993. – The death of Ajax in the storm after displaying once again his arrogance and *furor* (*Ag.* 552) anticipates and explains Agamemnon's later killing, as Seidensticker 1969, 128, n. 157 rightly stresses.

46 Tarrant 1976, 248.

47 For the term cf. Janka 2004, 49, 54.

48 The replacement of arms with oars (*Ag.* 423–25) is, of course, a symbolic act indicating the transition from war to peace.

tranquilla Zephyri mollis afflatu tremuit,
splendetque classe pelagus et pariter latet.
iuvat videre nuda Troiae litora,
iuvat relicti sola Sigei loca.

Then a breeze, gentle at first, slipped into the sails
and pushed the ships on; the calm waters, with scarcely any current,
were ruffled by the soft Zephyr's breath,
and the sea was both emblazoned and concealed by the fleet.
What a pleasure to see the empty shores of Troy,
to see the lonely terrain of deserted Sigeum!

In their eagerness to return home all the soldiers join forces and row at full speed (*Ag.* 437–39), so that "the furrowed waters glistened, the ships' sides hissed, and white foam sundered the dark blue sea" (*Ag.* 440–41: *sulcata vibrant aequora et latera increpant, / dirimuntque canae caerulum spumae mare*). Once a stronger wind blows, the men set down the oars (*Ag.* 442–43) and indulge in contemplating the landscape or telling each other war stories, before finally enjoying the appearance of a group of dolphins (*Ag.* 444–55).

As Caviglia has shown, Eurybates' description of the Greeks' happiness at their departure (*Ag.* 435–36: *iuvat videre nuda Troiae litora, / iuvat relicti sola Sigei loca*) closely recalls Aeneas' report of the Trojans' joy and relief over the (feigned) retreat of their enemy at the beginning of *Aeneid* 2 (*Aen.* 2.27–28: ... *iuvat ire et Dorica castra / desertosque videre locos litusque relictum*).[49] The intertextual resonance creates suspense, since it makes the audience realize that also the Greeks get carried away too soon and rashly believe that the danger is now over. Just as the Trojans succumb to the illusion of having won the war and later pay the highest price possible for this misjudgement, the sack of their city, so the victorious Greeks will be punished; in their case the price will be the destruction of almost the entire fleet. The connection is even further highlighted in the following lines picturing the carefree sailing, for as the Greeks leave their ships to the wind and pass the time telling each other war anecdotes (*Ag.* 443–48), so the Trojans in their last night abandon themselves to wine and sleep, while the Greek army approaches from the sea (*Aen.* 2. 252–65).[50] Moreover, the reference to the slaughter of Priam at the altar of Juppiter (*Ag.* 448) is an ominous reminder of the Greeks' many sacrilegious acts against both gods and men and of the punishment which normally follows such violations.[51]

Although the unsettling effect of these allusions is rightly stressed, I would like to point to a different kind of suspense that Seneca builds by integrating an extensive portrayal of the Greeks' joyous departure and the initial

---

49　Caviglia 1986–1987, 146–47.
50　*Ibid.*, 149–50.
51　Tarrant 1976, 259, cf. also Caviglia 1986–1987, 147.

pleasant phase of the journey. The seemingly good weather-conditions and a period of calm sailing are also frequently mentioned at the beginning of epic storm descriptions. Yet, the topic is usually passed over with a brief and general comment. Vergil, for instance, limits his description at the beginning of *Aeneid* 1 to one line (*Aen.* 1. 35):

vela dabant laeti et spumas salis aere ruebant.

They spread sail for the open sea, their spirits buoyant,
their bronze beaks churning the waves to foam.[52]

Seneca in the *Agamemnon*, on the other hand, devotes nearly thirty lines to this aspect, including in his account, as mentioned, numerous graphic details. In other words, he enlarges the traditional topic to an actual (epic) *ecphrasis* – an expansion that Vergil, as Richard Heinze has emphasized, deliberately refrains from in the *Aeneid*, being intent on advancing the plot of his story.[53]

The claim implicit in Heinze's statement is that Seneca by not following Vergil's model, but inserting a long description instead creates a sort of narrative pause or stand-still that is detrimental to the dramatic quality of the scene. However, I would argue that the exact opposite is the case. Eurybates' vivid account takes the spectator mentally back to the situation in which the Greeks were at the outset of their journey. The many details enable him to "see" the events he is being told before his (inner) eye, as if he had witnessed them himself. Even more, they draw him into the narrative: he shares the happiness of the Greeks about finally being able to leave Troy and enjoys with them the smooth voyage. This happens all the more easily as the messenger had (indirectly) asserted at the beginning of his speech that he will be giving an authentic and accurate report; and indeed, the numerous specifics of the journey seems to prove the authenticity of his speech.[54]

At the same time, the audience knows, of course, that almost all the ships of the Greek fleet have been destroyed by a massive storm, since Eurybates had told them so before his actual narration (*Ag.* 410a–13), and now expects him to recount just how this came about. They also know that this information will be of crucial importance to those listening to the messenger's report. The longer the messenger delays his description of the storm by minutely portraying the phase of peaceful and happy sailing beforehand, the greater is the effect of the sudden change, that is, in the case of the *Agamemnon*, the replacement of sunlight with pitch darkness and the gentle breeze with the

---

52 All translations of Vergil's *Aeneid* are taken from Fagles 2006.

53 Heinze 1957⁴, 76: "Virgil [...] beschränkt also die allgemeine Schilderung des Unwetters und der Not der Schiffe – wie er auch vorher (34f.) nur zwei Verse an die Schilderung der glücklichen Fahrt gewendet hatte – und erzählt, wie das Verderben fortschreitet und sich steigert."

54 Cf. also that here the narrative time (*Erzählzeit*) approximates the time narrated (*erzählte Zeit*), which similarly heightens the credibility of the report.

turmoil of the winds.[55] Thus, by amplifying the conventional brief reference to the "calm before the storm" into a long and pictorial *ecphrasis* Seneca heightens the suspense of the passage and increases its dramatic impact.

My second example of Seneca's "hyper-epicizing" the report of Eurybates is the description of the reaction of the men caught in the storm as well as the ensuing portrayal of the end of Ajax (*Ag.* 507–56). This section, covering some fifty lines, contains two direct speeches, which together take up more than one third of the account. Needless to say, a high incidence of speech is a typical characteristic of epic. The speeches increase the realism and vividness of the narrative – tellingly, the Homeric epics have been called "dramatic" for this very reason. Particularly in storm descriptions the epic poet regularly includes a lamentation speech of the hero that is at the mercy of rain, wind, and waves in order to emphasize his anguish and despair, but also his courage and strength (cf., e.g., Hom. *Od.* 5. 299–312, Verg. *Aen.* 1. 94–101). In the *Agamemnon*, Seneca adopts this practice, but simultaneously modifies it by integrating into Eurybates' *rhesis* not only a speech of a prominent hero, Ajax (even if in an inversed or perverted form), but also one of the anonymous crew (*Ag.* 517–26). This extension of the traditional motif once again is not a mere rhetorical elaboration inflating and prolonging the narrative, but on the contrary enhances the pathos of the scene.

In lines 510–11 Seneca stresses that fear and desperation drive Greeks and Trojans alike to beseech the gods to help, thus underlining the extraordinary proportions of the storm and the destruction it causes (*Ag.* 510–11):

in vota miseros ultimus cogit timor
eademque superos Troes et Danai rogant.

Extreme fear drove the wretches to prayer,
with Trojans and Danaans making the same request of the gods.

There are no differences anymore between the victorious and the conquered, between those who are happy to return home and those who will never see their native country again. Rather, the extremity has reduced Greeks and Trojans to the same level.

The actual prayer then shows that the Greeks and Trojans are, in fact, not only made equal, but that they have even exchanged roles. As the men attribute the storm to divine anger and conjecture that the Greeks are being punished for their crimes, they point out that the misfortune also affects the Trojans that are on board. For their sake the gods may calm down the violent sea – even if this means that also the Greeks will be spared (*Ag.* 522–26):

---

55 Cf. Stackmann 1949, 208–9: "Die idyllische Schilderung der Abfahrt von Troja, die durchaus der hellenistischen Dichtung anzugehören scheint, ist um des Kontrastes mit der folgenden Katastrophe willen eingeführt."

odia si durant tua
placetque mitti Doricum exitio genus,
quid hos simul perire nobiscum iuvat,
quibus perimus? sistite infestum mare:
vehit ista Danaos classis, et Troas vehit!

But if your hatred endures,
and you want the Dorican race destroyed,
why do you desire these people, on whose account
we are dying, to die with us? Calm the hostile seas:
this fleet carries Danaans, but it carries Trojans too!

Paradoxically, thus, the captive Trojans whose life so far depended on the Greeks' mercy become the (potential) saviours of their conquerors – a fact that highlights the utter despair of the men caught in the storm. By rendering their supplications in direct speech and, in so doing, further underlining their credibility, Seneca makes their misery even more perceivable and intensifies the emotional effect of the scene.

At the same time, their piety contrasts sharply with the bold arrogance of Ajax to whom the poet, using the transition formula *ecce alia clades* (*Ag.* 528), turns in the next section (*Ag.* 528–56). He is the only one who is not overcome by terror (*Ag.* 532–33: *solus invictus malis / luctatur Aiax*), although Athena renews the storm with her father's lightning-bolts (*Ag.* 528–32). Ajax gets his very "private" storm,[56] so to speak, initiated by Athena, whom he had insulted by raping Cassandra at the altar of the goddess. The sacrilege is not explicitly mentioned by the poet, but certainly present in the audience's memory. However, whereas everybody else has long dropped his equipment and resorted to pleading and praying (*Ag.* 507–11), Ajax still tries to meet the wrath of the weather with his *ars*, "straining on the ropes to shorten sail" (*Ag.* 533–34).[57] Even after another bolt of Athena smashes his ship, he is unmoved and, grasping the burning wreckage and eventually catching fire himself, sails on like a high stony crag[58] (*Ag.* 539–42):

nil ille motus, ardua ut cautes, salo
ambustus extat, dirimit insanum mare
fluctusque rumpit pectore et navem manu
complexus ignes traxit

Unshaken, though scorched like a lofty crag
he stood out from the saltwater, sundered the maddened sea,
broke the waves with his chest. As he grasped his ship tightly
he caught fire from it

---

56 Schindler 2000, 145.
57 Caviglia 1986–1987, 160.
58 The comparison is quite common, occurring frequently in epic as well as in tragedy, as Tarrant 1976, 277 points out.

His contempt of the gods is fully revealed in his subsequent speech, which is an inversion or perverted variation of the usual lamentation of the epic hero caught in a storm. Ajax jeers at Athena and "even offers to shout mockery and defiance of Jove"[59] (*Ag*. 545–52), before Neptune finally intervenes, knocking him into the sea and drowning him by dislodging the rock on which he was standing (*Ag*. 553–55: *tridente rupem subruit pulsam pater / Neptunus imis exerens undis caput / solvitque montem*). The intertextual echo of the first book of the *Aeneid*, in which the sea-god's appearance ensures the calming of the storm unleashed by Juno (*Aen*. 1. 125–27: *emissamque hiemem sensit Neptunus et imis / stagna refusa vadis, graviter commotus, et alto / prospiciens summa placidum caput extulit unda*) helps to emphasize Ajax's blasphemy, since in contrast to Aeneas he is not saved but destroyed by Neptune. Moreover, the last line of the narrative (*Ag*. 556):

> terraque et igne victus et pelago iacet.

> [he] lies conquered by earth and fire and sea.[60]

not only guarantees a nice rhetorical effect at the end of the account, but also stresses the cosmic dimensions of Ajax's *hybris*. His impious acts have violated the natural order and destabilized the universe, and it therefore takes the joint collaboration of all three elements, earth, fire and water, to eliminate him and re-establish order.

To sum up: I hope to have shown that Seneca in his messenger scenes adopts the same narrative practices that occur in Greek tragedy, and that their very narrativity is never "a handicap or disadvantage".[61] Rather, it is "often an instrument expertly wielded by the dramatist [...] and a means to create very special and impressive results",[62] thereby proving that messenger speeches – on- or offstage – are exciting and, what is more, immensely dramatic.

Bibliography

Amoroso, Filippo (1981), "Annunzi e scene d'annunzio nel teatro di L. Anneo Seneca", *Dioniso* 52, 307–38.

Agyon, Jean-Pierre (2004), *Pictor in fabula. L'ecphrasis – descriptio dans les tragédies de Sénèque*, Bruxelles.

---

59   Motto / Clark 1988, 201.
60   The line refers back to Ajax's boastful speech, claiming to have defeated sea, fire, heaven and Pallas herself (*Ag*. 545–46), which is strongly reminiscent of titano-machic imagery.
61   de Jong 1991, 177.
62   *Ibid*.

Barlow, Shirley A. (1971), *The Imagery of Euripides. A Study in the Dramatic Use of Pictorial Language*, London.

Barrett, James (2002), *Staged Narrative. Poetics and the Messenger in Greek Tragedy*, Berkeley / Los Angeles / London.

Brandt, Johanna (1986), *Argumentative Struktur in Senecas Tragödien. Eine Untersuchung anhand der Phaedra und des Agamemnon*, Hildesheim / Zürich / New York.

Benveniste, Emile (1971), *Problems in General Linguistics*, tr. M. E. Meek, Coral Gables, FL.

Bremer, Jan M. (1976), "Why Messenger-Speeches?", in: Jan M. Bremer / Stefan Radt / C. J. Ruijgh (eds.), *Miscellanea tragica in honorem J. C. Kamerbeek*, Amsterdam, 29–48.

Caviglia, Franco (1986–1987), "Elementi di tradizione epica nell'*Agamemnon* di Seneca", *QCTC* 4–5, 145–65.

Dingel, Joachim (1985), "Senecas Tragödien. Vorbilder und poetische Aspekte", in: *ANRW* II 32.2, Berlin / New York, 1052–99.

Erasmo, Mario (2004), *Roman Tragedy. Theatre to Theatricality*, Austin, TX.

Erdmann, Gerd (1964), *Der Botenbericht bei Euripides. Struktur und dramatische Funktion*, Diss. Kiel.

Fagles, Robert (2006), *Virgil. The Aeneid*, London.

Fischl, Johann (1910), *De nuntiis tragicis*, Wien / Leipzig.

Fitch, John G. (ed.) (2002–2004), *L. Annaeus Seneca. Tragedies*, Cambridge, MA.

François-Garelli, Marie-Hélène (1998), "Tradition littéraire et création dramatique dans les tragédies de Sénèque. L'exemple des récits de messagers", *Latomus* 57, 15–32.

Friedrich, Wolf-Hartmut (1956), "Episches Unwetter", in: *Festschrift Bruno Snell*, München, 77–87.

Giomini, Remus (ed.) (1956), *L. Annaei Senecae Agamemnona*, Roma.

Gregorio, Lamberto di (1967), *Le scene d'annuncio nella tragedia greca*, Milano.

Hall, Edith (ed.) (1996), *Aeschylus. The Persians*, Warminster.

Henning, Erich (1910), *De tragicorum Atticorum narrationibus*, Diss. Göttingen.

Janka, Markus (2004), "Senecas *Phaedra*: Des Dramas Kern und sein episch-elegischer Rahmen", in: Joachim Fugmann / Markus Janka / Ulrich Schmitzer / Helmut Seng (eds.), *Theater, Theaterpraxis, Theaterkritik im kaiserzeitlichen Rom*, Munich / Leipzig, 25–57.

Jong, Irene J. F. de (1991), *Narrative in Drama. The Art of the Euripidean Messenger-Speech*, Leiden.

Keller, Joachim (1959), *Struktur und dramatische Funktion des Botenberichts bei Aischylos und Sophokles*, Diss. Tübingen.

Lefèvre, Eckard (1966), "Schicksal und Selbstverschuldung in Senecas *Agamemnon*", *Hermes* 94, 482–96 [repr. in: E. Lefèvre (ed.), *Senecas Tragödien*, Darmstadt 1972, 457–76].

—— (1973), "Die Schuld des Agamemnon. Das Schicksal des Troja-Siegers in stoischer Sicht", *Hermes* 101, 64–91.

Liebermann, Wolf-Lüder (1974), *Studien zu Senecas Tragödien*, Meisenheim a. Gl.

Liedloff, Kurt (1884), *De tempestatibus, necyomanteae, inferorum descriptionibus, quae apud poetas Romanos primi p. Chr. saeculi leguntur*, Diss. Leipzig.

—— (1902), *Die Nachbildung griechischer und römischer Muster in Senecas Troades und im Agamemnon*, Grimma.

Michelini, Ann N. (1982), *Tradition and Dramatic Form in the 'Persians' of Aeschylus*, Leiden.

Morford, Mark P. O. (1967), *The Poet Lucan. Studies in Rhetorical Epic*, Oxford [repr. Bristol 1996].

Motto, Anna Lydia / Clark, John R. (1988), "*Fata mutata* and *fluctus varii* in the *Agamemnon*", in: Anna Lydia Motto / John R. Clark, *Senecan Tragedy*, Amsterdam, 163–214.

Pratt, Norman T. (1939), *Dramatic Suspense in Seneca and his Greek Predecessors*, Diss. Princeton.

Riemer, Peter (1997), "Zur dramaturgischen Konzeption von Senecas *Agamemnon*", in: Bernhard Zimmermann (ed.), *Griechisch-römische Komödie und Tragödie* II, Stuttgart, 135–51.

Rosenmeyer, Thomas G. (1989), *Senecan Drama and Stoic Cosmology*, Berkeley / Los Angeles.

Runchina, Giovanni (1960), "Tecnica drammatica e retorica nelle tragedie di Seneca", *AFLC* 28, 163–324.

Schiesaro, Alessandro (2003), *The Passions in the Play. Thyestes and the Dynamics of Senecan Drama*, Cambridge.

Schindler, Claudia (2000), "Dramatisches Unwetter. Der Seesturm in Senecas *Agamemnon* (vv. 421–578)", in: Susanne Gödde / Theodor Heinze (eds.), *Skenika. Beiträge zum antiken Theater und seiner Rezeption*, Darmstadt, 135–49.

Schmitz, Christine (1993), *Die kosmische Dimension in den Tragödien Senecas*, Berlin / New York.

Seidensticker, Bernd (1969), *Die Gesprächsverdichtung in den Tragödien Senecas*, Heidelberg.

Shelton, Jo-Ann (1983), "Revenge or resignation: Seneca's *Agamemnon*", in: A. J. Boyle (ed.), *Seneca Tragicus. Ramus Essays on Senecan Drama* [= *Ramus* 12], 159–83.

Stackmann, Karl (1949), "Senecas *Agamemnon*. Untersuchungen zur Geschichte des Agamemnon-Stoffes nach Aischylos", *C&M* 10, 180–221.

Stanley-Porter, D.-P. (1968), *Messenger-Scenes in Euripides*, Diss. London.

Tarrant, Richard T. (ed.) (1976), *Seneca. Agamemnon*, Cambridge.

Tietze (Larson), Victoria (1989), "Seneca's Epic Theatre", in: Carl Deroux (ed.), *Studies in Latin Liteature and Roman History* V, Bruxelles, 279–304.

—— (1994), *The Role of Description in Senecan Tragedy*, Frankfurt a. M.

Seneca and Pantomime

Alessandra Zanobi

1   Introduction

Seneca's tragedies are controversial, not least because they deviate in a range of formal characteristics from the compositional norms of fifth-century Greek tragedy. Their peculiar poetics include a pronounced looseness of structure, a striking freedom in the handling of the chorus, no scruples about the *mise-en-scène* of violent death, "running commentaries", i.e. sections in which one character describes the actions of another character while both are present on-stage, and the incorporation of lengthy descriptive narratives. Any of these aspects is hard to parallel in our surviving corpus of Attic scripts. In the past, Seneca's divergence from the dramatic practice of his classical Greek predecessors has often been interpreted as a sign of authorial incompetence. More charitably, Richard Tarrant has suggested that Seneca's break with fifth-century conventions simply reflects the ways in which the genre evolved during the Hellenistic period – a thesis difficult to prove, of course, since evidence for this chapter in the history of tragedy has almost entirely vanished.[1] Still, his basic point is well taken: a direct and exclusive comparison between Seneca's tragic corpus and the surviving scripts from fifth-century Athens can only result in a blinkered view of his dramatic art within the overall evolution of the genre. In fact, however, we need to broaden our historical and generic horizons even further. Thus, in a more recent intervention, Tarrant has emphasized the importance of the Roman tragic tradition, including the (now almost entirely lost) plays by Varius and Pomponius Secundus. He concludes that "Seneca's Augustan predecessors furnished him with a fully naturalized form of Greek tragic structure and language along with the poetic and thematic resources he employed to give what he had inherited a distinctively personal stamp."[2] In addition to this complex literary background, scholars have become increasingly aware of

---

1   See Tarrant 1978.
2   Tarrant 1995, 230.

the possibility that another genre of performance altogether, i.e. pantomime, ought to be factored into accounting for Seneca's poetics.

While issues of evidence again render it virtually impossible to reach certainty in the matter, Seneca's tragedies often seem to manifest what one may call "a pantomime aesthetics". Indeed, I would like to argue that positing the influence of pantomime would allow us to explain many of the formal peculiarities of his tragic *oeuvre*, which *prima facie* baffle.[3] That pantomime influenced Seneca's dramatic art should not come as a surprise: the genre was extraordinarily popular in imperial Rome, and the integration of some of its elements into tragic drama would appear to be a strategy not far-fetched for an author whom Tacitus once described as a man who had charming talent well suited to the taste of his age.[4] In addition, the "enrichment" of tragedy with components derived from pantomime chimes with the radical aesthetics and performative preferences that Nero cultivated at his court. To mention only one pertinent anecdote, according to Suetonius, the emperor vowed that, in addition to a variety of musical renditions, he would act out Virgil's Turnus as a pantomime dancer if he managed to retain his grip on power.[5] But these are, at any rate, circumstantial considerations: the pantomime thesis stands and falls with its ability to explain puzzling features in the tragedies themselves. After a brief sketch of the history of pantomime at Rome and a survey of the distinguishing features of the genre, I want to illustrate how passages from Seneca's tragedies that earlier critics have found puzzling acquire thematic point and dramatic power if we understand them as deliberate co-options of pantomimic customs and conventions.[6]

2   Pantomime: history and characteristics

Pantomime, which we may define, in its classical outlook, as a solo dance performance to the accompaniment of a chorus or flutist, started to flourish in Rome in the age of Augustus, after its supposed "invention" by Pylades of Cilicia, the author of a script on dance, and Bathyllus of Alexandria:[7]

---

3   See especially Zimmermann 1995.

4   Tac. *Ann.* 13.3: *fuit illi viro ingenium amoenum et temporis eius auribus accomodatum.*

5   Suet. *Nero* 54: *sub exitu quidem vitae palam voverat, si sibi incolumis status permansisset, proditurum se partae victoriae ludis etiam hydraulam et choraulam et utricularium ac novissimo die histrionem saltaturumque Vergili Turnum.*

6   In turn, Boyle 2006, 192 suggests that "extracts from the tragedies [of Seneca] could also have been used as libretti for *tragoediae cantatae* or for sung accompaniments (by a chorus or soloist) to *tragoediae saltatae*, the pantomimic dance."

7   On Pylades, see *RE*, s.v. Pylades, 2; on Bathyllus, see *RE*, s.v. Bathyllus, 7. The

the former tends to be credited with the invention of tragic pantomime, expressing passion and variety of characters, the latter with a more comic and light-hearted version.[8] As with all such ancient aetiologies that aim at pinpointing the *princeps generis*, doubts are in order as to the accuracy of the intelligence, and it seems more likely that the pair, rather than bringing into being a completely new theatrical genre, substantially transformed one already in existence.[9] A full genealogy of pantomime would have to include some passages in Plautus that show suggestive affinities with the genre, as well as Greek precedents.[10] Still, Pylades and Bathyllus seem to have given the pantomime repertory its imperial profile, thus putting their personal stamp on the city's dramatic entertainment culture. Their innovations may have consisted in amplifying the role of, or, indeed, introducing the chorus or flute player to accompany a dancer.[11] Intriguingly, the two artists were freedmen of Augustus (Pylades) and Maecenas (Bathyllus) and seem to have moved with some ease in the upper echelons of Roman society.[12] This tight nexus between pantomime and power should continue throughout the imperial period: emperors and common people became increasingly involved with the genre, and the habit of protecting and favouring dancers that started with Augustus' patronage of Pylades continued with his successors. Thus Caligula publicly showed his infatuation with the dancer Mnester and Nero favoured the pantomime Paris.

To identify the main features of the genre is not an easy task since the sources tend to be late and scattered, such as inscriptions and epigrams contained in the *Anthologia Palatina* and the *Anthologia Latina*, Lucian's dialogue *On the Dance* (written between 162 and 165 AD), or Libanius' oration *On Behalf of the Dancers* (c. 361 AD). There is thus a constant danger of anachronistic distortion if one mines these sources for evidence of early imperial performance practice – quite apart from the fact that one needs

---

genre as a whole has just received a magisterial treatment by Lada-Richards 2007. See also Jory 1981.

8   So Athenaeus *Deip.* 1.20–21.
9   See Goldberg 2005, 119–20. Jocelyn 1967, 21 notes that "according to Livy 7.2.9–10 the Roman *histriones* merely mimed the *cantica* while a singer accompanied the *tibicen.*" Finding it unlikely that this statement refers to the performance practice of tragedy and comedy, he suggests that "Livy may have been thinking of the contemporary pantomime."
10 See Zimmermann 1995 for Plautus and mime, and Gilula 2002, 211–3, Kokolakis 1959, 302, and Wüst 1949, 840–3 for the Greek background (esp. Xen. *Symp.* 9.2).
11 See Suet. *de Poetis*, fr. 3 and Macr. *Sat.* 2.7.18.
12 For Pylades see Dio Cass. 54.17.4 with Bonaria 1959, 133; for Bathyllus Tac. *Ann.* 1.54.2 and *schol. ad Pers.* 5.123: *Bathylli: pantomimus fuit libertus Maecenatis.* On the social status of stage artists in the Roman republic and early empire more generally, see Leppin 1992.

to reckon with a great fluidity in how pantomime was performed in any period.[13] Still, some basic facts seem reasonably certain. As far as we can gather, the song that accompanied the solo (and mute) performance of the pantomime dancer tended to be based on a libretto (the *fabula saltica*).[14] At the time of Lucian, the dancer was supported by an orchestra containing stringed, wind, and percussion instruments, and by a chorus. The rhythm was maintained by the *scabellum*, which was a wooden clapper attached to and operated by one of the musicians. The focus of the spectacle, however, was on the dancer and his movements, through which he interpreted and enacted a story, which was derived, in the majority of cases, from a mythological plot. Lucian reports that a single dancer danced all the roles in succession, changing his mask for each character he was playing – up to five in a single performance.[15] Usually, the dancing of tragic *sujets* aimed at portraying characters undergoing emotional strain, such as one would associate with the experience of love, madness, or grief. As Lucian puts it, "the dancer undertakes to present and enact characters and emotions, introducing now a lover and now an angry person, one man afflicted with madness, another with grief, and all this within fixed bounds."[16] His description is echoed in an anonymous epigram in the *Latin Anthology* about the art of the dancer: "He fights, he plays, he loves, he revels, he turns around, he stands still; he illuminates the truth, and imbues everything with grace."[17]

From a more technical point of view, the dancer relied on gesture and hand language (cheironomy), through which he described the story sung by the chorus; the artist used the movement of the fingers to express the words of the libretto or to convey the emotions experienced by the characters portrayed. Ancient writers place a lot of emphasis on the ability of the silently speaking hands of pantomime dancers.[18] Libanius (103) also states that well-formed fingers were a physical requirement of the profession. As to the content and structure of the libretto, we can infer from Lucian (67)

---

13 A point stressed by Hall 2002, 29.
14 Unfortunately, none of these *libretti* seems to have survived. Hall 2008, 258–82 proposes that the Barcelona *Alcestis* (a Latin hexameter poem perhaps composed in the fourth century AD) might be a pantomimic libretto. See Marcovich 1988 for an edition with commentary of the *Alcestis Barcinonensis*.
15 Lucian, *On the dance* 66.
16 Lucian 67.
17 *Latin Anthology*: "On the pantomime" (no. 110.7–10 ed. Shackleton Bailey): *pugnat, ludit, amat, bacchatur, vertitur, adstat; inlustrat verum, cuncta decore replet.*
18 Lucian 63, 69; Libanius, *Or.* 103; Sen. *Epist.* 121.6: *Mirari solemus saltandi peritos quod in omnem significationem rerum et adfectuum parata illorum est manus et verborum velocitatem gestus adsequitur.* ("We are accustomed to feeling wonder at skilled dancers because their gestures are perfectly adapted to the meaning of the piece and its accompanying emotions, and their movements match the speed of the dialogue.")

and Libanius (67) that, instead of presenting the development of the myth as a whole, it rather focused on its most emotionally climactic and spectacular moments. Thus a staged pantomime seems to have consisted in a sequence of scenes dramaturgically unconnected to one another, which chimes with the information that the solo dancer could use up to five changes of masks within a performance. Each scene most likely constituted a more or less self-contained tableau representing the very essence of a specific part of the mythological whole. Lucian (67), for example, notes that "the most surprising part of [a pantomimic performance] is that within the selfsame day at one moment we are shown Athamas in a frenzy, at another Ino in terror; presently the same person is Atreus, and after a little, Thyestes; then Aegisthus, or Aerope." We have a similar description in Libanius (67): "the theatre saw Deianeira, but also Oeneus and Achelous and Heracles and Nessus." This particular pantomime seems to have been concerned with the final segment of the saga of Heracles, and its thematic unity resides in the fact that all the characters have a relation with the hero. But since the episodes related to each character did neither happen at the same time nor in the same place, we have to infer that the transitions between single episodes of the myth were not subjected to a logical development. Rather, each episode appears to have been performed as a self-standing vignette and did not entail a proper dramatic sequence.

The costume commonly worn by the dancer was a light silk tunica (Lucian, 63) reaching down to the ankles; the light and silky fabric of the tunic was designed to follow and emphasise the movements of the dancer's body. The dancer also wore a *pallium*, which, according to Fronto, was used as an expressive and versatile prop to represent different objects according to the roles. For example, it could be the tail of a swan, then the long hair of the goddess Venus, and also the scourge of the Fury.[19] Archaeological findings indicate that the pantomimic masks had a closed mouth (understandably, since the actor did not speak), elaborated hair, and large holes for the eyes.[20] This last feature strongly suggests that the expression of the dancer's eyes remained visible through the eyeholes. Supporting evidence for this assumption comes from Cicero who describes a performance in which the eyes of the actor seemed to gleam to him from behind a mask.[21] He is probably re-

---

19 Fronto, *on Orations* 4: *ut histriones, quom palliolatim saltant, caudam cycni, capillum Veneris, Furiae flagellum eodem pallio demonstrant: ita isti unam eandemque sententiam multimodis faciunt.* ("As actors, when they dance clad in their mantles, with one and the same mantle represent a swan's tail, the tresses of Venus, a Fury's scourge....") See Csapo-Slater 1995, 383 no. V 38.

20 Jory 2001.

21 Cicero *de Orat.* 2.193: *Saepe ipse vidi, ut ex persona mihi ardere oculi hominis histrionis viderentur.*

ferring to a tragic show, but if the eyes were indeed visible through a tragic mask, *a fortiori* the same would have been the case for pantomime. The eye movements may have been suggested by emphatic movements of the head, to which a vivid expression of the eyes may have provided emotional intensity and the words of the libretto a more specific clue. It is not coincidental, then, that the ancient writers repeatedly praise the expressiveness of the dancers' eyes. Apuleius, for example, could claim that the dancer "would dance with her eyes alone". In a similar vein, St. Augustine affirms that actors "almost talk with their eyes".[22]

3   Seneca's pantomime aesthetics

The above survey ought to have shown that many of the features of Seneca's tragic art that diverge from the poetic practice of classical Greek tragedy can be paralleled in pantomime, in particular the lack of dramatic coherence, the emphasis on key moments in a larger mythic whole that does not necessarily yield a unified plot, and the disjunction between voice-over or musical accompaniment and acting. These striking similarities call for comment and explanation, and in what follows I want to explore how and why Seneca may have opted for integrating elements of what one may call the "pantomime aesthetics" into his tragedies. The focus will be on two areas of affinity: his dramatic art shares with pantomime a remarkable looseness of dramatic structure; and his plays feature "running commentaries", i.e. passages in which one character describes in the third person the movements of another one – descriptions, in other words, that, if the plays were staged, would involve a mute performance by one of the actors on stage.

---

22   Apuleius *Met.* 10.32: *nunc mite coniventibus nunc acre comminantibus gestire pupulis et nonnunquam saltare solis oculis* ("She gestured with her glances, now softly languid, now sharply threatening, and sometimes she would dance with her eyes alone."); St. Augustin *de Doctrina Christiana* 2.4.5: *histriones... cum oculis quasi fabulantur* ("the dancers almost talk with their eyes"). See also Nonnus *Dionysiaka* 5.107: "Polymnia nursing mother of the dance waved her arms, and sketched in the air an image of a soundless voice, speaking with hands and moving eyes in a graphic picture full of meaning" and 19.201: "he moved his eyes about as a picture of the story."

3.1   Structure

The dramatic structure of Seneca's tragedies is remarkably loose. Individual scenes possess an independence that would seem to weaken the dramatic coherence of the whole. Lengthy descriptions, during which the action of the main plot does not advance, frequently suspend dramatic time. The setting is fluid, transitions, which appear abrupt and unmotivated, link single scenes or acts, and the chorus has ceased to play a unifying role. Regenbogen summarizes the effect of these features as "a dissolution of the dramatic structure".[23] For several reasons, the *Trojan Women* offer an extreme example of this structural looseness, which is characteristic of Seneca's tragedies more generally. To begin with, there is the problem of location insofar as the play is not confined to a single setting. The actions of the first, second and third act are meant to take place in front of Hector's tomb, though the second scene of act two is set in the Greek camp; the action of the fourth act unfolds near Sigeum on the battlefield, in the vicinity of Achilles' tomb (893–5, 931); and in the fifth act Achilles' tomb is again off-stage, and the setting of the action is perhaps the shore of the sea.[24] Furthermore, Seneca has juxtaposed the acts, or even scenes within a single act, without connecting material or appropriate transitions. And finally, there are no consistent indications of entrances and exits of characters and chorus. On inspection, the play indeed consists of five main tableaux, which, apart from the fourth, are further divided into two scenes each that are only loosely connected to one another:

Tableau 1:
Location: at Hector's tomb
Scene 1: Hecuba mourns the fall of Troy.
Scene 2: Hecuba leads the chorus of Trojan women in a formal antiphonal lament over Troy, Hector, and Priam.

Tableau 2:
Location: at Hector's tomb, but change to the Greek camp in scene 2
Scene 1: Talthybius recounts the appearance of Achilles' ghost to the chorus of Trojan Women in the Greek camp, demanding that Polyxena be sacrificed to appease the dead hero.
Scene 2: Pyrrhus and Agamemnon discuss Achilles' demand. They summon Calchas, who appears in 353 and proclaims that not only Polyxena but also Hector's son Astyanax must be killed before the Greeks can set sail.

Tableau 3:
Location: at Hector's tomb
Scene 1: Andromache, warned by her dead husband Hector in a dream hides her son Astyanax in Hector's tomb chamber.

---

23   Regenbogen 1927/28 (reprinted 1961), 430.
24   See Fantham 1982, 39.

Scene 2: Ulysses arrives to fetch the boy; Andromache almost convinces him that the boy is dead, but her nervousness betrays her. Ulysses drags the boy away.

Tableau 4:
Location: near Sigeum (931); battlefield and Achilles' tomb (893–95)?
Scene: Helen is sent to collect Polyxena, on the pretext of preparing her for marriage; unable to maintain the pretence, she reveals the truth; finally Pyrrhus enters and silently drags Polyxena away.

Tableau 5:
Location: by the shore
Scene: A messenger recounts at length the deaths of Astyanax and Polyxena

Thus the first act begins with Hecuba's highly emotional soliloquy; afterwards a lyric interchange (in anapaests) between Hecuba and the chorus follows, performing a lamentation for the dead.[25] The second act is devoted to Talthybius' lengthy narration of the appearance of Achilles' ghost demanding the sacrifice of Polyxena. The third one revolves around Andromache's efforts to hide her little son from the Greeks; it achieves its pathetic and dramatic climax with Andromache's lyric monody (in anapaests 705–35), in which she pleads for Astyanax' life by compelling her son to act as a suppliant in front of Ulysses. (Interestingly, Andromache's lyric monody, which one would expect to be a surrendering lament of a mother faced with the cruel destiny of her son, actually describes the mute performance of Astyanax who acts out the gestures required in a supplication.) The fourth act deals with Polyxena's destiny. Even though Polyxena is the protagonist of the act she, too, does not speak a word: Helen and Andromache describe her reactions to the cruel destiny that is awaiting her. Just like Astyanax in the previous act, Polyxena thus delivers a mute performance – a dramatic choice of spectacular effect: "the silence of Polyxena throughout this act is a major aspect of the act's dramatic power".[26] The fifth act is occupied by the messenger's long description of the heroic deaths of Astyanax and Polyxena and the tearful reactions of both Greek and Trojan witnesses. The fact that the messenger's *rhesis* describes the deaths of the two children as well as the reactions of the crowd, which is described as an audience gathering in the theatre (the parallel is explicitly made at line 1125), makes this passage not only extremely peculiar with its two superimposed layers of spectatorship, but strives also for an accumulation of pathetic effects which provides a spectacular ending. Zwierlein summarises the overall effect thus:

---

25 In Seneca's tragic corpus this is the only lyric exchange between a character and the chorus, and clearly echoes the parallel one in Euripides' *Trojan Women* (153 ff.). Nonetheless Euripides' chorus is "less ritualistic and formal, focusing on the fates awaiting the Trojan women, not on the deaths of Hector and Priam or on Troy's tragic past" (Boyle 1994, 144–5).

26 Boyle 1994, 207.

Wo man also ein geschlossenes Ganzes hat sehen wollen, da müssen wir eine Folge von selbständigen Szenen erkennen: Klageprolog, Botenbericht, Fürstenstreit, philosophische Reflexion des Chores, Andromaches Kampf um ihr Kind gegen Ulixes, Helenes Trug; die Fugen bleiben jeweils deutlich offen.[27]

Seneca, in short, clearly threw to the wind dramatic norms of geographical and psychological continuity and dramatic coherence.

The organisation of the material around self-contained vignettes means that Seneca portrays only the most dramatic, pathetic, or spectacular episodes within this particular chapter of the Trojan saga. Concern for dramatic coherence or illusion seems to have been a secondary consideration. Explanations for this disinterest in an organic plot vary. Zwierlein sees it as evidence for Seneca's lack of interest in stage drama (as opposed to a drama of recitation); he is followed by Fantham, who notes that "if Seneca did not write for production he did not need to confine himself to a single setting, nor to identify the places of each separate scene."[28] Alternatively, we can attribute Seneca's approach to structure to the influence of pantomime. As Erasmo suggests, "Seneca's concentration on episodes, rather than on the dramatic structure as a whole, may be due not only to the influence of epic, but also to the success of the episodic mime productions of Publilius Syrus and to the influence of pantomime."[29] This seems an attractive proposition simply on the principle of critical benevolence: instead of explaining Seneca's pronounced looseness of structure in negative terms (Zwierlein talks of a *lack* of interest in dramatic performance), to posit a deliberate co-option of the aesthetics of pantomime implies an innovative and experimental author, who creatively engages with the contemporary theatrical repertory and its dramatic possibilities. The choice to pick only moments of high drama would thereby emerge as motivated by the desire to enhance the dramatic impact of the performance, offering, as it were, a highlight reel of powerful scenes and encounters to audiences well versed in the mythic material and able to appreciate the author's selectivity and essential concentration.

In addition to the dramatic possibilities that open up through a departure from the norm of a unified setting or plot (an aesthetic ideal as historically contingent as any other), Seneca may have been influenced by thematic considerations. It is well established that his tragedies are very much "cosmic" plays – in the sense that the entire universe, its order and its perversion

---

27 Zwierlein 1966, 93: "Where some wanted to see a coherent whole, we have to recognise a sequence of unconnected scenes: prologue devoted to mourning, messenger speech, strife between the princes, philosophical reflexion of the chorus, Andromache's struggle against Ulixes on behalf of her child, Helena's deception; the links remain clearly open."

28 Fantham 1982, 39.

29 Erasmo 2004, 134.

thereof, are implicated in the action that unfolds in the human sphere. Stoic philosophy and its view of the world as an ordered entity permeated by divine rationality constitutes the ideal backdrop, which tends to be invoked to no avail by minor characters, for events and deeds that show our world dissolving into moral and physical chaos.[30] Seneca's tragic art brings on stage *nefas* writ large and revels in the undoing of natural order.[31] *Natura versa est* is a distinct possibility, and all too often becomes a dire reality in his plays.[32] What Seneca stages is infernal, and in more than one of his tragedies the energy that drives the action comes from Hell. The *Thyestes* is the most obvious example, but the earth also splits open to unleash the forces of the underworld in the *Oedipus* (582–3: *subito dehiscit terra et immenso sinu/ laxata patuit*) and the *Trojan Women*. In his account of the appearance of Achilles' ghost, Thaltybius, after detailing the symptoms of nature under heavy, unnatural stress, announces that the earth has burst open, generating a path for the ascent of Hell.[33] In the light of these natural phenomena, which affect the entire cosmos, the precise delineation of specific setting takes on a rather secondary importance, or would even be distracting. The lack of precision arguably helps the audience to concentrate on, and appreciate the sublime impact of, the cosmic dimension of Seneca's plot. What Seneca wants to show is the sympathetic correlation of human action and the world at large, and for this purpose a dramatic structure resembling pantomime is arguably better suited than the dramatic conventions of classical Greek tragedy.[34] Seneca, in other words, partly innovated in matter of tragic form also for thematic reasons (and not just because of the popularity of pantomime), drawing on the aesthetic profile and possibilities of a cognate performance genre to enhance his message or, more generally, the view of the world that he wished to articulate.[35]

---

30 See e.g. Rosenmeyer 1989 and Schmitz 1993.
31 See especially and paradigmatically his *Thyestes* with Schiesaro 2003.
32 See Schmitz 1993, 196–200.
33 See *Tro* 178–80 with Schmitz 1993, 175–90.
34 For the cosmic perspective see e.g. *Hf* 1054–6, where the sky, God, the sea, and the sun are exhorted to cry a river, *Thy* 1069–71 (*audite maria, vos quoque audite hoc scelus,/ quocumque, di, fugistis, audite inferi,/ audite terrae*) or *Tro* 112 (*audiat omnis pontus et aether*). For Greek precedents see Griffith 1983 on [Aesch.] *PV* 88–92.
35 For the notion of generic enrichment see Harrison 2007.

3.2 Running commentaries

Running commentaries are passages in which the emotions, the actions, or the physical appearance of a character are described by the chorus or by another actor in the third person; usually, the character thus described remains mute and neither hears nor reacts to what is said to or about him or her. Running commentaries can accompany actions taking place onstage or offstage.[36] Briefly put, they consist of a speaking actor verbalizing the (mute) performance of a silent actor. In Greek tragedy, this technique hardly features at all: extraordinary emotional states (a favourite topic of Seneca's running commentaries), far from being articulated at length in discourse, tend to be projected in speech by whoever is experiencing them or by means of very brief and simple descriptions. In addition, observations about emotions are usually addressed to the character concerned and trigger some kind of response. Running commentaries belong to those features that have led scholars to suppose that Seneca's plays were not meant to be performed on stage, because if they were staged, there would have been no need to describe the action since it would unfold before the eyes of the audience. Thus, as Zwierlein maintains, "the spectator would get the impression that he is witness to a pantomime put into words in a troublesome and pedantic way by a third person, as if he were blind."[37] In a recitation (Zwierlein's preferred mode of performance), this problem of course disappears. More recently, however, Bernard Zimmermann has offered a completely different interpretation of the phenomenon. He proposes, picking up a cue provided unwittingly by Zwierlein himself, that these descriptive scenes betoken the influence of pantomime.[38] Seneca's characters would thus re-enact the relationship that pertains in a pantomimic performance between the (mute) dancer who embodies through movement, gesture, and facial expression the words sung or spoken by the narrator. To understand Seneca's 'running commentaries' as a deliberate adaptation of a pantomimic element does not resolve the intractable question as to whether Seneca designed his tragedies for performance or recitation. But it opens an exciting new vista on his poetic technique.

In what follows, I would like to illustrate this point by exploring several of these running commentaries. Here is Medea's nurse from the *Medea* (*Med* 380–96):

---

36 I here adopt the definition by Larson 1994, 31.
37 Zwierlein 1966, 58: "Der Zuchauer müsste den Eindruck bekommen, er werde Zeuge einer Pantomime, die ihm – lästig genug – auch noch pedantisch von dritten Seite beschrieben wird, als sei er blind."
38 Zimmermann 1990, 161–67.

Alumna, celerem quo rapis tectis pedem?   380
resiste et iras comprime ac retine impetum.
Incerta qualis entheos gressus tulit
cum iam recepto maenas insanit deo
Pindi nivalis vertice aut Nysae iugis,
talis recursat huc et huc motu effero,   385
furoris ore signa lymphati gerens.
flammata facies, spiritum ex alto citat,
proclamat, oculos uberi fletu rigat,
renidet; omnis specimen affectus capit.
haeret minatur aestuat queritur gemit.   390
quo pondus animi verget? Ubi ponet minas?
ubi se iste fluctus franget? exundat furor.
non facile secum versat aut medium scelus:
se vincet. Irae novimus veteris notas.
magnum aliquid instat, efferum immane impium.   395
vultum Furoris cerno. Di fallant metum!

[My child, where are you rushing in such haste from the house? Stop, curb your
anger, control your aggression! Like an ecstatic maenad taking erratic steps, crazed
and possessed by the god, on snowy Pindus' peak or Nysa's ridges, so she keeps
running here and there with wild movements, with signs of frenzied rage in her expression. Her face is blazing, she draws deep breaths, she shouts out, weeps floods of
tears, beams with joy; she shows evidence of each and every emotion. She hesitates,
threatens, fumes, laments, groans. Which way will the weight of her mind come
down? Where will she implement her threats? Where will that wave break? Her rage
is cresting. It is no simple or moderate crime she is contemplating: she will outdo
herself. I know the hallmarks of her old anger. Something great is looming, savage,
monstrous, unnatural. I see the face of Rage. May the gods prove my fears wrong!]

The passage begins with a direct address to Medea by the nurse, followed
by a puzzled question and three imperatives. Medea, however, appears to
ignore the communicative overtures. The text offers no indication why this
should be the case, but the nurse, at any rate, discontinues her efforts to engage Medea in dialogue, turning herself from a partner in conversation into a
marginal bystander and commentator, who simply verbalizes the solipsistic
display of the protagonist. For the rest of the quoted passage, the nurse describes what she sees Medea doing and offers her interpretation of it. As if to
mark the transition from dialogue to commentary, the nurse commences her
observation with a stylistic device typical of epic poetry: a simile.[39] The ensuing description of Medea's behaviour is extremely evocative and focuses
on movement (*recursat huc et huc motu effero*, picking up on *rapis pedem*
and *retine impetum*), facial features and expression (*ore, flammata facies,
oculos uberi fletu rigat, renidet*), and verbal and non-verbal sounds and nois-

---

39 This also means that the audience is not clued in on the change in perspective until
    the – surprising – third person *recursat* in line 385.

es (*spiritum ex alto citat, proclamat, renidet, minatur, queritur, gemit*). The dominant expression is one of utter insanity (*furoris signa lymphati, exundat Furor, vultum Furoris cerno*) that manifests itself in extreme swings in mood and conduct, an impression deftly underscored by the construction of the verses 387–90. After three lines with two verbs each, placed strategically at the beginning and end of the verse (*flammata* [sc. *est*] ~ *citat, proclamat* ~ *rigat, renidet* ~ *capit*), this section of the nurse's commentary concludes with the quick-fire enumeration of five successive verbs in asyndeton: *haeret minatur aestuat queritur gemit*. In short, if Medea embodies Madness visually, the nurse diagnoses and verbalizes the condition.

Overall, the passage has long baffled commentators. Hine sums up the problem: "The long description of the behaviour of Medea while she herself is on stage is regularly taken as a sign that the plays were not really meant for stage performance. Certainly if Medea is supposed to be acting out all the behaviour as the Nurse describes it, then the whole passage, and line 390 in particular, represents a histrionic obstacle course that in performance could well become comic; and if the actors wore masks, there could be no question of changes of facial expression. But it is possible to regard the Nurse's description … as a long aside."[40] This is a perceptive assessment of the crux, but the solution offered, i.e. that we are dealing with a long aside, is quite unsatisfactory. If the character playing Medea does not act out the behaviour as described by the Nurse, this entails an odd disjunction between the content of the "long aside" and the performance of the protagonist. And the apparent mismatch between discourse and action then raises the further question why Seneca would have opted for this technique in the first place.[41] In a milder form, the same question also dogs the thesis that Seneca did not mean his tragedies to be performed on stage. For the proposition that the plays were designed for recitation only explains why Seneca may not have felt *required* to ensure feasibility of performance; it does not explain why he *chose* to integrate passages into his plays that, *prima facie* (i.e. if assessed against the customs and conventions of fifth-century Greek tragedy) do not seem to lend themselves easily to being acted out.

The fact of the matter is, however, that in the pantomime tradition the split between a party responsible for the discourse and a party responsible for the acting is entirely normal and natural, indeed constitutive of the genre. The near-match would seem to suggest, if not encourage, the possibility that Seneca deliberately employed the running commentary as a technique well

---

40 Hine 2000, 155.
41 In the case of a performance, the gap between the action on stage and its verbalization disappears – and lines from comedy suggest that quick mood swings could indeed be acted out. Hine 2000, 155 appositely cites Pomponius *com.* 124 Ribbeck <*Flet*>, *fit desubito hilarus; tristis saltat; ridens ringitur* as a parallel for line 390.

known from pantomime – and this quite irrespective of whether or not we imagine the play performed on stage. The passage also contains a decisive cue as to why he may have been so fond of this device even if he intended his plays for recitation only. At one point in the midst of her observation, the nurse pauses and provides an overall assessment of what she sees as happening to Medea: *omnis specimen affectus capit*. The idiom is striking: *affectus* is the technical term used in Stoic philosophy for denoting the passions, which this particular school of thought deemed an ailment in need of therapy. We perhaps capture a further whiff of this 'medical' attitude towards the anatomy of a mind in the thrall of passion in the phrase *omnis specimen*. In other words, the nurse turns her account into a diagnosis of Medea's pathological state of mind, not unlike one, which a professional philosopher (such as Seneca) could have provided. Indeed, the passage bears a remarkable resemblance to the physiognomy of anger that Seneca develops in the *de Ira* (1.1.3–4):

> Vt scias autem non esse sanos quos ira possedit, ipsum illorum habitum intuere; nam ut furentium certa indicia sunt audax et minax vultus, tristis frons, torva facies, citatus gradus, inquietae manus, color versus, crebra et vehementius acta suspiria, ita irascentium eadem signa sunt: flagrant ac micant oculi, multus ore toto rubor exaestuante ab imis praecordiis sanguine, labra quatiuntur, dentes comprimuntur, horrent ac surriguntur capilli, spiritus coactus ac stridens, articulorum se ipsos torquentium sonus, gemitus mugitusque et parum explanatis vocibus sermo praeruptus et conplosae saepius manus et pulsata humus pedibus et totum concitum corpus magnasque irae minas agens, foeda visu et horrenda facies depravantium se atque intumescentium – nescias utrum magis detestabile vitium sit an deforme.

> [But you have only to behold the aspect of those possessed by anger to know that they are insane. For as the marks of a madman are unmistakable – a bold and threatening mien, a gloomy brow, a fierce expression, a hurried step, restless hands, an altered colour, a quick and more violent breathing – so likewise are the marks of the angry man; his eyes blaze and sparkle, his whole face is crimson with the blood that surges from the lowest depths of the heart, his lips quiver, his teeth are clenched, his hair bristles and stands on end, his breathing is forced and harsh, his joints crack from writhing, he groans and bellows, bursts out into speech with scarcely intelligible words, strikes his hands together continually, and stamps the ground with his feet; his whole body is excited and performs great angry threats; it is an ugly and horrible picture of distorted and swollen frenzy – you cannot tell whether this vice is more execrable or more hideous. (translated by John W. Basore, Loeb Classical Library, 1928)]

The running commentary, with its objectification of passion, thus has natural affinities with Seneca's Stoic leanings – it is an ideal dramatic form to make a philosophical point; and, given that the philosophical point is made by a rather marginal character in the play, its employment reinforces the impression of impotence of philosophy in the face of passion writ large. The exhortations by the nurse, at any rate, that conclude the cited passage have no bearings whatsoever on the protagonist of the unfolding plot of revenge. The prayer at the end remains ineffectual.[42]

The rhetorical and dramatic function of running commentaries in Seneca's other tragedies corroborate this interpretation. In the *Phaedra*, for instance, in a constellation virtually identical to the one found in the *Medea*, the nurse of Phaedra at one point diagnoses in minute detail the consequences of her mistress' suffering from the passion of love.[43] Throughout, the emphasis of her description is very much on empirical symptoms of a pathological state of mind, as she assigns verbal meaning to what Phaedra enacts. In this case, the running commentary does double duty as diagnosis and revelation because Phaedra, despite being beside herself, nevertheless wishes to deny and conceal her condition – to no avail. The suppressed and internal is all too apparent in her appearance and how she conducts herself (*Phae* 362–6):

> torretur aestu tacito et inclusus quoque,
> quamvis tegatur, proditur vultu furor
> erumpit oculis ignis et lassae genae
> lucem recusant; nil idem dubiae placet,   365
> artusque varie iactat incertus dolor.

[The fever silently burns her, and her inner madness, however much concealed, is betrayed in her face. Fire bursts forth through her eyes; her weary sight cannot bear the daylight. Nothing pleases her fickle mind for long, and her restless pain disturbs her body in various way.]

As in the running commentary from the *Medea*, the operative words to describe Phaedra's frame of mind is madness brought about by an attack of passion (*furor*). Like the nurse of Medea, Phaedra's nurse offers a diagnostic disquisition that reveals the state of mind of the protagonist while at the same time producing something akin to a choreography of enacted emotions: throughout her commentary, she foregrounds various body parts and movements of Love's victim. Phaedra betrays her insanity in her facial expression (363: *vultu*) as the fire of love bursts from her eyes (364: *erumpit oculis ignis*); anguish makes her skip about uncontrollably (366: *artusque varie iactat incertus dolor*); she collapses and cannot support her head on her neck (367–8: *nunc ut soluto labitur marcens gradu/et vix labante sustinet collo caput*); she is restless and constantly changing attitude and condition (372–3: *semper impatiens sui/mutatur habitus*); she walks with uncertain steps since she has lost all her strength (374–5: *vadit incerto pede/iam viribus defecta*); she is weak and pale (375–6: *non idem vigor,/non ora tinguens nitida purpureus rubor*); and she cries continuously and abundantly (381–2: *lacrimae cadunt per ora et assiduo genae/rore irrigantur*). Again, a philo-

---

42   For a parallel see Schiesaro 2003 on the role and function of Atreus' side-kick in the *Thyestes* (the ineffectual voice of reason).

43   See *Phae* 362–83.

sophical interest informs the commentary. As Tarrant has pointed out, the Stoics endorsed and elaborated the belief, widespread in the ancient world, that "the heart's construction could be read in the face".[44] Seneca, in his treatises and dialogues, repeatedly explores the "interface" between internal emotions and their somatic articulation.[45]

The passages from *Medea* and *Phaedra* share a common idiom that recurs in running commentaries from other plays. To illustrate Seneca's stereotypical design, it is worth looking at some further examples, such as the chorus' description of Cassandra in the *Agamemnon* (*Ag* 710–19):

> Silet repente Phoebas et pallor genas   710
> creberque totum possidet corpus tremor;
> stetere vittae, mollis horrescit coma,
> anhela corda murmure incluso fremunt,
> incerta nutant lumina et versi retro
> torquentur oculi, rursus immoti rigent.   715
> nunc levat in auras altior solito caput
> graditurque celsa, nunc reluctantes parat
> reserare fauces, verba nunc clauso male
> custodit ore maenas impatiens dei.

> [Suddenly Phoebus' priestess is silent: pallor spreads over her cheecks, continual trembling over her whole body. The holy ribbons stand out, her soft hair bristles. Her painting breast is loud with pent-up utterance; her gaze is unsteady and drooping; her eyes roll backwards, then again are fixed and rigid. Now she raises her head aloft, higher than usual, and walks tall; now she makes ready to unseal her reluctant mouth, now she tries in vain to hold in the words behind closed lips-a maenad unwilling to endure the god. (translated by John G. Fitch, Loeb Classical Library, 2004)]

The chorus here details the physical consequences of suffering from a bout of prophetic *furor*. In her frenzy, Cassandra exhibits the same symptoms as the enraged Medea and love-sick Phaedra. Her eye movements are described at length, she walks unsteadily, and she wavers as to whether or not to burst out in speech. The same devices are also on display in scenes where the character described is off-stage, as well as in more traditional messenger speeches. An example of the former is the nurse's description of how Deianira reacts to the arrival of Iole in the *Hercules Oetaeus* (241–53).[46] The passage starts out as a report of things past (240–5):

---

44   Tarrant 1976, 198 (*ad Ag* 128) with further passages and bibliography.
45   See e.g. *de Ira* 1.1.5: *Cetera licet abscondere et in abdito alere: ira se profert et in faciem exit, quantoque maior, hoc effervescit manifestius.*
46   For the latter, see e.g. the messenger in the *Oedipus*, who just like the nurse in *Medea*, resorts to a fairly conventional simile to illustrate the insanity of the protagonist, which is manifest in his eyes (*Oed* 919–42: *qualis per arva Libycus insanit leo,/ fulvam minaci fronte concutiens iubam;/ vultus furore torvus atque oculi truces,/ gemitus et altum murmur, et gelidus volat/ sudor per artus, spumat et volvit minas/*

stetit furenti similis ac torvum intuens
Herculea coniunx; feta ut Armenia iacens
sub rupe tigris hoste conspecto exilit
aut iussa thyrsum quatere conceptum ferens
Maenas Lyaeum dubia quo gressus agat
haesit parumper.

[Hercules' wife stood like a madwoman, glaring grimly. She resembled a whelped tigress, lying beneath a crag in Armenia, that leaps up at sight of the foe; or a Maenad, called to brandish the thyrsus, quickened and ridden by Lyaeus, who hesitates briefly, unsure where to direct her steps. (translated by John G. Fitch, Loeb Classical Library, 2004)]

Here again the emphasis is on madness (240: *furenti similis*), on the gaze (240: *torvum intuens*), and on uncertain movement (244–5); the comparison with a lioness and a Maenad is stereotypical imagery. But from a dramatic point of view, a sudden shift occurs in the middle of line 245 and the report turns into commentary. Up until *haesit*, the nurse has used the past tense; but she then suddenly switches in the present, which implies that she is actually seeing Deianeira acting out her fury off-stage (but in sight of the nurse). This prepares for Deianeira's entry (245–53):

... tum per Herculeos lares   245
lymphata rapitur, tota vix satis est domus:
incurrit, errat, sistit, in vultus dolor
processit omnis, pectori paene intimo
nihil est relictum; fletus insequitur minas.
nec unus habitus durat aut uno furit   250
contenta vultu: nunc inardescunt genae,
pallor ruborem pellit et formas dolor
errat per omnes; queritur implorat gemit.

[Then she rushed in frenzy through Hercules' house, the whole building scarcely giving room enough; she charged forward, swerved, stopped. All her pain came into her face, almost nothing was left hidden in her breast. Tears followed hard on threats. No single attitude lasted long, no single expression of rage satisfied her: now her cheeks flamed, now pallor expelled the colour. Her pain ranged through every possible form, she lamented, entreated, groaned. (translated by John G. Fitch, Loeb Classical Library, 2004)]

The similarities with the descriptions of Medea and Phaedra, which are quoted and analyzed above, are obvious: we get a full physiognomy of the pathology of passion.

---

ac mersus alte magnus exundat dolor.) In the case of Oedipus, of course, the focus on the eyes is particularly appropriate, as the entire report of the messenger works up to the climactic moment when they come out halfway – to meet the hands that would root them from their sockets: *Oed* 962–4: *at contra truces/ oculi steterunt et suam intenti manum/ ultro insequuntur, vulneri occurrunt suo.*

I want to conclude this survey with a passage where, just as in the *Medea*, the choice between interactive drama and the split between verbal articulation and action is thematized in the text itself, and in a particularly effective way. Towards the end of the *Hercules furens*, Amphitryon describes in "real time" how Hercules murders his wife and children before deciding, against the shocked intervention of the chorus, to turn himself into Hercules' last sacrificial victim. He addresses the hero directly, begging him to complete the butchering, but his attempt to interact with the madman fails. The scene turns into a running commentary (*Hf* 1039–50, Amphitryon speaking):

> Nondum litasti, nate; consumma sacrum.
> stat ecce ad aras hostia, expectat manum   1040
> cervice prona. praebeo occurro insequor;
> macta – quid hoc est? errat acies luminum
> visusque maeror hebetat; an video Herculis
> manus trementes? vultus in somnum cadit
> et fessa cervix capite summisso labat;   1045
> flexo genu iam totus ad terram ruit,
> ut caesa silvis ornus aut portum mari
> datura moles. vivis an leto dedit
> idem tuos qui misit ad mortem furor?
> sopor est; reciprocos spiritus motus agit.   1050

[You have not yet made full offering, son; complete the sacrifice. Look, the victim stands at the altar, his neck bent, and awaits your hand. I present myself, willingly, insistently: perform the killing! What is this? Are my eyes failing, and grief dulling my sight, or do I see Hercules' hands trembling? His eyes are closing in sleep, his head sinking, his weary neck drooping. Now his knees bend and his whole body collapses on the ground, as heavily as an ash tree felled in the woods, or a mass of masonry dropped in the sea to create a harbour. Are you alive, or killed by that same frenzy which sent your loved ones to their death? It is sleep: his breath comes and goes regularly. (translated by John G. Fitch, Loeb Classical Library, 2002)]

In this particular case, Seneca seems to flirt with a collapse between actor and commentator. Amphitryon, reduced to pleading for his death in view of the calamity that has hit his household, begs Hercules to accept him as a character with whom to interact – and be it as a sacrificial victim. But Hercules, in his madness, is incapable of doing so. The split between acting and commenting remains in place.

All of the passages considered deal with descriptions of characters under the effects of harmful emotions such as wrath (Medea), love (Phaedra); anger caused by jealousy (Deianeira); and prophetic frenzy (Cassandra). As we have previously said, the representation of a character in a state of extreme emotions was a typical theme of pantomimic performances.[47] Thus Seneca's potential interest in adopting the techniques of this theatrical medium may be

---

47   See above, p. 272.

due to the fact that the pantomimic genre was the most suitable one, thanks to its effectiveness in expressing many different *affectus*, to display the effects of passions, whose treatment had also a relevant place in Seneca's philosophical works. From Seneca's own words we know that his appreciation for pantomime was due to the dancer's ability to portray emotions. Furthermore, it is worth noticing the extensive presence of body parts contained in the passages which is suggestive of a poet producing verse with gestural and choreographic accompaniment in mind: the special emphasis on the movements of the eyes recalls the similar emphasis ancient writers give to the highly expressive and fundamental role of the dancer's gaze. Also, the descriptions of emotions and states of minds in the running commentaries are heavily stereotyped to the point that Seneca employs the same or very similar formulas and attributes to portray different characters affected by different passions, such as anger, love, or grief. If we compare the various descriptions, the recurrence of similar patterns of behaviour is evident. The characters all move with hasty or agitated movements and are affected by a constant change of attitude; their eyes are flashing and turning; the colour of their faces is in constant change; they cry and groan. Interestingly, even the range of comparison used in the descriptions is limited and repetitive. Particularly prominent are comparisons with a wild animal or a Maenad. The use of the same repertoire of either behaviour or expressions used in the descriptions seems to point to the fact that Seneca did not aim at variation or nuanced portrayal of different emotions and characters; on the contrary, running commentaries seem to stand as standard descriptions of passion, conceived as a stereotypical malaise.

To conclude, it is necessary to clarify that I am not suggesting that the influence of pantomime necessarily implies that Seneca meant his tragedies to be performed; my point is rather that he wrote them with pantomime in mind and explored the aesthetic possibilities of the genre to enhance the thematic and dramatic impact of his tragic plays.

Bibliography

Boyle, Anthony J. (1994), *Seneca's Troades*, Leeds.
—— (2006), *An Introduction to Roman Tragedy*, London and New York.
Bonaria, Mario (1959), "Dinastie di Pantomimi Latini", in: *Maia* 2, 224–42.
Csapo, Eric / Slater, William J. (1995), *The Context of Ancient Drama*, Ann Arbor.
Erasmo, Mario (2004), *Roman Tragedy: Theater to Theatricality*, Austin.
Fantham, Elaine (1982), *Seneca's Troades: a Literary Introduction with Text, Translation, and Commentary*, Princeton.
Gilula, Dwora (2002), "Entertainment at Xenophon's *Symposium*", in: *Athenaeum* 90, 207–13.
Goldberg, Sander (2005), *Constructing Literature in the Roman Republic: Poetry and its Reception*, Cambridge.

Griffith, Mark (1983), *Aeschylus, Prometheus Bound*, Cambridge.

Hall, Edith (2008), "Is the Barcelona Alcestis a Libretto?", in: Edith Hall / Rosie Wyles (eds.), *New Directions in Ancient Pantomime*, Oxford, 258–82.

Harrison, Stephen J. (2007), *Generic Enrichment in Vergil and Horace*, Oxford.

Hine, Harry M. (2000), *Seneca: Medea, with an Introduction, Text, Translation and Commentary*, Warminster.

Jory, John (1981), "The Literary Evidence for the Beginnings of Imperial Pantomime", in: *BICS* 28, 147–61.

—— (2001), "Some Cases of Mistaken Identity? Pantomime Masks and their Content", in: *BICS* 45, 1–20.

Kokolakis, Minos (1959), *Pantomimus and the treatise peri orcheseos*, Athens.

Lada-Richards, Ismene (2007), *Silent Eloquence: Lucian and Pantomime Dancing*, London.

Larson, Victoria T. (1994), *The Role of Description in Senecan Tragedy*, Frankfurt.

Leppin, Hartmut (1992), *Histrionen: Untersuchungen zur sozialen Stellung von Bühnenkünstler im Westen des Römischen Reiches zur Zeit der Republik und des Principats*, Bonn.

Marcovich, Miroslav (1988), *Alcestis Barcinonensis: Text and Commentary*, Leiden and New York.

Regenbogen, Otto (1927/28), "Schmerz und Tod in den Tragödien Senecas", in: *Vorträge der Bibliothek Warburg* 7, 167–218 [= *Kl. Schriften*, Munich 1961, 409–62].

Rosenmeyer, Thomas G. (1989), *Senecan Drama and Stoic Cosmology*, Berkeley, Los Angeles, London.

Schiesaro, Alessandro (2003), *The Passions in Play: Thyestes and the Dynamics of Senecan Drama*, Cambridge.

Schmitz, Christine (1993), *Die kosmische Dimension in den Tragödien Senecas*, Berlin and New York.

Tarrant, Richard J. (1976), *Seneca: Agamemnon, Edited with a Commentary*, Cambridge.

—— (1978), "Senecan Drama and its Antecedents", in: *HSCP* 82, 113–63.

—— (1995), "Greek and Roman in Seneca's Tragedies", in: Christopher P. Jones / Charles P. Segal / Richard J. Tarrant / Richard F. Thomas (eds.) *Harvard Studies in Classical Philology 97: Greece in Rome: Influence, Integration, Resistance*, Cambridge/ MA, 215–30.

Wüst, Ernst (1949), "Pantomimus", in: *RE* 18.3, 833–69.

Zimmermann, Bernhard (1995), "Pantomimische Elemente in den Komödien des Plautus", in: Lore Benz et al. (eds.) *Plautus und die Tradition des Stegreifspiels* (= ScriptOralia 75), Tübingen, 193–204.

Zwierlein, Otto (1966), *Die Rezitationsdramen Senecas, mit einem kritisch-exegetischen Anhang*, Meisenheim am Glan.

A Sophist's Drama: Lucian and Classical Tragedy

Thomas Schmitz

When we study the survival and reception of Greek tragedy, it may be apt to take a look at other genres and authors of classical antiquity in order to understand what an important role contingent factors may play in the history of reception. Lucian is an excellent case in point: during the Renaissance rediscovery of Greek literature, his writings were considered masterworks of Greek literature, and humanists such as Erasmus of Rotterdam or Thomas More were inspired by his witty dialogues. His irreverent treatment of religion and superstition made him one of the favorite authors of the European Enlightenment; he was read and admired by writers such as Henry Fielding or Christoph Martin Wieland.[1] In the nineteenth century, however, Lucian fell upon hard times: when classics was being established as an academic discipline in Germany, the Romantic movement and its ideology were the most important intellectual influence in Europe, and the Romantics were interested in poetry, not in prose, in "original" literature, not in imitation, and in early, "archaic" culture, not in late, "decadent" phenomena. On top of it all, Lucian had the misfortune of being descended from ancestors who were Syrians, not Greek; hence, a decidedly racist strand of criticism began to develop: it was not only pseudo-scholars like Richard Wagner's English son-in-law Houston Stewart Chamberlain (1855–1927) who wrote vitriolic anti-Semitic attacks against the "Syrian bastard", but even respectable scholars like the German Rudolf Helm for whom Lucian was a "nihilist" and "journalist", but not a writer who deserved to be read by serious people.[2] It took some time for Lucian to recover from these attacks. The last thirty years or so have witnessed a spectacular increase in interest in Greek literature during the first centuries C.E., and the sophisticated, multi-layered, and multi-faceted work of Lucian has profited from this renewed interest. Lucian is thus a good example for the changing nature of the classical canon.

Lucian provides a lot of autobiographical detail in his writings, but given the fictional nature of most of his works, his general flippancy, and his

---

1   On Lucian's afterlife, see Robinson 1979, Lauvergnat-Gagnière 1988, Braunsperger 1993, Marsh 1998, von Koppenfels 2007.
2   See Baumbach 2002 and Goldhill 2002, 93–107.

tendency to model his image on cultural clichés, it is impossible to say how much of his account is reliable; we have no contemporary evidence to verify his own version.[3] It appears that Lucian was born around 120 C.E. in the city of Samosata in Syria, the modern Samsat in Turkey. He claims that Greek was not his first language and that his father at first wanted him to become a sculptor. After some unfortunate experiences, however, Lucian studied rhetoric to become a declaimer. He claims that he became a celebrity in this business, travelling all over the world and declaiming to raptured audiences. Late in his life, he accepted a minor administrative post in Roman Egypt. The latest contemporary events to which his writings refer take place in 180 C.E.; we have no means of knowing how long Lucian lived after this date.[4]

Lucian's transmitted work fills four volumes. It is difficult to categorize because it is so varied: we find demonstrations of rhetorical showmanship such as *The Fly*,[5] there is a great number of pieces about the excesses of the so-called Atticism and about the second sophistic,[6] we have some fantastic novels and narratives,[7] a number of shrewd satirical descriptions of religious and political phenomena of his time,[8] and some popularizing philosophical treatises. His specialty and the part of his work that was most successful in his later reception were entertaining dialogues which make fun of the Greek mythological tradition, of would-be philosophers and frauds, and of human folly in general.[9]

Lucian's work must be understood against the cultural backdrop of his time. Its context is the so-called second sophistic, a cultural movement which was momentous all over the Greek-speaking world during the second and third centuries C.E. The last ten years have seen a renewed interest in this period and its literature; I can only give a very short summary of some of the

---

3   On Lucian's life, see Hall 1981, 1–63; Jones 1986; on the difficulties distinguishing between "real" and "fictional" elements in his writings, see Saïd 1993, Dubel 1994 and Raina 2001.

4   For references to Lucian's works, see the (uncritical) account in Schwartz 1965.

5   See Billerbeck/Zubler 2000 and Fuente 2004.

6   See Weissenberger 1996 and Dobrov 2002.

7   See Rütten 1997, Georgiadou/Larmour 1998, von Moellendorff 2000.

8   It will become clear in this article that Lucian's writings often look back to the "classical" past of Greek culture. Some critics have therefore concluded that he is a bookish author who deliberately turns his back on his own time; see esp. Bompaire 1958. More recently, critics have rightly warned against this tendency: Lucian was an astute observer of his own world, and he was particularly good at mirroring current affairs in the classical past. This satirical element has first been emphasized in magisterial studies by Louis Robert, see esp. Robert 1980, 393–436; more recent contributions are Jones 1986 and Follet 1994. However, we should not take this view to its extreme and view Lucian as a political pamphleteer or revolutionary writer, as Baldwin 1961 and Baldwin 1973 does.

9   See Branham 1989.

results of a vast amount of scholarship.[10] On its surface the second sophistic was almost obsessively concerned with the classical Greek past: sophists were public performers who visited cities in the Greek-speaking world and gave declamations about historical topics, in a language which tried to imitate as closely as possible the classical Attic idiom. This so-called Atticism (at which Lucian often pokes fun while being one of its most fervent and most successful practitioners) pervaded not only the rhetorical writings of this period, but almost all literary texts. While it may, at its surface, convey the impression of being resolutely "geeky" and a product of the ivory tower, scholars today agree that it served a quite precise social and cultural function. It was an instrument for constructing and enhancing the cultural identity of a consciously Greek elite in the Roman Empire, and it provided a means to compete and to demonstrate one's social status.

Lucian, in a way, was just one of the sophists who enthralled their audiences with their declamations. Yet it is clear that he was not quite in the same league as the big superstars in this trade, people like the multi-billionaire Herodes Atticus, the flamboyant Marcus Antonius Polemo, or the self-centered Aelius Aristides. Lucian was on the fringe of the sophistic movement, not in its center:[11] Philostratus, who wrote an anecdotal history of the great figures of the second sophistic, does not mention him; he seems to have lacked the band of loyal students and the pack of fierce competitors which were the hallmark of the great sophists. We may speculate whether this marginal position helped him gain a keen view of the more absurd aspects of the sophistic business, of the impostors and fake Atticists who tried to cash in on the cultural prestige that sophistic oratory conveyed: was Lucian in a better position to remark and describe these excesses because he was not one of the more successful sophists who were so caught in their own game that they completely identified with it? This biographical and psychological explanation is unverifiable, but there can be no doubt that Lucian's witty writings provide a keen and fascinating description of the culture of his times.

When we analyze the function of tragedy and theater in Lucian's works, we will see that in a number of points, his outlook is typical of a member of the cultural elite during the second century C.E. However, we will also see a number of points that appear to be specific to Lucian. In particular, I want to argue that Lucian was especially fascinated by the "theatrical", histrionic aspect of Greek tragedy, and that this should be seen in connection with the culture of his own time. The examples which I will present on the following pages will begin with passages that conform to the general usage

---

10 For some recent contributions, see Gleason 1995, Swain 1996, Schmitz 1997, Whitmarsh 2001, Goldhill 2001, Whitmarsh 2005.
11 Lucian's position as an outsider is well described by Swain 1996, 298–329.

of his period; I will then move on to examples which allow us more specific observations of Lucian's outlook.

Let us begin by taking a look at the ways in which Lucian uses the words "tragedy" and "tragic". As a good Atticist, Lucian imitates the metaphorical use of these words which can be found in classical prose.[12] Lucian was of course aware that Plato had already used the word "tragic" (τραγικός) to denote a particularly pompous and affected style,[13] so we find the same metaphorical use in his writings. When he complains, for instance, that some historians compose overly solemn proems that make readers expect grandiose books, while the historiographical works themselves are sober and minute, he uses the word τραγικός:

> Καὶ μὴν καὶ ἄλλους ἴδοις ἂν τὰ μὲν προοίμια λαμπρὰ καὶ τραγικὰ καὶ εἰς ὑπερβολὴν μακρὰ συγγράφοντας, ὡς ἐλπίσαι θαυμαστὰ ἡλίκα τὰ μετὰ ταῦτα πάντως ἀκούσεσθαι, τὸ σῶμα δὲ αὐτὸ τὸ τῆς ἱστορίας μικρόν τι καὶ ἀγεννὲς ἐπαγαγόντας ὡς καὶ τοῦτο ἐοικέναι παιδίῳ, εἴ που Ἔρωτα εἶδες παίζοντα, προσωπεῖον Ἡρακλέους πάμμεγα ἢ Τιτᾶνος περικείμενον.

> Again, you may see others writing introductions that are brilliant, "tragic", and excessively long, so that you expect what follows to be marvelous to hear, but for the body of their history they bring on something so tiny and so undistinguished that it resembles a child, some Cupid – you may have seen one playing and putting on a huge mask of Heracles or a Titan. (*How to Write History* 23)[14]

Lucian's use of the word τραγικά clearly alludes to the so-called "tragic" historiography,[15] but the main force of this polemical allusion is the style of these historical proems: it is inflated and verbose and thus raises expectations which the main body of the works will disappoint.

While "tragic" refers to literary style in this passage, Lucian also uses it as a metaphor describing events or actions. When he predicts that slander

---

12 For the metaphorical use of terms relating to the theater, see Trédé 2002; on τραγικός in Lucian, see Seeck 1990, 234–235.

13 I quote one example only: *Resp.* 545 e Ἦ βούλει, ὥσπερ Ὅμηρος, εὐχώμεθα ταῖς Μούσαις εἰπεῖν ἡμῖν "ὅπως δὴ πρῶτον" στάσις "ἔμπεσε", καὶ φῶμεν αὐτὰς τραγικῶς ὡς πρὸς παῖδας ἡμᾶς παιζούσας καὶ ἐρεσχηλούσας, ὡς δὴ σπουδῇ λεγούσας, ὑψηλολογουμένας λέγειν; "Shall we, like Homer, invoke the Muses to tell 'how faction first fell upon them,' and say that these goddesses playing with us and teasing us as if we were children address us in lofty, mock-serious tragic style?" (tr. P. Shorey). A good overview on the use of τραγικός in Plato can be found in Bluck 1961.

14 Lucian is quoted after the standard edition by M. D. Macleod, Oxford 1972–1987; the translations are taken from the Loeb edition, tr. A. M. Harmon, K. Kilburn, and M. D. Macleod. I have occasionally adapted these translations to stay closer to the original Greek text.

15 Some modern scholars have argued, with good reasons, that there was no such thing as a full-blown "school" of tragic historiography (esp. Walbank 1955, cf. Fornara 1983, 124–34). Nevertheless, Lucian's treatise is a clear sign that he was convinced of the existence of such a "tragic" style of historiography.

will trigger a "tragic outcome" (τραγικὰ [...] τέλη, *Slander* 10), this is almost identical to our clichéd metaphorical use of the word "tragic". In many cases, references to the style and to the content of a course of action are both present, as in this passage:

> Ἐχρῆν δέ, οἶμαι, μάλιστα μὲν περιμένειν τὸν θάνατον καὶ μὴ δραπετεύειν ἐκ τοῦ βίου· εἰ δὲ καὶ πάντως διέγνωστό οἱ ἀπαλλάττεσθαι, μὴ πυρὶ μηδὲ τοῖς ἀπὸ τῆς τραγῳδίας τούτοις χρῆσθαι, ἀλλ᾽ ἕτερόν τινα θανάτου τρόπον, μυρίων ὄντων, ἑλόμενον ἀπελθεῖν.

> What he should have done, I think, was first and foremost to await death and not to cut and run from life; but if he had determined to be off at all costs, not to use fire or any of these devices out of tragedy, but to choose for his departure some other form of death out of the myriads that there are. (*Peregrinus* 21)

Lucian here criticizes the overly theatrical manner in which Peregrinus staged his death in Olympia: he burnt himself in front of a large crowd. This is a "flight" from life, and it is a manner of death more befitting tragedy than real life. In a similar vein, Lucian calls the more grisly and pompous narratives of traditional myth a "tragedy":[16]

> Ἐμοὶ γοῦν πολλάκις αἰδεῖσθαι ὑπὲρ αὐτῶν ἔπεισιν, ὁπόταν Οὐρανοῦ τομὴν καὶ Προμηθέως δεσμὰ διηγῶνται καὶ Γιγάντων ἐπανάστασιν καὶ τὴν ἐν Ἅιδου πᾶσαν τραγῳδίαν [...].

> For my part it often occurs to me to blush for them when they tell of the castration of Uranus, and the fetters of Prometheus, and the revolt of the Giants, and the whole tragedy in Hades [...]. (*Philopseudes* 2).

Hence, when the Scythian Toxaris tells a couple of grandiose (and somewhat unbelievable) stories about friendship, his interlocutor Mnesippus calls them "tragic and myth-like" (πάνυ τραγικὰ [...] καὶ μύθοις ὅμοια, *Toxaris* 56).[17] Since classical tragedies usually treat mythical stories, the use of τραγικά here is almost indistinguishable from the use of "mythical" or "monstrous": all these terms refer to narratives which relate unbelievable events.[18]

In numerous passages then, Lucian uses words such as "tragic" or "tragedy" in a somewhat loose, stereotyped way, not unlike our modern use of these words. One aspect to which I want to draw attention is the fact that occasionally, the use of one word coming from the semantic field of "tragedy" triggers more words from the same field. A good example of this device can be found in the short speech *The Tyrannicide*. This is a typical text of the sort which sophists declaimed at their performances. The speaker has killed a tyrant's son. When the tyrant finds his son's dead body, he kills himself with the same sword. Now the speaker demands a reward for having killed the tyrant. Such purely fictitious speeches, set in a bizarre world that has its

---

16 See Karavas 2005 195.
17 See Karavas 2005, 198.
18 See, e.g., the use of μυθολογούμενα in *Timon* 6 or of τερατεία in *On Writing History* 8.

own rules (D. Russel has aptly called this world "Sophistopolis"[19]), were one
of the stock themes of sophistic declamations; our example with its tongue-
in-cheek reference to the myth of the Athenian tyrannicides Harmodius and
Aristogiton (and its subsequent deconstruction in Thucydides 6.53–59) adds
further layers of understanding and is thus typical of Lucian's special brand
of sophistic.

> Ἐγὼ γὰρ ἀπηλλαττόμην ποιητὴς μὲν τῆς ὅλης τραγῳδίας γεγενημένος, καταλιπὼν
> δὲ τῷ ὑποκριτῇ τὸν νεκρὸν καὶ τὴν σκηνὴν καὶ τὸ ξίφος καὶ τὰ λοιπὰ τοῦ δράματος.
>
> Before I slipped away, I had myself composed the whole plot of the tragedy, but had
> left to the actor the body, the stage-setting, the sword, and the remainder of the play.
> (*Tyrannicide* 20)

In this passage, the would-be tyrannicide calls himself "the maker of this
entire tragedy" (ποιητὴς τῆς ὅλης τραγῳδίας; with a playful allusion to
the ambivalence of the term ποιητής which means "perpetrator" as well as
"poet"). This first use of a metaphor taken from the theatrical sphere immediately provokes a series of similar metaphors: ὑποκριτής "actor", σκηνή
"scene" and δρᾶμα "drama". As I have argued elsewhere,[20] such series of
metaphors can be explained by the methods of rhetorical education that not
only sophists, but all members of the educated elite received. Since proper
use of a "correct" classical Attic was paramount in this training, students
would write exercises to enrich their vocabulary in a certain semantic field.
Tools such as the Atticist lexica give a clear idea of the ways in which such
exercises worked; in particular, the lexicon written by one Iulius Polydeukes
(better known in the Latinized form of his name, Pollux) is structured in sections that treat one semantic field. When we look at the way Pollux lists, e.g.,
words relating to "comedy", we can imagine that Lucian was remembering
just such exercises when he used this series of metaphors:

> Ἀπὸ δὲ κωμῶν κωμήτης καὶ κωμῆτις καὶ κώμαρχος, καὶ κωμοδρομεῖν καὶ
> κωμῳδεῖν, ἢ που δὲ καὶ κωμῳδία καὶ κωμῳδοδιδάσκαλος καὶ κωμῳδοποιὸς καὶ
> κωμῳδοποιητής, καὶ κωμῳδῶν, καὶ κωμικὸν δρᾶμα καὶ κωμῳδικὸν πρᾶγμα, ἐπεὶ
> κατὰ κώμας ἔστησαν τὴν πρώτην οἱ χοροί.
>
> From village (*kōmē*) is derived the word "village-dweller" and "village-chief" and
> "run through villages" and "play comedy", moreover "comedy" and "comic play-
> wright" and "comic writer" and "comic poet", and "comical", and "comic drama",
> and "comic subject" because at first, choruses were formed by villages. (Pollux,
> *Onomasticon* 9.11)

For a sophist like Lucian, language was the most important means of perceiving and interpreting reality. Hence, for him the world was, to a large
extent, structured like a thesaurus, a series of words related to each other

---

19   Russell 1983, 21–39.
20   See Schmitz 2004.

by synonymy or opposition. Every orator learned that there were certain "places" (τόποι, *loci*) where arguments and metaphors could be found (a process called εὕρεσις, *inventio*). Using a metaphor such as "tragedy" meant that one was visiting one of these "places" and would exploit, as much as possible, the rhetorical opportunities it offered. These rhetorical techniques, then, can be seen at work in such extended metaphors.

When we turn away from the use of tragedy as a metaphor, we have to bear in mind the cultural outlook of the second sophistic. For the entire elite of imperial Greece, the classical past was the most important part of defining and fashioning their identity. Given the preponderance of a predominantly linguistic and textual transmission of this classical past, it comes as no surprise that Lucian views tragedy primarily in this textual form, as a written book. When Lucian mentions the classical tragic poets, he thinks of their transmitted texts. Aspiring sophists are encouraged to *read* tragedies to become acquainted with pure Attic diction:

> Τὰ μὲν τοιαῦτα πάντα φεῦγε καὶ ἀποτρέπου, ἀρξάμενος δὲ ἀπὸ τῶν ἀρίστων ποιητῶν καὶ ὑπὸ διδασκάλοις αὐτοὺς ἀναγνοὺς μέτιθι ἐπὶ τοὺς ῥήτορας, καὶ τῇ ἐκείνων φωνῇ συντραφεὶς ἐπὶ τὰ Θουκυδίδου καὶ Πλάτωνος ἐν καιρῷ μέτιθι, πολλὰ καὶ τῇ καλῇ κωμῳδίᾳ καὶ τῇ σεμνῇ τραγῳδίᾳ ἐγγεγυμνασμένος·

> Avoid and shun all this sort of thing. After beginning with the best poets and reading them under tutors, pass to the orators, and when you have become familiar with their diction, go over in due time to Thucydides and Plato – but only after you have first disciplined yourself thoroughly in attractive comedy and sober tragedy. (*Lexiphanes* 22)

Comedy and tragedy are an important part of the sophistic curriculum, and all members of the educated elite (the πεπαιδευμένοι) could be expected to know these texts. Moreover, it is significant that our passage presents a close connection between both forms of classical drama, comedy and tragedy: as spectacles on the scene, comedy and tragedy were markedly different; as texts and embodiments of the classical past, they are closely related.

This view of tragedy as a text is particularly obvious in a passage from Lucian's *On Salaried Posts*. In it, he compares impostors who pretend that they are intellectuals to books that are splendid on the outside yet contain ghastly tragedies:

> Λογίζονται γὰρ ὡς ἐξαγορεύσουσιν αὐτῶν τὰ πολλὰ ἐκεῖνα τῆς φύσεως ἀπόρρητα ὡς ἅπαντα εἰδότες ἀκριβῶς καὶ γυμνοὺς αὐτοὺς ἐπωπτευκότες. τοῦτο τοίνυν ἀποπνίγει αὐτούς· ἅπαντες γὰρ ἀκριβῶς ὅμοιοί εἰσιν τοῖς καλλίστοις τούτοις βιβλίοις, ὧν χρυσοῖ μὲν οἱ ὀμφαλοί, πορφυρᾶ δὲ ἔκτοσθεν ἡ διφθέρα, τὰ δὲ ἔνδον ἢ Θυέστης ἐστὶν τῶν τέκνων ἑστιώμενος ἢ Οἰδίπους τῇ μητρὶ συνὼν ἢ Τηρεὺς δύο ἀδελφὰς ἅμα ὀπυίων. τοιοῦτοι καὶ αὐτοί εἰσι, λαμπροὶ καὶ περίβλεπτοι, ἔνδον δὲ ὑπὸ τῇ πορφύρᾳ πολλὴν τὴν τραγῳδίαν σκέποντες· ἕκαστον γοῦν αὐτῶν ἢν ἐξειλήσῃς, δρᾶμα οὐ μικρὸν εὑρήσεις Εὐριπίδου τινὸς ἢ Σοφοκλέους, τὰ δ' ἔξω πορφύρα εὐανθὴς καὶ χρυσοῦς ὁ ὀμφαλός. ταῦτα οὖν συνεπιστάμενοι αὐτοῖς, μισοῦσι καὶ ἐπιβουλεύουσιν εἴ τις ἀποστὰς ἀκριβῶς κατανενοηκὼς αὐτοὺς ἐκτραγῳδήσει καὶ πρὸς πολλοὺς ἐρεῖ.

They expect them to betray the many hidden mysteries of their make-up, inasmuch as they are thoroughly acquainted with everything and have looked upon them unveiled. That sticks in their throat, because they are all exactly like the finest of papyrus rolls, of which the knobs are of gold and the slip-cover of purple and the cover of purple leather, but the content is either Thyestes feasting on his children or Oedipus married to his mother, or Tereus debauching two sisters at once. They too are splendid and universally admired, but inside, underneath their purple, they hide a great deal of tragedy; in fact if you unroll any one of them, you will find an ample drama by an Euripides or a Sophocles, while on the outside there is a gaudy purple laticlave and a golden bulla. Conscious of all this, they hate and plot against any renegade who, having become thoroughly familiar with them, is likely to expose the plot and tell it broadcast. (*On Salaried Posts* 41)

Lucian here creates a contrast between the splendid exterior and the horrible interior of such uneducated people. When he compares them to works of art, he subtly alludes to and inverts a famous simile in Plato's *Symposium*, where Socrates is compared to an image of Silenus, ugly at the outside, yet containing a beautiful golden statue on the inside (Pl., *Symp.* 215 a–b). In Lucian's case, the object of comparison are elaborately ornate book rolls[21] containing tragedies about the most horrific Greek myths. While Lucian again uses "tragedy" in a metaphorical sense when he speaks of these rolls as "hiding a great deal of tragedy" (πολλὴν τὴν τραγῳδίαν σκέποντες), he visualizes these tragedies in the form which was most familiar to him, as papyrus rolls.[22]

Given the importance of this "bookish" aspect of tragedy, it is thus not surprising that quotations from tragedy abound in Lucian's work.[23] In accordance with a general tendency which can be observed since the Hellenistic period, Euripides is by far the most important source for such citations, followed by Sophocles; Aeschylus plays only a minor role. Many of these quotations are merely ornamental; they serve to demonstrate the writer's (or declaimer's) education and create a shared cultural ground between the writer and his audience. When Lycinus, the speaker in Lucian's dialogue *Symposium*, describes the violent end of the wedding party at which he was present, he uses a stock quotation from Euripidean tragedy:

---

21 Lucian uses similar imagery in *The Ignorant Book-collector*, where he mentions luxury editions which may contain a corrupted text; cf. Hopkinson 2008, 120; in both cases, the book roll serves to depict the contrast between splendid exterior and rotten core. For other allusions to Plato's *Symposium* in Lucian's works see Schröder 1999.

22 For another telling anecdote involving tragedy as a written book, see *The Ignorant Book-collector* 19: the cynic philosopher Demetrius tears up a book roll of Euripides's *Bacchae* which an uneducated person had been reading and added "it is better that Pentheus is ripped up by me once than by you repeatedly".

23 Karavas 2005, 137–170 offers a complete list, but hardly any interpretation of the phenomenon.

Τοῦτό σοι τέλος, ὦ καλὲ Φίλων, ἐγένετο τοῦ συμποσίου, ἢ ἄμεινον τὸ τραγικὸν
ἐκεῖνο ἐπειπεῖν,

πολλαὶ μορφαὶ τῶν δαιμονίων,
πολλὰ δ' ἀέλπτως κραίνουσι θεοί,
καὶ τὰ δοκηθέντ' οὐκ ἐτελέσθη·

Well, Philo, that was the end of the dinner-party: it would be better, though, to say
at the close as they do in the plays of Euripides:

In many shapes appear the powers above,
And many things the gods surprise us with,
While those we look for do not come about. (*The Banquet* 48)

A number of Euripidean tragedies ends with such bland, stereotypical lines;
since their relevance to the play's action is sometimes hard to see, most of
them have been suspected by modern scholars.[24] In the *Symposium*, Lucian
combines his quotation of this Euripidean cliché with an allusion to the end
of Plato's *Phaedo*. Lycinus' account of a wedding banquet turned sour (it
ends in a general brawl) is only mock-tragic; if he closes it with references
to tragedy and to the death of Socrates, this can be read as a tongue-in-cheek
wink to his audience, both the intradiegetic and the extradiegetic one, that
will emphasize the parodic element of this dialogue; at the same time, the
allusion to well-known classical texts creates a shared frame of reference
which is typical for literary culture in the second sophistic.[25]

Other quotations make use of the prestige of these classical texts and
quote them as an authority that can and will command respect, as in this
example:

ἡ μὲν γὰρ τραγῳδία καὶ σὺν μεγάλῳ ἐπαίνῳ μέμνηται τῆς μυίας, ὡς ἐν τούτοις,

δεινόν γε τὴν μὲν μυῖαν ἀλκίμῳ σθένει
πηδᾶν ἐπ' ἀνδρῶν σώμαθ', ὡς πλησθῇ φόνου,
ἄνδρας δ' ὁπλίτας πολέμιον ταρβεῖν δόρυ.

As for tragedy, it, too, mentions the fly with great praise; for example in these
words:

Tis strange that while the fly with hardy strength
Encounters man to sate itself with gore,
Stout men-at-arms should fear the foeman's lance! (*The Fly* 11)

The *Fly* is a typical mock encomium, a genre that has a long tradition in
Greek literature.[26] Quotations from classical texts fulfill an important function in these texts: in unexpected, humorous ways, they demonstrate that
the paradoxical subject of the encomium has already been mentioned and
praised in these great predecessors. In Lucian's text, there is a number of

---

24 See Roberts 1987.
25 See Schmakeit 2002–3.
26 See n. 5 above and Pease 1926, Pernot 1993, 2.532–68 as well as Fleury 2002.

passages which "prove" the excellence of the fly; the tragic quotation mentioned above[27] thus has an argumentative function.

Such quotations, then, must be understood in terms of the cultural prestige that tragedy, as part of the Greek classical heritage, conveyed. We have seen that linguistic classicism (Atticism) was the hallmark of the πεπαιδευμένος in imperial Greece. There is also a corollary of this attitude which we may term "material Atticism", an intense, sometimes almost obsessive look at and glorification of all aspects of classical Athenian culture.[28] Of course, tragedy was one of the most striking and visible features of this classical Attic heritage; accordingly, it plays an important role in the view of classical Athens which the second sophistic favored. An example can be seen in Lucian's *Zeus Rants*: in a philosophical discussion, the rather dull-witted Stoic philosopher Timocles claims that Euripides' plays are proof that gods exist because at the end of these dramas, the *deus ex machina* appears in order to punish the wicked and recompense the good characters. His Epicurean opponent Damis finds this argument preposterous: if this were the case, either the tragic actors themselves or their costumes and paraphernalia must be divine.

Ἀλλ', ὦ γενναιότατε φιλοσόφων Τιμόκλεις, εἰ ταῦτα ποιοῦντες οἱ τραγῳδοὶ πεπείκασί σε, ἀνάγκη δυοῖν θάτερον, ἤτοι Πῶλον καὶ Ἀριστόδημον καὶ Σάτυρον ἡγεῖσθαί σε θεοὺς εἶναι τότε ἢ τὰ πρόσωπα τῶν θεῶν αὐτὰ καὶ τοὺς ἐμβάτας καὶ τοὺς ποδήρεις χιτῶνας καὶ χλαμύδας καὶ χειρῖδας καὶ προγαστρίδια καὶ τἄλλα οἷς ἐκεῖνοι σεμνύνουσι τὴν τραγῳδίαν, ὅπερ καὶ γελοιότατον.

Why, Timocles, you doughtiest of philosophers, if the playwrights have convinced you by doing this, you must needs believe either that Polus and Aristodemus and Satyrus are gods for the nonce, or that the very masks representing the gods, the buskins, the trailing tunics, the cloaks, gauntlets, padded paunches and all the other things with which they make tragedy grand are divine; and that is thoroughly ridiculous. (*Zeus Rants* 41)

The tragic actors named in this passage are not contemporaries of Lucian's, but rather actors from the classical period.[29] Moreover, the long series of words describing the tragic equipment again demonstrates the sophistic method of exhausting a semantic field of related vocabulary. By listing all these details about tragic costumes, Lucian demonstrates his knowledge of classical culture.

This classicist outlook on tragedy had two consequences. As we have seen, tragedy was seen as a cultural manifestation of the venerated classical past and thus commanded respect, not only as a text that was read, studied, and put to use, but also as an antiquarian phenomenon, an integral part of

---

27   Adesp. 295 *TrGrFr*; cf. Gargiulo 2003 and Karavas 2005, 164.
28   See Delz 1950.
29   See Seeck 1990, 237.

this most important and most mythical of all sophistic places, classical Athens. Sophists lived, as it were, more in this quasi-mythical place than in their own time. It is important to note that this sophistic Athens was not meant to give a historically accurate picture; rather, as I have argued elsewhere, it provided a special, "invented" version of this classical past, which catered to the intellectual and emotional needs of imperial intellectuals.[30] Seen from the historical distance of half a millennium, classical Athens was a cozy and small place in which all the great cultural heroes of the Greek tradition rubbed elbows and lived the clichéd life that the rhetorical schools depicted. A good example for this phenomenon can be seen in Lucian's *Anacharsis*: in a discussion between Solon and the Scythian Anacharsis, the Athenian lawmaker explains customs and politics of Athens to his foreign visitor, and of course, he also refers to the functions of dramatic performances:

> Καὶ μέντοι καὶ εἰς τὸ θέατρον συνάγοντες αὐτοὺς δημοσίᾳ παιδεύομεν ὑπὸ κωμῳδίαις καὶ τραγῳδίαις ἀρετάς τε ἀνδρῶν παλαιῶν καὶ κακίας θεωμένους, ὡς τῶν μὲν ἀποτρέποιντο, ἐπ᾽ ἐκεῖνα δὲ σπεύδοιεν.

> Furthermore, assembling them in the theatre, we instruct them publicly through comedies and tragedies, in which they behold both the virtues and the vices of the ancients, in order that they may recoil from the vices and emulate the virtues. (*Anacharsis* 22)

For a second-century sophist and his audience, nothing could be more natural than this explanation of comedy and tragedy; since Lucian's dialogue is set in classical Athens, a reference to these striking phenomena (about which every educated Greek had heard in school) would be expected. From a historical point of view, however, Lucian commits an embarrassing blunder: Solon lived long before tragic and comic performances were institutionalized in Athens.[31] However, I have not quoted this passage for the somewhat pedantic pleasure of proving Lucian wrong, but because it is so revealing of the attitudes of his time: for the public in the second century, tragedy was so tightly integrated into their view of the classical period that Lucian could not imagine his mythical Athens without it; it was a necessary part of the cultural heritage, not a historically contingent factor that was subject to change. To put it bluntly: in sophistic Athens, Solon, Themistocles, and Demosthenes were all sitting together in the theater of Dionysus, watching plays by Aeschylus in the morning and by Aristophanes in the afternoon.

The second consequence of this classicizing outlook of material Atticism is the completely uncontroversial status of classical tragedy. For a modern observer, it is sometimes bizarre to see to which degree second-century classicists considered everything that was old and traditional as

---

30   See Schmitz 1997, 201–5 and Schmitz 2007.
31   See Seeck 1990, 239.

naturally superior.[32] Hence, we often see that sophists would only appreciate contemporary cultural phenomena if they found classical precedents for them. This is obvious, for example, in Lucian's small dialogue *On Dance*.[33] Lycinus and the philosopher Crato here discuss a very special form of dance, viz. pantomime. In what has become a classical paper, Louis Robert has shown that this form of theater was immensely popular in the second century C.E., not only in the Western, Latin part of the Roman Empire, but also in its Eastern half; as a popular pastime, it had replaced performances of classical tragedy.[34] Nevertheless, members of the educated elite often criticized pantomime severely because it was, by and large, a Roman development without a classical Greek pedigree. Pantomime did not even possess a classical name; it is most often referred to with blanket terms such as "dance".[35] This is visible in the way Lucian treats this dramatic form: he refers to it as something "barbarous" that "the Italians call pantomime".[36] He puts, so to speak, sanitizing double quotes around the word because he does not want to touch it with his hands. When he discusses the subjects of pantomime, Lucian is careful to name only subjects taken from classical tragedy. The same attempt at putting pantomime into a classical perspective is visible in inscriptions of the imperial period, where it is sometimes called a "tragic and rhythmic movement"[37]: it could become acceptable (to a certain degree) only by disguising itself as a classical form.

The aspects of tragedy in Lucian's work that we have seen so far tally well with what we know about Greek culture in the Roman empire. Πεπαιδευμένοι in this period would study tragedies in school, they would read them for their pleasure, they learned about tragic heroes by preparing and declaiming fictitious speeches (so-called μελέται) in their *persona*. They learned about and memorized aspects of the material context of classical tragedy and mastered lists of classical vocabulary relating to tragedy (that had already been collected by specialized lexicographers). Above all, tragedy was part of classical Athens, which conveyed a special value and a special status to all its manifestations. Lucian's view of tragedy, then, seems to confirm that this was indeed the ways in which he learned about tragedy

---

32 For some striking examples, see Schmitz 1997, 70–3.
33 I cannot do justice to this complex and fascinating work here; for a much fuller account, see now Garelli-François 2004, Lada-Richards 2007 and Schlapbach 2008
34 Robert 1930; on ancient pantomime, see now the contributions in Hall/Wyles 2008.
35 See Garelli-François 2001.
36 *On Dance* 67: Ταῦτα μὲν ὁ βάρβαρος. οὐκ ἀπεικότως δὲ καὶ οἱ Ἰταλιῶται τὸν ὀρχηστὴν παντόμιμον καλοῦσιν, ἀπὸ τοῦ δρωμένου σχεδόν. [Well, that is the way the barbarian viewed it. And the Italians quite appropriately call the dancer a pantomime, precisely in consequence of what he does.]
37 E.g., *IGRR* iv.1272 διὰ τῆς τραγικῆς ἐνρύθμου κεινήσεως (from Thyateira).

and that he expected his audience to share this attitude, to understand his allusions and in-jokes.

Does this mean that tragedies were only perceived as texts and as manifestations of the classical past and that no actual performances ever took place? Though we have some reports of tragedies being performed, most accounts show that this must have been quite exceptional events. A good example is provided by an anecdote that Lucian uses for the opening joke of his small treatise *How to Write History*; the same anecdote is also told by the historian Eunapius (fourth/fifth century C.E.):[38] a tragic actor comes to a Greek city and performs a tragedy. At first, the audience is shocked because of the unusual spectacle, but after a while, they get used to it; they even like it very much. However, a few days later, this tragic performance has bizarre side effects: the entire population of the city comes down with a fever, and in their madness, they all begin to recite lines from Euripidean tragedies at the top of their lungs. In Lucian's account, an important element is implied which is spelled out by Eunapius:[39] this must have been the first performance in a very long time, maybe the first performance that the spectators ever witnessed.

The fact that Lucian does not comment on or even mention this important detail is telling. If dramatic performances had been quite usual in his days, it would have been necessary to explain this fact to the audience. Obviously, they just accepted the premise that a performance was such an unusual event that it could trigger "dramatic" consequences. This seems to confirm what we have said before about the bookish, textual nature of tragedy in Lucian's writings.

Nevertheless, a number of references in Lucian's texts also refers to non-textual elements of tragedy, and we will now turn to these passages. Lucian is intensely, almost obsessively interested in the histrionic, deceptive quality of Greek tragedy. That tragedy was a kind of "deceit" was a view already current in the classical period, as witnessed by a famous fragment of Gorgias.[40]

---

38   See von Moellendorff 2001.

39   Eunapius, fg. 54 *Historici Graeci minores*: Καὶ συνελθόντων τὴν μὲν πρώτην ἡμέραν σφαλῆναι τῆς ἐπιδείξεως· οὐδὲ γὰρ τὴν ὄψιν ὑπομείναντας τοὺς θεατάς, ἅτε ἄρτι καὶ πρῶτον ἑορακότας, φεύγειν θλιβομένους περὶ ἀλλήλοις καὶ πατουμένους. [And when they gathered, the performance on the first day fell through, for the spectators could not even stand the view because they saw it just then for the first time, and they took flight, crushing and trampling each other.] On the question of tragic performances in Lucian's time, see Seeck 1990, 233–4.

40   Gorgias, fg. B 23 VS: [ἡ τραγῳδία παρέχει] ἀπάτην ἣν ὅ τ᾽ ἀπατήσας δικαιότερος τοῦ μὴ ἀπατήσαντος καὶ ὁ ἀπατηθεὶς σοφώτερος τοῦ μὴ ἀπατηθέντος [(tragedy offers) a deception where the man who deceives is more just than the man who does not deceive and the man who lets himself be deceived is wiser than the man who does not let himself be deceived.] On Gorgias and tragedy, see Schwinge 1997, Halliwell 2005, 396–7.

In Lucian's writings, we often find passages emphasizing the discrepancy between the insignificance of the actors and of the stage props on the one hand and their lofty roles within the tragic plays on the other hand. In his *Saturnalia*, Lucian has the god Cronus argue that the poor should not envy the rich because their life is much more miserable than one would think; it is full of dangers and worries. And if you look close enough, you see that they are much less vigorous and healthy than poor people who have to rely on their body to earn their daily bread. In this context, rich people are compared to tragic costumes: seen from a distance, they look all golden and venerable, yet when you come close, you realize that they are made up of worthless rags.

> Ἦ τίνα ἂν αὐτῶν ῥαδίως δεῖξαι δύναιο μὴ πάντως ὠχρὸν ὄντα πολὺ τὸ νεκρῶδες ἐμφαίνοντα; τίνα δὲ ἐς γῆρας ἀφικόμενον τοῖς αὐτοῦ ποσίν, ἀλλὰ μὴ φοράδην ἐπὶ τεττάρων ὀχούμενον, ὁλόχρυσον μὲν τὰ ἔξω, κατάρραφον δὲ τὰ ἔνδον, ὥσπερ αἱ τραγικαὶ ἐσθῆτες ἐκ ῥακῶν πάνυ εὐτελῶν συγκεκαττυμέναι;

> Again, would you find it easy to point out one of them who was not absolutely pale, looking very much like death? Or one who reached old age on his own feet and not carried on four men's backs, all gold on the outside, but with his inside cobbled like the costumes in tragedy, patched up out of quite worthless rags? (*Saturnalia* 28)

Tragedy and its paraphernalia thus symbolize deceptiveness; we have already seen a similar point in the passage from Lucian's *On Salaried Posts* discussed above where pretentious intellectuals were compared to splendid book rolls containing tragedies.

In a similar vein, Lucian looks at tragic actors and the masks they wear. In the dialogue *The Cock*, the poor cobbler Micyllus and his household cock discuss dreams and desires. Micyllus wants to be rich, but the cock shows him how dangerous and wretched the lives of rich and powerful people are. As in the *Saturnalia*, Lucian again uses a comparison involving tragedy.

> Οἱ δέ, ὡς φής, θανάσιμα εὐωχοῦνται, καὶ ταῦτα μυρίοις κακοῖς συνόντες. εἶτ' ἐπειδὰν πέσωσιν, ὅμοιοι μάλιστα φαίνονται τοῖς τραγικοῖς ὑποκριταῖς, ὧν πολλοὺς ἰδεῖν ἔνεστι τέως μὲν Κέκροπας δῆθεν ὄντας ἢ Σισύφους ἢ Τηλέφους, διαδήματα ἔχοντας καὶ ξίφη ἐλεφαντόκωπα καὶ ἐπίσειστον κόμην καὶ χλαμύδα χρυσόπαστον, ἢν δέ, οἷα πολλὰ γίνεται, κενεμβατήσας τις αὐτῶν ἐν μέσῃ τῇ σκηνῇ καταπέσῃ, γέλωτα δηλαδὴ παρέχει τοῖς θεαταῖς τοῦ προσωπείου μὲν συντριβέντος αὐτῷ διαδήματι, ἡμαγμένης δὲ τῆς ἀληθοῦς κεφαλῆς τοῦ ὑποκριτοῦ καὶ τῶν σκελῶν ἐπὶ πολὺ γυμνουμένων, ὡς τῆς τε ἐσθῆτος τὰ ἔνδοθεν φαίνεσθαι ῥάκια δύστηνα ὄντα καὶ τῶν ἐμβατῶν τὴν ὑπόδεσιν ἀμορφοτάτην καὶ οὐχὶ κατὰ λόγον τοῦ ποδός.

> But [the tyrants], as you say, do their feasting at the peril of their lives and live amid a thousand ills beside. Then when they fall they make no better figure than the actors that you often see, who for a time pretend to be a Cecrops or a Sisyphus or a Telephus, with diadems and ivory-hilted swords and waving hair and gold-embroidered tunics; but if (as often happens) one of them misses his footing and falls down in the middle of the stage, it naturally makes fun for the audience when the mask gets broken to pieces, diadem and all, and the actor's own face is covered with blood, and his legs are bared high, so as to show that his inner garments are miserable rags and that the buskins with which he is shod are hapless and do not fit the foot. (*The Cock* 26)

Similar descriptions of the discrepancy between the splendid outward appearance of the role that an actor is playing and his real, inner self (see the words τῆς ἀληθοῦς κεφαλῆς "his real head") are often applied to the situation of contemporary intellectuals, especially of sophistic performers: like a tragic actor who is always in danger of being unmasked, the sophistic declaimer constantly runs the risk of being exposed as a fraud, as someone who is assuming a role that is just too big and lofty for his small human body. This image can serve a polemical purpose and be addressed to an opponent, as in the following passage from the essay *Apology for "On Salaried Posts"*. In *On Salaried Posts*, Lucian had argued that accepting a position as a private tutor in a Roman household was a form of refined slavery that cannot fail to disgust a true intellectual. In the situation that this new essay presupposes, he himself had accepted a financially attractive position in the service of the Romans, and he now has to defend himself against accusations of hypocrisy, produced by an opponent named Sabinus.[41] Lucian's *Apology* first speaks in Sabinus' *persona*, and one of his polemical arguments is that acting in such a manner is being like a tragic actor who cannot sustain his lofty role but will be shown to be a mere servant who can be bought for money:

> Καίτοι τί δεῖ καινὴν ἐπὶ σὲ κατηγορίαν ζητεῖν μετὰ τὴν θαυμαστὴν τραγῳδίαν λέγουσαν μισῶ σοφιστήν, ὅστις οὐχ αὑτῷ σοφός;
>
> οὐκ ἀπορήσουσι δὲ οἱ κατηγοροῦντες καὶ ἄλλων παραδειγμάτων ἐπί σε, ἀλλ' οἱ μὲν τοῖς τραγικοῖς ὑποκριταῖς εἰκάσουσιν, οἳ ἐπὶ μὲν τῆς σκηνῆς Ἀγαμέμνων ἕκαστος αὐτῶν ἢ Κρέων ἢ αὐτὸς Ἡρακλῆς εἰσιν, ἔξω δὲ Πῶλος ἢ Ἀριστόδημος ἀποθέμενοι τὰ προσωπεῖα γίγνονται ὑπόμισθοι τραγῳδοῦντες, ἐκπίπτοντες καὶ συριττόμενοι, ἐνίοτε δὲ καὶ μαστιγούμενοί τινες αὐτῶν, ὡς ἂν τῷ θεάτρῳ δοκῇ.

> However, why need I look for a new charge against you when that splendid tragedy says: "I hate a wiseacre who's not wise for himself." Your accusers will find plenty more examples to quote against you. Some will compare you to tragic actors, on stage each an Agamemnon, Creon, or Heracles himself, but with their masks off a Polus or Aristodemus, playing a part for money, hissed and whistled off the stage, and sometimes some of them are flogged, if the audience wishes. (*Apology for "On Salaried Posts"* 5)

The reference to "splendid tragedy" (ἡ θαυμαστὴ τραγῳδία) works in two ways in this passage: on the one hand, it is used as an authority and quoted to prove the speaker's point;[42] on the other hand, as in the *Saturnalia* and *The Cock*, the perilous situation of the tragic actor is used as a metaphor for the perils of human life. In this case, the reference is more precise: like the tragic actors, the accused will be shown to be venal, a mere slave to the whims of his superiors.[43]

---

41 We have no means to tell whether this opponent, his accusations, or the entire situation of this treatise are real or fictitious.

42 The quotation is Euripides fr. 905 K.; the line was highly admired and was quoted by, e.g., Plutarch and Maximus of Tyre.

43 In the words ἐκπίπτοντες καὶ συριττόμενοι "hissed and whistled off the stage", Lu-

Yet this metaphor is not only used in such polemical contexts; we also find speakers who describe their own situation in similar terms. Lucian's dialogue *Nigrinus* presents its readers with an enthusiastic picture of a philosopher of this name. One of the two anonymous interlocutors recently visited Nigrinus in a big city (which is obviously Rome) and describes his discussion with the philosopher in vivid terms. Interpreters have often sought for irony in this small work, but so far, no convincing signposts for an ironic reading have been offered; it appears to be a genuinely enthusiastic philosophical dialogue.[44] At the beginning of his account, the speaker explains why he will not attempt to impersonate Nigrinus:

Καὶ ταῦτα μέν, ἃ σὺ διῆλθες, ἐβουλόμην ἂν εἰρῆσθαί μοι, κἀκεῖνα δέ, ὅτι οὐχ ἑξῆς οὐδὲ ὡς ἐκεῖνος ἔλεγε, ῥῆσίν τινα περὶ πάντων ἐρῶ· πάνυ γὰρ τοῦθ' ἡμῖν ἀδύνατον· οὐδ' αὖ ἐκείνῳ περιθεὶς τοὺς λόγους, μὴ καὶ κατ' ἄλλο τι γένωμαι τοῖς ὑποκριταῖς ἐκείνοις ὅμοιος, οἳ πολλάκις ἢ Ἀγαμέμνονος ἢ Κρέοντος ἢ καὶ Ἡρακλέους αὐτοῦ πρόσωπον ἀνειληφότες, χρυσίδας ἠμφιεσμένοι καὶ δεινὸν βλέποντες καὶ μέγα κεχηνότες μικρὸν φθέγγονται καὶ ἰσχνὸν καὶ γυναικῶδες καὶ τῆς Ἑκάβης ἢ Πολυξένης πολὺ ταπεινότερον. ἵν' οὖν μὴ καὶ αὐτὸς ἐλέγχωμαι πάνυ μεῖζον τῆς ἐμαυτοῦ κεφαλῆς προσωπεῖον περικείμενος καὶ τὴν σκευὴν καταισχύνω, ἀπὸ γυμνοῦ σοι βούλομαι τοὐμοῦ προσώπου προσλαλεῖν, ἵνα μὴ συγκατασπάσω που πεσὼν τὸν ἥρωα ὃν ὑποκρίνομαι.

I should have liked to say all that you mention, and also that I do not intend to quote him without a break and in his own words, in a long speech covering everything, for that would be quite beyond my powers; nor yet to quote him in the first person, for fear of making myself like the actors whom I mentioned in another way. Time and again when they have assumed the role of Agamemnon or Creon or even Heracles himself, costumed in cloth of gold, with fierce eyes and mouths wide agape, they speak in a voice that is small, thin, womanish, and far too poor for Hecuba or Polyxena. Therefore, to avoid being criticised like them for wearing a mask altogether too big for my head and for being a disgrace to my costume, I want to talk to you with my features exposed, so that the hero whose part I am taking may not be brought down with me if I stumble. (*Nigrinus* 11)

As in the polemical argument in the *Apology*, the actor and his role are again used as metaphors for the intellectual who falls short of the public image he adopts: assuming Nigrinus' *persona* may put the speaker in the position of a tragic actor who is wearing a mask that is "too big for his head". The difference between this assumed role and the real voice is here couched in

---

cian may be alluding to a passage in Demosthenes' most famous speech *On the Crown* in which he describes his opponent Aeschines as an actor who is "hissed off stage" (Dem. 18.256): ἐξέπιπτες, ἐγὼ δ' ἐσύριττον.

44 For an attempt to detect signs of irony, see Tarrant 1985 (who thinks Nigrinus is an unflattering portrait of the Platonic philosopher Albinus); for general assessments of this dialogue, see Clay 1992; Swain 1996, 315–7; Schröder 2000; Whitmarsh 2001, 265–79.

gender-specific terms of "male" and "effeminate" (μικρὸν καὶ ἰσχνὸν καὶ γυναικῶδες) voice.

I am well aware that with this metaphor of the actor and his mask and costume, Lucian is using a cliché that can be traced back to cynic philosophy; here is an example from the philosopher Bion of Borysthenes (third century B.C.E.).

Δεῖ ὥσπερ τὸν ἀγαθὸν ὑποκριτὴν ὅ τι ἂν ὁ ποιητὴς περιθῇ πρόσωπον τοῦτο ἀγωνίζεσθαι καλῶς, οὕτω καὶ τὸν ἀγαθὸν ἄνδρα ὅ τι ἂν περιθῇ ἡ τύχη. καὶ γὰρ αὕτη, φησὶν ὁ Βίων, ὥσπερ ποιήτρια, ὁτὲ μὲν πρωτολόγου, ὁτὲ δὲ δευτερολόγου περιτίθησι πρόσωπον, καὶ ὁτὲ μὲν βασιλέως, ὁτὲ δὲ ἀλήτου. μὴ οὖν βούλου δευτερολόγος ὢν τὸ πρωτολόγου πρόσωπον· εἰ δὲ μή, ἀνάρμοστόν τι ποιήσεις.

A good actor must act well whatever character the poet assigns him; in the same manner, a good man must act well whatever chance assigns him. Like a poet, it will, according to Bion, now assign the first role, now the second role, and now the role of a king, now of a beggar. When you play the second role, do not desire the mask of the first role, or else you will act incongruously. (Stobaeus, *Florilegium* 3.1.98 = Bion of Borysthenes, fr. 16a)

Lucian himself has made extended use of this philosophical topos "all the world's a stage" in his dialogue *Menippus*. In it, Menippus relates his journey to the underworld in the guise of Hercules. When he sees that after death, all human beings are exactly equal and nobody is richer, more powerful or more impressive than anybody else, he compares human life to a dramatic performance. Fortune (Τύχη) is the director, and everybody has to play her or his part; if the director wishes so, (s)he has to reappear in a different role on the spur of the moment:

Οἶμαι δέ σε καὶ τῶν ἐπὶ τῆς σκηνῆς πολλάκις ἑωρακέναι τοὺς τραγικοὺς ὑποκριτὰς τούτους πρὸς τὰς χρείας τῶν δραμάτων ἄρτι μὲν Κρέοντας, ἐνίοτε δὲ Πριάμους γιγνομένους ἢ Ἀγαμέμνονας, καὶ ὁ αὐτός, εἰ τύχοι, μικρὸν ἔμπροσθεν μάλα σεμνῶς τὸ τοῦ Κέκροπος ἢ Ἐρεχθέως σχῆμα μιμησάμενος μετ᾽ ὀλίγον οἰκέτης προῆλθεν ὑπὸ τοῦ ποιητοῦ κεκελευσμένος.

I think you have already seen the tragic actors on the stage: they have to play their roles according to the plan of the piece, and now they are Creon, now Priam or Agamemnon, and the same actor, if it so happens, who has just a moment ago loftily played the part of Cecrops or Erechtheus comes just a few moments later as a slave, if the poet tells him to do sc. (*Menippus* 17)

Hence, everything we think we own is just borrowed, and only stupid people will resent it when they have to give up what Fortune has lent them:

ἔνιοι δὲ ὑπ᾽ ἀγνωμοσύνης, ἐπειδὰν ἀπαιτῇ τὸν κόσμον ἐπιστᾶσα ἡ Τύχη, ἄχθονταί τε καὶ ἀγανακτοῦσιν ὥσπερ οἰκείων τινῶν στερισκόμενοι καὶ οὐχ ἃ πρὸς ὀλίγον ἐχρήσαντο ἀποδιδόντες.

When Fortune comes to them and tells them to give up these paraphernalia, some people, out of ignorance, become angry and upset as if they were being robbed of their own possession and not giving back what they had just borrowed for a short period. (*Menippus* 16)

We know that cynic influence on Lucian was quite strong,[45] so it is a reasonable assumption that it was the Cynics who drew his attention to this image. Nevertheless, I would argue that it is significant that it was precisely this image which caught Lucian's interest. As we have seen, tragic performances must have been pretty unusual in his time, so we should expect that this image would be rather unobtrusive in his writings – it referred, after all, to a spectacle with which neither he nor his audience was very familiar. Yet Lucian uses it several times, and he makes it a striking master metaphor at important turns in his writings. This fact needs explanation, and I would argue that Lucian was so fascinated with this Cynic topos because theatricality played a most important role in his own profession as well. Sophistic declamation was all about playing roles and wearing masks, and as we will see shortly, fear that these masks might be "too big", that the actor might not be up to his task, was ubiquitous in sophistic circles.

The most important part of a sophistic declamation was the so-called μελέτη, a speech in which the sophist would assume the role of and speak in the *persona* of a classical hero, thus inviting comparison between himself and this classical role. As the name (which roughly translates as "exercise") indicates, this rhetorical genre at first developed in schools. Students of rhetoric would train for their future profession by writing and declaiming fictitious historical pleas: what would Demosthenes say when he confronted king Philip of Macedon? How would he defend himself in the infamous Harpalus affair? Which arguments would Themistocles use to convince the Athenians to leave their city when king Xerxes approached? By the second century C.E., such school exercises had become a highly admired rhetorical form which gathered large audiences. And in the extremely competitive atmosphere of this society, these audiences were usually packed with connoisseurs, students of rhetoric, and envious colleagues who were just waiting for an occasion to trip the declaimer/actor up and prove that he was wearing a mask that was "too big for his head".

Sophists and their audiences were quite serious about these shows. Declaiming in the *persona* of Demosthenes meant really attempting to embody this greatest of all orators, to walk in his shoes. We can sense this seriousness when we remember that in imperial Greece, members of the cultural elite were fond of wearing names of these classical heroes; in inscriptions, we find numerous persons who were called "Demosthenes" or "Isocrates" or received sobriquets such as "New Xenophon" or "New Homer". I have described elsewhere that every sophistic performance can be described as a crisis, that sophists had to confirm and authenticate the classical author-

---

45 On imperial cynicism, see Goulet-Cazet/Goulet 1993 and Branham/Goulet-Cazet 1996; on Lucian's cynicism, see Nesselrath 1998.

ity they arrogated by embodying classical characters.[46] Members of the educated elite constantly had to prove their superiority, had to live up to the ideals of the classical heritage from which they derived their authority. This made them comparable to actors, as was already seen by Plutarch, who wrote about two generations earlier than Lucian. In his short treatise *Praecepta gerendae rei publicae*, Plutarch offers advice to a young man who is a member of the ruling elite and who wants to embark on a political career. One of the aspects he mentions is the fact that members of the elite led a life that was under constant observation, as if they were living on a stage:

Αὐτὸς δ᾽ ὥσπερ ἐν θεάτρῳ τὸ λοιπὸν ἀναπεπταμένῳ βιωσόμενος, ἐξάσκει καὶ κατακόσμει τὸν τρόπον· εἰ δὲ μὴ ῥάδιον ἀπαλλάξαι παντάπασι τῆς ψυχῆς τὴν κακίαν, ὅσα γοῦν ἐπανθεῖ μάλιστα καὶ προπίπτει τῶν ἁμαρτημάτων ἀφαιρῶν καὶ κολούων.

But do you yourself, since you are henceforth to live as on an open stage, educate your character and put it in order; and if it is not easy wholly to banish evil from the soul, at any rate remove and repress those faults which are most flourishing and conspicuous. (Plutarch, *Praecepta gerendae rei publicae* 4; 800 B; tr. H. N. Fowler)

A sophistic performance was an especially acute expression of this "theatrical" life: here, the sophist had to demonstrate his rhetorical brilliance, his secure knowledge of the classical language and culture, and above all his panache in front of a real audience. Such a crisis could fail, and Lucian's writings abound with examples of such failures. In his *Pseudologista*, Lucian tells us about a sophistic declamation he had heard at Olympia: instead of improvising his speech (as was expected from a successful sophist), this declaimer recited a work that had already been published, and instead of imitating the great classical models, he plagiarized modern sophists. The public detected his trickery, and in the end, just like the jackdaw in the fable, he was unmasked as decorating himself with false feathers.

Another example may suffice: Marcus Antonius Polemo was, together with Herodes Atticus, the most flamboyant and conspicuous of all second-century sophists. Nevertheless, he also suffered from severe stage fright. Philostratus relates one telling anecdote about him:

Σοφιστῇ δὲ ἐντυχὼν ἀλλᾶντας ὠνουμένῳ καὶ μαινίδας καὶ τὰ εὐτελῆ ὄψα "ὦ λῷστε," εἶπεν "οὐκ ἔστι τὸ Δαρείου καὶ Ξέρξου φρόνημα καλῶς ὑποκρίνασθαι ταῦτα σιτουμένῳ."

When [Polemo] met a sophist who was buying sausages, sprats, and other cheap dainties of that sort, he said: "My good sir, it is impossible for one who lives on this diet to act convincingly the arrogance of Darius and Xerxes." (Philostratus, *Lives of the Sophists* 541; tr. W. C. Wright)

---

46 See Schmitz 1999.

Polemo's aside reveals just how important and difficult sophistic self-fashioning could be: if you want to give a convincing performance in the *persona* of Darius and Xerxes, you cannot live on cheap fast-food. Sophists were expected to live up to their pretensions, not just on stage during their performances, but also in their private life. Given the almost religious veneration for the classical past and its cultural heroes which the second sophistic felt, it should be obvious that sophists lived under persistent pressure: the constant comparison with the towering idols of the good old times which their public performances invited must have made them anxious.

Social status, in the society of the Roman Empire, was not something you simply possessed once and for all; much rather, a member of the elite constantly had to demonstrate his superiority by performing in the public. These performances could be of different kinds (public offices or priesthoods, public generosity, sophistic declamation, or educated conversation in semi-public conditions, to name just a few examples), yet each one of them was a challenge in which there was a real danger of failing. As public figures, members of the elite constantly had to "fashion themselves in their competition for glory, like actors in the theatre".[47]

This self-fashioning was especially important for sophists. Recent scholarship has emphasized the often overlooked fact that in their dazzling rhetorical performances, outward appearance played an important role: flamboyant attire, appropriate gestures, a manly gait and demeanor, and of course a firm and resonant voice were not just a small part of sophistic declamations, but were as important as proper use of classical Attic and proper knowledge of classical history and literature.[48] Being successful as a sophistic declaimer was thus theatrical in more than one way: on the one hand, sophists were as much "on stage" as any member of the social elite who had to demonstrate his superior status; on the other hand, their status depended on elaborate role-playing, on being able to assume the *persona* of a classical hero.[49]

As I have tried to show, it was this theatrical aspect of sophistic performance which motivated Lucian to use all these metaphors emphasizing theatricality and duplicity, the possible discrepancy between outward appearance and inner value, and the danger and jeopardy that dramatic performances entailed. Tragedy, in this regard, embodies everything that classical culture was and meant to sophists: it was part of their identity that conveyed them power and authority, yet at the same time, it could be a trap and a pitfall that might unmask them as "too small" for the role they had assumed.

---

47 Plutarch, *Praecepta gerendae rei publicae* 2; 799 A: πρὸς ἅμιλλαν ἢ δόξαν ὥσπερ ὑποκριτὰς εἰς θέατρον ἀναπλάττοντας ἑαυτούς.
48 See esp. the brilliant contributions by Gleason 1995 and Connolly 2001.
49 See Connolly 2001, 85–8.

Bibliography

Baldwin, Barry (1961), "Lucian as a Social Satirist", *Classical Quarterly* 11, 199–208.
— (1973), *Studies in Lucian*, Toronto.
Baumbach, Manuel (2002), *Lukian in Deutschland: eine forschungs- und rezeptionsgeschichtliche Analyse vom Humanismus bis zur Gegenwart* (Beihefte zu Poetica 25), Munich.
Billault, Alain (ed.) (1994), *Lucien de Samosate : actes du colloque international de Lyon organisé au Centre d'études romaines et gallo-romaines les 30 septembre-1 octobre 1993*, Lyon.
Billerbeck, Margarethe and Zubler, Christian (2000), *Das Lob der Fliege von Lukian bis L. B. Alberti. Gattungsgeschichte, Texte, Übersetzungen und Kommentar* (Sapheneia 5), Frankfurt.
Bluck, R. S., (1961), "On τραγική: Plato, *Meno* 76 e", *Mnemosyne* 14, 289–95.
Bompaire, Jacques (1958), *Lucien écrivain. Imitation et création*, Paris [reprinted 2000].
Branham, R. Bracht (1989), *Unruly Eloquence. Lucian and the Comedy of Traditions*, Cambridge (Mass.).
Branham, R. Bracht, and Goulet-Cazé, Marie-Odile (eds.) (1996), *The Cynics: the Cynic Movement in Antiquity and Its Legacy* (Hellenistic Culture and Society 23), Berkeley.
Braunsperger, Gerhard (1993), *Aufklärung aus der Antike: Wielands Lukianrezeption in seinem Roman "Die geheime Geschichte des Philosophen Peregrinus Proteus"*, Frankfurt.
Clay, Diskin (1992), "Lucian of Samosata: Four Philosophical Lives (Nigrinus, Demonax, Peregrinus, Alexander Pseudomantis)", in: *Aufstieg und Niedergang der römischen Welt* II, 36, 5 Berlin, 3406–50.
Connolly, Joy (2001), "Reclaiming the Theatrical in the Second Sophistic", *Helios* 28, 75–96.
Delz, Josef (1950), *Lukians Kenntnis der athenischen Antiquitäten*, Freiburg.
Dobrov, Gregory W. (2002), "The Sophist on His Craft: Art, Text, and Self-Construction in Lucian", *Helios* 29, 173–192.
Dubel, Sandrine (1994), "Dialogue et autoportrait: les masques de Lucien", in: Billaut (1994) 19–26.
Fleury, Pascale (2002), "L'éloge paradoxal, entre virtuosité et construction idéologique: le cas de l'*Éloge de la négligence* de Fronton", *Rhetorica* 20, 119–32.
Follet, Simone (1994), "Lucien et l'Athènes de son temps", in: Billault (1994) 131–7.
Fornara, Charles W. (1983), *The Nature of History in Ancient Greece and Rome*, Berkeley.
Fuente, Jorge Marcos de la (2004), "El insecto como tema retórico y poético", *Minerva* 17, 85–102.
Garelli-François, Marie-Hélène (2001), "La Pantomime entre danse et drame: le geste et l'écriture", *Cahiers du groupe interdisciplinaire du théâtre antique* 14, 229–247.
Garelli-François, Marie-Hélène (2004), "La Pantomime antique ou Les mythes revisités: le répertoire de Lucien (*Danse*, 38–60)", *Dioniso* 3, 108–119.
Gargiulo, Tristano (2003), "Adesp. Trag. 295 TRGF (= Luc. Musc. Enc. 11): frammento tragico o paratragico?", *Lexis* 21, 179–199.
Georgiadou, Aristoula / Larmour, David H. J. (1998), *Lucian's Science Fiction Novel True Histories: Interpretation and Commentary* (Mnemosyne Suppl.179), Leiden.
Gleason, Maud W. (1995), *Making Men. Sophists and Self-Representation in Ancient Rome*, Princeton.
Goldhill, Simon (ed.) (2001), *Being Greek under Rome. Cultural Identity, the Second Sophistic and the Development of Empire*, Cambridge.

Goldhill, Simon (2002), *Who Needs Greek? Contests in the Cultural History of Hellenism*, Cambridge.

Goulet-Cazé, Marie-Odile / Goulet, Richard (eds.) (1993), *Le Cynisme ancien et ses prolongements. Actes du colloque international du CNRS (Paris, 22–25 juillet 1991)*, Paris.

Hall, Edith and Wyles, Rosie (eds.) (2008), *New Directions in Ancient Pantomime*, Oxford.

Hall, Jennifer (1981), *Lucian's Satire*, New York.

Halliwell, Stephen (2005), "Learning from Suffering: Ancient Responses to Tragedy", in: Justina Gregory (ed.), *A Companion to Greek Tragedy*, Malden, 394–412.

Hopkinson, Neil (2008), *Lucian. A Selection*, Cambridge.

Jones, Christopher P. (1986), *Culture and Society in Lucian*, Cambridge (Mass.).

Karavas, Orestis (2005), *Lucien et la tragédie* (Untersuchungen zur antiken Literatur und Geschichte 76), Berlin.

Lada-Richards, Ismene (2007), *Silent Eloquence. Lucian and Pantomime Dancing*, London.

Lauvergnat-Gagnière, Christiane (1988), *Lucien de Samosate et le lucianisme en France au XVIᵉ siècle: athéisme et polémique* (Travaux d'humanisme et renaissance 227), Geneva.

Marsh, David (1998), *Lucian and the Latins: Humor and Humanism in the Early Renaissance*, Ann Arbor.

Nesselrath, Heinz-Günther (1998), "Lucien et le Cynisme", *L'Antiquité Classique* 67, 121–135.

Oudot-Lutz, Estelle (1994), "La représentation des Athéniens dans l'œuvre de Lucien", in: Billault (1994) 141–48.

Pernot, Laurent (1993), *La Rhétorique de l'éloge dans le monde gréco-romain*, 2 vols. (Collection d'Études augustiniennes, série antiquité 136), Paris.

Raina, Giampiera (2001), "'Il sogno' di Luciano tra autobiografia e mitopoiesi", *Maia* 53, 399–409.

Robert, Louis (1930), "Pantomimen im griechischen Osten", *Hermes* 65, 106–22.

Robert, Louis (1980), *À travers l'Asie mineure. Poètes et prosateurs, monnaies grecques, voyageurs et géographie*, Paris.

Roberts, Deborah H. (1987), "Parting Words: Final Lines in Sophocles and Euripides", *Classical Quarterly* 37, 51–64.

Robinson, Christopher (1979), *Lucian and His Influence in Europe*, Chapel Hill.

Russell, Donald A. (1983), *Greek Declamation*, Cambridge.

Rütten, Ulrich (1997), *Phantasie und Lachkultur: Lukians Wahre Geschichten* (Classica Monacensia 16) Tübingen.

Saïd, Suzanne (1993), "Le « je » de Lucien", in: Baslez, Marie-Françoise / Hoffmann, Philippe / Pernot, Laurent (eds.), *L'invention de l'autobiographie d'Hésiode à Augustin: actes du deuxième colloque de l'Équipe de recherche sur l'hellénisme postclassique (Paris, École normale supérieure, 14–16 juin 1990)* (Études de littérature ancienne 5), Paris, 253–70.

Schlapbach, Karin (2008), "Lucian's *On Dancing* and the Models for a Discourse on Pantomime", in: Hall/Wyles (2008) 314–337.

Schmakeit, Iris Astrid (2002–3), "Tragödie und Parodie in der zweiten Sophistik: Euripides' Formelschluss am Ende von Lukians *Symposion oder Die Lapithen*", *Illinois Classical Studies* 27–8, 45–61.

Schmitz, Thomas A. (1997), *Bildung und Macht. Zur sozialen und politischen Funktion der zweiten Sophistik in der griechischen Welt der Kaiserzeit*, Munich.

—— (1999), "Performing History in the Second Sophistic", in: Martin Zimmermann (ed.), *Geschichtsschreibung und politischer Wandel im 3. Jh. n. Chr. Kolloquium zu Ehren von Karl-Ernst Petzold (Juni 1998 anläßlich seines 80. Geburtstags* (Historia Einzelschriften 127), Wiesbaden, 71–92.

—— (2004), "Alciphron's Letters as Sophistic Texts", in: Barbara Borg (ed.), *Paideia. The World of the Second Sophistic*, Berlin, 87–104.

—— (2007), "Die Erfindung des klassischen Athen in der zweiten Sophistik", in: Astrid Steiner-Weber / Thomas A. Schmitz / Marc Laureys (eds.), *Bilder der Antike* (Super alta perennis 1), Göttingen, 71–88.

Schröder, Bianca-Jeanette (1999), "Die 'Dichterweihe' eines Satirikers: Bemerkungen zu Lukians Bacchus", *Philologus* 143, 148–54.

—— (2000), "'Eulen nach Athen': ein Vorschlag zu Lukians Nigrinus", *Hermes* 128, 435–42.

Schwartz, Jacques (1965), *Biographie de Lucien de Samosate* (Coll. Latomus 83), Brussels.

Schwinge, Ernst-Richard (1997), *Griechische Tragödie und zeitgenössische Rezeption. Aristophanes und Gorgias: zur Frage einer angemessenen Tragödiendeutung* (Berichte aus den Sitzungen der Joachim-Jungius-Gesellschaft der Wissenschaften 15, 2), Göttingen.

Seeck, Gustav Adolf (1990), "Lukian und die griechische Tragödie", in: Jürgen Blaensdorf / Jean-Marie André / Nicole Fick (eds.), *Theater und Gesellschaft im Imperium Romanum. Théâtre et société dans l'empire romain* (Mainzer Forschungen zu Drama & Theater 4), Tübingen, 233–41.

Swain, Simon (1996), *Hellenism and Empire. Language, Classicism, and Power in the Greek World AD 50–250*, Oxford.

Tarrant, H. A. S. (1985), "Alcinous, Albinus, Nigrinus", *Antichthon* 19, 87–95.

Trédé, Monique (2002), "Le théâtre comme métaphore au IIᵉ s. ap. J.-C.: survivances et métamorphoses", in: *Comptes rendus de l'Académie des Inscriptions et Belles-Lettres*, 581–605.

von Koppenfels, Werner (2007), *Der andere Blick oder das Vermächtnis des Menippos*, Munich.

von Moellendorff, Peter (2000), *Auf der Suche nach der verlogenen Wahrheit. Lukians Wahre Geschichten* (Classica Monacensia 21), Tübingen.

—— (2001), "Frigid Enthusiasts: Lucian on Writing History", in: *Proceedings of the Cambridge Philological Society* 47, 116–40.

Walbank, Frank W. (1955), "Tragic History. A Reconsideration", *Bulletin of the Institute of Classical Studies* 2: 4–14.

Weissenberger, Michael (1996), *Literaturtheorie bei Lukian. Untersuchungen zum Dialog Lexiphanes* (Beiträge zur Altertumskunde 64), Stuttgart.

Whitmarsh, Tim (2001), *Greek Literature and the Roman Empire. The Politics of Imitation*, Oxford.

—— (2005), *The Second Sophistic* (New Surveys in the Classics 35), Oxford.

D. Late Antiquity and the Middle Ages

Christians and the Theater

Timothy Barnes

"The Church is not a theatre, where we listen merely for pleasure."
John Chrysostom, *Homilia de Statuis ad Populum Antiochenum*

Every self-respecting Greek city of the Roman East, however small and insignificant, had its theater, while larger cities also had an odeum, and still larger ones several theaters. A passage of Pausanias, the importance of which is not diminished by the fact that it is so frequently quoted, makes clear in a striking way how central a theater was to a city's self-esteem (10.4.1):[1]

> From Chaeronea two and a half miles bring you to the city of Panopeus in Phokis: if you can call it a city when it has no government offices, no gymnasium, no theater, no market-square, when it has no running water at a water-head and the inhabitants live on the edge of a torrent in hovels like mountain huts.

It could, perhaps, be argued that Pausanias presents too idealized a picture of Greece for this passage to count as probative, since his attitudes are those of a pilgrim more than of a dispassionate and accurate observer.[2] But archaeology abundantly confirms the ubiquity of theaters in all parts of the Greek world.[3] Moreover, many cities of the Latin West also had theaters, whether their culture had a strong Greek tinge, like that of Carthage, or was predominantly Latin.[4]

The central place that the theater still occupied in Roman society in the fourth century can be illustrated from a wide range of evidence, but I have selected two literary texts that are especially revealing because they mention the theater almost incidentally. The first is Eusebius' *Life of Constantine* (2.61.5). Describing the controversy over the theological views of Arius that

---

1   My translation combines elements from the translations by W. H. S. Jones in the Loeb edition ([London/New York, 1935], 4:383), and by Peter Levi, *Pausanias' Guide to Greece* (Harmondsworth, 1971), 1:410. Levi's version is on the whole superior, but I do not like his rendering of *archeia* as "state buildings" and of *gymnasion* as "training-ground".
2   Elsner 1992; cf. Gogos 1988.
3   See esp. de Bernardi Ferrero 1966–74, Mitens 1989, Green 1989, 14–24, Moretti 1991 and 1992.
4   See esp. Frere 1970, Fuchs 1987, Landes 1989, 23–90, Zervetti 1991, Gianotti 1991.

erupted before Constantine defeated Licinius, Eusebius observes that the fire of discord spread from Alexandria through the whole of Egypt and even into other provinces:

> it was possible to see not only the leaders of the churches disputing but also the congregations divided as the people inclined to one party or the other. The spectacle reached such a pitch of absurdity that the solemn <truths> of the divine teaching were now enduring the vilest mockery in the very theaters of the unbelievers.

Theaters, of course, were, and always had been, places of public assembly as well as places for dramatic performances;[5] hence, it is not clear whether Eusebius means that the theological squabbles of the early 320s were ridiculed on the stage (presumably in mimes) or mocked by pagans when they assembled in the theater on public business. But what is significant about the passage is that Eusebius simply assumes without reflection that theaters are a natural venue in which contemporary pagans would either discuss or hear about the quarreling Christians in their midst.

The second passage comes from Libanius' panegyric on the dead Julian (*Or.* 18.66). After his victory over the Alamanni near Strasbourg in 357, Libanius remarks, the Caesar did not allow success to divert him into pleasure or idleness:

> Any other man, after such an overwhelming victory, might have disbanded his army, retired to his capital and feasted his eyes on horse races and theatrical amusements, and sought mental relaxation. But not he![6]

The main contrast intended is far more precise than the indefinite generalization seems to imply. Libanius is comparing Julian specifically to Constantius, whom he later stigmatizes as more interested in horse races and charioteers than in defeating the Persians (*Or.* 18.207); Antioch was especially famous for its *circenses*, as is noted in a text written while the emperor was residing in that city (*Expositio totius mundi et gentium* 32).[7] However, Constantius is not known to have been an aficionado of the theater or even to have taken any interest in it – hence this aspect of the comparison is general and, as such, an indication of the popularity of the theater in fourth-century Antioch.[8]

Similar illustrative examples could easily be multiplied, but they would neither advance the argument nor help to pose more precisely the main problem in the history and culture of late antiquity to which this chapter

---

5   On the earliest theaters, see Kolb 1981, esp. 100–2.
6   Translated by A. F. Norman, *Libanius: Selected Works*, Cambridge/ Mass 1969, 1.321.
7   The date of the original Greek of the *Expositio* is argued to be the late 340s in Barnes 1993, 311 n. 7.
8   On 'routine entertainment' in the city, see Liebeschuetz 1972, 144–7, who notes that imperial letters were read out in the theater (106; cf. Libanius *Or.* 1.157).

addresses itself. Christian attitudes toward the theater have been discussed ably and often by a series of scholars, who have fully documented the fact that, from the Severan age onward, Christian preachers and Christian writers regularly condemned the theater, theatrical performances, and those who attended them.[9] But such condemnations are entirely predictable and therefore uninteresting – except as evidence that Christians habitually indulged in the behavior condemned. Although I shall say something about several works directed against the theater (and draw gratefully on the excellent modern scholarship devoted to them), my theme is a different one. I wish to ask, rather, what effect such condemnations and Christian attitudes in general had on the theater in late antiquity. The relationship between preaching and actual conduct is rarely straightforward, and it is not always easy to evaluate what effect the teaching of the church had on ordinary Christians. It will suffice to allude to the use of contraception and abortion by contemporary Catholics to illustrate how wide a divergence there can be between what is preached from the pulpit and what happens in real life.

When the Roman Empire became Christian, theaters were neither torn down nor closed. They continued to be used as places of entertainment.[10] Indeed, so strongly did the assumption that cities needed theaters persist in the fourth century that theaters were built in Constantine's new and aggressively Christian city of Constantinople,[11] and some new theaters were still constructed: in 373 the praetorian prefect Petronius Probus was able to fortify Sirmium rapidly by using material assembled for building a theater (Ammianus 29.6.11). The theater did not go into terminal decline until two centuries after Constantine, presumably as part of that fundamental shift of cultural attitudes in the sixth century that Averil Cameron has done so much to map out precisely over the last twenty-five years.[12]

---

9   Jürgens 1972, Weismann 1972, Schnusenberg 1988, Sallmann 1990. (Schnusenberg's book is a "corrected, slightly enlarged and revised version and English translation" of her Chicago doctoral thesis, which was written in German, accepted in 1976, and subsequently published in the series *Europäische Hochschulschriften*, Reihe 23, Theologie 141, Bern, Frankfurt, and Las Vegas 1981.) It is often asserted that "the mime frequently satirized Christianity and its practices, parodying its most sacred rituals (such as communion) and beliefs (including the Trinity, the divinity, the virgin birth of Christ, and reincarnation)" and that this explains why it was so fiercely denounced (e.g., recently and following a respectable line of scholars, Beacham 1991, 138). The evidence normally adduced for this assertion consists entirely of bogus and fictitious hagiographical documents: I shall accordingly disregard it entirely, even though Christians were undoubtedly sometimes mocked on the stage (Gregory of Nazianzus Or. 2.84).

10 On the difficulty of evaluating the archaeological evidence for theaters falling out of use, see Green 1994, 161ff.

11 Dagron 1974, 316.

12 Camron 1969, 1981, 1985, 1991, 189–229, 1993, 128–51.

In the early decades of the sixth century, theaters – in some cities, at least – were still used for stage performances: besides archaeological evidence at Gerasa and elsewhere, there is explicit literary evidence for Edessa around 500, for Gaza in the reign Justinian, and for Thessalonica even later.[13] Moreover, Procopius includes in his *de Aedificiis* the claim that when the emperor Justinian rebuilt Antioch after the Persian sack of 540 (2.10.22):

> he laid it out with stoas and market-places, and diving all the blocks of houses by means of streets, and making water channels and fountains and sewers, all those of which the city now boasts, he built theaters and baths for it, ornamenting it with all the other public buildings by mean of which the prosperity of a city is wont to be shown.

H. B. Dewing, whose Loeb translation I have quoted, duly cited the passage of Pausanias quoted earlier:[14] the basic assumption that Procopius voices here about the amenities needed to support city life seems to be virtually identical to that enunciated by Pausanias four centuries before. Moreover, the same assumption surfaces in two other passages by the same author. The small city of Apsarus in Colchis, in ruins at the time of writing, used to be adorned with "a theater and a hippodrome and all the other things by which a city's size is normally displayed" (*Bella* 8.2.14); and before the emperor Anastasius fortified it, Melitene in Armenia had shops, streets, stoas, baths, theaters "and whatever else contributes to adorning a great city" (*Aed.* 3.4.18).

It might be concluded from these passages that, apart from the obsolescence of the gymnasium, which Procopius omits, nothing fundamental had changed in the normal forms of civic life in the Greek city between the pagan second century and the age of Justinian. But that would be a hasty and mistaken inference. The passage quoted is (I believe) the sole passage in Procopius' *de Aedificiis* that attributes the construction of new theaters to Justinian. Procopius' silence is significant. For the *de Aedificiis* is an extended panegyric to which the invective against Justianian and Theodora in the *Secret History* (6–18) provides a foil and an antithesis: had Justinian been in the habit of buildings theaters, both works would have given this trait prominence – the one as an imperial virtue, the other as a vice showing him besotted with the mime and virtual ex-prostitute Theodora, who had made a career in the theater (*Arc.* 9.10–20).[15] The theaters at Antioch of which

---

13   See the brief survey by Claude 1969, 74–5, who argues that most theaters, especially in Africa, had passed out of use by 500. In Aphrodisias, the theater was still in use at the very end of the sixth century; see Rouché 1989, 218–26.
14   H. B. Dewing, *Procopius*, New York and London 1940, 7.171 n. 2.
15   On the complementary nature of the two depictions of Justinian, see Cameron 1985, 49–112. The inference drawn in the text stands even if the *Secret History* consists of three separate essays by Procopius that were only combined together and equipped with a preface long after his death, as is persuasively argued by Adshead 1993.

Procopius speaks were not really new theaters, since they merely replaced old ones recently destroyed by the Persians.[16] Outside Constantinople, there is so little evidence for the construction of new theaters after A.D. 300 that it must be concluded that few were built after that date.[17] Despite Procopius, the theater, with its tradition of live performance, was no longer generally considered an essential part of urban life in the Christian Roman Empire. When Justinian honored his home village by building there the new city of Justiniana Prima, it contained churches, official residences, stoas, market-places, fountains, streets, and baths (Procopius *Aed.* 4.1.19–27) – but no theater.

So far I have deliberately spoken somewhat vaguely about 'theater' and 'the theater', while suggesting that any changes brought about by Christian-ity were probably slow, subtle, and difficult to detect over the short term.[18] It is now necessary to discuss what was normally performed in the theaters of the Roman Empire after the classical period. For when Christians be-gan to become socially respectable and prominent around 200, a significant change of taste had already occurred. Theaters continued, as before, to be used for political gatherings – it is this aspect of the theater that first ap-pears in Christian literature, when the *Acts of the Apostles* describe Paul's adventures in Ephesus (19.31). And theaters continued to be used on occa-sion for gladiatorial games – until these were prohibited by Constantine, with evident success, except in a few large cities where such shows were too well established to abolish easily.[19] During the second century, however, there occurred a significant change in the nature of theatrical performances, as something closer to vaudeville displaced serious drama from the public stage. Pantomimes and mimes had long existed and had been fashionable in Rome and Campania at least since the days of Augustus; the classic descrip-tion of Roman life and manners by Ludwig Friedländer sets out abundant

---

16 Downey 1961; cf. ibid., 443–6. John Malalas registers the rebuildings of public are-nas at Nicomedia by the younger Theodosius after an earthquake and of the theater of Sykai by Justinian when he rebuilt it as Justinianopolis (pp. 363, 420 Bonn).

17 The plan of Cyrene in Roques 1987, 47 fig. 2, describes one buildings as 'théâtre byzantin', but its date seems to be uncertain – and could be before 300; cf. Good-child 1971, 138, with plan facing p. 200 ('Spätes Theater' [Theater IV]).

18 On the nature of the problem of defining such changes in another important area of ancient life, see Temkin 1991, esp. 134–5.

19 The classic treatment is Ville 1960; cf. Gregori 1991, 330–5. Since Ville's conclu-sions have often been misreported, it is necessary to reiterate them: in brief, (1) Ville argued from the silence of the canons of the Councils of Elvira and Arles in the West and of Libanius in the East that gladiatorial games had already disappeared almost everywhere by 325, and (2) Ville found plentiful evidence for such games after 325 only in Rome, though there is sporadic evidence for them elsewhere in Italy, in An-tioch (in 328), and at Carthage (shortly after 410).

evidence for them in the early Roman Empire.[20] In the course of the second century, however, pantomimes and mimes took over the theatrical stage and became the normal forms of public entertainment in the theater.

Aelius Aristides noted the change and lamented it in an open letter to the city of Sparta denouncing dancers.[21] Aristides' work is, unfortunately, lost. But three later works survive that take a different view of the matter – Lucian's dialogue *de Saltatione*, written in Antioch in the 160s, and Libanius' oration *Against Aristides on behalf of the pantomimes* (*orchêstai*), also written in Antioch, apparently in 361, defend the art of the *pantomimus*, while Choricius' *Apologia mimorum*, which was written in Gaza in the early sixth century, undertakes the altogether harder task of defending the mime.[22] Although these works span four centuries, what all three report about *mimi* and *pantomimi* on the stage corresponds so closely that the nature of the two types of performance can be reconstructed in details. This task was undertaken by the young Greek scholar Georgios Theocharidis in a thesis written in Munich, under the supervision of Franz Dölger, which showed how the many remarks about the theater in the homilies of John Chrysostom around 400 mesh with what is to be found in Lucian, Libanius, and Choricius.[23] Theocharidis' conclusions have never, to the best of my knowledge, been contested; on the contrary, they are confirmed and strengthened by Greek inscriptions that refer to theatrical performers, especially the rich epigraphical and archaeological evidence relating to them from Aphrodisias in Caria.[24] However, the fact that Theocharidis' conclusions are widely accepted by scholars who study the ancient theater and ancient drama does not mean that their significance is universally appreciated. It will be worthwhile, therefore, to summarize them, as the most effective way of putting before the reader what the theatrical shows were that the Christians of the Later Roman Empire condemned – and attended.

In John Chrysostom and the other evidence, Theocharidis found frequent reference to three types of dramatic performance:

---

20 Friedländer 1922, most conveniently consulted in the English translation of the seventh edition by J. H. Freese and L. A. Magnus, *Roman Life and Manners under the Early Empire*, vols. 2 and 4. London 1908 and 1913, 2:90–117; 4.535–47; cf. now Leppin 1992.

21 For what is known about the work, see Mesk 1909, Jones 1986, 70.

22 The following editions are used: (1) Lucian, *de Saltatione*, ed. M. D. MacLeod (Oxford 1980) 3.26–54; (2) Libanius *Or.* 64, ed. R. Foerster (Leipzig 1908) 4.420–98; (3) Choricius, *Apologia Mimorum*, ed. R. Foerster and E. Richtstieg (Leipzig 1929) 344–80. I do not accept the breezy dismissal of the second of these works as "a rhetorical display, not a development of Libanius' opinions" by Liebeschuetz 1972, 14 n. 5. On the precise cultural context, see Mary 1993.

23 Theocharidis 1940.

24 See esp. Robert 1936, 1939, 1970, 1983, Roueché 1993.

1. Excerpts from tragedy performed by a *pantomimus*, that is, a performance includ-ing the three elements (a) the dance of the *pantomimus*, (b) a song sung by others to which he danced, and (c) accompanying music;

2. Excerpts from tragedy performed by tragic actors (*tragôidoi*);

3. The mime.

The performance of the *pantomimus* was fundamentally different from that of the mime. The *pantomimus* was a solo performer, always a man, who played both male and female roles; he danced, without speaking or singing, to the accompaniment of a choral ode; and the subject matter was mainly mythological, though it might sometimes be historical (as had been the case with Athenian tragedy). In contrast, mimes were performed by several play-ers, female as well as male; the performers spoke and sang, usually without a chorus, but did not dance; and the plots were taken from or modeled on everyday life. The *tragôidos* was the poor relation of the *pantomimus*. Like the latter, he was a solo performer who took both male and female roles, and he might well employ nonspeaking assistants as part of his act. Unlike the *pantomimus*, however, the *tragôidos* did not dance but merely gestured; he wore a mask and long sleeves; he sang solo, without chorus and without musical accompaniment; and he performed on stilts or at least in high boots. There is also evidence in John Chrysostom for performances by *kitharôidoi* and *kômôidoi*.

Inscriptions add the important fact that all these four types of solo per-former frequently performed as competitors in contests, specifically in the numerous games that are attested for almost every Greek city of any size in the second and third centuries. By good fortune, the rise of the *pantomimus* can be dated quite precisely. In the 120s, when Julius Demosthenes founded he *agôn* at Oenoanda, whose foundation charter survives in full and was published by Michael Wörrle in 1988, there was no contest or prize for *pan-tomimi*. The act of foundation provides prizes for trumpeters and heralds, for writers of prose encomiums, for poets, for choral flautists, for comic actors, for tragic actors, for harp-singers, and for overall prizes for the outstand-ing performers among all these categories. It then adds a sum to provide performances without prizes, among which are to be mimes, recitals, and spectacles (*mimoi kai akroamata kai theamata*). These recitals and those that Demosthenes goes on to call "the other *akroamata* that give pleasure to the city" must include *pantomimi*.[25] It is clear, therefore, that contests of *pantomimi* were not a normal part of the games in the Greek world during the reign of Hadrian.

A generation later, when Lucian wrote the dialogue conventionally known under the Latin title *de Saltatione*, there was a lively controversy

---

25 Wörrle 1988, 4–16; cf. ibid., 227–58 (Das Fest des Demosthenes); Mitchell 1990.

over whether contests of *pantomimi* should be added to the traditional program of Greek festivals. In Lucian's dialogue, it is taken for granted that
the art of the *pantomimus* is not part of the normal cycle of contests (32: εἰ
δὲ μὴ ἐναγώνιος ἡ ὄρχησις). But in the same context, Lucian alludes to a
Greek city in Italy (clearly Naples) where a competition for *pantomimi* does
exist – presumably under Roman influence.[26] Moreover, he tells an anecdote
about a *pantomimus* playing the madness of Ajax, apparently in Antioch,
who really became deranged, jumped into the audience, and sat between
two ex-consuls, who were afraid that he would treat them like the sheep of
the plot. When he came to his senses, his supporters (*stasiôtai*) asked him
to dance Ajax again. He refused, partly at least because he was irritated by
his opponent (ὁ ἀνταγωνιστὴς καὶ ἀντίτεχνος), who danced a similar Ajax
but observed all the rules of the pantomimic art without straying into acting
(83–4).

The popularity of *pantomimi* and the mime, and the occasional performance of tragic extracts are well documented. But were whole plays also
still written or, at least, still performed? Christopher Jones has recently collected and set out clear evidence from Aelius Aristides and inscriptions for
the composition and performance of new plays during the second century,
and Margarete Bieber, in her standard history of the Greek and Roman theater, deduces from varied archaeological and iconographical evidence that
"comedy and tragedy continued into at least the third century".[29] But it is
hard, perhaps impossible, to find similar evidence for real drama after the
Severan period. What is found in this period is, rather, the turning of plays
into some other literary genre. The Medea of Hosidius Geta, to which Tertullian applies the term tragedy around 200 (*de Praescriptione Haereticorum*
39.4: *Hosidius Geta Medeam tragoediam ex Virgilio plenissime exsuxit*), is
less a real play than a Virgilian cento;[30] and the Barcelona *Alcestis*, which

Louis Robert long ago collected Greek inscriptions that show both
that men of respectable social status might become *pantomimi* and that, by
the end of the second century, contests in what was grandiloquently called
"rhythmical tragic motion" formed a standard component of the program in
Greek festivals, even the most prestigious.[27] Moreover, mimes too were admitted to competition by the Severan period, although they are only attested
as competing in the lower tier of contests – those that offered money prizes
– not in the prestigious sacred contests.[28]

---

26   Leppin 1992, 169–76.
27   Robert 1930; cf. *Rev. phil.* n.s. 32, 1958, 52 n. 1. (= OMS 5.192 n.1).
28   Roueché 1993, 23.
29   Jones 1993, Bieber 1961, 227–53, esp. 250.
30   For the text, see E. Baehrens, *Poetae Latini Minores*, Leipzig 1882 4.219–37; A.
     Riese, *Anthologia Latina*, Leipzig 1893, 1.61–79.

renders Euripides' play into Latin hexameters with clear borrowings from Lucretius, Virgil, Horace, Propertius, Ovid, Tibullus, Lucan, Silius Italicus, Statius, and popular funerary verse, should probably be regarded as belonging to the literary genre of the *ethopoeia*.[31] The absence of drama proper (except the mime) from the standard handbooks of Greek and Latin literature in late antiquity need not in itself prove that there was none, but if there is evidence for real drama as a living art form after about 230, let it be produced.

Some examples of the performance of old plays are admittedly sometimes alleged for this period. But all the examples that I have examined disappear under close scrutiny. For example, Arnobius refers to Sophocles' *Trachiniae* and uses the present tense as if reporting actual performance of the play: *Hercules ... miserabiles edere inducitur heiulatus* (*Adv. Gent.* 4.35); *tragoedia Sophoclis, cui Trachiniae nomen est ... actitatur* (7.33). Yet, although Arnobius clearly refers to Sophocles, not to a pantomimic representation of the plot, he draws his observation and much of his wording from an identifiable literary model.[32] Again, Albert Müller confidently asserted that Augustine saw tragedies as a young man in Carthage and that a reference in one of his sermons to a *histrio* alongside a *mimus* and a *pantomimus* can only designate a tragic or comic actor (*Sermo* 198.3 [*PL* 38.1026]).[33] When the passages are analyzed closely, however, they turn out to have nothing to say about whole tragedies as opposed to excerpts. Augustine's *Confessions* speak of *spectacula theatrica* (3.2.2), which is indeed often translated as "stage plays".[34] But Henry Chadwick's "theatrical shows" more accurately conveys the lack of specificity in the Latin.[35] As for the sermon, the phrase *pro mimo, pro histrione, pro pantomimo* is a tricolon crescendo that takes up a preceding *turpitudines variae theatrorum*, and again it may apply to an actor who declaimed tragic excerpts, though at least once elsewhere Augustine uses *histrio* to mean *pantomimus* (*de Magistro* 3.32). Augustine refers to the theater about two hundred times in total: although most of these permit no specific inference, it seems to me that those that do all tend to confirm, rather than to contradict, the picture drawn by Theocharidis from the relevant Greek evidence.[36] Let me give just one example. In one of his tracts on Saint John's Gospel, Augustine utters a

---

31 See Marcovich 1988, esp. 4–14, 96–101. He argues that the poem was composed in Alexandria ca. 350.
32 That is, Cicero *Tusc.* 2.20; cf. Jürgens 1972, 10–11.
33 Müller 1909, 40.
34 As in the classic translation of 1631 by William Watts, reproduced in Saint Augustine: *Confessions*, Cambridge/ Mass. 1919, 101.
35 H. Chadwick, *Saint Augustine: Confessions, translated with an introduction and notes*, Oxford 1991, 35.
36 I rely on a search in the CD-ROM of the *CETEDOC Library of Christian Latin Texts* published by the Université Catholique de Louvain.

wish that the *fabulae* of the foolish and reckless woman of *Proverbs* 9.13–17 had not been directed against God but might instead have been such *fabulae*, (*Tractatus in Johannis Evangelium* 97.3 [CCL 36.574])

> quales in theatris sive cantantur sive saltantur sive mimica scurrilitate ridentur

Again, this passage is most naturally construed as a reference to the three types of theatrical performance which are well attested in the later Roman Empire – a *tragôidos* performing dramatic excerpts (*cantantur*), a *pantomimus* (*saltantur*), and the mime.

In the West, as in the East, the *tragôidos* faded out. Procopius refers to popular acclamations in theaters and at horse races as a common occurrence both in the cities of the East and at Rome in the early decades of the sixth century (*Arc.* 7.13; *Bella* 5.6.4), and he refers to theaters and hippodromes as constituents of the luxurious existence that the Vandals enjoyed in Africa (*Bella* 4.6.7). He thus assumes that theaters were still in use. For what was normally performed in them, Cassiodorus provides a valuable indication. Between 507 and 511 he composed a letter for Theodoric to send to a man who was about to repair a theater (*Variae* 4.51). Cassiodorus passes easily from Attic tragedy and comedy to Pompey's theater and from Pompey to the performances that graced the contemporary stage. It is the *pantomimus* and the *mimus* who alone appear, just as they do in Libanius' speech *To the Antiochenes on the Emperor's Anger*, which professed to reconcile the parting Julian with the city in 363 (*Or.* 16.41):

> Let us close the theater for a short time and request the *pantomimi* and *mimi* here to let our neighbors share the blessings they provide, and allow us to pass the summer without amusements.

Perhaps the point has been labored and illustrated in excessive detail. But it is important to stress that the norms of theatrical performance had already changed markedly before the Christians were in any position to influence their development and before Christian views on the subject are documented. Two works survive in which Christian writers before 300 deal with the moral and practical questions posed by the theatre – Tertullian's *de Spectaculis*, written shortly before 200 in Carthage,[37] and Novatian's work of the same name, which is a letter written half a century later and largely modeled on Tertullian.[38] Both writers address the question whether Christians

---

37 On which, see Barnes 1971; Turcan 1986, esp. 34–7 (the structure), 62–8 ('resultat et survie').

38 Edited by W. Hartel, CSEL 3.3 (1871): 3–13; G. F. Diercks, CCL 4, 1972, 167–79. Novatian's authorship of this work, which is transmitted under the name of Cyprian, was proved by Weyman 1892; Demmler 1894; Melin 1946. A defense of the transmitted attribution was attempted by Wölfflin 1893; but he recanted in his review of Demmler, *Archiv für lateinische Lexicographie* 9, 1894, 319.

may attend games and shows in general, and both answer with a resounding negative. Countering the plea that watching *spectacula* is a harmless pleasure, Tertullian deploys an argument that has two stages. First, he contends at length that every sort of public entertainment is idolatrous by nature as a result of its origin: hence every Christian's baptismal vow to renounce the Devil, his entourage, and his angels includes a renunciation of the theater. Then Tertullian argues that the *spectacula* themselves corrupt those who watch them by arousing base and immoral emotions. Novatian repeats the same twofold argument in a more restrained manner that avoids both Tertullian's quirkiness and his rhetorical sparkle.

Both Tertullian and Novatian assumed that theatrical performances were inherently idolatrous. That seemed a natural view to take in 200 or 250, especially when account is taken of the context in which *tragôidoi* and *pantomimi* normally performed in the third century, that is, in dramatic contests that formed part of festivals in honor of traditional divinities, festivals whose essential elements were a procession in honor of a god or goddess, a sacrifice, and a series of contests. Every Greek city had its local cult or cults, which were normally the focus of a festival or festivals held at regular intervals and celebrated by a procession, a sacrifice, and games consisting of athletic competitions, of competitions in the performing arts, or of a combination of the two.[39]

Despite appearances, Tertullian and Novatian were mistaken. For the obvious idolatry of the theater could be removed just as easily as the pagan veneer in the imperial cult, which survived into the fifth century in an expurgated form.[40] It required merely a change in the surrounding ceremony, not an alteration in the nature of performance. In Rome, in the middle of the fourth century, there were one hundred and seventy-five days of games each year – ten of gladiatorial *munera*, sixty-four of horse racing, and one hundred and one of dramatic *ludi*. In the new city of Constantinople, the newly instituted games were attached not to pagan festivals, of which there were none, but to the appointment of magistrates, the celebration of triumphs, and imperial anniversaries.[41] In other cities, festivals and shows could continue as before, provided that they no longer commenced with sacrifice to traditional deities, and provided that explicitly pagan elements were removed from the procession and any other attendant ceremonies. Hence the old festivals could survive in a purified form as long as cities could support them.

Charlotte Roueché has recently described the serious problem that confronts any attempt to understand what happened to the innumerable *agones*

---

39 Roueché 1993, 4–5.
40 On the imperial cult in Africa in the fifth century, see Clover 1982, 661–74; 1979–80, 121–8.
41 Müller 1909, 37–8.

of the Greek world after 300. The problem can be stated simply. Our main source of information for the games in the second and third centuries is epigraphic, and the types of inscription that provide this documentation dry up in the fourth century. Hence, if evidence for games disappears from the surviving record after 300, it does not necessarily follow that the games themselves disappeared with any rapidity.[42]

The legislation of the Christian emperors recognized the necessity of providing public entertainments and attempted to reconcile it with the demands of Christian morality.[43] This emerges most clearly from the chapter in the *Codex Theodosianus* relating to the *maiouma*, which was a festival of Syrian origin held at night, centered on mime and pantomime performances, and associated with water.[44] Successive imperial constitutions in the chapter, addressed to the praetorian prefect of the East in 396 and 399, read as follows (*Cod. Th.* 15.6.1, 2):

> It pleases our clemency that the joyfulness of the *maiouma* be restored to the provincials, yet in such a way that propriety and modesty be preserved by chaste morals.

> We allow the skills of actors to be exercised, lest sadness be created as a result of excessive restrictions of them. But we forbid that foul and indecent spectacle that wanton license has claimed for itself, the *maiouma*.

The fact that the two constitutions take different views of the *maiouma* is less important in the present context than the fact that they both balance the same moral standard against the same practical or political necessity. It should also be noted that Arcadius did not change his mind about whether or not to permit the *maiouma*: rather the two documents reflect the views of the praetorian prefects Caesarius and Aurelianus, the consuls of 398 and 400, to whom they were formally addressed in 396 and 399. In his *de Providentia*, Synesius used Aurelianus and Caesarius as the models for his hero and villain, respectively, the virtuous Osiris and the wicked Typhos, brothers but bitter enemies. Significantly, it is Aurelianus, whom Synesius presents as a good Hellene, who takes the stricter view of the *maiouma* and receives instructions to abolish it entirely. John Chrysostom surely approved.[45]

Christians were not alone in regarding the theater of imperial times as immoral. Several passages of the lost work of Aristides that Libanius quotes for rebuttal state this point of view in a forthright fashion, at least as regards the art of the *pantomimus* (*Or.* 64.31, 37, 59):

> It is the ruin of cities and households, and whoever watches them is lost, and his inability to escape them is the worst of disasters.

---

42   Rouché 1993, 5–7.
43   For a recent brief general treatment, see Blänsdorf 1990.
44   Roueché 1989, 71–3.
45   On the piety of Aurelianus, see Cameron and Long 1993, 71–84.

They themselves live dishonorably, and they also corrupt the spectators by dragging them toward what it is worse <to do>.

A nod of theirs is more capable of producing moral corruption than the war-engines of others are of forcing the surrender of a city.

Aristides depicted *pantomimi* as sexually promiscuous, no better than male prostitutes, to which Libanius replied – truthfully, if rather lamely – that they were neither all paragons of virtue nor all monsters of depravity (*Or.* 64.38–43). The denigration of *pantomimi* that Aristides employed was inherently appealing to Christian moralists, who could easily give it a distinctively Christian twist by appeal to Jesus' saying that "If a man looks on a woman with a lustful eye, he has already committed adultery with her in his heart" (Matthew 5.28). John Chrysostom duly quotes this proof-text in his sermon "against those who abandoned his church and deserted to the horse races and theaters" (*Contra ludos et theatra* [*PG* 56.263–70]).[46]

John was provoked by injured pride: some of his congregation in Constantinople preferred watching horses and mimes to deriving moral benefit from his oratory. But his main argument is general and repeats Aristides. Those who watch such spectacles, he asserts, allow their souls to be dragged hither and thither by irrational passions; when they see adultery depicted on the stage, their minds become full of adultery, and their intelligence is enslaved to passion. The spiritual damage suffered in the theater, John contends, is permanent:

Even if you have not lain with the whore [i.e., the actress], you have copulated with her in desire, and you have committed the sin in intention. Not only at that moment but also when the show ends and the actress exits, her image remains in your soul – her words, her gestures, her glances, her walk, her rhythm, her tone of voice,[47] her seductive limbs – and you return home with countless wounds.

Accordingly, John announces, he will not in the future allow anyone who sets foot in a theater to enter his church or share in Christian communion.

It is significant that, whereas John's ire was initially aroused by Christians who went to the hippodrome and the theater, he explicitly excludes from communion only the theatergoers. Imperial legislation made a similar distinction between those professionally engaged in the two types of entertainment. The first imperial constitution in the chapter *de Scaenicis* in the *Codex Theodosianus* was issued in 367 to the *praefectus urbi* at Rome: it ordains that *scaenici* may take the sacrament only at the point of death; if they recover, they are forbidden from returning to the stage (*Cod. Th.* 15.7.1^S [371 mss.]). These rules were not new in 367, since the main purpose of the extract from the constitution preserved in the *Codex Theodosianus* is to safe-

---

46 For fuller discussion of John's attitude towards the theater, see Vandenberghe 1955, Pasquato 1976.

47 The meaning of *hê diakrisis* is uncertain: I follow Montfaucon's interpretation (*PG* 56. 267 n. a).

guard the supply of actors by ordering inspectors to ascertain that *scaenici* allowed to take the sacrament really were in danger of dying. For Christian legislators were confronted by a constant conflict between the morality that they officially espoused and the practical need to ensure the provision of popular entertainment. Daughters of actors and actresses had a legal obligation to perform on the stage, but a consistent commitment to Christianity was held to free them from this statutory duty (*Cod. Th.* 15.7.2 [371], 4 [380], 9 [381], 12 [394]). Potential performers were often far from eager to take up a stage career, and there were serious problems of recruitment. Accordingly, in 413, the emperor Honorius informed the *tribunus voluptatum* in Carthage that

> we order that female mimes who have been freed by various rulings should immediately be recalled to their proper function, so that there should be no adornment lacking to the pleasures of the people and the days of festivities (*Cod. Th.* 15.7.13).

It is tempting to infer that Christian disapproval of the stage helps to explain the growing popularity of chariot racing in the fourth and fifth centuries[48] – and the apparent conversion of theaters for the exhibition of water spectacles.[49] The Council of Arles in 314 excommunicated both theatrical performers and charioteers, so long as they continued to perform or to race (*Canons* 4,5); and the ruling was repeated verbatim at a later Council of Arles in the second half of the fifth century (*Canon* 20).[50] But the relative standing of stage and hippodrome diverged widely in the Christian Roman Empire. On the one hand, chariot racing became closely associated with imperial ceremony.[51] On the other hand, theatrical performances and contests were subjected to constant disapproval: the Council of Laodicea in the middle decades of the fourth century forbade Christians to dance even at wedding parties and instructed clergy of all ranks to leave such celebrations before the musicians (*thymelikoi*) entered (*Canons* 53, 54). Roman law had long treated actors as technically *infames*, and Roman society had always regarded their profession as demeaning;[52] Christianity sharpened that prejudice, reinforcing a social and moral contempt that already existed, by excluding actors, at least in theory, from membership in a religious community that normally admitted both sinners and the lowborn.

---

48 Cameron 1976, 214–18 invokes a "genuine change of popular taste" and imperial patronage – both of which were affected by religious change.

49 Traversari 1960, esp. 107–17.

50 *Concilia Galliae A. 314–A. 506*, ed. C. Munier, *CCL* 148 (1963): 5, 10, 118. Hefele and Leclercq (1907) vol. 1, pt. 2, 1023, note that the prohibition was reiterated at the council in Trullo in 691 and thence made its way into Gratian's handbook of canon law.

51 Cameron 1976, 249ff., McCormick 1986, 35–79.

52 Kaser 1956, Levick 1983.

The third defense of the theater that survives from late antiquity is Choricius' defense of the mimes, to which he gave the significant programmatic title *On Behalf of Those Who Represent Life in the Theater of Dionysus*. This speech, which is very relevant to what 'Hellenism' meant in late antiquity, appears to need a thorough reevaluation.[53] Choricius held the municipal chair of rhetoric at Gaza in the reign of Justinian. All who have discussed him recently present him as a Christian in a Christian city.[54] If that were true, then the speech would be highly anomalous in light of the evidence for attitudes toward the mime presented so far. For Choricius not only defends the mime at length as morally harmless but even suggests that watching it is morally beneficial. He directly confronts and contradicts the argument, familiar from John Chrysostom, that spectators especially young and impressionable ones, fall victim to an unquenchable passion for pleasures because their reason is corrupted or destroyed by what they see (32.30):

> But, my good sir, when you watch adultery, then you also see the magistrate's court: the husband of the woman caught *in flagranti* makes an accusation, the man who rashly committed adultery is tried with his lover, and the judge threatens both with punishment.

Since condign punishment is always meted out to evil deeds, Choricius argues, the mime does not subvert morality; it reinforces it.

Both Choricius and his milieu have (I believe) been misinterpreted. Gaza is held to have been converted from paganism to Christianity around 400 by bishop Porphyrius, whose biography by Mark the Deacon has usually been taken as the authentic account of how Porphyrius found only 280 Christians in the city when he was consecrated bishop in 395 but left a congregation of 2,647 when he died twenty-five years later.[55] On this showing, Gaza became thoroughly Christian a century before Choricius, and presumably it remained so. Unfortunately, Mark's *Life of Porphyrius* is a fraudulent and inauthentic document: although it purports to give an eyewitness account of events seen by its author as an adult in the 370s, it copies Theodoretus' *History of the Monks in Syria*, which was written in the 440s, and it systematically contradicts known facts from the period about which it writes – on virtually every occasion where independent evidence exists.[56] It is not necessary here either to establish the real date of composition or to assess the

---

53 For a full discussion of the speech but one based on several premises that are rejected here, see Reich 1903, 1.204–30.
54 E.g. Downey 1961a, 109–39.
55 On the long controversy over the value of the text, see Grégoire and Kugener 1930, vii–lxxxix, who are widely regarded as having proved that the biography is an authentic eyewitness account that was later expanded and dramatized (see, e.g., Holum 1982, 55).
56 Peeters 1941, MacMullen 1984, Barnes 1989.

validity of a recent attempt to answer the arguments of Paul Peeters – who maintained that the *Life of Porphyrius* belongs to the seventh century – by propounding the hypothesis that it is a careless reworking in around 450 of a deliberately misleading document originally composed in 415.[57] It will suffice to note that since the *Life of Porphyrius* is not what it purports to be, it cannot legitimately be adduced as proof that Gaza was largely Christian in the fifth century: the religious complexion of the city remains to be delineated from genuine evidence.

Choricius himself is styled a Christian by Photius, who (it is assumed) ought to have known. But it is clear that Photius knew nothing precise about Choricius except what he inferred from his writings (*Bibliotheca* 160). His belief that he was a Christian is deduced from Choricius' two panegyrics on Bishop Marcianus of Gaza, especially the earlier one, with its description of the Church of Saints Sergius and Stephanus (*Or.* 1). This speech is indeed full of Christian terminology and allusions to the gospels, but there is hardly any similar Christian terminology in Choricius' other speeches, and he alludes to the New Testament nowhere else except in his funerary speech on Maria, the mother of Marcianus (*Or.* 7). On the contrary, as Wilhelm Schmid put it long ago in his still standard treatment of the author, Choricius moves in a pagan thought-world: he expounds Homer and evaluates myths like a conservative pagan, he studiously avoids mentioning Christian customs and attitudes, he speaks of Zeus as the creator of the world and of the Fates as the arbiters of human life, and he describes the Islands of the Blessed, where one might expect to hear something about personal immortality.[58] The fact that an official poet, orator, or panegyrist in a Christian city cannot avoid on occasion using the religious language of the people whom he praises is not good evidence for his real beliefs. What Choricius reveals, perhaps inadvertently, of his deepest assumptions about life and death surely stamps him as a pagan.

Choricius' defense of the mime remains surprising even if it was penned by a pagan. For, although his model, Libanius, whom he uses heavily throughout the speech, defended *pantomimi* and declared that their arts was "the most useful of all things" and that it had no evil consequences whatsoever (*Or.* 64.103–20, esp. 115, 119), he regarded the mime in a very different light – as totally and irredeemably disreputable. Libanius scolded Aristides for attempting to discredit the respectable art of the *pantomimus* by associating *pantomimi* with the mime, with which he proclaimed they had virtually nothing in common (*Or.* 64.10–11). Choricius defends the mime by using

---

57 Trombley 1993, 1.246–82. He bases his picture of the Christianization of Gaza exclusively on the biography (188–245).

58 Schmid (1899) 2426–7. Despite the observations summarized here, Schmid pronounced him "ohne Zweifel Christ" (2426).

praise very similar to that which Libanius had lavished on the art of the *pantomimus*. Choricius' speech is a calculated apologia for something that he knew Christians in theory condemned: perhaps, therefore, he intended it as a deliberate provocation, an implicit criticism of the contradiction between the theoretical demands of Christian morality and the actual behavior of the Christians whom he observed in Gaza. For, although the theater disappeared not long after Choricius, the arts of the mime and the *pantomimus* persisted into the Byzantine period, and it is the mime, not one of the higher forms of dramatic art, from which modern drama is lineally descended.[59]

Addendum:

The discussion of Choricius requires significant modification in light of G. W. Bowersock, *Mosaics as History. The Near East from Antiquity to Islam* (Cambridge, Mass. and London, 2006), esp. 59–63. Bowersock argues that Late Antique mosaics from the Near East depicting the god Dionysus, whom Choricius praises, and scenes from Greek mythology reflect contemporary performances of mimes and "demonstrate a shared enjoyment of the ancient and undying tradition of ancient myths": since Dionysus was "the encompassing, enabling inspiration for the mimes and, through them, for the mosaists who evoked the entertainments of their cities", he holds that my attempt to deny that Choricius was a Christian is fundamentally misconceived.

Bibliography

Adshead, K. (1993), "The Secret History of Procopius and its Genesis", in: *Byzantion* 63, 5–28.
Barnes, Timothy D. (1971), *Tertullian: a Historical and Literary Study*, Oxford.
—— (1989), "The Baptism of Theodosius II", in: *Studia Patristica* 19, 8–13.
—— (1993), *Athanasius and Constantius: Theology and Politics in the Constantinian Empire*, Cambridge/ Mass.
Beacham, Richard C. (1991), *The Roman Theater and its Audience*, London.
Bieber, Margarete (1961), *History of the Greek and Roman Theater*, 2nd edn., Princeton.
Blänsdorf, Jürgen (1990), "Der spätantike Staat und die Schauspiele im *Codex Theodosianus*", in: id. (ed.), *Theater und Gesellschaft im Imperium Romanum* (= Mainzer Forschungen zu Drama und Theater 4), Tübingen, 261–73.
Cameron, Alan (1976), *Circus Factions: Blues and Greens at Rome and Byzantium*, Oxford.
Cameron, Alen and Long, Jacqueline (1993), *Barbarians and Politics at the Court of Arcadius*, Berkeley, Los Angeles, and Oxford.

---

59   Reich (1903) 616–93, 744–900.

Cameron, Averil (1969), *Agathias*, Oxford.
—— (1981), *Change and Continuity in Sixth-Century Byzantium*, London.
—— (1985), *Procopius and the Sixth Century*, London.
—— (1991), *Christianity and the Rhetoric of Empire: the Development of Christian Discourse*, Berkeley and Los Angeles.
—— (1993), *The Mediterranean World in Late Antiquity A.D. 395–600*, London.
Claude, Dietrich (1969), *Die byzantinische Stadt im 6. Jahrhundert* (= Byzantinisches Archiv 13), Munich.
Clover, Frank M. (1979–80), "Le culte des empereurs dans l'Africa vandale", in: *Bulletin archéologique du Comité des Travaux historiques et scientifiques*, n.s. 15–16, 121–8.
—— (1982), "Emperor Worship in Vandal Africa", in: *Romanitas-Christianitas: Untersuchungen zur Geschichte und Literatur der römischen Kaiserzeit*, Berlin, 661–74.
Dagron, Gilbert (1974), *Naissance d'une capitale: Constantinople et ses institutions de 300 à 451*, Paris.
de Bernardi Ferrero, Daria (1966–74), *Teatri classici in Asia Minore*, 4 vols., Rome.
Demmler, A. (1894), *Über den Verfasser der unter Cyprians Namen überlieferten Traktate 'De bono pudicitae' und 'De Spectaculis'*, Munich.
Downey, Glanville (1961), *A History of Antioch in Syria*, Princeton.
—— (1961a), *Gaza in the Early Sixth Century*, Norman.
Elsner, Jaś (1992), "Pausanias: a Greek Pilgrim in the Roman World", in: *Past and Present* 135, 3–29.
Frere, Sheppard S. (1970), "The Roman Theater at Canterbury", in: *Britannia* 1, 83–113.
Friedländer, Ludwig (1922), *Darstellungen aus der Sittengeschichte Roms in der Zeit von Augustus bus zum Ausgang der Antonine II*, 10th edn, Leipzig.
Fuchs, Michaela (1987), *Untersuchungen zur Ausstattung römischer Theater in Italien und den Westprovinzen des Imperium Romanum*, Mainz.
Gianotti, G. F. (1991), "Letteratura e spettacoli teatrali in età imperiale", in: M. Verzár-Bass (ed.), *Il teatro romano di Trieste: monumento, storia, funzione* (= Contributi per lo studio del teatro antico: Bibliotheca Helvetica Romana 25), Rome, Geneva, and Mainz, 284–329.
Gogos, S. (1988), "Das antike Theater in der Periegesis des Pausanias", in: *Klio* 70, 329–39.
Goodchild, Richard G. (1971), *Kyrene und Apollonia*, 3rd edn., Zurich.
Green, John R. (1989), "Theater Production, 1971–1986", in: *Lustrum* 31, 7–95.
—— (1994), *Theater in Ancient Greek Society*, New York and London.
Grégoire, Henri / Kugener, M.-A. (1930), *Marc le diacre: Vie de Porphyre évêque de Gaza*, Paris.
Gregori, G. L. (1991), "Il teatro di Trieste quale sede di spettacoli gladiatorii nel tardo impero", in: Monika Verzár-Bass (ed.) *Il teatro romano di Trieste: monumento, storia, funzione* (= Contributi per lo studio del teatro antico: Bibliotheca Helvetica Romana 25), Rome, Geneva, and Mainz, 330–5.
Hefele, Charles Joseph / Leclercq, H. (1907), *Histoire des conciles*, Paris.
Holum, Kenneth G. (1982), *Theodosian Empresses: Women and Imperial Dominion in Late Antiquity*, Berkeley.
Jones, Christopher P. (1986), *Culture and Society in Lucian*, Cambridge/ Mass.
—— (1993), "Greek Drama in the Roman Empire ", in: R. Scodel (ed.), *Theater and Society in the Classical World*, Ann Arbor, 39–52.
Jürgens, Heiko (1972), *Pompa diaboli: die lateinischen Kirchenväter und das antike Theater* (= Tübinger Beiträge zur Altertumswissenschaft 46), Tübingen.

Kaser, Max (1956), "*Infamia* und *ignominia* in den römischen Rechtsquellen",
in: *ZSS* Romanistische Abteilung 73, 220–78.

Kolb, Frank (1981), *Agora und Theater, Volks- und Festversammlung*
(= Archäologische Forschungen, vol. 9), Berlin.

Landes, Christian (ed.) (1989), *Le goût du théâtre à Rome et en Gaule romaine*, Lattes.

Levick, Barbara (1983), "The *Senatus Consultum* from Larinum", in: *JRS* 73, 97–115.

Liebeschuetz, J. H. W. G. (1972), *Antioch: City and Imperial Administration in the
Later Roman Empire*, Oxford.

MacMullen, Ramsay (1984), *Christianizing the Roman Empire*, New Haven.

Marcovich, Miroslav (1988), *Alcestis Barcinonensis* (= Mnemosyne Suppl. 103).

Mary, L. (1993), "Les captives et le pantomime: deux rencontres de l'empereur Julien
(Ammien Marcellin 24,4,25–27)", in: *Revue de études augustiniennes* 39, 37–56.

McCormick, Michael (1986), *Eternal Victory: Triumphal Rulership in Late Antiquity,
Byzantium, and the Early Medieval West*, Cambridge.

Melin, Bengt (1946), *Studia in Corpus Cyprianeum*, Uppsala.

Mesk, J. (1909), "Des Aelius Aristides verlorene Rede gegen die Tänzer",
in: *WS* 30, 59–74.

Mitchell, Stephen (1990), "Festivals, Games, and Civic Life in Asia Minor",
in: *JRS* 80, 183–93.

Mitens, Karina (1988), *Teatri greci e teatri ispirati all'architettura greca in Sicilia e
nell'Italia meridionale (circa 350 –50 A.C.)* (= Analecta Romana Instituti Danici,
Supplementa 13), Rome.

Moretti, Jean-Charles (1991), "L'Architecture des théâtres en Grèce (1980–1989)",
in: *Topoi* 1, 7–28.

—— (1992), "L'Architecture des théâtres en Asie Mineure (1980–1989)",
in: *Topoi* 2, 9–32.

Müller, A. (1909), "Das Bühnenwesen in der Zeit von Constantin d. Gr. bis Justinian",
in: *Neue Jahrbücher* 23, 36–55.

Pasquato, Ottorino (1976), *Gli spettacoli in S. Giovanni Crisostomo: paganesimo e
cristianesimo ad Antiocha e Costantinopoli nel IV secolo* (= Orientalia Christiana
Analecta 201), Rome.

Peeters, Paul (1941), "La vie géorgienne de Saint Porphyre de Gaza",
in: *Analecta Bollandiana* 59, 65–216.

Reich, Hermann (1903), *Der Mimus: ein litterar-entwicklungsgeschichtlicher Versuch*,
Berlin.

Robert, Louis (1930), "Pantomimen im griechischen Osten", in: *Hermes* 65, 106–22.
[reprinted in his *Opera Minora Selecta*, Amsterdam 1964–90, 1.654–670].

—— (1936), "Archaiologos", in: *REG* 49, 235–54 [reprinted in his *Opera Minora
Selecta*, Amsterdam 1964–90, 1.671–90].

—— (1939), *Mélanges syriens offerts à René Dussaud*, Paris, 735–8
[reprinted in his *Opera Minora Selecta*, Amsterdam 1964–90, 1.607–10].

—— (1970), "Deux concours grecs à Rome", in: *CRAI* 6–27 [reprinted in his *Opera
Minora Selecta*, Amsterdam 1964–90, 5.647–68].

—— (1983), "Une vision de Perpétue martyre à Carthage en 203", in: *CRAI* 228–76
[reprinted in his *Opera Minora Selecta*, Amsterdam 1964–90, 6.791–839].

Roques, Denis (1987), *Synésios de Cyrène et la Cyrénaïque du Bas-Empire*, Paris.

Roueché, Charlotte (1989), *Aphrodisias in Late Antiquity* (= *JRS* monograph 5), London.

—— (1993), *Performers and Partisans at Aphrodisias in the Roman and Late Roman
Period* (= *JRS* monograph 6), London.

Sallmann, Klaus (1990), "Christen vor dem Theater", in: J. Blänsdorf (ed.), *Theater und Gesellschaft im Imperium Romanum* (= Mainzer Forschungen zu Drama und Theater 4), Tübingen.

Schmid, W. (1899), "Chorikios", in: *RE* 3, 2424–31.

Schnusenberg, Christine (1988), *The Relationship between the Church and the Theater Exemplified by Selected Writings of the Church Fathers and by Liturgical Texts until Amalarius of Metz – 775–852 A.D.*, Lanham.

Temkin, Owsei (1991), *Hippocrates in a World of Pagans and Christians*, Baltimore and London.

Theocharidis, G. J. (1940), *Beiträge zur Geschichte des byzantinischen Profantheaters im IV. und V. Jahrhundert, hauptsächlich auf Grund der Predigten des Johannes Chrysostomus, Patriarchen von Constantinopel* (= Laographia: Parartema 3), Thessaloniki.

Traversari, G. (1960), *Gli spettacoli in acqua nel teatro tardo antico*, Rome.

Trombley, Frank R. (1993), *Hellenic Religion and Christianization c. 370–529*, Leiden.

Turcan, Marie (1986), *Tertullien: Les Spectacles (De Spectaculis)*, (= Sources chrétiennes 332), Paris.

Vandenberghe, Bruno H. (1955), "Saint Jean Chrysostome et les spectacles", in: *Zeitschrift für Religions- und Geistesgeschichte* 7, 34–46.

Ville, Georges (1960), "Les jeux de gladiateurs dans l'empire chrétien", in: *MEFR* 72, 273–335.

Weismann, Werner (1972), *Kirche und Schauspiele: die Schauspiele im Urteil der lateinischen Kirchenväter unter besonderer Berücksichtigung von Augustin* (= Cassiaciacum 27), Würzburg.

Weyman, Carl (1892), "Über die dem Cyprianus beigelegten Schriften *de Spectaculis* und *de Bono Pudicitiae*", in: *Historisches Jahrbuch* 13, 737–48.

Wölfflin, Eduard (1893), "Cyprians *de Spectaculis*", in: *Archiv für lateinische Lexicographie* 8, 1–22.

Wörrle, Michael (1988), *Stadt und Fest im kaiserzeitlichen Kleinasien: Studien zu einer agonistischen Stiftung aus Oinoanda* (= Vestigia 39), Munich.

Zervetti, N. (1991), "Osservazioni su significato e funzione del teatro nella cultura romana', in: Monika Verzár-Bass (ed.) *Il teatro romano di Trieste: monumento, storia, funzione* (= Contributi per lo studio del teatro antico: Bibliotheca Helvetica Romana 25), Rome, Geneva, and Mainz, 264–83.

The Tragedy of the Middle Ages

Carol Symes

The story goes like this. The fall of Rome and the rise of Christianity, which Edward Gibbon notoriously construed as one and the same, destroyed the rich heritage of antiquity.[1] Theatres were relegated to obscurity or ransacked as quarries. Professional entertainers went underground, died out, buried without sacrament or ceremony. Gradually, a specifically Christian (but artistically inferior) mode of theatricality came into being, the liturgy; and occasionally, an isolated monastery might produce something that could be called drama. That took a long time, however: while the germ of medieval theatre might be found in the tenth century, it would not flower until the late twelfth or thirteenth, when a few isolated texts suggest that medieval man was stepping beyond the confines of the Church and into the secular sphere. But it was only with the Renaissance that Europe would be freed from the religiosity and cant of such pastimes. Finally, secular themes were re-introduced, and classical models re-employed.[2] At long last, the death of Greek tragedy, a cultural crime for which the Christian Middle Ages has long stood accused, was avenged.

This familiar teleology has shaped the historiography of theatre for centuries, and has predetermined the ways that the medieval reception of ancient practices has been (mis)understood. The fulminations of Tertullian, or Augustine's oft-cited anxieties, have usually been taken at face value. Meanwhile, the relative scarcity of early records documenting the activities of those who made a living as theatre professionals (playwrights, actors, musicians, mimes) has been viewed as evidence of theatre's eradication when juxtaposed with the relatively voluminous condemnations of a few medieval critics, whose remarks have been read as proof that dramatic activity could be stifled by an authoritarian Church, and that the theatricality indigenous to the Middle Ages represents (at best) an impoverishment of the classi-

---

1   Gibbon 1776, vol. 1, cc. XV and XVI.
2   For a summary of the scholarship contributing to this grand narrative from the seventeenth to the late twentieth century, see Vince 1984, 89–96. For a series of critical essays on medieval drama – many of which call for a revision of this narrative – see Simon (ed.) 1991.

cal tradition.[3] With respect to Byzantium, where the texts of ancient Greece were actually preserved for posterity, a similarly prejudicial reading of the record has led scholars to the ironic conclusion that the society to which we owe our knowledge of tragedy was ignorant of its dramatic possibilities. Supposedly, plays were copied in an atmosphere of arid pedantry, never enlivened by performance. Moreover, it is commonly argued that the Eastern Roman Empire produced only a single dramatic document in the course of a thousand years, the Χριστὸς πάσχων, invariably dismissed as a ham-fisted pastiche, allegedly unsuitable and unintended for performance.[4]

In order to dismantle this tragic paradigm, this essay will begin by debunking the myth of Greek tragedy's murder by the Middle Ages. It will then go on to survey the ways in which medieval intellectuals in the Latin-speaking West understood and invoked both the genre and the concept of tragedy, translating it into terms suited to their own times.

Who Killed Greek Tragedy?

One recent assessment of tragedy's post-classical history may be taken to represent the prosecution in the case against the Middle Ages. Although "a vestigial knowledge of tragedy was preserved through the medium of pantomime" in the eastern Roman Empire, the barbarous practices of the copyists who preserved the texts of canonical plays during the ninth century made this "tragedy's darkest hour." Meanwhile, "the situation in the West was understandably much bleaker." "Considered with the general decline of the performing arts which dates from the early Byzantine age, no Greek tragedy, so far as we know, was performed on a stage throughout this long period, though informal readings might have taken place in private houses," and "[p]recisely what function the plays served in the schools is impossible to determine; though it is probable that they were used in the teaching of basic grammar and the principles of rhetoric. ... Most students, however, would have studied only set speeches and set scenes; very few can have had the expertise or the staying power to read a whole play." Thankfully, though, everyone suddenly became much smarter, so that "scribes with genuine pre-

---

3   My own (very different interpretation) of the evidence has been developed in Symes 2002, 2003, 2004, 2007. In what follows, I engage the arguments of Kelly 1993 and Dox 2004.

4   The only study cited with any regularity among Anglophone scholars is LaPiana 1936, a distillation of LaPiana 1912, whose argument is driven by the same pseudo-Darwinian model of theatrical evolution that informed the scholarship of Young 1933, which has long been subject to critique. For a welcome antidote, see the essay by Andrew Walker White in this volume. See also Puchner 2002.

tensions to being scholars now began to take an interest in classical texts" in the thirteenth century. But this was too late to resuscitate tragedy's stifled corpse, until the sixteenth century fostered its revival.[5]

The premises underlying these allegations can be summarized as follows. (1) There was an unbroken tradition of tragedy's preservation and enactment from the fifth century B.C.E. until the dawn of the Christian era, when that living tragedy was suffocated. (2) The prejudices of Christians in powerful positions succeeded in radically limiting and censoring the texts of tragedy in the Greek-speaking East, while in the West there was no received tradition at all. (3) Only fully-staged productions of plays matter when it comes to studying the history of theatre. (4) Medieval people alone lack "the expertise or the staying power to read a whole play." (5) "Genuine pretensions to scholarship" are only to be observed at the dawn of modernity. (6) Fundamental information about performance praxis is always and everywhere best conveyed through textual media. (7) It is the task of each subsequent era to preserve, unchanged and intact, the heritage of a classical past, and not to introduce inventions and updated understandings.

While the counsel for the defense of the Middle Ages could easily expose the fallacy of each of these premises in turn, we will focus on two main points of contention: the exigencies of tragedy's transmission and the reception of tragedy in a Christian context.

The oldest manuscript witness to the *Bacchae* is a fourteenth-century codex now in two parts in two different Italian libraries, the product of a chancy and contingent process of conveyance that began at least 1700 years earlier, at the time of its composition.[6] In fact, the appreciation of any extant Greek tragedy cannot be separated from an appreciation of the ways in which new writing technologies, reading habits, and practices of documentation affect what is preserved, how, and why.[7] Taking Euripides' *Iphigenia in Aulis* as an example, Denys Page long ago showed how much the "original" play produced in Athens at the Dionysia of 404 must have differed from the play left unfinished by the author at his death in 406.[8] And thereafter, according to William Slater, we know "even less about ancient scholarship than we think we do." What actually happened during the first five hundred years of tragedy's transmission, or for that matter in the next five hundred years?[9] Plays and other performance pieces usually circulated orally down

---

5   I summarize the remarks of Garland 2004, 65, 78–80, 84–5.
6   *I.e.* Rome, Biblioteca Vaticana cod. Palatinus graec. 287; and Florence, Biblioteca Laurenciana conventi soppressi 172. See Turyn 1957, 258–267.
7   See, *e.g.*, Herington 1985, Tarrant 1989, Clanchy 1993, Williams 1993, Bowman and Woolf (eds.) 1994, Nagy 1996, Yunis (ed.) 2003.
8   Page 1934, 1–10.
9   Slater 1989, 38. On the fixing of the canon, see also E. Wilson 1968, 123.

to the late fifth century,[10] and Aristotle's reliance on the standards of an oral tradition still shape the way he defines tragedy in the middle of the fourth.[11] At the same time, though, a new vogue for reading tragedy assisted in the apotheosis of three tragic poets, and the selective citation of their plays in political and legal rhetoric implies "an evaluative difference regarding their respective usefulness as persuasive and authoritative paradigms of popular culture," in the words of Peter Wilson. Moreover, the threat to Athenian cultural hegemony posed by the Macedonian conquest and occupation of Attica spurred "legislation to establish the texts of the canonical fifth-century tragedians and to deposit them in the *polis* archive," indicating both "their importance to the city's identity" and "a perceived need to preserve the great masters of the past from the ravages of the present." Thereafter, whenever these "old" tragedies were revived at the Dionysia, they did not compete; they were literally "beyond judgment."[12]

Originally, tragedy's purpose had been to address "central issues of fifth-century Athenian society and ideology for a very largely Athenian audience." Its new role, as Marco Fantuzzi and Richard Hunter put it, was "to be invoked in Athens for its moral and social authority" and elsewhere "for its gnomic wisdom," meaning that this fossilized Athenian tragedy was "often revived as univocal in meaning and less provocative than the original plays," while new tragedies benefited from "a particular and recognisable generic resonance" that lent them authority and *gravitas*.[13] Of this select group of "old tragedies," the few to survive today are those further selected for editing and circulation by the librarians of Alexandria in the third century B.C., where booksellers' trade in the new editions "rapidly eclipsed all other current texts." In turn, these popular play texts would be amended by actors according to their own preferences, or be glossed by schoolmasters and readers in a "live process of transmission," distancing them even more from their Athenian origins.[14] For classicists, accordingly, *this* is "the dark period" of Greek tragedy, the third and second centuries B.C.E.[15] Now, observed Eric Havelock, "tragedy would become obsolete. Drama became what it has largely remained in literate societies ever since, an ingenious entertainment, not a contribution to the social encyclopædia."[16] Subsequently, in Republican Rome, the varied fortunes of tragedy and comedy were driven by profit rather than the ritual demands of state-sponsored religious contests, as well

---

10 Thomas 1989, 49.
11 Melia 2005; Halliwell 2006.
12 P. Wilson 1996, 316.
13 Fantuzzi and Hunter 2004, 432–3.
14 Zuntz 1965, 250, 252–3. Page 1934, 1–3.
15 Fantuzzi and Hunter 2004, 444.
16 Havelock 1982, 266.

as by the hard-and-fast choices of individual actor-managers gauging and reacting to audience expectations.[17] By the third century C.E., the only "classic" tragedies still available to the public had ceased to be plays at all; they were "literature."[18]

It was thus that the remains of Athenian tragedy were received in Byzantium, "the guardian, throughout a thousand years, of Greek traditions,"[19] as one should remember. There, in the ninth century C.E., the narrow selection of texts inherited from antiquity was gathered together and copied using the new scribal technology of miniscule cursive, codification being facilitated by the patriarch John the Grammarian's effort to bring books from the empire's fast-shrinking hinterland to the capital. These texts, in turn, became the exemplars used in the great copying campaigns of the Paleologan Renaissance, after Michael VIII recaptured Constantinople in 1261 and attempted to reverse the devastation wrought by the Crusades – another era when scholarly activity was spurred by a fresh flow of books to the capital, this time carried by refugees from the cities in Asia Minor seized by the Ottoman Turks.[20] Then, after the fall of Constantinople in 1453, a year or two before Johannes Gutenberg printed the 42-line Bible at Mainz, the manuscript witnesses resulting from this long process were transferred to Italy by another set of refugees, later to form the basis for *editiones principes* disseminated by that new medium. Yet for all that, the much-touted revival of tragedy in the sixteenth century owed its impetus to a passion for Seneca, not Attica.[21]

To summarize: there never was a golden age of unmediated access to tragedy in textual form. The division between what was seen at the Dionysia and what was transmitted to posterity began at the moment of tragedy's inception, and continues up to the present day. As Slater observes, "I venture to ask whether we will find any error in antiquity that we cannot parallel in modern times," and he goes on to say how silly it is to point fingers of blame at any era in order to favor another, "as if one practised ancestor worship by abusing other people's ancestors."[22] Or, to quote the young poet-philologist A. E. Housman, as depicted in Tom Stoppard's *The Invention of Love*: "To be a scholar, the first thing you have to learn is that scholarship has nothing to do with taste."[23]

---

17 Lebek 1996; Brown 2002.
18 Falkner 2002.
19 Zuntz 1965, xix; Fantuzzi / Hunter 2004, 433.
20 Devreesse 1954, 25–32; Turyn 1957, 311–12; Erbse 1961; Zuntz 1965, 261, 281–3; Harlfinger (ed.) 1980; Treadgold 1981.
21 Boyle 1997, 10–11, 211–12. See also Smith 1988.
22 Slater 1989, 41 and 61.
23 Stoppard 1997, 69.

Yet it is hard to discipline taste – and its parent, desire – when one wants something from the past. Even Nigel Wilson's authoritative "account of what happened to Greek literature from the end of the ancient world until the time of its reappearance in western Europe during the Renaissance"[24] – which conclusively demonstrates that Byzantine scholars were *not* given to censorship, and that the pagan authors of antiquity were more assiduously copied than the copyists' Christian contemporaries – betrays an occasional tendency to treat these scholars as though they should have had the same standards as his Oxbridge contemporaries. So he dismisses Michael Psellos' assessment of Euripides "as superficial in the extreme," sniffs at a thirteenth-century edition of *Œdipus Tyrannos* that offers "nothing of value whatever to modern scholars," and deems that Manuel Moschopoulos' "alleged re-censions of Sophocles and Euripides have not stood up to investigation," faulting the Byzantines generally for "not maintaining the theatre as an art form."[25]

Having acquitted the Middle Ages of willfully bowdlerizing Greek tragedy, it is relatively easy to dismiss the other capital charge against it, that the Church actively and successfully stamped out (what little remained of) tragedy. Cyril Mango is astute: "Historians have blindly followed the Church Fathers in denouncing the shameful licentiousness of the Late An-tique theatre," ignoring the fact that their dramatic invective was part of the attempt to rival "a dangerous competitor."[26] Hence John Chrysostom tells his audience that "the church is not a theatre, where we listen merely for pleasure" and Eusebius assumes that the theatre will be a meeting-place in which Christian doctrine is discussed.[27] As Edith Hall insists, "the very vehemence of the discussion of singing" in the early Church "testifies more strongly than any pagan source to the intense appeal of the solo songs of the ancient theatre" and invites us to imagine how the craft of the singing actor – never learned from books – would not be dependent on the produc-tion of texts and therefore even harder to suppress.[28] Furthermore, Timothy Barnes notes, "Any changes brought about by Christianity were probably slow, subtle, and difficult to detect over the short term" and, in any case – as we have seen – "a significant change of taste had already occurred" which informed the Church fathers' attitude to theatre. Tragedy had long since found new avenues of expression in pantomime (extracts from tragic stories sung and danced to music), performance by individual tragic singers

---

24 N. Wilson 1996, 1, 12–13, 18–27, 204.
25 N. Wilson 1996, 177–9, 238, 254–5.
26 Mango 1980, 64. Negative attitudes toward theatrical activity are usually an excel-lent index of its prosperity: see Barish 1981.
27 Barnes (this volume), p. 316.
28 Hall 2002, 37. See also Lightfoot 2002, Hall / Wyles (2008).

(like St. Augustine: see below), or mimes, who worked in groups. Thereafter, what medieval people knew or did not know about tragedy would be the legacy of long-term developments in the Greco-Roman world, where "the norms of theatrical performance had already changed markedly before the Christians were in any position to influence their development."[29]

With this in mind, we can compare the edict of a *Christian* emperor desirous of *safeguarding* Roman theatrical traditions, however debased, with that of a pagan emperor who showed no desire to maintain or revive them. In 342, Constantius II (337–361), Constantine's second son and successor, was not so prejudiced in favor of Christianity that he was willing to see Rome's heritage destroyed.

> Although all superstition should be entirely eradicated, nevertheless we will that the edifices of the temples that are situated outside the walls [of Rome] shall remain untouched and uninjured. For since plays and spectacles of the circus and athletic contests derive their origin from some of these temples, it is not suitable that they be torn down, since from them are produced celebrations of longstanding enjoyment to the Roman people.[30]

While it is not clear whether these spectacles "derive their origin" from performances in the actual temple structures or from religious practices represented by these temples, Constantius is dedicated to honoring the memory of these traditions because of their obvious civic importance. By contrast, Emperor Julian the Apostate was so disgusted by the decadence of those traditional practices, and their ill effects on the old Roman religion he was attempting to restore, that he made the following pronouncement in a letter to the High Priest of Asia in 363 A.D.

> No priest should, in any place, attend these licentious theatrical shows (τοῖς ἀσελγέσι τούτοις θεάτροις). ... Indeed, if it were possible to expel such shows from the theatres and give back pure offspring (καθαρὰ γενόμενα) to Dionysus, I should certainly have attempted to carry this out zealously; but since I thought that this was impossible, and that even if it were possible it would, for other reasons, not be expedient, I abstained entirely from this ambition. I do expect, however, that priests should withdraw themselves from the lewdness of the theatres and leave them to the crowd. Therefore let no priest enter a theatre, nor have for a friend either an entertainer or a charioteer (θυμελικὸν μηδὲ ἁρματηλάτην); let no dancer nor mime (μηδὲ ὀρχηστὴς μηδὲ μῖμος) approach his door."[31]

---

29   See Barnes in this volume, 319, 319, 324.

30   *Codex Theodosianus* 16.10.3. "Quamquam omnis superstitio penitus eruenda sit, tamen volumus, ut aedes templorum, quae extra muros sunt positae, intactae incorruptaeque consistant. Nam cum ex nonnullis vel ludorum vel circensium vel agonum origo fuerit exorta, non convenit ea convelli, ex quibus populo Romano praebeatur priscarum sollemnitas voluptatum." See Krueger and Mommsen (eds.) 1905, I (pt. 2), 898. I am grateful to Gregor Kalas for drawing my attention to this edict.

31   Bidez and Cumont (eds.) 1922, 172–3 (Ep. 89). See also Wellesz 1961, 84.

The pagan emperor himself exonerates Christians, by showing himself to be more zealous (and more effective) in his attempted suppression of theatre than contemporary Christians were either inclined or empowered to be.

The verdict? Allegations of criminal neglect or censorship regularly leveled against Christian theologians or the scholars of Byzantium are groundless. The canon of Greek tragedy had been drastically circumscribed long before Constantine's conversion to Christianity and the founding of a New Rome in the East. If we locate the discomfiture of the early Church fathers in the prior conditions of theatre under the Roman Empire, where other varieties of entertainment and spectacle had long since relegated tragedy to a place of antiquarian obscurity, we recognize that even the most Hellenized Romans would have had no experience of Athenian tragedy in performance, and few would have had access to or interest in the texts of the remaining tragedies. Viewed in this light, the attitudes of subsequent medieval intellectuals toward tragedy, and their curious opinions as to its purpose and production, can be seen as the logical outgrowths of this different cultural climate. Moreover, as I have argued elsewhere, the sparse textual record of the Middle Ages does not indicate that theatre was silenced, merely that the formal scripting of performance practice was unusual, and hence the number of scripts cannot be used to measure the vibrancy of medieval theatrical activity or the extent of its disjunctions with antiquity.[32] More attention could be paid to the circumstances of textual transmission in the Greek-speaking world and in the West, as well as to the changing methods of inscription, preservation, circulation, editing, and anthologizing from antiquity to the earliest editions in print. For the time being, this brief survey of the problem clears the way for a preliminary re-evaluation of tragedy's medieval heritage and the meanings attached to it by teachers, theologians, historians, poets, and performers.

The Uses of Tragedy in the Medieval Latin West

The Patrologia Latina Database offers a complete electronic version of the 221 volumes published by Jacques-Paul Migne as the *Patrologia Latina* in 1844–1855 and 1862–1865. A search for the word *tragoedia* (or *tragedia*) and its grammatical variants yields some 400 separate instances of its use by the patristic or medieval authors included in the corpus.[33] (A search for the

---

32 I develop this argument further in "Prescription, Proscription, Transcription, Improvisation: Deciphering the Written and Unwritten Evidence for Pre-Modern Performance Practice" (forthcoming).

33 This number is not the same as the total number of "hits," which is much larger and

related adjective *tragicus – a – um* yields about 130 uses, mostly by the same authors and in similar contexts; a detailed examination of these instances does not form a separate part of the analysis offered here.) Bearing in mind the obvious caveats – that we are dealing only with the opinions of medieval intellectuals writing in Latin, who were chosen by modern codifiers as representative of a period that is itself the product of modernity – what do the uses of tragedy in these sources reveal about its indigenous meanings and associations during a thousand years, from the time of Tertullian (c. 155–230) to the advent of written European vernaculars around 1200?

Both a quantitative analysis of the data and a qualitative consideration of specific examples reveal some interesting trends. Below, I discuss the five main categories into which references to tragedy can be organized, in order of frequency, although not necessarily of significance: (I) value-neutral or historical references to the genre understood to have arisen in ancient Athens; (II) negative references to tragedy as a pagan practice; (III) tragedy as a metaphor for dangerous divisions within the Church, including the errors of Jews and heretics; (IV) tragedy as denoting a disruptive event in the history of a community or a way of reporting past events; and (V) the uses of tragedy as a means for commenting (approvingly or anxiously) on contemporary performance practices.

I. Value-neutral, historical references to tragedy as the poetic and performative genre of classical antiquity, or references to certain person as the composers of tragedies or to the fate of a character in one of these plays: 130 (33%).[34] The clear majority of references to tragedy as a product of ancient

---

reflects multiple uses of the word within a single passage, whereas a global search also counts references to tragedy made by modern editors and commentators. All the translations which follow are my own, unless otherwise specified.

34 *E.g. PL* 3:335–336,715 (Marcus Minucius Felix); 6:140 (Lactantius); 13:481,516 (Pacatus Drepanius); 15:2187 and 16:85,614,891,1184 (Ambrose of Milan); 19:553 (Coelius Sedulius); 22:528,1095 and 23:278, 739 and 25:322; 26:528 and 27:433 ,443,447,451,453,499,509,511,587 (St. Jerome); 31:1076 (Orosius); 49:330,1102 (John Cassian); 51:554 (Prosper Aquitanus); 58:376,603,701 (Sidonius Apollinaris); 59:775,871,969,1073 and 60:230,443,529,744,806 (Prudentius and Dracontius); 63:664,705,843,907,912,956–957,1055 and 64:1343,1347,1373,1392 (Boethius, with the commentary by Gilbert de la Porée); 69:643,1040,1056,1221 (Casssiodorus *et alia*); 74:9 (Theodoretus of Cyr); 80:304 (Goldastus); 95:801,868, 875 (Paulus Vinfridus); 103:829 (Benedict of Agnani); 106:397, 989,994,996,999,1001,1032,1045,1131 (Fréculf of Lisieux); 111: 419,485,585,666–669 (Rabanus Maurus); 118: 834 (Haimo of Halberstadt); 123:51,80 (Ado of Vienne); 139:528,530 (Abo of Fleury); 147:649 (Marianus Scotus); 154:547–559,608–622 (Ekkehard of Aura); 176:768 (Hugh of Saint-Victor); 177:247 (Hugh of Fouilloy); 178:1258 (Peter Abelard, quoting Boethius and paraphrasing Honorius in the *Theologica Christiana*); 105:161,188 (Peter the Chanter); 199:633,644,707,723,802 (John of Salisbury).

Athens and its dramatic poets, one third of the total, suggest that its interest for medieval intellectuals was primarily historical, and moreover that it carried a certain cultural *cachet*. Somewhat surprisingly, only a fraction of these references are found in Isidore's *Etymologies* or citations of this well-known work, so the data is not skewed in favor of a single author's perspective – as it is to tragedy's detriment when glimpsed in the writings of Tertullian, whose negative attitude has been wrongly regarded as normative among early Christians (see below).[35] In this context, tragedy is most frequently invoked to bolster authority, to showcase classical learning, or to allow an author to make favorable comparisons between his own time and the distant past, sometimes in order to raise the æsthetic profile of Christianity or to embed it in an historical continuum. For example, Cassiodorus Senator (c.485–c.585), writing on behalf of Theodoric the Ostrogoth to the Roman senator Symmachus, depicts the urbane Byzantine-educated monarch as looking forward to the rebuilding of the theatre of Pompey, where tragedies had once been mounted;[36] while elsewhere he notes approvingly that Basil the Great and Gregory of Cappadocia had imitated Homer and the classical genres of comedy and tragedy in their eloquent writings.[37] Once, with very self-conscious irony, he describes Marcus of Arethusa's zealous destruction of a pagan temple (and his zealot's subsequent martyrdom) as "deeds that might have provoked the talents of Aeschylus and Sophocles, so that the acts of that tragedy could have been performed in a worthy and orderly fashion."[38]

Ambrose of Milan (c. 338–397) not only makes several casual references to tragedy, but on one occasion compares the inscription of King David's songs to other products of oral composition: "Also as regards secular writings, there were some who wrote [performance pieces] and others who were wont to sing them on stage, whether songs, comedies, or tragedies."[39] His awareness of the process by which tragedy was conveyed to posterity is striking, and so is his equation of the Psalms' original performance with the arts of the theatre.

---

35 Isidore of Seville, *Etymologies* in *PL* 82:97,120,132,164,226,309,658,704; *cf.* 93: 685,1033,1041. On the reception and influence of Isidore's works, see Kelly 1993, 37–67 and Dox 2004, 29–42.

36 Cassiodorus Senator, *Variarum libri duodecim*, *PL* 69:643.

37 *Historia tripartita*, *PL* 69:1056.

38 *Historia tripartita*, *PL* 69: 1040. "Porro Marci Arethusii episcopi gesta vel passio Aeschyli et Sophoclis concione noscitur indigere, ut digne actus illius tragoediae ordine recitentur."

39 Ambrose of Milan, commentary on Psalm 38, *PL* 14:1039: "Denique etiam in saecularibus scriptis alii erant qui scribebant, alii qui in scena, vel cantica, vel comoedias, vel tragoedias, canere consueverant." *Cf. PL* 14:709,713; 15:2187; 16:85,614,891,1184.

A similar comparison is made by the Venerable Bede (673–735) in his treatise *De arte metrica*.

> The dramatic, or active, is the genre, in which speaking characters are introduced, without the interruption of the poet, as is the case in tragedies and plays. ... [A]nd in our scriptures, the Song of Songs is written in this genre, where the alternating voice of Christ and the Church is evidently on display, even without interruption by the poet.[40]

Bede's poetic categories are based on those articulated by Roman grammarians, but his decision to classify the Song of Songs as a form analogous to tragedy is a deliberate innovation. Like Ambrose, he thereby elevates the artistry of Scripture by comparing it to the drama of antiquity. And like Ambrose, he is alive to the challenge of conveying the dynamism of performance in writing, since he places even more emphasis on the difficulty of communicating vital information about the mimetic effects of one culture's dramatic art to the readership of another culture. (Although Bede's library contained at least a few Greek books, and he himself appears capable of writing a rough, old-fashioned Greek hand, he had no direct access to Greek drama; the only other time he mentions tragedy, in his *De temporibus*, the reference is to Seneca.[41])

The salient point is that both of these devout churchmen could have avoided mentioning tragedy at all, had they considered it an inappropriate *comparandum*. Instead, they use it to validate Christian poetics. When we focus on *how* and *why* medieval commentators bring tragedy into their writings, then – and not on what they knew (or did not know) about it – it appears that most considered it to be an important part of their heritage, even though it was destined to remain somewhat mysterious. It is reasonable to suggest, in fact, that tragedy's bad press in some patristic texts may have worked to heighten its transgressive appeal, since the mere mention of it not only bespoke the writer's sophistication but provoked a *frisson* of worldly collusion in the reader. Thus the generations of adolescents raised on Priscian's Latin grammar as redacted by Rabanus Maurus (784?–856) were given a tantalizing description of tragedy's subject-matter that must have tickled the schoolboy imagination: "comedy differs from tragedy because in tragedy heroes, leaders, and kings are touted; in comedy it is humble and even private matters: in the one, sor-

---

40 Bede, *De arte metrica* (c. 25) in *PL* 90: 174: "Dramaticum est, vel activum, in quo personae loquentes introducuntur, sine poetae interlocutione, ut se habent tragoediae et fabulae. ... Quo apud nos genere Cantica canticorum scripta sunt, ubi vox alternans Christi et Ecclesiae, tametsi non in hoc interloquente scriptore, manifesta reperitur." On Bede's sources, see Kelly 1993, 40–41.

41 *PL* 90:280. For a codex thought to feature Greek annotations in Bede's hand (Oxford, Bodleian, Laud gr. 35), see N. G. Wilson 1973, 10, 12 and plates 4 and 10. See also Reynolds / Wilson 1991, 88–9 and 118–21; and Riché 1976, 387–90.

row, banishment, and bloodshed; in the other love-affairs and the abduction of virgins."[42] This was accompanied by Rabanus' anthropological report of the curious circumstances in which the genre had emerged. "Tragedy [*tragoedia*], as some have it, comes from *trago* and *ode*, because it is said that at one time the tragic authors would be awarded a *tragos*, that is a goat, as a prize for their song."[43] In the contemporary chronicle of Fréculf, bishop of Lisieux (825–851), tragedy's earliest beginnings are more soberly tied to the dating of the Babylonian Captivity, when Alkman and Stesichoros were regarded as famous poets and Sappho flourished on Lesbos: "In those days, a *tragus* was given as a prize to those who strove with each other in competition, that is, a goat, whence they are said to be called *tragoedoi*."[44]

By contrast, Sedulius Scotus (*fl.* 848–860), an Irish grammarian and *bona fide* scholar of Greek resident in Liège, rings all the imaginative changes on the history of tragedy's invention and social function in his commentary on the grammar of Donatus.

> Tragedy is derived from the Greek word τράγος, that is "he-goat," since whoever composed a song would receive a goat as a reward – whence the poet: *Carmine nam* [sic: *qui*] *tragico vilem certavit ob hircum* [Horace, *Ars poetica*, v. 220]. Alternatively, tragedy derives from the Greek *traconodon* [cf. τραχύνω], that is a harsh and lamentable song, for it is made up of battles and the killing of men. Tragedy indeed might be said to be 'a song named after goats' in two ways: either because the ancients Greeks, when they returned from war, had the habit of sacrificing as many goats as they killed men; or because he, who composed a song about a battle, received a goat as a reward. Or, tragedy may be derived from the Greek τρυγία, that is 'dregs,' since when they composed that sort of song, they received dregs; whence Horace: *peruncti faecibus ora* [*Ars poetica*, v. 277]. Thence τὰ τραγήματα, the tiny little favors which in Latin are called 'desserts.'[45]

---

42   Rabanus Maurus, *Excerptio de Arte grammatica Prisciani, PL* 111: 668. "Igitur comoedia a tragoedia differt, quod in tragoedia introducuntur heroes, duces, reges; in comoedia, humiles atque privatae: in illa luctus, exsilia, caedes; in hac amores, virginum raptus."

43   *PL* 111:667–8. "Tragoedia, ut quidam volunt, a *trago* et *ode*, dicta est, quod olim auctoribus tragicis *tragos*, id est, hircus, praemium cantus proponebatur."

44   Fréculf, *Historiae* 3.17, *PL* 106:989–90: "Quibus temporibus in agone certantibus tragus dabatur in praemio, id est, hircus, unde aiunt tragoedos nuncupatos... Alcman et Stesichorus poetae clari habentur. ... Per idem tempus Sappho mulier in diverso poemate claruit."

45   Sedulius Scotus, *In Donati artem maiorem*, Book II. This text is not included in the *PL*, although other works of the same author are – a reminder that this rich sample of data is incomplete and not necessarily representative of all medieval perspectives on tragedy, or anything else. I have consulted the edition of Löfstedt 1977, 115–18. "Tragoedia dicitur a Greco verbo, quod est τράγος, id est 'hircus' quia qui illud carmen componebant hircum in mercede accipiebant; unde poeta: *Carmine nam* [sic: *qui*] *tragico vilem certavit ob hircum* [Horace, *Ars poetica*, v. 220]. Vel tragoedia dicitur a Greco, quod est traconodon, id est durum et lamentabile carmen. est enim

Sedulius, whose works include the only known Latin commentary on Por-phyry's *Isagoge*, was unlike many of his contemporaries in that he might actually have read a Greek tragedy – or at least have read more extensively about them. He certainly has fun flaunting his superior knowledge, and pull-ing a few legs, in a context where a discussion of tragedy would seem to be irrelevant. For unlike Bede and Rabanus, Sedulius is not dealing with po-etic forms in this passage, but with proper nouns of composite gender – the *comoedia Eunuch*, the *tragoedia Orestes*, the (female) ship named *Centaur* – so that his meditation on the genre (which includes a synopsis of family dysfunction in the House of Atreus) is really an extended gloss on the rather gratuitous statement, "When I say 'I'm reading Orestes,' you understand that I mean a play, which is written about him by Terence, the kind which is called a tragedy" (*quia cum dico 'Orestem lego' intelligis fabulam, quae de eo scripta est apud Terrentium*) *Quae tragoedia vocatur*. Since he has taken the trouble to adduce it as an example, it is necessary to offer an explanation. Yet he need not have referred to tragedy at all; he could have contented him-self with that quick reference to Terence, with whose comedies all medieval schoolboys were familiar. So far from treating tragedy as taboo, Sedulius manufactures an excuse for this colorful ellipsis.

II. Negative references to tragedy as a genre of the pagan theatre: 92 (23%). Of these, however, the writings of the second-century Christian Tertullian, whose disapproval of Roman spectacle is well documented, account for 69 (that is, 17% of *all* references to tragedy in the database, and 75% of the negative citations, can be traced to a single source).[46] Furthermore, quo-tations from Tertullian by Lactantius and others account for another five condemnations,[47] while later citations of other patristic texts chosen to repre-sent tragedy in a negative light account for ten,[48] and references to Jerome's somewhat ambiguous statement that "Whole tragedies of Euripides are nay-sayings against women" gain goliardic currency in the twelfth century.[49] If

---

de proeliis et interfectione hominum compositum. Tragoedia quoque dicitur carmen de hircis editum duabus pro causis: sive quia antiqui Grecorum de bello remeantes quotquot homines necarent, tot hircus mactabant, sive quia illi, qui carmen de pro-elia edebat, hircus pro mercede tribuebatur. Vel tragoedia dicitur a Greco quod est τρυγία, id est faeces, quia illud carmen componebant, faeces recipiebant; unde Hora-tius: *peruncti faecibus ora* [*Ars poetica*, v. 277]. Inde τὰ τραγήματα dicuntur vilia munuscula, quae Latine 'bellaria' vocantur."

46 Tertullian, *PL* 1:258–660.
47 *PL* 3:1027, 6:599, 708–9, 1074.
48 *PL* 13:356, 48:814, 851, 862, 1075; 53:41; 67:924; 176:1205; 199:752; 207:243.
49 Jerome, *Adversus Jovinianum* I.48, PL 23:278. "Totae Euripidis tragoediae in mu-lierum maledicta sunt." *Cf. PL* 176:1205 (anonymous treatise *De nuptiis*); 199:752 (John of Salisbury); 207:243 (Peter of the Blois). See also below.

we place Tertullian and his followers to one side, then, acknowledging both the immediacy and the inconsequentiality of their opinions in the centuries before Christian hegemony, we are left with only a dozen or so references to classical tragedy as something inherently bad, most of which (not surprisingly) date from the early years of the institutional Church.

Indeed, it should be noted that Jerome elsewhere endows the mention of tragedy with the neutral or historicist connotations discussed above,[50] also using it once as a simile for a lamentable story (see below),[51] and once for heresy within the Church (see below).[52] Augustine, whose perspective on contemporary theatre was particularly well-developed and influential – he mentions it over 200 times[53] – actually invokes tragedy itself on only seven occasions: once in the famous confession of his youthful devotion to the stage and its spectacle of "sorrowful and tragic things" (*luctuosa atque tragica*),[54] twice in the *City of God*,[55] three times as a simile for a sorrowful event,[56] and once in his commentary on the Sermon on the Mount (Matthew 6:2–5; see below). Another, indirect reference to tragedy occurs in the *Confessions*, when Augustine brags about his own skill as a tragedian in performing his party-piece, *The Flying Medea* – which Edith Hall has called "a fascinating window on the late Roman theatre, where famous songs on mythical themes were still being sung by expert singers, more than eight centuries since the first actor to impersonate Euripides' Medea had flown off to Athens." [57]

Of these references to tragedy in Augustine's writings, the discussion of the Sermon on the Mount was the most likely to have influenced the ways that subsequent commentators dealt with a *locus classicus*: the passage that would seem to reveal Christ's own attitude to theatre in general and tragedy in particular.

> *Thus, when you give alms,* he said, *sound no trumpet before you, as the actors* [hypo-critae] *do in the synagogues and in the streets, that they may be praised by men.* No one, he said, should wish to become known as actors do. It is obvious, moreover, that actors do not cherish that in their hearts what they display before the eyes of men. For actors are deceivers insofar as they publicly take on the characters of other people, as in theatrical plays. For someone who acts the part or Agamemnon in a tragedy, for instance, or of any other person involved in the story or myth that is

---

50   E.g. *PL* 22:528,1095.
51   *PL* 22:1203.
52   *PL* 25:262.
53   Barnes (this volume) p. 323.
54   Augustine of Hippo, *Confessions* III.2, *PL* 32:893. See Dox 2004, 12–29.
55   *PL* 41:53,55.
56   *PL* 32:937, 959, 1013.
57   *Confessions* III:6 in *PL* 32:687–688. See Hall 2002, 3. Typically, Kelly is much more skeptical about the value of this episode for the history of performance: Kelly 1993, 18, 30–31.

enacted, is not truly himself, but takes on the appearance of the character and is called a *hypocrita*.[58]

As Donnalee Dox has observed, "Augustine understood theatre as a social reality in a way later Christians could not,"[59] which is one of the reasons why he found it so powerful – and potentially problematic; for him and for his contemporaries, the word *hypocrita* retained its primary meaning and conjured up images of professional actors. These associations were both less lively and less immediate for later theologians. Moreover, the word *hypocrita* quickly took on its secondary meaning, the meaning ascribed to it by Jesus and analyzed by Augustine; it was no longer a technical term for "actor" but a word designating a pretender to virtue, a lover of pious display. As such, it no longer required explanation. Perhaps this is why only one medieval author, Rabanus Maurus, follows Augustine in implicating tragedians, explicitly, in his discussion of this passage from Matthew's gospel.[60]

Furthermore, apart from a handful of other direct borrowings from patristic authors (as I noted above), there are few additional references to tragedy understood as a nefarious practice of the pagan past. The historian Gregory of Tours (c. 538–594) underscores the villainy of Nero by alleging that he sang tragedies while Rome burned.[61] Aldhelm of Sherborne (c. 640–709) somewhat equivocally describes the spectacle of Christian martyrdom at Rome as a tragedy in his treatise "In Praise of Virginity."[62] In a long didactic poem, Marbod of Rennes (c. 1035–1123) includes a misogynist riff on Jerome's assessment of Euripides when naming female wrongdoers from sacred history (Jezebel) and from the stories "tragedians are apt recite to the people" (Helen, Clytæmnestra).[63] And in the early twelfth-century bestiary attributed to Hugh of Fouilloy, the seductive effects of sirens' songs are made analogous to the moral dissolution experienced by lovers of drama, "who are ravished by the delights of the world, the pomp and pleasures of

---

58 Augustine, *De sermone Domini in monte libros duos* II:2,5, *PL* 34:1271. "Cum ergo facis elemosynam, inquit, noli tuba canere ante te, sicut hypocritae faciunt in sinagogis et in vicis, ut glorificentur ab hominibus. Noli, inquit, sic uelle innotescere ut hypocritae. Manifestum est autem hypocritas non quod oculis praetendunt hominum id etiam corde gestare. Sunt enim hypocritae simulatores tamquam pronuntiatores personarum alienarum sicut in theatricis fabulis. Non enim qui agit partes Agamemnonis in tragoedia verbi gratia sive alicuius alterius ad historiam vel fabulam quae agitur pertinentis vere ipse est, sed simulat eum et hypocrita dicitur." I have also consulted Mutzenbecher (ed.) 1967, 95–6.
59 Dox 2004, 13.
60 Rabanus Maurus, *Commentarium in Matthaeum* II:6, PL 107:815.
61 Gregory of Tours, *Historia* VI.46, *PL* 71:412.
62 Aldhelm of Sherborne, *De laudibus virginitatis, PL* 89:135.
63 Marbod of Rennes, *De apto genero scribendi* ("De meretrice"), *PL* 170: 1699. See Kelly 1993, 77.

the theatre, undone by tragedies and comedies."[64] But both quantitatively and qualitatively, these references are of negligible interest when compared to the richer and more complex uses of tragedy in other contexts.

III. "Tragedy" as a way of describing the errors of Jews, the evils of heresy, or the effects of schism within the Church: 82 (20%).[65] Much more significant than any negative connotations attached to tragedy's pagan heritage is its vital function within narratives of Judeo-Christian history, both in the Biblical past and the contemporary (medieval) present. In Fréculf's world chronicle, as I noted above, tragedy's genesis is linked to the Babylonian Captivity of the Jews, while its further development over time is traced alongside the events of the Old Testament down to the first century C.E, so that it functions as a useful chronological marker.[66] Yet the eleventh and final time Fréculf introduces the word into his narrative, it designates the "lamentable tragedy" (*luctuosa tragoedia*) of the Jews as related in the histories of Flavius Josephus (c.37–c.101 C.E.). Tragedy's new valence thus coincides exactly with the change in the human condition brought about by the birth of Christ, and to commemorate this event it is applied to the failed revolt of 66–73 C.E., construed as a punishment for the Jews' rejection of the New Testament.

Similarly, in the sermons of Peter Chrysologus (c.400–c.450), archbishop of Ravenna, the word "tragedy" is twice invoked to describe the martyrdom of John the Baptist in the early days of Jesus' ministry. In one sermon, he manages to allude to tragedy's classical origins while at the same time implying that it had been re-invented as a Jewish genre by the impieties of Herod's birthday feast, where Salome "had sung a wicked tragedy" and requested the head of the prophet as a prize for her performance.[67] In another sermon, his description of the scene is reminiscent of the messenger's speech in the *Bacchae*.

> The house turns into an arena, the table transfers to the auditorium; diners become spectators, the dinner-party is transformed through madness; the food becomes slaughter, wine turns into blood, the birthday celebration comes to an end; in birth,

---

64 Hugh of Fouilloy, *De anima, PL* 177 :78: "qui deliciis hujus saeculi, et pompis et theatralibus voluptatibus delectantur, tragoediis et comoediis dissoluti."

65 In addition to the specific cases discussed below, these include: *PL* 7:134,257 (Lactantius); 14:18,63 (Ambrose); 18:355 (Symmachus); 20:1046 (Bachiarius); 25:262 (Jerome); 49:510 and 50:160 (John Cassian); 50:599 (Sixtus III); 52:549,609, 650 (Chrysologus); 63:536 (Trifolius); 71:716 (Gregory of Tours); 74:25,31,69 (Theodoretus of Cyr); 80:158 (Paulus Emeritanus); 110:782,836 (Rabanus Maurus); 130:964, 969,971 (Isidorus Mercator); 148:791 (Gregory VII).

66 Fréculf, *Historiae, PL* 106:989, 994 ,996,999,1001,1032,1045,1131.

67 Peter Chrysologus, *De D. Joanne Baptista et Herode* (Sermon 173), *PL* 52:653: "tragoediam nefandam caneret."

death is on display; a party is transformed into murder, the musical instruments ring out a worldly tragedy.[68]

Three centuries later, Paschasius Radbertus (c. 790–860), abbot of Corbie, also represented "this tragedy about John" (*haec tragoedia de Joanne*) as the aboriginal instance of Jewish violence against Christianity. "More profane even than Herod and Herodias was she, the one who danced, who as a prize for her tragedy demanded, not a goat, but the head of a prophet."[69] For him, too, the household of the incestuous and adulterous King Herod bears a family resemblance to that of Oedipus or Agamemnon.

Citing a parallel incident in the Old Testament, Rupert of Deutz (*c.* 1075–1129) drew the following lessons from the story of Joseph's rejection of Potiphar's wife and her vengefully false accusation of rape in Genesis 39:1–20.

> Such is the literal sense. In other respects, it is symbolic of the Lord, the Savior; the tragedy of the woman is the madness of the Synagogue. For Our Lord, when taken by his Jewish brothers, had suffered derision and hatred through the night; afterward, he was taken from the grove and brought before the governor, when he was accused by false witnesses. One thus ought to learn what the Synagoge desired in Christ, and why, in grief of not having attained it, she handed Christ over to the governor.[70]

As in the analyses of Salome's fatal performance, the traditional themes of classical tragedy – influentially characterized by Jerome as *mulierum maledicta* – are shown to be played out in the malevolent workings of Synagoga, portrayed as a lustful Jewess who seduces Ecclesia's susceptible clergy.[71] So in the later twelfth-century *vita* of St. Reginard of Liège, the healing unguent flowing from the body of the holy man is offhandedly contrasted with the

---

68 *De decollatione D. Joannis Baptistae* (Sermon 127), *PL* 52:552. "In arenam vertitur domus, mensa migrat in caveam; fiunt de pransoribus spectatores, furore mutatur convivium; fit cibus caedes, vinum transit in sanguinem, finis apponitur natali; in ortu exhibetur occasus, convivium in homicidium commutatur, organa tragoediam personant saecularem."

69 Paschasius Radbertus, *Expositio in Matthaeo. Libri XII, PL* 120:515. "Quanto sceleratior in facto Herodes et Herodiadis, necnon et puella quae saltavit, et in pretium tragoediae suae, non hircum, sed caput postulat prophetae." I have also consulted Paulus (ed.) 1984, II: 734 (VII:1399–1400).

70 Rupert of Deutz, *Commentariorum in Genesim* VIII.33, *PL* 167: 520. "Haec de sensu litterali. Ceterum in typum Domini salvatoris illa feminae tragoedia synagogae vesania est. ... Nam Dominus noster, cum a Iudaeis fratribus suis comprehens et tota nocte irrisiones et opprobria passus fuisset, subsecuta luce ante praesidum adductus et cum testibus falsis accusatus est. Discendum igitur quid in Christo synagoga concupierit, quid non adeptem se esse dolens Christum praesidi suo tradiderit." I have also consulted the edition of Haacke (ed.), I: 521.

71 Rupert repeats this allegorical reading verbatim in his treatise *De Sancta Trinitate, PL* 167:519.

seductive perfumes of the Queen of Sheba, which caused tragedy rather than miracles.[72]

Rupert's modern biographer, John Van Engen, has called him "the most prolific of all twelfth-century writers,"[73] and he was certainly prolific in his allusions to the Jews' tragic history. In his treatise "On the Workings of the Holy Spirit," their role in Jesus' crucifixion is described as an act of *hubris* punished by the destruction of the Temple, foretold by the Jews' own prophets, standing in for the oracles of Greek tragedy.[74] According to Rupert, the warning in Isaiah 2:22–3:3 ("For behold, the Lord, the Lord of hosts, is taking away from Jerusalem and from Judah stay and staff") foreshadows the account of Josephus, which he reads as "the tragedy of your [the Jews'] calamity,"[75] a "miserable tragedy" also inscribed in the prophecies of Jeremiah.[76] Indeed, Josephus appears throughout Rupert's writings as a kind of tragic poet. His history is "that tragedy" which was "witnessed by Josephus",[77] "the tragedy documented by Josephus,"[78] "the tragedy witnessed in the writing by Josephus,"[79] "the tragedy witnessed in the description by Josephus,"[80] "the marvelous and yet miserable tragedy written out fully by Josephus in seven volumes,"[81] supreme among "the histories or tragedies of nations."[82] For "we read Josephus reporting the miserable tragedy of that downfall, which because of its magnitude is always renewed in readings of it,"[83] and is thus more instructive and immediate than the earlier "tragedy of the kings of Israel, which is transmitted in a few words."[84] Rupert also sees the tragedy of the Jews' unbelief mirrored in the tragedies of the early Church and in the Investiture Controversy of his own day, as well as in the necessity for his own real and rhetorical disputations with the Jews of

---

72 *PL* 205:133.
73 Van Engen 1983, 3.
74 Rupert of Deutz, *De operibus Spiritus Sancti, PL* 167: 1719.
75 *in Isaiam, PL* 167:1286: "[l]egent qui volent vestrae calamitatis tragoediam."
76 *in Jeremiam, PL* 167:1417: "et illam legenti miserabilem tragoediam satis claret."
77 *Liber Genesis, PL* 168:355: "quam verum sit testis est Josephus, qui tragoediam illam describens."
78 *De operibus Spiritus Sancti, PL* 167:1718: "tragoediam a Josepho conscriptam."
79 *Commentaria in duodecim prophetas minores, PL* 168:152: "tragoedia testatur Josepho scribente."
80 *Commentaria, PL* 168:175: "tragoedia Josepho describente testatur."
81 *Commentaria, PL* 168:205: "mirabilem atque miserabilem tragoediam plenius scribit Josephus septem voluminibus."
82 *Commentaria, PL* 168:510: "quantum vel quale in nulla gente vel natione habuisse legitur, si cunctas gentium historias sive tragoedias recenseamus. Legamus Josephum ..."
83 *Commentaria, PL* 169:954. "Legamus Josephum miserabilem excidii illius tragoediam referentem, quae pro sua magnitudine legentibus semper nova est."
84 *Commentaria, PL* 168:510: "tragoedia regum Israel brevibus verbis insinuatur."

the Rhineland.[85] Events prefigured in the Old Testament – tantamount to the world's "grimmest and bloodiest tragedies"[86] – are not only fulfilled in the New but continue to be re-enacted in perpetuity. As Van Engen has argued, Rupert's account of humanity's salvation was the most ambitious since Augustine's *City of God* and "perhaps the first to carry the story down to the present age."[87] Hence the Whore of Babylon, costumed as a wicked queen in Revelation 17:4–5, is a graphic reminder that "books are full, indeed even now the theatres of all the countries of the world are glutted, with the tragedies of kings."[88]

No other medieval author so firmly equates tragedy with the role of the Jews in history, yet the renewed tensions of the eleventh and twelfth centuries – pivotal in "the formation of a persecuting society," according to historian R.I. Moore – certainly contributed to the more frequent use of the term in this context.[89] Gerhoh of Reichersberg (1093–1169) quotes Fréculf's *luctuosa tragoedia* in his commentary on Moses,[90] and so does John of Salisbury (c.1115–1176) in his *Policraticus* (c.1115–1176).[91] Peter the Venerable (1092–1156), abbot of Cluny, denounces Jewish learning as "profound stupidity" and declares the study of the Talmud to be less edifying even than that of tragedies and comedies.[92]

Some twelfth-century authors, however, preferred to equate tragedy with the Fall of Man and the persistence of Original Sin. In his commentary on the Song of Songs, Abbot Wolberus of St. Pantaleon (near Cologne) contrasted this "new song" – *i.e.* the godly relationship between Christ and the nuns to whom he addressed this work – with the "old song" (*vetus canticum*) of "the old man Adam" (*vetus homo Adam*) whose pride had destined subsequent generations to sing "the woeful tragedy of this song."[93] Another abbot, Henry of Marcy, echoes these sentiments when alluding to that primeval story: "Not only is it fit to be read, it should be imprinted on the hearts of men, a tragedy bewailed in the singing of it."[94]

---

85 *Commentarius in Job*, *PL* 169:1062: "tragoedias illorum temporum." Rupert wrote a formal dialogue between a hypothetical Christian and a Jew, the *Anulus*, in 1126. See Van Engen 1983, 241–248.

86 *Commentaria*, *PL* 168:565. "Quis illas legens historias, imo tragedias truces et sanguineas non exhorrescat atque admiretur quomodo mundus subsistat?"

87 Van Engen 1983, 87–88, 94.

88 Rupert of Deutz, *Commentarius in Job*, *PL* 169:1132. "Pleni sunt libri, imo satiata jam sunt theatra orbis terrarum regum tragoediis." Cf. 169: 1447.

89 Moore 1987.

90 Gerhoh, *Expositio in canticum Moysis II* (Deuteronomy 32:24–25), *PL* 194:1057.

91 John of Salisbury, *Policraticus* II. 5, *PL* 199:421.

92 Peter of Cluny, *Adversus Judaeos*, *PL* 189:606.

93 Wolberus of St. Pantaleon, *PL* 198: 1273: "hujus cantici flebilem tragoediam."

94 Henry of Marcy, *De peregrinante civitate Dei*, *PL* 204:361. "Non solum legitur, sed et ut cordibus humanis utilius imprimatur, etiam cantando tragoedia eadem deploratur."

Tragedy could also be applied to lapses from orthodoxy within the Church, or even represented as the cause of such lapses. In recounting the miracles of St. Mansuetus (d. 375), the first bishop of Toul, Adso of Montier-in-Der (930–992) tells how a child was drowned in the course of a festival that seems to have included the performance of plays (*ludi*), so that the lamenting parents are said to have "embodied the tragedies of the women" that had been enacted there. The implication is that those who fall back into pagan ways are destined to live out the tragedies they ape.[95] Rabanus Maurus later implies something similar when describing the dangerous effects of over-indulgence in the enjoyment of secular poetry.[96] And in the annals of Lambert of Hersfeld (c.1024–c.1088), the impious deeds of those resistant to Gregory VII's reforms bring to mind the hypocrisy of actors, so that he makes an explicit analogy to the world as a stage and to the state of the Church as a "woeful tragedy" or "just like a tragedy."[97] These sentiments are echoed by the reformers Peter Damian and Gerhoh of Reichersberg,[98] as well as by the opposing imperial party.[99]

According to Manegold of Lautenbach (d. c.1103), doctrinal errors are actually linked to indulgence in illicit activities, including the antics of jongleurs and the performance of lyric poetry, comedy, satire, and tragedy.[100] The equations of heresy with tragedy in a more metaphorical sense can be traced back to the letters of Pope Leo I (r. 440–461), who railed against "the whole Manichean tragedy" threatening the unity of the Roman Church and who dubbed the thwarting of his apostolic authority "this woeful tragedy."[101] The word is used in similar contexts by popes Gelasius I (r. 492–496) and Leo II (r. 682–683).[102] In the canons of the Council of Carthage (255–56), tragedy refers to the unjust deposition of a bishop from his see,[103] and the Carolingian archbishop Hincmar of Reims (806–882) uses it three times to refer to abuses of episcopal authority.[104] In the twelfth century, by contrast,

---

95   Adso of Montier-in-Der, *Vita S. Mansueti PL* 137:625: "tragediae personant mulierum."
96   Rabanus Maurus, *PL* 111: 419,485,585,666–9.
97   Lambert of Hersfeld, *PL* 146:1107,1200–1 ("lugubrem tragediam"), 1211 ("consimilem tragediam").
98   Peter Damian, *PL* 144: 241,254; Gerhoh, *Syntagma, PL* 194: 1459.
99   See the open letter of Emperor Henry V to Abbot Hugh and the monks of Cluny, *PL* 159:936: "Sed jam tempus est tam longae miseriarum nostrarum tragoediae finem imponere."
100 Manegold of Lautenbach, *Contra Wolfelmum, PL* 155:157.
101 Leo I, *PL* 55:876,878: "totam Manichaicam tragoediam; 55:1144: "lugubrem hanc tragoediam."
102 Gelasius I, *PL* 59:61,80,90; Leo II in *PL* 96:393.
103 Council of Carthage, *PL* 3:1027.
104 Hincmar of Reims, *PL* 126:428,455,498; cf. Flodoard of Reims, quoting Hincmar, *PL* 135: 208.

a spirited defense of Peter Abelard's theology by Berengarius Scholasticus likens Bernard of Clairvaux's accusations of heresy to a *tragoedia*, but one so frivolous that it should be dismissed as a joke.[105] One man's heresy is another's orthodoxy: perhaps this is why Isidore of Seville's only metaphorical use of the term describes any schism within the Church.[106]

Cassiodorus also calls doctrinal divisions "tragedies" on two occasions,[107] just as in three letters written on behalf of Theodoric he calls crimes committed within a kin group "tragedies," underscoring the fact that schism is a crisis of kinship within the Christian community.[108] This is nicely illustrated in the ninth-century chronicle of Anastasius the Librarian, which invokes the term seven times when speaking of rifts within the early Church.[109] Anastasius also repeats an interesting anecdote about St. Demetrius of Thessalonica, who is said to have had a vision that he was standing in the city's theatre with a great crowd of his friends – and while he was wondering how he had come to be seated there, "he saw that a tragedian was standing in the logia where plays were performed, who said to him: 'Wait, because I have to lament for you and for your daughter.'" During the ensuing exchange, the proconsul comes to realize that the tragedian is referring to the city as his "daughter," and "he realized that the tragedy had no good significance." [110] Sure enough, a barbarian invasion devastated Thessalonica a few days later, realizing the tragedian's warning of violence against the fledgling Christian family.

IV. "Tragedy" as a synonym for a story of dramatic reversal or as an historiographical style: 71 (18%).[111] During the Middle Ages, as in our own day,

---

105 Berengarius Scholasticus, *PL* 178: 1863

106 Isidore of Seville, *De viris illustribus, PL* 83:1085.

107 Cassiodorus, *PL* 68:941,1104.

108 *PL* 69:521: "quod totius tragoediam reatus exsuperet." *Cf. PL* 69:451,600.

109 Anastasius the Librarian, *Historia de vitis pontificum Romanorum, PL* 128: 114,219,243,306, 328,398,665.

110 *Passio S. Demetrii martyris, PL* 129: 772. "[V]idit tragoedum stare in logio ubi fabulae recitantur, dicentem sibi: Exspecta, quia te et filiam tuam habeo lamentari. Qui dixit ei: Ne labores, ego enim neque filiam habeo, neque in me est lamentum. At ille: Vere et filiam habes, et multorum filiorum matrem; et oportet te illam lamentari. Tunc intellexit praesul quod civitatem diceret filiam ejus, et ait: Adjuro te per Deum ut non me nec illam lamenteris. Cumque tertio repetere vellet lamentum, et ab episcopo non sineretur, a somno excitus, intellexit tragoediam non bonam habere significationem."

111 In addition to the specific uses discussed below, these include: *PL* 4:354 (Cyprian of Carthage); 15:2015 (Ambrose); 22:1203 (Jerome); 63:38,96,263 (Ennodius); 68:1006,1042 (Liberatus of Carthage); 104:964 (Agobard of Lyons); 138:386 (Henry of Auxerre); 143:437 (Wibertus); 146:487,492,602 (Adam of Bremen); 153:1061 (Alexander of Canterbury); 173:1470 (Landulph the Younger); 182:149, 377 (Bernard of Clairvaux); 194:1459 (Gerhoh of Reichersberg); 195:565 (Aelred of

"tragedy" could be used to designate a fall from a position of prominence or a drastic turn of events. And occasionally, then as now, such uses seem banal or excessive. Eleanor of Aquitaine describes the captivity of her son, Richard the Lionheart, as a tragedy in a letter to Pope Celestinus III in 1192. But given that Richard was the royal hostage of the Duke of Austria and enjoying the hospitality of Schloss Dürnstein, this is tragedy as melodrama.[112] Rupert of Deutz – who usually reserved the word "tragedy" for the historical condition of the Jews, as we have seen – once described history itself as an endless series of slaughter perpetrated by the devil "for sport" (pro ludo). Yet he declared that it was not his duty, as a theologian, "to recite the horrible and diabolical tragedies of the wars of the pagans. Who wishes, or who has the leisure, there are histories galore: let him read them."[113]

And in fact, the employment of "tragedy" as a powerful lens through which to view and interpret certain critical moments in the past tends to be the province of historians, and most historians of this era were sparing and careful in their invocation of it. Most often, an event or series of events is associated with tragedy only when it results in the dissolution – the public dissolution – of a community through civil unrest. For example, Paul the Deacon (c.720–799) refers on four occasions to the unfolding of internecine warfare among the Lombards as the "acts of a tragedy" (actae tragoediae) or "the scene of a tragedy" (tragoediae scoenam);[114] and Guibert of Nogent calls the bishop of Laon's assassination at the hands of his own congregation in 1115 a tragoedia.[115] Very cannily, William of Malmesbury (d. c.1143) applies the term to the untimely death of the heir to the English throne in the wreck of the White Ship on 25 November 1125 – not merely because the loss of a young life is tragic, but because in this case it precipitated a crisis of succession and the terrible civil wars he was chronicling. His usage is doubly apt, in fact, since "tragedy" here refers not only to the event itself but to the story of it, told by the sole member of the ship's crew to have "lived to portray the whole proceeding of the tragedy."[116]

Rievaulx); 204:943 (Laurentius de Leodio); 204:1169 (Petrus Bernardus); 212:1056 (Hélinand of Froidmont).

112 Eleanor of Aquitaine (via Peter of Blois?), PL 206:1262.

113 Rupert of Deutz, De victoria verbi Dei, PL 169:1396. "Millia centena, et plus quam millia centena dietim bello caesa, nimirum diabolo pro ludo habentur. Non est praesentis propositi horribiles et diabolicas recitare gentilium bellorum tragoedias. Qui vult, vel cui vacat, sunt historiae multiplices, legat illas."

114 Paul the Deacon, De gestis Langobardorum, PL 95:498,501,547,562 .

115 Guibert of Nogent, De vita sua, PL 156:907, 931; cf. PL 162:1169.

116 William of Malmesbury, Gesta regum Anglorum, PL 179:1372: "mane totius tragoediae actum expressit." For other uses, see 179:1432,1446. For a rather different reading, see Kelly 1993, 91–92.

Clearly, these historians had absorbed the lessons they learned in grammar school from commentaries like those of Rabanus and Sedulius. However little they actually knew about Athenian tragedy, they understood that it is was supposed to come about through some breach of family bonds or some violation of the social contract, and that its mimetic power should lie in its skillful *reporting* of events. Thus the historian Gildas uses the word only once in his dark account of "The Ruin of Britain," when British emissaries bring such dreadful news of the ravages wrought by Picts and Scots that Rome's senators are "moved by the story of such a tragedy."[117] At the same time, the capacity of the historian (like the tragic messenger) to elicit pity or horror through the skillful practice of his craft was discomfiting to some medieval chroniclers. Liutprand, bishop of Cremona (c.922–972), interrupts a particularly fraught segment of his narrative to complain that "the quality of this present time requires of me something more tragedic than historiographic." According to him, the historian's mandate requires him not to be swept along in the current of events. If God's plan remains inscrutable, it is better not to write at all.[118] Cosmas of Prague (c.1045–1125) is so anxious to avoid histrionics in his history that he refuses to describe certain events taking place in Poland and Hungary, even though "we have ample material for writing, lest it seem as though we are performing tragedy in a goatsong."[119] Sigibert of Gembloux (c.1030–1112) also refrains from enumerating the "many very unfortunate things that happened" to his monastery after the death of a beloved abbot, "because it is enough that such tragedy is sung in the theatre of the world": neither the cloister nor the chronicle is an appropriate venue for it.[120]

One of the greatest of medieval historians, Orderic Vitalis (1075–c.1142), bases his very claim to authority on the avoidance of *pathos* and unseemly exhibitionism, equating tragedy with a style detrimental to rigorous historical inquiry. Writing about the death of William the Conqueror,

---

117 Gildas, *De excidio Britanniæ, PL* 69: 340: "commoti tantae historia tragoediae."
118 Liutprand of Cremona, *Antapodosis, PL* 136: 893. "Temporis instantis qualitas tragoedum me potius quam historiagrophum quaerere, nisi pararet Dominus in conspectu [corrected ; text has "conspectus"] meo mensam adversus eos qui tribulant me. Explicare enim non possum, quot peregre profectus incommoditatibus quatiar, juvatque hominem exteriorem potius lugere quam scribere."
119 Cosmas of Prague, *Chronicon Bohemorum, PL* 168:211. "Caeteri vero qui superstites fuerunt ex gente illa, delituerunt fuga; alii in Poloniam, alii fugientes in Pannoniam, de quorum excidio simul et discidio licet amplam habeamus ad scribendum materiam, sed ne videamur velut hircino cantu explicuisse tragediam, redeamus unde paulo digressi sumus, ad chronicam."
120 Sigibert of Gembloux, *Miraculi S. Wicberti, PL* 160:689. "[M]ultae et magnae adversitates occurrerunt nobis. ... Quam tragediam quia satis cantata est in mundi theatro hic referre supersedeo, cum proprium locum desideret ejus plena relatio."

he proclaims: "Behold, I have accurately investigated and truly explained what orderly arrangement of God was predisclosed in the fall of the Duke. I do not sell invented tragedy nor do I value the loud guffaws the ground-lings give to comedy's chatter, rather, I truthfully report manifold events for learned readers."[121] His near contemporary, Gerhoh of Reichersberg, also advocated the expository over the dramatic when "writing history in the plain style," the better to ensure the author's clarity and the listener-read-er's understanding.[122] Yet even these medieval historians' vocal distrust of emotive language and poetic hyperbole calls to mind the methodology of Thucydides, who noisily rejected the lies of poets and mythmakers while artfully deploying the structure and dialogue of tragedy in his analysis of the Peloponnesian War.

V. Tragedy as a vehicle for commenting on contemporary performance prac-tices and genres: 25 (6%). We have already seen that tragedy, in its several meanings, functioned as a comparative crux for medieval intellectuals seek-ing to connect or contrast their world(s) with that of the pre-Christian past. Even though the theatre of the Middle Ages was very different from that of classical Athens, the Hellenistic world, or imperial Rome, references to the enactment of tragedy and its imagined effects on audiences are regularly introduced into writings that deal with contemporary performance practices.

Jerome provides an early instance in his commentary on Ezekiel 33:31–32: "And they come to you as people come, and they sit before you as my people, and they hear what you say but they will not do it. ... And lo, you are to them like one who sings love songs with a beautiful voice and plays well on an instrument, for they hear what you say, but they will not do it."[123] Somewhat predictably, he extends the simile "to those who are entertained by the songs of the theatre" and who, "whether they hear tragedies or com-edies," take pleasure in this but are not moved to action. More surprisingly, he goes on to say that such men are also like the charismatic preachers of

---

121 Orderic Vitalis, *Historia ecclesiastica* , PL 188:554 (*cf.* 188:576). "Ecce subtiliter investigavi et veraciter enucleavi quae in lapsu ducis praeostendit dispositio Dei. Non fictilem tragoediam venundo, non loquaci comoedia cachinnantibus parasitis faveo, sed studiosis lectoribus varios eventus veraciter intimo." See also Kelly 1993, 90–91.

122 Gerhoh of Reichersberg, *Commentarius aureus in Psalmos et cantica ferialia, PL* 193: 631–632: "Genus exagematicum convenit historiographis currens plano stylo per res gestas, quarum penes auctorem esse debet indubitata veritas, et penes audi-torem sive lectorem facilis credulitas."

123 Here, and below, I quote from the Revised Standard Version of the Bible. The key clause in the Vulgate is: "est eis quasi carmen musicum quod suavi dulcique sono canitur et audient verba tua et non facient ea."

whom people say, "'Let's go hear that one or that one!'" and whose audiences "are carried away with applause, and cry out, and throw up their hands,
and who pay no heed to good works."[124] This does not reflect badly on tragedy alone, however; the comparison implicates all vain performers and all
frivolous audiences. By contrast, Cassiodorus asks, "Is there anything to be
heard in the staging of tragedies such as there is to perceive in health-giving
psalmodies in the choirs of the Church?"[125] Although we have seen that Cassiodorus usually spoke of tragedy approvingly or metaphorically, here he
weighs secular theatricals against sacred song to the detriment of the former.

In a similar vein, writing at a time that coincides with the Carolingian
reform of the liturgy, Agobard of Lyons (c.779–840) quotes Jerome's commentary on Paul's Letter to the Ephesians 5:19, where Paul advocates "singing
and performing psalms in your hearts to God." He then launches into a rant.

> The young men should listen to these things, those should listen for whom the chant-
> ing of the psalms in the Church is a duty: God ought to be hymned not with the
> voice, but the heart. For the gullet and the throat must not be anointed with sweet
> appliances in the manner of the tragedians, so that theatrical measures and songs are
> heard in the Church, but in fear, in workmanship, in the wisdom of the Scriptures.[126]

Cassiodorus had found the pleasures of the liturgy more wholesome than
those of the theatre; by Agobard's time, three centuries later, the histrionics
of some young singers are perceived to have collapsed any distinction. Three
centuries later still, the concordance of canon law attributed to Gratian is
resigned to this; it quotes Agobard's remarks in full, but only to footnote a
much more practical ruling that deacons serving at Mass should be excused
from singing and psalmody "lest, while concentrating on modulating their
voices, they neglect the ministry of the altar."[127] Rather than attempting to
eradicate operatics, the canonist advocates a division of labor in which some
clerics concentrate on their music, others on the consecration of the Eucharist.

---

124 Jerome, *PL* 25:322. "Istiusmodi mihi videntur eorum similes, qui theatralibus ludun-
    tur carminibus: et vel tragoedos audiunt, vel comoedos, et ibi cum voluptate palpan-
    tur. …Tales sunt usque hodie multi in Ecclesiis, qui aiunt: Venite audiamus illum et
    illum, mira eloquentia praedicationis suae verba volventem: plaususque commov-
    ent, et vociferantur, et jactant manus, et quae operibus neglexerant."
125 Cassiodorus, *Expositio in Psalterium, PL* 70:289: "Nunquid tale est scenicas audire
    tragoedias, quale est in choris Ecclesiae salutiferas cognoscere psalmodias? "
126 Agobard of Lyons, *Liber de correctione antiphonarii, PL* 104:334 (*cf.* 26 :528).
    "Audiant haec adolescentuli, audiant hi quibus psallendi in Ecclesia officium est,
    Deo non voce, sed corde cantandum; nec in tragoedorum modum guttur et fauces
    dulci medicamine colliniendae sunt, ut in Ecclesia theatrales moduli audiantur et
    cantica; sed in timore, in opere, in scientia Scripturarum."
127 Gratian, *Concordia discordantia canonum* (Distinctio XCII), *PL* 187:429. "Ab of-
    ficio autem cantandi et psallendi diaconi inveniuntur exemti, ne, dum vocis modula-
    tioni student, altaris ministeria negligant."

In the eleventh-century musical handbook by Aribo Scholasticus, awareness of similarities between liturgical and theatrical performance is also expressed matter-of-factly. Harmonious (elevated) modes are "like those who
process in a tragedy" while inharmonious (base) modes are like "those who
buzz in a comedy."[128] Sicard of Cremona (d. 1215), too, is comfortable with
the invocation of tragedy in a Christian context. Expatiating "On the organization and casting of ecclesiastical characters," he links the liturgical roles
played by Christian clergy with those of their ancient Hebrew and Roman
counterparts, among whom there were "comedians, tragedians, historians,"
just as there are in the Church.[129]

Both strains of comparison, then, the favorable and the critical, run
through the references to tragedy as a mode of performance and a model
for liturgy. And these remarks are colored not only by the acknowledged
similarities – or desired distinctions – between the classical past and the
Christian present, but by changing attitudes toward tragedy's reception in
more worldly contexts. In the ninth century, Paschasius Radbertus (whose
commentary on the story of Herod and Salome we have already noted) chided those who preferred "the inanities of the tragedians and the fictions of
poets" to the study of divine eloquence.[130] However, the Carolingian revival
of classical learning in which he participated resulted in the increased dissemination of information about these texts, as well as their revival. By the
tenth century, the hagiographer of the Blessed Bruno – duke of Lotharingia,
archbishop of Cologne, and brother of Emperor Otto the Great – can invoke a princely court enlivened by staged readings of favourite plays whose
subject-matter and dubious pasts matter little compared to the delights of
their performance – though he is anxious to distance Bruno from such do-
ings, portraying him as only reading the scripts that others watch on stage,
and doing so not for entertainment, but to improve his grasp of style.[131] This
scenario helps to explain the achievement of one youthful participant in such
revels, the future canoness Hrotsvit of Gandersheim (935–1001/2), whose

---

128 Aribo Scholasticus, *PL* 150:1315. "Concordant discordantque autenti et plagales
   sicut divites et pauperes: quia licet hi in alto hi in humili degant loco, quamvis isti
   ambullentur [sic] in tragoedia, illi mussitent in comoedia."
129 Sicard of Cremona, *Summa de officiis ecclesiasticis (De institutione et habitu personarum eccclesiasticarum)*, *PL* 213:57: "comoedi, tragoedi, historiographi."
130 Paschasius Radbertus, *PL* 120:183. "Unde miror satis quid divina eloquia quorum-
   dam mores offenderunt, quod non velint mystica Dei sacramenta ea diligentia per-
   scrutari, qua tragoediarum naenias et poetarum figmenta sudantes cupiunt investig-
   are labore, et si per theatralia mimorum plausus hominum excitare."
131 Ruotger of Cologne, *Vita Brunonis, PL* 134: 946–947. "Scurrilia et mimica, quae in
   comoediis et tragoediis a personis variis edita quidam concrepantes risu se infinito
   concutiunt, ipse semper serio lectitabat: materiam pro minimo, auctoritatem in verborum compositionibus pro maximo reputabat."

Terence-inspired comedies are among the first surviving examples of a popular medieval genre.[132]

Bruno's court was not content to read tragedies and comedies. They wanted to make ancient dramas their own, they wanted to experience feigned mirth and mock sorrow. And part of what fed medieval intellectuals' approval or disapproval of tragedy as a *contemporary* practice was precisely its capacity to voice multiple perspectives and to provide mimetic access to emotions. As Bede had explained it, poetry comes in three forms: active "which the Greeks called dramatic," imitative, and narrative. Narrative features the poet speaking alone, as in most of Virgil's *Georgics* or, "among us," in the books of Proverbs and Ecclesiastes. Imitative poetry includes other characters, as in the *Iliad* and *Odyssey* of Homer, the *Aeneid*, and the book of Job. But in dramatic poetry, Bede says, the characters confront us directly, as in the Song of Songs.[133]

In the twelfth-century, however, Gerhoh of Reichersberg would borrow Bede's typology to express anxiety about the similarities between the drama of Scripture and the poetics of "secular authors in comedies or tragedies," for whom "this type of speech is more useful for conveying either sorrow, or joy, or other conditions of the soul when it is moved by emotion." Echoing, perhaps consciously, the sentiments of Cassiodorus, he celebrates the affective impact of psalmody's stichomythia, whether said or sung, yet strongly insists that its emotional and aesthetic impact must always be greater than that aroused by pagan or secular drama, whose emotional displays are fake.[134] He does not condemn the strong feelings elicited by the beauty of liturgical performance, but he wants them to remain uncorrupted by the self-important, worldly posturing of those condemned by Agobard. We hear strains of Augustine here, too, as we do in Gerhoh's comment on the same Psalm 39 [40]

---

132 Symes 2003.

133 Bede, *De arte metrica*, *PL* 90:174. "[P]oematum genera sunt tria; aut enim activum vel imitativum est, quod Graeci dramaticon vel micticon appellant; aut enarrativum, quod Graeci exegematicon vel apangelticon nuncupant; aut commune vel mixtum, quod Graeci coenon vel micton vocant. ... Exegematicon est, vel enarrativum, in quo poeta ipse loquitur sine ullius interpositione personae, ut se habent tres libri Georgici toti, et prima pars quarti; item Lucretii carmina, et his similia. Quo genere apud nos scriptae sunt Parabolae Salomonis et Ecclesiastes, quae in sua lingua, sicut et Psalterium, metro constat esse conscripta. Coenon est, vel micton, in quo poeta ipse loquitur, et personae loquentes introducuntur, ut sunt scripta et Ilias et Odyssia Homeri, et Aeneidos Virgilii; et apud nos historia beati Job, quamvis haec in sua lingua non tota poetico, sed partim rhetorico, partim sit metrico vel rithmico scripta sermone."

134 Gerhoh of Reichersberg, *Commentarius aureus*, *PL* 193: 631–633: "Genus dramaticum variis personis contextum convenit carminibus nuptialibus, ut sunt Cantica canticorum. Hoc etiam in comoediis, vel tragoediis agendis observatum est a saecularibus auctoribus; quia hoc genus loquendi magis commodum videbatur vel tristitiae, vel laetitiae, vel alterius qualitatis animi movendis affectionibus."

that had inspired Cassiodorus, when he glosses the injunction not to stray after "false gods" as a warning against "playthings, or theatrical or staged shows," whether "they simulate weddings and youthful love-affairs, as in the comedies, or bitter histories, as in the tragedies."[135]

Here and elsewhere in contemporary writings, it is clear that the living liturgy of the present is not being compared to the dead drama of the past, but to the plays read, taught, and performed in every cathedral and monastery school. (Gerhoh even names some of the eponymous characters familiar from the plays of Terence and their many contemporary spin-offs: Davos and Phormio, Thaïs, Thraso.[136]) Some of these new plays were supplied by the statesman Peter of Blois (c. 1153–c.1203) and his brother William, a prominent abbot whose surviving comedy, *Alda*, was remembered admiringly in one of Peter's letters, alongside a lost "tragedy about Flaura and Marcus" and among sermons and theological tracts.[137] Peter himself was chided for wasting his time "in writing comedies and tragedies" in a letter from John of Salisbury,[138] pastimes that a letter of Peter the Venerable also testifies to being particularly attractive to young monks, who loved reading comedies aloud, weeping over tragedies, and other "stupidities" (*stultitiae*).[139] In John of Salisbury's own *Policraticus, sive de nugis curialium et de vestigiis philosophorum* ("On the Trumperies of Courtiers and the Tracks of the Philosophers"), composed around 1159 during his exile from the court of Henry II of England, "this worldly comedy, or tragedy" of the court itself becomes an index of his own era's artistic and moral impoverishment, a force that "effeminizes the virility of the mind" and leads to hysterical behavior. Tragedy's prevalence in the age of Nero is adduced as proof of this, along with Jerome's lapidary remark about Euripides' *mulierum maledicta*.[140]

---

135 *Commentarium in psalmos, PL* 193:1439: "id est ludicras, vel theatrales ac scenicas, in quorum spectaculis est quidem insania vera, sed ob hoc recte dicitur … quod, dum aut similantur nuptiae, amatoriaeque naeniae, ut in comoediis, aut amarae historiae, ut in tragoediis, personae larvatae". See Dox 2004, 87.

136 Symes 2003.

137 Peter of Blois, *PL* 207:291. "Nomen vestrum diuturniore memoria commendabile reddent tragoedia vestra de Flaura et Marco, versus de pulice et musca, comoedia vestra de alda, sermones vestri, et caetera theologicae facultatis opera, quae utinam diffusius essent ac celebrius publicata!"

138 John of Salisbury, *PL* 207:234: "in scribendis comoediis et tragoediis."

139 Peter the Venerable (Epistolae IX), *PL* 189:78. "Quid inani studio cum comoedis recitas, cum tragoedis deploras, cum metricis ludis, cum poetis fallis, cum philosophis falleris?"

140 John of Salisbury, *Policraticus* III.8, *PL* 199: 488: *"De mundana comoedia, vel tragoedia"*; and VIII.6–7 (*cf.* I.7) in *PL* 199:724 (*cf.* 405): "virilitatem mentis effiminat." See also *PL* 199: 730,755,787. Five further references to tragedy as an ancient dramatic genre are either noncommital or approving and another designates the *luctuosa tragoedia* of the Jews: see above. See also the discussion in Dox 2004, 87–92.

These denunciations of theatre were far from new, but they were provoked by a new Latin poetics, as well as by the new challenge to Latin hegemony posed by various European vernaculars, whose contributions to medieval performance practices were now being preserved in writing.[141]

Yet not all views were negative. In Peter of Blois' treatise on the sacrament of confession, tales of tragedy drawn from popular genres are actually used to illustrate the nature of sacramental contrition.

> Often in the tragedies and other songs of the poets, or in the ditties of the jongleurs, some man is described: wise, handsome, strong, lovable, pleasant in every respect. It is told, then, that through pressures or injuries, that same man is cruelly afflicted, as in the stories of Arthur and Gawain and Tristan, the fabulous tales the actors tell, which when heard shake to compassion the hearts of the audience, and even move them to tears. You, therefore, who are roused to sympathy through the telling of tales, if you should hear anything pious to be read about the Lord that should wrench tears from you, shouldn't you be able to write down something meaningful from this experience about the love of God? You who are compassionate with God are also compassionate for Arthur.[142]

Although Peter concludes that all vicarious suffering is empty if there is no true devotion to God and no true repentance, he does not condemn the pity inspired by the tragic heroes; on the contrary, he considers it a form of spiritual training. At the same time, he shows that the human being's limited capacity for mercy is only a pale reflection of the divine compassion inspired by the real spectacle of human fallibility. This opinion differs significantly from that featured in the *Speculum caritatis* of Aelred of Rievaulx (1109–1167), a dialogue in which the abbot's young monastic interlocutors warn against attaching any meaning whatsoever to either the passions aroused by the tragedies of Arthur or the equally passionate – but potentially hypocritical – shows of piety displayed in the performance of monastic prayer.[143]

Yet another perspective on contemporary tragedy and its relationship to affective piety is revealed in an anonymous Latin sermon preached in northeastern France during the thirteenth century.

---

141 Symes 2002 and 2003. See also Kelly 1993, 92–110.
142 Peter of Blois, *Liber de confessione sacramentali*, PL 207:1088–9. "Saepe in tragoediis et aliis carminibus poetarum, in joculatorum cantilenis describitur aliquis vir prudens, decorus, fortis, amabilis et per omnia gratiosus. Recitantur etiam pressurae vel injuriae eidem crudeliter irrogatae, sicut de Arturo et Gangano et Tristanno, fabulosa quaedam referunt histriones, quorum auditu concutiuntur ad compassionem audientium corda, et usque ad lacrymas compunguntur. Qui ergo de fabulae recitatione ad misericordiam commoveris, si de Domino aliquid pium legi audias, quod extorqueat tibi lacrymas, nunquid propter hoc de Dei dilectione potes dictare sententiam? Qui compateris Deo, compateris et Arturo."
143 Aelred of Rievaulx, *Speculum caritatis* II :17, PL 195:565–6. For a different view, see Kelly 1993, 85–6.

When in the voice of the jongleur, sitting in the public square, it is recited how those errant knights of old, Roland and Olivier and the rest, were killed in war, the crowd standing around is moved to pity, and oftentimes to tears. But when in the voice of the Church the glorious wars of Christ are daily commemorated in sacrifice – that is to say, how He defeated death by dying, and triumphed over the vainglory of the enemy – where are those who are moved to pity?[144]

Here, in a text that reaches beyond the purview of the *Patrologia Latina*, we catch a glimpse of what was at stake in a new era of vernacular literacy and cultural production, an era in which the forms of entertainment most accessible and attractive to the laity were deflecting attention away from those of the institutional Church, even though the Church was placing increased emphasis on evangelism and lay participation in the sacraments.[145]

It is in this context that the most striking and complete meditation on the relationship between Greek tragedy and Christian ritual was articulated, by the theologian Honorius Augustodunensis (1075/80–c. 1156).

It is known that those who recited tragedies in the theatres represented to the people, through their actions, the movements of men in fight. So our tragedian represents the battle of Christ to the Christian people in the theatre of the church through his actions, and teaches them to the victory of his redemption. Thus when the celebrant says, "Pray," he portrays Christ who underwent trials [*agonia*] on our behalf, as when he exhorted the apostles to pray. By the silence of the *Secreta* he signifies Christ as if he were a lamb without a voice, being led to the sacrifice. By stretching out his hands, he imitates the extension of Christ on the cross. By the singing of the preface, he expresses the cry of Christ, hanging on the cross (for he sang ten Psalms, that is from *Deus meus respice* up to *In manus tuas commendo spiritum meum*, and thus breathed his last). Through the secret words of the canon he implies the silence of the Sabbath. By the peace, he signifies the sharing and the peace bestowed after the resurrection of Christ and the sharing of joy. In concluding the sacrament, peace and communion are bestowed upon the people by the priest, because our opponent has been overthrown by our champion [*agonotheta*] in this contest; so peace is announced to the people by the judge, and one is invited to a feast. Then, by the *Ite missa est* they are told to return home in joy, they shout "thanks be to God," and come back home rejoicing.[146]

---

144 Paris, Bibliothèque nationale, fonds latin 14925, fol. 132 ; *cf.* lat. 3594, fol. 192. See Hauréau (ed.) 1891, 317.

145 Symes 2007, 154–74.

146 Honorius, *Gemma animae* I.83, *PL* 172: 570. "Sciendum quod hi qui tragoedias in theatris recitabant, actus pugnantium gestibus populo repraesentabant. Sic tragicus noster pugnam Christi populo Christiano in theatro Ecclesiae gestibus suis repraesentat, eique victoriam redemptionis suae inculcat. Itaque cum presbyter *Orate* dicit, Christum pro nobis in agonia positum exprimit, cum apostolos orare monuit. Per secretum silentium, significat Christum velut agnum sine voce ad victimam ductum. Per manuum expansionem, designat Christi in cruce extensionem. Per cantum praefationis, exprimit clamorem Christi in cruce pendentis. Decem namque psalmos, scilicet a *Deus meus respice* usque *In manus tuas commendo*

Honorius' discussion of tragedy, as Dox remarks, "stands out as unusual in its approach to explaining how the entire Mass works effectively as ritual."[147] Yet it was also influential, and was quoted approvingly in the decades just before the Fourth Lateran Council of 1215 made pastoral care and public outreach major goals for the Church.[148] Eventually, it became available to a wider public in vernacular translations and adaptations.[149]

Placing Honorius' reading of the Mass as tragedy alongside other references to tragedy as a synecdoche for both the ceremonies and the entertainments of the Middle Ages, we can see that it participates in a long and complex history of transmission, reception, and re-use. Indeed, this conceptualization can be fruitfully compared to the (roughly contemporary) Χριστὸς πάσχων, which also enacts a fascinating transubstantiation of Greek tragedy. Honorius strips the ancient genre down to its essential skeletal structure and then clothes it freshly with Christian garments, so that the body of a tragic hero can become the regenerative Body of Christ.[150] By contrast, the author of the tripartite Byzantine Passion play, who makes masterful use of the late antique *cento* technique, dismembers the still-living verses of Euripides – much as the maenads dismember the living body of Pentheus – in order to fashion a sacramental drama whose full impact would depend on the audience's shared familiarity with those verses in their original tragic context.[151]

Conclusion

"[I]t is clear that Honorius' idea of tragedy is more medieval than classical," opines Henry Ansgar Kelly in *The Ideas and Forms of Tragedy from Aristotle to the Middle Ages*, and he goes on to expose the theologian's ignorance

---

spiritum meum cantavit, et sic exspiravit. Per Canonis secretum innuit Sabbati silentium. Per pacem, et communicationem designat pacem datam post Christi resurrectionem et gaudii communicationem. Confecto sacramento, pax et communio populo a sacerdote datur, quia accusatore nostro ab agonotheta nostro per duellum prostrato, pax a judice populo denuntiatur, ad convivium invitatur. Deinde ad propria redire cum gaudio per *Ite missa est* imperatur. Qui gratias Deo jubilat et gaudens domum remeat."

147 Dox 2004, 75–6. See also Bestul 1996, 1–68.
148 Sicard of Cremona, *PL* 213 :145.
149 Dox 2004, 74–85. Symes 2007, 168–74.
150 See also the discussion of Honorius, and the question of Christian tragedy, in the paper by Domenico Pietropaolo.
151 The edition of Brambs 1885 makes it easy to trace the sources woven together from the plays. On the structure of the play, see Tuilier 1969, 20. On the larger cultural and theological context in which this transubstantiation became possible, see Puchner 1997.

of what tragedy *really* was – just as he criticizes Isidore of Seville's "conjectures" while praising "the more enlightened views of twelfth-century writers," as opposed to those "totally in the dark" at "low points" in the history of tragedy's reception. Although Kelly's avowed aim is "to see what authors of the past meant by the word as a literary or dramatic term," he measures these meanings against the yardstick of the *Poetics* or the later achievements of Dante, Chaucer, and Shakespeare.[152] My very different goal has been to argue that the tragedy of the Middle Ages is worthy of consideration in its own right. It should not be dismissed because it does not fulfill an impossible, anachronistic desire for direct access to the theatre of antiquity. And with the assistance of a tool only recently made available to scholars, it has actually been possible to prove that the medieval uses of tragedy are *not* confined to a "rather limited number of writers in the Middle Ages," as Kelly alleges. Many, if not most, of the principal authors considered representative by the editors of the *Patrologia Latina* have something to say about it, or with it. Moreover, the vast majority of these authors do *not* "consider it to refer to an obsolete genre," as Kelly claims, but regard it as useful for understanding their own ever-changing presents.

First and foremost, the Latin-speaking intellectuals active in the West between the second and twelfth centuries considered tragedy to be an important part of their cultural heritage and an object of intense curiosity (category I). If their curiosity was ill-informed, that was the result of historical accidents and processes that began long before the Middle Ages – as demonstrated in the first portion of this essay – and to which modern scholarship is still subject. It is a problem they inherited, not one that they caused. Secondarily, tragedy was spoken of as a dangerous pagan rite, but mainly by a few select critics whose perspectives made it symbolic of threats to their fledgling Church (category II). For a much larger and more diverse group of early and medieval Christians, tragedy had a specifically Christian meaning of its own, and was frequently used to describe a time of crisis within the history of human salvation, broadly or narrowly construed: the condition of the Jews, a heretical practice, a schism (category III). For another large and diverse group, tragedy was synonymous with a certain type of historical event, designating a breach of trust within a family or community, the tidings of civil strife, or a style of historical reportage shunned by some chroniclers as over-determined and manipulative (category IV). Finally, tragedy was part of a lively discourse surrounding modes of performance throughout the period, from the chanting of the Psalms and the celebration of the Mass to the pastimes of those who strove to recreate the tragedies of yore or to create new tragedies for the age.

---

152 Kelly 1993, xiii, 36, 111.

Whether any of these medieval tragedies were "accurate" attempts to re-vive "authentic" tragedy does not matter. What matters is the vital work that tragedy continued to accomplish beyond the theatre of Dionysus, in states unborn and accents yet unknown to the citizens of ancient Athens.

Bibliography

Augustine, *De sermone Domini in monte libri duo*, ed. Almut Mutzenbecher (1967), *Corpus Christianorum* Series Latina 35, Turnhout.

Barish, Jonas (1981), *The Antitheatrical Prejudice*, Berkeley and Los Angeles.

Bestul, Thomas (1996), *Texts of the Passion: Latin Devotional Literature and Medieval Society*, Philadelphia.

Bidez, Joseph / Franz Cumont (eds.) (1922), *Imp.Caesaris Flavii Claudii Iuliani epistulae, leges, poemata, fragmenta varia*, Paris.

Bowman, Alan K. / Greg Woolf (eds.) (1994), *Literacy and Power in the Ancient World*, Cambridge.

Brown, Peter G. (2002), "Actors and Actor-Managers at Rome in the Time of Plautus and Terence", in: Easterling / Hall (eds.), 225–37.

Boyle, A. J. (1997), *Tragic Seneca: An Essay in the Theatrical Tradition*, London and New York.

Clanchy, Michael T. (1993), *From Memory to Written Record: England 1066–1307*, 2nd edn., Oxford.

Christus patiens: Tragoedia christiana, quae inscribi solet Χριστὸς πάσχων *Gregorio Nazianzeno falso attributa*, ed. Johann Georg Brambs (1885), Leipzig.

Devreesse, Robert (1954), *Introduction à l'étude des manuscrits grecs*, Paris.

Dox, Donnalee (2004), *The Idea of the Theater in Latin Christian Thought: Augustine to the Fourteenth Century*, Ann Arbor.

Easterling, Patricia E. / Hall, Edith (eds.) (2002), *Greek and Roman Actors: Aspects of an Ancient Profession*, London and New York.

Erbse, Hartmut (1961), "Überlieferungsgeschichte der griechischen klassischen und hellenistischen Literatur", in: Herbert Hunger *et al.* (eds.), *Geschichte der Textüberlieferung der antiken und mittelalterlichen Literatur*, I: *Antikes und mittelalterliches Buch- und Schriftwesen. Überlieferungsgeschichte der antiken Literatur*, Zurich, 207–83.

Falkner, Thomas (2002), "Scholars versus Actors: Text and Performance in the Greek Scholia", Easterling / Hall (eds.), 342–61.

Fantuzzi, Marco / Hunter, Richard (2002), *Muse e modelli: La poesia ellenistica da Alessandro Magno ad Augusto*, Rome and Bari; rev. and trans. (2004) as *Tradition and Innovation in Hellenistic Poetry*, Cambridge.

Garland, Robert (2004), *Surviving Greek Tragedy*, London.

Gibbon, Edward (1776), *The Decline and Fall of the Roman Empire*, vol. 1, London.

Hall, Edith (2002), "The Singing Actors of Antiquity", in: Easterling / Hall (eds.), 3–38.

Hall, Edith / Wyles, Rosie (2008), *New Directions in Ancient Pantomime*, Oxford.

Halliwell, Stephen (2006), "Plato and Aristotle on the Denial of Tragedy", in: Andrew Laird (ed.), *Oxford Readings in Ancient Literary Criticism*, Oxford, 115–141.

Harlfinger, Dieter (ed.) (1980), *Griechische Kodikologie und Textüberlieferung*, Darmstadt.

Hauréau, Barthélemy (ed.) (1891), *Notices et extraits de quelques manuscrits latins de la Bibliothèque nationale*, vol. 3, Paris.

Havelock, Eric A. (1980), "The Oral Composition of Greek Drama", *Quaderni Urbanati di Cultura Classica* n.s. 6 [35], 61–113; repr. (1982) in: *The Literate Revolution in Greece and Its Cultural Consequences*, Princeton, 261–313.

Herington, John (1985), *Poetry into Drama: Early Tragedy and the Greek Poetic Tradition,* Berkeley and Los Angeles.

Kelly, Henry Ansgar (1993), *Ideas and Forms of Tragedy from Aristotle to the Middle Ages*, Cambridge.

Krueger, P. and T. Mommsen (eds.) (1990), *Theodosiani Libri XVI cum constitutionibus Sirmondinis* in: *Codex Theodosianus*, vol. 1, Hildesheim.

LaPiana, George (1912), *Le rappresentazioni sacre nella letteratura bizantina dalle origini al sec. IX, con rapporti al teatro sacro d'Occidente*, Grottaferrata.

—— (1936), "The Byzantine Theatre", *Speculum* 11, 171–211.

Lebek, W. D. (1996), "Moneymaking and the Roman Stage", in Slater (ed.) (1996), 29–48.

Lightfoot, Jane L. (2002), "Nothing to Do with the *Technītai* of Dionysius?", in Easterling / Hall (eds.), 209–224.

Mango, Cyril (1980, repr. 2005), *Byzantium: The Empire of the New Rome,* London.

Melia, Daniel F. (2005), "Orality and Aristotle's Aesthetics", in: Mark C. Amodio (ed.), *New Directions in Oral Theory*, Tempe, 91–124.

Moore, Robert I. (1987), *The Formation of a Persecuting Society: Power and Deviance in Western Europe, 950–1250*, Oxford.

Nagy, Gregory (1996a), *Homeric Questions*, Austin.

—— (1996b), *Poetry as Performance: Homer and Beyond*, Cambridge.

Page, Denys L. (1934), *Actors' Interpolations in Greek Tragedy, Studied with Special Reference to Euripides' Iphigeneia in Aulis*, Oxford.

Paschasius Radbertus, *Expositio in Matthaeo. Libri XII*, ed. Beda Paulus (1984) in *Corpus Christianorum, Continuatio medievalis* 56, Turnhout.

Patrologia Latina, ed. Jacques-Paul Migne *et al.* (1844–55, 1862–5), Paris.

Puchner, Walter (1997), *Akkommodationsfragen: Einzelbeispiele zum paganen Hintergrund von Elementen der frühkirchlichen und mittelalterlichen Sakraltradition und Volksfrömmigkeit*, Munich.

—— (2002), "Acting in the Byzantine Theatre: Evidence and Problems", in: Easterling / Hall (eds.), 304–24.

Reynolds, Leighton D. / Wilson, Nigel G. (1991), *Scribes and Scholars: A Guide to the Transmission of Greek and Latin Literature*, 3rd edn., Oxford.

Riché, Pierre (1962), *Éducation et culture dans l'Occident barbare, 6e–8e siècles*, Paris; trans. John J. Contreni (1976) as *Education and Culture in the Barbarian West, from the Sixth through the Eighth Century*, Columbia, S.C.

Rupert of Deutz, *De Sancta Trinitate et operibus eius*, ed. Hrabanus Haacke (1971) in *Corpus Christianorum, Continuatio medievalis* 21–24, Turnhout.

Sedulius Scotus, *In Donati artem maiorem*, ed. Bengt Löfstedt (1977) in *Corpus Christianorum, Continuatio medievalis* 40C, Turnhout.

Simon, Eckehard (ed.) (1991), *The Theatre of Medieval Europe: New Research in Early Drama,* Cambridge.

Slater, W. J. (1996), "Problems in Interpreting Scholia on Greek Texts", in: Slater (ed.), 37–61.

—— (ed.) (1996), *Roman Theatre and Society: E. Togo Salmon Papers I,* Ann Arbor.

Smith, Bruce R. (1988), *Ancient Scripts and Modern Experience on the English Stage, 1500–1700*, Princeton.

Stoppard, Tom (1997), *The Invention of Love,* New York.

Symes, Carol (2002), "The Appearance of Early Vernacular Plays: Forms, Functions, and the Future of Medieval Theatre", *Speculum* 77, 778–831.

—— (2003), "The Performance and Preservation of Medieval Latin Comedy", *European Medieval Drama* 7, 29–50.

—— (2004), "Theatre", in: Kristen M. Figg and John Block Friedman (eds.), *Arts and Humanities through the Eras, V: Medieval Europe (814–1450)*, Farmington Hills, Mich., 377–417.

—— (2007), *A Common Stage: Theatre and Public Life in Medieval Arras*, Ithaca and London.

Tarrant, Richard J. (1989), "The Reader as Author: Collaborative Interpolation in Latin Poetry", in: John N. Grant (ed.), *Editing Greek and Latin Texts,* New York, 121–162.

Thomas, Rosalind (1989), *Oral Tradition and Written Record in Classical Athens,* Cambridge.

Treadgold, Warren, (1981) "Photios and the Reading Public for Classical Philology in Byzantium", in: Margaret Mullett and Roger Scott (eds.), *Byzantium and the Classical Tradition,* Birmingham, 123–126.

Tuilier, André (1969), *La passion du Christ: Tragédie*, Sources chrétiennes 149, Paris.

Turyn, Alexander (1957), *The Byzantine Manuscript Tradition of the Tragedies of Euripides,* Urbana.

Van Engen, John (1983), *Rupert of Deutz*, Berkeley and Los Angeles.

Vince, Ronald W. (1984), *Ancient and Medieval Theatre: A Historiographical Handbook*, Westport, Conn.

Wellesz, Egon (1961), *A History of Byzantine Music and Hymnography*, 2nd rev. edn., Oxford.

Williams, Ralph G. (1993), "I Shall Be Spoken: Textual Boundaries, Authors, and Intent", in: George Bornstein and Ralph G. Williams (eds.), *Palimpsest: Editorial Theory in the Humanities*, Ann Arbor, 45–66.

Wilson, Eric G. (1968), *Greek Papyri*, Princeton.

Wilson, Nigel G. (1973; repr. 1995), *Medieval Greek Bookhands: Examples Selected from Greek Manuscripts in Oxford Libraries,* Cambridge, Mass.

—— (1996), *Scholars of Byzantium,* rev. edn., Cambridge, Mass.

Wilson, Peter J. (1996), "Tragic Rhetoric: The Use of Tragedy and the Tragic in the Fourth Century", in: Michael S. Silk (ed.), *Tragedy and the Tragic: Greek Theatre and Beyond,* Oxford, 310–31.

Young, Karl (1933), *The Drama of the Medieval Church*, 2 vols., Oxford.

Yunis, Henry (ed.) (2003), *Written Texts and the Rise of Literate Culture in Ancient Greece*, Cambridge.

Zuntz, Günther (1965), *An Inquiry into the Transmission of the Plays of Euripides*, Cambridge.

Adventures in Recording Technology:
The Drama-as-Performance in the Greek East

Andrew White

We operate in a culture where human presence has become increasingly marginalized by a variety of media. As a performer who has spent the bulk of my life on-stage, I still find it odd to sit in front of my laptop, type and edit slide shows and use DVDs and videos to teach theatre history. And I am not alone; theatre scholars now routinely contrast "materialized" with "dematerialized performance,"[1] and talk of "speech acts" – as if speech could be anything but.[2] And yet from its inception, drama has been about real people going onto a real stage and actually *doing* something. Although often distinguished from theatre because of its literary qualities, and although associated with the advent of literacy in antiquity,[3] dramatic compositions assumed the presence of a live interpreter; whether performed on-stage by a sizeable cast, read aloud in the classroom or (after the demise of traditional theatre) for private *soirées*, they were experienced primarily as public events, and only rarely as words on a page.[4]

In discussing the fate of drama among Greek speakers in the Eastern Roman Empire, a period spanning from Late Antiquity through the Fall of Constantinople in 1453, it is helpful to begin with the "how" of cultural transmission in those days, to better understand the "what" that has been the traditional focus of theatre history. For the better part of two thousand years written drama was more an *aide-répétition* (to borrow the French term for 'rehearsal') than an *aide-mémoire*. And it is the written word's subservience to the performed word that renders it, in a sense, a mode of recording

---

1   The term "dematerialized performance" has been applied to the experience of listening to recorded popular music, but applies to other mediated experiences as well. For a brief discussion of this concept see Auslander 2006.
2   See especially Bakhtin's "The Problem of Speech Genres" in Bakhtin 1986, 60–102.
3   See for example Ong 1982, 139–55.
4   "Deeply typographic folk forget to think of words as primarily oral, as events, and hence as necessarily powered: for them, words tend rather to be assimilated into things, 'out there' on a flat surface" (Ong 1982, 32–3).

technology.[5] In the days before iPods and DVD players, Greek drama was transmitted primarily through live interpretations of handwritten scripts; and the drama's music was preserved through pitch-specific notation that endured for centuries into the Common Era. Even in a non-theatrical context the drama was generally experienced through the reader's vocal inflections, further enhanced by facial and corporeal gestures.[6]

What also distinguishes the fate of drama in Byzantium is the survival of Classical Greek as a spoken language. This continuity was, of course, tempered by changes in melodic and linguistic dialect. But Classical Greek's unique status as a living tongue throughout the Middle Ages, and its direct use in contemporary discourse are its distinguishing features. As Byzantine historian Ihor Ševčenko explains:

> Antique literary and scientific culture was endemic in Byzantium, and the Byzantines were too familiar with it to react to antiquity as violently as did the West, which had almost forgotten it for centuries. What we call Byzantine renaissances are just intensifications of the elite's contacts with antiquity – which were never lost – rather than rediscoveries of ancient culture.[7]

Ancient drama was preserved, read aloud and otherwise embodied for two thousand years in a culture whose language continued to function at multiple registers simultaneously. Educated Byzantines lived and moved in an environment where the Greek of Aeschylus and Euripides was in constant interaction with the *koinē*, or common, street Greek.[8]

Drama was also preserved and transmitted in a culture that placed a premium on human memory. Classes in grammar involved learning the vocabulary and key passages of Greek classics by heart.[9] In this way, Plato's nightmare of literacy killing off the memory would not become a reality until the advent first of print media and eventually the computer.[10] Today we read passively and in silence from books and the Web; when done, our inert reading material is either put on the shelf or set adrift in the ether for future reference. The only people expected to memorize and perform these plays, and briefly at that, are actors; such is progress.

---

5   "Recording technology" here is generically defined as any medium designed to ensure the accurate re-performance of a given composition.

6   Ong's theories have been criticized for privileging verbal at the expense of gestural communication (see for example Theall 1992). For the purposes of this essay, it is assumed that verbal and non-verbal communication are of a piece.

7   Ševčenko 1975, 19.

8   Robert Browning points out that in Byzantium, as a practical matter, people spoke and wrote at a number of different linguistic levels, even though Byzantium's writers often preferred to write in more elite forms. See Browning 1989, 103–33.

9   See Law 1996, 37–52. For a collection of readings on the art of memory from Antiquity see Hermann and Chaffin 1988.

10 On the endurance of orality in literate cultures see for example Ong 2002, 109–13.

The purpose of the present paper is to show how the fate of drama in Byzantium and the Greek-speaking East is best understood as an interplay between manuscript production and the enduring orality and musicality of Greek culture.[11] Drama remained a central motif of Greek culture through its musical, manuscript and rhetorical traditions. The Eastern Roman Empire may have been our bridge to the drama of the ancient world, and it may have facilitated the rebirth of traditional theatre in the West; but being Greek and a millennium in the making, this bridge is of unique construction.

1   The Legacy of Dramatic Music

Theatre scholars have largely ignored the melodic aspect of dramatic compositions – this in spite of evidence that music was the main attraction at the *Dionysia*, and remained an important component in Greek education.[12] Exemplars of musical notation from ancient drama are fragmentary, and hence do not reflect all the nuances of the original melodies of the fifth century BCE.[13] But there is a wealth of information, both anecdotal and theoretical, about the mechanisms by which Greek "composers" – a more apt translation of the word *poiētēs*, 'poet' – created their work.[14] The musical theory and practice of Ancient Greece remained part of the standard schoolboy curriculum throughout Byzantium's history.[15]

Descriptions of tragic and comic music tend to reveal less about the subject than about the misconceptions we bring to it, the traditional position being, as one scholar puts it, that "ancient tunes were repetitive and conformed to traditional melodic patterns."[16] Although melodic patterns, like metric patterns, lay at the heart of traditional Greek composition, what gave these patterns life and distinguished one composer's work from another's were the *variations* on these themes.[17] And as the debate over Euripides' mu-

---

11   In some regions oral tradition has thrived into modern times. For an account of recent encounters between print and oral culture in Greece see Romanos 2004, 29–87.

12   Auslander points out that theatre scholars tend to dismiss music as "non-mimetic"; see Auslander 2006, 261 and n. 1). A welcome exception to this tacit rule of divorcing music from drama is Wilson 2005.

13   For a transcription and facsimile of these fragments see Pöhlmann and West 2001.

14   The chief reference for primary sources on ancient Greek music is Barker 1984. For detailed studies see Comotti 1989, West 1992 and Mathiesen (1999).

15   I have detailed the Attic roots of Byzantine chant in White 2007.

16   Hall 2002, 18.

17   A useful comparison might be with Alexandrian verse in French drama: the 12-syllable, rhyming-couplet, one-thought-per-line model can seem tedious, but these rules also made the genius of Racine and Molière possible. It can be argued that these dramatists thrived precisely because of these rules, not (as with Victor Hugo) in spite of them.

sical reforms in Aristophanes' *Frogs*, let alone Plato's extensive treatment of music in the *Republic* would indicate, tragic music was a highly contested cultural practice with profound implications for its audiences.[18]

The key to ancient music was the melody. With performers behind masks and unable to reveal emotion through facial expression, melodic patterns unlocked the secrets of a character's emotions and moral character.[19] Melodic patterns – *harmonia* – offered the audience a sense of action, of a journey, as well as a specific mood comparable in some ways to an operatic *Leitmotif*. Certain patterns, apart from having regional associations – the Dorian, the Phrygian, etc. – were associated with personal qualities like courage, despair, cowardice, hope, etc., and provided crucial information about the state of the action on-stage. Hence the ancient understanding of music's mimetic and "ethical" qualities. As Aristotle observed:

> Melodies themselves do contain imitations of character. This is perfectly clear, for the *harmoniai* have quite distinct natures from one another, so that those who hear them are differently affected and do not respond in the same way to each.[20]

Adherence to certain melodic norms, then as now, provided a foundation for artistic innovation. Athenian audiences would have been attuned to specific auditory cues provided by the melody's shape, and this would have made it possible for them to appreciate each composer's innovations. Complex melodies became the chief focus of music theorists, with great attention paid to *metabolē* or "modulation" between different registers and melodic patterns.[21] Ancient Greek theorists came up with general *schemata* for notes, known as the "Greater" and "Lesser Perfect Systems," that enabled com-

---

18 For a recent analysis of the politics of tragic music see Csapo 2004.

19 See Barker 1984, 1.163–164, for a description of the *harmoniai* and Aristoxenus' now-lost attempt to create a system of *tonoi* (a term that encompasses *harmoniai* but is closer in spirit to what we might call a "key signature"). See also *ibid.* 2.17–27 for a more detailed discussion incorporating post-Aristoxenian treatments of the *tonoi*. For the ancients, notes only had meaning as part of a specific sequence. The sequence of notes in the traditional hymn *Dies Irae*, for example, would constitute its *harmonia*, and would form the basis for all compositions trying to evoke its unique, fateful mood. A music theorist, attempting to reconcile the notes of *Dies Irae* to those used in other melodies, would derive its *tonos* or set of notes in the abstract, without an eye to their sequencing, which is as close as ancient theory would get to what we would call the "key" of D minor.

20 *Pol.* 1340a, translation from Barker 1984, 2.175. Plato's discussion of musical ethics, or character, is concerned chiefly with which melodic patterns are most suitable for his ideal city-state; Aristotle points out elsewhere in the *Politics* that Plato's standards are inconsistent, and that musical response is a subjective matter. For the purposes of this study, the term *ēthos* can be understood in dynamic terms: "character" is realized through actions of a specific quality.

21 See for example Aristox. *Harm.* 7.10–8.2, translation in Barker 1984, 2.131.

posers and musicians to identify the ideal places for modulation within and between specific *harmoniai*.[22]

The first performers of tragedy and comedy, being educated male citizens, brought to the stage a rare sense of musicality. Available evidence indicates that the music of the *Dionysia* used melodic patterns that were enharmonic, i.e. that used microtones, intervals of less than a western half-step.[23] The diatonic and chromatic modes – comparable to what we can pick out on a piano today – were known but rejected as effeminate and fit only for women or slaves. As Aristotle's protégé, the music theorist Aristoxenus put it:

> Of these [modes] the diatonic, since human nature comes upon it first, must be reckoned the first and oldest, the chromatic second, and the enharmonic third and most sophisticated, since perception becomes accustomed to it at last, with difficulty, and through much hard work.[24]

It is somewhat ironic to realize that the ancients would have regarded much of our modern repertoire as beneath their dignity. And their pitch-specific musical notation system, created most likely during the fourth century BCE, provides concrete evidence of ancient music's sophistication.[25] Conceived as two parallel systems, one for instrumentalists and one for singers, each tone in the scale is assigned three different symbols; the center of the vocal register requires all 24 letters of the Greek alphabet to cover a single octave.[26]

With Alexander the Great's conquests and the construction of new, Greek urban centers throughout the Mediterranean and beyond came a need for performers to fill theatres on a truly international scale. A sacred fraternity, the "Artists of Dionysus," quickly replaced the citizen-amateurs of

---

22 See West 1992, 218–253 for a summary of the basic concepts of ancient Greek music theory, too complex to be addressed here in any detail. See especially fig. 8.1 (222), for the Greater and Lesser Perfect Systems, with the terminology (unfortunately) transliterated and untranslated. The terms are actually quite simple – "topmost, index-finger, next-bottom," etc., and speak to their roots in musical practice.

23 Here, the term *genus* refers to a method of tuning. On the three ancient modal *genera* – enharmonic, chromatic and diatonic – see West 1992, 164.

24 Aristox. *Harm.* 19.22–29, from Barker 1984, 2.139. Aristoxenus goes on to say that previous theorists "dealt only with the *enharmonic*, and never gave a thought to the other genera" (*Harm.* 2.6–7, Barker 1984, 2.126).

25 For ancient pitch-specific notation, its rough western equivalents, and its (probable) associations with specific melodic types (Dorian, Phrygian, etc.) see West 1992, 256–257.

26 The notation for an ode from Euripides' *Orestes* uses immediately adjacent letters, which can make for awkward transcriptions in half-step-based Western notation. See West 1992, 284; Pöhlmann and West 2001, 13; and Mathiesen 1999, 117–118. Recordings by western-trained musicians have difficulty in approximating these intervals: listen to Halaris, track 1 and Paniagua, track 2.

the original *Dionysia*.[27] Unfortunately for this fraternity's musicians, there is evidence that even as the international theatre scene was taking shape, tastes were changing.[28] Known colloquially as *banausoi* or "mechanicals", professional musicians were presumably trained in microtonal music but were confronted by Hellenistic audiences who no longer cared for it. The evidence for changing tastes comes from contemporary theorists: Aristoxenus, whose career coincided with the formation of the Artists of Dionysus, describes how microtonal melodies in his day were re-tuned into chromatic ones.[29] And if the commentary of a theorist from the Early Roman Empire is any gauge, it would appear that almost all theatre music was diatonic by the dawn of the Common Era.[30]

This change in musical tastes parallels the development of a simpler form of spoken Greek, and with similar implications; the emergence of a *koine* or "common" language did not mean that people stopped speaking Classical Greek. The elite linguistic registers of antiquity – Ionian, Doric, Attic, etc. – became the marker of the literate ruling class, and were used routinely in interactions, both written and spoken, with other educated Greeks. It is likely that the *enharmonic* melodic patterns of ancient drama endured in much the same way, as a part of the educated Greek-speaker's cultural heritage, useless in the streets but of vital importance in the palaces and salons of the Hellenistic, Roman, and Byzantine Empires.

27　Sir Arthur Pickard-Cambridge finds the first extant reference to the artists of Dionysus in Egypt under Ptolemy Philadelphus (282–246 BCE) (Pickard-Cambridge 1988, 287); Paulette Ghiron-Bistagne dates the formation of the first professional guilds to ca. 320 BCE, when actors in Alexander the Great's entourage in Asia Minor suddenly found themselves without his protection upon his untimely death (Ghiron-Bistagne 1976, 67–68 and 163–4); for more recent scholarship see Ceccarelli (2004).

28　For the purposes of this study, I assume a more dynamic model of cultural transmission along the lines of Prauscello 2006. Rejecting past models of transmission based on stability and consistency, Prauscello assumes "the 'true' form of survival and persistence of a [dramatic] text through different periods seems to have been its inner capability of being *adapted* to changed performance practices without losing its own identity" (Prauscello 2006, 5, emphasis mine). I would like to thank Ingo Gildenhard for bringing this fascinating study to my attention.

29　Aristox. *Harm.* 23.10–23, Barker 1984, 2.141–142.

30　Mathiesen cites the theorist Gaudentius (third-fourth century CE), who confines himself to discussions of diatonic music because "the use of the remaining two *genera* seems to have lapsed" (Mathiesen 1999, 502). The situation bears comparison to the current state of globalized pop culture. Consider the television series *American Idol* and its derivatives, or the *Euro-Vision* song contest, which consists of musicians from dozens of countries competing with the same limited repertoire of diatonic melodic models, and a heavy reliance on clichéd English lyrics.

Early Christian hymnography, emerging as it did in Roman times, was born in a diatonic milieu; the simplicity of these *harmoniai* suited the tastes of the more ascetic Church Fathers. But early hymnography was also informed by "pagan" musical practice and theory, so there was room for more sophisticated fare: the earliest extant sheet music for a Christian hymn was written with ancient notation, and transitional figures from Late Antiquity like Bishop Synesius of Cyrene (ca. 370–413 CE) continued to enjoy pagan odes even as they composed new hymns for their congregations.[31] Meanwhile the introduction of castrati into the imperial church of Hagia Sophia during the same period confirms the desire for more sophisticated hymnographic forms.[32]

With Constantinople as the capitol of a culturally Greek yet spiritually Christian Roman Empire, the music of antiquity remained a dominant theme in Christian education, dramatic music included. Ignatius, Deacon of Hagia Sophia, in his biography of Patriarch Nicephorus I (806–815) stresses his subject's facility with music studies.[33] Photius, a highly regarded academic and sometime Patriarch of Constantinople (858–867 and 877–886), wrote a *Bibliotheca* or "Library" of suggested readings for his brother that includes a critique of certain scholars' knowledge of music and musical instruments.[34] Two etymological dictionaries from this period, one associated with Photius, include musical vocabulary; these dictionaries, in turn, seem to have formed the basis for the famous *Suda* Lexicon.[35] Together, these works offer a number of ancient musical references – tragic composers included – that are unattested elsewhere.[36] Sometime later a letter on tragedy attributed to Byzantine courtier, monk and professor Michael Psellos (11th century) devotes much of its discussion to music, describing in detail the modes, melodic patterns, and ethical associations of works by composers like Sophocles and Euripides.[37]

As esoteric as these concerns may appear to the modern reader, they laid the foundation for traditional Greek Orthodox hymnography; and the perception of kinship between ancient and Byzantine music became even stronger from the thirteenth century onward. A description of a music theory

---

31   For a transcription of this Christian hymn see West 1992, 324–326; see also Wellesz
      1998, 148–152 on Synesius and other early hymnographers.
32   On the history of *castrati* in the Eastern Empire see Moran 2002.
33   See Lemerle 1986, 150. Lemerle critiques this passage as out of place, but he was
      not aware of the value a musical education had during Ignatius' time.
34   See Treadgold 1980, 99 and n. 11.
35   See Suda 1928–1938. The *Suda* has been the subject of an online translation project
      for a number of years, see Suda 2009.
36   Mathiesen 1999, 643 n. 109 acknowledges his debt to these three sources.
37   See Browning 1963.

class at a boy's school in the Church of the Holy Apostles (Constantinople's most elite academy prior to the Latin conquest of 1204) makes clear that ancient theory was a part of the standard curriculum.[38] Graduates of the Holy Apostles School would have gone onto careers in both the court and church, becoming either composers or patrons of the arts.[39] In the years immediately after the restoration of the Greek emperors to Constantinople in 1261, music theorists like George Pachymeres argued that the *octoechos*, the "eight-tone" (or "eight-melody") system of Orthodox chant, was rooted in the *harmoniai* of antiquity;[40] and it was understood that some of these *harmoniai* were previously associated with ancient drama.[41]

For all this musical activity, it is not until the creation of a new system of musical notation for Orthodox chant (ca. the ninth or tenth century) that we can find any concrete relationship between antiquity and Byzantium. Ancient, pitch-specific notation appears to have died out with the demise of the professional theatre musician, perhaps as late as Emperor Justinian's time (522–545 CE) when he withdrew state theatre funding.[42] And because Orthodox chant was purely vocal, early iterations of the Church's new recording technology simply traced out the basic shape of the melody in imitation of the *cheironomia*, or hand gestures given by the choir leader.[43] The resulting musical silhouette provided the trained chanter with the information needed to perform and embellish the melody to the best of his or her ability.

---

38 See Downey 1957, 895f. Egon Wellesz's interpretation of this passage (Wellesz 1998, 63) is dated and misinformed.

39 Roughly contemporary to this, in a commentary on the Ecumenical Church Councils, the scholar Theodore Balsamon contrasts the disreputable mime-shows of antiquity with the "dignified royal plays" (*epitimia basilica paignia*) of his day; we have only their titles, *Octoechos* among them, which suggests that they were at least quasi-dramatic oratorios (see Migne 1979, 137.693a–b). The possible relationship between Byzantine court musicals and Italian Renaissance drama has not yet been explored, to my knowledge.

40 See Tannery 1940, 146.

41 A *caveat* is in order here; although there is agreement about the ancient roots of the *octoechos*, there is little or no agreement on which *harmonia* was related to which Byzantine *echos*. See Richter 1964, 195 for a chart of correspondences according to three Byzantine theorists, as well as the "Gregorian" eight-tone system. The chief problem seems to be that theorists disagree about whether to name the ancient *harmoniai* by their relative pitch-levels or by their ethical qualities. The subjectivity of Byzantine musical response in these treatises is yet another complicating factor.

42 According to West, the last extant piece in ancient notation is the Christian hymn, about which see n. 31 above (West 1992, 283). On the final "closing of the theatres" see Procopius 1966, 169. Procopius' narrative of Justinian shifting arts funding to the military might seem eerily familiar to modern readers.

43 See Wellesz 1998, 287–288.

In later years the basic notation system, consisting of signs known as *somata* and *pneumata*, was enhanced by the creation of a more precise class of musical signs called *hypostaseis*,[44] an innovation in recording technology that coincides with the codification of *kalophonic* or "beautified" chant. Court composers and theorists like John Koukouzeles and Manuel Chrysaphes began to use *hypostaseis* to record the nuances of their live performances in the Great Church of Hagia Sophia (and upon their retirement, the monasteries of Mount Athos), enabling chanters throughout the Orthodox world to perform melodies previously known only to a select few. In an echo of ancient theorists, Chrysaphes's musical treatise specifically addresses the art of modulation – known now as *parallage* – and comes to much the same conclusions as his ancient predecessors.[45] Although the Byzantine notation system lacked pitch-specificity and was to that extent an inferior technology, it provides hard evidence of the refinement of Byzantine hymnography during the thirteenth through fifteenth centuries – a refinement grounded in Church composers' training in ancient Greek music theory and practice.

Barring the discovery of more musical manuscripts, it is doubtful we will know exactly how the music of ancient drama sounded beyond a few small snippets. And evidence presented here for continuity is tempered by the many changes in musical tastes from antiquity to Byzantine times; even if they had survived into the Middle Ages, it is safe to assume that melodic patterns from antiquity would have undergone significant changes. But the survival of key elements of ancient music theory, coupled with the later development of a new notation system for Orthodox hymnography, enables us to explore the basic principles of dramatic composition through performances (and now recordings) of Byzantine chant. By identifying the specific characteristics of each of the Church's eight modes, and listening closely to the modulations and variations in hymns written by Medieval masters like

---

44 Wellesz 1998, 285–6. By design the names for musical signs in Orthodox chant had theological meaning: *somata*, "bodies", indicated movements of one tone, *pneumata*, "spirits", movements of two or more tones. *Hypostaseis*, a reference to the Orthodox Trinitarian formula *mia ousia, treis hypostaseis* ("One Being, Three Substances"), covered the dynamics, rates and manners of movement from one note to the next. The mystical significance of each member in this last class of signs was outlined by a Late Byzantine theorist, see Schartau 1998.

45 See Chrysaphes 1985. The term *parallagē* in Patristic Greek, has the sense of "deterioration", and the class of musical signs for modulation, *phthora*, carries with it a sense of "corruption" (see Lampe 1961 s.vv. *parallagi, phthora*). The idea of chant as a spiritual journey is reinforced through the sense of modulation as a departure from, followed by a return to the right path.

Koukouzeles and Chrysaphes, we can come closer to the experience of dramatic music than previously thought possible.[46]

2   The Legacy of Dramatic Letters

In the Greek East there is evidence for dramatic competitions at public festivals well into the second century CE, although the evidence disappears soon afterwards.[47] Meanwhile in the West, learned Latins continued to write closet dramas for private readings through at least the fifth century CE; the *Querolus* offers a fascinating glimpse of comedy in Late Antiquity, a hybrid of contemporary political commentary and Menandrian urban stereotype whose development was cut off by Rome's final collapse.[48]

The knowledge that some dramatic manuscripts were designed specifically for actors, and that actors and scholars routinely interacted in places like second century BCE Alexandria (where a substantial number of extant commentaries, or *scholia*, were composed) raises the question: how reliant were the Byzantines on manuscripts written for the stage? Thomas Falkner points out that the scholarly canon of ancient drama, from its earliest days, relied on the repertoire established by the Hellenistic actors' synods. And the frequency of early scholars' complaints about inauthentic passages (the result, they claimed, of actors' oversimplifications and interpolations) implies that they relied heavily on stage-scripts for their own work.[49] The drama's earliest scholars openly admitted that theirs was an unstable, performance-based tradition, in which the niceties of Classical Greek (like those of Classical melody) were often lost in their adaptation for the contemporary stage. Their work, like those of their Byzantine and modern successors, consisted of trying to restore what the composers "actually" wrote, as opposed to what worked before a contemporary popular audience.

What has complicated discussions of drama in the Greek East is that from the Hellenistic period onward, an ever-expanding field of discursive

---

46   Listen, for example, to the Greek Byzantine Choir directed by Lycourgos Angelopoulos, one of Byzantine chant's most widely known exponents.

47   See Roueché 1993, 173, for an inscription offering a prize for *kaine tragodia*, "new tragedy" in the late second century CE, and 223–7, for the honors bestowed on the second-century composer Gaius Julius Longianus.

48   On the social context for *Querolus* and a translation of its dedication see Mathiesen 2003, 1.17–19. Originally attributed to Plautus, arguments for its authorship have varied from "Gallic" rhetor Axius Paulus (Dezeimeris 1881, 8–31) to an African (Jacquemard-Le Saos 1994, vii and n. 1). Dr. Mathiesen is currently preparing a new translation with commentary, to be published by Johns Hopkins University Press.

49   See Falkner 2002.

and performance practices were labeled as "drama".[50] Walter Puchner and Iosef Vivilakes have demonstrated how over time, the vocabulary of the theatre came to be applied to a wide range of phenomena.[51] It has taken some time for scholars to distinguish between traditional and non-traditional uses of terms like "drama", "tragedy", "comedy", etc.[52]

This fluidity of terminology can be seen as the natural consequence of an oral culture whose compositions were experienced as live recitations from manuscripts that, by virtue of their format, displayed *all* genres identically. The written drama in its earliest form bore no resemblance whatsoever to the neat translations we see today, consisting instead of capitol letters, "uncials", bunched together on the page without spacing between words, let alone diacritical marks to aid the reader in breathing or stress. In only a few cases do manuscripts designate changes of speaker, but even these fail to give the characters' names.[53] The absolute neutrality of the page, without any internal directions on how to group let alone read the letters aloud, ensured that the page itself had little or no authority; that authority resided in the reader/performer.[54]

When compared with ancient musical notation the medium of plain uncial characters seems crude; but the preference for uncial versions of the drama demonstrates how educated amateurs – the first composers and performers – privileged the spoken word over the written, and embraced the drama as a rich resource for contemporary discourse.[55] From a Byzantine perspective, this was the optimal arrangement for drama's transmission; Byzantine educators drilled ancient drama into their students' heads, with the goal of

---

50 George La Piana's application of cultural Darwinism, the "ritual-to-theatre" model of cultural development, confused matters further by claiming homilies and hymns were eventually staged as plays. See his dissertation, La Piana 1912, summarized in English in La Piana 1936. As pointed out by Mary Cunningham, however, La Piana had no evidence to back up his thesis (see Cunningham 2003, 102 and n. 6).

51 See Puchner 2002, 307–9, and Vivilakes 1996, 49–307; Vivilakes provides a lexicon of theatre-related terms and the varieties of their usage in Early Byzantine Greek.

52 See for example George La Piana's attacks on Konstantinos Sathas in La Piana 1936, 172–4; for his attacks on Venetia Cottas, 189–201. For further misunderstandings see Vogt 1931, refuted by Cyril Mango (Mango 1981).

53 Examples of extant dramatic papyri can be found in Turner 1971, 54–79, plates 24–43; see also 64–5, plate 32, for a dialogue from Euripides' *Chresphontes* annotated for *a'* and *c'* (first and third actor).

54 M. B. Parkes argues that this was the chief virtue of what in the West was known as *scriptio continua*: see Parkes 1993, 11. Latin writers, under Greek influence, abandoned the use of interpuncts (points to divide words) in favor of *scriptio continua* by the end of the first century CE (*ibid.*, 10).

55 On the uses of poetry at the earliest stages of education in the Greek East, see Webb 1994. Webb's Late Byzantine sources routinely cite Late Antique and Early Byzantine authorities.

ensuring that its vocabulary, sentiments and key passages would become an inseparable part of their live discursive practice. This use of drama may seem "inauthentic", in that it is an open invitation for variation and corruption;[56] but the experience of dramatic poetry lay at the foundation of every Greek grammar and rhetoric school, from antiquity through Byzantine times.[57]

At some point, Byzantine grammarians appear to have settled on a curriculum of three dramas written by each of four ancient composers, known as the "Triads": [58]

Table 1: The Byzantine Triads

Poet	Play 1	Play 2	Play 3
Aeschylus	Prometheus Bound	Persians	Seven Against Thebes
Sophocles	Ajax	Electra	Oedipus the King
Euripides	Hecuba	Orestes	Phoenician Women
Aristophanes	Wealth	Clouds	Frogs

The selections for this "core curriculum" can be understood in any number of ways; some, like *Oedipus*, may have recommended themselves as representative works, while ongoing political tensions along the Empire's eastern border may help to explain *Persians'* enduring appeal. Aristophanes' *Wealth* with its paean to poverty had a certain appeal to professional scholars (see below).[59] *Clouds* offered an amusing portrait of Socrates, a figure central to the philosophy curriculum, while *Frogs* provided valuable information about how tragedy and its music was composed – evidence of Byzantine education's fundamental interdisciplinarity. This interdisciplinarity, in turn, had implications for the future uses of drama beyond its original theatrical context (see part 3 below).

It would not be until the early ninth century that copyists finally adopted a more detailed mode of recording drama with the introduction of lower-case letters – "miniscule" – and markings above the letters to guide the speaker's performance of words that, finally, became distinct entities on the

---

56 A contemporary example of the dynamic relationship between oral and written traditions can be found in Lord 1967, 1199–1206.

57 Dinoysius Thrax, the grammarian most cited as an authority by Byzantine sources, defines grammar as the "experience of what composers [poets] and writers usually say". See Webb 1994, 90.

58 From Marciniak 2004, 37. Marciniak posits that the triads were developed during the transferal of dramatic texts from the large, uncial script of antiquity to the new miniscule script, during the tenth century. See also Turyn 1943, 15 and Turyn 1957, 19.

59 N. G. Wilson found that it was the most commonly read comic play in Byzantium for a number of years (see Wilson 1996, 112).

page.[60] Motivations for this change are hard to discern. One popular scenario notes that this was an age when papyrus was no longer available. Egypt had been lost to the Caliphate and, as some scholars have argued, miniscule enabled you to fit more material onto pages of more costly animal skin – parchment or vellum.[61] On the other hand, separating words and specifying their pronunciation was time-consuming, involving as it did transliteration, interpretation and embellishment of unaccented uncial originals. To top it off, miniscule copyists (after upwards of fifteen hundred years) took it upon themselves to attribute lines to specific dramatic characters.

Spatial economy, then, does not account for the adoption of miniscule; there were simply too many innovations involved in the change. Nor did these innovations suddenly burst upon the scene in the Middle Ages; miniscule, separate words and accent systems had been developed in the third century BCE, and writers had used them ever since in official and other non-'literary' documents.[62] The decision to apply the miniscule system to drama, then, speaks more to the desire for greater cheirographic control over this specific genre.[63]

Throughout the Eastern Empire, annotated manuscripts of this kind had been prized for their ability to ensure that the reader/performer could realize the "presence" of an absent writer.[64] And in the case of dramatic manuscripts, the immediate impact of the miniscule system would have been plays read aloud with "higher fidelity" to the language's proper pronunciation. But the timing of this change was awkward because by the Middle Ages certain traditions associated with ancient drama were long lost. The metric system was now based on stress rather than quantity (i.e., accents instead of a system of long and short vowels), and by the Middle Ages ancient musical notation – which could have offered an even more nuanced reading of ancient dramatic diction – had been long out of use. For all its seeming authority, the finished product had more to do with the Byzantine reader's contemporary mode of speaking Ancient Greek – the medieval equivalent of "received pronunciation" – than with ancient dramatic performance.

---

60 The element of word separation, taken for granted by the modern reader, was not regarded as necessary until quite late; see and Gamillscheg and Ševčenko 1991, 2.1377–1378.

61 See for example the Introduction to Barbour 1981, xviii.

62 Aristophanes of Byzantium (*fl.* 260 BCE) is credited with creating the system of punctuation, breathings and accents, but they were only irregularly used prior to the Middle Ages; see Thompson 1912, 60–3, and van Groningen 1963, 51–3.

63 Carol Symes recently discussed the challenges faced by Medieval western scribes in creating a suitable manuscript format for drama, a difficulty rooted in transcribing significant aspects of oral performance (see Symes 2002). Eastern scribes faced similar challenges.

64 For a discussion of evidence for this phenomenon of reader-as-*simulacra* see Cavallo 2006, 47–55.

Once cheirographic control over the drama was established there was a natural shift in the direction of the play as a visual phenomenon. Dramas were now integrated with commentaries that had been written separately from antiquity, and these *scholia* came to encircle the plays in a visual format not unfamiliar to students of Byzantine sacred art. In the Orthodox tradition it is common to find icons of saints which consist of a central figure surrounded by smaller images from the person's life, their miracles, and even stories of the discovery and transportation of their relics; icons being, by design, an object of silent contemplation.

The *scholia* addressed a variety of topics: stage blocking, melodies, alternative readings, sources of errant passages, critiques of style, etc. And their placement around the play created a multilayered experience that, it can be argued, privileged the eye. On the page, the simultaneity of narrative (the play) and metanarrative (the *scholia*) may have distracted the live reader from her/his task.

There is a sense in which the emergence of what we would call "Byzantine drama" was predicated on the introduction of this new manuscript format. Byzantine composers now had a new way to organize their works visually, and the fact that this organizational scheme was associated with the latest editions of ancient drama gave it even greater *caché*. Because there had been other avenues for dramatic expression among educated Greeks in the form of rhetorical show-pieces (as discussed below), the return to writing dramas may have been a deliberate if nostalgic choice.

Roughly contemporary with Michael Psellos is perhaps the most famous closet drama written in Byzantium, the *Christos Paschon*. Initially attributed to the fourth-century poet and homilist St. Gregory of Nazienzus – fake attributions, then as now, being a popular literary sport – a rough consensus now dates it to the eleventh century.[65] Its status as an appropriation of ancient drama is stated explicitly in the prologue: "I shall now recite the world-saving Passion in Euripides' style (*kat' Euripidēn*)."[66] Given the *Christos Paschon's* subject, it is no surprise that tragedies in which mothers and sons come to grief receive the most attention: *Medea*, *Bacchae*, and *Hippolytus* account for the overwhelming majority of citations.[67] In at least two manu-

---

65   There is a substantial bibliography on this play, both regarding its authenticity and
     approximate dates of composition. See for starters Tuilier 1969, 117–21; Tuilier pro-
     vides a critically edited Greek text and French translation. For a synopsis and over-
     view of its history see also Sticca 1974, 25–41. Sticca argues in favor of Gregory of
     Nazienzus' authorship.
66   *Christos Paschon* 3–4, after Tuilier 1969, 124–5.
67   For a comprehensive list see Tuilier 1969, 343–55. In his study, Marciniak (2004,
     89) finds about 542 lines are adapted from Euripides, 188 of them direct quotes.
     Given disagreements on the poem's length (there are two distinct traditions), Eurip-

scripts, the author appears to have added a postscript stating that he has written a "real drama" that is "unsullied by the horseshit of mythical trash (*ou ... pephyrmenon te mythikōn lērōn koprō*)"[68] – a sign that classical drama's value in Byzantium depended, at least in part, on its adaptability to Christian concerns. Walter Puchner has pointed out that the author of the *Christos Paschon* had no practical experience with staging a play, only how it should look on the page;[69] his analysis would make sense if the author were a professional writer who produced the *Christos Paschon* on commission from a client with archaic tastes – including, perhaps, the conceit of attributing it to St. Gregory.[70]

Secular writers in the twelfth century continued to turn their hands to drama; Theodore Prodromos, a satirist who (to hear him tell it) was always on the verge of starvation,[71] has earned his place in future theatre history books as the author of *Katomyomachia*, "The Cat and Mouse War". Not unlike Peter Quince's ill-begotten "Pyramus and Thisbe", the solemn language of "Cat and Mouse War" is completely undermined by its satiric context: the action centers on Kreillos ("Fleshy" or "Fatty"), a long-suffering patriarch who has lost children to the "all-devouring" cat.[72] The mice form an army, make sacrifices to the gods, and march off to battle. There is the inevitable messenger from the front – Kreillos loses another son to the cause – but with a nod to Euripides' *deus ex machina* the cat is killed miraculously by a chunk of wood that falls off the roof. Prodromos, being Byzantine, also reveals his familiarity with patristic and contemporary works in "Cat and Mouse War," and there is evidence that he had also read, if not authored, the *Christos Paschon*.[73] There is no evidence that Prodromos' mock-tragedy was intended for the stage, but it would have been a joy to read aloud.

Shortly after Prodromos' time Michael Haplucheiros wrote a few verses in dramatic form about the plight of the learned man. This 123-verse playlet (named *Dramation*, "Little Drama", by its first Renaissance editor) contrasts the good fortune of *Agroikos*, "Ignoramus", with the miserable poverty of *Sophos*, "Wise Man"; the cast is rounded out by the Muses, the goddess

---

ides accounts for anywhere between one third and nearly one half of the total.

68 *Christos Paschon* colophon, 1–2, as found in Parisinus gr. 2875. Tuilier questions the authenticity of this passage, because of its (perceived) crudity (Tuilier 1969, 30–2). Tuilier seems unaware that pious Orthodox historians did not hesitate to heap manure-based invective on enemies like iconoclast emperor Constantine V, who is known to this day as *Kopronymos*, "Mr. Horseshit", a term that features even in modern Greek school-room posters of Byzantine royalty.

69 Puchner 2004, 318.

70 Marciniak 2004, 92 n. 35 argues for a monastic author.

71 For a brief sketch of his career and work see Vasiliev 1964, 500–2.

72 Tyrokleptos = "cheese-thief".

73 Marciniak 2004, 95–100.

Fortune, as well as a Chorus.[74] The vignette begins when Fortune, intending to give Wise Man her blessings, pays a call on Ignoramus' house by mistake (the goddess is portrayed as something of a blind twit); Wise Man castigates her, and soon after the Muses arrive in the guise of a Chorus. Wise Man, not fooled, calls out the real chorus and demands that the Muses be thrown out, begging for any line of work that, unlike his present one, will put food on his table.[75] Haplucheiros drew from a number of sources, chief among them Aristophanes' *Wealth* – a play that ironically points out the consequences of too much good fortune. He also quoted extensively from Prodromos, who (like Haplucheiros) made a career out of griping about his rotten luck.

Ironically, the same Byzantine scholarship that preserved the drama for posterity and inspired these Byzantine dramas has been the target of an academic cleansing campaign. When not separating drama and *scholia* into separate editions (and neglecting to translate the *scholia*) classicists used to complain about how hard it was to identify Byzantine interpolations – so that they could be erased.[76] There has been a tendency to contrast the "purity" of the Italian Renaissance with the "interpolation libido" of the same Byzantine editors who made the Renaissance (let alone the modern field of Classics) possible.[77] The agendas of eastern and western scholars have always been at odds, however, and the enduring orality of Attic Greek, and the continued use of manuscripts as recording technologies, lies at the root of their misunderstanding.

The rediscovery of Greek philosophy and literature may have created a new world of ideas in Italy, but they were never lost in Byzantium. The chief concern in the East was to produce better, more reader-friendly editions of already-familiar classics in their original elite dialects.[78] The emphasis here is on reader-friendliness: it is one thing to edit a text in a long-forgotten dead language, but quite another to edit a text whose language remains alive and well. The element of orality lay at the heart of the Byzantine editor's work, and the expectation that her/his edition of a dramatic manuscript would be interpreted live (albeit as a solo reading before a circle of your peers) was predominant. Byzantine dramatic manuscripts, in all their bewildering variety, are the product of Greek speakers applying their knowledge of the original language to available manuscript sources, tempered by the aural experience of contemporary, spoken Classical Greek. Even in Byzantium's last years, deriving an authoritative version of the drama from sources in

---

74   See Romano 1999, 409–35.
75   Synopsis from Marciniak 2004, 101–2.
76   See Turyn 1957, 17–18.
77   See Turyn 1952, 120–1.
78   Fryde 2000, 197.

varying states of corruption was a subjective, creative process; and the rules for interpretation were as fluid as the language itself.

More recently, critics have begun to appreciate the role of Byzantine editors like Demetrius Triclinius (*fl.* early fourteenth century), who among other accomplishments re-assembled Aeschylus' *Agamemnon*, the first play in the *Oresteia*, and thus bequeathed to us Antiquity's lone surviving dramatic trilogy. Triclinius has come to be regarded as the first modern philologist, whose editions laid the foundation for print editions throughout the Italian renaissance.[79] Complete translations of editions like Triclinius', drama and *scholia* included, would go a long way towards rehabilitating Byzantium's reputation, and reveal much that has been deliberately obscured about the experience of the dramatic manuscript in pre-Gutenberg times.

The dramatic manuscripts of Byzantium's later years represented a triumph of the written over the spoken word, and it is possible that they mark the twilight of an era in which live recitation was the chief mode of a play's transmission. The much-vaunted invention of the printing press, in this regard, was merely the industrialization and alienation of a manuscript tradition that had placed an increasing emphasis on cheirographic control over the drama. From a Byzantine perspective, the Renaissance was more a matter of heathen Latin warlords and merchants finally learning how to read; much was lost in the translation,[80] and the nature of Classical Greek as a living, organic phenomenon would be obscured by Western scholars for centuries to come.

3   The Rhetorical Legacy of Drama

The most immediate use for Ancient drama was as the foundation for a performance genre that had developed in parallel with it: rhetoric.[81] But the symbiotic relationship between drama and rhetoric, noted with varying degrees of acceptance and alarm from Antiquity onward, has been obscured by two habits of contemporary thought: first, Darwinian theories of cultural

---

79 For a survey of Triclinius' life and work see Fryde 2000, 268–294. N. G. Wilson goes so far as to say that Triclinius' edits, usually referred to as "interpolations" (i.e., needless changes), should really be considered "recensions" (i.e., legitimate, modern-style corrections) – see Wilson 1996, 250.

80 Ruth Webb notes that Greeks looked down on the Italian fashion for conducting Classical Greek classes in Latin, instead of the traditional "immersion method" (Webb 1994, 90).

81 On the relationship between drama and rhetoric see for example Goldhill 1997, 127–50. On the ways in which Aristotle's *Poetics* positions dramatic poetry as rhetorical see also Cole 1991, 15–17.

development that privilege the drama as the marker of a fully-developed society; and second, the academic tradition of specialization and the cantonization of the arts and sciences. Cultural Darwinists fail to consider that a genre which, by Aristotle's own witness, was already fully developed[82] might continue to develop in new directions; and that those new directions were the inevitable result of the Greek education system's interdisciplinary approach.

Although drawn from the same stock as the drama's original performers – the educated male elite – rhetors usually distanced themselves from actors even as they memorized their most popular monologues and coveted their skills, developing performance styles that (to rhetors, at least) were distinct from that of the "rude mechanicals" of the theatre.[83] Although the Roman rhetor Quintilian (first century CE) believed actors had a corrupting influence on a young man's morals, he still found them useful for training in the *minutiae* of oral delivery – posture, diction, pacing, hand gestures (so long as they were not too stagy), even how to produce appropriate emotions when pleading a case in a court of law.[84] Joseph Roach has pointed out how Quintilian's approach to oratory is rooted in classical beliefs about emotions, and typifies what he calls "the combat between technique and inspiration in performance theory".[85]

The distinction between technique and inspiration took on a new aspect with the rise of Christianity and its heightened awareness of "hypocrisy", i.e. social play-acting.[86] Classically-trained rhetoricians avoided controversy by portraying theirs as a manly craft requiring careful study; and Church authorities, drawn since Christianity's earliest days from the educated urban

---

82 *Poetics* 1449a7–30.
83 For a recent analysis of the relationship between actors and rhetors in Roman times see Gunderson 2000, 111–48. Gunderson points out that no matter how rhetors constructed and presented themselves, it was impossible to create any hard and fast barrier between themselves and their "lesser" cohorts.
84 "The comic actor too should be given some part, but only in so far as the future orator needs a knowledge of Delivery. I do not want the boy we are educating for this purpose to have a weak and womanish voice or to quaver like an old man. Nor ought he to mimic the failings of drunkenness, be taught the cringing manners of a slave, or learn the emotions of love, greed, or fear. These things are not necessary for an orator, and they infect the mind, especially in the early years when it is malleable and unformed" (*Inst.* 1.11.1–2 trans. by D. A. Russell).
85 Roach 1993, 26.
86 Jesus' famous denunciations of *hypocrisia*, a term that refers to both acting and rhetoric, is part of a long Jewish tradition of hostility to Greek-style theatrics and oratory, first introduced to the Holy Land in Hellenistic times. See for example the Septuagint rendering of *Job* 36:13–14, "Those who are actors at heart prefer anger; they will not be helped when they need it. Let their soul die, then, in its arrogance." Ceslas Spicq points out that in the Septuagint "*hypokrinomai* (Hebrew *ānâh*) becomes a sin" (Spicq 1994, 3.408).

elite, continued to regard training in rhetoric as an important step on the ecclesiastical ladder, with drama as an acceptable component of their education. The incorporation of dialogue into early sermons and hymnography, mischaracterized as 'proto-dramatic' by early Darwinist scholars, has its origins in classrooms where bishops and patriarchs-to-be had their first lessons in the art of public speaking – an art that included the creation of character monologues and dialogues.[87]

Students of rhetoric worked from *progymnasmata*, preliminary exercise books which included exercises in composing character monologues: three genres, *ethopoeia*, *eidolopoeia* and *prosopopoeia* required students to craft speeches by persons living or dead, real or fictional.[88] Teachers like Aphthonius (fourth century CE) would encourage students to compose and perform passages in the spirit of tragedy and comedy, even portraying female protagonists at their most histrionic.[89] Eventually students were expected to create such speeches *extempore*, under conditions not unlike those of an improvisational drama studio. Trained in Aphthonius' methods, mature rhetors continued to practice the art of *ēthikai meletai* – "character studies" – and compete for honors with them.[90] Rhetors would perform in accordance with available information on the character's speaking style, and include introductions explaining both the subject matter as well as how the speech's delivery was put together.[91] These character monologues, when taken together with the imaginary court cases, encomia on trivial themes and other epideictic or "show" pieces demonstrate how citizen-amateurs developed a new, socially acceptable way to exercise their dramatic and histrionic skills after they were forced to yield the stage to professional actors. As George Kennedy puts it, rhetors became:

---

87 George La Piana is chief among the older, Darwinian school (see n. 50 above); for an analysis of dialogue in Orthodox homilies and hymns see White 2006, 59–62.

88 *Ēthopoieia* is an imitation of a known person, *eidolopoeia* that of a person now dead, while *prosopopeia* concerned completely fictional characters (see Kennedy 2003, 115f.). For a detailed analysis of these genres see Lausberg 1998, 366–72.

89 *Inst.* 1.8.6–7, see also Aphthonius The Sophist's monologue "What Niobe Might Say When Her Children Lie Dead," in Kennedy 2003, 116f. That Greek educators saw nothing wrong with young boys assuming the *persona* of histrionic females is, naturally, problematic; it is equally problematic when the sympathetic portrayal of women in the classroom is contrasted with their presumed attitudes towards "real" women. One way to understand this rhetorical cross-dressing (albeit from a Western Medieval perspective) can be found in Woods 2001, 143–66.

90 As D. A. Russell notes, "Whether improvised or not, [character studies], at least those intended for a wider audience, required the skills of an actor. They were essentially dramatic monologues" (Libanius 1996, 7).

91 Kennedy gives an example of an introduction to Libanius of Antioch's *prosopopoeia* (creating characters based on Homer) in Kennedy 1994, 250.

... the great performers and entertainers of their time; their speeches can be approached in the way that listeners today appreciate musical compositions, whether classical or popular.[92]

By the sixth century some rhetors openly positioned their craft as mimetic and performed mime routines on the public stage at festivals;[93] one rhetor, Choricius of Gaza, took the unprecedented step of defending the dignity of mimes as equals and colleagues – the same mimes who for centuries had endured near-slave status in the Roman Empire.[94]

Perhaps the most striking evidence of rhetoric's status as what we might consider a para- or even post-dramatic genre of performance is in the Byzantine institution of the *theatron*. From the Eastern Empire's earliest days when rhetors weren't competing in public contests, advocating in the courts or lobbying the imperial bureaucracy, they regaled each other with stand-up performances as entertainment – and, in some cases, as a means of social advancement.[95] More in the spirit of the ancient *symposium*, the *theatron* was very likely performed in normal "street" or court dress, without any of the trappings we associate with traditional theatre. By the Middle Ages the term *theatron*, "theatre", had become synonymous with live performances, the bulk of which were now performed before a circle of court-connected intellectuals; the term also designates the places where these performances took place, and their audiences.[96] The speeches were sometimes written in advance, sometimes improvised, and not always read by the author him/

---

92   Kennedy 1994, 232.
93   See Choricius of Gaza *or.* 8.95. Choricius describes a theatre festival in the suburbs of Caesaria Maritima, and the theatre has been tentatively identified as the one near the city's chief water source (a probable Maiouma site). See Tsafrir, Di Segni and Green 1994, s.vv. 'Kefar Shuni, 'Ramat ha-Nadiv,' and 'Syna Mons' (165, 211 & 238). Recent excavations in the theatre have confirmed it was renovated and expanded in the fifth century CE; see Abumokh 2001, 34 and 44f.
94   *Or.* 8.1 "No-one here should think this case would disgrace me if, imitating everything through set-speeches, I have come here as an ally to those who have taken *mimesis* as their name".
95   See for example Cavallo 2006, 57–66 and Medvedev 1993. On the role of rhetoric in career advancement consider Kennedy 1999, 170: "knowledge of the right language and right forms was the prerequisite for a career in church and state." For rhetoric's uses among would-be emperors see Vinson 2003, 12f.
96   See Puchner 2002, 308 for the various connotations of *theatron* in relation to public and private speeches. For more concrete examples see also Michael Italikos 1972, 145–6 where *theatron* is translated as *"parterre"* (stalls, or orchestra seating) and 153–4 where *logikon theatron* is rendered "a distinguished, extended circle".

herself.[97] The audience could be sober and reflective, or as rowdy as those at the traditional theatres of antiquity.[98]

Conclusion

It is a commonplace among theatre scholars and Byzantinists alike to dismiss the Eastern Empire as a culture without a drama. But given the definitions and assumptions imposed on the genre, it has been impossible to see it otherwise. Only within the past few years have we begun to reassess this vital, performance-rich empire and understand it on its own terms. Classical Greek survived as a spoken language through the Fall of Constantinople in 1453, and ancient drama remained a dominant concern in both educational and performance contexts. The "after-life" of the drama in the East, however strange it may look to us, was regarded by the Byzantines as a natural outcome of their process of cultural development.

The music that was central to the dramatic experience remained an object of study and imitation throughout this period; and the rich legacy of Byzantine chant allows us to explore – albeit in a more somber, conservative way – the aural atmosphere of the original *Dionysia*. Dramatic manuscripts were not merely studied but read aloud, memorized, and incorporated into the daily operations of the Byzantine elite (a "consummation devoutly to be wished" for modern dramatists). Only with the switch from uncial to accented miniscule, and the incorporation of *scholia* in the Middle Ages did drama begin to assume the literary *persona* we now take for granted.

The drama's most direct and enduring legacy in the Greek performing arts was in the field of rhetoric, through its in-depth study of the emotions and especially its entertaining *ethopoieia*. Rhetoric may have been more prosaic in form, but the variety of works grouped under this general category – indeed, it has been argued that rhetoric covers nearly everything written in Byzantium – indicates a potentially fruitful avenue of study for future historians of the drama. Rhetoric provided what Margaret Mullett aptly calls the "screenplay" of the Eastern Empire,[99] and the many *personae* adopted by

---

97 On improvisation see for example Michael Italikos 1972, 145–6; for a "review" of a letter written by Nicephorus Bryennius and performed by a mutual friend see *ibid.* 153–4. On the uses of rhetoric in social advancement see also Kennedy 1983, 291–325.

98 For a more sober *theatron* see Emperor Manual II Palaeologus' letter to Triboles of Mistras (*Ep.* 9.1–8, in Manuel II Palaeologus 1977, 24). For signs of a more vigorous atmosphere see also Medvedev 1993.

99 Mullett 2003, 151.

its writer/speakers give the lie to our notions of Byzantium as a moribund, fossilized society.[100]

With the fall of Byzantium to the Ottoman Turks, and the mass-emigration of Greek intellectuals to the city-states of Italy, western elites once again had an opportunity to study and perform ancient drama. This re-transplantation, however, ultimately required translation into Latin and the vernacular. Greek drama would lose its place in daily conversation – Latin had supplanted Greek as the West's learned language – so the genre went from being a familiar, living oral phenomenon to a foreign, primarily written one. Still, the West embraced ancient drama at a time when the society that had created and nurtured it for two thousand years was being torn apart. And the Renaissance's experiments in dramatic form, inspired by the Byzantine manuscript tradition and conducted in some cases under Byzantine tutelage, would prove to be an essential component in the West's cultural revival.

Bibliography

Abumokh, K. (2001), "Shuni", *Hadashot Arkheologiyot–Excavations and Surveys in Israel* 113, 34 and 44–45.

Adler, Ada (ed.) (1928–1938), *Suidae Lexicon*, 5 vols., Leipzig.

Angelopoulos, Lycourgos (Dir), *Ioannis Koukouzèlis: Le Maïstor Byzantin*, Jade C 129, Compact Disc.

Auslander, Philip (2006), "Music as Performance: Living in the Immaterial World", *Theatre Survey* 47.2, 261–70.

Bakhtin, Michael (1986), "The Problem of Speech Genres", in: Michael Bakhtin, *Speech Genres & Other Late Essays* (trans. Vern W. McGee), Austin, TX, 60–102.

Barbour, Ruth (1981), *Greek Literary Hands A.D. 400–1600*, Oxford.

Barker, Andrew (1984), *Greek Musical Writings*, 2 vols., New York.

Browning, Robert (1989), "The Language of Byzantine Literature", in: Spiros Vryonis Jr. (ed.), *The Past in Medieval and Modern Greek Culture*, Malibu/ CA 1978, 103–33 [reprinted in Robert Browning, *History, Language and Literacy in the Byzantine World*, Northampton, 1989].

—— (1963), "A Byzantine Treatise on Tragedy", in: L. Varcle / R. F. Willetts (eds.), *ΓΕΡΑΣ: Studies Presented to George Thomson on the Occasion of his 60th Birthday*, Prague, 67–82.

Cavallo, Guglielmo (2006), *Lire à Byzance* (translated by P. Odorico / A. Segonds), Paris.

Ceccarelli, Paola (2004), "'Autour de Dionysos': remarques sur la dénomination des artistes dionysiaques", in: Christophe Hugoniot / Frederic Hurlet / Silvia Milanezi (eds.), *Le statut de l'acteur dans l'antiquité grecque et romaine*, Tours, 109–42.

---

100 Ruth Webb points out that the earliest Italian students of Classical Greek regarded themselves as rhetoricians and orators in the Byzantine tradition – not "humanists" (Webb 1994, 98).

Chrysaphes, Manuel (1985), *The Treatise of Manuel Chrysaphes, the Lampadarios* (translated by Dimitri E. Conomos), Vienna.

Cole, Thomas (1991), *The Origins of Rhetoric in Ancient Greece*, Baltimore, MD.

Comotti, Giovanni (1989), *Music in Greek and Roman Culture*, Baltimore, MD.

Csapo, Eric (2004), "The Politics of the New Music", in: Murray Penelope / Peter Wilson (eds.), *Music and the Muses: The Culture of 'Mousikē' in the Classical Athenian City*, Oxford, 207–48.

Cunningham, Mary (2003), "Dramatic Device or Didactic Tool? The Function of Dialogue in Byzantine Preaching", in: Jeffreys (2003) 101–13.

Dezeimeris, Reinhold (1881), *Études sur le Querolus*, Bordeaux.

Downey, Glanville (1957), "Nicholas Mesarites: Description of the Church of the Holy Apostles at Constantinople", *Transactions of the American Philosophical Society* 47, 855–918.

Easterling, Patricia / Hall, Edith (eds.) (2002), *Greek and Roman Actors: Aspects of an Ancient Profession*, Cambridge.

Falkner, Thomas (2002), "Scholars versus Actors: Text and Performance in the Greek Tragic Scholia", in: Easterling / Hall (2002), 342–61.

Fryde, Edmund (2000), *The Early Palaeologan Renaissance (1261–c. 1360),* Boston.

Gamillscheg, Ernst and Ševčenko, Ihor (1991), "Miniscule", in: Alexander P. Kazhdan (ed.), *The Oxford Dictionary of Byzantium*, New York, 2:1377–8.

Ghiron-Bistagne, Paulette (1976), *Recherches sur les Acteurs dans la Grèce Antique*, Paris.

Goldhill, Simon (1997), "The Language of Tragedy- Rhetoric and Communication", in: Patricia Easterling (ed.), *The Cambridge Companion to Greek Tragedy*, Cambridge, 127–50.

Gunderson, Erik (2000), *Staging Masculinity: The Rhetoric of Performance in the Roman World*, Ann Arbor.

Halaris, Christodoulos (prod. & dir.), *Hellenic Elegies*, Orata Ltd. ORM 4012, Compact Disk.

Hall, Edith (2002), "The Singing Actors of Antiquity", in: Easterling / Hall (2002) 3–38.

Hermann, Douglas J. / Chaffin, Roger (eds.) (1988), *Memory in Historical Perspective: The Literature Before Ebbinghaus*, New York.

Jacquemard-Le Saos, Catherine (1994), *Querolus (Aulularia) ou Le Grincheux (Comédie de la Petite Marmite)*, Paris.

Jeffreys, Elizabeth (ed.) (2003), *Rhetoric in Byzantium: Papers from the Thirty-Fifth Spring Symposium of Byzantine Studies, Exeter College, University of Oxford, March 2001*, London.

Kazhdan, Alexander P. (ed.) (1991), *The Oxford Dictionary of Byzantium*, 3 vols., New York.

Kennedy George (2003), *Progymnasmata: Greek Textbooks of Prose Composition and Rhetoric*, Atlanta.

—— (1999), *Classical Rhetoric and its Christian and Secular Tradition from Ancient to Modern Times*, 2nd ed., Chapel Hill, NC.

—— (1994), *A New History of Classical Rhetoric*, Princeton.

—— (1983), *Greek Rhetoric under Christian Emperors*, Princeton.

Lampe, G. W. H. (ed.) (1961), *A Patristic Greek Lexicon*, Oxford.

La Piana, George (1912), *Le Rappresentazioni Sacre nella Litteratura Bizantina dalle Origini al Secolo IX, con Rapporti al Teatro Sacro d'Occidente*, Grotteferrata.

—— (1936), "The Byzantine Theatre", *Speculum* 11, 171–211.

Lausberg, Heinrich (1998), *Handbook of Literary Rhetoric: a Foundation for Literary Study* (transl. by Matthew T. Bliss), Boston.

Law, Vivien (1996), "The Mnemonic Structure of Ancient Grammatical Doctrine", in: Pierre Swiggers / Alfons Wouters (eds.), *Ancient Grammar: Content and Context*, Paris, 37–52.

Lemerle, Paul (1986), *Byzantine Humanism: the First Phase* (transl. by Helen Lindsay and Ann Moffatt), *Byzantina Australiensia* 3.

Libanius (1996), *Imaginary Speeches: A Selection of Declamations* (transl. by D. A. Russell), London.

Lord, Albert Bates (1967), "The Influence of a Fixed Text", in: *To Honor Roman Jakobson: Essays on the Occasion of His Seventieth Birthday (11 October 1966)*, Paris, 1199–1206.

Mango, Cyril (1981), "Daily Life in Byzantium", in: *Jahrbuch der Österreichischen Byzantinistik* 31/1, 337–53.

Manuel II Paleologus, Emperor (1977), *The Letters of Manuel II Palaeologus* (transl. by George T. Dennis), Washington.

Marciniak, Przemysław (2004), *Greek Drama in Byzantine Times*, Katowice.

Mathiesen, Thomas F. (1999), *Apollo's Lyre: Greek Music and Music Theory in Antiquity and the Middle Ages*, Lincoln.

Mathisen, Ralph W. (ed.) (2003), *People, Personal Expression, and Social Relations in Late Antiquity*, 2 vols., Ann Arbor.

Medvedev, I. P. (1993), "The So-Called θέατρα as a Form of Communication of the Byzantine Intellectuals in the 14th and 15th Centuries", in: N. G. Moschonas (ed.), *I epikoinonia sto vyzantio: praktika tou B' Diethnous Symposiou, 4–6 Octovriou 1990*, Athens, 227–35.

Michael Italikos (1972), *Michel Italikos; Lettres et Discours* (transl. by Paul Gautier), Paris.

Migne, J.-P. (ed.) (1979), *Patrologiae Cursus Completus, Series Graeca*, 161 vols., reprint, Brepols.

Moran, Neil K. (2002), "Byzantine castrati", *Plainsong and Medieval Music* 11.2, 99–112.

Mullett, Margaret (2003), "Rhetoric, Theory and the Imperative of Performance: Byzantium and Now", in: Jeffreys (2003) 151–70.

Ong, Walter J. (2002), "Orality and Literacy: Writing Restructures Consciousness", in: David Finkelstein and Alistair McCleery (eds.), *The Book History Reader*, New York, 109–13.

—— (1982), *Orality and Literacy: The Technologizing of the Word*. London.

Paniagua, Gregorio (prod. & dir.), *Musique de la Grèce Antique*, Harmonia Mundi HMA 1951015, compact disk.

Parkes, Malcolm Beckwith (1993), *Pause and Effect: An Introduction to the History of Punctuation in the West*, Berkeley.

Pickard-Cambridge, Sir Arthur (1988), *The Dramatic Festivals of Athens*, 3rd ed. (by J. Gould / D. M. Lewis), Oxford.

Pöhlmann, Egert / West, Martin L. (eds.) (2001), *Documents of Ancient Greek Music: Extant Melodies and Fragments Edited and Transcribed with Commentary*, Oxford.

Prauscello, Lucia (2006), *Singing Alexandria: Music Between Practice and Textual Transmission*, Boston.

Procopius of Caesaria (1966), *Procopius: The Secret History* (transl. by G. A. Williamson), New York.

Puchner, Walter (2002), "Acting in the Byzantine Theatre: Evidence and Problems", in: Easterling / Hall (2002) 304–26.

Richter, Lucas (1964), "Fragen der spätgriechisch-byzantinischen Musiktheorie: die Erforschung der byzantinischen Musik", in: Johannes Irmscher (ed.), *Byzantinische Beiträge*, Berlin, 187–230.

Roach, Joseph R. (1993), *The Player's Passion: Studies in the Science of Acting*, Ann Arbor.

Romano, Roberto (ed.) (1999), *La Satira Byzantina dei secoli XI–XV*, Turin.

Romanos, Christos S. (2004), *Human Boundaries: Oral Song, Text, Hypertext*, Minneapolis.

Roueché, Charlotte (1993), *Performers and Partisans at Aphrodisias*, London.

Schartau, Bjarne (ed.) (1998), *Anonymous Questions and Answers on the Interval Signs*, Vienna.

Ševčenko, Ihor (1975), "Theodore Metochites, the Chora, and the Intellectual Trends of His Time", in: Paul A. Underwood (ed.), *The Kariye Djami*, vol. 4, *Studies in the Art of the Kariye Djami and Its Intellectual Background*, Princeton, 17–84.

Spicq, Ceslas (ed.) (1994), *Theological Lexicon of the New Testament*, volume: *pai-pseu* (transl. by James D. Earnest), New York.

Sticca, Sandro (1974), "The *Christos Paschon* and the Byzantine Theatre", *Comparative Drama* 8, 25–41.

Suda On Line: Byzantine Lexicography (2009), David Whitehead et al. (eds.), http://www.stoa.org/sol/ (accessed 10/16/2009).

Symes, Carol (2002), "The Appearance of Early Vernacular Plays: Forms, Functions, and the Future of Medieval Theater", *Speculum* 77, 778–831.

Tannery, P. (1940), *Quadrivium de Georges Pachymere*, Vatican City.

Theall, Donald F. (1992), "Beyond the Orality/Literacy Dichotomy: James Joyce and the Pre-History of Cyberspace", *Postmodern Culture* 2.3 (1992), http://muse.jhu.edu/journals/postmodern_culture/v002/2.3theall.html (accessed November 11, 2006).

Thompson, Sir Edward Maunde (1912), *An Introduction to Greek and Latin Palaeography*, Oxford.

Treadgold, Warren (1980), *The Nature of the* Bibliotheca *of Photius*, Washington, D.C.

Tsafrir, Y. / Di Segni, Leah / Green, J. (eds.) (1994), *Tabula Imperii Romani: Iudaea Palaestina*, Jerusalem.

Tuilier, A. (1969), *La Passion du Christ*, Paris.

Turner, Eric Gardner (ed.) (1971), *Greek Manuscripts of the Ancient World*, Oxford.

Turyn, Alexander (1957), *The Byzantine Manuscript Tradition of the Tragedies of Euripides*, Urbana.

—— (1952), *Studies in the Manuscript Tradition of the Tragedies of Sophocles*, Urbana.

—— (1943), *The Manuscript Tradition of the Tragedies of Aeschylus*, New York.

van Groningen, Bernhard Abraham (1963), *Short Manual of Greek Palaeography*, Leyden.

Vasiliev, Alexander A. (1964), *History of the Byzantine Empire 324–1453*, 2 vols., Madison.

Vivilakes, Iosef (1996), " *I Theatriki Orologia stous Pateres tis Ekklisias: Symvoli sti Meleti tis Scheseos Ekklesias kai Theatrou*", Ph.D. diss, University of Athens.

Vinson, Martha (2003), "Rhetoric and Writing Strategies in the Ninth Century", in: Elizabeth Jeffreys (2003) 9–22.

Vogt, Albert (1931), "Le Théâtre a Byzance et Dans l'Empire du IVᵉ au XIIIᵉ Siecle", *Revue des Questions Historiques* 115, 257–296.

Webb, Ruth (1994), "A Slavish Art? Language and Grammar in Late Byzantine Education and Society", *Dialogos* 1, 81–103.

Wellesz, Egon (1998), *A History of Byzantine Music and Hymnography*, 2nd ed., Oxford.

West, Martin L. (1992), *Ancient Greek Music*, Oxford.

White, Andrew W. (2007), "From Euripides to Koukouzeles and Back: A Survey of Greek Musical Culture from Antiquity to Late Byzantine Times", in: Iosef Vivilakes (ed.), *Stephanos. Tribute to Walter Puchner*, Athens, 1367–1380.

—— (2006), *The Artifice of Eternity: a Study of Liturgical and Theatrical Practices in Byzantium*, Ph.D. diss., University of Maryland, College Park.

Wilson, Nigel G. (1996), *Scholars of Byzantium*, rev. ed., Cambridge, MA.

Wilson, Peter (2005), "Music", in: Justina Gregory (ed.), *A Companion to Greek Tragedy*, Malden, MA, 183–93.

Woods, Marjorie Curry (2001), "Boys Will Be Women: Musings on Classroom Nostalgia and the Chaucerian Audience", in: Robert F. Yeager and Charlotte C. Morse (eds.), *Speaking Images: Essays in Honor of V. A. Kolve*, Asheville, 143–66.

Whipping Jesus Devoutly:
The Dramaturgy of Catharsis and the Christian Idea of Tragic Form

Domenico Pietropaolo

In a moving passage of the *Divine Comedy,* Vergil takes Dante by his hand and leads him to a bush whose leaves have been scattered by savage hounds. Pouring out at once words and blood from its injuries, the bush cries out its pain, asks that its mutilated leaves be brought back to it as an act of pity, and describes itself as the transformed soul of a suicide from the city of Florence. He must have been one of those who, in a mysterious impulse to commit suicide that threw the city into mourning at the end of the thirteenth century, succumbed to unknown despair and took their lives in the secrecy of their own homes. His anonymity, suggests Boccaccio lecturing on Dante in the Florentine church of St. Stephen, leaves the readers free to imagine that the tormented soul imprisoned in the branches and leaves of the bush is that of a suicide they may have personally known in their community. The number of those who hanged themselves in Florence at this dark hour of its history seemed to Boccaccio to be large enough to be unintelligible other than as evidence of the wrath of God, delivering terrible punishment upon the city for some unconscionable and unredeemed sin. The wayfarer is so moved to pity that he gathers the scattered leaves and gently places them at the foot of the bush inhabited by the soul of his unhappy compatriot.[1]

The moral culture of the transitional period between the Middle Ages and the Renaissance was a profoundly troubled one, in a manner and to a degree that may at times be obscured in our historical consciousness by the magnitude of its aesthetic expression in art and literature. Paul Tillich described the condition as a contagious moral disease, a general anxiety of guilt, experienced as an existential urgency to ward off the prospect of

---

1   *Inferno* XIII 130–151 and XIV 1–3. Textual citations are from *La Divina Comme-dia,* testo critico stabilito da Giorgio Petrocchi (Torino: Einaudi, 1975). Boccaccio's gloss is in his *Esposizioni sopra la Comedia di Dante* (Milano: Mondadori, 1994) II p. 629f.

despair before death and the risk of eternal damnation in the afterlife.[2] That
was certainly a reason why many joined religious orders, practised conspicuous penance, participated actively in sacred rituals, made pilgrimages to
holy places, became self-torturing mystics, and purchased indulgences. It
seems that, at the hour of their death, they all wanted to be in the odour of
sanctity, or, failing that, in a state of moral purity sufficient for them to enter
purgatory. Some, however, were unable to overcome their despair and, their
religious education notwithstanding, committed the terrible sin of taking
their own lives.

Narrating the story of the anonymous suicide as a stern theologian,
Dante is careful to say that, as the wayfarer, who experienced the narrated
action as its protagonist, he was impelled by love of country ("carità del
natio loco" *Inf.* XIV, 1), and not by charity for an unrepentant sinner, to perform his moving gesture of piety. The theologian is quick to provide us with
proper hermeneutical coordinates at every step of the journey through hell,
lest we be fooled by the damned into commiserating them for their tragic
fate, blinding ourselves to the justness of their suffering and falling prey to
a process of reverse catharsis that would cause us to sin under the cloak of
mercy. The medieval theologian knows nothing of the Willy Lomans of the
modern world and would not be moved by their plight. Despair, for whatever reason, is a sin. However tragic the fate that led them to hell may still
appear to them, the damned are all unrepentant and are fixed forever in their
will-to-sin. The souls of the damned are generally aware of the fact that human beings, prone as they are to commiserate the tragic fate of others, can be
swayed to feel pity for them without realizing that such pity is actually tantamount to contempt for divine justice. When it is considered in isolation from
its surrounding presentational narrative, the represented action of the *Divine
Comedy* is structured as the dialogue of an episodic play, to be performed
on an imaginary stage with many mansions, while the narrative assumes the
role of the stage directions needed to govern its proper enactment and its
correct interpretation by the reader. As he advances in his journey through
hell, the wayfarer can be seen occasionally yielding to human passions, in
ways that the theologian, who knows better because he has completed his
journey, would not. The fullness of our visualization of the action depends to
a very large extent on our ability to hear both voices simultaneously, while
our emotional and our intellectual response to it depends on our willingness
to let our interpretative consciousness slide without interruption back and
forth along the dialectic by which presentation and representation are linked
in the poem.

---

2   Tillich 1968, 228.

The episode of the anonymous Florentine suicide – a small detail, to be sure, on the large and complex canvas of the *Inferno* – is a convenient point of departure for the question that I intend to examine in this paper, which is how, in the transitional period between the Middle Ages and the Renaissance, Christian culture understood the issue of moral catharsis before dramatic re-enactments of the supreme spectacle of suffering. This is not the suffering of a great hero, morally or intellectually responsible for his own downfall, but the suffering of the Lamb of God for the iniquities of mankind. To enter this arena is to raise once again the question of the possibility of a Christian tragedy that is grounded in, or analogous to, classical tragedy. The issues to be considered are basically three: whether there can be a tragic hero without *hamartia,* a tragic action without a downfall, and a tragic plot that does not cause the catharsis of compassion, since Christ and his martyrs are flawless heroes and, in the transcendent order, always triumph over the immanence of reality, and since compassion remains a supreme Christian virtue. These questions, however, are here, and generally elsewhere, posed from the perspective of Athenian tragedy and Aristotle's *Poetics,* on the principle that they represent with sufficient clarity the distinctive features of the genre as a whole. For modern criticism, with its grasp of the western dramatic tradition in its full historical development, it makes good sense to begin with questions such as these, since it is on the ideas that they presuppose that the conventional theory of tragedy is generally based. Scholars are nonetheless divided on the issue because they are not all equally willing to regard the defining traits of Athenian tragedy as the informing principles of tragedy as such. A larger textual base and a wider purview could lead us to a variety of definitions and relativize the Athenian concept of tragedy. The same approach would certainly make less sense in a period of western history in which the classics were less perfectly known, and in which the Greek origins of the genre were still a matter of contention. In high Renaissance Italy, as late as 1556, the Jewish scholar Leone De' Sommi could surmise with confidence that the cultural origins of western drama were Hebrew rather than Greek, the first great tragedy being the *Book of Job,* "la elegantissima et filosofica tragedia di Iobbe."[3]

If the defining features of tragedy as such were derived from the story of Job, we would have, of course, a different concept of tragedy, the large Greek corpus of the genre notwithstanding. Among modern scholars, Sidney Lamb would surely agree, since for him the *Book of Job,* which he classifies as a proto-tragedy, dramatizes the principle of the incompatibility of suffering and justice, which is "at the basis of all tragic situations."[4] The tradition

---

3   De' Sommi 1968, 14.
4   Lamb 1965, 7.

of considering the book of Job a tragedy is at least as ancient as Theodore of Mopsuestia, who suggested that it was an imitation of classical Greek tragedy, but it was only after Theodore Beza divided the book into acts and scenes in 1587 that a succession of scholars pointed out similarities, until the early twentieth century, when Horace Meyer Kallen argued the unlikely thesis that the Book of Job was consciously written in the manner of Euripides.[5] More to our point, however, is the earlier observation by George Goodspeed that the story of the Hebrew sufferer, though not consciously patterned on any dramatic work, was nonetheless a prototype of both that of Prometheus, "the Greek Job," and that of Hamlet, "Shakespeare's Job."[6] The conception of the *Book of Job* as a tragedy that is typologically comparable to *Prometheus Bound* has weighty implications for a theory of Christian tragedy in the late Middle Ages. For, in the first place, the interpretation of Prometheus by early Christian apologetics and iconography as a classical type of the biblical creator – the "verus Prometheus," in the words of Tertullian – eventually led to his allegorical identification with Christ.[7] A fourteenth-century preacher could speak the name of Prometheus with confidence in a sermon because "Dei sapienciam signat, qui Christus est,"[8] while his torment on the Caucasus came to be viewed as a classical adumbration of Christian martyrdom.[9] In the second place, Job was typologically regarded by the religious culture of the Middle Ages, principally on the authority of St. Jerome and Gregory the Great, as a prefiguration of the *Christus patiens,* the suffering Christ of the Passion and, by extension, as a symbol of suffering Christians everywhere, all part of the mystical body of Christ, which is his church: "beatus Job passiones Redemptoris nostri, ejusque corporis, id est Sanctae Ecclesiae, et passione sua significavit et nomine."[10] ("Blessed Job has signi-

---

5   Kallen 1918, 7.
6   Goodspeed 1892, 105 and 109.
7   Tertullian, *Apologeticus* 18.2, *P. L.* 1, col. 434: "hic enim est verus Prometheus."
8   Wenzel 1989, 296.
9   On the relationship between Prometheus and Christian martyrs, an obvious bridge was Martial's *De Spectaculis,* in which the torment of Prometheus on the rock is comparatively invoked in the description of an execution combining the sentences of crucifixion and *ad bestias* in the Coliseum. In a gloss of Farnciscus Bivarius on epigram 7, appended by him to the *Chronicon* of Flavius Lucius Dexter, who mentions a theatrical miming of such an execution, the relationship is made explicit: "quo martyris cujusdam Christiani passionem veram, simulatam agentis Laureoli Latronis fabulam, refert." See *Flavii Lucii Dextri Barcinonensis, Chronicon Omnimodae Historiae, una cum commentariis Fr. Francisci Bivarii, P.L.* 31, col. 251.
10 Gregory the Great, *Moralia in Job, P. L.* 75, col. 533; Jerome, *Expositio interlinearis libri Job, P. L.* 23, col. 1475 ("Job dolens interpretatur Jesus Christus, qui dolores nostros portavit"). The name of Job was etymologized as "the one who suffers" by Isidore of Seville, *Etimologie o origini,* a cura di Angelo Valastro Canale (Torino: Unione Tipografico-Editrice Torinese, 2004), I p. 586: "Iob in Latinum vertitur dolens."

fied the sufferings of our Redeemer, and of his body, that is the Holy Church, with his suffering and name.")

The Possibility of Christian Tragedy

The question of the possibility of Christian tragedy in the late Middle Ages is historically prompted by the hermeneutical association of the suffering of Prometheus and Job with the Passion of Christ. It now remains to be seen whether the same question can be ontologically grounded in the theology of the Passion, for without such grounding the question can have little interest for Christian thought. If such a thing as Christian tragedy exists, its principle of being and its principle of explanation must be sought in the foundation of Christian thought itself. We must therefore inquire under what hermeneutical aspect medieval theology might lend itself to such a possibility. In this context Honorius of Autun, whose *Gemma animae* was probably one of Dante's sources for the theatrical pageant he witnesses in Eden, offers us a reliable theoretical orientation: "Tragicus noster pugnam Christi populo Christiano in theatro Ecclesiae gestibus suis repraesentat eique victoriam redemptionis suae inculcat."[11] ("Our tragic actor portrays the struggle of Christ to the Christian people in the theatre of the Church with his gestures and teaches them the victory of his redemption.")

Honorius is not speaking of a dramatic work in the ordinary sense of the word, but of the originary Christian tragedy, understood at the highest level of generality and at the deepest level of profundity possible. It is the tragedy in which the meaning of all ordinary Christian tragedies must be ultimately rooted. From the perspective of a developing theory of Christian tragedy, the orientation offered by this definition could not be clearer: the foundations of Christian tragedy are located entirely in the Mass, which is the sole source of its ontological clarity. This term does not mean logical or linguistic clarity but clarity of substantiation, whether or not that is understood by observers. This is the sense in which the late medieval Schoolmen used it. For scholasticism ontological clarity represents a principle of substantiation that includes intelligibility and mystery simultaneously, since there is always mystery where the mind is invited to reach out to something beyond what is apparent to it in contact, especially when that beyond is deep within the observer's conscience.[12] The Mass is the source of ontological substantiation of tragedy also with respect to its mode of performance, by which it must signify in the manner of the liturgy, that is rememoratively and transfor-

---

11   *P. L.* 172, col. 570.
12   Maritain 1962, 28.

matively. The place of performance is the Church, a material area of focus for the ubiquity of God, a place visible to us either as a real church or as an architectural trope of one. The audience are the faithful, that is members of the mystical body of Christ, impelled to take part in the celebration by their need for redemption. The achievement of consciousness of redemption, in the here and now of the communal experience, is the intended cathartic effect of the performance.

We are here at the very heart of the question of Christian tragedy, for in the hermeneutics of Honorius the theory of Greek classical tragedy and the theology of the Eucharist are made explicitly to intersect. Hardison has observed that, throughout his interpretation of the Mass as a dramatic form in performance, Honorius uses the vocabulary of the classical theory of drama "with considerable sophistication."[13] Ultimately the contact between the classics and Christianity in his analysis of the Mass is, in a certain sense, philological, in that it presupposes a concatenation of texts, echoes and citations from the dramatic theory of antiquity to the allegorization of the liturgy in the late Middle Ages. It is not possible to know with precision just how far the surviving classical tradition had permeated medieval consciousness, inducing it to think of the Mass in terms of Greek tragedy, but we can determine the dimensions and character of the contextual classicism that made such an association meaningful. In the pursuit of this determination Dante is a good reference point. His knowledge of the classics is unmatched by anyone in Europe prior to the Renaissance, as is the degree to which he manages to weave classical allusions and citations directly into his own language in relation to analogous borrowings from the Bible. A quantitative analysis of relevant textual citations in Dante's works and a simple census of the characters assigned to the three spiritual realms of the *Divine Comedy* may be regarded as good indicators of the extent of his contact with the classics, direct or indirect though that contact may have been, and may safely be considered the upper limit of the classicism of his age. Against the 500 or so citations of the Vulgate, there are more than 300 textual references to Aristotle, around 200 to Vergil, approximately 100 to Ovid, about 50 each to Cicero and Lucan, somewhere between 30 and 40 to each of Statius and Boethius, and between 10 and 20 to Horace, Livy and Orosius, plus a few each to Plato, Homer, Juvenal, Seneca, Ptolemy, Aesop, Lucretius, Galen, Suetonius, Vegetius, Euclid, and Valerius Maximus. As for the census of the characters in the netherworld of the *Divine Comedy*, we know that of the 332 mentioned, a total of 89 are classical, almost twice as many as the 48 of biblical origin.[14] Among the characters of classical origin, we find the most

---

13   Hardison 1965, 40.
14   The figures on textual citations are based on Moore 1896, 4–5, whereas those on the

famous protagonists of classical tragedy, whose stories had reached the late Middle Ages through non-dramatic sources, though it is safe to assume that Dante had direct knowledge of the tragedies of Seneca, which had started to circulate in the eleventh century.[15]

Something of the overall perception that the late Middle Ages had of the classical world may be surmised from the fact that Dante placed most of the great spirits of antiquity in a special part of limbo, a castle bathed in light where the only punishment suffered by the pagan souls is privation of the sight of the true God. As the wayfarer and his guide approach the castle, which Vergil had temporarily left in order to succour Dante, they are met by Homer, Horace, Ovid and Lucan who come to welcome Vergil back among them, and, after their reunion, they all invite Dante to become the sixth member of their company. By joining their *bella scola*, Dante shows that he understood the imaginative universe of his poetry to stand in a direct line of continuity with the classics, almost as the Christian *eschaton* to which the enlightened minds of pagan antiquity were unknowingly reaching out. Such vision of continuity was a direct function of the power of assimilation that informed medieval hermeneutics, in which historical exegesis and allegorical eisegesis flowed freely into one another. Among the classical authors, Vergil became early an unknowing prophet of Christ in his fourth eclogue, Seneca found his way into St. Jerome's list of Christian saints chiefly on the strength of his presumed friendship and correspondence with St. Paul, while in Dante's vision Statius converted secretly to Christianity, largely under the salvific influence of Vergil's poetry, and was secretly baptized during a persecution ordered by Domitian. Moreover, Cato Uticensis is the guardian of Dante's purgatory and is idealized to such an extent that, in the *Convivio*, he alone among all men is said to be worthy of signifying God by his very existence, his suicide being allegorically sublimated into an act of martyrdom in the name of freedom.[16]

Beyond the world of literature the disposition of medieval culture to Christianize the classical tradition may be observed in the Mass, the very heart of Christian worship, where it is expressed forcefully in two brief texts

---

characters of the *Divine Comedy* are based on the lists compiled by Simons 1918, 371–380.

15   The E text is from the eleventh century, but it was not transmitted in many other copies. However, the text that appeared in the twelfth or thirteenth century (the A text) was copied very frequently, contributing, among other things, to the developing thought on the nature of cruelty; it has come down to us in almost 300 manuscripts. Cf. Baraz 1998, 195–215 (especially p. 210). For a detailed account of the transmission of Seneca's tragedies in the late Middle Ages, see Rouse 1971 and Zwierlein 1989.

16   *Convivio* IV.28.15–19. Edition used: *Il Convivio*, ridotto a miglior lezione e commentato da G. Busnelli e G. Vandelli, seconda edizione (Firenze: Le Monnier, 1968).

of the period: the *Dies irae,* the famous sequence of funeral services, in a line of which the Hebrew David and the pagan Sybil join voices ("teste David cum Sybilla") to prophesy the Christian day of judgement, and the *Ad Maronis Mausoleum,* a hymn chanted in the service for the feast of St. Paul in Mantua, which describes the Apostle weeping with grief over the tomb of Vergil for having lived too late to bring the noble pagan to the Christian fulfilment of his calling.[17] The Mass at the time was the Franciscan Mass, and in that context it may be worth recalling that, according to a contemporary hagiographic legend, St. Francis of Assisi would lovingly pick up all discarded pieces of written parchment that he might find on the ground, indiscriminately, showing as much care for relics of classical works as for those of Christian works, because all good things eventually lead the mind back to their origin, which is God. "Litterae sunt," he apparently explained to a disciple who was puzzled by his care for written fragments of a pagan culture, "ex quibus componitur gloriosissimum Dei nomen."[18]

It is within such a reconfiguration and transfiguration of classicism that the Mass can be considered functionally equivalent to the religious sources of classical tragedy. In contemporary theology there was general agreement that the Mass was an allegorical ritual of the Passion in dramatic form, but there was some variance of opinion concerning the nature of the relationship between the enacted representation and the historical event at its origin. The majority view was the one upheld by St. Thomas Aquinas, who argued that, in so far as the reality of the death of Jesus is concerned, the relation between the Mass and the event is one of simple signification. The celebrant (*tragicus noster*) signifies by his words and actions the essential aspects of the Passion but does not himself suffer it in the process. However, in so far as the salvific effect of the celebration is concerned – its sacramental value – the Mass and the event are for St. Thomas functionally equivalent.[19] To attend Mass with the right disposition is to benefit spiritually from the celebration, anywhere and at any time. Viewed against the background of Honorius' superimposition of the theory of classical tragedy, the argument advanced by St. Thomas brings into great prominence the notion of the spiritual impact of the Mass as a form of sacramental catharsis. The suffering and death of Jesus are present only symbolically, but the spiritual effect of their enactment is as real as the original event, and is equally real each time that it occurs before a congregation of believers. The analogy with classical tragedy is clear and does not

---

17 On the *Dies Irae* see Ong 1947, 321. The text of the Mantuan hymn may be found in Ziolkowski and Putnam 2007, 412.
18 Th. da Celano, *Vita prima,* 83.2–4, in *S. Francisci Assisiensis Vita et Miracula,* ed. E. d'Alençon (Rome, 1906).
19 *Summa Theologiae,* III.83, Cura Fratrum eiusdem Ordinis (Madrid: Biblioteca de Autores Cristianos, 1965), and cf. Marsili 1987, 257–258.

call for detailed commentary: for each person in attendance, the catharsis is real in both cases, the only difference being that at Mass the experience is spiritual rather than merely psychological, since the Mass is a sacred liturgy of salvation and not a secular play with a paraliturgical function in festivities.

As a sacramental ritual, the Mass is both timeless and unlocalized. At the signifying level, the struggle of Christ is enacted in the here and now of any particular celebration, but at the signified level it takes place in the minds and hearts of the people present, individually incorporated into the mystical body of Christ by virtue of their spiritual disposition to be thus united. But when the boundary between ritual and representation is crossed, the signifying elements of the Passion move into the imaginative world of localized space, linear time, sequential narrative, and structural particularity. It is at this point that Christian drama emerges as an art form in its own right, and that the analogy with classical tragedy can be on the same plane of meaning.[20] In the composition of such works, the selection of a particular gospel as the controlling narrative is significant. For although in the collective religious imagination the four canonical accounts of the Passion are generally fused into a single narrative, in a dramatic perspective it is useful to keep them apart as much as possible and to read one without being influenced by the others. If the story of the Passion is taken from Mark or Matthew, the tragic dimension of the suffering and death of Jesus emerges with overpowering force. In these two gospels – especially in Matthew, in whom the tragic end is prepared with a greater abundance of *hubris*[21] – Jesus dies in utter desolation, abandoned by his disciples and forsaken by God. There is no attenuating acceptance of the divine plan that calls for his death on the cross, such as we find in Luke when he commends his spirit to God, and no tenderness of human concerns, such as we see in John, when he commends his youngest disciple to his mother. In John and Luke, Jesus dies at peace, "a fellow to Socrates."[22] In Mark and Matthew he dies a tragic hero of the greatest magnitude, titanic in his solitude and in his suffering. Here he is a fellow to Prometheus.

The cry of forsakenness issued by Jesus from the cross in Aramaic (*Eli, Eli, lamma sabacthani*) is the ultimate argument against all theories of the presumed incompatibility of tragedy and Christianity. Hans Urs von Balthasar reminds us that in proclaiming the death of tragedy at the beginning of the Christian era, scholars such as George Steiner and philosophers such as Karl Jaspers failed to take into account that Jesus does not die in the

---

20 Cf. Hardison 1965, 271.
21 Mandel 1961, 114.
22 Mandel 1961, 114.

knowledge that with his death he was fulfilling the divine economy of salvation, but really forsaken, his final question remaining unanswered.[23] The fact that the crucifixion of Jesus is followed by his resurrection, that Good Friday is followed by Easter Sunday, does not attenuate the tragedy of his death as a man but only invests it with the meaning of the divine plan for the reconciliation of all to God. The tragedy is fully contained in the Passion; the Resurrection is the hermeneutical ground on which Christians are asked to stand in order to interpret it correctly. In the scholastic culture of the late Middle Ages, the form of any object, including sacred narratives, was understood as an internal principle of clarity, a metaphysical source deep within that warranted the object's intelligibility. The form of Christian tragedy, the retelling of the story of the crucifixion or of another modelled on it, is distinguished by the fact that at every point of its unfolding two distinct principles of intelligibility are simultaneously operative, warranting what Maritain calls its intelligibility *in itself* and its intelligibility *for us*.[24] Though they work in unison, these are radically different principles. The first principle is grounded in the mystery of the forsakenness of Jesus and is perceived as an invitation, issued silently from within the story, to listen more attentively and to look more carefully, for there is always more to know at every stage of reflection. Why does God abandon Jesus at the point of his death? What implication does this have for the meaning of other details of the Passion? Questions such as these are generated by what we might call the Promethean principle of the Christian idea of tragic form, according to which the metaphysical clarity of the narrative is warranted by the darkness of God's silence. On the other hand, the principle that generates the narrative's clarity for us is grounded in the light of the Resurrection. This principle of Christian tragic form has a Socratic character, in that it throws the light of understanding onto the Promethean tragedy on the cross, and it makes every detail of the Passion available to us as something revelatory of meaning in our own lives.

Equipped with these two principles of form, we can see, among other things, that no despair can be attached to the humanity of Jesus on the cross, not even when he emits his final cry. Unlike the classical and the modern worlds, in which the psychology of despair may easily figure as a legitimate part of the aesthetic substance of tragedy – at least in the sense that, though it does not lend particular grandeur to the hero that yields to his despair, it can generate in the commiserative experience of the audience a definite sense of ethical nobility – medieval culture had no positive use for it. Despair was a terrible sin against the goodness of God and an outright rejection of the economy of salvation. As an expression of the psychology of discourage-

---

23   Balthasar 1988, 71.
24   Maritain 1962, 28.

ment and anxiety, despair elicits compassion and solidarity in all periods of history. But as a voluntarily accepted metaphysical perspective that sees the finitude of contingency as absolute, despair denies the very foundations of Christian thought, namely the transcendence and love of God. Its gravest consequence is suicide, from which it is virtually inseparable. In the Scrovegni Chapel, Dante's contemporary Giotto painted the allegory of despair as a woman in the act of hanging herself from a beam in the ceiling, much like the Florentine suicides recalled by Boccaccio in his gloss on the lines of the anonymous suicide in the *Divine Comedy*. Medieval theology is not moved by either despair or suicide and sees no artistic potential in them, other than in an aesthetics designed to condemn them both. The rhetoric of desperation, which plays so memorable a role in Sophocles (e.g. *Ajax,* 430–80) and Euripides (e.g. *Alcestis,* 935–61), appears only as a distorted logic of self-delusion in Pier delle Vigne's account of the apparently rational argument that led him to commit suicide at *Inferno* XIII, 72: *ingiusto fece me contra me giusto.*[25] Despair and suicide transform innocence into guilt.

Medieval Christianity took much from the moral philosophy of antiquity and prefigured much of the moral philosophy of the post-medieval world, but not the philosophical justification of suicide by Roman Stoicism nor the moral acceptance of it by the returned Stoicism of the Renaissance. The only form of voluntary death acceptable to it was martyrdom. Soon after the fall of Edessa, St. Bernard sent a fiery letter to pope Eugenius III, urging him to raise another crusade against the enemies of Christ, who was once again suffering crucifixion in the place where he was first put to death.[26] The warriors who have died – and, by implication, those who will die in the crusade – defending and proclaiming his Word participate fully in his Passion by way of their martyrdom. Their death is a typological recurrence of the Crucifixion. St. Bernard begins his exhortation of the pope by quoting to him from Seneca's letter to Lucilius on the futility of halfway measures in the face of difficulty, arguing that the spirit should rise heroically to the occasion. In this letter Seneca also tells his disciple that, if he cannot do anything to come out of his predicament, suicide remains the logical option. By quoting Seneca's words on the need to respond with courage to the adversities of life, St. Bernard is not advocating Stoic suicide, of course, but the urgency to rise in one's spirit high above one's attachment to earthly life. Yet there is a level

---

25 Fowler 1987, 13 argues that speeches of despair were a "typical feature" of classical tragedy. On the psychological state of the character conveyed by the syntax of Pier Delle Vigne, see Spitzer 1942, 96.

26 *Epistola CCLVI ad Dominum Papam Eugenium*, in *P. L.* 182, 463d. The words quoted by St. Bernard are: "non est vir fortis, cui non crescit animus in ipsa rerum difficultate." The modern critical text, by L. D. Reynolds (OUP, 1991) is "non est vir fortis ac strenuus qui laborem fugit, nisi crescit illi animus ipsa rerum difficultate."

on which the martyrdom of warriors, in so far as it consists of walking into
the spears of the enemy, may appear as a form of heroic suicide grounded
in faith. However, because it is not a seeking of death in order to prevent
a humiliation of life but the free relinquishing of life in order to prevent a
violation of the spirit, martyrdom is not reducible to Stoic suicide in any
perspective that values the sanctity of the spirit.

The reverse is also true. Suicide can be raised to the order of martyrdom
only if, through subtle hermeneutical manoeuvres, its immediate cause is
given a theological dimension, analogically or figuratively. In such cases, the
sin of suicide vanishes, and what remains is the allegorical value produced by
the interpretative act. This is how Cato becomes the guardian of purgatory:
his suicide is viewed as an act of martyrdom suffered for the sake of freedom,
and the spiritual nobility of his sacrifice is such as to elevate him to the role
of guardian of purgatory, the realm through which all souls of the saved must
pass in order to achieve their ultimate freedom. This is the result of the principle of anagogic interpretation applied to the exodus motif from within the
heart of Christian thought, which is the theology of the death and resurrection
of Jesus, ritualized in the feasts of Good Friday and Easter. Cato's suicide, in
other words, is ontologically grounded in the story of the Passion, and by this
fact achieves the status of a potentially tragic act, analogous to the martyrdom
suffered by many heroic individuals who confessed their faith by their acceptance of suffering and violent death. Cato's salvation is figured as a product of
Christian typology, and that is why he can represent God himself.

The typological linkage of events in salvation history is the result of a
hermeneutical operation conventionally called rememorative allegory, one
of the chief tools used in the Middle Ages to describe the ritual of the Mass
as sacred drama. From Amalarius of Metz, who wrote in the ninth century,
to Durandus of Mende, who wrote in the thirteenth, the mass was allegorically interpreted by means of rememorative techniques in order to show that
the nature and placement of most of its components actually brought the
historical elements of the Passion to renewed presence in the mind of the
faithful.[27] Educated to this method by rote in their observance of the liturgy
itself and, no doubt, made familiar with the doctrine of the mystical body
by the homiletic tradition, the faithful would naturally allow the rememorative dimension of the Mass to recast as Christological figures all the martyrs
whose story they had cause to recollect. As a ritual form of drama, the Mass
is not restricted to the temporal linearity of secular dramatic actions but is
endowed with a dimension of timelessness that enables both the priest and
the congregation to move back and forth in the history of salvation, understanding the significance of distant events as typological functions of each

---

27   On rememorative allegory see Thibodeau 1993, 77f.

other and anchoring them all to the significance that the actual celebration of the mass has for the individual in attendance *hic et nunc*.

That significance is not, and cannot be, tragic in its entirety. It is tragic, in the classical sense of the term, in so far as the Passion and its typological associations are recalled for the suffering that they entail; but it is positive, and therefore comic, in the Dantean sense of the term comedy, in so far as the Passion is regarded as the necessary condition for the salvation of all mankind, pagans and other enemies of Christianity included. The overall dramatic form of Christianity must embrace the Resurrection, and in that sense cannot be other than comic, just as surely as it is tragic in dramatizing the cry of forsakenness from the cross.[28] The liturgy of Maunday Thursday in particular shows that the Promethean element in the tragedy of the Passion is attenuated by the overall Socratic hermeneutics that is grounded in the doctrine of salvation. Couched between Wednesday and Friday, the days in which the Church, among other things, utters prayers for the salvation of her enemies, and including as it did a Mass for the penitents, Maundy Thursday stood in medieval faith as a reminder that the ritualistic enactment of grief must also ring with the note of prayer for the forgiveness of all, the emotional and intellectual basis of which is the cathartic purport of the ritual.

Passion Plays and Tragedy

In fourteenth-century Italy this message was made especially clear with enacted scenes from the first stages of the Passion embedded in a homiletic frame that could guarantee their correct interpretation. This type of Christian drama is a hybrid genre in which scenes of performed action are summoned forth, one at the time, by a preacher from the pulpit and are incorporated, in the manner of illustrative quotations, in an expository homily that controlled both their performance and their interpretation. The thematic material of the plays in the genre, which are generally known as *devozioni* or devout representations, comes from the historical account of the Passion in the gospels and from a variety of other works of popular piety that reinforced basic theological principles. It is in this genre that the suffering of Jesus, from just before his arrest to the moment of his execution, is dramatized at the end of the Middle Ages in Italy. The cathartic objective of passion plays must consequently be viewed against the background of the relationship between history and faith, and must be interpreted in relation to the function of the liturgy in the salvation of mankind. My method will be to identify the principal issues involved in the cathartic aspect of the spectacle of suffering and

---

28   On the comic dimension of the mass, see Hardison 1969, 46.

to sort them out for dramaturgical interpretation. I therefore propose to consider them chiefly in relation to the idea of a production script, in which the representation of a given action is governed by the presentational narrative given in the form of stage directions, in much the same way the poet controls the reader's understanding of the actions performed by the protagonist as he moves about the imaginary set of the *Divine Comedy*.

The relative newness of dramaturgy as an instrumental science of theatre history calls for a word or two of commentary. Dramaturgy is not a self-contained area of study, endowed with a sophisticated technical tradition and susceptible of positive definition without reference to adjacent fields of inquiry. On the contrary, it is a relational discipline, concerned, in the first place, with the possibilities of emplotment and characterization available to the playwright in the writing process, as he transforms an action and a theory of drama into a production script. In the second place, it is concerned with the possibilities of enactment available to the director in the staging process, as he or she transforms the production script into a performance text. And in the third place, it is concerned with possibilities of interpretation and emotional response available to the audience in the reception process, as they transform the performance text into an experience both aesthetic and intellectual. Though it is frequently convenient to separate these components of dramaturgy, almost as if they represented three autonomous and sequential moments of operation, in fact they are simultaneous and interdependent activities, governed by the same purpose, which is to consider the possibilities of development available at each stage of the process and to understand how and why only one possibility among them tends to become a necessity.

In a dramaturgical treatment of the spectacle of the Passion, the cathartic moment belongs to the last of the three sets of possibilities, those concerned with the ethical and emotional impact of reception. In this context we can speak of a theology of catharsis, that is to say a theory of the intended impact of the re-enactment of the suffering of Jesus derivable from the stage directions or the embedding narrative of the script. Borrowing the words of St. Paul, who worked out the Christian theology of suffering, we can quickly summarize the impact of all passion plays: to suffer along with Jesus for the redemption of man and to triumph in the experience: *gaudeo in passionibus*.[29] This places the concept of catharsis in a non-Aristotelian dimension. For though the theology of the late Middle Ages was everywhere permeated by the teaching of *il maestro di color che sanno*, Aristotelian catharsis is not a technical term of the vocabulary of Christianity. To be sure, the root of the term occurs in various lexical forms in the New Testament and a few times

---

29 Colossians 1.24, in *Biblia Sacra* iuxta vulgata clementinam nova editio (Madrid: Biblioteca de Autores Cristianos, 1977).

even in the *Patrologia Latina*, but Christian theology has paid little or no attention to the concept in Aristotle's *Poetics*. Moreover, catharsis is not a significant term of the Aristotelianism of the late Middle Ages, which flourished despite its almost complete lack of interest in issues that, under this rubric, were to burden much Aristotelian research in later periods of history.

Two factors can be cited to account for this: (i) the so-called context editorial tradition of the works of Aristotle, and (ii) the interpretation of the *Poetics* by Islamic scholars. The first factor refers to the hermeneutical impact of the editorial work of Simplicius, who, around 533, first grouped the *Poetics* and the *Rhetoric* with Aristotle's logical works, thereby casting them epistemologically as instruments for the attainment of knowledge, rather than primarily as constructive arts and objects of knowledge, and blurring out of focus concepts such as catharsis, which had little relevance for epistemology. The second factor refers instead to the Aristotelianism of Arabic scholars, which was itself conditioned by the context theory of the editorial tradition. The fundamental assumptions of the Arabic interpretation of the *Poetics* are that drama is a type of lyric poetry, that tragedy is a species of lyric poetry devoted to the encomium of great heroes, and that the *Rhetoric,* by virtue of its editorial association with the *Poetics,* represents a valid point of access to its central issues, on the principle that there is a substantive analogy of purpose and method between the poet and the orator.

One of the most significant consequences of this position is that the careful elucidation of catharsis is neither an interesting nor a necessary pursuit for medieval Aristotelianism. The term was variously glossed as a modification of emotional behaviour by means of pity and fear (Abu Ishr Matta), or as the healthy excitation and development of pity and reverential fear (Avicenna), and as the moderation of emotional excess by means of pity and fear (Averroes).[30] Some of the factors involved in this commentary tradition were of a philological order, since the transmission of the text in Arabic was sadly wanting. But other factors were of the more strictly hermeneutical type, concerning as they did the idea of poetry of encomium. Averroes, for example, made a concerted effort to adhere to the text more closely than his predecessors, but in doing so he ended up with an interpretation of catharsis that was more deeply rooted in his major assumption: "poetry of praise moves people to noble emotions because it portrays people who themselves are normally pure and noble."[31] The ideas of the Arabic commentators were assimilated

---

30   The commentaries of Avicenna and Averroes are available in English: Dahyat 1974 and Butterworth 1986.

31   Gutas 1990, 97. Among transformations of the original text is the notion of *opsis* at 1450a8–10, which is understood by Averroes as "theoretical investigation," though, as Gutas points out, in the translation by Butterworth it appears as "spectacle" (p. 98).

by Christian Aristotelians of the late Middle Ages and echoed again and again until well into the Renaissance. In the end, the received wisdom was that tragedy achieved its effects by the excitation of pity and fear, understood as positive and edifying Passions rather than negative dispositions to be purged away. When the process of Christianization was over, pity had become commiseration (*misericordia*) or the impulse to alleviate the pain of others by suffering along with them, while the purpose of the dramatic action was to strengthen belief in Christian virtues, to encourage intelligent participation in the liturgy, and to illuminate the principles of faith. Once the edifying function of the representation of suffering is firmly established, the other passion involved in catharsis, fear, is not especially problematic. It too is to be viewed positively, on the principle that, if we were ourselves guilty of the same sin, we would naturally visualize the punishment of typical sinners as our own. Fear has an alienating dramaturgical function, in that it causes the members of the audience to resist the temptation to identify too closely with a particular character, while encouraging them to be prepared to sit in judgment of him.

Of course no such consideration of fear needs to be made for re-enactments of the suffering of Jesus and the martyrs. They are neither morally nor intellectually guilty, since they are in possession of the truth and their will is equal in all respects to the will of God. In an authentically Christian response to spectacles of their suffering, the audience is expected to experience sorrow, exaltation and enlightenment at the same time. "The true martyr," says T.S. Eliot's archbishop in *Murder in the Cathedral,* "is he who has become the instrument of God, who has lost his will in the will of God, and who no longer desires anything for himself, not even the glory of being a martyr."[32] For that reason the church "mourns and rejoices" at the same time. This double experience, coupled with a fuller understanding of faith, is the only catharsis possible for Christians at the performance of the supreme forms of Christian suffering.

In order to understand how this experience can be achieved, it is necessary to examine closely the dramaturgical governance of the theme of redemptive suffering in the construction and delivery of the performance text. To do this, we need first to look at the idea of performance style. Now the problem of how to study the performance style presupposed by religious medieval play texts has never found a satisfactory solution and probably never will. In the absence of technical manuals and production data, students of performance style are naturally compelled to resort to conjecture and analogy, rather more frequently than scholars working in later periods of theatre

---

32   T. S. Eliot, *Murder in the Cathedral*, ed. H. Voaden (Toronto: Kingswood House, 1959), p. 58.

history. Religious iconography from the period is, of course, plentiful, but its relation to the drama of a particular time and place is at best oblique. Most attempts at shedding light tend to revolve around the degree of historical precision that is needed in the interpretation of the verbal text and the degree of verisimilitude that can be assumed in producing it – both ideas no doubt due to the fact that the modern rediscovery of medieval drama occurred in the age of naturalism, a time when it became fashionable for directors to control the meaning of the text while pretending to serve it. Since the nineteenth century the question has been studied in a variety of contexts, but on the whole, comparatively little has been done from a dramaturgical perspective, that is to say from a perspective consciously anchored to the principle that the play texts that have come down to us, whatever else they may be considered, are first of all production scripts, either real or only intended, and must be read as such. "Scripts" are conceptually different from "play texts" in that they automatically bring to the foreground of consciousness a sense of their built-in intentionality to be staged in a particular way and in that they invite reflection on other possible stagings. Scripts are performance texts in a state of latency and are therefore more easily envisioned as performances from within the text itself.

This apparently innocent principle has serious implications for the study of the drama of Christian suffering. The first and most important is that, in a play, stage directions have the same textual status as the dialogue, and that what we call the dramatic text is an indivisible whole of which dialogue and stage directions are equally essential parts, philologically as well as aesthetically. In a dramaturgical purview the meaning of the dramatic text is no more, but also no less, than the structured relationship of reciprocal dependency by which the stage directions and the dialogue are linked, visually and vocally throughout the play during performance and in our recollection of the play when the performance is over. The theories of drama predicated on the ontological hierarchy of primary and secondary texts, with the stage directions, explicit or implied though they may be, relegated to the secondary level, are incompatible with the dramaturgical principle of the equivalence of their textual status, and, consequently, with the analysis proposed in this paper.

Principles, however, are always easier to define than to observe, and this one is no exception. A company that proposes to retrieve on stage a play of Christian suffering, as a living work of art endowed with a message that needs to be reckoned with, must filter the dramatic text through the creative imagination of a director, and it is hardly necessary to recall that, for a director, preparing a production plan is largely a matter of writing new or additional stage directions that restrict the range of possibilities available to the actors and designers. Whether by the playwright or the director, stage directions are, among other things, textual devices by means of which plays protect themselves from spurious production concepts, chiefly by controlling the freedom of interpretation available to actors and designers in constructing the performance text. Such restrictions are especially significant when the intent is to protect not only the aesthetic integrity of the play but also the doctrine that it teaches and the effect that it is intended to have on the audience.

Two Scenes of Supreme Christian Suffering

In the rest of this paper I will examine how this dramaturgical control of the performance and audience response is exercised in two scenes of supreme Christian suffering, one with and one without externally inflicted violence: The agony of Jesus in the garden and his flagellation at the column. They are taken from two relatively unknown Passion plays known as *Devotione de Zobiadí sancto* and *Devotione de Venerdí sancto*, that is *A Devout Representation of Holy Thursday* and *A Devout Representation of Good Friday,* plays which were designed to be structurally embedded into homilies on the Passion and obviously meant to be produced in church with conspicuous visual allusions to the liturgy.[33] Preserved in a manuscript dated 1375, but written probably fifty years earlier, within a few years of the *Divine Comedy*, these are the oldest Italian plays in the vernacular. Very briefly the first play dramatises the return of Jesus to Jerusalem and his agony in the garden, both episodes in the vernacular of early fourteenth-century Umbria, and ends with his arrest, dramatised in Latin as a variation on the *Quem quaeritis* trope. The second play, entirely in the vernacular, begins with the flagellation, focuses on the principal stages of the Passion, includes a few extravagant theatricals complete with demons and resurrections of the dead, and ends with a truly powerful scene, in which Mary moves towards the audience showing everyone the nails used to crucify her son.

The stage directions are long and detailed in some scenes and little more than generic indications in others. Yet if we were to separate them, artificially, from the dialogue and print them in a separate column, we would have no difficulty following the narrative that they tell gesturally and visually, alongside the one that is told verbally in the speeches of the characters. At times the two narratives overlap, while at other times they seem to go in opposite directions, like two melodic lines whose movement of convergence and divergence gives rise to a pattern aesthetically and semantically richer than either considered by itself. There is an important lesson in method for

---

33   The two *devozioni* were first published by Alessandro D'Ancona in *Rivista di filologia romanza* II (1875), pp. 14–19 (*Devotione de Zobiadí sancto*) and pp. 19–28 (*Devotione de Venerdí sancto*). Further references in the text.

us here, and it is that, where the gestural narrative is thin or uncertain on account of the sketchiness of the stage directions, we cannot freely and reliably use the dialogue as a base from which to infer the nature of the presupposed gestures, following the faulty convention of attributing to the verbal text narrative dominance over the visual one, since we might be seeing convergence where in fact we should see divergence.

Having thus separated the stage directions from the dialogue, our first observation concerns the frequency with which expressions like *more consuetudinario,* in the usual manner, occur in the scripts, in various forms, such as "come è consueto" (pp. 19, 25) and "secondo che è consueto" (p. 25). These expressions refer to the fact that the script was written in the context of an uninterrupted performance tradition that was thoroughly familiar to the actors before rehearsal. The actors therefore did not require detailed stage directions on every point of the action. They already knew what costumes to use, what gestures were appropriate, and to what degree they could legitimately feel free to improvise. This accounts for the brevity of the stage directions in many scenes, scenes which in all likelihood recurred frequently in other dramatisations of the Passion. On the other hand it seems safe to assume that long and detailed stage directions, specifying hand gestures, facial expressions, stage properties, blocking, and exact movements, with a degree of precision not inferior to that of nineteenth-century texts – such stage directions are likely to signal an action so peculiar to the logic of the narrative and so crucial to the play that it had to be prescribed in detail in the script.

The relationship of these stage directions to the iconographic tradition is naturally quite different, as is the use that the theatre historian can make of it in studying the dramaturgical structure of the play. It is here useful to outline a working typology of the relevant visual culture, by which I mean images as well as descriptions of images. In the first place, we have a visual culture produced before the composition of the script and depicting a received tradition in the visualization of the gospel narratives, a tradition familiar to actors and audiences alike. For the theatre historian this corpus of visuals constitutes an archaeological base from which to give fullness of stage direction to the script, integrating the stage directions that are too cryptic to stand on their own and generating new ones where stage directions are silently presupposed, in order to render the visualisation of the action dramaturgically possible from within the script. In the second place we find a body of imagery painted or described after the performance by artists and writers intimately familiar with it or, more probably, by artists acquainted with productions of the same general type. These images can be further divided into two categories, depending on whether they are focused on the material surface of the production, regarded as opaque to viewer's gaze, or whether they are focused on the original narrative, as seen through the prism of the production itself, which is regarded as transparent and used as a matrix for the visual interpretation of the story. In the images produced before the performance, theatre history finds a useful philological base from which to elucidate the aesthetic materiality of the performance text, whereas in images produced after the performance it finds a convenient hermeneutical base from which to assess its reception history.

The scene of the agony in the garden depends heavily on the iconographic tradition for its role in the dramaturgical economy of the script. In contrast with the original account in the Gospel, in which Jesus speaks to God metaphorically of his imminent death when he asks him to take away the chalice of his passion, the script dramatises both the metaphor and its message. The metaphor becomes a visible stage property, a chalice to be discovered on location by the actor playing the role of Jesus, while the metaphorical words of the evangelist are rendered by simple non-metaphorical language. In the script Jesus, without the slightest recourse to figurative language, asks God to spare him his cruel death, if it be His will that this be done. He does not mention the chalice at all and does not allude to it verbally. But he speaks his prayer while holding a chalice in his hands, kneeling on the ground, and looking upward. The stage directions are very specific: "e stando inzenochiato è pilgia lo calice in mano cun li occhi levati su, e dice al suo padre" (p. 18). The episode narrated verbally is the historical event of the prayer in the Garden, but the one symbolised gesturally is clearly the celebration of the Eucharist, in the context of which the play was meant to be performed. The dramatisation of the historical event, in other words, is performed in a manner that alludes visually to the liturgy in which that event is celebrated *sub specie aeternitatis*. The result is that, in this dramatisation of the passion narrative, the relationship between the liturgy and history is neatly reversed, the liturgy being here not the agent but the object of anamnesis.

In the theatre of verisimilitude stage properties and accessories handled by the actors are material aids to performance that have normally a descriptive nature and a referential function, representing as they do the equally tangible objects of the characters in the text by a mechanical association of ideas, though, of course, the mechanism of association may vary considerably, from literal and metaphorical likeness to ironic difference. But this is clearly not the case of the chalice in our dramatisation of the scene in the garden, which is not in the least based on the aesthetics of verisimilitude. Here the object held by the actor in his hands cannot be regarded as either descriptive or referential with respect to the story, since in the Gospel narrative Jesus spoke of a chalice but did not have one in his hands, whereas in the speech assigned to the actor impersonating him in the play no chalice is mentioned. But since its function is to bring silently to consciousness, on the one hand, the physical metaphor through which God the father manifested his will to Jesus in the Gospel, and, on the other hand, the paradigm for the proper interpretation of that metaphor, both of which are outside the story told in the verbal text of the play, the chalice can be regarded as performative and evocative, thematically with respect to Jesus in the play and theatrically with respect to the audience in the church.

Now Jesus and the audience are both confined to the finitude of humanity, a fact much exploited in the fourteenth century – though, to be sure, not nearly as much as in our own unhappy times – for the purpose of arousing empathy. In our story Jesus walks to his place of prayer, and there he finds a chalice waiting for him. In a dramaturgical context, the scene would have little sense if the audience did not know who put the chalice there for Jesus to find, to kneel before it, to take into his hands, and to pray with it for possible deliverance. But the context leaves no doubt: the chalice has been left there by God himself, and the iconographic tradition allows us to conjecture comfortably that God accomplishes this through the agency of the angel mentioned by Luke. The richness and consistency of the visual tradition on this point enables the theatre historian to add a silent character to the cast, to put him on the platform depicting Gethsemane where he is to place the chalice for Jesus. Though in actuality a stage property for the actor, the chalice is thematically a stage property for God, used by him invisibly from within the realm of eternity to make manifest his will in the realm of history, to which Jesus is still confined.

In the there and then of the story in the script, the chalice is for Jesus a material channel through which his human imagination may come into more intimate contact with God, from within the limits of his existence as a man – it is a material point of contact through which he, overcoming the greatest temptation of his humanity, accepts from his Father the mandate of his crucifixion. In the here and now of the implied performance text, described by the theological voice of the narrative and the theological echo of the iconographic tradition, the chalice found in the set of Gethsemane is for the audience a visual evocation of the one on the altar, while the actor playing Jesus is also an evocation of the priest celebrating the Eucharist. In this correlation of the liturgy with the story of the garden in the script, the play is on safe ground, since it offers us nothing more than a then very popular interpretation of the mass, as described by William Durandus in his *Rationale Divinorum Officiorum*: when the priest walks towards the centre of the altar, Durandus says, he symbolizes Jesus going to his place of prayer in Gethsemane; when he bows his head, he symbolises Jesus suffering before the prospect of his death; and when he looks up, he symbolises Jesus uttering his prayer.[34] The dramatic form of the play simply reverses the order of

---

34 Guillelmus Durantius, *Rationale officiorum Divinorum, I–IV,* ed. T.M. Thibodeau (Turnhout: Brepols, 1995), section 1.5.

signification: when the actor goes to the platform representing Gethsemane, he re-enacts the movement of Jesus but symbolises the priest approaching the altar; when he picks up his stage property, he symbolises the priest raising the chalice, and so on with his other movements and gestures. The verbal text is the diachronic vehicle of signification; the liturgy, the synchronic sacramental reality signified. The mechanism of signification is visual allusion.

This correlation of the script with the liturgy has significant implications for the visual dimension of early passion plays, since the colours, blocking and gestures of the liturgy were codified in great detail and at times represented in diagrams and illustrations in perspective. If the chalice in the garden scene is an allusion to the chalice on the altar, it cannot be made of glass or wood, but must be gold plated – as it is, in fact, in the iconographic tradition. If the actor playing Jesus is also playing the celebrant, the hillock of Gethsemane must be the altar, and the actor's movement towards and about it must be studied in relation to what was prescribed for movement around the altar.

On the question of gestures and costumes, something dramaturgically analogous occurs in the scene of the flagellation, with which the Good Friday play opens. The script begins with a long stage direction on how to perform it:

> Quando lo predicatore ave predicato fin a quello loco quando Pilato comanda che Cristo sia posto a la colonna, lo Predicatore tase, e vene Cristo nudo con li Frustatori, e vano a lo loco deputato dove sta la colona, e portenlo per mezo de la zente tanto homini quanto femine, si se può fare; e Iohanne sta con Cristo; e posto che l'ano a la colona li Frustatori lo frustano un poco devotamente, e poi stano in pace, cioè quando Cristo vole parlare a Iohanne, e Iohanne sta ante Cristo inzenochiato, e Cristo dice a Iohanne. (p. 19)

> (When he reaches in his sermon the point where Pilate orders that Christ be brought to the column, the preacher stops talking. Then Christ comes out, naked, with his scourgers, and together they go to the set where the column is located. They bring him through the crowd, which should consist of men and women, if this can be done. John is with Christ. And having brought him to the column, the scourgers whip him a little, devoutly, and then, when Christ motions that he wants to speak to John, they remain there peacefully. John kneels before Christ, and Christ speaks thus to him.)

With respect to the number of soldiers whipping Jesus, the scene called for in this stage direction is essentially the same as the standard iconographic version of the time, which tends to limit it to two, a fact corroborated by the properties list of confraternities that staged passion plays routinely in the area of Perugia using only two whips. But the question of the nudity of Jesus and of the visible attitude of his tormentors is not easily disposed of. The verbal text of the script calls for a naked Jesus, but in the performance text this means only that the actor wore a costume for nudity, which was typically a body suit made of flesh coloured leather with wounds and drops of blood painted upon it – hardly capable of arousing empathy with its presumed realism.[35] The visual culture of the passion is of little help in this regard, since it tends to paint Jesus either wearing only a loin cloth or else, less commonly, totally naked. To the extent that such paintings were inspired by real productions, as some of them undoubtedly were, the performance text was for them a transparent medium of expression: the artist could see right through it to the image verbally suggested by the script. This is true of most of the iconography, but by no means of all of it. The flagellation scene in the large stained glass window of the Sacraments Chapel in the cathedral of Cologne shows Jesus wearing what appears to be a nudity costume. Here the artist clearly regarded the performance text as opaque and depicted its materiality, documenting for us what this costume might have actually looked like.

As far as the acting style of the intended performance text is concerned, the flagellation is strikingly different from the style called for by more famous passion plays, in which, it is generally assumed, the scourging needs to be carried out with a considerable degree of realism. In our play there is no doubt that the torturers whip Jesus devoutly and that, having whipped him, remain peacefully on the platform for the rest of the scene. These adverbial qualifiers, *devoutly* and *peacefully*, are laden with implications for our understanding of the gestural action carried out and of the theory of performance presupposed. The actors are expected to play and yet not to play the roles of the historical torturers. They must perform the action of scourging Jesus, while speaking words of savage cruelty to him, but they must appear to do so as an act of piety rather than as an act of cruelty. And when they have performed their action, they must appear on stage as men who are now at peace with themselves and with God. The stage directions, in other words, call for a very complex and very demanding style of acting. In pretending to whip Jesus, the actors mime the flagellation as an event in history; in pretending to do so devoutly, they perform the scourging as a ritual of atonement; in pretending to be at peace with themselves and with God for having done so, they perform the efficacy of the ritual. The flagellation thus enacted is at the same time a visualization of sacred history, a lesson in moral theology, and an invitation to penitential practice. At no time must the actors pretend to transport the audience into the reality of the past, so that they might experience more intensely the horror of that moment of sacred history and be overcome by an upsurge of hatred for the scourgers. This would be a spurious production concept decidedly excluded by the stage directions. On the contrary, their effort must be to transport the past into the present, wherein the same event, recognizable for its uniqueness, can occur rememoratively and efficaciously as a moment, both horrible and redemptive, in their own

---

35   On contemporary nudity costumes, see Meredith and Tailby, 1983.

lives. Viewed from the perspective of Christian theology, the purpose of theatre is to enable man "to recollect himself and to remember who he is."[36] In
a place of performance that is nothing more than an architectural signifier for
the mystical body of Christ, tragic catharsis is an act of self-recognition and
participation in the signified metaphysical substance of that body rather than
in the material one that signifies it. The audience must not be made to feel
that, in the actors performing the flagellation, they can imaginatively see the
cruelty of the historical torturers. They must instead be enabled to see that
these torturers are projections of contemporary Christians like themselves,
in pursuit of atonement through a sacred ritual.

In order to transport the past into the present and yet to respect its historical distinction from the present, the actors must perform their roles from
outside the imagined self-understanding of the characters, in the alienated
mode of one who does not make his character's emotions his own. But in
order to superimpose on the characters of the scourgers appropriate projections of typical spectators in the audience, they must perform their roles
from inside the presumed self-understanding of typical members of the
congregation in attendance. Their bodies and their voices must be protean
enough, and their understanding of their roles must be clear enough to them,
for them to fuse the two levels of reality and to produce them in an indivisible act of performance, like the vowels of a diphthong pronounced with a
single issue of breath. We may recall that the iconographic tradition of the
flagellation is divided on this point: in some cases the soldiers are caught in
a posture of savagery, while in other cases they are shown more or less at
peace – an indication, perhaps, that passion plays with intended performance
texts in the liturgical mode were not as rare as the surviving scripts would
lead us to believe.

Some Final Reflections

As we make our final approach, it may be instructive for us to reflect for
a moment on these issues from the perspective of the concept of time involved in them. It may seem from the verbal text that passion plays, being intentional recollections of historical events, are concerned chiefly with
ways of turning our gaze to the past, by way of the spectacle of suffering.
But recollection is an activity of the mind in the present, and to remember
is simply to live the present moment performing that activity, as a species
of meditation, on the assumption that it may fulfil our present yearning for
meaning. As St Augustine observed, recollection is but the present time of

---

36   Balthasar 1998, 86.

things past, just as hope is the present time of things future, and perception the present time of things present. The chief concern of the plays and, we may add, of the liturgy in which the same events are celebrated, is not with the magnitude of the suffering of Jesus as a man in history but with the here and now of the community in attendance. The dramaturgical task of ensuring that the audience retain throughout full consciousness of their location in the present does not fall to the speeches in the text but to the stage directions that support them. By prescribing the right properties, costumes, and gestures, they ensure that the community does not get catapulted by the language into the reconstructed spectacle of violence and is not confused by the desire to pursue a more intimate knowledge of the passion as an end in itself – propelled, perhaps, by that unhealthy spiritual disposition that medieval theology called *mala curiositas*. Sacred history, the visual text of the stage directions tells the members of the audience, is not meaningful in itself if it is not meaningful for each of them at that particular moment of their lives.

The conception of dramaturgy to which my argument reaches out is of considerable sophistication in the history of the theatre: the dramatic form with which the plays are invested is at once bifocal with respect to the representation of history, and ambivalent with respect to intended response. The complexity of this idea of drama may not be immediately clear to scholars easily persuaded that popular art forms are of necessity technically crude and intellectually shallow, even at their most majestic. Such an attitude – which Vico might call the conceit of scholars – is ultimately the result of an unwitting infantilisation of the unschooled, thought to lack all tools of sophistication because of insufficient access to intellectual apprenticeship. Yet I would submit that the uneducated congregations of the time, accustomed by preachers to reflection on a Bible that they could not read, deriving their education from the walls of a church that imparted moral theology by means of architecture and imagery, were likely to be in more intimate contact with the theological principles underlying the art of Passiontide drama, and with the way in which script and performance text were related to their Scriptural and liturgical referents, than modern audiences are with the ideological principles that inform the popular art forms of our times.

To be sure, we may never find out what sort of preparatory exercises the medieval player had to go through in order to make himself ready to represent at the same time a soldier whipping Jesus and a member of his own community performing an act of devotion and redemption. We can, however, say with some confidence that the theoretical basis for such a conception of religious dramaturgy was an aspect of contemporary culture familiar not only to the preacher, who probably made routine use of it in his sermons, but also to the congregation listening to him. The double historical focus and the intended ambivalence of response are ultimately rooted in the contemporary apparatus for the conceptual interpretation of the Bible and the liturgy. In the account of William Durandus each component of a liturgical act is subject to a fourfold interpretation: historical, allegorical, tropological, and anagogic.[37] For the art of preaching and for the dramaturgy of sacred catharsis the central moment of this hermeneutic is the tropological one, when each member of the congregation – which is to say, each member of the audience – seeks to discover the meaning that the scriptural event has for him, at that particular moment, in his life as a private individual and as a member of his community. The call of tropology is a call to theological introspection and redemptive practice, and it is issued to the individual as well as the community. In a tropologically clear dramaturgy of the passion, Jesus cannot be naked other than through a body suit, he cannot be whipped other than devoutly, and he cannot hold a chalice that is not also the one on the altar.

These considerations enable us to draw at least two inferences, both significant for the study of passion drama: one concerning the structure of the play text and the other the structure of its perception as a sacred tragedy, in so far as the structure of perception can be governed from within the text. The first inference is that the direction of narrative dependency normally assumed to exist between the dialogue and the stage directions should be reversed, the higher degree of semantic autonomy belonging to the stage directions and not to the verbal speeches of the characters. The play's primary narrative voice is the visual one of the stage directions, and the story that it tells, with the help of the surrounding visual culture, is the host narrative into which the other is inserted in the manner of a corroborating quotation. The primary narrative is a story of sacramental spirituality, and it is necessarily conceived in the present tense. It uses the visual rhetoric of the liturgy, it is focused on the theology of the Eucharist, and it carries a message of reconciliation with God. The dialogue, on the other hand, consists of supporting scriptural material, enriched with details from pious apocryphal sources, transformed into rhythmical verse, and offered in the manner of a rhapsodic quotation in the present tense, though it is semantically confined to the preterit. The primary narrative voice is presentational, and therefore speaks from the present to the present. The quoted narrative voice is representational, and speaks from the reconstructed past for the benefit of the present. The material of the presentational narrative is neither historical nor emotional but openly theological and sacramental. In this sense it is analogous to the theological vision of the authors of the gospels, the vision within which they redacted the parables and episodes of the life of Jesus, boldly adapting them to the different theological goals by which they knew to be governed.

The second inference is that the audience's perception of the play is structured as an oscillation of consciousness between the presentational and

---

37 Durantius (fn. 34), pp. 8ff.

the representational objects of the performance text. This mode of experience is necessarily dialectical, since the mind, other than by abstraction, cannot move towards one of the semantic dimensions of the play without responding to the magnetism of the other, both being present at every moment of the action. Were this not the case, the representational story would have no necessary relation to the liturgy and would be formally indistinguishable from any other historical drama of suffering. By the same token, the presentational dimension would be no more than a dramatisation of a sermon on the Eucharist.

These two dimensions of the text give rise between them to a structured semantic space, an intertext flanked by the spoken narrative of the passion and the visual discourse on the Eucharist, within which the audience can experience the performance both aesthetically and hermeneutically. On the aesthetic side, the dialectic governs our experience of the play by showing that the place in which it operates is the ultimate origin of its form, the source of both its conceptual organization and its ontological clarity. On the hermeneutical side, the same dialectic governs our understanding of the play, by showing that neither dimension of the text is self-contained and by directing us to the inference that history and faith are thereby related by continuity and reciprocal implication.

Bibliography

Balthasar, Hans Urs von (1998), *Theo-Drama: Theological Dramatic Theory,* vol. 1: *Prolegomena,* tr. Graham Harrison, San Francisco.

Baraz, Daniel (1998), "Seneca, Ethics, and the Body: The Treatment of Cruelty in Medieval Thought", in: *Journal of the History of Ideas* 59, 195–215.

Butterworth, Charles E. (1986), *Averroes' Middle Commentary on Aristotle's Poetics,* Princeton.

Dahyat, Ismail M. (1974), *Avicenna's Commentary on the Poetics of Aristotle,* Leiden.

De' Sommi, Leone (1968), *Quattro dialoghi in materia di rappresentazioni sceniche,* a cura di Ferruccio Marotti, Milano.

Gutas, Dimitri (1990), "On Translating Averroes' Commentaries", in: *Journal of the American Oriental Society* 110, 92–101.

Fowler, Robert (1987), "The Rhetoric of Desperation," in: *Harvard Studies in Classical Philology* 91, 5–38.

Goodspeed, George S. (1892), "The Book of Job in Other Literatures, II," in: *The Old and New Testament Studies* 15, 105–114.

Hardison, Jr., O. B. (1965), *Christian Rite and Christian Drama in the Middle Ages,* Baltimore.

Kallen, Horace Meyer (1918), *The Book of Job as Greek Tragedy,* ed. George F. Moore, New York.

Lamb, Sidney (1965), *Tragedy,* Toronto.

Mandel, Oscar (1961), *A Definition of Tragedy,* New York.

Maritain, Jacques (1962), *Art and Scholasticism* and *The Frontiers of Poetry,* tr. J.W.Evans, Notre Dame and London.

Marsili, Salvatore (1987), *I segni del mistero di Cristo: Teologia liturgica dei sacramenti*, Rome.

Meredith, Peter / Tailby, John E. (1983), *The Staging of Religious Drama in Europe in the Later Middle Ages*, Kalamazoo (Michigan).

Moore, Edward (1896), *Studies in Dante,* first series, *Scriptures and Classical Authors in Dante*, Oxford.

Ong, Walter J. (1947), "Wit and Mystery: a Reevaluation in Medieval Hymnody", in: *Speculum* 22, 310–41.

Rouse, Richard H. (1971), "The A Text of Seneca's Tragedies in the Thirteenth Century", in: *Revue d'histoire des textes* 1, 93–121.

Simons, Dorothy Lister (1918), "The Individual Human *dramatis personae* of the *Divine Comedy*", in: *Modern Philology* 16, 371–380.

Spitzer, Leo (1942), "Speech and Language in *Inferno* XIII", in: *Italica*, 81–104.

Thibodeau, Timothy M. (1993), "*Enigmata Figurarum*: Biblical Exegesis and Liturgical Exposition in Durand's *Rationale*", in: *The Harvard Theological Review* 86, 65–79.

Tillich, Paul (1968), *A History of Christian Thought*, New York.

Wenzel, Sigfried (1989), *Fasciculus Morum: A Fourteenth-Century Preacher's Handbook*, University Park and London.

Ziolkowski, Jan M. / Putnam, Michael C. J. (2007), *The Virgilian Tradition: The First Fifteen Hundred Years*, New Haven and London.

Zwierlein, Otto (1989), "Spuren der Tragödien Senecas bei Bernardus Silvestris, Petrus Pictor und Marbod von Rennes", in: *Mittellateinisches Jahrbuch*, 22 (for 1987), 171–96.

List of Contributors

Annette M. Baertschi is an Assistant Professor at the Department of Greek, Latin & Classical Studies at Bryn Mawr College. She has just finished co-editing *Die modernen Väter der Antike: Die Entwicklung der Altertumswissenschaften an Akademie und Universität im Berlin des 19. Jahrhunderts* (Berlin and New York 2009) and is currently at work on a book entitled *(Re)interpreting the Underworld: necyia scenes in Neronian and Flavian epic.*

Timothy D. Barnes is Emeritus Professor of Classics at the University of Toronto. His *Constantine and Eusebius* (Cambridge 1981) was awarded the Philip Schaff Memorial Prize by the American Society of Church History and the Charles Goodwin Award of Merit by the American Philological Association (1984). In 1985 he was elected Fellow of the Royal Society of Canada.

Paola Ceccarelli is Leverhulme Reader in Greek cultural history at Durham University. She has written a monograph on the ancient weapon dance (*La danza pirrica nell'antichità greco-romana*, Pisa-Rome 1998) as well as numerous articles on the cultural poetics and epigraphy of the Greek theatre.

Ingo Gildenhard is Reader in Latin Literature and Roman culture at Durham University and Director of the Durham Centre for the Study of the Classical Tradition. He is the author of *Paideia Romana: Cicero's Tusculan Disputations* (Cambridge 2007) and has co-edited a volume on the history of classical scholarship: *Out of Arcadia: classics and politics in Germany in the age of Burckhardt, Nietzsche and Wilamowitz* (London 2003).

Johanna Hanink is a doctoral student at Queens' College, Cambridge, where she is completing a thesis on the reception of tragedy in fourth-century Athens (provisionally entitled 'Classical Tragedy in the Age of Macedon'). As of July 2010 she will be an Assistant Professor of Classics at Brown University.

Jennifer Ingleheart is Lecturer in Classics at Durham University. She is the author of numerous articles on Augustan poetry, in particular the exile poetry of Ovid, and is currently completing a major commentary on *Tristia* 2 for Oxford University Press.

Alison Keith is Professor of Latin Literature at the University of Toronto, with a cross-appointment in Classics and Women Studies. She is the author of *The play of fictions: studies in Ovid's Metamorphoses Book 2* (Ann Arbor 1992) and *Engendering Rome: women in Latin epic* (Cambridge 2000).

Domenico Pietropaolo holds the Emilio Goggio Chair in the Department of Italian Studies at the University of Toronto. He is the author of *The enlightenment in a Western Mediterranean context* (1984). His many edited volumes include *The performance text* (1999), *Goldoni and the musical theatre* (1995), *Writing and the growth of culture in the Mediterranean* (1991), and *The science of buffoonery: theory and history of the Commedia dell'Arte* (1988).

Martin Revermann is Associate Professor in Classics and Theatre Studies at the University of Toronto. His research interests lie in the cultural history of Greek drama, performance analysis, iconography, theatre sociology and theories of drama. He is the author of *Comic business: theatricality, dramatic technique, and performance contexts of Aristophanic comedy* (Oxford 2006) and the editor (with Peter Wilson) of *Performance, iconography, reception: studies in honour of Oliver Taplin* (Oxford 2008).

Thomas A. Schmitz is Professor of Greek Language and Literature at the University of Bonn and a founding member of the Bonner Zentrum für Antike und ihre Rezeption (Centre for the Classical Tradition). He is the author of *Bildung und Macht: Zur sozialen und politischen Funktion der zweiten Sophistik in der griechischen Welt der Kaiserzeit* (1997) and *Moderne Literaturtheorie und antike Texte: Eine Einführung* (2002) (translated into English, Blackwell 2007).

Carol Symes is Helen Corley Petit Scholar in the College of Liberal Arts and Sciences at the University of Illinois, where she teaches in the Department of History and the Program in Medieval Studies. Her first book, *A common stage: theater and public life in medieval Arras* (Ithaca, 2007), which explores the role of performance in shaping the public sphere of a prominent urban community, recently received the David Pinkney Prize of the Society for French Historical Studies. She is also the author of numerous articles on the transmission of pre-modern performance practices, notably "The appearance of early vernacular plays: forms, functions, and the future of medieval theater" (*Speculum 77*, 2002).

Andrew W. White is currently Professorial Lecturer with the Performing Arts Department of American University and recently completed his dissertation *The artifice of eternity: studies of representational practices in the Byzantine theatre and orthodox church* at the University of Maryland, College Park. A former Fulbright scholar, he has taught at the University of Maryland and University of South Carolina's Washington Semester Program. Throughout his academic career White has continued to work as a theatre artist in the Washington, D.C. area, producing, directing and performing for several years as a member of the mime-based, francophone company, Théâtre Le Neon.

Alessandra Zanobi obtained her PhD from the University of Durham in 2009, for a thesis entitled *Seneca and the aesthetics of pantomime*.

Index

Abo of Fleury, 343
Ado of Vienne, 343
Abu Ishr Matta, 411
Accius, 10, 22, 161–162, 166–167,
 169–170, 180, 197
 Amphitryo, 189
 Atreus, 161–162, 166–167
 Bacchae, 189, 197
 Clytemnestra, 169–170
 Epigoni, 189
 Phoenissae, 189
 Stasiastae (*vel Tropaeum liberi*), 189
 Tereus, 10
 Thebais, 189
Achaios, 123
Achilles, 10–11, 73, 163, 175, 177–178,
 275–276, 278
actors, acting, 5–6, 7, 18, 19, 22, 41–42,
 105, 107, 129, 123, 129, 143–144,
 160, 168, 171, 273–274, 279, 281,
 286, 294, 302, 304–307, 308, 321,
 326, 328, 335, 340, 348–349, 363,
 372, 380, 388, 389, 413–420
 actor-managers, 339
 comic, 139, 323
 guilds, 146
 negative perception of, 23–24, 165,
 327–328, 354
 social status of, 154, 165
 tragic, 123, 138–139, 298, 301, 303,
 321, 323, 401
 travelling troupes, 83
 see also pantomime and mime
Acts of the Apostles, 25, 319
Adaeus of Mytilene, 55
Adso of Montier-in-Der, 354
Aelius Aristides, 291, 320, 322
Aelred of Rievaulx, *Speculum Caritatis*,
 363
Aeschines, *Against Ctesiphon*, 106–108,
 112–113

Aeschylus, 6, 7, 10, 12, 15, 47–53,
 253–254, 296, 299, 344, 372
 Aetnaeae, 49, 59, 62, 99
 Agamemnon, 253, 255, 387
 Athamas, 189
 Bacchae, 189
 Eumenides, 73, 79, 81, 192
 Laius, 189
 Lycurgeia, 189
 Nurses of Dionysus, 189
 Oedipus, 189
 Oresteia, 165, 192, 387
 Pentheus, 189
 Persians, 100, 250, 252, 256–257, 382
 Prometheus Bound, 382
 Semele, 189
 Seven Against Thebes, 189, 192, 382
 Sphinx, 189
 Toxotides, 219
 Wool-carders, 189, 196
 biography, 39–40, 42, 45, 49, 53,
 55–59, 62–63, 99–100
 epitaph, 53
 and the dissemination of Athenian
 tragedy, 99–100
Aesop, 402
Agathon, 100
Agobard of Lyons, 359, 361
agon, agones, 102–104, 109–117,
 121–135, 141, 144–145, 325–326
Aldhelm of Sherborne, *In Praise of
 Virginity*, 349
Alexander IV, 126
Alexander the Great, 8, 101, 124, 375
Alexander of Pherae, 24
Alkman, 346
allegory, Christian, 25, 26, 351–355, 400,
 403–404, 407–408, 422,
  see also Christianity and tragedy,
 Greek political, 171
 in painted vessels, 86, *see also vase
 paintings*

allusion, 20, 163, 180, 187–214, 223–224, 227, 239, 414
Amalarius of Metz, 408
Ambrose of Milan, 344
Ammianus, 317
Amphiklos of Chios, 62
Anastasius (the emperor), 318
Anastasius (the Librarian), 355
Anthologia Latina, 271
Anthologia Palatina, 271
Antioch, 316, 318–320, 322
Antipater of Thessalonica, 53
Antoninus Liberalis, 199
Aphthonius, 389
Aquinas, Thomas, 26, 404
Arcadius, 326
Archelaus of Macedon, 49–52, 55, see also Euripides
Archilochus, 63
Areopagus, 159
Aribo Scholasticus, 360
Aristides, Aelius, 291, 320, 322, 326–327, 330, see also sophists, Second Sophistic
Aristodemus, 298, 303, see also actors, acting
Aristophanes (dramatist), 6, 9, 10, 11, 12, 15, 41, 44–45, 118, 119, 189, 299, 374, 382, 386
  Birds, 10
  Clouds, 382
  Frogs, 6, 11, 12, 15, 41, 44–45, 374, 382
  Thesmophoriazousae, 189
  Wealth, 382
Aristophanes of Byzantium (scribe), 383
Aristotle, 7, 11, 12, 26, 42, 146, 199, 338, 374–375, 388, 399, 402, 411
  Poetics, 11, 26, 146, 399, 411
  Politics, 374
Aristoxenus, 375–376
Arius, 315–316
Arnobius, 323
Artaud, Antonin, 21
Artists of Dionysus, guild of, 6, 139, 143, 375–376
Asia Minor: announcement of honours in, 132–138, see also honorific decrees
  choruses from, 141
  choral performance in, 145, see also chorus

transmission of texts from, 339
Athens: archives of, 12
  Fifth-century, 3–4, 7–8, 12, 143
  Athenian dramatic festivals, see festivals; Athenian reperformance, see reperformance; Athenian tragedy, see tragedy, Greek
Attic elocution, 291, 294–295
  socio-cultural function of, 291; see also sophists, Second Sophistic and orators, oration
Atticism, 290–291, 298
audience, 8, 17, 20, 26–27
  Athenian, 39–40, 374–376
  Christian, 402, 406, 410–423
  of comedy, 205
  festival, 119
  of Greek tragedy, 196
  and messenger speeches, 250–251, 261–262, see also messenger
  Roman, 154–155, 160; 162–163, 165, 167, 169, 170–175, 180
  of vessels, 87, 90, see also vase paintings
Augustine, 24, 26, 274, 323, 335, 341, 348–349, 353, 361, 420
Augustus, 220–245, 270–271, 319
  Letter to Augustus, see Horace
aulos, aulos player, 122, 134–136, 139, 143–144, see also music
Aurelianus, 326
Averroes, 26, 411
Avicenna, 26
Axionicus, *Euripides Lover*, 43–44

Bacchus, 20, 55, 187, 191, 196–202, 204, 208–214
  Bacchants, 189, 196, 210, 231
  Bacchic ritual, 210, 214
  themes of, 214
Bacchylides, 61
barbarism, barbarian, 4, 73, 86, 90, 91, 153, 222–224, 228–231, 234–236, 240, 241, 243, 300, 336, 355
Basil the Great, 344
Bathyllus of Alexandria, 270–271
Battle of Mice and Frogs, 12
Bede, Venerable, 345, 347, 361
  De Arte Metrica, 345
Benedict of Agnani, 343
Berengarius Scholasticus, 355

Bernard of Clairvaux, 355, 407
Beza, Theodore, 400
Bible, Biblical, 339, 358, 400, 421
biography, *see lives of authors*
Bion of Borysthenes, 305
Boccaccio, 397, 407
Boethius, 402
Bruno, the Blessed, 360–361
Byzantium, 12, 26
    continuity of Greek cultural elements
      in, 26, 372–373, 378, 386, 391
    drama in, 371–392
    manuscript tradition, 373, 380–381,
      383–384, 386–387, 391–392
    and transmission of texts, 12, 26, 41,
      336, 342

Caesar, 181, 245
Caesarius, 326
Caligula, 271
Callimachus, *Aetia*, 241
Carcinus, *Medea*, 83
Cassiodorus, 324, 344, 355, 359, 361–362
catharsis, 26, 398–399
    and Christian culture, 399–423
Catullus, 20, 155
celebrity, 46, 56–57, 62, 290
Celestinus III, 356
Chaucer, 366
Choricius, 320, 329–331, 390
Chorus, choral, 11, 60, 123–124, 127, 136
    137, 138–139, 141, 145, 213, 232,
    269–272, 275, 279, 284, 286, 321,
    329, 386
    citizen, 141–142
    competition, 16, 104, 118, 122,
      128–136, 138
    dramatic, 83, 126, 138–139
    hired, 141
    of Bacchants, 196, 210, 213
    performance, 106, 129, 133–135,
      141, 143, 145
    tragic, 105, 138–141, 196, 232, *see*
    also tragedy, Greek,
    travelling, 141–142
Christians, Christianity, 4, 12, 13, 19,
    24–25
    Christian liturgy, 25
    Christian morality and public enter-
    tainment, 325–328
    Christian tragedy, 23–27, 401–409

condemnation of theater, 317,
    327–328
    early Christian hymnography, 377
    education, 377
    and pagan theater, 24–25, 315–331
    parallels between Christian Church
    and ancient theater, 340, 344–345,
    349, 351–355, 401
Christos Paschon, 384–385
Chrysaphes, Manuel, 379–380, *see also*
    music
Chrysostom, John, 315, 320–321,
    326–327, 329, 340
Cicero, 9, 159, 166–167, 169, 171, 175,
    180–181, 238, 273–274, 402
    pro Caelio, 180
    de Haruspicum Responso, 181
    de Inventione, 9
    pro lege Manilia, 180
    de Officiis, 181
    de Oratore, 9
Cleveland Medea,16, 70–93
    contextualizing, 85–91
    perversion of sacrifice, 79–80
    representation of women, 86, 90, 92
Clodia, 180
Clodius, 181
Codex Theodosianus, 326–328
comedy, 9, 14, 23, 43–44, 58,129, 133,
    135, 138, 205, 294–295, 299, 322,
    324, 338, 344–345, 354, 358, 360,
    362, 389
    comic tradition, 118
    contests, 117–118
    first performers of, 375
    in Late Antiquity, 380
    middle, 43, 46
    new, 44, 133
    old, 44, 133
    vase paintings inspired by, 74, 77–78,
      87–88, *see also vase paintings*
Constantine, 316–317, 319, 341–342
Constantius, 316, 341
Correr, Gregorio, *Progne*, 10
Cosmas of Prague, 357
Council of Arles, 328
Council of Carthage, 354
Council of Laodicea, 328
Crates of Mallos, 179

Dante, 366, 397–398, 401–403, 407, 409
    Divine Comedy, 263, 397–398,
    402–403, 407, 410, 414
    Inferno, 399, 407
David (King), 344
De'Sommi, Leone, 399
Demetrius Ixion, 204
Demetrius Poliorketes, 6, 114
Demetrius of Thessalonica, 355
Demetrius Triclinius, 387
Demosthenes, 51, 57–58, 101 107–108,
    112, 118, 119, 299, 306, 321
    Olynthiacs, 51
    On the Crown, 51, 112
    Philippics, 51
Didaskaliae, 113–114
Diodorus of Sardis, 53
Dionysia, Great, 5, 113, 339
    and conferment of crowns: 101,
    108–120, 122–124; *see also festivals*
Dionysus, 44, 165, 188–189, 192–194,
    196–197, 199, 201–202, 207–214
    theater of, 299, 329, 367
Dionysius I of Syracuse, 41, 46–48, 51, 57
Donatus, 346
Dracontius, 343
Drama: tragic, 1–3, 5–8, 17–18, 23, 49,
    60, 70–72, 92, 93, 118, 120, 123, 129,
    141, 143, 159, 174, 192, 270, 320, 380
    Attic, 100
    Christian, 405, 408–409, 413, 422
    closet drama, 380, 384
    cultural origins of, 399
    Dionysiac origins of, 194
    displacement by pantomime and
    mime, 319, *see also pantomime and
    mime*
    dramatic choruses, 83, 138–140, *see
    also chorus*
    dramatic contests, 122, 325, 380, *see
    also festivals*
    dramatic music, 373–380, *see also
    music*
    dramatic performance, *see perfor-
    mance*
    dramatic structure, 192, 237, 249,
    269, 274–278
    dramatic subjects, 188–189, 192
    dramatic tradition, 2, 13
    and epic narrative, 249–266
    founder, 189

    god of, 188, 196
    in the Greek East, 371–373, 381–
    389, 391–392, *see also Byzantium*
    interactive, 286
    historical, 423
    at the *Ludi Romani*, 156
    of the Middle Ages, 335, 338
    modern, 331
    New, 141
    old dramas, 112–113
    performative nature of, 371
    reception of, 41, 90, *see also recep-
    tion*
    Roman, 167, 171, "preliterary", 154,
    158
    sacramental, 365
    and Scripture, 345, 361–362
    Senecan, 22, *see also Seneca*
    sociology of, 90–91, *see also vase
    paintings*
    staged, 194, 277
    sophist drama, *see sophists, Second
    Sophistic*
    theory of, 410–411, 421
dramatists, *see playwrights*
Durandus of Mende, 408

Eastern Roman Empire, *see Byzantium*
Ekkehard of Aura, 343
Eleanor of Aquitaine, 356
elegy, 8, 241
    elegiac influence, 20, 62, 200–201,
    238, 240–241, 244
    mythological narrative in, 240
    origins of, 241
    romantic, 201, 240
Ennius, 173–175, 178, 180, 189, 197, 203
    Achilles, 175
    Athamas, 189
    Medea, 173–175
Ennodius, 355
Ephesos, 103, 114, 116, 120, 133–134,
    143
Erasmus of Rotterdam, 289
Erinyes, 80–82, 86, 91, 225–226
    Eumenides, 59, 192
    Furies, 223, 225, 273
Etruscans, 92, 156
Eubulus, 88, 90; *Dionysius,*46
Euclid, 402
Eunapius, 301

Euripides, 6–9, 12, 21, 25. 100, 123, 189, 210, 213
  Alcestis, 86
  Andromeda, 44
  Antigone, 189
  Antiope, 189
  Archelaus, 49, 58–60, 62
  Bacchae, 25, 189, 192, 199, 210, 213
  Cadmus, 189
  Erechtheus, 43, 50, 86
  Heracles, 86
  Hippolytus, 192, 384
  Ino, 189
  Iphigenia Among the Taurians, 21, 219–245
  Medea, 72, 74–77, 79–84, 86, 90, 173–175, 348, 384
  Oedipus, 189
  Phoenissae, 8, 86, 181, 189, 193, 251, 382
  Suppliants, 189, 251
  adaptation of Euripidean model to Roman culture, 240
  biography, 15, 39–40, 42–60, 62–63
  in Byzantium, 372–373, 377, 382, 384–385
  comparison with Seneca, 249, 251, 253
  features of Euripidean tragedy, 231
  reception in the Middle Ages, 337, 340, 347–349, 362, 365
  Renaissance reception of, 296–298
  Roman reception of, 173–174, 181
  transcultural adaptation, 173–174, 323, 400, in Ovid, 193–194, 196, 197, 199, 210, 213, 219–227, 232–235, 237–238, 240, 242–245
  in vase paintings, 72–77, 79–84, 90, *see also vase paintings*
Eusebius, 24, 340
  Life of Constantine, 315–316
Ezekiel, *Exagoge*, 7

fabulae praetextae, 157–158, 161, 164
Fasti, 5, 113
Festivals: *Antiocheia*, 137
  Apollonia, 128–129
  Asclepieia, 130
  Great Dionysia, 112, 115, 127
  Herakleia, 139–140
  Klaria, 136–137

  Lenaia, 5, 165
  Panathenaia, 115–117, 119, 131, 143
  Posideia, 127
  Ptolemaia, 100, 115, 119, 139, 140
  Seleukeia, 131
  Soteria, 100, 120–122, 145
  Athenian, 5
  dramatic, tragic, 5, 61, 99–102, 322
  festival culture, 4
  inscriptions, 3, 14, 16, 99–146, 321–322, 326
  outside of Athens, 99–146
  Roman, 165, 167, 180, 211
  as a venue for civic announcements and honorific decrees, 102–106, 109–112, 114–146
Flavius Josephus, 350, 400
Fréculf, 346, 350, 353
  Luctuosa Tragoedia, 353
Fulvius Nobilior, 157
funeral, funerary, 15, 19, 53–54, 168, 404
  art, 8
  context of painted vessels, 15, 70, 84–88, 92
  games, 165
  oration, 19, 54, 85–86
  verse, 323, 330
Furies, *see Erinyes*

Galen, 45, 402
Games, 89, 101, 117, 117–119, 126–127, 133, 135, 139–140, 325–326
  and Christians, 325
  gladiatorial, 22, 168, 319, 325
  ludi publici, 154
  Ludi Romani, 17, 156, 159
  and pantomime, 321
  Roman, 159–160, 165, 168–169, 176–177 *see also agon, agones*
Gawain, 363
Gelasius I, 354
Gellius, Aulus, 55, 62
  Attic Nights, 55
Gerhoh of Reichersberg, 353–354, 358, 361–362
Gibbon, Edward, 335, 367
Gildas, 357
Giotto, 58, 407
Gratian, 359
Gregory VII, 354
Gregory of Cappadocia, 344

Gregory the Great, 400
Gregory of Nazienzus, 384, 386
Gregory of Tours, 349
Guibert of Nogent, 356
Gutenberg, Johannes, 339, 387

Hadrian, 6, 321
Haimo of Halberstadt, 204, 343
Haplucheiros, Michael, 385–386
Hélinand of Froidmont, 356
Hellas, Hellenes, concept applied in repa-
    triation of Euripides, 53–54, 56
  Hellenistic audiences, 376
  Hellenistic period, 5, 16, 61, 104,
    120, 138, 140, 144, 270, 380
  Hellenistic precedent applied to Ro-
    man education, 179
  Hellenocentrism, 156
  literature and society, 45, 208,
    99–146
Henry of Auxerre, 355
Henry of Marcy, 353
heresy, 348, 354–355
Hermesianax, 62–63
Hermippus of Smyrna, 41, 46–47, 57
Herod, 350–351, 360
Herodes Atticus, 291, 307, see also soph-
    ists, Second Sophistic
Herodias, 351
Herodotus, 51, 224–225, 233
Hieron, 49, 50, 51, 52, 59, 99
Hieronymus of Rhodes, 41, 56
Hincmar of Reims, 354
Hippocleas of Thessaly, 61
historiography, 9, 292, 335
Homer, 1, 9, 11, 40, 51, 61, 63, 168, 175,
    177–178, 199, 202, 206, 261, 264,
    306, 330, 344, 361, 402, 403
Honorific decree, 99–141
Honorius (emperor), 328
Honorius Augustodunensis (Honorius of
    Autun), 364–365, 401–402
  Gemma Animae, 25, 401
Horace, 12, 179, 323, 346, 400, 402, 403
  Ars Poetica, 12, 346
  Letter to Augustus, 170–171
Hosidius Geta, 322
Hrotsvit of Gandersheim, 360–361
hubris, 162–163, 352, 405
Hugh of Fouilloy, 349, 350
Hugh of Saint–Victor, 343

human sacrifice, 224, 233–237
hymnography, early Christian, 26,
    377–379, 389
hypocrisy, 363, 388–389
  of actors, 348–349, 354
Hypodikos of Chalcis, 123, see also cho-
    rus, choral competition

Ignatius, Deacon, 377
inscriptions, Greek, 3, 16, 61–62, 102,
    108, 111–113, 117, 122, 126–127,
    129, 133–136, 139–140, 271, 300,
    306, 320–322, 326, 342, 344
interpolation, 41, 380, 386–387
intertextuality, see also allusion
inventio, 295, see also orators, oration
Ion of Chios, 53
Isaiah, 352
Isidore of Seville, 344, 355, 366
Isidorus Mercator, 350
Isocrates, 108, 306, Aeginetikos, 127

Jeremiah, 352
Jerome, 347–349, 351, 358–359, 362,
    400, 403
Jesus Christ, 327, 345, 348–350, 351–
    353, 364–365, 399–406, 407–408,
    410, 412, 414, 416–422
Jews, Judaism, 343, 350–353, 356, 362,
    366, 388, 399
Job, 13, 399–401
  Book of Job, 361, 399–400
John the Grammarian, 339
John of Salisbury, Policraticus, 353, 362
Josephus, 350, 352
Julian the Apostate, 316, 324, 341
Justinian, 318–319, 329, 378
Juvenal, 402

Kolophon, 117, 120, 136–137
Koukouzeles, John 379–380, see also
    music

Lactantius, 206, 347
Lambert of Hersfeld, 354
Landulph the Younger, 355
Laurentius de Leodio, 356
Leo I, 354
Leo II, 354
Leontinos of Chalcis, 126
Lesbos, 139, 346

letter-writing, 239–240, 242
Libanius, 271, 272–273, 316, 320, 324, 326–327, 330–331
Liberatus of Carthage, 355
library of Alexandria, 12, 45
    Athenian archive, 42
libretti (*fabulae salticae*), 270, 272, 274, *see also pantomime and mime*
Licinius, 316
literary history, 5, 17, 55–56, 155–156
    transmission of texts, 12, 45, 48, 206
liturgy, 25–27, 335, 359–362, 401–402, 405, 408, 412, 416–418, 420–423
    of Maunday Thursday, 409
    visual allusions to, 414, *see Christians, Christianity*
Liutprand, bishop of Cremona, 357
lives of authors, 40, 41, 49–64, 289–290
    ancient biographers, 46, 58, 62
    patronage, 41, 49–53, 58–59, 62, 271
    comparison of Aeschylus, Euripides, and Sophocles, 56–58
Livius Andronicus, 17, 19, 153, 156–157
Livy, 168, 402
Lucan, 323, 402–403
Lucian, 23, 46–47, 271–273, 289–308, 320–322
    Anacharsis, 299
    Apology, 303
    How to Write History, 292, 301
    Lexiphanes, 295
    Menippus, 305
    Nigrinus, 304
    On Dance, 271, 300, 320
    On Salaried Posts, 295–296, 302
    Peregrinus, 293
    Philospeudes, 293
    Pseudologista, 307
    Saturnalia, 302
    Slander, 293
    The Banquet, 296–297
    The Cock, 302, 303
    The Fly, 297
    The Ignorant Book–collector, 46, 296
    Toxaris, 293
    Tyrannicide, 293, 294
    Zeus Rants, 298
    biographical information, 290
    cynic influence, 305–306
    metaphorical use of 'tragedy' and 'tragic'; transmitted work, 290

Lucretius, 323, 402
ludi, see games
Lycophron, 7, 192
Lycurgus, *Against Leocrates*, 42

Macedonia, Macedonians, 7, 15, 49, 51–52, 54–55, 58–59, 62–63, 10, 122, 338
    court of, 100
Macrobius, 49
Magnesia, Magnesians, 62, 100, 125, 133, 137
Manegold of Lautenbach, 354
Mansuetus, 354
Manuscript, 12, 40, 55, 59, 206, 337, 373, 379, 381, 384, 386, 388
Manutius, Aldus, 12
Marbod of Rennes, 349
Marcianus of Gaza, 330
Marcus of Arethusa, 344
Marianus of Scotus, 343
Mark the Deacon, 329
    Life of Porphyrius, 329–330; *see also Porphyrius*
masks, 8, 19, 21, 70, 73, 76, 89, 281, 298, 302, 303, 306, 374
    comic, 74
    pantomimic, 273
    tragic, 75, 303
mass, 25, 359, 365–366, 401–405, 408–409, 417
    Christianization of the classical tradition, 403–405
    foundations of Christian tragedy, 401–402
Matthew, 327, 348, 349, 405
Maximus of Tyre, 303
Megale Hellas, 70, 78, 82–83
Menander, 50, 380
Michael VIII, 339
Middle Ages, 3, 4, 5, 12–13, 23–27, 335–367
    defense of, with respect to tragedy, 335–340
    perceived paucity of theatrical instantiation, 336
    status of the Greek language in, 372
mime, *see pantomime and mime*
mimesis, 23, 24
    mimetic, 345, 357, 361
    mimetic poetry, 48

Minucius Felix, 343
Mithridates, 180
Mnester, 271
Mnesippus, 293
Moschopoulos, Manuel, 340
Moses, 353
Muses, 46, 47, 53, 54, 61, 101, 385–386
music, 26
    competitions, 104, 122, 132, 136,
       143–144
    dramatic, 373–380
    musical *agon*, 135, 144
    musicians, 272, 328
    notation, 375, 378–379, 381
    songs, 89, 90, 142, 340, 344, 348,
       349, 353, 358, 359, 363
    theory, 373–379
    tragic, 26, 321, 373–374, 377
Mynniskos, 123, *see also actors, acting*
myths, mythology, 10, 20, 23, 73–76,
    189–196, 206, 219–245, 273
    Greek and Roman, 10–11, 157–171,
       179–180
    Greek mythological tragedy, 158,
       160, 170, 180
    mythic heroes, heroines, 10, 158,
       164, 194, 236, 240, 299
    mythic narrative, 227–228, 231–234,
       236, correlation between mythic
       narrative and local history, 224, 231,
       233, 236
    myth–telling, mythical stories, 76, 93

Naevius, *Lycurgus*, 189
    Trojan Horse, 189
Nauplius, 254
Neophron, 83
Nero, 270, 271, 349, 362
Nicander, 199
Novatian, 324–325

Old Testament, 350–351, 353
orators, oration, 388, 411
    Fourth-century BCE, 42–43, 50, 52
    Christian, 327, 330
    cultural prestige conveyed, 291–292
    distinction between orator and actor,
       18, 24
    funeral, 87
    Roman, 155, 180, 181
    sophistic oratory: 291, 295, 306

themes of sophistic declamation,
    293–294
Orchomenos, 100, 195–196, 206
Orderic Vitalis, 357–358
Oropos, 100, 103
Orosius, 402
Otto the Great, 360
Ovid, 10, 20–21, 22, 25, 155, 167,
    187–214, 323, 402–403
    Epistulae ex Ponto, 21, 219–245
    Metamorphoses, 10, 20–21, 187–214
    Tristia, 21, 219–245
    adaptation of sources, 206
    autobiographical engagement with
       Greek tragedy, myth, 219–245
    derivations from Roman tragedy, 238
    framing of scenes, 207
    identification with tragic figures,
       219–220
    Roman theme of friendship, mutual
       love, 236–239
    thematic debt to tragic models, 189

Pacatus Drepanius, 343
Pachymeres, George, 378
Pacuvius, 180, 239
    Antiopa, 189
    Pentheus, 189, 190
    Chryses, 239
paganism, 24–25, 316, 318, 325,
    329–330, 340–344
    pagan drama, 361
    pagan musical practice, 377
    tragedy and, 343, 347, 349, 350, 354,
       356, 366
Panathenaia, 101, 111, 115–117, 119, 131,
    143
Pantomime and mime, 6–7, 22–25, 89,
    171, 205
    actors, 24, 273–274, 279, 281, 286
    dance and dancers, 271–274, 287
    defense of mime, 320, 390
    expression of tragedy, 340–341
    history and characteristics of,
       270–274
    and Christianity, 25, 326–331
    in the early Roman Empire, 319–322
    female mimes, 328
    prizes, 321, 322
papyri, 14, 83, 86, 381, 383
Paschasius Radbertus, 351, 360

Passio Perpetuae, 25
Passion Play, 26, 365, 409–410, 414–421
Paul (the Apostle), 319
  Letter to the Ephesians, 359, 403, 410
  Feast of St. Paul, 404
Paul the Deacon, 356
Paulus Emeritanus, 350
Paulus Vinfridus, 343
Pausanias, 50, 53, 55, 315, 318
Peregrinus Proteus, 293
performance, 1, 14, 16, 25, 74, 82,
    92, 100, 104, 145, 158, 194, 205,
    319–320, 336–337, 350–351, 360
  Athenian, 84, 342
  Byzantine, 382, 390–391
  choral, 134–135, 141, 143, 145, 383
  Christian, 344, 401–402, 409,
    412–413, 416, 420–421
  disapproval of, 328
  dramatic, 101–102, 126, 129–130,
    138, 156–157, 167–168, 205, 299,
    305, 316–318, 322–325
  history of, 23
  imperial, 271
  liturgical, 361, 379
  medieval, 361
  modes of performance, pantomime,
    270, 272, 321, 326, *see also panto-
    mime and mime*
  performance culture, context, 100,
    154, 156, 179, 391
  performance praxis, 337
  performance theory, 388
  performance text, 12, 76, 79–80, 410,
    413–414, 417–419, 423
  performance tradition, 9, 157, 415
  of poetry, 89, 354
  Roman "preliterary", 172
  sophistic, 293, 306–308
  tragic, 2, 5–7, 8, 24, 34, 105–107,
    112–113, 115, 120, 124 132, 138,
    165–166, 171, 301, 306, 340
  see also spectacle
Pericles, 54
Peter Abelard, 355
Peter of Blois, 362–363
Peter the Chanter, 343
Peter Chrysologus, 350
Peter Damian, 354
Peter the Venerable, 353
Petronius Probus, 317

Petrus Bernardus, 356
Philemon, 44
Philip Arrhidaios, 126
Philip II of Macedon, 51, 58, 101, 306
Philippides, 44, 114, 118–119
  Euripides Lover, 43–44
Philochorus, 41
philosophy, 9, 24, 26, 48–49, 89, 155,
    278, 282, 287, 290, 298, 305, 382,
    386, 407
Philostratus, 291, 307, *see also sophists,
    Second Sophistic*
Photius, 330, 377
Pindar, 56, 61
pity, 24, 26, 27, 165, 357, 363–364,
    397–398, 411–412
Planudes, 206
Plato, 11, 24, 48–49, 91, 123, 292,
    295–297, 372, 374, 402
  Ion, 11
  Phaedo, 297
  Republic, 11, 48, 374
  Symposium, 11, 91, 296
Plautus, 20, 155, 178, 271
Playwrights, Greek, 39–63, 143, 144, 178
  Roman heirs of, 189
  Roman, 153, 154, 161–162, 164, 165,
    172–175, 179–180
Pliny the Elder, 176–177, 199, 210–211
Plutarch, 50
poetry, poetics, 5, 7, 8, 9, 13, 18, 21, 22,
    93, 166, 173, 188, 189, 195, 196, 200
  exile poetry, 219–245
  in symposium, 89–90
Polemo, Marcus Antonius, 291, 307–308
  see also sophists, Second Sophistic
Policoro Painter, 73
polis, 43, 62, 99, 102–104, 106–107,
    121–122, 125, 127, 130, 134, 137,
    142, 144–148, 165, 338
Pollux, 294
Polybius, 168, 177
Pompey, 169–171, 180, 324, 344
Pomponius Secundus, 269
Porphyrius, 329, 347; *Isagoge*, 347
  Life of Porphyrius, see Mark
Priene, 16, 110, 120, 135–137
Priscian, 345
Procopius, 318–319, 324
Prodromos, Theodore, 385–386
  Katomyomachia, 385

Progymnastmata, 389, *see also rhetoric*
Pronomos Vase, 83
Propertius, 192, 323
Prosper Aquitanus, 343
Prudentius, 343
psalmody, 359, 361
Psellos, Michael, 340, 377, 384
Publilius Syrus, 277

Queen of Sheba, 352
Querolus, 380
Quintilian, 180, 388
Quintus Smyrnaeus, 254

Rabanus Maurus, 345–347, 349, 354, 357
Reception: of Athenian playwrights, 39–63
    contextual,1–4, 14–15
    in late antiquity and the Middle Ages,
    5, 23–27, 41, 42, 335–336, 345
    in the Hellenistic period, 5
    intercultural, 46, 153–181
    intermedial, 3, 8, 15, 72–82, 84–93
    modes of, 3–4, 166–167
    popular tastes, 239
    Roman, 5, 17–18, 20, 21–23, 240
    of Greek tragedy, 20, 153–181
    through Ovid's exile poetry,
    219–245
    secondary receptions of tragedy,
    154–155
    synchronic, 14
recording technology, 371–392, *see also*
    music, notation
Reginard of Liège, 351
religious practice, Greco–Roman, 208
    Greek, 4, 80, 92, 102, 104, 106, 165,
    290
    Roman, 175, 241, 328
Renaissance, 3, 4, 11–12, 21, 26, 289, 335,
    340, 385, 392, 397, 399, 402, 412
    Byzantine, 372
    Italian, 386–387
    Stoicism of, 407
reperformance, 3–7, 14, 42, 100, 119, 155
Rhesus, 7, 105
rhetoric, 8–9, 21–21, 24, 26, 42, 48,
    51, 155, 167, 179, 250, 290–291,
    294–295, 299, 306–307, 329, 336,
    373, 382, 384, 387–392
    rhetors, 388–390
Rhetorica ad Herennium, 9

Rhodes, 41, 43, 56, 107, 120, 124–125,
    128–129, 131–132, 144
Richard the Lionheart, 356
Rome, Roman, 1–5, 8, 9, 17–23, 24
    and the 'Greek turn', 154, 157–160
    Christian Roman Empire, 319, 328,
    377
    Imperial, 22, 205, 270, 358
    Republican, 153–181
    society, 155, 181, 271, 315, 328
    tragedy, *see tragedy, Roman*
    Trojan heritage, *see Troy, Trojans*
    women writers, 240
Ruotger of Cologne, 360
Rupert of Deutz, 351–353, 356,

Saint John's Gospel, 323
Salome, 350–351, 360
Samos, 40, 100, 120, 124–126, 132, 145
Sappho, 63, 346
satyr plays, 77, 79, 88, 113, 189, 209
Satyrus (biographer), 51–53, 56–57
scholia, 26, 59–62, 189, 380, 384,
    386–387, 391
Sedulius Scotus, 346–347, 357
Seneca, 1, 7, 10, 17, 21–23, 167, 249–266,
    269–287, 339, 345, 402–403, 407
    Agamemnon, 22, 249–266, 284
    Hercules Oetaeus, 284–286
    Medea, 279–286
    Oedipus, 249, 278
    Thyestes, 10, 249, 278
    Trojan Women, 275–276, 278
    contrast with Athenian tragedy, 269,
    274
    influence of Stoic philosophy, 278,
    282–284
    and pantomime: influence of, 270,
    274
    structural comparison, 275–278
    theatrical devices employed,
    284–286
    thematic considerations, 277–278
    use of running commentaries,
    279–287
Servius, 161, 204
Shakespeare, William, 2, 10, 11, 13, 22,
    366
Sicard of Cremona, 360
Sicily, 7, 8, 46, 48–49, 50, 52–53, 59, 63
Sidonius Apollinaris, 343

Sigibert of Gembloux, 357
Silius Italicus, 323
Simonides, 50–51, 61
Simplicius, 411
Siphnos, 126, 132
Sithon, 208–209
Sixtus III, 350
Socrates, 48–49, 56–57, 296–297, 382, 405
Solon, 299
Song of Songs, 345, 353, 361
sophists, Second Sophistic, 23, 290–291, 293–295, 297–300, 303, 306–308
    classicist outlook on tragedy, 298–299
    identification with classical Athens, 299
    performance, 291, 301, 306–307
    pedagogical purpose of, 299
    rhetorical education, 294–295
    sophistic oratory, see orators, oration
    rarity of performed tragedies, 301
    use of metaphor, 292–295
    view of tragedy, tragic actors as deceptive, 296, 302–303
Sophocles, 4, 6, 7, 9, 10, 11, 12, 13, 14, 15, 39–42, 47, 56–63, 154, 157–160, 189, 192, 249
    Ajax, 165, 192, 407
    Amphitryon, 189
    Antigone, 189
    Epigoni, 189
    Oedipus at Colonus, 59–60, 61, 62, 189
    Oedipus the King, 4, 86, 189, 192, 249, 382
    Peri chorou, 11
    Tereus, 10
    Trachiniae, 323
    biography, 55–58
    dedication to Athens, 56, 58–60
South Italy, 15, 72, 85, 92, see also vase paintings
spectacle, 4, 21, 164, 165, 167, 170–171, 194, 205, 256, 272, 294, 301, 306, 316, 321, 326, 327, 341, 342, 347, 348, 349
    and piety, 363
    of recognition and reversal, 188–191
    of suffering, 26, 399, 409–412, 420
    of violence, 22, 421
    as voyeurism, 190–191, 194, 205

Statius, 323, 402–403
Stesichoros, 346
Suda, 55, 377
Suetonius, 270, 402
Symmachus, 344
symposium, 390
    contextual use of theatre-related vessels, 16, 70, 85, 87–93
Synesius, 326, 377
    de Providentia, 326

Tacitus, 270
Tanagra, 100, 101, 139
Teos, 100, 137
Terence, 347, 361–362
Tertullian, 24, 26, 322, 324–325, 335, 343, 344, 347–348, 400
    de Spectaculis, 324–325
Thasos, 103, 125, 130
theater: and Christianity, 317, 325–328, 331
    recognition of civic importance, 340–341
    role in Roman civic identity, 315–316
    theatrical performance in the Roman Empire 319–325
    uses of theaters in the Roman Empire after the classical period, 319–320, 324
Theatre of Pompey, 324, 344, see also Pompey
theatricality, 77, 90, 205
    Christian, 335
    conveyed through gesture and proxemics, 75–76
    metaphorical emphasis of, 308
    non-theatricality, 76
    of political life, 8
    signs of, 73–75
Thebes, Theban, 51, 60, 189, 192, 204, 210
    epic,192–193
    narrative, 187–189, 193, 194–195, 198, 200, 206, 209, 213
    themes, 193
    tragedy, 189
    women, 196, 200–20, 207–208
Themistocles, 299, 306
Theocharidis, 320–321, 323
Theocritus, 209
Theodora, 318

Theodore of Mopsuestia, 400
Theodoretus of Cyr, 329, 343
Theodoric the Ostrogoth, 324, 344, 355
Theodotus, archonship of, 5, 113
Theophrastus, *Enquiry into Plants*, 208
Thespiai, 100, 121, 143
Thespis, *Pentheus*, 189
Thessalonike, 53, 63, 101, 128, 318, 355
Thucydides, 53–55, 294–295, 358
Tibullus, 323
tragedy, Greek, 1–5, 23, 39–46, 48–50,
    59–60, 62–63, 188, 189, 324, 402
    and ancient romantic tales, 200–201
    audiences, 196
    changes in, 141
    and Christianity: 4, 12, 13, 19,
    24–25, 315–331, 397–422
    and Christian ritual, 364
    as a source of metaphor for Christian
    historical narrative, 351–355
    to validate Christian poetics, 345
    and civic identity, 42–43, 50, 99, 104,
    315–316
    and civic life, 99–146, 340–341
    competitions, 110, 117, 119, 139,
    132, 144
    contemporary dialogue about, 9–10,
    20
    creative appropriation of, 72, 219, 227
    and cultural competence, 87, 91
    cultural history of, 72, 78
    cultural significance of, 15, 45, 366
    Dionysian origins of, 188–189
    dissemination of, 7–8, 17–26, 39–41,
    48, 99–100, 120–138
    distinction between old and new,
    112–113
    divine inspiration, 47
    evolution of, 7, 241, 269
    expression through mime and panto-
    mime, 341–342
    and Greek cultural life, 70, 76, 82,
    84, 88–91, 93
    historicization of, 42, 343–347
    intercultural context, 39, 100,
    155–158, 166–181, 219–245
    intermedial interpretation, *see recep-
    tion, intermedial*
    in late antiquity, 23–27
    and literary and cultural theory,
    11–12

    and material culture, 8–9, 45–48
    in the Middle Ages, 335–367
    music in, *see music*
    myth and the classical tradition,
    10–11, 157–174; 179–180
    negative reference to, 347–350
    Ovid's engagement with, 188,
    219–245
    and paganism, 347–350, 354
    performance of, 5–7, 14, 100
    and politics, 2, 8, 48–53, 57, 95–101,
    99
    problems of defining, 105, 399
    representations in art: figurines 14
    funerary, 8
    wall paintings, mosaics, 8
    vases, *see vase paintings*
    ritual language of, 197
    and Roman identity politics, 154,
    161–163
    and aristocratic self–promotion,
    159–160, 164, 168–169, 180, 344
    Roman reception of, 4, 5, 8, 17–21,
    154–181, 315–331, 335–367
    and Roman societal evolution, 155,
    179–181
    staging tableau, 79
    tragic competitions, 73, 110–115
    tragic plots, 86–87, 169, 172, 178,
    219, 221, 236, 244, 250, 253, 399
    tragic themes, 5–13, 21, 192, 197,
    209, 219, 230, 237, 240, 351, 352,
    399
    transhistorical and cross-cultural
    perspectives, 13, 17–21, 156–160
    translation of, 17, 155–156, 160, 165,
    172–175, 179, 387
    transmission of texts, 12–3, 20,
    41–48, 156 295, 337–339, 371–372,
    371–392, 411
tragedy, Roman, 3, 17, 21–23, 155, 162,
    153–181, 196, 200, 238–239
    civic function of, 157, 164–167,
    171–172
    authenticity, realism in, 253, 263–264
    entertainment value, 166–167
    and influence of Greek mythological
    tragedy, 158, 170, 180
    lack of extant texts, 153–154
    social and political significance,
    157–158, 160–172

tragic messenger, 21–22, 232, 238, 249–266, 284, 357
    development of tragic theme, 260
    epic narrative strategies, 261–266
    epic nature of, 259–262
    theatrical function of, 251, 266, 276–277
tragic scripts, 1, 12, 17, 20, 45, 72, 75, 155, 173
    Athenian reproduction of, 6
    Christian use of, 25, 377
    civic interpretation of, 99
    in Greco–Roman education, 4, 8, 25, 86, 155, 179–180, 299–300, 373
    preservation of, 44–45
    in Rome, 18, 21, 160–171, 172, 173
    semantics of in relation to Roman society, 155, 172–179
Triclinius, 387
Trifolius, 350
Tristan, 363
Troy, 73, 162, 164, 169, 249, 253–255, 258, 263, 275
    Trojans, 162–164, 169, 258, 262, 264–265

vase paintings, 3, 8, 14, 15, 69–93
    interpretation, 72–82
    comedy, 71, 74, 77 87, 88
    funerary context, 70, 84–88
    iconography of, 71, 74, 76–85, 87, 89–90
    infanticide, theme of, 68, 77, 79, 83–85, 86, 90
    markers of theatricality, 74
    non-theatricality of tragic scenes, 76
    painters, 66, 73, 77–82, 84, 88
    paradox of surviving vessels, 92–93
    problems of identifying tragedy, 74–78
    reception, 84–87
    symposium context, 87–93
    see also Cleveland Medea
Vegetius, 402
Virgil, 20, 22, 24, 155, 167, 188, 193, 204, 261–263, 266, 270, 322, 323, 361, 397, 402–404
    Aeneid, 188, 261–263, 266
    Georgics, 361

Wagner, Richard, 289
Wibertus, 355
Wieland, Christoph Martin, 289
William of Blois, *Alda*, 362
William of Malmesbury, 356
Wolberus, Abbot of St. Pantaleon, 353
Wolf, Friedrich August, 153

Xenophon, 89, 91, 201, 306
Xerxes, 252, 306, 308

Zenobius, 209